UNDER THE EDITORSHIP OF

Leonard Carmichael

SECRETARY, SMITHSONIAN INSTITUTION, FOR-
MERLY PRESIDENT, TUFTS COLLEGE, AND
DIRECTOR, TUFTS RESEARCH LABORATORY OF
SENSORY PSYCHOLOGY AND PHYSIOLOGY

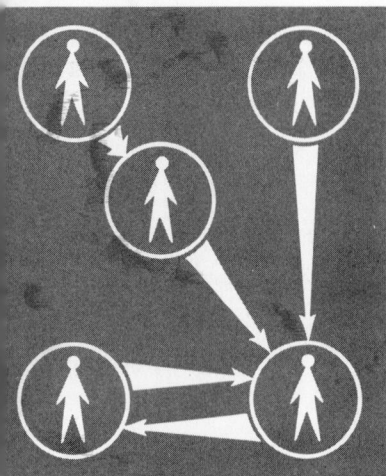

PSYCHOLOGY IN

THOMAS A. RINGNESS

UNIVERSITY OF WISCONSIN · MADISON

HOUGHTON MIFFLIN COMPANY

THEORY AND PRACTICE

HERBERT J. KLAUSMEIER

UNIVERSITY OF WISCONSIN · MADISON

ARTHUR J. SINGER, JR.

SAN DIEGO STATE COLLEGE

BOSTON · The Riverside Press Cambridge

Key to color plates inside front cover.

	Normal usually sees	Red-green blind usually sees
Top of left page	8	3
Bottom of left page	6	5
Top of right page	29	70
Bottom of right page	57	35

A totally color-blind person may see no numbers.

Editor's Introduction

The editor of this book once asked a nice girl cousin of his, who was an undergraduate in one of America's great state universities, how she liked the introductory course in psychology that she had just taken. "Oh, it was the dullest course I ever took," she said. "It was just facts about the eye and the ear and how rats run through little tunnels." As I listened to this statement, I could only think that the psychologists who had taught this bright girl had not been very psychological in their approach. No doubt her teachers had presented a good, formal course, but they had forgotten something that is psychologically important: All learning involves the modification of the individual as he is at the time that learning begins. People's interests and skills are not always what we wish they were. More and more teachers, like modern advertisers, are coming to remember that, as they set about changing human reactions or "imparting knowledge," they must start with people as they are.

In the present book the authors talk directly to active, living American college students. The book begins, after its introductory chapter, with a consideration of some of the social and psychological factors involved in meeting the challenge of college life. Its pages take up genuine everyday problems of the university classroom and of the increasingly complex social patterns of undergraduate living. The suggested solutions to these immediate problems in human behavior are then related to established principles of scientific psychology.

In this book the student does indeed learn how sense organs work and how white rats learn, but these facts are presented in a context that gives them a personal and immediate meaning that has not always been clear, at least to some students, in more formal courses.

This book is thus intended to contribute to the general education of the college undergraduate and at the same time to lead the student into the technical understanding of modern psychology. In achieving this objective, the authors explain the intimate relationship between psychology and other academic subjects and the importance of psychological facts and principles in solving some of the basic problems of the social sciences.

As its Glossary and Index show, this volume deals with what may be called the standard topics of psychology. For example learning and perception are given quite full consideration, but even in dealing with such topics as these, the book emphasizes applications that the student himself can make. Thus, in speaking of reading, the authors stress the basic psychology of reading, but they also explain the steps that can be taken to improve the individual's own reading rate. They even suggest the relationship that they see between psychology and humanistic wisdom and formal philosophy. The book also considers the role in each life of self-accepted and socially approved sets of ethical and moral standards.

Biologists, physiologists, neurologists, physicists, and chemists, as well as professional psychologists, have in the last decades gained great new insights into the bodily mechanisms that underlie behavior. Similarly many of the recent advances in the social sciences and especially in psychiatry throw new light upon the make-up of human nature. In the present volume these now very large and involved sets of facts and principles are brought together in a novel way. By centering their focus upon the problems of the immediate environment of the college student, the authors work out a new synthesis of this important material. For some students the realism of this method of introduction will make the subject of psychology a live one from their first day of study. The authors have woven into a new tapestry the general factual and theoretical material found in standard introductory courses in scientific psychology.

Early in this book the student is asked to think about such questions as the social factors that make student clubs successful. Soon, however, he is also learning why good statistical procedures are important in psychological research and how to use dozens of technical terms, such as "mental age," "whole-part-learning," and "schizophrenia." Thus gradually he comes to see for himself what modern scientific psychology is about.

It has sometimes been said that a good elementary course in psychology is really an initiation into a secret society. Certainly many students do learn from psychology to understand themselves and their associates better than they could without a knowledge of this subject. The present volume thus may be thought of as a new type of initiation into the fraternity of those who think of human behavior and of mental life in scientific terms. Not only, therefore, will this interesting and substantial book assist many students in acquiring for themselves a factual knowledge of psychology, but also it may help some of them to gain a new stability and even a new energy in their own personal lives.

LEONARD CARMICHAEL

Preface

Psychology is of very recent origin in comparison to most physical and biological sciences. Nevertheless, a large number of important psychological facts, principles, and methods have emerged and are becoming stabilized and being put to use. These, in turn, are useful for building further theories, and also as tools in dealing with the more immediate and practical situations of life. Much as the study of chemistry and physics in a first college course contributes to understanding aspects of the physical world in which the student lives, so a first course in psychology should yield increased understanding of human behavior — one's own and that of others, and of self–other relationships.

From this point of view, we present major principles and theories rather than an encyclopedic body of specific facts, and we give considerable attention to the application of principles and methods. Most of the material presented in this book is drawn from major fields of psychological research — experimental, clinical, developmental, educational, and industrial. As necessary, we have included ideas from other sciences, particularly biology and sociology, and from other disciplines, including philosophy.

We believe that most important in a first course in psychology are the students themselves — their expanding knowledge of self and others, their methods of identifying and attacking the problems of young adulthood, and their emerging goals for college and life. In this conviction, and especially in Part One, we discuss principles and theories and give many practical suggestions. These suggestions are partly inferred from research, but are also based upon our own experiences as professors, advisers of undergraduates, consultants to various groups, and as parents. The suggestions are not intended as prescriptions but as ideas for consideration by students who may not already have given them serious thought. Depending upon the orientation of the course and the characteristics of the students, the instructor may give more or less class time to the chapters in Part One and to the related material in the Workbook.

Part Two discusses such central areas of psychological theory and investigation as purposeful learning, sensation and perception, thinking and communication, motivation and emotions, and intelligence. Part Three opens with an examination of human behavior as a partial product of cultural and more immediate social forces. Then follow chapters on group dynamics, psychology in various social settings and institutions, and mental health. The broader aspects of personality integration are considered in Part Four. Deciding upon or considering seriously a life career and stabilizing a value system are discussed in the broad framework of developing a mature personality.

This book is not a compendium but an introduction. We recognize that psychological theories and principles will come to function in the lives of students only with excellent instruction. The instructor may wish to present factual information in lectures, or by other means, to supplement the text and Workbook; he may assist the students in gathering and analyzing information about themselves, arranging small-group discussions and experiments, counseling with some students, helping them find and use various sources of information, and introducing them to experimental and clinical procedures in the laboratory or classroom. The many graphic and pictorial illustrations in the textbook, along with the Suggested Activities, indicate a variety of useful instructional approaches. The Suggestions for Further Reading at the end of each chapter, and most of the chapter References, were selected on the same three criteria: to supplement the text and Workbook, to be understandable to lower-division students, and to include points of view from various psychological orientations. We recognize that the second course taken by students who major in psychology or in other fields may be in any of such areas as experimental, clinical, developmental, educational, and industrial psychology.

We have given the usual acknowledgements in footnotes and references. In addition, we acknowledge the helpful suggestions of our students and colleagues who used the book in mimeographed form. Finally, the editorial and art staff of Houghton Mifflin Company deserve our plaudits for improving the readability of the book and for its excellent design and illustrations.

THOMAS A. RINGNESS
HERBERT J. KLAUSMEIER
ARTHUR J. SINGER, JR.

Contents

PART TWO • Psychology and the Individual

PART FOUR • Psychology and Your Future

PSYCHOLOGY IN THEORY AND PRACTICE

Introduction

The word psychology stems from two Greek words which together have come to mean "the study of mind." More broadly, psychology is now accepted as the science of behavior. It is mainly concerned with the mental workings of man, individually and in groups, and while it frequently makes use of animals for experimental purposes, it usually does so to shed light on human behavior.

THE NATURE OF SCIENCE

Before we can see how the study of psychology can help us, we must first understand that it is a science and gain some idea of what a science is. A science is a systematic method of inquiry and a related body of knowledge and theory about some aspect of the physical world or the creatures in it. Thus the science of physics deals with matter and motion. The science of chemistry deals with the nature and composition of substances and with changes in them. Biology deals with the structure and organization of plants and animals. Astronomy deals with the solar system, the stars and galaxies, and the motions of these bodies. Geology deals with the nature of rocks and their formation, with mountain building and the action of wind and water on the land.

These are the so-called physical and life sciences. There is another group known as the social sciences. These include economics, or the study of money,

What Psychology Is

What is a science? In what ways is psychology a science? What are the methods used by psychology? What are the aims of psychology? What can you expect to gain from your study of psychology?

finance, and the exchange of goods and services; sociology, or the study of societies or of man in groups; anthropology, or the study of human cultures and civilizations; and psychology, which is mainly concerned with the study of man and of the human mind as it manifests itself both in individual and in group behavior.

A science, we said above, is a systematic method and body of knowledge and theory. There are many kinds of knowledge in the world which have value but which are not sciences — literature, for instance, and the other arts; and religion and philosophy, two of the greatest of human preoccupations throughout history. These methods of inquiry — the scientific, literary, artistic, religious, and philosophical — are related in that man has devised all of them to find and express some aspect of truth about himself and the world he lives in. But they go about it in vastly different ways. Literature and art seek to express an intuitively perceived truth of human experience in terms of a story, poem, painting, or statue. Religion seeks by logic and speculation to answer ultimate questions about the nature of God, of good and evil, of the origin of the universe and the earth, of the reason for the existence of man and the other creatures, of the possibility and nature of a life after this life. Philosophy is interested in many of these same questions. It is also concerned with the nature of knowledge and the processes of thought as a means of gaining knowledge.

These modes of exploring life and experience are of incalculable human

3

value, but they are not sciences. For they do not deal primarily with questions which can be answered by observation and measurement of some aspect of the physical universe. The scientist speculates on the nature of his subject, but also the astronomer *watches* the stars, the chemist *observes* and *reports* on the behavior of solids and gases, the physicist *experiments* with the motions of bodies and *formulates laws* which describe their behavior. The philosopher, on the other hand, can speculate on the nature of good and evil, and the religionist can speculate on the nature of the soul, but neither can observe the subject of his speculation, weigh or measure it in the laboratory, or subject it to experiment. Hence his conclusions cannot be checked against facts; they are not, in the scientific sense, verifiable. The advantage of these disciplines is that they can deal with questions which science cannot touch, for science is limited to what can be checked and verified. The advantage of the sciences is that they can verify and check a great many facts which had not been observed or discovered before.

As a science, psychology is young, though speculation about the nature of man and mind is probably as old as the human race. Until little more than seventy-five years ago psychology was largely speculative, and hence more a branch of philosophy than a science in its own right. As far back as the fourth century B.C. Aristotle speculated very acutely that mind is not a mysterious spiritual entity but a function of the body. But he saw it as linked to the body by "an organ of the soul," an unverifiable and unscientific notion. Christian thinkers speculated that mind and body were separate, were joined at birth, and separated at death. As late as the sevententh century the French mathematician and philosopher René Descartes thought that the nerves were hollow tubes filled with a substance called "animal spirits," and that it was these spirits which carried sensations and messages. In the same century the Eng-

Wilhelm Wundt. *The beginning of psychology as a formal science in its own right is marked by Wundt's opening of the Psychological Institute at the University of Leipzig in 1879. (Keystone View Co. Inc. of N. Y.)*

Sigmund Freud. *A Viennese physician who had worked with neurotics, Freud developed the methods and concepts now known as psychoanalysis. (Keystone View Co. Inc. of N. Y.)*

lish philosopher John Locke proposed a very influential theory that at birth the mind is blank, that experience is the source of all knowledge, and that thoughts and sensations grow out of this source. But all this was speculation. It was philosophy, not psychology as we think of it today.

PSYCHOLOGY AS A SCIENCE

Psychology as a formal science in its own right originated when Wilhelm Wundt opened the Psychological Institute at the University of Leipzig in 1879. Wundt's principal aim was to apply to problems of the mind the findings of other sciences, chiefly medicine and physiology, which had been making great strides. To do so he used the laboratory methods and equipment of physics and physiology, and accomplished a good deal toward describing such aspects of mental behavior as sensations, images, and emotions. His students came from all over the civilized world, and many of them returned to their homes and established schools of psychology much like the parent Institute. Thus psychology, as a science, came quickly into prominence.

The next great step in the development of psychology came with the study of mental functions, such as habit and learning. By the end of the nineteenth century experimental psychology — the use of the laboratory and the experimental method — was well established. Since then many new areas of study and methodology have evolved. The study of learning led to the investigation of memory, this to the nature of intelligence, and this in turn to the development of standardized tests and the measurement of intelligence. Meanwhile the nature of mental illness was being intensively studied. Today the science of psychology has many specialized branches, each dealing with one specific aspect of the whole. Some of these are experimental psychology, animal psychology, developmental psychology, social psychology, industrial psychology, abnormal psychology, educational psychology, and the study of tests and measurements.

THE METHODS OF PSYCHOLOGY

In the search for factual understanding of human behavior, psychologists use a variety of research methods, each of which has both merits and limitations. Learning the various methods used in psychological studies will help you to evaluate statements and theories about human behavior which you encounter in books, journals, radio and television programs, and everyday conversation. It will also give you further insight into the nature of science, and of psychology specifically.

The essence of scientific procedure is 1. systematic observation with a view to answering a specific factual question; 2. performing controlled experiments to find the answer to such a question; 3. communicating one's methods and findings objectively. The scientist is impersonal in his search for truth. He seeks information to test his ideas, opinions, and hypotheses, not to prove or verify ideas he already has. However long and strongly he may have held a theory, he is always willing to discard it if new facts do not support it. He is willing to say "I don't know," and to have no theory rather than cling to one which facts do not maintain. Moreover, he is interested that others should be able to repeat his observations under substantially the same conditions.

Naturalistic observation

The easiest place in which to observe many scientific phenomena is the laboratory. For there it is possible to set up an experiment precisely as one wishes, and to observe every stage of it. The physicist and the chemist can do this a great deal of the time. But it is in the nature of the materials which the psychologist works with — human life and behavior — that much of it cannot be closeted in the laboratory and there neatly run through its paces. It has to be observed in its natural environment. Many questions of child development, group behavior, and other branches of psychology have to be studied largely through systematic observation of human beings in relatively uncontrolled situations, such as the home, school, neighborhood, factory, and hospital.

The experimental method

But whenever possible, systematic observation is supplemented with experiments carefully controlled, and often carried out under laboratory conditions.

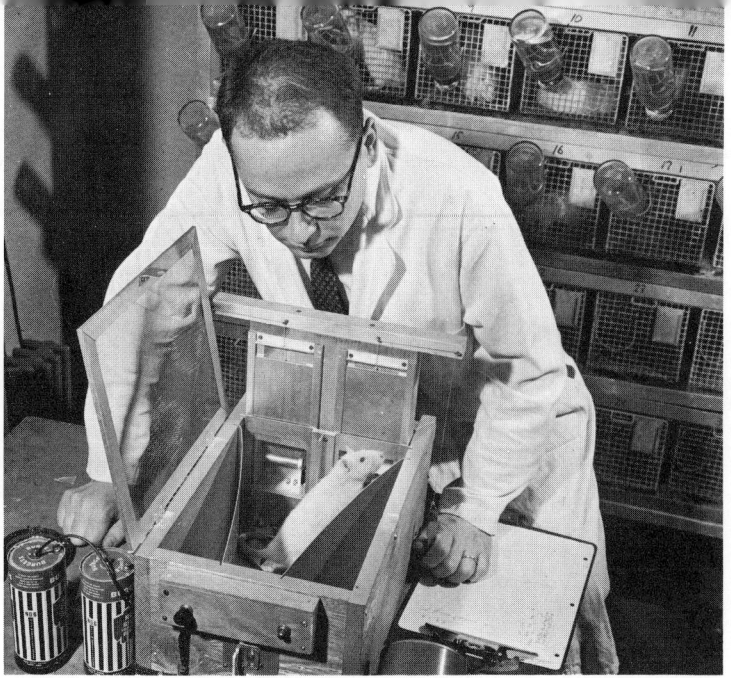

Psychology as a laboratory science. *Using scientific methods of experiment and investigation in studying and observing animal behavior, psychologists can often discover principles and information concerning human behavior. (Merrim, from Monkmeyer.)*

In its ideal form, a psychological experiment involves a situation in which the investigator controls every significant factor and varies only a single factor in order to see whether this variable affects behavior. For example, let us suppose that an investigator wishes to find out whether reward is important to accomplishment. To answer this question he may set up a number of possible experiments. He may have pre-school children carry buckets of sand from one side of a room to another; he may have older persons memorize nonsense syllables; or he may have persons of any age take a test of mechanical or verbal skills. To answer his question, he divides his subjects into two groups, and promises to reward one group for superior performance but does not promise to reward the other. He then measures the performance of the two groups and records his findings. The rewarded group is known as the experimental group, the other as the control. Without the control the experiment would have little significance.

As another example, Stanley and Klausmeier (1) wanted to find out whether playing roles (the conscious assumption of a "character" or "personality") in harmony with originally expressed opinions fixed the opinions more strongly, and vice versa. As subjects, they chose 145 university students, and tested their opinions before and after the role playing. The first test results were divided according to high and low scores, and from these were drawn at random eight groups of eight persons each, with four high and four low scorers in each group, and an equal number of men and women in each group. Of the eight groups, four were role playing, two observed the role playing, and two knew nothing about the experiment. After the role playing, a second test was administered. Changes in test scores indicated that role playing for a short period of time, fifteen minutes, did not alter prior opinions in the direction of the role played.

HYPOTHESIS
The amount of learning is increased when the subject is rewarded for learning

A group of average college students is chosen for the experiment

The group is divided in half

CONTROL GROUP   EXPERIMENTAL GROUP

Fra-Tow-Na
Con-Tas ——

Fra-Tow-Na
Con-Tas ——

Both groups are given the same nonsense syllables to learn without reward

← X →

Both groups do equally well and learn x number of nonsense syllables

Tak-Ya-Tay
Pe-Ja-Cor ——

Tak-Ya-Tay
Pe-Ja-Cor ——

Both groups are given another set of nonsense syllables to learn

No reward

Reward of 10¢
for each syllable learned

The INDEPENDENT VARIABLE is the reward given to the experimental group for each syllable learned

X number of nonsense
syllables learned

Y number of nonsense
syllables learned

The DEPENDENT VARIABLE is the number of syllables learned by the experimental group

In this case they learn more syllables than the control group. Since all the other conditions are the same for each group, the experimenter assumes that this change is caused by the INDEPENDENT VARIABLE

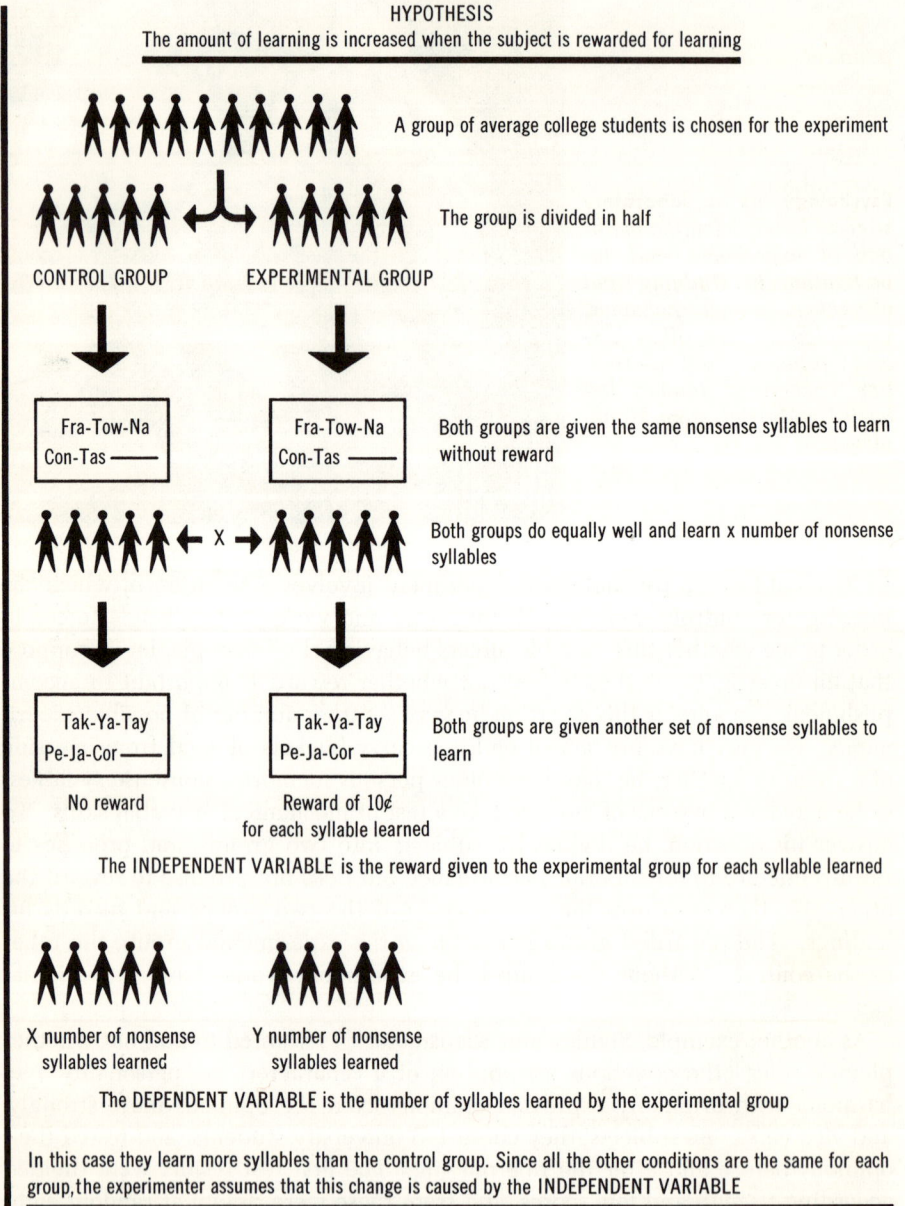

The experimental method. *In this experiment note how all the significant factors are controlled except one (the reward element) which may be interpreted as the cause of any change in behavior. Why is the control group so essential? Why difficult to maintain?*

The experimental method employs what are known as *independent* and *dependent variables*. The independent variable is a condition which is varied by the investigator, and the dependent variable is allowed to vary as it will. Conditions other than those related to the particular independent variable are held constant, so that any changes in the dependent variable must result from manipulation of the independent variable.

Because some conditions may be inadequately controlled or perhaps overlooked in an experiment, a *control group* is often used. That is, certain subjects go through all the experimental procedures except for certain treatments of the independent variable. If these subjects show no change in the dependent variable, it is reasonably certain that the independent variable causes or at least is definitely related to the dependent variable.

In the Stanley and Klausmeier study described above, the independent variable was the treatment given to the subjects: some subjects played roles consistent with their opinions, others played roles opposite to their opinions. The dependent variable was the effects of the role playing as measured by change in test scores from first to second administration. Control groups were those students who went to the library, having no knowledge of the experiment, and, to a lesser extent, those who were observers. Thus the degree to which the independent variable — role playing, observing, or being absent — affected change in opinion, the dependent variable, could be observed.

Experimental studies in psychology often have the following characteristics:

1. A clearly stated hypothesis.

2. Carefully defined conditions for the experiment.

3. A carefully controlled situation in which only the independent and dependent variables are allowed to change — the former manipulated by the researcher, with any variations in the latter observed and noted.

4. A control group of subjects, as a check on factors influencing observed changes in the dependent variable. If this technique is not used, statistical methods of control may be introduced.

5. An experimental group of subjects, in relation to which the independent variable will be manipulated, and whose resulting behavior may be attributed to that variable.

6. Carefully drawn conclusions, based on the conditions of the experiment.

The experimental method has many values when conditions are carefully controlled and observations are accurate. Due to the objectivity and accuracy of the experiment we may infer that whatever changes we find in our subjects are related to whatever conditions are varied. We have clearly indentified our problem, secured precise results, and others can repeat the experiment.

However, in experiments with human subjects there are many aspects of people's lives which we cannot control for a sufficiently long period of time to draw significant conclusions in many areas of human behavior. Furthermore, the experimental situation may not be like situations in real life, and conclusions covering behavior outside the laboratory cannot always be reached.

White rats and other animals are often used as experimental subjects in animal psychology laboratories because their performance gives us many clues which may be used to investigate human behavior in later studies. Just as the medical profession uses first animals and then human subjects for experiments before drawing conclusions about the use of certain drugs, so also psychologists often study both animal and human subjects before generalizing from subhuman to human behavior, especially with complex behavior which involves learning. Animal studies may provide clues to human behavior, and animals are easily controlled subjects whose environment can easily be manipulated. However, the results obtained must be tested on human beings before they can be confidently applied to human behavior by psychologists, educators, and others.

The clinical method

Clinical methods are used in the analysis and treatment of behavior problems of all kinds, ranging from the school difficulties of children to the marital difficulties of adults. The clinical psychologist frequently uses standard tests to diagnose the problem, reconstructs the individual's life story through a series of interviews, and gathers additional information about him from persons who have known him. On the basis of all the dependable information he can get, from whatever sources, he then formulates a program of therapy or treatment and follows up the patient as long as may be necessary.

Clinical methods are often applied by teams of trained investigators working in different areas of psychology to study a problem in human behavior as it is reflected in one or a group of subjects. One such study (2) was made to discover whether mentally retarded children vary more than normally developing children in the emotionality with which they face unfamiliar learning situations. That is, the investigators posed to themselves the question: Do the mentally retarded tend to feel inadequate in learning situations and approach such situations with emotional stress? If so, does this increased emotionality interfere with the children's efficiency in learning the task? Does an attempt to relieve emotional stress improve learning efficiency? How do the mentally retarded children compare with normally developing and gifted children in these respects?

One of the problems was to discover the usual level of emotionality of all the subjects — retarded, normal, and gifted. Another was to determine whether any of these children were emotionally disturbed from causes other than those attributable to the learning situation. Did the subjects have realistic ideas of their own abilities? Did they approach learning situations with confidence, fear, anger, or frustration?

A first step in this study was to gather clinical information about all the subjects, making an effort to determine why the mentally retarded children *were* mentally retarded. In order to assess personal adjustment, adequacy of the self-concept, and the general level of confidence of the children, as well as their approach to new situations, psychologists assessed the mentally retarded chil-

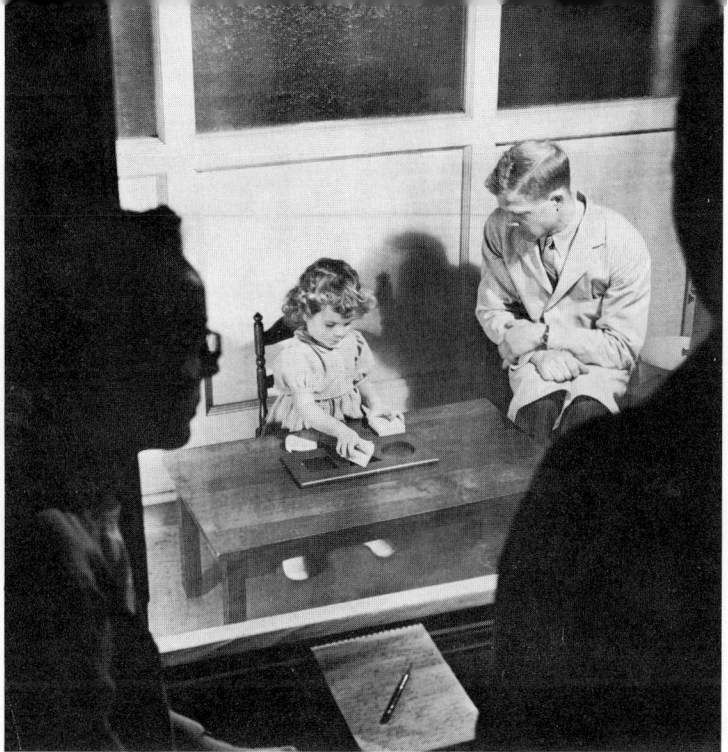

The clinical method. *This method of investigation frequently uses observation of behavior to gain information for use in diagnosis and therapy. Important aspects of this method are interviews and testing. (Edmund Gerard.)*

dren, using interviews, figure drawings, and the Rorschach test in which the subject responds to a number of ink blots. To gain a better understanding of the reasons for the mental retardation, medical examinations were given and the children's family backgrounds were investigated. To get a better understanding of the child's habitual approach to learning situations, records of achievement and teacher ratings were employed. To learn about the emotionality of the children in new learning situations, the galvanic (electric) skin response was measured. To make sure that the learning situations involved in the study were new to the children, especially devised tasks in arithmetic were developed. Intelligence was assessed by use of the Wechsler Intelligence Scale for Children (see chapter 9.)

Thus this clinical study required investigators representing various areas of specialization to work together in securing complete clinical information to answer what might appear to be quite simple questions: Do mentally retarded children learn inefficiently in part because of becoming emotionalized when presented with a novel learning task? Can relieving the mentally retarded child of emotional stress improve his learning efficiency? Some controlled experimentation was, of course, needed within the clinical study to arrive at answers to these questions, but without the clinical information the investigator could not adequately describe his subjects in the first place.

Opinion sampling

The information in the Kinsey reports (3, 4) on the sexual behavior of human males and females was obtained mostly by interviewing subjects. Such informa-

Opinion sampling. *Accurate and useful information for psychological research is often provided by polls, opinion surveys, and other methods of discovering ideas and obtaining statements about behavior and attitudes.* (St. Louis Post-Dispatch, *from Black Star.*)

tion portrays current conditions, at least as far as these subjects are concerned, and supplies hypotheses for further study. Polls, opinion surveys, and other methods of discovering the ideas of people through obtaining their statements of their own behavior utilize large samples of the population. When carefully executed, this research provides accurate and useful information concerning facts and opinions at a given time. The accuracy of the information obtained depends on the frankness and willingness of the subjects to answer questions, their own knowledge of their attitudes and opinions, and their understanding of the meaning and intent of the questions. Further, people's opinions may change, even during the course of gathering the data, because of factors which the investigator does not know about or cannot control. Despite these difficulties, opinion sampling can increase our knowledge of human behavior. Opinions on such subjects as race, higher education, religion, politics, and many others can be reliably estimated by investigators who choose their samples scientifically. In this as in other kinds of psychological research, statistical methods are of great importance.

Other methods

Special combinations of observation, interviewing, clinical methods, and laboratory techniques are known as the *longitudinal* and *horizontal* methods of study. The former studies its subjects over a period of years, while the latter reports on a group of subjects at a given point in time. Terman's (5) study of gifted persons was longitudinal in that it followed about 1,000 persons from childhood through middle age. A variety of techniques was used, including tests, interviews, questionnaires, clinical data, and analyzing the information by statistical techniques. Because of the span of time covered, this method discovers relationships among such factors as intelligence, achievement, and emotionality in childhood, adolescence, and adulthood. The chief difficulty of the method is following up the experimental subjects in a population which is becoming increasingly mobile.

A typical horizontal study (6) ascertained the factors that influenced choice of career among a group of prospective teachers who were college sophomores at the time. It was found that those who planned to enter elementary teaching were mainly interested in working with children, whereas those who planned to teach in high schools were primarily interested in a major subject field. By this method questionnaires and interviews yield the desired information quickly, but it is not particularly useful in discovering the causes of behavior or controlling it. Many psychological studies employ a combination of experimental, observational, and clinical methods.

WHAT CAN YOU EXPECT FROM PSYCHOLOGY?

You may well ask, at the beginning of this course, what you can expect to get from the study of psychology. Will it help you to solve your own problems? Will it help you to understand other people better? Will it help you get along with others, and succeed in the world? Of course, it is impossible to answer these questions precisely, partly because a good deal of the answer depends on you. If you apply the principles of psychology as you learn about them to your own situations and problems, and try to evaluate yourself clear-sightedly in the light of what you learn, the chances are that psychology will help to increase your understanding of both yourself and others. But don't expect miracles. If you hope that all your troubles will suddenly evaporate, you are in for disappointment. If you expect that you will learn to see so deeply into the motives and emotions of others that all your problems of personal relations miraculously disappear, be assured that they won't. And if you think you are going to learn so much about other people that you can manipulate them for your own purposes, that won't happen either. But *within reason,* if you study intelligently, you should make real headway in all the fundamental aims of psychology. These are:

To understand human behavior, both your own and that of others;

To describe that behavior in precise and objective language;

To predict human behavior, especially your own, on the basis of what you have learned of the principles of psychology; and

To control human behavior particularly in the sense of improving your own, by the application of these principles.

As you have noticed, this book bears the title, *Psychology in Theory and Practice.* The chief subject on which you will be asked to "practice" is yourself, in relation to your life in college and in after years. It is our aim to help you make the most of both. The first three chapters, as practice, deal mainly with your own adjustment to college life and the problems it raises. These are, in a sense, first aid. The remainder of the book is more concerned with the principles of psychology — though practice is never far from the center of our attention and concern.

REFERENCES

1. J. Stanley and H. Klausmeier, "Opinion Constancy after Formal Role Playing," *J. Soc. Psychol.,* 1957, 46, pp. 11–18.
2. T. A. Ringness, "A Study of the Relationships between Emotional Reactions to Learning Situations and Learning Efficiency of Mentally Retarded Children" (in progress under support from the United States Office of Education, Department of Health, Education, and Welfare).
3. A. C. Kinsey, W. B. Pomeroy, and C. E. Martin, *Sexual Behavior in the Human Male,* Saunders, Philadelphia, 1948.
4. A. C. Kinsey, W. B. Pomeroy, C. E. Martin, and P. S. Gebhart, *Sexual Behavior in the Human Female,* Saunders, Philadelphia, 1953.
5. L. M. Terman and M. Odom, *The Gifted Child Grows Up,* Stanford Univ. Press, Stanford, 1947.
6. H. Klausmeier, A. Luker, and S. Stromswold, "Factors Affecting Choice of Teaching Career among College Sophomores," *J. Educ. Res.,* 1951, 45, pp. 24–32.

PART ONE •

PSYCHOLOGY AND

STUDENT LIFE

Psychology in the

College Setting

Is college life what you thought it would be? Are you getting everything you want from college? Not everyone can say "Yes" to these questions. Yet you, and many students like you, are in the midst of experiences which can influence your lives for happiness and success, both now and in the future. Going to college is one of the most important series of experiences you will ever have, and a great deal depends upon your making the most of your college years — which may be the final years of your formal education. You are presented with a challenge of the highest order. We hope you accept this challenge with enthusiasm.

Increasing numbers of young men and women are graduating from high school. Many of them go on for higher education. More and more they are finding that a college education is valuable for various reasons — personal, social, and economic. Higher education is more than ever able to provide opportunities for young people to achieve the important life-goals of understanding the world we live in, understanding ourselves, learning about social groups, and learning how to deal with the many problems characteristic of a rapidly changing society like ours. The rapid changes in our whole civilization lead not only to better opportunities for each succeeding generation but also to more problems and more intense conflicts in personal adjustment and group living.

This book was written to help college students get more from their college living and also to help them form a basis for more useful and happy lives in the future when, as parents and citizens, they take their places in the communities in which they will live. Some college students will be more happy

16

Meeting the Challenge of College Life

In what ways are the demands of college greater than those of high school? What are some of the problems you may meet in college? How can psychology help you to understand yourself and others? What are the steps in solving a problem? How can this book help you to attack some of the biggest problems of college life and begin to achieve some of your major goals?

and successful than others, of course, but *all* can learn principles and ideas which will help them come closer to achieving their life-goals. The study of psychology can provide some of these principles and ideas. Is such study necessary? Let us look at some students you may know.

Sue is preparing to become a teacher. She finds classes interesting, she studies hard and makes good grades. She finds her instructors interesting and friendly, and she enjoys her relationships with other students. Her roommates are congenial, and she likes to be with them. Boys ask her for dates and most of them are "smooth." Sue is finding college life stimulating and rewarding in practically every way. It is everything she dreamed it would be, and just as her parents hoped it would be for her; for Sue was always a happy person, meeting life with enthusiasm, poise, and intelligence.

Jean, too, is a high-spirited, popular college freshman. She never seems to lack friends, and her days are a round of social activities — pleasant meetings on campus, in the library, or at the coffee shop. Being bright, Jean does not have to study hard to get good grades. Her social "know-how" enables her to make the best possible impressions on her fellow students and on her instructors.

But early in life Jean suffered family disappointments. Her mother remarried and Jean has not felt part of the new family group. Her stepfather not only seems unable to understand Jean but fails to provide a pleasant and secure home for her mother and her younger brother. Jean has seen that managing a home and bringing up children are not as easy as they sometimes appear to be, and she doubts her own ability to do it successfully. Although she is popular,

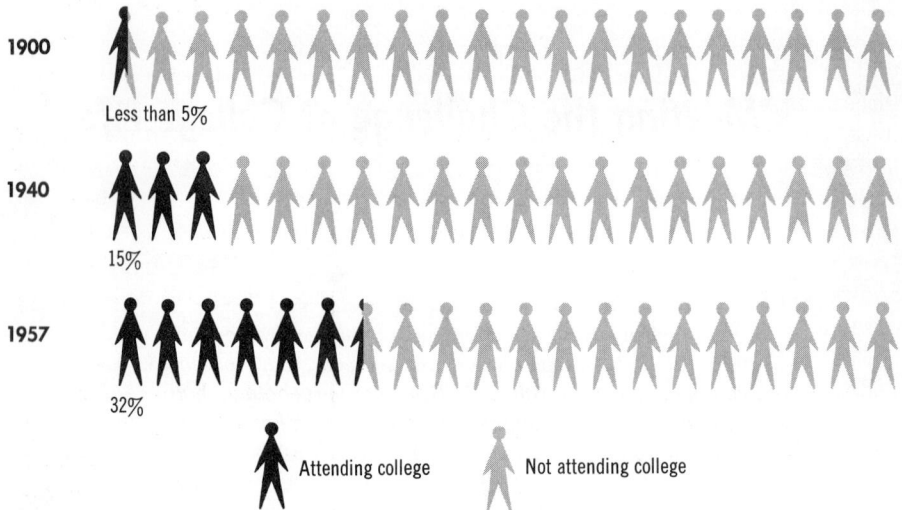

College attendance. *The percentage of young people attending college has increased markedly since 1900. In 1958 there were more than 3 million students in college. Record-breaking enrollments should continue until about 1965, when the greatest number of "war babies" will be of college age. (Statistics from Office of Education, U.S. Department of Health, Education, and Welfare.)*

Jean thinks she may never marry. She may not have had this thought consciously, but she does not date any one boy very long. She seems to distrust them all.

As for Peter, he studies incessantly. He is not a brilliant student, but his hard work and willingness to plug away at a tough job have carried him through school thus far. Peter never has found much time to play. His parents prize a college education and have pushed him to get good grades. He has a scholarship to college, but his keeping it depends on his ability to maintain a high average; and since his work is harder now than it was in high school, Peter is not sure he will be able to keep his scholarship. Besides, he isn't quite sure that so much study is really worth the effort.

Harry, as a freshman, would have been good enough to make the varsity football team if the rules permitted. He has more than his share of good looks, good health, plenty of money to spend, and the good wishes and help of the coaches. Anyone would think Harry had about everything he could desire.

But Harry's teammates could tell you that he can't seem to settle into college life. Keeping him eligible is a coach's nightmare. He doesn't date or go to parties, either. He says he doesn't feel at home in his college and probably will leave after this year. Harry is not too sure what he will do then — maybe take a job, or join the Army, or try another college. More than anything else, he is homesick.

So, if we can judge by the lives of these four people, it looks as if getting a college education is not as simple as merely doing the assignments and taking part in college activities. It has been estimated that about one out of every three high school graduates enters a college or a university, but only half of these young people ever get college degrees. Many young men and women find college a means to a happy and more useful life, but for too many others difficulties arise. Some have financial problems. Others have academic difficulties. Illness, marriage, jobs, and military service cause many to withdraw. Lack of success with their studies causes some to lose interest in college life and perhaps to feel that the things they are studying are not valuable enough to warrant their staying in college. Some find that their social expectations are not realized, and give up in disappointment.

Why do students encounter these difficulties or need to change their plans after they enter college? How is going to college different from going to high school? Why do almost half of the entering college freshman fail to graduate? How can you learn most from your college experiences? And how can psychology help you?

● A. COLLEGE LEARNING AND MATURITY

In many respects college life is like other ways of living, for you naturally will be carrying on the functions of eating, sleeping, breathing, and the other biological processes. As in high school, you will study and take part in certain social activities. You will have friends and belong to different groups. It is not so much that college life is completely new as that *college demands changes in the ways you see yourself and your surroundings.* As in any change of locale you will find some completely new experiences; nevertheless, you will

Percentage of college students who graduate. *Note how many students fall by the wayside, and how few transfer. (Office of Education, U.S. Department of Health, Education, and Welfare.)*

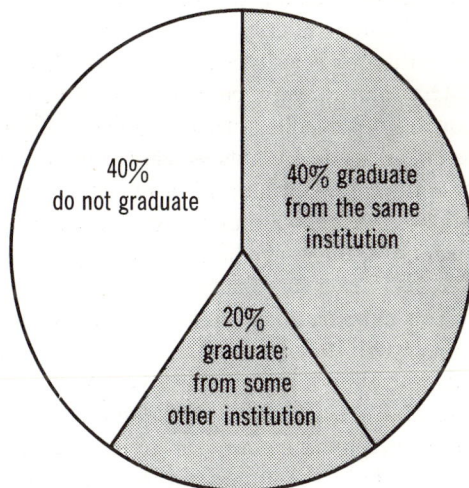

40%
do not graduate

40% graduate
from the same
institution

20%
graduate
from some
other institution

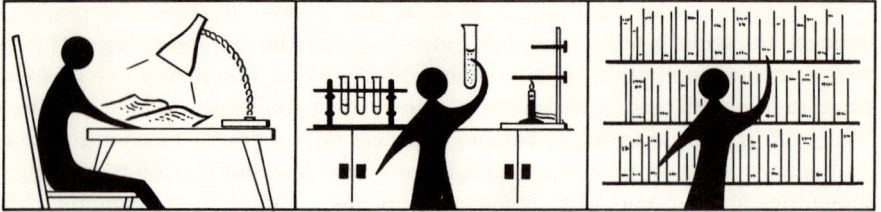

Learning on your own. *In individual activities such as study or extra library research, you must take the responsibility for success or failure. No one will tell you when to do certain tasks or even demand that you do them. What you achieve is up to you.*

be your old familiar self all along. Is that self going to be adequate to this new environment? Let us look at some differences between college and high school.

College studies are usually more demanding. Much more than in high school you can extend your knowledge in almost any field you choose — English, foreign languages, science, social science, music, art — any area in which your college offers instruction. But because you are more mature than you were in high school (and because you are with more mature people) you will be expected to learn more "on your own." You will have the privilege of working with your college library, laboratories, and instructors (who are likely to be specialists of stature in their fields), and all these resources can give you a better understanding of the physical and social world you live in. You will have the opportunity to go more deeply into subjects which interest you and to cultivate a broader view of their relationships to other fields. In college, perhaps more than in any other environment, you will have the chance to increase your creative abilities and to come into contact with newer and more stimulating ideas and modes of thought. You may lay a basis for making a real contribution to our society through a career for which college can prepare you. Many would say that this is one of the greatest opportunities of a college education and perhaps the most worthwhile goal you can strive for.

One aim of your college education is to develop your ability to learn by yourself after college days are over. Another is to enable you to examine different ideas and points of view, not merely to provide you with specific skills or information. The ability to get ideas from people and books, and then to think these ideas through to your own conclusion, is perhaps one of the greatest accomplishments in life. If you are to be successful in your chosen career, it is also necessary that you be able to communicate your ideas to others, and so you must be able to write and speak clearly and efficiently. Your reading in college will be broad, not confined to a single textbook. You should learn to be thoughtful and independently critical in your acceptance of the authors' views. The ability to organize your thinking, reading, writing, and speaking is for all these reasons immensely important. Finally, the ability to apply your ideas to life will help you immeasurably toward success.

College associations can enrich life. You often hear people speak of friendships made during college days. In examining autobiographies of juniors and seniors in college, the authors of this text have found that many students believe living in a dormitory, taking part in clubs and social organizations, and assuming responsibilities in academic groups have proved as valuable to them as many of their classes. As a case in point, we quote from Mary's autobiography:

> Since I have come to the University I have become close with several of my previous high school friends and have also gained more good friendships through my sorority, not only in the one I belong to, but in many others. Through these associations I have learned the value of true friendship and what one expects from a real friend. The real friends are the ones who are willing to help you, the ones you can help, too, and trust. I have met people from all over the country and other countries and from all types of homes. From these associations I have come to realize some of the things which mean so much to me.

While you may or may not agree with everything Mary says, you probably will agree that friendships and social contacts should play an important part in your college life.

But you have not had time to develop friendships yet, for you are new to the campus, and social conditions there are different from those you knew before. For some students the campus represents a smaller social group than did their high school. For others, college is a larger and more heterogeneous society. Everyone finds a *new* group, in which he must start afresh to make his way; and entering a new social group is often disconcerting. Other students may seem already to have friends and to know their way around. They may seem to be organized and ready for work or play. But the new student may feel he is "just a number," especially after standing in line to register or buy books. College authorities recognize these problems and try to make every new student feel at home; so they have counseling systems, advisers, New Student Week, and mixer parties. Of course, in the last analysis responsibility for getting acquainted rests with the student himself — that is, with *you*. If you wait to receive personal invitations to the mixers or other all-student activities, you are likely to wait unnoticed. Actually, students are a friendly lot, and, if you are willing to take some initiative, you can readily make new friends.

College requires greater maturity. High school students are often called "boys" or "girls," but college students are known as young "men" or "women." Only a summer's vacation usually separates the college freshman from the high school senior, yet the high school boy or girl and the college man or woman are considered as people in two different stages of maturity. This indicates that the students, too, should regard themselves in a different way. Others recognize that college students have taken a step toward adult freedom and its accompanying adult responsibilities, and students should also be aware of this change in their status. Many college students accept this step as a matter of course.

College students are treated as responsible adults in nearly all respects. Yet no college can permit students to do entirely as they please, for colleges have responsibilities to parents and to the public for their students' health, morals, and attention to studies. Most students are able to manage their own affairs and most colleges foster the development of independence and responsibility. Yet in any group of new and untried students there may be some irresponsible people. Some may not have been away from home before, and many will not be legally "of age." For these reasons some regulations must be set up to protect everyone, just as it is necessary to have local or state laws.

Consider for a moment the idea of adult freedom. In college one's personal life is treated as his own. Unless he gets in trouble, he will not be asked how he spends his leisure time or his money, where he eats, or whether he has dates. He need not be in a study hall, as he was required to be in high school. Whether he gets passing marks is entirely up to him, and his instructors will not hound him to do better work. The student's freedom to come and go, work or play, loaf or study, is much greater than ever before.

But freedom entails responsibility. If the college does not prescribe study halls, neither can it permit academic standards to be lowered. If the college does not supervise finances, neither can it permit unpaid library accounts. If it does not prescribe uniform clothing, neither can it permit flagrant violation in dress, for the college is judged by the public according to the actions of the student body. In the minds of the townspeople *you* represent the college. Your behavior affects enrollment, job placement of graduates, and the budget.

The college student has an enviable place in society. In the minds of many the stamp of such an institution conveys a sort of authority upon the bearer. His words are considered more weighty and his opinions more valuable than before he entered college. His behavior is copied by younger people. He is considered to have some understanding of moral and social issues and is expected to take an active interest in community problems.

To help students reach the maturity these expectations imply, many colleges emphasize the high quality of the student body. Thus students may be carefully selected for admission. In most colleges students are admitted as freshmen on the basis of high school grades. Some colleges use entrance examinations to select their students and also to help the students plan their course work. And as you know, all through high school the students who find the work very difficult tend to drop out before graduation, so that only above-average students are likely to enter college. The academic company you are now in has much greater ability than any you have been in before, and you will have to work harder to get marks as high as those you got in high school.

Your classmates are likely to be interested in the things that are learned at your college. There will be students who enjoy reading difficult books or solving very abstract mathematical problems. Many will have well-formed ideas of the careers they wish to follow and will have begun to specialize to that end; their interest in their work is more than superficial. More and more you will be working with students who like the things they are studying and who seek learning experiences beyond the minimum assignments.

College students often come from families that prize higher education and are willing to make sacrifices to provide it for their children. Many students come from homes of considerable culture. Some desire more than mere training to help them make a living or prepare for a specific career. Rather, they wish also to learn a better way of life and do not insist that all their studies be "practical." Some have done serious reading and thinking, have traveled, had jobs, or engaged in hobbies and sports requiring concentrated effort. Many students are earning part or all of their college expenses.

Generally, every college student has some well-developed interest or skill; but college work requires *many* interests and skills, especially during the first two years when there are requirements to be met in several subject-matter areas. In this way a college education not only provides opportunities for developing the student's mature self but also demands that he be grown up enough to see himself in a larger perspective — to relate himself to many fields of knowledge and, in the process, become a better-informed and more self-reliant person.

Suggested activities

1. Think back to your anticipations of college. Compare the ideas you had with your first impressions after arriving on campus. What impressed you most vividly? How is your college life different from your high school life?

2. Are you satisfied that you are getting acquainted as quickly as you wish? Discuss some techniques you have seen your classmates use for getting acquainted on campus.

3. What activities does your college provide? How do you go about joining them? (See your student handbook, the college catalog, etc.)

4. List your most pressing college problems. Can you classify them? Is your list similar to that of other students?

5. Keep a list of problems currently bothering you. Later in the semester, look back over this list. At that time you may wish to ask yourself whether your problems are still the same and what steps you have taken to solve them.

6. Where in your college can you get help with your academic problems? Your social problems? Financial aid? Family difficulties? Health needs? Job counseling? (See your student handbook, the catalog, etc.)

A.   COLLEGE LEARNING AND MATURITY

● B.   PROBLEMS OF ADJUSTMENT

Most, if not all, college graduates will tell you that their college education did help them to learn more efficiently, to develop social skills, and to manage their lives better. Of course, not all who started as freshmen graduated, and many of those who did graduate encountered some of the adjustment problems common to young adults. Another area in which college can help is in learning to adjust to life in different environments. Let us examine some of the more typical problems of adjustment encountered by college students.

Such problems may relate to our goals, our attitudes, and our emotions. They embody difficulties we face in trying to achieve our individual aims and satisfy our needs while we are trying at the same time to meet the demands of society. There are available data on many problems which college students bring to their counselors. The list can be made very long, but you can get a good idea of the scope of actual student difficulties from the following illustrations.

Lack of plans: "I imagine my problems represent those of most any other person in my circumstances and at my age. I am nearing the age of twenty, and although I realize that having no definite plans for the future is not a catastrophe, it leaves me with a sense of insecurity. At times I believe I should like to be a career woman in business. At other times, a business education teacher. And at still other times my mind wanders off into other areas I think might interest me."

Social relationships: "One of my biggest problems is moodiness. I am always very, very happy or very, very sad. When I am sad and crabby I know that I am jumping on everyone, but that doesn't help any. I have always been this way."

Dating: "Dating bothers me to some extent, but I sometimes feel abnormal because I have no overpowering desire to date. I am interested in my work and in my family at home, yet I feel I should have social life here too."

Insecurity: "I feel that one of my biggest problems has been, and still is, having too many responsibilities piled on me all at once. When I was fifteen I lost my parents and I was left with a ten-year-old sister. From then on, although I was under age, I was forced to make decisions for my sister and myself. It put me under a severe strain and I was constantly wondering whether the decisions I made were the best ones."

Being liked: "One of my most pressing problems is the feeling that the majority of people I associate with don't like me, even though I try to be friendly with them. I have no confidence in what I do; therefore I am always expecting the worst. I feel extremely shy in many situations and have a difficult time thinking of the right things to say to people, even though I want to make a good impression."

Codes of conduct: "My biggest problem is my roommate's attitude toward smoking and drinking. She thinks that no girl under any conditions should smoke or drink. We can't have certain mutual friends because they smoke. She doesn't like them and won't associate with them. Yet she and I are very good friends and like to room together."

Other problems are frequent — family, studies, finances, military service, health. Nearly all students appear at some time or other to have a problem to discuss with the counselor or with their friends.

A common denominator in these problems is that each comes about in a particular situation in which an individual interacts with his social and physical environment. For example, Mary may have found her last year in a small high school most satisfying in every way — family life, friends, school, religion, and recreation. Now, at college, in a different environment, she may experience an adjustment problem stemming from a change in *any* of these areas. This brings us to a discussion of ways in which *psychology* can be of service.

    A.   COLLEGE LEARNING AND MATURITY
    B.   PROBLEMS OF ADJUSTMENT

● C. PSYCHOLOGY AS AN AID TO ACHIEVEMENT

The word "psychology" probably means something a little different to every one of us. It may be just a vague word you have heard somewhere, or it may be a term you use to describe an understanding of yourself and others. It may suggest a technique for getting others to do your will, or it may represent a vigorous laboratory discipline. Regardless of what the word means to you, psychology has some effect upon your life. Your study of psychology can aid you in achieving your most important goals in life.

Psychology is the science of human behavior. Psychology seeks to understand the relationships of man to his environment — what man can do, how he does it, and why he does it. Inherent in such an inquiry is the necessary attempt to understand human habits, attitudes, abilities, and motives. The psychologist wants to know what we inherit and what we learn. The nature of intelligence, the ways in which we sense and perceive the world, how we learn and remember, and how personality develops are interesting questions to psychologists. Why are some people in good mental and emotional health while others are not? Psychology seeks the answers to these questions and many others like them.

As a science, psychology is related to certain other social sciences, such as sociology and anthropology, and to biology and other natural sciences. It makes some use of their knowledge and ideas, and it produces knowledge and ideas of its own. Let us see why that should be.

Consider any life situation; for example, sitting in the classroom. To it we bring our biological selves — our sense organs, our brains and nervous systems, and our muscles. We bring our needs for food, air, and rest. We also have with us our personalities, involving things we have learned — our ways of looking at situations, our social habits and desires, our purposes, goals, and values. We see that both the biological and the social sciences are already involved in understanding how we meet a given situation.

But the environment in which we find ourselves — in this case, the classroom — imposes certain controls on our behavior. We can either adjust to this environment or try to make it adjust to us; probably in most instances we work out some sort of compromise. In this environment are the instructor, the students, furniture, temperature, light, and ventilation — that is, both biological and social factors.

To understand human behavior then, we must try to understand the *interaction* of the various forces within and outside ourselves. The study of psychology is an attempt to reach this kind of understanding.

If we were in a classroom in Greenland, would we act as we do in a class in the United States? Is normal behavior there the same as it is here? To assess our behavior, we need to know something of *anthropology*. To measure it more accurately, we need to know something of the mathematics of *statistics*. To know whether it is normal or average we need to know something of the *value system* in which we find ourselves; here *philosophy* comes to our rescue.

Such studies are tremendously broad. Specialized areas within psychology have therefore been developed in order to bring some organization to the many questions asked and the researches that have been made. As we have seen, there are many areas within psychology, and more uses for this science are being found as time goes on. One may spend a lifetime as a professional worker in any one of these areas, and for such a career he needs extensive training and many specialized courses.

But as you know, this book is for all college students — not just for those who will have careers in psychology. How, then, can psychology be useful to the *typical* student?

Psychology applies techniques of problem-solving. One of the many contributions of psychology is the application of problem-solving techniques. Getting the most from college requires effective problem-solving. To get the most from studying this book, you must practice problem-solving all along the way. To get off to a good start, examine the following problem-solving activity:

John is about to fail a course even though he is working hard in it. He wishes to employ useful problem-solving techniques to help him get out of his difficulty. What may he do?

To begin with, we can say that "John is not passing the course." Have we identified the real problem? Probably not; such statements are often so broad that they are almost meaningless. If we were John, we might ask ourselves questions like these: "Do I fail my tests? Is my written work satisfactory? Do I contribute well to class discussions? Am I doing enough outside reading? Do I understand the aims of the course? The terms used?"

Let us assume that John has talked with the instructor and that, after thinking things over, he has defined his problem as "How can I improve my test scores?" We notice that even before he could pin his problem down, he had to gather some data. He did this through a conference with his instructor.

Now John can make some guesses (he can formulate hypotheses) about why he has trouble with tests and about possible ways to help himself. He can assume, if he likes, that he should read the text more carefully, and therefore he may resolve to spend more time studying. On the other hand, John may feel that he is being unfairly graded by the instructor and ought to complain. (Of course, John has little basis for forming hypotheses at this time, but he is attacking the problem

PSYCHOLOGY

BIOLOGY	Maturation and development	**PHILOSOPHY**
CHEMISTRY	Learning Perception	**ART**
SOCIOLOGY	Thinking Communication	**MUSIC**
ANTHROPOLOGY	Emotion Motivation	**LITERATURE**
POLITICAL SCIENCE	Personality Intelligence	**SPEECH**
EDUCATION	Special abilities Group dynamics Mental illness	**HISTORY**

How psychology relates to other studies. *In the box are listed major areas of psychological investigation. Each of these areas — as well as psychology in general — has some relation to other college courses. Draw lines connecting related areas.*

as well as he can in the light of his past experience. He really needs more information.)

John decides to get out the tests which were handed back to him, and he looks them over carefully. He discovers that in several instances he has missed the question entirely, apparently because he misunderstood it. He also finds that in each test he failed to finish one or more of his answers. John can now make a new attack on the problem, formulating more hypotheses. He finds two that seem sensible: (1) "I write too much on some questions and therefore I never finish a test." (2) "I do not read the questions carefully and therefore do not really know what the instructor is after." As a possible solution he thinks, "I must organize my time better when taking a test, so that I can read the questions more carefully and write at least something in answer to each one."

Next John can take steps to see whether this solution is the correct one. In any case, he has learned something — he has discovered some possible solutions and will find which will and which will not work in his own case. He has gathered data which he did not have before. He has tried to interpret his situation, focusing on aspects which had not come to his attention before this problem arose.

If John's solution is correct, results will show it. If he gets better grades in future tests, his solution probably has merit. But if his grades do not improve he should continue to look for further data and try to form new hypotheses. He may, of course, find that his goal is unrealistic, that he does not have the ability to get high marks in this course. That too may be an important partial solution, and his problem will then be to set a goal consistent with his abilities.

We see that in the usual problem-solving situation it is necessary to work back and forth in our attempt to find a solution. We define and redefine our problem. We suggest answers and proceed to check them. Let us now take a closer look at the nature of problem-solving activity.

Problem-solving is essentially a form of learning activity. We have to learn the correct solution, the best behavior in a given set of circumstances. We may first have to discover what our problem really is, and then to gather data for its solution.

A problem does not arise until the way to some goal is blocked and the situation is recognized as a problem. Once this happens, the learner will try to interpret the situation and attack the problem in terms of his past experience. Some results — either positive or negative in terms of progress toward the goal — will occur. The learner will either then be satisfied (in which case learning activities will cease) or, if his results are negative, he will find it necessary to reinterpret the situation to find a basis for further attacks on the problem.

The steps in problem-solving may then be outlined as follows:

1. Progress toward a goal is blocked; a problem is found to exist.

2. The problem must be recognized and defined carefully, for it is necessary to discover the true nature of the problem.

3. Data to help solve the problem are either found at hand or specially gathered.

4. Tentative solutions (hypotheses) are formulated.

5. In terms of previous learning and present interpretation of the problem, one or more of the hypotheses is tried.

6. Results of the attack or attacks on the problem are noted. The solution may be found quickly, or it may be necessary to reinterpret the problem, re-examine the solution, gather more data, formulate and try more hypotheses.

7. Problem-solving activity ceases when the problem is solved, or when the learner accepts a substitute goal, or when he is so frustrated that he no longer attempts to find a solution. In the latter instance problems of an emotional

nature may arise. Thus, if problem-solving techniques are applied to daily living, they can be a valuable contribution to health and happiness.

Psychology develops principles of human behavior. It follows that another main value of psychology is that it develops principles useful in understanding one's own behavior and that of others. Again we present an overview of some of these principles so that you may begin to use them early in your study:

1. *The mature individual for the most part controls his own destiny within the broad limits set by his culture.* For example, Bill likes football and engineering. His previous education and activities provide an excellent background for each. He has the needed abilities to become a teacher of physical education and a coach, or to become a good engineer. He can hardly become both. In our society Bill should make his own decision. He may wish advice from parents, vocational counselors, or others, but the decision should be his own.

What cultural limitations might affect his decision? One very common limitation is that of military service. This may or may not seriously affect Bill's decision and his progress toward his goal, but, in any case, required military service limits Bill's freedom to decide on how he will use a portion of his life and in this respect limits the scope of his decision-making.

2. *Most, if not all, behavior of mature persons is purposeful, and everyone does at a particular time what he thinks is best for him at that time.* Again, consider Bill's situation. After weighing the evidence, he decides one way or the other, and the question uppermost in his mind is what is best for him. Having made a decision, Bill works purposefully toward achieving the goal he has set for himself.

Of course, time may prove that Bill acted unwisely. Hindsight is often better than foresight. But Bill must learn not to regret having made wrong decisions at various times during his life if, in view of the knowledge and experience available at those times, he acted as well as he was able.

One of the purposes of studying psychology, then, is to provide sounder bases for making whatever decisions must be made throughout life.

3. *Living in modern times presents the mature individual with frequent problems of adjustment, some of which may be threatening to him.* Bill had to decide between two goals — preparing for a career in teaching and coaching, or for a career in engineering. Both these goals were attractive to him. Having to decide between the two may have been something of a threat to Bill, because he may have felt that either choice would force him to give up something else he desired. If military service should actually prevent Bill from achieving his goal, he would probably see such service as threatening also.

Making decisions often forces an individual to face unpleasant situations in which he feels threatened. Learning how to overcome the fear of such situations is a necessary accomplishment of the mature individual.

4. *The mature individual uses a variety of techniques in dealing with*

threatening problems of adjustment. Jean, who was discussed at the beginning of this chapter, does well with her classes. She has many social activities and is popular with friends and teachers. But because of her earlier home life, she has a strong distrust of men. She recognizes that in our culture marriage is keenly desired by most young women. This leads her to date frequently, but not with the same boy for very long at a time. Jean recognizes the situation as threatening, so she always withdraws before she can be seriously hurt by falling in love and marrying. Other girls might use different techniques if they perceived the situation in the same way. One might not date at all; another might date quite steadily, then "break up" and thus deliberately hurt the young man; still others might immerse themselves in intellectual work.

Perhaps you are beginning to see that behind certain behavior there may be hidden reasons and motives. A person may not always know why he behaves as he does, but always inherent in his actions is the principle that one does what seems to be best for himself. To others his behavior may appear unintelligent, wrong, or immature. But if we make such judgments quickly without first trying to see further into what is behind his behavior, we may never really understand him.

5. *The response which the mature individual makes to a situation results from what he has learned previously, from his analysis of the situation, and from his interpretation of the consequences of his response.* Why does Jean respond as she does? In part, because of what she has learned in life at home, in part, because of the way she interprets dating, and in part, because of what she thinks may be the result of falling in love and marrying. It is entirely possible that Jean, hurt deeply in earlier life, sees in the present situation the danger of being hurt again by a man; yet she wishes to continue dating in the hope of overcoming her distrust. She may consciously try to forget some of her unhappy home experiences, and she may be partly successful. Though this mode of reacting to previous experiences may prove successful in relieving the threat some of the time, it will probably not be successful for an extended period.

Thus our attempt to understand Jean will be more successful if we can understand her previous experiences and how she feels about them. If we know how she relates her past to her present experiences, how she views the present situation, and what she thinks may come of her present behavior, we shall begin to understand her better.

6. *The mature individual can to some extent modify his behavior.* Just how much a young adult can do so is unknown, but it is certain that some college students can and do change their attitudes about economic, social, political, and religious matters. Some learn to study more effectively, to make wise decisions on a variety of problems, and to build physical and mental skills of a higher order.

But can a person who has been severely injured in an automobile accident ever feel perfectly safe in a car again? Can a person who has been knocked down by a bolt of lightning ever feel comfortable in a thunderstorm? Can a person who has been rejected by his playmates as a child ever give and receive affection freely among adult friends? The answer to these questions is that some people can and some cannot. The extent to which an individual can modify his behavior is an individual matter. Generally the person who has been brought up at home and in school with the emphasis on being ready to accept changes and modify his behavior is more flexible than one who has developed in a more rigid environment. Since a more flexible person has at his command a variety of techniques for meeting any situation, we can conclude that the more mature person is one who is trying to attain this sort of flexibility.

We have seen that psychology can help us with problem-solving, and can provide us with a set of principles to help us understand human behavior. It offers other benefits, too. Techniques for specific situations — such as studying — can be of immediate help. Questions may be raised by some of the findings we present to you, and you may even find yourself embarking on a career in one or another of the areas of psychology. This book, we hope, will help you in some, if not in all, of these ways.

A. COLLEGE LEARNING AND MATURITY
B. PROBLEMS OF ADJUSTMENT
C. PSYCHOLOGY AS AN AID TO ACHIEVEMENT

● **D. THE PLAN OF THIS BOOK**

During each quarter or semester, especially during his freshman year, the student must accomplish certain tasks. He must manage his work so that he passes his courses with satisfactory grades; he must meet new instructors and classmates and profit from social experiences; he must gain a better understanding of himself as a college student so that he can make wise decisions. In Chapters 2, 3, and 4 of this text, each of these areas is surveyed so that you may have the opportunity to apply important principles to accomplishing these tasks and so that you may intelligently tackle the problems you meet.

In Part Two, "Psychology and the Individual," the purpose is to develop a more complete understanding of learning, so that you may realize your academic goals. Because the authors of this book fully realize that some students may find it necessary to change goals at one time or another during college, the intent here is not only to supply information and principles to those who will complete four years of college work, but also to assist those who do much of their adult learning outside the college environment. In Chapter 5, we study the ways in which learning occurs. In Chapter 6, the learning process is examined in further detail, with special attention to sensing and perceiving, while Chapter 7 takes up thinking and communicating. Chapter 8 deals with motivation and the emotions, and Chapter 9 gives information about intelligence and various abilities.

Part Three, "Psychology and Society," will aid you in understanding group living and may help you to achieve some of your important social goals. Chapter 10 discusses the kinds of human needs which can be met only in social groups. Chapter 11 brings in some of the more recent information concerning group dynamics, public opinion, and group leadership. Chapter 12 deals with the role of psychology in society.

Part Four, "Psychology and Your Future," examines three areas: building and maintaining mental health, planning for the future, and developing a life philosophy.

Throughout the book, the authors have deliberately chosen to report studies dealing with human behavior, particularly those in which college students have been the subjects. While much of the controlled experimentation in psychology has taken place in animal laboratories and many of the best designed experiments have utilized animals, there has been enough investigation of human behavior to provide an adequate body of psychological information for our purposes. The student who plans to take further courses in psychology will find it useful to supplement his study by reading the reports of investigations in the areas in which he is most interested.

Throughout this book we shall attempt to help you examine possible goals you may set for yourself, problems you may encounter on your way to these goals, and ways to achieve your goals and overcome your problems. For the most part we shall cite for further reading psychological investigations which provide evidence about human beings in situations much like your own.

In using this book it is suggested that you, the student, (*a*) read the questions at the beginning of each chapter so that you will see the purposes for which it is written; (*b*) read the text material, asking yourself about its meaning, vocabulary, and implications for everyday life, and writing down questions that arise from your thinking; (*c*) try to recite to yourself the basic ideas of each section of a chapter and then re-read to check your recitation; (*d*) try the suggested activities, either in class or by yourself; (*e*) discuss with others the ideas presented in the chapters, raise questions, and do supplementary reading when possible.

Perhaps you would like to review this chapter with these suggestions in mind. Can you summarize this chapter? The headings were as follows:

> A. College Learning and Maturity
> B. Problems of Adjustment
> C. Psychology as an Aid to Achievement
> D. The Plan of This Book

Suggested activities

1. Summarize the rules and regulations of your college. In what ways do they reflect expectations of student maturity?

2. What is your complete program? In what ways are you providing for

general education? Professional education? Social education? What courses contribute to each? What activities?

3. Consider a problem you have met and (preferably) solved. Relate this to the problem-solving techniques discussed in this chapter.

4. Examine briefly some textbooks in professional courses in psychology — experimental, clinical, industrial, animal, etc. Compare them with the book you are now reading insofar as type of writing and kinds of research included are concerned.

5. Take any practical life situation. Show how physical, emotional, social, and intellectual aspects are present. Demonstrate the interaction of the individual with his environment. In what ways are heredity, learning, motives, and emotions involved?

Special project for the class

Here is a common college problem you may wish to discuss:

WHY COLLEGE ANYWAY?

At the cafeteria the other day, as a small group of girls lingered over their coffee, the conversation went something like this:

Sally: "You ask why we came to college? As a daughter of graduates of this college, I came to please my parents. Mother wanted me to come here because this is where she and Dad went to school and they want me to carry on the tradition. They think it's a very romantic sort of place — it's where they got engaged, you see. They think that college life for a girl ought to be a round of parties and dances and football games where you see your boy friend make the winning touchdown. And they told me to be sure to get some classes under Miss Kate. She's such a *lady*. I was supposed to take a lot of art and literature and music and things. But not so I could be an artist — just to get 'culture' with a capital C. College is a place, they think, where you get polish and make a lot of contacts So here I am."

Mary: "I can see their point, Sally, and I believe in gaining a cultural education too. In fact, that's my main interest in coming here. And I'm taking art and music and literature and drama and such things too. But I'm also taking science and history and economics — oh, not all at once, of course — and lots of different things. Getting a cultural education, to me, means getting to understand people, and the kind of country we live in, and getting to appreciate good things. And I think it means learning how to think and how to be creative. Yes, and getting interested in things you didn't even know about before. I spend lots of time just talking to people who know interesting things — and I don't mean gossip, either. I am fascinated in learning about myself, too. I guess it's true, isn't it, that there isn't anything as interesting to you as you yourself."

Joan: "Well, you can get a lot of education at dances and parties and social activities, too. Yes, and living in a dorm and being in organizations help. But to me, that is all frosting on the cake. I'm going to be a career girl. There's only one thing that counts when all is said and done, and that's your future occupation. I don't just want to make money. But I do want to learn to do some job well —

something I like and that interests me. I take a lot of satisfaction in doing a good job at something that is worth doing. My main purpose at college is to prepare for a profession. They do a good job of that here and you can always get a position when you graduate."

Carol: "I should say that all of you had good reasons. But you also have to learn what people are like. You have to develop a personality and social know-how. After all, what good is a doctor without a decent bedside manner? No patients. What good is it to be smart and well-rounded if you haven't any friends to talk to? No, for me, I've got to have a social education. Learn how to enjoy myself, meet people, get along in a group. And find ways to operate on committees so I can be a better community member. And I want to be happy — that's my main goal. But you can't do that without friends. So I stress activities and service organizations and clubs and so on. It pays off, too. You should see my calendar."

Helps for solving this problem

The problem has been well defined for you. We might state it in this way: "What are some possible goals of a college education?"

Several hypotheses have been suggested in the above conversation and you and your friends will undoubtedly have others. You need to check all these hypotheses, both in general terms and in terms of what they mean to you personally.

In the last analysis, a solution to this problem lies within the realm of philosophy — it is concerned to a great extent with your goals and values, and you will have to make your decisions in relation to the following questions, gathering data as needed:

a. What are the reasons for people's success or failure at their jobs? (See books on job counseling, etc.)

b. What is the likelihood that you will or will not work? What do statistics show about the number of women working? (See census reports, etc.)

c. Have segments of our society changed in their ways of living since the days of our parents? If so, how? Read such books as Frederick Lewis Allen's *Only Yesterday* and *Since Yesterday*.

Your classmates and you will probably come up with some general statements on what one should get from college. (To see how groups operate, watch how the discussion is handled by the leader and how various members contribute.)

But now you have some sub-problems:

a. Are the general class goals applicable to my personal situation?

b. Can this college satisfy my needs?

c. Is my schedule of classes and activities planned so that I can achieve my goals?

d. How can I improve my program? What activities shall I participate in?

It is possible that finding the answers to these questions will require the gathering of further data from sources such as college catalogs, freshmen hand-books, and other college publications.

Apply and check your solution. How? By examining from time to time your own ideas. Have your goals changed or are they the same? What evidence can you see of progress toward achieving your goals? Consider people's attitudes toward you, the knowledge you have gained, and the satisfactions you have achieved. If you haven't changed to some extent — for the better, we hope — maybe you aren't being educated!

SUGGESTIONS FOR FURTHER READING

Abstracting. The writings of psychologists include books, ranging from broad to narrow content, and articles in which research is reported or discussed, ideas are criticized, humorous anecdotes are presented, case studies are given, and many other treatments are used. Familiarity with psychological books and articles is useful in many ways: to gain an idea of the comprehensiveness and depth of the field, to read and evaluate various works critically, to discover points of view on many problems, to read original research reports rather than interpretations, to write correctly and concisely.

The suggestions for further reading listed at the end of each chapter in this book are a sampling of psychological works — some reports of research, some philosophical writings, some books, and some critiques. Some are more difficult to read and interpret than others and you may need the help of your instructor in interpreting the content. The listing includes recent writings appropriate for each of the chapters.

No one library is likely to have *all* of the books and articles we list. Further, no one student is likely to read all of those which may be available to him. But whatever one reads, the process of *abstracting* the information is useful. Abstracting is a process of getting the "meat" of the article into a condensed form, the length and form of abstract varying with the purpose of making it and the material read. Abstracts may be duplicated for the use of other class members or reported orally. Not only do they provide information, but they are also useful hints to determine whether one's purpose might be well suited by reading the entire original article from which the abstract was made.

The authors have found the following form for abstracting useful in their classes:

1. Identification of the book or article in correct bibliographical form.
2. A brief statement of the author's purpose in making the study.
3. A brief statement of the kind of study and procedure followed. This may include the setting for the study, number and description of subjects, methods of gathering and analyzing data.
4. A report of the findings of the study.
5. The significance of the study to *your* purposes or work.
6. *Your* evaluation of the study.

The points listed above refer to articles in which scientific or research studies are discussed. They may be modified to relate to other types of writings. Points 5 and 6 are not always used in professionally written abstracts which are usually informative rather than evaluative in nature.

A sample abstract follows:

Mull, Helen K., "The Ethical Discrimination of Various Groups of College Women," *J. Soc. Psychol.*, 1952, 35, pp. 69–72.

An experimental attempt to measure the improvement of social values during the four college years was undertaken by Mull. The study included 440 students in Sweet Briar College in the spring of 1950. Hollingsworth's Scale of Ethical Insight was used. The average scores for the classes on the test as a whole (perfect score being 100) were: seniors 81; juniors 79; sophomores 78; freshmen 73. The study, which is quite reliable, shows that there is a gain in ethical insight during the four years. How largely college education is responsible for this increase is not here determined, but it appears evident that it has some influence.

Several studies, thus far, have concluded that education is a vital factor in influencing people towards favorable attitudes. Further studies reviewed in this paper reveal that democratic attitudes, liberal viewpoints, and social values improve among college students as they progress through the college program.

Articles and Books.[1]

Cronbach, L. J., "The Meaning of Problems," *Supplementary Education Monographs*, No. 66, Univ. of Chicago Press, Chicago, 1948, pp. 32–43.

DeRidder, L. H., "Factors Influencing Probationary Students," *J. Higher Educ.*, 1954, 25, pp. 95–97.

Freedman, M. B., "The Passage Through College," *J. Soc. Issues*, 1956, 12, pp. 13–28.

Hanna, J. V., and A. Crossman, "The Problems of Freshmen Entering Washington Square College, New York University," *Counseling*, 1954, 7, pp. 2, 3.

Hilgard, E. R., *Introduction to Psychology*, Harcourt, Brace, New York, 1953, Chapter 1.

Hunter, E. C., "Attitudes of College Freshmen, 1934–1939," *J. Psychol.*, 1950, 30, pp. 281–296.

Jensen, R. E., "Student Feeling about Counseling Help," *Personn. Guid. J.*, 1955, 33, pp. 498–503.

Jervis, F. M., and R. G. Congdon, "Student and Faculty Perceptions of Educational Values," *Amer. Psychologist*, 1958, 13, pp. 464–466.

Karn, H. W., and J. Weitz, *An Introduction to Psychology*, Wiley, New York, 1955, Chapter 1.

Lowenstein, N., and V. Yates, "How Freshmen Feel about College," *Personn. Guid. J.*, 1955, 33, pp. 379–380.

[1] So that you may familiarize yourself with the standard abbreviations for scholarly journals which apply to your study of psychology, we are using them throughout our references and suggestions for further reading. In order to help you get acquainted with them, we have included a list of the full titles with their abbreviations at the end of the book. We suggest that you refer to this list during the early chapters until they become familiar.

Munger, P. F., and R. W. Goeckerman, "College Persistence of Upper- and Lower-Third High School Graduates," *J. Counseling Psychol.*, 1955, 2, pp. 142–145.

Rogers, C. R., "Persons or Science? a Philosophical Question," *Amer. Psychologist*, 1955, 10, pp. 267–278.

Smith, K. U., and W. M. Smith, *The Behavior of Man: Introduction to Psychology*, Holt, New York, 1958, Chapter 1.

Snygg, D., and A. W. Combs, *Individual Behavior*, Harper, New York, 1949, Chapters 1, 4.

Webster, H., "Changes in Attitudes During College," *J. Educ. Psychol.*, 1958, 49, pp. 109–117.

Wolfle, D., "Factors Determining Who Goes to College and Who Succeeds in College," in W. L. Layton, *Selection and Counseling of Students in Engineering*, Univ. of Minnesota Press, Minneapolis, 1954, pp. 3–21.

Effective Study

and Academic

Success

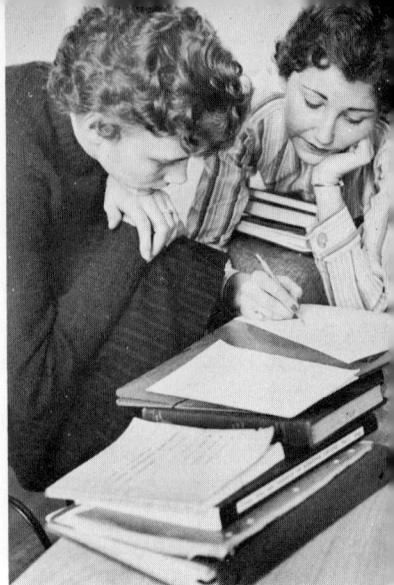

In Chapter 1 we saw that students come to college with some goals more clearly in mind than others. Each strives throughout his college career to attain his goals, both in and outside the classroom. Depending on his abilities and how he uses them, college may help the student with his total adjustment — in securing knowledge he might not otherwise gain and in becoming more at ease socially, more secure emotionally, and more adept physically. This chapter is aimed at helping you achieve success in perhaps the most important area of college life — in your various college courses.

According to a study conducted by Summerskill and Darling (1), many students are unsuited for academic life. They either do not get enough outside help or they do not help themselves. Records of 1818 students who enrolled as freshmen at Cornell University in September, 1948, were studied again in June, 1952. Forty per cent had left without graduating. Academic difficulties clearly led to about 25 per cent of the withdrawals; 50 per cent had received no "probation" or "warning" statements about low grades; and for the remaining 25 per cent, low grades may or may not have been a contributing factor. The percentages of women among the outright failures, inferior scholars, and non-participants in campus activities were disproportionately low, whereas the percentages of women among the non-academic withdrawals, superior scholars, and students in poor health were disproportionately high.

These figures indicate, among other things, that academic progress is not always smooth and easy. Applying the principles set forth later in this chapter will help you over the rough spots — but only you can apply them.

2

Making the Most of Your Time and Ability

What do you want from your college work? At what stage are you in deciding on a career? What are some conditions which make learning and study easier and more effective? How can you improve study techniques? Can you improve your reading ability? Do you take class notes which are helpful in studying for exams? What are the advantages of a time schedule?

What are some of the main problems in achieving academic success?

1. One problem is to decide what you want to learn; that is, what program of studies you will pursue and what you want to gain from each course.

2. Another is to maintain the necessary environment and motivation for effective learning.

3. A third is to develop techniques for efficient learning through reading, class work, and written work.

4. And a fourth is to plan and use your time wisely in study and in out-of-class activities including recreation, rest, earning money, and the like.

These problem areas are the subject of this chapter. As we look at them individually we shall see that some of them can be solved ahead of time through good advance planning, while others can be solved as one goes along.

● A. DECIDING YOUR PROGRAM OF STUDY

When does a student choose a career? The time of decision seems to vary. Bill wanted to become a chemist ever since he had his first general science studies in grade school. He eventually succeeded in becoming a good chemist and made significant contributions to our scientific knowledge. Henry, a college junior, has not yet chosen a specific career; but the liberal arts course he is pursuing, with major emphasis on political science, is fascinating to him. He is learning very efficiently. Arthur, another junior, is equally undecided about a career; he cannot seem to relate any of his college courses to a definite aim in life. Most of Arthur's courses are meaningless to him, and registration days are almost a source of dread. Then there is John, who was so undecided about a career that none of his work was interesting, and he finally dropped out of college entirely.

Generally, the student who has a fairly definite idea of the career he wishes to follow can more readily select a program of courses meeting his interest than one who has no definite aim. It is equally important, however, to note that some students, by following the suggestions of others, force themselves into a program leading to a career about which they know little and care less. College education is designed in great part to prepare you for a particular occupation — teaching, engineering, medicine, law, business — or for a variety of careers which are furthered by following a liberal arts or general college program.

It should be pointed out that, although a liberal arts education may serve as a foundation for careers, the immediate goal of some students of liberal arts is simply to become an educated person, i.e., to gain some knowledge of our Western culture. For such students, training for a career comes later, usually in graduate school.

If you have already decided upon a career. Though you may have known precisely the career for which you wish to prepare, even before entering college, you may find that during your first two college years there are so many required subjects that you have little time left for work in the area of your major interest. In many colleges and universities a large number of courses are required of everyone, regardless of future career. Everybody, for example, may be required to take a certain amount of English composition and literature. Other required courses may include science, mathematics, and social studies, as in high school. You may find that in your first two college years you have only one or two courses completely elective. However, within the entire four-year program, you will have considerable choice. Within the general areas of required courses some will be more appropriate for you than others. Take science, for example. If you are required to have three years of science, you can choose from chemistry, physics, physical geography, geology, botany, zoology, or other sciences which your college offers. Depending on your interests and talents, some of these will clearly be more useful and congenial than others.

Even if you have decided upon a career, then, you still must take required courses, at least within certain areas. You will be with students with other plans for a major course and with other careers in mind. What happens to students in these required courses?

You will have few problems if you try to relate the course content to your plans for a career or if you like to master facts and principles for the sheer pleasure of learning. If you have a reasonably adequate background and at least an average ability to learn you should have little difficulty. Thus a student intending to major in psychology may find English, science, and social studies of value to him as general background and can readily relate them to his career interests.

But what if you have trouble with those required courses? If we assume that your difficulty stems from lack of interest or inability to see the usefulness of these courses, there are things you can do to help yourself. Suppose, for example, you are a student preparing for medicine and find English composition dull and trite: You can go to a member of the medical staff to get his opinion on the usefulness of English in the practice of medicine. You can go to a medical journal to see how English is of use. You can go to a practicing physician and talk to him about the importance of good English in the profession. (After all, in your practice you will meet persons of culture who will immediately sense your cultural level.) It is easy to see how a subject which may at first seem to have little relationship to your career can actually be extremely valuable.

People who lack interest in what they are doing often fail. It is only natural that, if you fail to see value in a given course, you will tend to study it less and will find concentration difficult. In turn, being poorly prepared, failing to participate in class discussions, or listening inattentively to lectures leads to further lack of interest. We can take a tip from baseball. When a major-league player experiences a hitting slump, he does not usually quit practicing. On the contrary, he may practice more than ever and seek coaching aid to get him out of his slump. Many college students who find classes uninteresting have not done enough thinking to develop the background necessary for real interest. They may quit before they really get started. The solution is to work at courses which may originally seem dull, even if you must force yourself to do so. Very often, with more background and with success in your studies, the interest will develop.

The late Guy Sundt, successful university football coach and director of athletics at the University of Wisconsin, used to say to his athletes:

1. Never miss a class unless you are physically ill or otherwise officially excused.
2. Always go to your classes prepared to take a quiz on the assigned material.
3. There is not a course required of you in this university which will not make you a better man and athlete if you do your best in it.

This is good advice. One of the sound psychological facts about motivation is that we tend to like to do things we can do well. Good preparation, active class participation, and sound scholarship lead to success and make almost any class useful — and enjoyable as well.

If you thought you had decided upon a career but are now uncertain. Carol was sure that she wanted to become a physical therapist. Possessing a strong interest in children, a warm personality, and a keen desire to learn, she did well both in her studies and in her social activities. In her sophomore year Carol had her first chance to work in a hospital ward for physically handicapped children. She saw this as an opportunity to get started in the field of her choice.

Carol's coming was a joyful occasion for the children. She radiated hope and enthusiasm, and soon — under supervision, of course — she was massaging taut muscles, helping with corrective exercises, and teaching children to walk again. Carol was friendly with all and loved some of her patients deeply.

Unfortunately, not all children recover from serious physical handicaps. During the semester Carol learned that some would never be well again. Some might live only a few months, and others would be bedridden for years. One child with whom Carol was working grew worse steadily, and Carol was unable to help. She reacted as keenly as if she were the child's parent. She was deeply hurt — her interest in learning and living was dulled. She decided that she could not go through such experiences again because she became too deeply involved emotionally. She recognized that she was a girl who gave freely of herself and was sensitive to the tragedies these youngsters were facing.

So Carol examined her choice of a career anew. During the next semester she decided to change her plans and prepare to teach normally developing children. But while she was making her decision, rather than dropping all work and study, she worked harder than before, since concentration helped to take her mind off her unpleasant experiences. She became more active in college groups. Although she had to make up a course or two because of changing her major field, she pitched in and proceeded to learn to become a teacher.

We are not debating here whether Carol was wise in changing from physical therapy as her program of study. From the little information we have, her choice of teaching seems reasonable, since she could not be happy and hence could not do her best with seriously ill or severely handicapped children.

Most students do not have such intense emotional experiences which lead them to change their plans. Many have only vague feelings of uneasiness; they are not entirely sure they are following the right program but may not know exactly why they feel such uncertainty. Generally, such students need more information about vocations, just as we need information in order to solve any problem. The college staff, counseling center, library, parents, classmates, and friends all may be able to help. If you have any misgivings about your present course, it is important that you assess yourself in all respects in relation to the program you are following. If you are not sure that you are suited to that particular study or would be satisfied in the career to which it leads, you must be willing to make a change. It is folly to continue studying for a life work that would make you unhappy.

(We should like to insert a word of caution about the weight you should give to the advice you obtain. If you have not yet discovered it, you may soon find that instructors in whose classes you are doing well will attempt to influence you toward a career in their areas of interest. Professors are generally very observant of "A" students, and come to feel that such young people are potentially topnotch prospects for successful careers in their fields. If you were such an instructor, having high interest and enthusiasm for your subject, you too would be interested in trying to get your best students to think about careers in your field. This would also serve the best interests of your profession, and, you would naturally feel, would also serve the best interests of the better students. We don't want you to be suspicious. But you should keep in mind that you must decide on your career in view of your own interests, abilities, and plans and not upon the suggestions of others.)

If you are uncertain about a career. Some eminent modern psychologists did not major in psychology as undergraduates. Some of our top Air Force generals did not take up aviation at West Point. Some of our best teachers had other careers before they became teachers. If you do not know exactly what career you wish to follow, the situation is not too serious. Many students wisely change their choice of career at some time during their college years, and others make the choice for the first time when they enter college. Nevertheless, it is helpful to have a definite purpose as soon as possible, for an early choice may prevent backtracking, changing courses and making up for lost time, and it will provide a goal toward which you can see yourself progressing. A later chapter will provide more information on choosing a career, but for the present you might consider a few leading questions: What sort of person are you? Daring? Self-sufficient? Comfortable in the company of other college students who know what they want to be doing five or ten years from now? Do you like to explore many different areas of knowledge? If so, maybe you are wise, for the present, to continue a general college course without specializing. Numerous opportunities are open to the college graduate in such fields as transportation, communication, the distribution of goods, and in many other fields besides the specific professions — and for such positions specialized college education is unnecessary. There is a potential risk in ending college unprepared for any career, but if you are competent in the humanities, physical sciences, or social sciences, you may have sufficient breadth so that, with inservice training in industry or with creative effort "on your own," you can carve out a career for yourself which you will enjoy and can handle with competence and pleasure. Many, if not most, industries provide periods of orientation and specialized education on the job, and a few even prefer to train their own men "from scratch."

But, as we suggested earlier, one problem you may have to face if you do not choose a major field until late in college is a corresponding lack of interest in many of the courses you may take. This in turn can lead to inefficient study and low marks. A second problem is that, if you eventually wish to prepare for a specific vocation, you may find that certain courses must be made up.

It is probably wise, if you are undecided about a career, to seek constantly for information about job opportunities, programs of study related to careers, requirements for various positions, and the abilities which are needed. You can get some clues about your interests by reviewing your high school experi-

TABLE 2.1

Size, Current Demand, and Supply-Demand Prospects in the Principal Areas of Specialization

Field	Estimated number employed at professional level, 1953	State of 1953 demand	Adequacy of prospective graduates in 1953–1957 to meet anticipated demand
Natural sciences	237,000	high	insufficient at both A.B. and Ph.D. levels
Psychology	22,000	increasing	insufficient at Ph.D. level; inadequate at lower levels
Social science	47,000	increasing	moderate shortage at Ph.D. level; adequate at lower levels
Humanities	114,000	increasing	insufficient at Ph.D. level; adequate at lower levels
Engineering	633,000	30,000 year	insufficient
Applied Biology	246,000	variable	sufficient in agriculture and forestry; insufficient in home economics
Health Fields Dentistry Medicine Nursing Pharmacy	 84,000 185,000 340,000 91,000	 more needed more needed more needed moderate	 insufficient insufficient insufficient sufficient
Business and Commerce	1,372,000	flexible	will absorb many grads. from other fields
School teaching	1,141,000	160,000 year	insufficient by 60,000 year
College teaching	200,000	increasing	insufficient
Other professions Law Ministry Social work Other prof.	 202,000 168,000 77,000 118,000	 moderate moderate variable variable	 sufficient sufficient variable variable

By permission of Dael Wolfle, *America's Resources of Specialized Talent*, Harper & Brothers, New York, 1954, p. 77.

ences. You can learn which activities proved of most interest and which gave you most success. Your work experiences may also help you to decide. Counseling interviews, trying out various jobs in summer vacations, or visiting industries may help. Table 2.1 may supply some suggestions (2).

The counseling center or the student personnel office of your college is useful in helping students to make decisions. One main aim of the skilled psychological counselor is to assist the student in increasing his knowledge about himself so he can make decisions more wisely. Torrance (3) reported a study in which college freshmen were asked to predict how well they would do on certain achievement tests, a scholastic ability test, and in college courses as measured by grades. Five weeks later the freshmen came back for interviews and re-evaluated their predictions. The self-estimates of most students were more accurate in the interview than in the earlier assessment. Torrance concluded that the interview helped the student to get a better understanding of himself. Interesting, too, was the marked tendency for students to overestimate themselves more during the first prediction than during the second.

Matteson (4) conducted a similar study. Four hundred nineteen entering freshmen responded to a questionnaire on which each indicated (*a*) how he saw himself at that time, (*b*) as he hoped to be two years hence, and (*c*) as he thought others saw him. The areas questioned included academic aptitude, interest, temperament, personality, and adjustment. No statistically significant differences were found between men's and women's responses. But a statistically significant relationship was found between the grades students predicted for themselves and the grades they actually obtained. That is, students tended to achieve as they had predicted they would.

A.   DECIDING YOUR PROGRAM OF STUDY

● B.   CONDITIONS OF EFFECTIVE STUDY

Having decided upon your program of studies, the next step is to get yourself in the best personal condition for attacking them. Here we might think in terms of physical condition, morale, and motivation.

Illness interferes with successful college work just as it does with any other work. Although college students are usually in excellent physical condition, still there are times when you may not be up to par. Common colds, the "flu bug," and other relatively minor ailments may occasionally attack you; and lack of exercise, rest, and recreation may lead to fatigue and a worn-down physical condition that can prevent you from doing your best work. We shall not discuss at length the need for adequate rest, exercise, or nutrition; these ideas have undoubtedly been presented to you in many ways in your earlier school years. Moreover it would be difficult to suggest programs for individual students, for people vary greatly in their requirements. And many colleges provide excellent health services at little or no cost to the student. The reasonable thing to do is to make use of those facilities any time you are feeling below par.

Physical health is closely related to another personal condition for success — morale. What lowers the morale of a person so that he no longer particularly wants to continue his work? Many things contribute, of course — repeated failures in classwork, discouraging social relationships, homesickness, worry about parents or brothers and sisters, anxiety about health, the breaking-up of a romance, involvement in so many activities that the pressure is unbearable, and many other factors.

Each of these conditions may lead to lowered morale and decreased interest in studying. Of course, if you have a problem, your solution may differ considerably from someone else's. But the basic problem-solving techniques outlined in Chapter 1 and restated briefly here may be of help:

1. Recognize and accept the problem as such. Try to discover its true nature. Stop rationalizing.

2. Secure needed information, starting with the most logical and accessible sources. Utilize the services of college counselors, instructors, and other persons with special training.

3. Identify some possible solutions and concentrate on the most reasonable one.

4. Get more information while working toward a solution.

5. Try to determine the success of your solution. If it was not successful, get more information and try a new method.

Most adults (including college professors) meet problems that cannot be solved without specialized assistance. When such problems arise, competent help must be sought.

In this connection Maier (5) conducted an experiment with college students to study the effect of the discussion leader on decisions made by the group. A seven-man assembly line, being slowed down by "Joe," who was unable to keep up with the others, served as the problem situation. Groups attempted to find a solution to the problem under four experimental conditions. Under one condition, students worked in groups of seven without a leader and without knowledge of the roles of the seven men in the assembly line. Under the second condition, students worked alone in groups of seven with knowledge of the roles of the seven men. Under the third experimental condition, students worked together in groups of seven, again with knowledge of the roles of the seven men and with an untrained discussion leader. In the fourth situation, the groups worked the same way except that they had a trained discussion leader. The results showed that students working with a trained discussion leader and with knowledge of roles achieved the best solutions to the problem — and solved it most often. The trained leader in this case offered the specialized help needed for successful solution of the problem.

Obviously, many adults do not solve their problems completely even when leadership and specialists are available. As a world civilization we have not yet solved the problems of destructive war, extreme poverty, prejudice, discrimination, and crime. As individuals, with or without leadership or counseling, many adults fail to find solutions to the various problems which rise in their daily living. Consequently, most of us anticipate that some of our desires will be frustrated, and try to accept such frustrations as part of the challenge of living in the modern world. A considerable number of persons in and out of college get an actual thrill out of overcoming difficulties and achieving success in the face of adverse conditions. Most students are willing enough to face such challenges, although some become discouraged and leave college when too many serious problems remain unsolved.

The principles we have been discussing can be summarized as follows:

1. The student who knows what he wants from college and from life in general can find his academic work more meaningful and can achieve greater success than the one who has not set his goals.

2. The student who tries to relate his classes to his goals will probably be better motivated and do better work than the one who does not seek such relationships.

3. Good physical, mental, and emotional health and high morale are conducive to academic success.

4. Applying problem-solving techniques to college difficulties is more efficient than making no effort to resolve them or using blind trial-and-error techniques.

5. When one's own resources are not sufficient for achieving his goals, it is only reasonable to seek expert help.

The next two sections of this chapter discuss other areas related to academic success: developing efficient techniques for learning through reading, class participation, and written work; and planning for the efficient use of time.

A.   DECIDING YOUR PROGRAM OF STUDY
B.   CONDITIONS OF EFFECTIVE STUDY

● C. IMPROVING STUDY TECHNIQUES

Some of your college experiences will consist of working *with* things directly — in the laboratory, on field trips, or in the shop. Others will consist of reading and talking *about* things, and perhaps the greatest part of your time will be given to this sort of activity. A great deal of one's education is gained from the material he reads in the various subjects he is studying, since books make it possible to learn things which other people have discovered and thus eliminate the necessity for the student to discover everything for himself. Note the emphasis we place on reading. Although lectures, discussions, and other forms of learning activity are common, they are much less important in some college subjects than others. As opposed to elementary and high school practices, the use in college classes of drill sessions, blackboard practice, supervised study, and other controlled study sessions is very slight. Therefore the ability to learn through independent reading is extremely important for sucess in college.

Good reading and study habits are learned. Marvin D. Glock, in *The Improvement of College Reading* (6), points out that most, if not all, college students *can* learn to read well, and that many who are already good readers can improve. Carmichael (7), in the introduction to Glock's book, finds that

> in the silent reading of an interesting novel, for example, university students have been found to differ markedly. The slowest read about 2.5 words per second. The fastest average more than 10 words per second. If one had to walk his way, rather than read his way through college, the fact that some students were four times as fast as others would surely be the subject of comment and action.

Glock finds that one out of every five college freshmen reads less efficiently than the average eighth-grade pupil. Many upperclassmen read no better than ninth-graders. Some students can read as many as 18,000 more words per hour than others. Thus such rapid readers can master in sixty minutes an assignment which their slower-reading classmates may not complete even after a full evening's work. Poor reading is obviously a severe handicap. Many slow readers fail, while others who succeed do so only by sacrificing nearly all social and physical activities.

Jackson (8) studied the records of all 3053 freshmen at Michigan State University during one year and found that scores on a reading achievement test administered during orientation week had a higher correlation with subsequent grade-point averages than did scores on intelligence, English usage, and arithmetic proficiency tests. Women received significantly higher grades than men and tended to achieve more in accordance with their ability as measured by the intelligence (scholastic aptitude) test. Molloy (9), studying freshmen pursuing engineering courses at Marquette University, found that reading test scores were not so closely related to grade-point averages as scores on the Minnesota Paper Form Board Test. He pointed out, however, that the Minnesota Test includes items somewhat, if not directly, related to courses in the engineering curriculum. The mathematics tests, administered to engineering freshmen, were *less useful for predicting success than was the reading achievement test.*

Research has generally shown a significant relationship between reading ability and scholastic success. We now consider that the following factors affect improvement in reading, the first five having to do with comprehending what is read and the sixth with increasing the speed of reading:

1. Ability to select main ideas, supporting statements, and non-essential details.

2. Ability to follow the organization of the author's ideas.

3. Ability to improve vocabulary — use of context, prefixes, suffixes, use of the dictionary and other reference books.

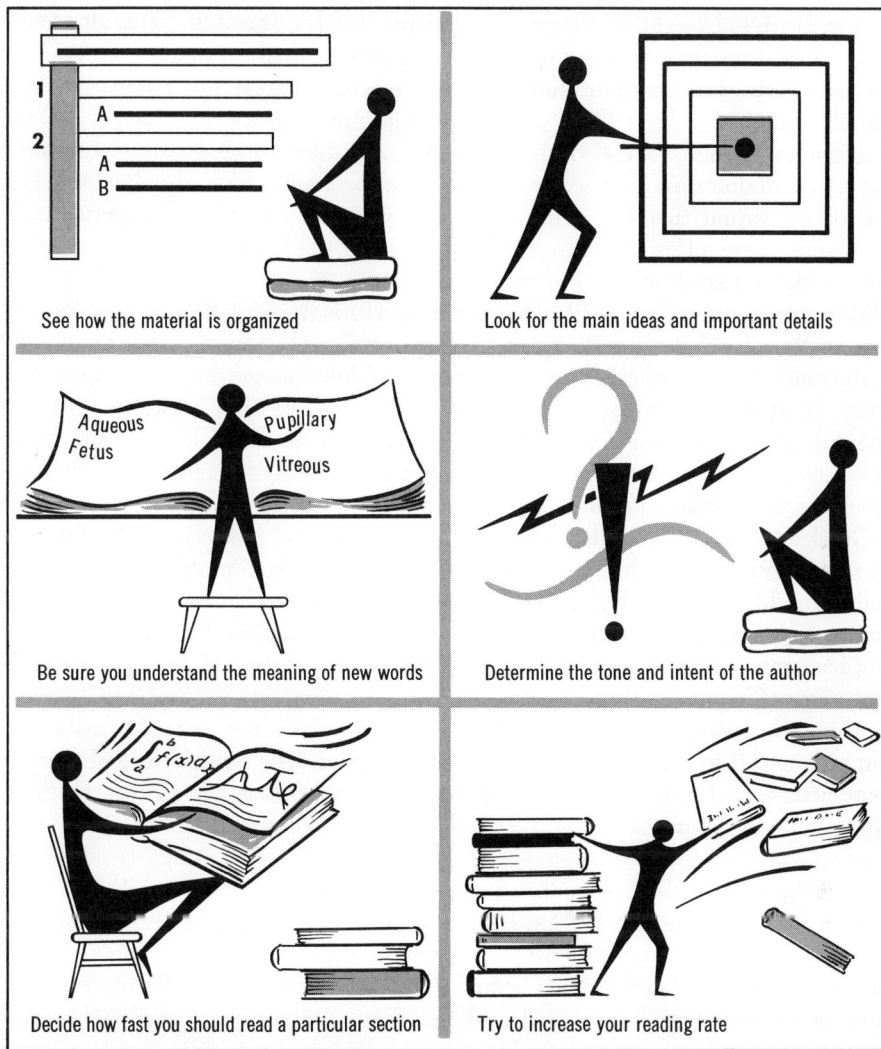

See how the material is organized

Look for the main ideas and important details

Be sure you understand the meaning of new words

Determine the tone and intent of the author

Decide how fast you should read a particular section

Try to increase your reading rate

How to improve your reading. *Most people can learn to read more quickly and efficiently as well as with more enjoyment. Some ways of doing this are included in the above suggestions. By following these simple rules, you should improve not only your reading but your whole academic work.*

4. Ability to determine tone and intent of the author.
5. Ability to adjust reading method to content.
6. Improvement of reading rate.

Let us first examine motivation in reading and studying. Most learning is purposeful. The stronger your desire to learn, the more you are ready to achieve real understanding and to retain what you learn. Probably the first step in studying ought to be getting yourself set for learning. This does not mean "mood-setting" or babying but a straightforward approach.

Carter (10) has corroborated what other recent researches have revealed, namely that not only is there a positive relationship between study methods and grades earned, but also that students' attitudes toward study are more important in determining success than are the mechanics of study. Brown (11) and others found that low-achieving college students tended to procrastinate and were more often unwilling to try to meet academic requirements than high-achieving students.

Motivation, including attitude toward work, is related to the problem of concentration. If you really want to concentrate, you must interest yourself in the material you are studying and ignore possible distractions such as outside noise, competing motives, and distaste for hard work. For make no mistake about it, concentration *is* hard work, and it may take considerable self-discipline to get started. But which would you rather do — study half-heartedly for two hours, or work efficiently and complete the job in thirty minutes?

Glock (12) points out that sometimes concentration is hindered by fatigue, worries, and fears. This confirms our statements that problems related to college and to life must be solved or at least attacked so that morale will permit one to do his best. We shall say more later about conditions for effective study, emphasizing here the need for proper motivation as an aid to concentration and more efficient reading.

Although an aid to efficient study, reading rapidly is not merely a matter of forcing oneself to speed up in a mechanical manner. The ability to read rapidly is of little use if one does not comprehend or remember what he is reading. How can you improve your comprehension and retention of what you read?

As indicated by the first point in the outline on page 48, the ability to spot main ideas and distinguish them from supporting statements and non-essential details can increase comprehension and thus improve reading. In this textbook this problem of selection has been partly solved for you. We have used various sizes of type, numerical and aphabetical indicators, and various indentations to help you determine the main and subordinate points of the chapters. Closely related to the ability to recognize main ideas, supporting statements, and non-essential details is the ability to follow the organization of the author's ideas as an aid to comprehension. In this book, as the more important points are presented, the preceding main ideas of the chapter are brought forward in the headings in this manner:

> Deciding Your Program of Study
> Conditions of Effective Study
> Improving Study Techniques

Thus as you glance through a chapter and reach the summary, you should be more readily able to detect and follow the organization of material. However, the organization of some books is not so clearly marked, and you must discover the plan for yourself.

It should be pointed out that the organization of an author's ideas is important in that it tends to build his argument or support his thesis. Now, how can you discover and follow the organization of ideas? One method is to make an outline of the chapter as you read. By numbering and underlining main and sub-points as they occur, you can gain a fair idea of the organization. Summarizing is also useful and has the added advantage of helping you to organize the material in your mind as well as on paper. Some students find that marking the book itself is a useful technique — it amounts to outlining the book *in* the book. These methods may at first be somewhat slow, but practice will enable you to improve your ability to discover organization in writing, and the time may come when you can do this job mentally and dispense with most of the writing.

Another aid to understanding the organization of ideas is in the paragraph structure itself. Normally each paragraph contains a complete idea, and a new paragraph is used when the author changes the subject. Sentences are intended to contain a complete thought, contributing to the paragraph as a whole. Does the author stress any points in particular? Does his style of writing change? Such stresses and changes may be clues to his thinking.

So far, we have discussed ways to discover main and sub-points and non-essential details and thus to follow the organization of ideas. Now we wish to review the manner in which these points are brought together in order to produce a complete and organized coverage of the subject.

Have you discovered what the author is "getting at?" Do you follow his argument? Are his points valid and acceptable to you? Are there fallacies or half-truths? How does what this author is saying agree with what you have heard or read elsewhere? If you realize that a book is primarily the author's way of "talking" with you, you can put yourself in the frame of mind you would be in if he were actually with you. That is, you can begin to ask him questions. What is his purpose? Why did he say this? What did he mean there? Did he contradict himself? Is this point a fact or merely an opinion? None of these questions need be antagonistic, but good reading and thinking demand that the reader be critical. Not only will such questions aid you in following the author's ideas, but also they will broaden your understanding, aid you in coming to an opinion of your own, and help you to remember what you have read.

The third point pertaining to improvement in understanding is the development of an adequate vocabulary. One of the authors of this book once watched a high school home economics class for a few minutes. The teacher had discussed at some length the cooking of eggs — ways and means, and timing. She made the point that usually eggs are cooked when the whites have coagulated. Finally, after fifteen minutes of discussion, one member of the class timidly raised her hand and asked, "Miss Green, what is the meaning of 'when the whites have coagulated'?" Obviously, if the meanings of the words are not clear, the meanings of sentences, paragraphs, and chapters cannot be clear either. In the back of this book is a glossary in which a number of psychological terms are defined for you. We hope you will use it, for even such an apparently simple word as "learning" means different things to different people.

But there are other ways of discovering word meanings than using the glossary or dictionary. The use of context can be helpful. Knowledge of prefixes and suffixes is useful, as well as knowledge of the roots from which many English words come. Since the study of any new subject involves learning a vocabulary, such aids as keeping a notebook of definitions, practice in spelling new words, practice in discovering the root of a word, surrounding it with whatever associations you can and using it frequently, can be helpful.

Take the word "baroque" as an example. What does it mean? The *New College Standard Dictionary* (13) says, in part, "Irregularly shaped; fantastic in style; grotesque; specif. denoting a style of architecture and decoration common to the first half of the 18th century, rococo." Does this help? Yes, but we still ask ourselves, *how shaped? What kind of architecture? In what way grotesque?* For additional meaning we may look at the context in which the word is used. For still more complete meaning we may have to consult the encyclopedia, the art department, or the architectural library. For most purposes, however, the dictionary is enough, but in this case finding a meaning from a prefix or suffix is not likely. Our point is that there are many ways of finding word meanings, and all should be used if necessary — comprehension and retention are directly related to the ability to understand the meaning of words.

The fourth factor in the improvement of understanding is the ability to determine the "tone" or intent of the author. This is almost a matter of "reading between the lines." The author says certain things, but *how* does he say them? Is he sincere? Sarcastic? Humorous? Subtle? Is he playing "the devil's advocate" — that is, building up the opposite side of the argument from the one he really believes so that he can knock it down later? Some materials, such as the poems of Edgar Allan Poe, depend as much on the sound of the words as the sense to convey what the author intended. Textbooks, contrary to popular opinion, do not always present purely factual information. Some are written to convey a specific point of view and to influence the reader to adopt certain attitudes. Such books sometimes omit certain materials which might provide a more rounded and deeper understanding of the subject. They may stress certain ideas which others might give less emphasis. These "slants" or "biases" in writing are difficult to avoid, especially when the author is trying to present his material concisely. But the fact that books are written from differing points of view is one of the reasons why your college instructor wishes you to read various books on many assignments, rather than basing all your learning on a single text. Practically all books are somewhat biased, of course. The author would have little reason for writing a book, especially in a field which is already well covered by existing books, if he were not striving to present new information or develop a fresh point of view. Aside from purposeful slanting of material, an author has a real problem in remaining objective and keeping his own personal prejudices off the printed page. Thus as you read you will want to keep in mind the tone of the writing, the point of view of the author (which you may gain in part from your instructor, other books by the same writer, or your knowledge of the author's life), and possible biases.

The fifth factor in improved understanding is the ability to adjust one's method of reading to the kind of material. We tend to think of ourselves as having developed a way of reading which is suitable for almost any material, yet a moment's thought will make it obvious that we cannot read a mathematics book in the same way we read a novel. The purposes are different. So is the nature and manner of writing, the difficulty of content, and the ease of reading. Some books are difficult to read and demand slow and thoughtful progress. Of these, some are difficult because of the vocabularly and style. "Big" words and involved style do not necessarily make a book scholarly, because many ideas can be expressed in simple language; and if the intent of the author is to be read and understood he will often achieve his purpose best by keeping his writing simple, clear, and to the point. On the other hand, some ideas cannot be expressed in simple language. It would be hard to popularize many of the ideas of higher mathematics, the sciences, or philosophy, although certain writers have tried to do this with varying degrees of success. The only justifiable reason for using a "big" word where a "little" word might do is that the more difficult language may contain shades of meaning and a degree of precision not offered by the simpler expressions. We suggest that you carefully consider the purpose of your reading and try to adapt your speed of reading to it. If it is necessary to stop in order to "think through" some of the ideas or to look up some of the vocabulary, do so; only in this way will you be able to understand the precise meanings intended by the author.

Improvement of reading rate, the sixth point in our list of factors in the improvement of reading, can be attempted in several ways. As you may know, the eyes stop and fixate several times as they move across the printed page. They do not see while they are in motion. If we practice trying to see a greater amount during a single fixation, we can speed up our reading. Although reading clinics possess mechanical devices which help to speed reading through forcing one to "take in" more at a glance, you can work on this by yourself. Practice seeing as many words as you can at glance, but make sure you comprehend their meanings. In time practice will probably bring results — that is, make it possible for you to see and understand larger groups of words at a glance.

There is another problem in what we term "word-calling." Often people who first learned to read orally will find themselves inadvertently pronouncing the words they are reading, either with small movements of throat, tongue, and lips (sometimes unobservable) or mentally. This word-calling tends to pull the speed of reading down to the speed of speaking. Conscious effort to reduce word-calling should eventually result in speeding your reading.

Finally, timing yourself as you read and actually attempting to speed up may help to increase your reading rate.

All these ways of improving reading depend upon motivation and continued practice. As you try them, it is conceivable that temporarily, because of the change of reading habits, your reading speed may be lowered. However, if you continue your efforts over a period of time, your reading efficiency will almost certainly improve. When the cause of a reading problem is obscure, or improvement does not take place through individual effort, a visit to the reading clinic, an eye specialist, or another qualified professional is indicated.

Suggested activity

1. This is a sample reading-rate and comprehension test. *Do not read this until you are ready to be timed by a friend. When ready to start, arrange signals so that your rate can be accurately timed.*

Mexican Love (14)

There are not many Mexican towns that still organize promenades, those courting parades in which the girls walk one way around the town square, the men another, both making eyes and eventually pairing off. They are a dying custom, fading as the language of the fan faded. But in the hot lowlands, people still stroll in the evening after supper while their houses cool, and the plaza is still the best place to go. And in the little towns on Sunday nights the local band still mounts the kiosk in the middle of the square to toot out brave *paso dobles* and tender songs like *Valentine,* war songs that do not mention war, but love. Under such sociable conditions, promenades, or *noches de ronda,* as the Mexicans call them, still spontaneously spring up.

Even in Veracruz, relatively a metropolis, they still have *noches de ronda* of sorts at fiesta time. Though the crowd that strolls to canned music blared from the government palace is rapidly forgetting the old ways, and is peppered with strangers who never knew the rules, and though the square is surrounded with blatting automobiles and shoeshine boys, a lot of the old magic still exists.

Folding chairs are brought out from the union halls to fill the gaps between the stone park benches, making places for the old ladies, the mothers and aunts, to sit with prim crossed ankles and panting fans, and for the old wizened, bright-eyed men who are too stiff to walk but are not too old to look. In front of them their daughters stroll clockwise around the park, in twos and threes, with plump arms linked and flowers in the hair. On the outside of the women's ring, and circling counterclockwise so that they will meet the women heart to heart, march the men. They are dressed in pleated *guayaberas,* shirts as formal and as necessary as dinner jackets at a Harvard prom.

Stop reading. Call time!

Now, figure your reading rate by dividing the number of seconds into 323, the number of words in the above paragraph. Multiply by 60 to find the words per minute. How does your speed compare with that of others?

Now, can you answer the following questions?

1. What is one town where promenades still take place? When?
2. What is a *noches de ronda?*
3. Who sits on the benches? Why?
4. Describe the circling of the promenade.
5. What is the purpose of the promenade?
6. What music is used nowadays?
7. How are old ways changing?
8. What is in the hair of the girls?
9. What is a *guayabera?*
10. What used to be in the kiosk? (What *is* a kiosk?)

Efficient Study Habits

People are funny. They invent and use labor-saving devices in almost every kind of work, yet students can hardly be influenced to save themselves study time and energy. We are a nation which employs the telephone, the automobile, the time clock, and the typewriter — both as labor-saving devices and to gain speed of production — yet the person who prefers a telephone call to writing a letter often still attacks his studies inefficiently. College students usually have received advice in earlier years about efficient study, yet many appear perfectly willing to spend several hours working haphazardly instead of finishing quickly and being free to spend the rest of their time in other activities. This may be because each person has developed his own way of studying, and the suggestions he has received for study improvement have appeared useless or complicated. Perhaps he has tried them and they have not borne fruit.

A good environment for study. *These girls are studying in a well-lighted room with few distractions (Northern Illinois University.)*

But consider some of the problems of study. One common complaint is, "I can't concentrate." Although this problem is related to motivation, it has several other aspects also. We quote the University of Colorado student handbook on this point (15).

It's not the time you put into study that makes you a good student. It's what you accomplish in that time . . .

1. Prepare your environment: When you have a satisfactory condition, try to study under those same conditions all the time. A change of study habits and environment is psychologically disturbing and may slow up the process. Be sure the room is well lighted, neat and quiet.

2. Define your purpose: Decide what you wish to accomplish and work toward that end.

3. Don't just read your lesson: Understand it. Keep a dictionary handy. It can be a big help.

4. Don't skip graphs, drawings, tables, etc. Learn to read the graphs which you come across and take in their essential points.

5. Decide when you are going to study and stick to your decision. Time has a mysterious way of slipping by, and you may find yourself having to study on the night you planned on going to that show.

6. Learn to take notes. Good notes can be much more helpful than the text when exams roll around at the end of the course.

7. Review periodically. This will help you to avoid congestion at exam time and will fix the material more firmly in your mind.

Scheduling time is important. A few persons seem automatically to schedule their time wisely. Most do not. To get into the week everything that must be done and to prevent some things from taking more than their share of time, a time schedule is helpful. The first requirement is that there be adequate time for study. Preparation of a particular subject is often most efficient shortly after the class period for that subject, since the assignment, terminology, lecture, and other details are clearly in mind, and motivation may be higher than it will be later. Generally, it is wiser to complete one assignment than to shift from one subject to another. A warming-up period for study may be necessary, just as it is in sports, and by consistent study until the preparation is completed you can take advantage of this fact. On the other hand, working too long may create fatigue, boredom, or other conditions causing inefficiency. A helpful practice is to break up your studies into manageable units which can be completely covered at a reasonable sitting and to spread out these sittings through the day, rather than do *all* your studying in one session at night when you are likely to be tired.

Daily assignments

"Let's see, we were supposed to study pages 15 to 35, weren't we? Or was it pages 50 to 70? Something about Washington's life at Mount Vernon. Here's an article about George Washington. It refers to that old fable about chopping down the cherry tree. Wonder if that is why there are so many cherry trees in Washington, D. C.? I've been there once. Visited the Capitol. Oh, well, I've forgotten just what we were supposed to study anyway. I'll ask Margie when I see her. Class isn't until day after tomorrow. . . ."

Does this sound familiar? We think it adds point to the contention that recording assignments carefully is a good practice. The habit of asking for clarification of assignments from the instructor is a good one, if you are not sure just how to proceed. Checking the assignment with your fellow students may work sometimes, but they may be as vague as you are.

A notebook section set aside for assignments is essential. Here the assignments should be entered clearly and carefully each day with the date on which it was made and should be completed, for this is one place where abbreviations and omissions are not likely to be helpful.

Keeping up with daily assignments, rather than leaving them until the end of the week, is desirable, too. All too soon the laggard begins to trail far behind the rest of the class and eventually will not be able to catch up. Furthermore, lectures and class discussions are likely to have little meaning unless one has read and studied the material ahead of time. Again: relatively small bits of material are more efficiently studied than large sections, but these "bits" should be units of thought — main divisions or sub-divisions of the topic, not just arbitrary divisions which may interrupt the continuity of an idea or a body of information.

Notebooks

Two high school courses which many students are later grateful they took are shorthand and typewriting. Unfortunately many of us never studied shorthand and can only look with wonder at people who can take notes in that manner, but many of us have owned a typewriter for a long time. As we look at a typical notebook, we may find that it is a collection of hastily scribbled assignments, a lecture note or two, some mimeographed material handed out by the instructor, and perhaps a few doodles. Here's where the typewriter comes in. The best practice is to take class notes in whatever way seems most appropriate to you — either as topics, in outline form, or in full sentences. If your notes tend to be sketchy, you should as soon as possible after class organize them and transcribe them into a durable notebook. Typewriting (or careful pen-and-ink handwriting) makes them permanently legible. There is the further advantage that organizing and transcribing helps you to remember the material. Time spent in review can then be minimized. And you will not waste time trying to decode "cold" notes.

How can you learn to take notes? Primarily *by taking notes*. But it must be done purposefully. Ordinarily the instructor will tell you, or in some way clearly emphasize, the main points of his lecture. Some instructors use a mimeographed or blackboard outline which will help you to organize your

Revolutionary Movement of 1848-49
and Its Collapse

1830 – <u>Paris Rev. in July</u> – Louis Philippe
　　　"Citizen King"
　　　bourgeois, business prosperity aim of the regime
　　　discreet foreign policy to avoid war
　　　"Peace without honor"
1840 – <u>Thiers resigns to Guizot</u>
　　　more conservative
　　　regime unprogressive, criticism muffled
　　　dull and respectable, pleased bourgeoisie
　　　　　Opposition to regime divided 5 ways
　　　　　　　1. Legitimists
　　　　　　　2. Bonapartists
　　　　　　　3. Clericals
　　　　　　　4. Republicans
　　　　　　　5. Socialists
1843 – <u>Republicans and Socialists form</u>
　　　　　<u>fusion party</u>
　　　sought wider franchise, abolition
　　　　　of property qualifications
　　　St. Simon and Fourier – early Socialists –
　　　　　utopian schemes,
　　　but working classes preferred more
　　　practical scheme of Louis Blanc's

Good notes. *What makes this set of notes one which will aid the student in study and achievement? Note its outline form, neatness, legibility, and accuracy.*

Rev. Movement   July -
Citizen king - boorjoisee? bourgoi -
Thiers — KING
Guizot (Gee-zo, Gwee-zo ---
5 opponents to regime — legitamists
Ashes of Napoleon brought to Paris - 1840
Republicans - Socialists
      Louis Blank
Foreign policy - "peace without ___"
Thiers was more conservative....
      unprogressive
1843 - Parties fuse
Radicals were for labor ——
Gout. didn't like all the banquets
Guizot more conservative —
5 divisions: 1. legitimists
      2. Bonapartists
      3. Clericals
      4. ——— ? ———
      5. Soc.
St. Simon   Simple simon
St. Simon   St. Simon   Simon   Mmmm!
Working classes liked Louis Blanc
NAPOLEON   FRANCE
Next wk: Read pp. 516 — 600 —

R.S.
G.C.
Let's go to the coop after class   OK
John
Who said this? "Let them eat cake!"   John   John
When is the next quiz? Tuesday!
Did you see Susie last night?
What was that last name? I dunno — Guizot, I think
What was this one?
Got a date tonight?
Going home this weekend? Have you got a ride?   I'm bored! me, too

Bad notes. *Will the student who took these notes be likely to find them helpful in studying for an exam? What about the misspelled words, the disorderly appearance, the lack of organization, missing information, vagueness, and distractions?*

notes. Learn to listen carefully. It is usually not hard to follow an instructor's comments and to put down main points, sub-topics, definitions, formulae, dates, and other important facts and ideas.

Students sometimes complain that if they follow the instructor carefully, it is impossible to take good notes at the same time, because — they say — if they get wrapped up in note-taking they miss part of the lecture. The use of abbreviations, making outlines instead of writing full sentences and paragraphs, and learning what to write down and what to leave out can help you to listen and write at the same time.

Finally, notes help you to remember other things besides lectures. It is often wise to take notes during class discussions. Many points made and questions answered may become hazy or be forgotten if not written down immediately. Information and opinions gained from other students are often worth keeping, and notes can preserve them for you. Note-taking can be useful in keeping discussions on the right track, too.

Term papers

This book will not treat all phases of student work in detail, but there are some important things about term papers which should be said. For one thing, a term paper is likely to be judged just that by the instructor. To him it represents work done during a term or course. Such a paper is usually the culmination of the course experience and indicates collected knowledge and thought about some phase of the course. Most instructors feel that a term paper should show evidence of careful thought and attention to detail and should not show signs of being written in haste the night before it was due. A paper may have various purposes, but it should give evidence of constructive thought. The practice of raiding the works of "authorities" and making a hasty patchwork of their facts, opinions, and even of their words is usually unacceptable for a variety of reasons. A long bibliography means little unless thought goes into the reading and is reflected in the paper. A host of quotations, an undigested array of authoritative comments, a train of references to out-of-date materials are pitfalls to avoid. For they show that you have not really thought your material through but have merely gone through the motions.

The form of the paper is important to many instructors. There are good reasons for this, the most important being that following the approved form helps to attain clarity and good organization. The reader can tell from the footnotes where the material in the paper came from. He knows where to look for the sources of the student's argument. Most instructors evaluate term papers in part by the skill and sureness with which students follow the approved form.

Neatness, accurate typing or clear handwriting, and absence of erasures are desirable in all written work. In spite of himself, an instructor tends to be more favorably impressed by a paper which looks neat, though neatness in itself is never a substitute for thought or good work. In writing, it is best to state your points once, simply and clearly. Padding to fill space is clearly recognizable. Usually a paper should be written in as concise a manner and in as simple a vocabulary as possible. Schedule your papers so that you have ample time for gathering information, writing, correcting errors, and handing the papers in on time. The grade on a term paper is often weighted heavily in the calculation of the final mark in a course and should reflect your best work.

Tests

Tests are of many kinds, but techniques for preparing for tests and taking them can be learned. A "test wise" student will often do better on an examination than a student who has equal knowledge but lacks these techniques.

To begin with, most tests and examinations are scheduled far enough in advance so that the student has opportunity for review. Sometimes an instructor will indicate the material to be covered or will even conduct a review in class. The study of how learning takes place indicates that practicing something in short but concentrated study periods, spaced over a period of time, provides more efficient learning than study or practice in a single longer period. By and large, the person who reviews frequently during the semester will be better prepared for his examinations than the one who waits to cram the night before the final. Except when a test is given without warning, you have a chance to review, and how you do it influences your score or grade.

Preparation for the two main types of examinations — essay and objective — is somewhat different. Although there are exceptions, these tests are likely to have different purposes. In an essay examination, the student has latitude in which to discuss, organize, qualify, and otherwise answer the questions which are asked. Essay tests let the student show the depth and breadth of his knowledge and demonstrate his organizing ability. They also let him demonstrate his ability to write good English and to make his ideas available to others. For the easy questions first. This gives you confidence, facilitates your thinking, and principles. Attention should be given to finding ways of applying the material and to using the facts in reasoning and creative thought. Techniques such as reciting to oneself or friends, having informal discussions or arguments, outlining, reviewing methods of solving problems, debating with the authors, working extra exercises, and making summaries can be very helpful.

In objective tests, on the other hand, the answers are much more restricted. Multiple-choice, true-false, matching, and similar types of question give little opportunity to discuss, qualify, or in other ways explain the answer. Such tests *can* be constructed to indicate knowledge of principles or the ability to apply them, but *generally* they test the ability to recall facts. This puts a premium on one kind of memorization in reviewing. Purposeful practice — with a view to adding meaning to the memory work — is useful. Mere repetition of words or phrases is of little help. Here also spacing review periods regularly over the course is much more effective than trying to cram everything into your head at one sitting. So-called memory aids can be more confusing than helpful, and they may slow down responses in taking the test. Good organization of material will always aid in reviewing effectively.

Should you guess on objective examinations? Arvo Juola,[1] in an unpublished study, examined the effect of instructions to guess and not to guess on test scores of 150 graduate students at the University of Wisconsin. Subjects were asked to guess at answers to examination questions in which they were not sure of the answers, and to indicate which questions these were. Test scores including guessed questions were compared with scores obtained on non-guessed questions only. He found that for students ranking in the upper third of the class generally, guessing was useful in improving test scores; that students in the middle third of the class neither benefited nor received poorer scores when guessing; and that for students ranking in the lower third of the class, test scores were lowered by guessing. He concluded that the better students had a residual knowledge of the material which improved their chances of guessing correctly and that the middle students' scores corresponded roughly to what we might expect from the law of averages; but that for poor students, inaccurate knowledge and confusion actually made guessing a hazard. When taking an objective examination, be sure to find out whether your test score depends upon the number correct, only, or whether you are penalized for wrong answers by some formula such as Score-Right minus Wrong.

When we hear that someone has failed a test, we usually assume that he did not know the material. But other reasons may contribute to a failure. Some students do not finish the test, perhaps because they spend so much time on certain questions that they have too little for others. It is often wise to answer the easy questions first. This gives you confidence, facilitates your thinking, and aids you in seeing possible relationships to other questions. Answering these easy questions — the ones whose answers you know well — may provide clues to other questions and will leave you more time for the harder ones. Plan to have time to write at least something on all questions.

Some students fail because they misread or misinterpret test questions. Tests are not to be scanned, but read carefully. Making sure that you understand the questions eliminates the need for the old excuse, "I knew the answer but I just didn't know what he wanted." Usually an instructor will clarify doubtful issues before a test begins. If he does not, questions may be in order. Neatness and clarity often affect a test grade, especially in essay questions. A balance must be struck between verbosity and conciseness in the answers.

Finally, having taken a test and received your mark, make use of what your answers tell you. Where are your errors? Where do you need to place more emphasis in your study? Do you have the proper technical vocabulary? Is your organization good? Don't let the test merely say that you are doing well or poorly. Make it tell you something definite.

[1] Arvo Juola, University of Wisconsin, Department of Education, 1956.

Class instruction

Many instructors, especially in small classes, permit and expect students to raise questions and contribute to the discussions. Often taking part in class discussions not only helps you learn but also affects your grade in the course. By the way they participate in class discussions, several types of students are easy to identify.

There is Type A, who never seems present, in body or soul. He seldom is heard and takes the attitude that he knows the answers to the test questions and that is all that can be expected of him.

Type B talks most of the time. He may argue, air his opinions, or give information based on reading or experience — but he talks continuously, using more than a fair share of the group's time.

Type C talks only when called upon. He may or may not be timid, but he certainly does not push himself forward.

Type D feels that student contributions to the discussion are a waste of time. He goes to class to hear the instructor. He may even take a combative attitude toward his classmates — especially those who do talk.

Most satisfactory is Type E. He helps discussion along with a good comment or query. When talk gets out of hand or off the track he tries to help the instructor bring it back to the point. He is also a good listener. He is unemotional — he does not take things personally, and he does not get angry or feel hurt. Type E carries his share of the discussion but does not monopolize it.

Class discussions have many possible advantages. Often you can get better acquainted with a subject by approaching it from various angles and by asking pertinent questions. Discussion may lead to group problem-solving. Instructor and students may get to know each other better. Discussion may sharpen thinking, increase mastery of special materials and facts, and clarify their application to real situations. Don't waste your opportunities for discussion; your thoughts are as worthy of expression as those of anybody else in the class.

Some classes use projects or other forms of laboratory experience. If the class "team" is to operate successfully, every student in the group must be willing and able to contribute his time and talents. To develop group morale, each student should submerge his own interests to further the larger interests of the group. This takes dependability and cooperation. Willingness to attend meetings, to share in writing and developing reports, to search out information, and to accept responsibility — all these are essential to satisfactory group experiences. Students in various colleges have successfully handled such projects as radio programs, panel discussions, writing and producing plays, making social surveys, and even teaching their own classes. Such activities make their work much more interesting and meaningful.

Instructional practices tend to vary with the ability and preferences of the instructor as well as with the nature of the subject and the size of the class. But each kind of presentation has peculiar advantages, and it is worth while to know something about them.

The lecture can give a maximum of authoritative information in a well-organized, stimulating, and interesting form. It is primarily suited to supplying knowledge, and does little to develop problem-solving skills, creative effort, or group activity. The lecture is often used to introduce a new subject and to develop interest in it. It can also describe a manner of approaching a study. The instructor sometimes gives an opportunity for the students to ask questions and is often willing to spend some time on subjects of special interest to the class. Very large classes can best be handled in lecture sessions. Study for lecture classes requires careful attention to note-taking and to reading assigned material.

We have already considered the discussion method. To study for discussions you should not only read but also attempt to formulate and develop ideas of your own and work out ways of presenting them to the class. Besides a presentation of knowledge, the discussion method requires applications, generalizations, and problem-solving skills.

Some colleges have small quiz sections devoted to the discussion of lectures given in large classes and to preparation for tests. These sections may be handled by an assistant or junior instructor, and are designed to permit ample opportunity for clarification of specific problems. Preparation for a quiz section often means listing questions about points which were not clear in the lectures or reading, or on which amplification is needed.

Laboratory work and field trips provide active, real-life situations related to the class work. In them you find applications of the more theoretical material you have read or discussed. But labs and field trips also require creative thinking. You can study for such sessions by securing theoretical knowledge of the topic to be covered in the laboratory or in the field as well as by understanding the purposes and procedures of the experiment or field observation.

Instructors differ greatly in their nature and interests, and one ability which you, as a student, must master is how to discover the qualities of each professor and adapt your work to him. Some professors are known to be specialists in restricted areas, whereas others have broader interests. Some are noted for research, others for lecturing, and many do exceptional work in counseling students. Some professors present a strongly biased point of view — quite correctly, in view of their background. Others may make a point of bringing out different sides of controversial questions. Some prefer general concepts and broad understanding, while others insist upon more attention to details than to generalizations.

Instructors also have various goals in their teaching. Some may desire to develop in their students the ability to solve their own problems and to be creative; others mainly seek to impart a thorough knowledge of subject matter. Some will press the student to get his work in, and will go over problems in detail; others will not seem to care whether the student is present in class and will leave it up to him whether his work comes in at all.

Generally speaking, each instructor has a fairly definite pattern of teaching.

You should analyze this pattern so that you can get the best from its strong points and supplement the weaker points in other ways. Many instructors will give you a course outline and bibliography which will help you in your analysis and in your supplementary work.

Finally, instructors can help you in ways other than their teaching. They may give special help and counseling. They can make recommendations for jobs and help you find openings. They chaperone dances and sponsor student organizations. They direct research, write, study, lecture, and hold open house. Staff members make surveys and work with committees. They do research in their own field and work in the community. In short, they are busy folk. Learn to recognize their various talents and interests, consider their busy lives, and make good use of the time they give you.

A. DECIDING YOUR PROGRAM OF STUDY
B. CONDITIONS OF EFFECTIVE STUDY
C. IMPROVING STUDY TECHNIQUES

● **D. SCHEDULING YOUR TIME**

We touched upon time schedules earlier, in discussing techniques for study. Perhaps this topic does not seem very important to you as a student. But instructors will tell you that their advisees typically overestimate their abilities and underestimate their loads. Your college undoubtedly has set a maximum number of courses or credit-hours which it will permit you to take, and only in certain cases will deviations be allowed. There is a reason for this. As you progress through college, courses become more and more difficult. The senior college or upper-division courses are more difficult than the lower-division or junior college courses, and graduate courses are even more difficult than those. Generally you are expected to spend one to two hours in preparation for every hour you spend in class. Thus if you carry an average load and spend sixteen hours a week in class, you should be spending from sixteen to thirty-two *more* hours in study. This is quite a load in itself. Of course, an exceptional student may require less time and a slower student more, but to do the job properly — reading, review, exercises, and the like — simply demands a great deal of study! If you use less time than indicated above, you may be slighting some of your work. You may be reading hurriedly, scanning where you should be carefully following the details in the text; you may be omitting certain outside readings expected of you; you may be failing to do your best on your homework, failing to review for tests, or otherwise not doing all that is required for successful college work. Before you try to schedule more than the normal number of classes, you must be sure that you are considerably above average in ability and background.

Besides trying to pack too many subjects into one semester, some students try to arrange all their classes for a given time of day — morning, perhaps. This, they feel, gives them all afternoon for study and other activities. What all too often follows, however, is that this packed morning schedule soon bores or tires them, so that they "need a rest," and the afternoon comes to be used for almost everything except study.

While we have emphasized the need for out-of-class activities, for both social and recreational reasons, some students overdo it badly. Although the desire to cooperate and to be active (and perhaps to gain prestige or recognition) is normal, one must learn to say "No" if he is in danger of assuming too many such responsibilities. Part-time or full-time work for pay may also take too much time and energy. While it is admirable that many students — perhaps half of all in college — earn part or all of their expenses, it is hardly necessary to skimp on study time in order to keep up the payments on an automobile. What happens, of course, is that students who take on too much extra work are either burning the candle at both ends and later may suffer ill health, or are scanting the college program which is expected to prepare them to earn a good living the rest of their lives. The writers have seen such instances as these:

Mrs. Anderson, a housewife of about thirty, is interested in finishing the college degree she dropped when she married. She now wants to help support the family and improve their standard of living. To this end she has registered for a class load of sixteen credit hours. In addition, she keeps house for her husband and two school-age children. She is also active in her home community — church, woman's club, and parent–teacher association. She has a social life to maintain for herself and her husband. Transportation takes between one and two hours a day.

Helen Kaye is a junior in college. Her family is happy to have her in school, but they haven't the money to keep her there. Helen works six hours a day in town for her room and board. On top of a full academic load she is active in the student council, girls' chorus, and the dramatic club, and she occasionally types a thesis for pay.

George Olsen commutes, traveling forty miles each way every day. At home on the farm he helps with the chores and does occasional special jobs. He not only carries a full academic load but also is active in athletics.

In Chapter 13, on mental health, we shall discuss personal problems in greater detail, but we must note here that a college student can do his best work and enjoy his college years only if he has enough time for rest, exercise, proper eating, recreation, and miscellaneous activities such as letter-writing and clothes-pressing — as well as going to class and studying. This fact is recognized by colleges and government as a problem demanding attention, and most colleges have scholarship programs to aid the student who has ability but needs money.

A time schedule should provide not only *a* time for each activity, but the *most appropriate* time for each. Thus, if the college library is near one of your classrooms, you could save both time and energy by arranging to do your library work immediately before or after that class. Do you schedule your

	SUN.	MON.	TUES.	WED.	THUR.	FRI.	SAT.
7							
8							
9							
10							
11							
12							
1							
2							
3							
4							
5							
6							
7							
8							
9							
10							
11							

Scheduling your time. *To help you allow enough time for each of your daily activities, make out a time schedule. Fill out the chart on this page, if you wish — or copy it — and plan to follow it as regularly as possible. It should make your life run more smoothly and efficiently.*

classes so that on some days you can eat lunch only at 2 P.M.? Must you run from a class on campus over to the gymnasium so rapidly that you arrive out-of-breath and with little time to change into gym clothes? Do you keep your energy level in mind so that your hardest work will be done when you are most "pepped-up," and easier work or recreation can come when you are less rested? Is there flexibility and free time in your schedule so that you are not always under pressure to be at a definite place every hour of the day?

As you see, we recommend that you actually draw up a time budget and set it down on paper. It will have to be revised in terms of experience, of course, as you find that you have allowed too much time for this activity and too little for that — perhaps forgetting some duties entirely. But, aside from making provision for each activity and regulating your load, scheduling has an added advantage due to the tremendous force of habit in our everyday lives. If we get into the *habit* of studying at given times of day, studying will tend to come quite naturally to us at those times; but if we study at any odd times available, we may never be in the mood for careful work.

In making a time schedule it is wise to provide first for major items. There will be some over which you have little control; for example, certain required classes may be listed at only one hour of the day, or laboratory periods may take up half a day at a time. Next you must consider the problems of eating and sleeping. In this connection, is it necessary to wait in line at the cafeteria? Are there problems in catching a bus to the place where you room? What about times and places for studying?

You will also want to think in terms of social activities, campus organizations, and recreation. Finally, what about the little but time-consuming activities such as getting a haircut, visiting the dentist, or mailing letters? Some unscheduled time should be provided for classes which take more preparation than you had allowed for, studying for unexpected tests, or just visiting friends. If you keep not only a weekly time budget but also a calendar, you can plan for such things as trips home, field trips, and special events, and you can make notes indicating dates when assignments are due.

Does this sound like a great deal of trouble? Actually, it is time-saving in the long run, as you will agree if you have had the experience of suddenly discovering there were three or four places you should be at precisely the same time.

SUMMARY

Purposeful behavior is essential throughout life in setting goals and in preventing and solving problems. It is just as important in academic achievement as in any other area — especially to the college student, because his main purpose in attending college is to learn, either for general culture or to prepare for an occupation. Since learning in college is more demanding than in elementary or high school, it is often in college that major problems first arise.

The first step in purposeful problem-solving is to determine goals. A specific purpose or goal is a requisite of successful problem-solving behavior, for the student with a purpose not only tends to learn more efficiently but also has ways of assessing his progress. Setting a goal involves a consideration of how you may best fit into an occupational pattern, what courses are appropriate for you, how large a load and what extra-class activities you can carry.

Colleges tend to prescribe most courses for the first two years. These required studies may lead to lack of motivation if the student sees them as entirely unrelated to his goals, but they can be very meaningful and useful if he makes a real attempt to see how they contribute to his plans for the future. To help him see the relationship, he can obtain advice from various sources.

After deciding on your goals for academic achievement, you can improve your study efficiency by creating the conditions necessary for effective work. Physical health, rest, recreation, work for pay, emotional health, and morale must be taken into account. Problems should be solved, or at least an attack on them begun, if you are to get the most from your academic life.

Techniques for study can be learned. Since college places heavy premiums on reading ability and since most of us *can* learn to read better, we can profitably give attention to our ability to read rapidly and well. Especially important, of course, is the ability to comprehend and remember what we read. Learning from context, using the dictionary, outlining, using various sources, and other methods of improving comprehension are helpful. Speed can often be increased, but it is secondary in importance to comprehension.

Study habits can be improved. Included as aids to efficient study are such devices as careful reading, understanding the purpose of the lesson, scheduling study time, careful reviewing, preparing for tests, noting assignments carefully, taking notes, preparing papers properly, and making best use of the various types of classes one may attend. Class instruction varies with the purpose of the lesson and with the instructor. Class work also includes participation in group work, projects, and laboratory and field experiences, along with counsel from the instructor.

To help students avoid the common practice of overloading themselves and to aid in forming efficient habits of study and personal living, time schedules are recommended.

Suggested activities

1. How is your study environment? Check the following list:

   a. Light (direction and brightness)?
   b. Radio or TV on?
   c. Distractions by roommates and other friends?
   d. Dictionary handy?
   e. Room to study at desk or table?
   f. Chair neither too hard nor too soft?
   g. Ventilation?
   h. Eyesight? Need glasses?
   i. Street noises? House noises?

Are *you* ready for study?

   j. Motivation, purpose?

  k. Health?
  l. Tired? Worried?
  m. Background? Review needed?
  n. Vocabulary adequate?
  o. Materials provided?

2. How would you prepare for a test with such questions as these?
  T F Reading is a matter of eye fixations.
  T F Speed is more important than comprehension in reading.
  T F One should read different material at different rates.
  Factors in reading efficiency include:
    a. Vocabulary
    b. Comprehension
    c. Reading habits
    d. All of these
  Tests are either:
    a. Objective or essay
    b. Objective or subjective
    c. Essay or objective-subjective
    d. Textbook or teacher-made

How would you prepare for these questions?

  a. Discuss the importance of reading efficiency.
  b. Discuss teaching techniques and their uses.
  c. Outline this chapter from memory, showing main headings and sub-headings.
  d. Evaluate your own study habits and suggest ways of improvement.

REFERENCES

1. J. Summerskill and C. D. Darling, "Sex Differences in Adjustment to College," *J. Educ. Psychol.*, 1955, 46, pp. 355–361.

2. See T. R. Cross, "An Exploratory Investigation of the Personality and Background Factors Characterizing Entering College Men Who Possess a Low Intensity of Vocational Interests," *Dissert. Abstr.*, 1955, 15, pp. 2467–2468.

3. E. P. Torrance, "Some Practical Uses of a Knowledge of Self-Concepts in Counseling and Guidance," *Educ. Psychol. Measmt.*, 1954, 14, pp. 120–127.

4. R. W. Matteson, "Self-Estimates of College Freshmen," *Personn. Guid. J.*, 1956, pp. 280–284.

5. N. R. F. Maier, "The Quality of Group Decision as Influenced by the Discussion Leader," *Human Rel.*, 1950, 3, pp. 155–174.

6. Marvin D. Glock, *The Improvement of College Reading*, Houghton Mifflin, Boston, 1954, p. 5.

7. L. Carmichael in Marvin D. Glock, *The Improvement of College Reading*, Houghton Mifflin Company, Boston, 1954.

8. R. A. Jackson, "Prediction of Academic Success of College Freshmen," *J. Educ. Psychol.*, 1955, 46, pp. 296–301.

9. J. P. Molloy *et al.*, "Predicting Attrition-Survival in First Year Engineering," *J. Educ. Psychol.*, 1955, 46, pp. 217–221.

10. H. D. Carter, "Development of a Diagnostic Scoring Scheme for Study Methods," *Calif. J. Educ. Res.*, 1955, 6, pp. 26–32.

11. W. F. Brown, N. Abeles, and I. Iscoe, "Motivational Differences Between High and Low Scholarship Students," *J. Educ. Psychol.*, 1954, 45, pp. 215–223.

12. Marvin D. Glock, *op. cit.*, p. 24.

13. *New College Standard Dictionary*, Funk and Wagnalls, New York, 1946.

14. H. Casteel, "Mexican Love," *Holiday*, September 1954. Copyright, The Curtiss Publishing Company, 1954.

15. *Student Handbook*, University of Colorado Press, Boulder, Colorado, 1952.

SUGGESTIONS FOR FURTHER READING

Understanding the meaning of measurements used in abstracts or original writings. You will encounter various statistical and measurement terms in following our suggestions for further reading. We cannot pretend to include a course of statistics within this text, but it is our hope that we can help you understand the meaning of a few commonly used terms.

To begin with, research studies employ subjects — whether human beings or white rats. This group of subjects is termed the *sample*. Because we ordinarily wish to generalize our conclusions to a wider group than the sample itself, we try to pick these subjects at *random* from a larger *population*. For example, if we wished to try to find the relationship between height and sex in growing children, we would pick a sample of boys and girls in such a way that any boy or girl in the school, grade, town, or state we are studying would have as good a chance of being chosen as any other youngster. One way would be to list all of the names of the children, and number them. By using a mathematical table of random numbers, we could choose our sample from the total population we listed. Since every person in the population had an equal chance of appearing in the sample, we reason that what is true for the sample is true for the population as a whole, within certain statistical limitations.

The trouble is, many of the things we try to study are more restrictive in sampling than this. Many studies are conducted with volunteer college students, for example. The generalizations which can be made cannot be drawn beyond the parent population of college students. However, within this population, randomization can be pursued.

Now, it is *possible* that in studying the heights of boys and girls that our sample happened to contain all of the taller boys and shorter girls — that is, that while random, it is not representative. This is a source of bias to our results, for we might find that the difference in height in our boys and girls is greater than it would have been if we had taken our entire population and measured it. Chance errors have crept in. We can, through statistical formulae, predict the likelihood that such errors have appeared in our study, using tests of statistical significance. These tests tell us the chance of our finding the same differences between boys and girls if we drew another sample from our population, still another, and so on. Thus we can, through formulas, say that the results we have gained are significant at the 5% level (P = .05) or at the 1% level (P = .01) or some other figure, meaning that there is less than 1% chance in 20 or 1 chance in 100 that chance accounted for these results. In our illustration, if we found a difference in the mean or average height of the boys over the girls of 2″ (P = .01), we would feel that less than one time out of a hundred would this difference be due to a biased sample of unusually tall boys or short girls or both.

The correlation coefficient "r" is often used to indicate the relationship between two sets of test scores or other data. This is a measure of the degree to which the subjects in one test situation hold the same relative position in the other test situation. If the highest man in test 1 were also the highest man on test 2, the next highest on test 1 also next highest on test 2, and so on all the way through the sample, we would have perfect positive correlation (r = 1.00). If the highest man were *lowest* on the second test, etc., we would have perfect negative correlation (*r* = −1.00). Often correlation coefficients are somewhere between + .50 and − .50. An *r* of .50 is of moderate value in prediction; an *r* of .60 is of considerable practical value, but an *r* of .15 shows almost no relationship between two variables.

In many reports *means* and *standard deviations* are listed. The mean is merely the average of the set of test scores or other data being used. The standard deviation is a measure of dispersion from the mean, that is, its variability. We may have two sets of measures to compare, such as scores of the same subjects on two different tests. The means or averages for each test may be exactly the same. Yet on one test we may have had many of the subjects' scores centering around the mean, and on the other test there may be many high and many low scores. The standard deviation (S.D. or σ) is a measure of this — the larger the S.D., the farther the scores are dispersed from the mean.

Other measures are frequently used. To understand their use and meaning requires education in statistics. However, do not skip the figures listed in tables or in results of studies you read. Your instructor will help you interpret them, and as you gain a wider knowledge, you will be able to do so yourself. These are the bases for much of the text or verbal material you read in scientific studies — they are the mathematical foundations for the conclusions and interpretations that are drawn.

Articles and Books.

Blue, J. T., "The Effect of Group Study on Grade Achievement," *J. Educ. Psychol.*, 1958, 49, pp. 118–123.

Drews, E. M., and J. E. Teahan, "Parental Attitudes and Academic Achievement," *J. Clin. Psychol.*, 1957, 13, pp. 328–332..

Garber, R. B., "Influence of Cognitive and Affective Factors in Learning and Retaining Attitudinal Materials," *J. Abnorm. Soc. Psychol.*, 1955, 51, pp. 384–389.

Garrett, H.E., *General Psychology*, American, New York, 1955, Chapter 9.

Klare, G. R., J. E. Mabry, and L. H. Gustafson, "The Relationship of Human Interest to Immediate Retention and to Acceptability of Technical Material," *J. Appl. Psychol.*, 1955, 39, pp. 92–95.

Munn, N. L., *Psychology: The Fundamentals of Human Adjustment*, Houghton Mifflin, Boston, third edition, 1956, Chapter 10.

Thompson, C., "Anti-Intellectualism in the Individual," *J. Soc. Issues*, 1955, 11, pp. 48–50.

Voas, R. B., "Personality Correlates of Reading Speed and the Time Required to Complete Questionnaires," *Psychol. Rep.*, 1957, 3, pp. 177–182.

Webb, W. B., and E. J. Wallon, "Comprehension by Reading versus Hearing," *J. Appl. Psychol.*, 1956, 40, pp. 237–240.

Group Living

Living in isolation from other people has many disadvantages. Admiral Richard E. Byrd (1), alone in the Antarctic for a time, accidentally suffered from carbon monoxide poisoning when his stove failed to function properly. Not only did he have to contend with the carbon monoxide generated by the stove but also he had trouble obtaining food, water, and warmth when forced to let the fire die out because of the danger involved. Because of sickness and privation, he could not communicate effectively by radio with his base camp and experienced difficulty in thinking logically and maintaining emotional balance. He found that his habits of living, his ways of thinking, and even his personality tended to change because he was living alone. Byrd makes it evident that living alone can be dangerous to physical existence, to maintaining rational thought, and to keeping contact with reality. His thrilling account of his experiences must be read to be appreciated, but from this brief description alone you can easily see that a solitary existence may present many serious problems.

You may feel that living in the Antarctic presents highly unusual conditions, and we agree. But, we also find accounts of prisoners who have experienced similar sharp changes in personality during solitary confinement. "Cabin fever," a form of reaction to the emotional stress of loneliness (and perhaps fear), may afflict people isolated in the cold north woods. Talking to oneself, treating birds and animals as human, experiencing hallucinations and illusions — all may be symptoms of personality changes which occur when one has lived alone too long.

3

Problems and Values in Human Relations

What are the advantages of being a member of groups? What are the roles of different members in a group? In what ways is it sometimes difficult for students to adjust to group living at college? How can a person evaluate a group and decide whether or not to join it? How can psychological principles be applied to group living?

Social life provides more security than we can gain by ourselves, and furnishes companionship and emotional outlets. Furthermore, it gives us yardsticks by which to judge our own behavior. The evaluations which other people make of us help us to understand ourselves as we really are. Those who lack the opportunity for social interaction may form a very narrow and biased conception of themselves and of others.

While periods of privacy for thinking and working without interruption are essential to academic success, life is enriched by sharing goals, interests, and duties with others. Sociability and group activity of students need not interfere with academic success. Though intelligence and other abilities enter into successful completion of studies, Willerman (2) found that college women who were active in sorority affairs achieved higher marks, had more self-confidence, and made more friends than the less active women students. We cannot be sure whether being active promoted the efficiency of these women or whether they were naturally more active in sorority affairs. Nevertheless, a positive relationship was found between grades and social activities. As you read further in this chapter, you will find that groups offer advantages to students which may help them in academic achievement as well as aid them to be happier and better adjusted. Social organizations like sororities or fraternities are not the answer in every case, but identification with some group or groups is valuable.

As you read, try to clarify the values of group living at college and reach a better understanding of what group living is. As you know, some students

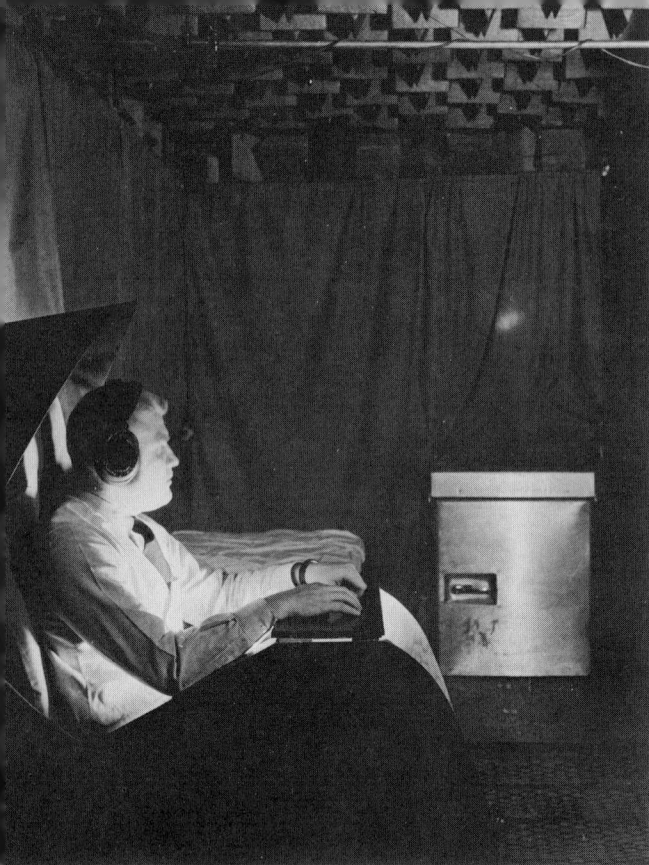

Effects of being alone. *To study reactions to isolation, the Air Force uses a light-proof, sound-proof room in which subjects remain as long as they can. At right is a refrigerator, with food packages coded for recognition in the dark. Subjects have remained in isolation up to 44 hours. (Official U.S. Air Force Photo.)*

tend to isolate themselves, either by choice or by their inability to find ways to integrate themselves into group life. At the opposite extreme, others make effective social interaction their main goal; they appear to attend college only for the "contacts" they make. A happy balance can be found between these extremes. Such a balance can enable you to reach your life-goals satisfactorily and at the same time make life more meaningful and pleasant for others.

● A. VALUES OF GROUP LIVING

For most people, living represents a mutual adjustment between themselves and the rest of their society. Individual needs for food, air, rest, and security from danger must be satisfied. If a person should take some of the more direct and primitive means of satisfying them, however, society as a whole might suffer. Living, then, is a process of learning to satisfy individual needs *within a framework* which contributes to society, and, in turn, helps the individual to satisfy his needs more successfully than he could unaided.

Consider the child of two as he attempts to satisfy his needs in a direct and self-centered manner. If he wants another child's toy, he may simply grab for it. If the other child is aggressive, a battle for possession results. The tiny infant cries for food when he is hungry, at three o'clock in the morning as readily as at six in the evening. He does not know that his parents need sleep. Still, even small children soon learn that the consequences of attempting to satisfy their needs directly, without considering others, may be even more grave than the original needs; battles, spankings, and cross parents, are almost sure to result. Fortunately, children learn methods of satisfying their needs in socially acceptable ways.

If a society is to remain cohesive, it must successfully meet the needs of its individual members. Our Pilgrim forefathers left their homeland to set up their own government, because they felt that some of their needs were not being met in England. Minority group members continually struggle not to be overlooked in economic and in legislative affairs. Others whose needs are not met may become enemies of society, as is the case with some delinquents and criminals. Or they may turn into wards of society, like some alcoholics.

The process of satisfying one's individual needs within a social framework should not be in the nature of a compromise, for compromises may result in satisfaction to no one. Rather, the individual's social behavior should be a matter of manipulating the environment to suit himself, with benefit to others or at least without harm to them. When neither benefit nor lack of harm to others is possible, he must consider his specific goals in relation to the limitations imposed by the social and physical environment and perhaps give up some desires while altering others. Consider the following example:

George Jones takes a job with a company which he feels offers real opportunity. He soon finds, however, that his immediate superior "steals" his ideas and passes them off as his own. His superior is highly critical, even carping. Apparently, success with that company depends on George's adjustment to the disagreeable superior. However, there are other ways to meet the situation. He can attempt to move to another position within the company, he can attempt to bring his achievements to the attention of higher superiors, or he can perhaps enlist the friendship of the disagreeable boss. He might even get a job with another company, utilizing his former experience to achieve his goals. Such adjustments are not compromises. They are partly a manipulation of the environment.

In many areas of life, however, social limitations on our actions are rigidly prescribed. If we wish to own property, we must obtain it legally or face the power of the law. A marriage is not recognized unless a proper license has been obtained. The practice of medicine requires conformity to the laws of the state. In some colleges freshmen cannot join social fraternities or sororities and must meet certain academic standards to remain in school. If a person cannot accept and meet such social limitations, he must either alter his goals or change his social context for a new one.

Recently we have been hearing much about "adjustment," with the implication that one must conform to the group's desires and codes of life. If this form of adjustment is carried to its final conclusion, individuality would probably be lost. We might find all people as alike as peas in a pod (3).

Thus, adjustment to others can be overemphasized and esteemed too highly. As an idea, it contrasts with the teachings of past generations which urged young people to strive to shape their environment to meet their needs. We too stress the importance of remaining an individual and the dangers of constant willingness to conform and adjust uncritically to the demands of others. College students feel a need to conform, and it may be advantageous to be somewhat like others in regard to clothing, language, and certain social customs. But the uniqueness of the individual should not be sacrificed. The world has seen progress through the efforts of people like Semmelweiss, Gandhi, and Einstein who were willing to stake their own ideas against those of others. These individuals did satisfy some of their needs in groups and they did contribute to community living — but they did not always conform to the ideas of others.

College living offers many opportunities to develop individuality while at the same time working with both formal and informal groups. Various kinds of socially oriented intellectual, academic, and recreational groups are available to students. Indeed, the rich variety of possibilities for joining with people of varying interests is seldom duplicated elsewhere. The problem of deciding what to join and how best to use one's talents is worth consideration.

To decide whether to join a group, consider membership in relation to the values which you can derive from the group.

1. Groups can broaden our ability to get along with others. By developing sets of standards, implying value systems, and providing practice and examples, group members can help us to see ourselves as we appear to other people and aid us in improving our relationships with them.

2. Groups can help us solve problems. The problems which groups can work on successfully are likely to be problems of the groups themselves. However, when several people, rather than only one, contribute to the thought on an issue, more creative ideas, more careful consideration of all aspects of an issue, and more fair and usable solutions may result.

3. Groups can widen our horizons. Because members of college groups have varying backgrounds, interests, and goals, we can often learn a great deal about the values of various individuals and cultures. For example, some students may come from foreign countries, from Army posts, from ranches, or from the seacoast. Some may represent highly specialized cultures, and others may have particular talents. All can contribute new views on living.

4. Groups can help us discover or consolidate our goals. Many students come to college with clear goals in mind. Others are not certain what they are striving for. By associating with others and learning some of their plans, we can often clarify our own goals.

5. Groups can help us satisfy our emotional needs (4). We all need affection, recognition, self-esteem, new experiences, and group status. The group can provide a sustaining force which enables us to see ourselves as successful and desirable persons. We have only to think of the power of high school crowds and cliques to see how this important function figures in the life of an individual.

6. *Groups can provide us pleasure and recreation.* Although reading and other solitary forms of recreation can be fruitful, most of us also enjoy social activities such as games, sports, and dances — or just sitting and talking. The student who does not belong to any organized group may often feel that he is missing a great part of the fun of being at college.

7. *Groups can give us opportunities to serve society.* Most students feel a need to be useful to others, to give "point" to their lives. They want to contribute something of value to the lives of others as well as to achieve things for themselves. Groups can provide such opportunities to be of service. Developing loyalty, offering friendly help to others, learning to advance group purposes — all are aided by belonging.

Since we have stressed the idea of clarifying your purposes in regard to groups, questions may now arise as to the ways in which groups operate and the main problems they encounter. You may also be wondering how you can find time for group activities and how you can retain your individuality while promoting group goals.

A.   VALUES OF GROUP LIVING

● B.   WAYS IN WHICH GROUPS OPERATE

Some of the more apparent characteristics of groups and group membership are discussed here so that you can clarify some of your immediate goals. Chapter 11 provides more detailed information about group dynamics and will help you further, but here is certain information that may be of immediate use.

Groups are associations of individuals who have something in common — goals, backgrounds, and interests. A group may consist of persons who have been accidentally placed together in the same geographical area and thus act largely as a collection of individuals, such as shoppers in the supermarket or people walking on a crowded street. Our present focus, however, is not upon these accidentally or loosely organized groups, but upon *primary* groups — that is, groups which involve face-to-face relationships, community of purpose, and some consideration of the needs of others. Primary groups tend to develop *structure*. That is, leaders and followers emerge, and interaction among individuals occurs — along with the development of some sort of patterning, customs, and habits of behavior. Acquaintanceship and friendship appear. Common problems may be discovered and group solutions attempted; for example, dormitory residents may form house organizations and carry out projects together. Even the little crowd that habitually meets for coffee and doughnuts at the campus "hang-out" tends to become somewhat structured, although the organization is informal and implied rather than recognized consciously by the members.

When a primary group is formed, various roles are assumed by the members sometimes consciously but often with no deliberate intent, although they can be identified by skilled observers and often by untrained ones (5). Chapter 11 will attempt to provide more insight into group roles. At present you may wish to try to recognize some of the following roles in your own groups:

1. Leadership roles. Groups usually are "sparked" by leaders who make suggestions, initiate projects or problems, provide organization, and help to assign member functions. Leadership is of many different kinds, and its form may vary from person to person, depending on the group's activities.

2. Supportive roles. Some members tend to support leadership and group policy and exhibit loyalty, although they themselves may not initiate the thinking or planning. Such members are often called the "ones you can count on."

3. Negativistic or destructive roles. Some people are "agin" everything. They may have various motives, such as jealousy, desire for attention, or a wish to be independent. However, they are not always mere "knockers" or trouble-makers; they may have good criticisms which should be considered.

4. Clowns. These people are cast as entertainers. They may not assume real responsibilities as group members, but act as leavening factors when situations get tense. They often act as scapegoats and may be the perennial butt of jokes. Sometimes they are almost pets or mascots. They may be tolerated for their entertainment value alone.

5. Devil's advocate roles. Persons who assume this role are likely to be in accord with group thinking but act as if they were on the other side of the fence in order to clarify issues and make sure that group actions are considered carefully.

6. Passive roles. These are played by members who will contribute services (or opinions) when pressed but rarely venture anything voluntarily. Their reactions may be caused by shyness, inertia, or the fact that having to be coaxed draws attention. They sit back in their chairs and hardly ever comment on anything. Sometimes, when highly interested in a group project, they may assume real leadership.

Roles in a group. *In almost any group, one or more members will usually assume each of the roles shown here. One will tend to be the leader, in practice if not in name. Usually at least one is passive; doing little or nothing to further progress. And so on.*

7. Absentee members. It could be argued that these people do not even have a "role." At least it is not a positive one. They are good "joiners" but are not always prompt or even present at meetings. They may shrug off responsibility and, if given a job to do, usually need prodding or supervision.

You will recognize many of these membership and leadership roles and perhaps even think of a few we have not mentioned.

As you consider joining various groups, you may wish to ask yourself about the roles the present members play and the role you may assume. As you work in groups and study group dynamics, you will gain more insight into group techniques and behaviors. To begin with, you might study groups in terms of the following questions:

1. Who are the leaders? Why are these particular people in the position of leadership? Are they successful? How do they lead — democratically or autocratically? Does the group depend entirely on one or two leaders, or are the members active and do they contribute to decisions?

2. What are the purposes of this group? What might I contribute? What might I gain? What background, talents, or other qualifications are necessary for active membership?

3. What roles are the members assuming? How would I work with each of these people?

4. What role would I have? How could I best approach my relation with this group?

5. Do we communicate well with each other? When with this group, do I understand what the members are saying? Do I listen to the opinions of others, weigh them, and help to formulate group opinion through discussion? Am I easily swayed by this group? Do I feel "at home" here?

6. What plans has this group? How can they be carried out? Are they reasonable, realistic, and desirable?

7. What is my motivation in attempting to join?

You may enjoy this tongue-in-cheek list of principles presented by Dr. Marvin Rife (6).

THIRTEEN WAYS TO WRECK A CLUB

1. Encourage the formation of cliques within the club. They are extremely effective in breaking down morale and a sense of belonging to a democratic group.

2. When you assume responsibility in the club, put off carrying it out until the latest possible moment. This increases anxiety and frustration on the part of leaders of the club.

3. When you serve on a committee, don't bother to understand clearly the scope or functions of the work of the committee. This will help to insure that you and your fellow committee members will accomplish nothing.

4. Don't worry about getting or giving progress reports on the work of committees in the club. The longer their work slides along, the more miserable and confused everyone will become.

5. At club meetings, be sure you do a lion's share of the talking. You are perhaps the only one in the group who has any worthwhile ideas.

6. If you are an officer in the club, never prepare in advance for the meeting. Just come in huffing and puffing and make comments "off the cuff." This helps to keep the meeting spontaneous and superficial.

7. By all means, don't come to a meeting on time. No one else does, so why bother? Only the early and prompt birds have to sit around and wait.

8. See that the meetings drag out beyond a reasonable length of time. There's nothing like a stuffy business meeting where everyone is asleep or bored stiff.

9. Above all, hog the major credit for any of the club's achievements. The other club members just love to hear you brag.

10. Don't give recognition for work well done by others. Just assume that loyal club members operate entirely upon motives of pure altruism.

11. When you have the floor in a meeting, be sure to mumble your words. What difference does it make if only the guy next to you can hear what you say?

12. When you meet other club members in between meetings, be sure to talk shop and worry about how the club is going to pieces. Make certain that you stress all the negative aspects of the club, in spite of the progress it is making.

13. If none of the above succeeds in wrecking the club — be a sourpuss. You will then be an eloquent walking advertisement of all the club stands for, and others will be eager to join and become more like you.

A.   VALUES OF GROUP LIVING
B.   WAYS IN WHICH GROUPS OPERATE

● C. PROBLEMS OF GROUP LIVING

Group living, we have seen, offers opportunities to satisfy many needs. It also may create problems. The fact that entering college students have to begin living in social situations different from those in high school or at home may call for readjustment in their ways of thinking and acting. A delay in forming close friendships and integrating themselves satisfactorily into college groups may cause difficulties. During this period some may lose efficiency in their work, seek desperately to form friendships even though their choices may later seem unsuitable, visit home frequently, write many letters, spend an undue amount of time and money seeking fun, or even think seriously of dropping out of college altogether. The problems of orientation to college living, of finding new friendships, of joining suitable groups, of learning customs and mores, and of becoming a real part of college society are real problems for many students. Some find satisfactory answers with little difficulty, but others spend much time in the early months of college attempting to discover workable solutions. Here are some problems counselors find:

1. Home and family relationships. Dominance by parents, lack of parental control, lack of home fellowship, broken homes, too many or too few home duties, sibling rivalry, family disapproval, poor cooperation at school.

2. Leisure time conditions. Lack of interests, inability to engage in desired activities, limited financial resources.

ROLES IN THE LIFE OF A COLLEGE STUDENT.

Each student plays many different roles. How do his roles differ? What conflicts may arise?

MEMBER OF A FAMILY. A girl who is a leader on the campus may find it hard to assume a more subordinate role at home. (A. M. Love, Jr.)

ON A DATE. A boy and a girl have specific roles to play. For example, the boy opens doors for the girl, guides her to a seat in the theatre, helps her with her coat. (Delmar Lipp, from Monkmeyer.)

MEMBER OF A TEAM. How does the student relate to others in sports, as a member of a group working for a common goal? (A. M. Love, Jr.)

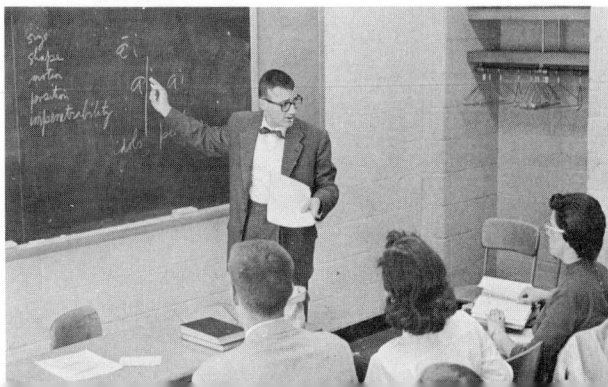

MEMBER OF A CLASS. In a classroom the student concentrates seriously on a subject. What is his role in relation to the professor — to other students? (Hays, from Monkmeyer.)

3. School conditions. Budgeting time, ineffective study habits, lack of application, lack of independence, too much help by teacher, boredom, fear of failure, unwillingness to put forth effort, dislike for teacher or classmates, impatience with slower students, work unadjusted to mental ability, too much attention to athletics or other student activities.

4. Religious life. Doubts and conflicts, extreme religious attitude of parents, conversion, excessive religious activity.

5. Moral, civic, and other conditions. Cheating, lying, stealing, lack of moral standards, manners, antisocial tendencies, prejudice, insufficient social life, excessive social life, unwise use of leisure, smoking and drinking, discourtesy, rebellion, intolerance, choice of friends of opposite sex, petting and necking, flirting, disappointment in love, being in love, unreasonable restrictions on friendships with opposite sex, sex perversions, double standards of morality, unwillingness to assume citizenship duties, inability to choose leaders wisely, unwillingness to follow chosen leaders, unwillingness to accept leadership responsibility.

6. Vocational conditions. Unwise choice of vocation, inability to get along with employer, inability to please a superior, difficulty in obtaining a job, difficulty in preparing for a job, difficulty with fellow workers.

Most, if not all, of these problems reflect problems in social adjustment. In some cases, they could have been prevented by early social training and adjustment. In other cases, the problem is one that needs to be solved — right now! In line with the problem-solving approach discussed above, it would be valuable to take a few fairly common, illustrative sources of problems and suggest types of procedure in solving them.

Homesickness

Leaving home for the first time is difficult. The student no longer has the counsel and friendship of his parents and intimate high school friends. He no longer has the security of a familiar environment — his own room, his old school, well-known neighborhoods. Not only is he in a new and strange environment but he must also face the problems of adapting himself to new faces, new activities, and new ways of behaving. Homesickness can indicate a definite lack of security, but it may have varying causes.

As we mentioned above, one first needs to examine the nature of the problem. For example, one person may be anxious because he feels a lack in his ability to meet people. Another may feel he is in the wrong college or preparing for the wrong career. Someone else may think he could be of more use at home, helping to support the family, while his roommate may simply feel incapable of doing college work. Any of these situations may be sufficient cause for feelings of insecurity, which in turn can cause one to resent his college environment and feel that home is a more suitable place to be — and thus result in his longing for his home environment.

The problem of homesickness obviously cannot be solved in any single way. For one student, merely making friends may be the solution. Another may need to re-examine his goals and abilities and their relationships to his particular program and college. Perhaps a third may find that dropping school for a while and helping at home is the best solution.

Often a change in viewpoint may be the answer. Deliberately fostering a positive point of view can be useful. After all, one must have been enthusiastic about coming to college or he never would have taken the steps necessary to get there. Too, there is something good about leaving home for college. In the first place, even if one remains all his life in his home environment it will change. People whose families move frequently sometimes feel as if they had no roots, but those whose families seldom move find that the neighborhood itself is continually changing: even though they themselves do not move, their friends and neighbors do. Stability is no longer the rule in neighborhoods; Americans are a very mobile society.

In the second place, one must break certain home ties sooner or later if he is to become mature. Otherwise, he is likely to be an immature, dependent adult who is increasingly afraid of making decisions for himself. One of the writers attended college in his home town. After graduation he left for a position in a distant city. The first few weeks were difficult. He had to make the adjustment that most students make when they first go away to college. Thus he was confronted with the problem of homesickness, plus the difficulty of learning a new job and orienting himself to the new community. The writer now feels that, for many people, a college away from home where there are counselors, other students with similar problems, and many activities to promote maturity and independence eases the adjustment of breaking away for the first time.

Finally, college represents a great deal of fun and makes acquaintance with others relatively easy. It is a society where there are many others of one's own age, activities aimed at the interests of young people, and orientation programs for new students.

Some of the following generalizations may be of value if you are trying to solve a homesickness problem.

1. The student who keeps busy with his studies, independent sports and hobbies, and group activities has little time to feel homesick.

2. The student who attempts to govern his emotions and seek positive outlets for feelings of anxiety or insecurity is more likely to develop a beneficial frame of reference.

3. The student who seeks counseling when unable to solve his own problems is often able to obtain useful information and advice.

Getting acquainted

The authors have reason to thank some unknown writer for a paragraph or two which appeared in a daily paper a few years ago. The commentator began by saying that riding to and from the city on a commuter's train could be a pretty dull sort of thing — folks often read the paper or stared out the window. A few tried to organize a bridge game — anything to while away the time spent in train-riding. Commuting was a chore and a waste of time. The article then went on to say that people are always interesting and that one often gets new understanding of life by talking to new acquaintances. The problem is: How does one get into conversation with people in a casual way?

According to the article, we must remember that, while we do not know how the other fellow will act, neither does he know what we are like. Someone has to start the getting acquainted, if it is to be done at all. Usually if we take the attitude that the other will not be stand-offish and if we use a little initiative in starting a conversation we will find the other person willing and happy to discuss the weather, the ball game, the freshman picnic, or any number of general topics.

Perhaps not all of us could accept the idea of breaking into conversation with perfect strangers as easily as the article indicates. Yet for new students there are devices fostered by the college for just that purpose — helping them to make new friends. Mixer dances, freshman week affairs, college clubs, and even teas work to that end. Churches often have get-togethers for college students, and dormitories hold open-house evenings.

Once the student has found places where he can make new acquaintances his next problem is to decide whom to get acquainted with. Here he should rely on the principles stated on page 78. He must also bear in mind that. as a convenience, people often tend to prejudge through stereotyping others. That is, instead of taking the trouble to look at a person closely to see what he is like, they may make a snap-judgment and place him in a certain category without even trying to be accurate. First impressions are important because of this tendency. It is these superficial judgments that account for such remarks to persons with whom we are well acquainted as "You certainly aren't like what I first thought you were," or "George is quite a person, after you get to know him."

What factors influence the way we appraise strangers? Surface appearance, of course — that is, grooming, clothes, posture, and facial expression; also the person's language reflects his cultural background and his intelligence. We are often attracted to those who seem to be interesting, approachable, and friendly.

Whether acquaintanceship ripens into friendship depends upon many factors. The old saying "Birds of a feather flock together," is merely another way of indicating that similarity of interests, goals, and backgrounds — or other bonds which allow each acquaintance to feel that the other has something to offer him — enhance the formation of friendships and small groups. Particularly during the earlier stages of acquaintanceship, small matters are influential. Such things as repayment of favors, consistency, promptness, cheerfulness, helpfulness, and consideration seem important. Old friends can overlook the lack of certain virtues because they have seen a person's good points demonstrated, but in beginning an acquaintance we tend to be more critical.

Some persons cultivate various devices for getting attention. They may wear extreme clothing, talk loudly, or practice an individual manner of speech. Some discuss their athletic ability or brag about their families or personal possessions. They may try to get a reputation for being radical or for not obeying rules. Some keep "fast" company. Such attention-getting is often a substitute for a more desirable form of winning recognition. Those who employ it may be compensating for feelings of inadequacy, or they may feel a lack of friendship and affection in their lives and prefer almost any kind of attention to being ignored. In other cases this behavior may simply indicate social ineptitude (7). Many times, after one gets to know such people, he finds that they are really little different from others — the only difficulty is that he may be afraid to risk his own reputation by being associated with them.

Living together

In college one of the important experiences you may have is living with a roommate in a dormitory, fraternity or sorority house, or private rooming-house. Often graduates number their roommates among their best friends. There may be many occasions when roommates or dorm fellows operate almost like little teams in double-dating, attending sports and other college functions together, sharing books and even clothes. There is often a degree of close friendship among college roommates which is absent among other social groups — a sharing of secrets, discussion of philosophies, airing of problems, and the like. Due to the closeness of the relationship, the selection of a place to room and the discovery of congenial house-fellows can become a problem.

Mary and Jean who had never met before, found themselves living together in a room of one of the big college dorms assigned by the house mother. During the days before college started in the fall, each had wondered at home what life in the dorm would be like. Jean arrived on campus first, her parents full of desire to help her get properly settled. Since the rooms were bare of curtains, pictures, bed linen, and the little things that make a room homelike, Jean and Mother and Dad got to work promptly. Out came Jean's favorite pictures of members of her family, along with some of her high school efforts at painting. Twin bedspreads, taken from her room at home, were trotted out and drapes were quickly purchased downtown. Jean's clothes filled the closet, and her radio, lamps, favorite novels, and the various toys with which a girl likes to decorate her room soon made the place homelike. She hoped Mary would like it as well as she did.

Mary arrived, bag and baggage, and knew she would like Jean at once. The two girls found much in common — similar interests, quite similar backgrounds, similar courses, and so on. But where was Mary to put *her* pictures, books, radio, lamps, bedspreads, drapes, clothes, and some of her favorite knick-knacks? Eventually a compromise was worked out, but at first the room didn't quite seem like home to either girl. Each missed some of her own possessions.

As time went on, other problems developed. Mary wakened at the crack of dawn and liked to throw up the blinds and cheerfully parade the room while dressing. Jean wanted to sleep late. Jean liked to type out her class notes while listening to the late radio programs, and Mary retired early. Jean was a borrower — with or without permission. Mary liked to keep her possessions to herself. Jean was disorderly in picking up after herself, but Mary was the soul of neatness.

Eventually they worked out techniques of living happily together. Jean and Mary discovered that quarrels or complaints should be brought out into the open and settled as quickly as possible. Repressed feelings, sulking, and avoiding the other person would merely lead to a more complete blow-up later on. Most things, they found, could be settled merely by talking them out. Both girls learned to be more tolerant and considerate of each other. They found that neither personality was likely to change, and they discovered that it is not necessary for everyone to live in exactly the same way. Having a roommate turned out to be fun. Jean and Mary — as a team — got acquainted with the other girls easily and helped each other become oriented. They shared friends and experiences. They talked over their work, planned recreation together, and enjoyed having each other to share confidences and problems. They also learned not to become too dependent on each other. Each decided to have some activity and friends apart from the other. The two girls showed a good deal of maturity in working out their problems. The problem-solving approach works as well in social relationships as it does in other areas.

To join or not to join

At most colleges several kinds of student organizations exist. There are the social organizations such as fraternities and sororites, church-affiliated groups and organizations whose primary aim is service to society (such as the campus Red Cross, YMCA, and YWCA), professional or semiprofessional organizations (such as Psi Chi, journalism clubs, Future Teachers of America, engineering or science fraternities), and the extra-class activities (such as band, newspaper, drama, chorus, debate, and athletics). Each has a place in your plans for your college education (8). The authors hope they show no biases in regard to the benefits or worth of any of them; indeed, organizations may vary in character and activities from college to college, even though carrying the same name.

Let us consider the various kinds of organizations from the viewpoint of how they can help the student set and achieve important goals. We shall begin with social organizations.

Fraternities and sororities. In this regard we are referring to the "Greek letter" social organizations. Although these groups ordinarily have high ideals expressed in their constitutions and hold purposes such as the fostering of special virtues, their activities may be largely social in nature.

Exponents of fraternity life point out many possible advantages for the fraternity member. They feel that he is closely associated with congenial men of similar tastes, backgrounds, and qualifications. The organization lends itself to fellowship, security, group solidarity, and prestige. Members are carefully chosen, indoctrinated, and led to conform to standards set by the group (9). The member is acquainted with people of various talents and abilities. He makes friends and "contacts" which may stand him in good stead later in life. He meets alumni, many of whom may be prominent. He enjoys rites and rituals, dances and parties. He may be introduced to girls whom he otherwise might not meet. And he may take part in college politics and help good causes backed by the fraternity.

Opponents of fraternity life say there are disadvantages in "cliques" — a person may tend to conform too much. He may find his circle of friends more narrow than he would prefer, and he may be under undue pressure to keep up financial obligations he really cannot afford — clothes, dues, parties, jewelry, and the like. He may even become snobbish. Certainly, fraternity life demands a certain amount of time, as there are obligations to fulfill for the good of the group — planning activities, attending functions, and providing services for the organization.

Literature on the subject indicates that scholarship of such groups may be either above or below average. Opinions differ in regard to the desirability of the friendly competition often sponsored by them. The writers tend to feel that — as is usual with any kind of college experience — there may be things to be said on both sides. To join or not to join must be a decision based on one's own preferences and motives and the nature of the organizations in question (10). Fraternal orders are usually neither as good nor as bad as they are alleged to be. In making the choice of joining or not joining, the student ought to examine his goals for his college career to see how they fit into Greek or non-Greek living. He must base his opinions on the particular groups he is considering and must inquire rather thoroughly into what would be expected of him. Since the fraternity or sorority will be carefully examining him in his turn, he should take the same privilege and examine them. In other words, rushing season shouldn't become too much of a rush.

1. How do your goals compare with those of the organization?
2. What can you gain by joining? What will you lose?
3. What can you contribute? How can you be of service to the group?
4. What would be the financial obligations? Time obligations?
5. How is this organization regarded on the campus?
6. Who are the members? What do they stand for?
7. Are the backgrounds, tastes, financial status, etc., of the members similar to your own?
8. What do others think about your joining this group (parents, alumni, other students)?

Service organizations. Such organizations as church-affiliated student groups, YMCA and YWCA, and similar organizations may have two purposes — to perform a service to the college and/or community, and to provide fellowship and service to the members. Each college provides a list of such organizations, with the hope that they will be well supported. Opportunities to join are almost unlimited, for the usual qualification for membership is simply an expressed willingness to live up to accepted standards and to be of service to the organization by participating in its activities.

These organizations may offer a chance both to make a contribution to your social groups and at the same time to learn how service groups operate. College-educated people usually take an active part in such groups in the communities where they later make their homes. Leadership and followership learned in college help to make such endeavors satisfying. The largest problem here may be that of budgeting time. A tendency of some students is to get involved in more activities than they can handle without neglecting something. Some students, of course, are mere "joiners" who contribute little but their names to an organization, partly in the hope that they will meet people they like, partly because they want to be able to say that they belong to this or that group, and partly because it may look good in their records. On the other hand, one who is really willing to contribute time to an organization can receive the benefits of fellowship and participation in useful and enjoyable activities.

Professional and semi-professional organizations. Most career groups have organizations on campus. There are groups for those who will become psychologists, engineers, teachers, businessmen, journalists — in fact, nearly every type of career is represented in some way. Many of the student organizations will be affiliated with professional groups in society at large. Advantages of such groups may include the opportunity of increasing your knowledge about the particular profession, making contacts among its members, aid in obtaining a position after college, actual professional activities (such as working on the college paper, putting on dramatic entertainments,) engaging in fellowship activities, and supporting college programs.

Other extra-class activities. These include the various sports, musical organizations, speech and dramatic groups, journalism activities, hobby groups, and the like. Their advantages are similar to those already listed for other kinds of activities. It should be clear that if college is to be of maximum benefit, you must be aware of and participate in the activities it offers. A well-rounded program is necessary for mental health and the development of personality. For each student the proper amount of study, rest, recreation, fellowship, and service is a necessity. Personnel men in industry sometimes wonder about the one-sided college man who has placed nearly all his emphasis on one or two aspects of college life (11). Finding the proper balance is likely to be a matter of experience at first, but everyone should soon be able to find his special aptitudes and interests in order to develop for himself a congenial, well-rounded program.

Traditions and customs of life at college. One of the finest accomplishments of a college is the encouragement of a high morale and feeling of unity among its students. What links you and your fellow students to those of the past? What gives your school its individuality? What sets your own classmates

TRADITIONS AT COLLEGE. *Customs and traditions help immeasurably to bind students together in loyalty and school spirit, making each one feel that he is a part of the college and its history.*

FRESHMAN BEANIES. Freshmen at Washington University in St. Louis, Missouri, must wear beanies to indicate their low status to upperclassmen. Here they are shown at a traditional picnic given annually for new students. (Washington University News Bureau.)

ACADEMIC PROCESSIONAL. The ceremonial procession is a tradition of college life. The academic gown historically is a symbol of scholarship and learning. (Northern Illinois University.)

PEP RALLY. At Whitman College students join in building a giant bonfire for a pep rally before an important game. (Whitman College.)

apart from college students elsewhere? What gives you that "we" feeling which is so necessary? The answer lies in the campus itself, the faculty, the organizations you join, or other persons and activities — but it is sure to include *traditions.*

Washington University (12), for example, asks freshmen to wear their "beanies" and carry their Freshman Bibles at all times. They must attend all special assemblies and events for freshmen. They must know the words and music of the Alma Mater and the Fight Song. They are to "button" whenever commanded to do so by upperclassmen and whenever passing members of the Freshmen Police Corps.

Another college, DePauw University (13), presents information about traditions in its handbook. Seniors there have a special stone seat for them alone along the walk leading up to East College. In February there is a Gold Diggers' Ball when women make the dates, call for the men, buy their corsages, carry all the paraphernalia, and in general show the men how things ought to be done.

At Annapolis midshipmen toss a penny to the statue of Tecumseh before exams.

It is this sort of thing which makes *your* college life different from college life elsewhere. Traditions help to bind the student body together and add to the fun of college days. Enjoy your traditions and live up to them. They are part of the reason a student thinks there is no place quite like his own school.

    A.   VALUES OF GROUP LIVING
    B.   WAYS IN WHICH GROUPS OPERATE
    C.   PROBLEMS OF GROUP LIVING

● D. APPLYING PSYCHOLOGICAL PRINCIPLES

As your study of psychology continues, you will discover many psychological principles that are useful in terms of group living as well as for individual behavior. At first they may seem hard to apply, but if you keep them in mind they will begin to come naturally. Two major principles will be discussed here.

1. We tend to perceive a situation in terms of our own backgrounds, motivations, and emotions, as well as in terms of environmental factors. This principle, developed further in Chapter 5, indicates that reality is not the same for each person — that is, each of us to some extent lives in a world of his own making. The reason is that each person interprets situations in terms of what he *expects* them to be, and such expectations are based on his past experiences. Furthermore, each of us tends to see what he *wants to see;* the particular aspects of the environment we focus on depend in part on our motives and goals.

In attempting to apply this principle to group living, we find many implications. For example, we may misinterpret group feelings or actions by reading into them too much of our personal expectations. We must try to judge a person's actions not only on the basis of what we expect or desire, but also on the basis of that person's expectations and desires. For example, let us assume that one person in a certain group seems friendly and pleasant but does not volunteer to do any work. If you are a volunteer and an eager worker, you may expect the other person to be the same, failing to take into account his already overloaded schedule. Thus you have misinterpreted his actions, and you may be led into making an incorrect judgment about him.

The ability to sense other people's emotions without necessarily sharing in them is called *empathy* (14). Some students, through experience, have more empathy for some groups or individuals than other students have. We are finding that the more one is like other people whom he is trying to understand, the better he can understand them. If they are very different in background, ability, or other ways, he may misjudge them completely (15).

Other interesting examples of this same principle are beginning to emerge from psychiatric studies and work in social–psychological laboratories. In trying to categorize human behavior as deviant or as nearly normal, we apparently do not have an empirical basis but depend to some extent on our own recent experiences (16).

To help you interpret this statement, we call to your attention the lifting and judging of weights. If one lifts several heavy weights and then a light one, the light weight will be estimated to be even lighter than it really is. But if one lifts several light weights and then a heavy one, the heavy weight seems heavier than it really is. That is, weights are judged in part in relation to immediate past experiences. (Try this as a classroom "experiment" to see for yourself.)

In applying this idea to group behavior, we begin to see for example that, if a psychologist has been associating with a number of highly deviant personalities while diagnosing the nature of severe behavior problems in a clinical setting, subjects with lesser personality defects may seem quite normal. In comparison with severely disturbed individuals, such people might really *be* quite normal. However, if one had been working with normal people, a subject with a relatively minor personality defect might seem even more deviant than was actually the case.

Understanding and rating others is not always consistent from person to person or from time to time. When judgments of behavior are repeated, they sometimes are not in agreement — even with the same judges and subjects. Furthermore, those whose backgrounds are much like those of the persons being rated tend to be better judges than people who are vastly different. That is, students generally can rate other students better than can their parents or other adults (except teachers probably, who have both education and experience in this area).

Since the basis for judging human behavior depends on relative judgments or comparisons rather than absolute standards, our judgment of group climates and group behavior should be made cautiously. That is, if we are accustomed to informal and congenial people and then meet some who are reserved, we may classify the latter as more cold and formal than they really are. If we have attended several classes with rather uncritical and perhaps mediocre students, high-achieving students in another class may seem more superior than they really are. Knowing these tendencies in our perception of others, we should be careful in forming our opinions about persons or groups.

2. *When the way to a goal is blocked, behavior may be in the direction of removing the block, setting a new goal, circumventing the barrier, or emotional activity reflecting frustration.* This psychological principle may help you to understand group and individual behavior involving frustration. When a group is trying to solve a problem, progress may occasionally be blocked. Probable ways around the difficulty are sought, a new goal may be set, or the old one altered. Possibly, however, emotional behavior will result. Let us illustrate:

Club X, one of the college service organizations, has agreed to hold the state convention at your college. The commitment has been made without adequate checking with the college authorities. Brother clubs have accepted the invitation to attend, but when you request permission of your dean to hold this meeting, he refuses. He tells you there is no room in the calendar, and that commitments of this sort should always be preceded by a request to his office. You must recall your invitations.

The dean's decision is a barrier to your goals. But to tell the other clubs that you cannot hold the convention at your college will result in a loss of status for your group.

You attack the problem. First, you try to get the dean to rescind his decision. When this fails, you try to change the date, ask some other club to take the convention this year, consider holding the convention in town rather than on campus, and use other methods with all your ingenuity to try to circumvent the barrier. None of them appear successful.

You now attempt to change your goal by offering to entertain merely the officers of your brother organizations, but they remind you of your promise to hold the entire convention. Now emotion enters the scene. There may be blaming and recriminations. Scapegoating, name-calling, ostracizing, withdrawal from the club, anger, disgust, levity, or other emotions may be manifest. The authors do not know how to resolve the situation, but they have confidence the group will find a way. Before any progress can be made, however, someone must help the group to relieve emotional pressure and start thinking constructively again.

Apply this same idea to individual behavior. When someone gets angry, why is he angry? Perhaps he is angry at something someone has done, but it may be that he is simply exhibiting symptoms of frustration because of a situation he cannot cope with. If he acts silly or tries to be funny in a situation where such behavior seems improper, perhaps here again he is attempting to relieve emotional tension. Why do you sometimes give vent to emotions, rather than work constructively? What can be done to control your emotions?

Refer now to some of the principles stated in Chapter 1 and, as you continue reading the following chapters, keep trying to find ways to apply psychological principles to various types of situations. Not only will your understanding of psychology be improved but you will also be able to make use of your knowledge.

Suggested activities

1. Attempt to judge weights as discussed on page 93. Now construct a rating scale for some particular kind of behavior (for example, an oral recitation), and see whether you can apply the same type of tests to your judgment of this behavior as you did in judging the weights.

2. Study what is meant by "halo effect." How might this affect your estimates of people or situations?

3. What is your classroom "society" like? How does your judgment of this group compare with that of others in the class?

4. Keep note of what happens in some groups of which you are a member. Characterize the groups. Interpret the behavior and roles of individuals. Interpret your own roles.

5. Try role-playing in a problem situation. Try to analyze how individual class members aid the group in advancing toward a solution of a group problem.

Group problem-solving

A few years ago one of the authors was an instructor in a college which lacked sufficient dormitory space. Many students were obliged to obtain rooms off campus. On one occasion, a college girl came to him, her adviser, with considerable distress. Ellen, it appeared, was about to lose her room. The landlady, who was renting four rooms to eight sophomore girls, had become "disgusted with their behavior" and had decided that at the end of the semester she would no longer rent space. Since rooms were very scarce, Ellen and her friends were apparently going to be forced to drop out of college for a while. What could they do?

Here was where problem-solving techniques were useful. First, of course, the problem had to be defined. What was the "disgusting behavior" the girls had engaged in? It turned out to be nothing more serious than washing some of their clothing and leaving it to dry in the bathroom and occasionally failing to tidy up their rooms before going to class in the morning. Was this the landlady's real reason for not wanting to rent rooms any longer? Was there any other reason for animosity? What was the attitude of the girls? Did they really want to keep the rooms? Would they bear ill will against Mrs. Kane?

More information was needed. The problem needed careful definition. As a means of gathering data it was suggested to Ellen that the girls first sit down together to try to figure out whether any of them had at any time done other things for which they had been criticized. Were they teasing the landlady or being deliberately antagonistic? Were their habits really as bad as they sounded? Then they might approach the landlady to see whether she had other grievances or other reasons for wanting to close the rooms.

The girls conferred. It was decided that a girl who was known to be tactful should try to pin down the problem further with Mrs. Kane, if possible. Ellen was chosen to do this. Ellen gained Mrs. Kane's confidence after helping her clean the upper floor one morning. Mrs. Kane then invited her into the kitchen for coffee, and the girl and her landlady began to talk. In the course of the conversation it became apparent that Mrs. Kane had problems other than the ones she mentioned. Her rest and reading had been disturbed by one girl in particular, who had a particularly loud voice and used the hall telephone at length. Probing further still, Ellen found that her landlady was being repeatedly urged to visit her sister in Florida and even to make her home there. She had thought not only of "closing out" the roomers but also of selling her home and moving south.

The girls tried problem-solving as a group. First they decided to try harder to make a good impression. They removed the causes of complaint by asking the girl who used the telephone to cut her conversations short or else make them from a different phone. They worked at keeping their rooms and the bath tidied up. When they could, they tried to help Mrs. Kane and to visit with her once in a while. In time, they were much better accepted. However, this did not solve the problem of Mrs. Kane's wanting to sell her home. The girls considered various hypotheses.

Could they rent the home, install a house mother, and operate as a sort of dormitory? Would the college buy the home? Would a new owner rent rooms to them? Could they possibly find other quarters?

The attempt to answer these questions led to visits with the Dean of Women, who had charge of housing, discussions with people who could advise them about finances, talks with Mrs. Kane about these possibilities, and consultations with their parents. But for one reason or another, the various solutions had to be rejected. Finally someone had a bright idea. She went to the Dean and discovered that there was no college regulation in regard to the number of women who could occupy each room in the dormitory. The college policy was to try to have no more than two girls to a room, but the Dean agreed to permit three temporarily — providing the resident students did not object.

Ellen knew some of the girls who were active in the dormitory student organization. Putting the problem up to them, she asked if they could possibly find space for her and her friends. This they proceeded to do. Calling a meeting of the dorm girls, they stated the problem and asked for volunteers to share a room with a third girl, stressing the financial advantage of a third party to share expenses. In this way space for six girls was found; the other two displaced girls were lucky enough to find a room in town.

Probably the main advantage of the problem-solving approach in this instance lay in clarification of the problem itself. At first, you recall, the surface problem was animosity between landlady and girls, with what —to the girls — appeared to be insufficient cause. As the problem was clarified, attempts at solution took a much more fruitful course.

SUMMARY

We have tried in this chapter to remind you of some of the values of living in groups — and, in fact, that living alone presents real problems. As we saw, Admiral Byrd's experiences show that one's behavior may change when living alone, even to the point where he might feel his personality itself might change. Social life presents physical and emotional security, it is true, but it also provides a mirror for evaluating one's own behavior. Among the values most readily derived in groups are those of becoming more able to get along with other people, improving skill in solving problems, widening horizons, consolidating goals, satisfying emotional needs, gaining pleasure and enjoyment, and obtaining opportunities to serve society. Probably the attitude a person should form is that of trying to achieve satisfaction of personal needs within a social framework, contributing to the good of society while also, insofar as possible, enhancing his own best interests. When this can be done, a person is considered well-adjusted. On the other hand, he must not sacrifice the values of original talents and ideas in blind conformity to the group.

To make this sort of adjustment, a knowledge of group behavior is useful. We were able to identify roles played in various groups by leaders and by other members. It was evident that some people were of more use to the social group than others and that people act according to a consistent pattern. We considered some of the questions which might well be answered before one identifies with a group: Who are the leaders? What are the group purposes? What roles do the members play? How could one approach the group? Can one communicate well with the members? What is a possible reason for wanting to join? We gave a few suggestions of how one can best further club or social group purposes.

Although it was evident that groups have many potential values to the individual student, group living was found also to involve possible problems. At college such problems may include home and family relationships, use of leisure time or lack of it, school and religious difficulties, and moral, civic, and vocational conditions. Common areas of difficulty include homesickness, getting acquainted with others, living in rooms with other students, joining or not joining social organizations and other groups, and making use of the particular traditions and customs of one's college.

Psychology presents principles which aid in preventing and solving group problems. We found, for example, that persons tend to perceive a situation in terms of their own backgrounds, motivations, and emotions as well as in terms of environmental factors. As we developed this principle, it was evident that some people are good judges of the motives and behavior of others whereas some are relatively poor judges. Various factors enter into our judgments. A second principle was that of frustration. We found that when the way to a goal is blocked, behavior may be directed toward removing the block, setting a new goal, circumventing the barrier, or reflecting itself in emotional activity. Which behavior results is dependent upon the maturity, experience, and abilities of the group and of its individual members, as well as the situation itself.

Finally, we illustrated problem-solving by citing the experience of a group of girls who were being forced to leave their rooming-house. We saw how some of the principles we had discussed entered into this situation. We found that group problem-solving was effective in this instance, and we saw some of the ways in which members of the group operated to further the solution to their problem. As you live in the college environment, we hope you will improve your skill in dealing with groups and at this particular time begin to study this aspect of your education more consciously and purposefully.

Suggested activity

Record the interaction of members in one of the groups you belong to. Provide yourself with a chart on which each person present is allotted a horizontal line with the leader of the discussion on the top line. Draw vertical lines on which to make a mark at each comment or contribution by any of the persons opposite their names. Keep a running graph (from left to right), utilizing these lines and indicating how the flow of conversation went. As you become skilled with this technique, you may wish to insert letters such as "A" to indicate that the subject asked for information, "G" to indicate that he gave information, "J" for a joke or quip, "I" for a rude interruption, and so on, for varying kinds of participation in that situation.

Guides to better relationships

Dr. Marvin Rife, who wrote "Thirteen Ways to Wreck a Club" quoted on page 81, has a very good guide list toward better human relationships. This, however, is not "tongue-in-cheek" like the earlier rules. On the contrary, these are sound and straightforward principles which will add to your knowledge of people and psychology. As a conclusion to your study of this chapter, read and consider the following material (17).

TEN PRINCIPLES OF GOOD HUMAN RELATIONS
1. Most people resent being dominated.
2. Almost all of us want to have a fair hearing

3. We tend to agree with persons we like.
4. Sympathy and sentiment play a large role in personal relations.
5. We all want to feel we are important, at least in some areas.
6. Most people like to be informed about their status and progress.
7. We gain satisfaction through solution of problems.
8. We are all different, even though we are much alike.
9. Most progress comes by "one thing done well along one line at one time."
10. Most of us desire credit and reward for a job well done.

REFERENCES

1. Adm. R. E. Byrd, *Alone*, Putnam, New York, 1938.
2. B. Willerman, "The Relation of Motivation and Skill to Active and Passive Participation in the Group," *J. Appl. Psychol.*, 1953, 37, pp. 387–390.
3. You will be interested in reading R. Lindner, *Must You Conform?* Rinehart, New York, 1956.
4. See also J. R. Christiansen, and T. R. Black, "Group Participation and Personality Adjustment," *Rur. Sociol.*, 1954, 19, pp. 183–185.
5. P. E. Slater, "Role Differentiation in Small Groups," *J. Human Rel.*, 1955, 3, p. 76.
6. Marvin Rife, unpublished classroom materials, University of Wisconsin, Madison, 1951.
7. J. W. Kidd, "Personality Traits as Barriers to Acceptability in a College Men's Residence Hall," *J. Soc. Psychol.*, 1953, 38, pp. 127–130.
8. P. Benson, and R. McMullin, "Student Motives for Extra-Curricular Activities," *J. Higher Educ.*, 1954, 25, pp. 437–439.
9. E. M. Abernethy, "The Effect of Sorority Pressures on the Results of a Self-Inventory," *J. Soc. Psychol.*, 1954, 40, pp. 177–183.
10. See J. A. Smith, "Sororities, A Psychiatric Appraisal," *J. Nerv. Ment. Dis.*, 1955, 122, pp. 603–605.
11. C. Dickinson, "What Employers Look For in the College Graduate," *Personn. Guid. J.*, 1955, 33, pp. 460–464.
12. *Student Handbook*, Washington University, St. Louis, Missouri, 1952.
13. *Student Handbook*, DePauw University, Greencastle, Indiana, 1951.
14. For a treatment of the effects of empathy, see S. Hayden, "Some Behavioral Correlates of Empathy," *Dissert. Abstr.*, 1955, 15, pp. 875–876.
15. R. Taft, "The Ability to Judge People," *Psychol. Bull.*, 1955, 52, pp. 1–23.
16. J. E. Gilchrist, Unpublished Studies, Group Behavior Laboratory, University of Wisconsin, Madison, 1956.
17. Dr. Marvin Rife, Office of Advisement and Counseling, University of Rhode Island, Kingston, 1955.

SUGGESTIONS FOR FURTHER READING

Crutchfield, R. S., "Conformity and Character," *Amer. Psychologist*, 1955, 10, pp. 191–198.

Hayes, M. L., and M. E. Conklin, "Intergroup Attitudes and Experimental Change," *J. Exp. Educ.*, 1953, 22, pp. 19–36.

Hilgard, E. R., *Introduction to Psychology*, Harcourt, New York, 1953, Chapter 7.

Holmes, D. C., "Students' Attitudes Toward the Worth and Dignity of Others," *Educ. Res. Bull.*, 1952, 31, pp. 63–66.

Lehner, G. F. J., and E. Kube, *The Dynamics of Personal Adjustment*, Prentice-Hall, Englewood Cliffs, N.J., 1955, Chapter 2.

McKeachie, W. J., "Individual Conformity to Attitudes of Classroom Groups," *J. Abnorm. Soc. Psychol.*, 1954, 49, pp. 282–289.

Pepinsky, P. N., et al., "Attempts to Lead, Group Productivity, and Morale Under Conditions of Acceptance and Rejection," *J. Abnorm. Soc. Psychol.*, 1958, 57, pp. 47–54.

Plant, W. T., "Changes in Ethnocentrism Associated with a Four-Year College Education," *J. Educ. Psychol.*, 1958, 49, pp. 162–165.

Pressey, S. L., and R. G. Kuhlen, *Psychological Development through the Life Span*, Harper, New York, 1957, Chapter 11.

Rasmussen, G., and A. Zander, "Group Membership and Self-Evaluation," *Hum. Relat.*, 1954, 7, pp. 239–251.

Ruch, F. L., *Psychology and Life*, Scott, Foresman, Chicago, fourth edition, 1953, Chapter 14.

Selltiz, C., et al., "The Effects of Situational Factors on Personal Interaction between Foreign Students and Americans," *J. Soc. Issues*, 1956, 12, pp. 33–44.

Smith, A. J., et al., "Productivity and Recall in Cooperative and Competitive Group Discussions," *J. Psychol.*, 1957, 43, pp. 193–204.

Smith, K. U., and W. M. Smith, *The Behavior of Man: Introduction to Psychology*, Holt, New York, 1958, Chapter 14.

PART TWO •

PSYCHOLOGY AND

THE INDIVIDUAL

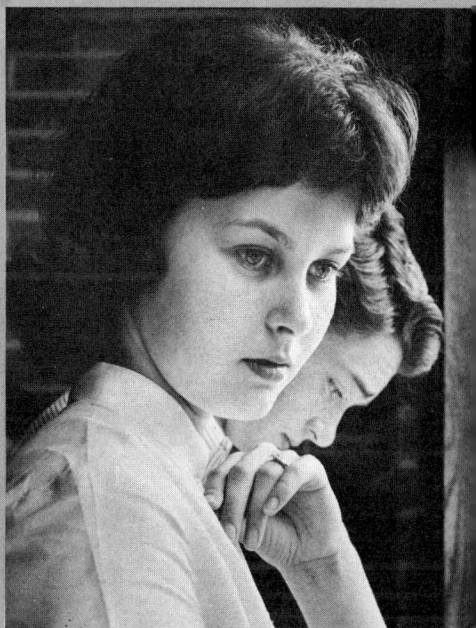

Maturing and

Developing

Do you consider college students mature? What criteria do you use for making this sort of judgment? Obviously, there is disagreement on when a person is mature. College men and women are usually considered sufficiently mature physically to marry, even though some are so young that they require their parents' consent. Some who are still growing taller, and some who have not yet acquired their wisdom teeth, may be old enough to vote, while others — physically mature — may not. The men are usually of "draft age"; that is, they are mature enough to do work required by the Armed Forces. Some students, however, cannot be legally bound by business contracts. And while the actions of some may be considered delinquencies, for others who are slightly older these same acts are crimes.

The problem of determining maturity cannot be resolved by simply assuming, as legal authorities may, that women of age eighteen and men of age twenty-one are mature or adult. Physically we mature at different rates. And, in a behavioral sense, even some middle-aged or older persons are not mature emotionally or intellectually. Some may not have developed a healthy moral sense. Some act irresponsibly and refuse to accept the responsibilities along with the privileges of maturity.

Chapter 1 mentioned briefly some of the characteristics of mature behavior. Here we shall further examine such behavior as a background for discussing physical growth. We assume that if people are to function successfully in our society their behavior must be mature and that the development of mature be-

4

The Growth of the Total Human Individual

What are the characteristics of a mature person?
What are some characteristics unique to human beings?
What is the effect of heredity on an individual?. What
are some of the biological bases of our behavior? How
can growth, maturation, and development be defined?
What are the stages of human development? What are
the principles of development?

havior is a process which continues into adulthood. In this sense probably very few students are mature — except perhaps physically. But before concentrating on growth toward physical maturity, let us briefly consider certain other kinds of maturity in order to see later how they are interrelated with the physical factors of heredity, growth, and development. The person who is really grown up is mature intellectually, emotionally, socially, and morally as well as physically.

● A. KINDS OF MATURITY (1)

Intellectual maturity

The intellectually mature person does not shirk making his own decisions. Although it is sometimes necessary to gather information and listen to advice, the mature person makes up his own mind and takes responsibility for his actions. He is not vacillating and does not put off making decisions.

> Whereas some students always seemed to hang around their instructors, trying to get help with their work and suggestions for using their time wisely, Arnie was independent. He did not feel a need to get others to make his decisions for him and was able to plan and carry out work on his own, some of it quite creative and original. At the fraternity house Arnie was the same. Although others would ask what suit or tie to wear or when to study, he used his own judgment and made his own decisions. His behavior suggests intellectual maturity.

The intellectually mature person tries to be unprejudiced. He sizes up each situation as objectively as possible and weighs each person on his own merits. He does not live in logic-tight compartments like people who cannot be reasoned with.

> Joe, in contrast to Arnie, "knew" in advance that certain courses were tough and that the instructors were trying to "kill off" all but the best students. Although his classmates believed him for a time, they soon came to see that his opinions were not based on facts. But they could not tell Joe anything. He *knew* that he was right. Joe was prejudiced. He was not intellectually mature.

The intellectually mature person tries to be objective about himself. He recognizes both deficiencies and talents in his make-up. He is willing to examine his own motives. He wishes to see himself as he really is.

> When people did not seem friendly, Ronald sought *reasons*, instead of dismissing the matter by merely feeling that they were snobbish. When others were more successful than he, instead of believing they were lucky or enjoyed favoritism, he sought reasonable explanations for success in their abilities and behavior. He tried to examine his own personality objectively and to improve himself on the basis of what he observed. Ronald was intellectually mature.

Emotional maturity

The emotionally mature person has learned adult ways of expressing emotion. Instead of throwing temper tantrums he has learned to use restraint in expressing himself. He realizes that a display of emotion often engenders the counterpart of that emotion in others. He knows it is possible to get so upset that he cannot act rationally. He does not try to repress emotions permanently but seeks socially acceptable outlets.

> Karl had a bad night. He got caught in the rain and ruined a pair of slacks. Then he found he had locked himself out of the house and had to wake his roommate in order to get in. Not being particularly sleepy, he decided to shave, only to find his supply of razor blades exhausted. Yelling, stamping around, and making a fuss were bad enough, but when he spoke harshly to his landlady she became angry and put him out of the house. Needless to say, Karl was not mature.

The emotionally mature person reacts to stimuli in an adult manner. He is not seriously or long upset by such things as being called names, and the childish behavior of others does not trouble him unduly. He does not laugh at the discomforts of others. Many things which bothered him when he was younger no longer cause him to react strongly, for he sees the world through adult eyes.

> Two girls, sorority sisters and good friends, began by quarreling over a lost lipstick. Soon came an orgy of name-calling. We hope you would not recognize

these young ladies by their descriptions of each other. They followed with slaps, squeals, and tears, but finally they "made up." They were not emotionally mature.

The adult can put off expressions of emotion until a suitable time arises. For example, when students complain about their tests or assignments as they walk down the halls, they are probably displaying more mature behavior than if they had expressed anger in the classroom.

Control of emotional expression can be learned. External control in turn helps one to control the inward emotional state. Of course, the person who is *too* controlled seems cold and uninteresting; so it is an adult *expression* of emotion, rather than *repression,* which is desired.

The mature person is no longer moody, as he may have been during adolescence. He analyzes his mental states and tries to find ways to moderate his moods. He finds ways of easing tension. (There is something to be said for the farmer who chopped a cord of wood every time he became angry with his wife.) Cheering at football games, class "sings," sports, dancing, reading, and music — all can help relieve pent-up emotions. Even just acting silly may help at times, and talking things out is useful.

Social maturity

The socially mature person has adequate family relationships. He has affection for his parents and can recognize their virtues. At the same time, he does not expect them to be paragons of virtue, for he can see that they are human beings and have faults just like other people. He is independent in his thinking but values his parents' advice. He does not have many family conflicts.

Although George knew that his father was not as successful as he could have wished and that his parents favored his not going to college, he respected and loved them for what they were. Even though he had to earn his entire way through college when they would have preferred to have him help at home, he was able to resolve the difference of opinion gracefully. He worked at home during vacations and on some weekends and earned his education during the week by assisting in the laboratory. George was socially mature.

The socially mature person has a practical view of the worth of others. He makes friends, fully realizing that they have their faults as well as their virtues. He does not idolize anyone blindly and is willing to study others a bit before giving his close companionship too freely. Some people may have greater ability than he, but it does not make him feel inferior so long as he uses his own ability well. He enjoys his friendships, sharing his friends with others, and making himself useful to them whenever he can.

Peter had many friends after only a week at college. One reason was that he was always ready to do someone a favor. He helped with studies, lent his clothing, and took time for a joke with anyone. He did not, however, take part in gossip sessions and, although he recognized some of the faults of his friends, he insisted that he and others also recognize their good points. Peter was socially mature.

The socially mature person achieves security with his peers. He attempts to make himself successful and accepted. Although he is concerned with his relationships to older and younger persons, he primarily attempts to have sound relationships with members of his own age group, with whom he has most in common. He does not strive to ingratiate himself or seek attention, preferring to make his way on his own merits.

Although Jean was a model of perfection to her mother and her mother's friends, she had few close friends of her own age. She seemed to enjoy working with children and played games with them, to their great delight. She enjoyed her instructors and loved her classes. Probably no one knew how much she would have appreciated a date or two or a feminine pal to whom she could confide her wishes and plans. Jean had somehow failed in social maturity.

The socially mature person places sex in its proper perspective. His desires are sublimated into useful channels such as work or sports. When he is married, he expects a normal and satisfying sex life. He achieves a sense of proportion and, realizing that sexual desires are normal, adjusts to the mores of his society. He tries to find acceptable outlets for expression.

Probably counselors have seen few students who were subjected to as much emotional tension as Harry. His main problem was an inability to accept normal sexual thoughts and desires in himself, so that his feelings of guilt and his conflicting desires were causing him sleepless nights and a great deal of anxiety that was transferred to most of his waking life. Coming from an extremely strict home in which thoughts of sex were considered shameful, he found the change to a stimulating college environment hard to make. Harry in this way was not socially mature.

The socially mature person is practical about customs and conventions. He adjusts to society as it exists. He usually accepts conformity to the group mode as the most practical way of getting along with others. Careful consideration must precede any deviations from the established ways of behaving. Blind conformity is not demanded, however; in certain instances it may be better to be unconventional.

Herman, coming from a foreign country, found his American college social life quite different from that abroad. His manners and customs were different as well as his values and standards. Even his religious and political ideas were different. However, he was able to adjust. He accepted being different as part of the game and was able even to make jokes about some of his manners, ideas, and ways of expressing himself. As time went on, Herman was able to find much good in the new culture as well as to promote some of his own ideas. Sometimes, although he did not agree in principle with what was said or done, Herman went along with the crowd if he could without doing basic injustice to his personal sense of values. Herman was mature.

The mature person is not a rabid reformer, nor does he continually feel frustrated by social practices unlike his own. He recognizes that freedom is relative, as are some ideas of right and wrong. Insofar as he can satisfy his own ends within the framework of society, he does so; but usually he prefers to fall short of attaining his goals rather than to leave the social milieu. Working with other people, instead of against them, is important to him.

Moral maturity

The morally mature person has a deep regard for the rights of others. He recognizes that his own conduct must provide satisfaction for his needs but not deprive others of *their* satisfactions. He considers the consequences of his behavior and its effects on other people.

Ken was certainly the demanding type. If a girl went on a date with him, she went where he wanted to go and danced if he wanted to dance. He would swear, drink, or smoke if he wanted to, regardless of how his companion felt. If it was convenient for him to make use of his friends' homework for classes, he used it. Naturally, he had few friends after his reputation became known. He could hardly be called mature in any moral sense.

The morally mature person accepts moral codes only after due consideration. He seeks reasons for behaving as others expect and does not accept any dictum with blind obedience, recognizing that customs may become outmoded, that certain groups may be attempting to preserve the status quo, and that even criminals have their codes of behavior.

Sue was uncertain whether she should join the A's. For one thing, she heard that they had a code of one for all and all for one, and that whatever any of the girls did, the others must stand by to defend her. They seemed to be a fast crowd, too. If she joined she would have to change some of her ideas on proper behavior. Her thoughtful consideration of the possible problems involved indicates maturity.

Finally, the mature person needs *a philosophy of life.* He needs to have definite ideas about the greatest values in living. A satisfactory religion, carefully considered, is important to him. He bases his philosophy on past teachings, the writings of great thinkers, talks with his peers, and studies of the lives of great individuals. He thinks about the world as he finds it and thereby gains a greater understanding of the values of mankind and of himself. He does not search blindly. While certain aspects of life may seem confusing, he settles them at least on a temporary basis.

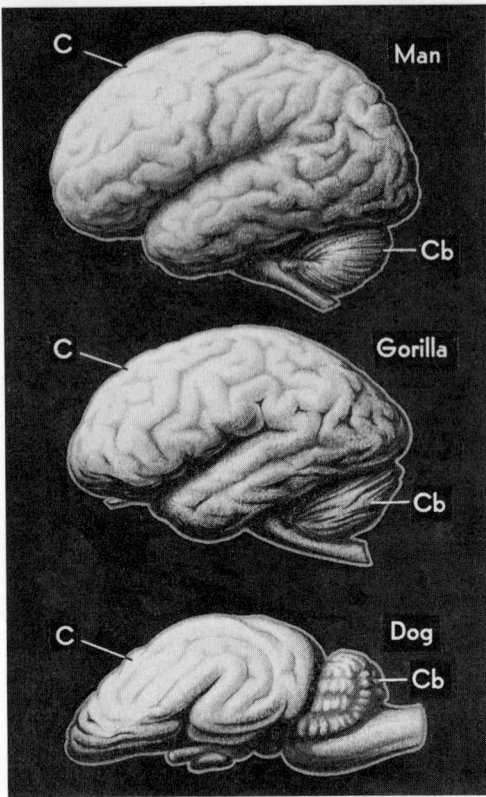

C — Man
Cb

C — Gorilla
Cb

C — Dog
Cb

INVAGINATIONS IN THE CEREBRAL CORTEX. The structure most important to intelligence is the brain — especially the *cerebral cortex*, the external layer of the *cerebrum* (*C*). In lower mammals, this cortex is small and smooth. In higher forms it is larger and has invaginations which give it a wrinkled appearance. The invaginations, which increase the area of gray matter are evident in the cat and dog but pronounced in monkeys, higher apes, and man. The cerebral cortex comprises billions of nerve cells. The cerebellum (*Cb*) is concerned mainly with bodily coordination. The brains above are pictured as of the same length to show detail. Actually there is a marked difference in size. (Drawing by Elmer Smith, from Munn, *Psychology*, Houghton Mifflin.)

MAN'S ADVANTAGE OVER ANIMALS. *Human beings as a species have certain structural advantages which distinguish them from other animals and make them superior.*

SIZE OF THE BRAIN. The size of the brain in relation to the size of the spinal cord is a factor in intelligence. A frog's brain weighs no more than its spinal cord while man's brain is 55 times as heavy as his spinal cord. (From the Encyclopedia Britannica film, "The Nervous System.")

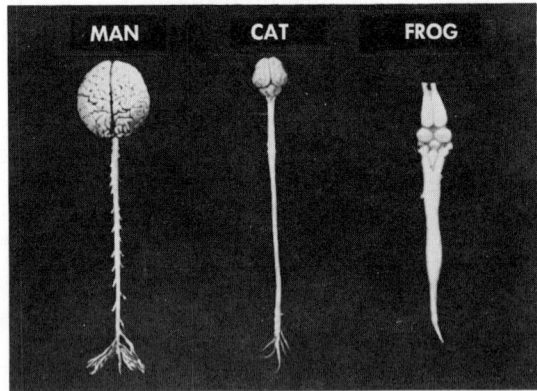

MAN   CAT   FROG

THE OPPOSABLE THUMB. Man can grasp and manipulate objects with great skill because of the shape of the thumb and its position in relation to fingers. The gorilla's thumb is less useful. Animals with paws do not have even this structural differentiation. (From G. Revesz, *The Psychology and the Art of the Blind*, Longmans, Green & Co.)

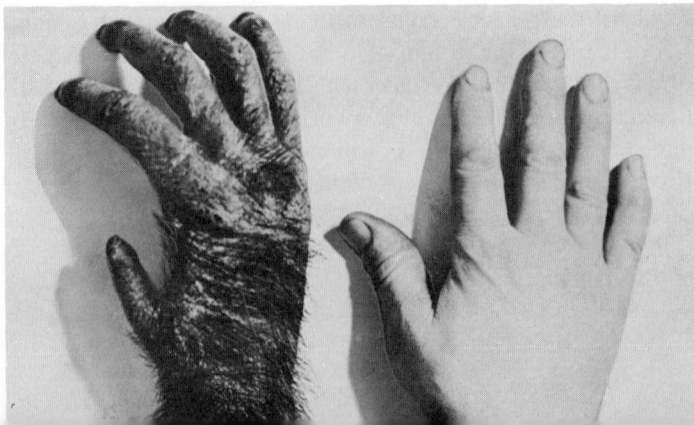

These paragraphs have contained ideas to be developed in more detail in later chapters. At this point, however, you should begin to think in terms of definite goals in your life at college and to work out ways of achieving them.

A.   KINDS OF MATURITY

● B.   HEREDITARY CHARACTERISTICS OF MAN

Do human beings think and act in a way basically different from other animals? How are we like other animals? What is the biological basis of human behavior?

Scientists have studied questions like these for many years. Some have concluded that human superiority is primarily the result of greater intelligence. Perhaps, however, if some of the higher animals were carefully educated, they might become more like human beings.

Dr. W. N. Kellogg (2), formerly of Indiana University, was one of those who studied this question. For a time he tried to bring up a baby chimpanzee with his own small son, Donald. The baby chimp, Gua, was seven and a half months old at the start of the experiment; Donald was ten months old. The two babies were dressed similarly. Gua was placed in a high chair, just as Donald was, and fed with real utensils. Her teeth were brushed and she, along with Donald, was helped to perform many of the activities that little children learn. She practiced walking on two feet, turned lights on and off, and opened and closed doors. She learned to use the bathroom quite well. After extensive training she could do many other things a small child can do. She even learned to respond to about ninety-five words.

But Gua could not do some things because of the nature of her physical structure. For example, she could not build with toy blocks, for she did not have the use of a thumb like a human child's. And even though she learned to make noises which had meaning to others, she did not learn to speak.

The chimpanzee's behavioral development soon reached a limit where she could perform many simple activities but nothing more complicated. Her growth was rapid, but she stopped growing at an early age. At this time her mental ability appeared to be about that of a two and one-half year old child. Although she was stronger than Donald, the little boy, and more adept at certain physical tasks, she did not advance beyond what would be very elementary behavior for human beings.

Dr. Kellogg's experiment indicates that with proper training some animals can learn many types of human behavior, but it also seems to show that there is something lacking in the mental and physical equipment of these animals which prevents their ever reaching the level of an adult human personality. Since physical structures are determined largely by heredity, and since many psychologists feel that heredity in large measure helps to determine intelligence, we are led to conclude that heredity also plays an extremely large part in determining what we *can* learn. The function of environment (which includes training as well as surroundings *per se*) appears to be largely that of determining which of the types of our potential behavior we will actually learn.

We know that animals can reason to some extent. Lions cooperate in hunting, some driving the game toward the others. Dogs can learn to tend sheep or do certain kinds of police work, and some have appeared to use reasoning in saving human lives. But if we investigate circus acts in which horses are apparently able to spell or count, we discover that they are actually responding to small cues given to them by their trainers. This is not to say that animals cannot reason at all or that they do not exhibit intelligent behavior. Nevertheless, whenever we see such behavior in animals, we *remark* about it — not because it would be intelligent for humans but because it is intelligent for animals. Animal intelligence is actually meager when compared to that of human beings. The four-year-old child can organize games, pretend he is a fireman or a cowboy, and invent and tell long stories. Even a very young boy can co-operate with his friends in playtime projects, use his father's tools, and invent his own.

Man is able to perform mental activities which are quite different in degree, and possibly in kind, from those of even the highest animals. Training and learning account for some of these differences; structure, for others. As we proceed with the chapters on perception, emotions, intelligence, and learning, we shall be considering the effects of both environment and heredity. Since the early life of man, like that of all biological organisms, is characterized by physical growth and maturation, we may well consider some of the physical structures which are determined largely by heredity and see how they affect a person's life. But first, we should define three important terms — growth, maturation, and development.

First, *growth*, broadly speaking, may be considered to be an increase in size or development of a structure or a function. Thus we may speak of the growth of a child as he becomes taller and heavier, or we may speak of the growth of the power to learn or of some similar ability. However, in this book we shall use the term in a more limited sense to denote simply an increase in the size of a structure; *i.e.*, an increase in length, weight, or mass. Second, *maturation* is, in a sense, the result of growth. When a structure — for example, the hand, the speech mechanism, or the glands controlling sex activity — grows to the stage at which it begins to perform its proper function, maturation has taken place. It has been a process independent of specific learning but dependent on hereditary processes of growth. And third, *development*, another commonly used term, is a more inclusive word which describes the interactive processes of learning and maturation. It represents not only the physical changes which may result from heredity, but also the changes in behavior resulting from all forms of learning. As man grows, matures, and develops, he is able to master his environment to a greater extent than any other creature. Thus he is particularly well-equipped for life on earth.

Adaptability of man

While man shares with all other animals the biological functions of food-gathering, digestion, circulation, respiration, assimilation, excretion, sensation, and reproduction, he is definitely superior to other creatures in almost all areas of physical development. He is not the weak, ill-adapted creature some writers have portrayed. The size of a human being, to mention one character-istic, is considered to be ideal (3). Man is neither so large that he has diffi-culty in obtaining enough food to support his bulk, nor so small that he cannot protect himself from his enemies. Man's brain is larger in proportion to his body size than that of other animals, and a greater share of nervous tissue is given over to the higher mental processes, with relatively less tissue needed for the more automatic control of breathing, circulation, and similar processes. Man (or more specifically, woman) is one of the longest-lived of animals. Man is provided with a long period of life during which he can learn. Because child-bearing ceases long before old age begins, man enjoys a period of independ-ence, freed from the demands of raising a family that enables him to channel some of his activities into fields which will aid society as a whole. Many of our most important studies, political undertakings, and business activities are guided by persons in their forties or older.

Living in family groups is another major characteristic of man. Since he matures slowly, the period during which he needs close association with his parents is long, compared to that of other creatures. Human offspring require more parental training and attention than the young of any other animal, and they receive it in the home, that is, the dwelling of several human beings who form a family. Family life offers to human beings the opportunity to exchange opinions and viewpoints, to learn from each other, to cooperate and work together. Continuous family life provides for the sexual needs of the parents (who, unlike some animals, are not limited to particular seasons or periods for mating) and also helps to fit the child for independent life as an adult. Besides fulfilling basic biological needs, it gives to man a foundation for the emotional, social, ethical, and religious concerns which other animals do not experience.

Human beings also enjoy structural advantages over other organisms. For instance, man's hands are so developed that he can use them for grasping and manipulation; thus he can use tools adeptly. Although his sense organs are no better than those of other animals, his sensations are generally excellent. He sees well and has the rare gift of binocular vision, which enables him to judge distances with considerable accuracy. He has comparatively good hearing and adequate senses of smell and touch. The use of the word "adequate" may sur-prise you unless you have read of some of the feats of primitive tribesmen in tracking animals, of the delicate skills of coffee tasters and perfume blenders, and of the sense of touch of skilled surgeons.

Man is extremely hardy. He can eat many forms of plant and animal life. Because of his excellent central nervous system he can learn and remember, and thus has been able to build upon the experience of earlier generations and to develop such tools as fire, clothing, shelter, and communication. Thus it is possible for him to live in almost any kind of climate. Human beings range over a greater area of the earth's surface than any other creature, with the possible exception of birds. Man's powers of recuperation after accident or illness, and his abilities for endurance are tremendous. How these characteristics are passed on from generation to generation through a combination of the hereditary process, learning, and teaching is one of the wonders of nature.

Heredity provides the basis for man's adaptation. In many ways we are all alike. That is, we all look and act like human beings. We all have much the same needs to maintain our physical existence. But each one of us, while acting in some ways like every other, is also a unique being. Each acts in his own particular ways to satisfy his needs. Each looks different enough from other persons to be recognized as a particular individual. Each has an odor or scent which enables a dog to distinguish him from other people. Voices sound individual, even over the telephone. And yet there are family resemblances, and racial and ethnic characteristics which can be broadly distinguished.

Each of us is a product of many varying factors. First we are provided through heredity with the potential to mature as human beings. Parents to child, the patterns are set at the moment of conception. But also, at the beginning of life, environment begins to chart the course of individual development. We are what we are because of the interaction of both these forces — our inherited tendencies and the forces of the environment in which we grow and develop. Since heredity and environment do not operate independently, it is clear that we cannot say whether heredity or environment is the more important. Heredity provides us with a basis for development; environment acts to shape our lives within the limits provided by heredity.

The science of genetics offers essential information about heredity, the ways in which certain capacities and tendencies are passed on from parent to child. As in any sexual reproduction, human conception occurs when the ovum (the egg cell) produced by the female unites with the sperm cell, produced by the male. When the two unite, the sperm penetrates the ovum, and the nuclei, the essential central portions of the two cells, combine. The ovum thus fertilized, begins to divide and subdivide, and to form specialized tissues later to become bone, muscle, and nerve cells, eventually forming the embryo which eventually becomes a child. It is at the time of conception that our hereditary characteristics are determined for life. No other opportunity ever occurs for providing different hereditary influences which might affect the characteristics of the child. Environment, of course, is another matter, and continues to be of profound effect.

The nuclei of ova and sperms, like all other cells, contain small rod-shaped bodies called *chromosomes*. During a ripening process in which ovum and sperm are readied for reproduction, the full number of chromosomes divides by half. It was long thought that the full or *diploid* number in man was 48 and the reduced or *haploid* number 24; but recent evidence, largely photographic, sug-

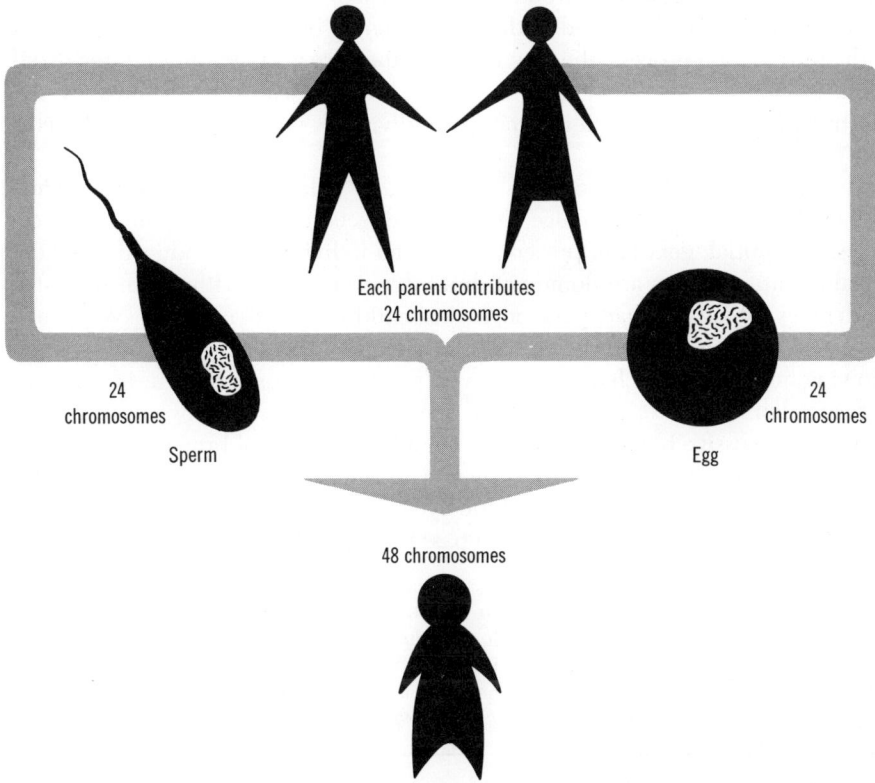

The heredity process. *The fertilized egg, which will develop into a child, receives half its chromosomes from each parent, 24 (or perhaps 23) from the sperm and the same number from the ovum or egg. The resulting total number of chromosomes comprise the child's entire hereditary equipment.*

gests that these numbers should be 46 and 23 respectively. Whichever the number, when ovum and sperm unite in fertilization, the diploid number is restored to the fertilized egg and to each cell in the embryo which develops from it.

The ripening process, known as spermatogenesis, is extremely important in determining our hereditary tendencies. Chromosomes occur in homologous, or "matched," pairs, *i.e.*, pairs in which the two members are similar, one being of maternal, the other of paternal origin. In this complicated ripening process of chromosome reduction, each 48-chromosome nucleus actually produces four 24-chromosome nuclei. The process involves not merely the separation of homologous chromosomes but also an interchange between the two members of a pair so that the ripened ova and sperms come to differ among themselves as from the ones from which they were derived. Thus variations in hereditary endowment have already begun to occur within the separate parents, even before fertilization.

The actual carriers of hereditary traits or tendencies are the *genes*, small bodies of protein molecules located in the chromosomes. Each of us has many thousands of genes which produce or influence special characteristics. But since the genes become mixed both in the ripening of the sperm and ovum and in the fertilization process, the way in which they are arranged in each fertilized ovum is unique. It is evident that, except for identical twins formed by the splitting of a single fertilized egg, no two individuals will have the same hereditary endowment.

Moreover, some genes are more *dominant,* or influential, than others. They overshadow others and produce their own effects, even though the *recessive,* or less influential, genes are present. Hence an individual is produced in whom certain characteristics are dominant, but who also carries within him recessive tendencies which he may pass on to his children. If two people who have similar recessive characteristics for a particular trait marry, a family strain showing only recessive characteristics will result. For example, genes for brown eyes are dominant over genes for blue eyes, and thus some brown-eyed people may carry recessive blue-eye genes. As a result some pairs of brown-eyed parents may have blue-eyed as well as brown-eyed children. However, two people with blue eyes will produce only blue-eyed children, since these parents cannot have genes for brown eyes and so pass on a "pure" recessive inheritance for eye color.

Dominance and recessiveness in genes. *A gene for brown eyes is dominant; a gene for blue eyes, recessive. Any combination with a dominant gene B (e.g., BB or Bb) therefore yields brown eyes. What would result from a brown-eyed mother with genes BB and a blue-eyed father with bb? A brown-eyed mother with Bb and a brown-eyed father with BB?*

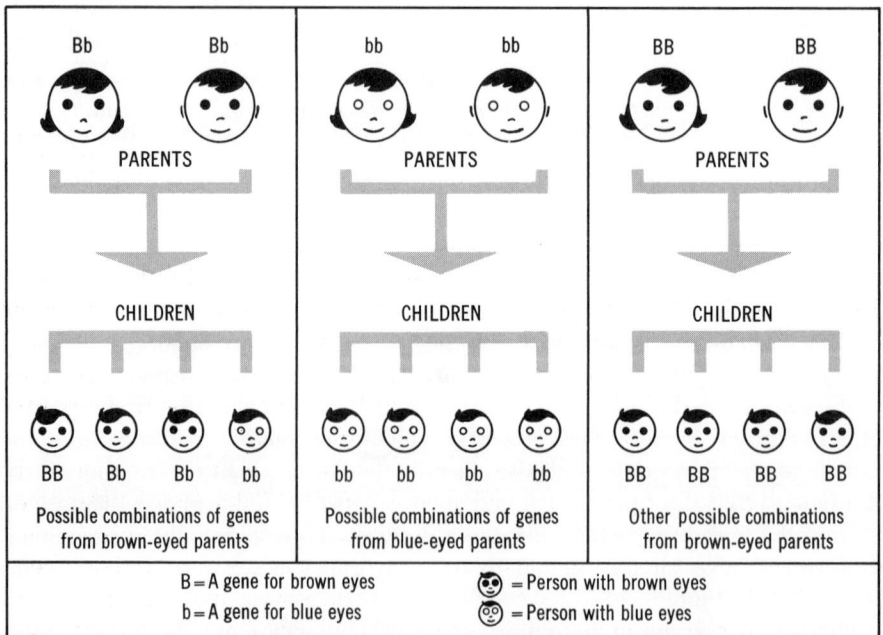

Bb Bb	bb bb	BB BB
PARENTS	PARENTS	PARENTS
CHILDREN	CHILDREN	CHILDREN
BB Bb Bb bb	bb bb bb bb	BB BB BB BB
Possible combinations of genes from brown-eyed parents	Possible combinations of genes from blue-eyed parents	Other possible combinations from brown-eyed parents

B = A gene for brown eyes
b = A gene for blue eyes
= Person with brown eyes
= Person with blue eyes

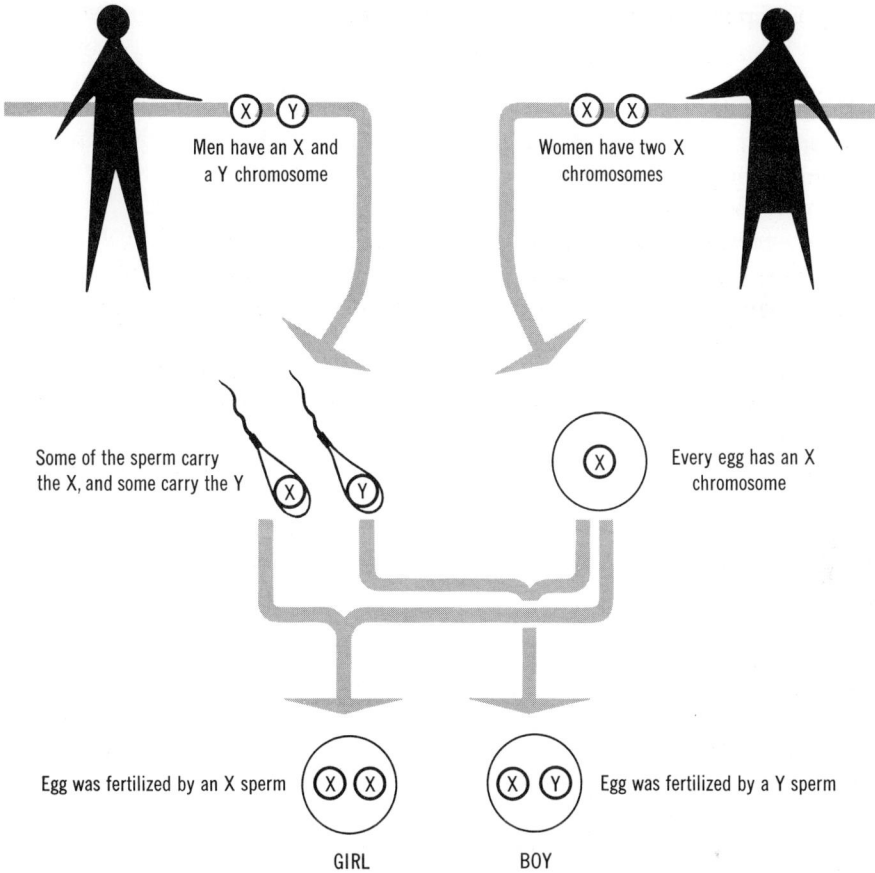

Men have an X and a Y chromosome

Women have two X chromosomes

Some of the sperm carry the X, and some carry the Y

Every egg has an X chromosome

Egg was fertilized by an X sperm

Egg was fertilized by a Y sperm

GIRL   BOY

Determination of sex. *The father is the sole determiner of sex. Every ovum contains the female X chromosome, but while some sperm have an X, others have a type known as Y. Any egg fertilized by a sperm carrying a Y chromosome will produce a male child.*

But some tendencies to dominance and recessiveness do not follow this simple pattern. For instance hemophilia, a condition characterized by the inability of the blood to clot, is a tendency recessive for women but dominant for men. This character is transmitted from parent to daughter, and from this daughter to her sons in turn. On the other hand, certain forms of baldness are transmitted to sons, but not to daughters.

The sex of a child is determined at the moment of conception, and the sperm cell from the father is the sole determiner. All female reproductive cells contain an X or female chromosome and contribute only that kind to conception. The male, however, has two kinds of sperm cells, occurring in different numbers in different men. The sperm may, like the ovum, contain an X chromosome, in which case the child is female; or it may contain a Y chromosome, in which case the child is male. The fact that some families have all girls or all boys does not mean that the father possesses only one of these types of chromosomes, but that somehow due to chance the same kind of sperm has fertilized the egg in each case. A relatively few more boys than girls are born each year, but the mortality rate for boys is higher, and thus the number in each sex is generally evened out until later life, when women outnumber men.

Some genes affect body build, size, weight, height, or general features and shape. Some influence the size or shape of mouth, nose, and chin. Others affect the color of the skin, texture of the hair, color of the eyes, blood type, and hormonal or glandular characteristics.

Certain tendencies to diabetes or other diseases may be inherited, although it does not necessarily follow that an individual will have these diseases because his parents have had them.

Intelligence, to the extent that it must depend upon quantity and quality of brain tissue, also seems to be inherited.

Genes usually act in conjunction with each other in producing inherited characteristics. That is, a single gene, acting by itself, does not usually appear to be the sole determiner of any particular trait. Here again the element of chance enters the picture and plays its part in determining individual characteristics. Environment during the period of embryonic development can also affect the genes. Experimentation with animals (4) has shown that variations in the number of legs of fruit flies can be produced by changing the temperature in which the flies develop, and that certain fish may have either one or two eyes depending upon the chemicals in the water where the larvae develop (5). Some human abnormalities, too, may be due to the environment of the developing embryo; these are described as *congenital,* as distinct from *hereditary* effect, due to the genes. Such disorders may include abnormalities of the skeleton, certain kinds of mental retardation, and inability to control the muscles properly. Environment obviously affects our normal development from the very beginning of life.

Genes, acting with each other, may strengthen tendencies appearing in the families of both the mother and the father. On the other hand, if the families of the parents possess opposing tendencies, the children produced may show leanings either way, or may have "in-between" characteristics. Children and parents resemble each other less than do brothers and sisters (siblings). Children and their grandparents are even less alike.

Suggested activities

1. Peter, aged 12, who had a very high IQ, attended classes at X college. In terms of maturity, how would you expect him to fare? Experiments are being made in which students younger than the average are attending various universities. Can you gather evidence about their success?

2. When something goes wrong, the crowd often finds a scapegoat. Do you consider such behavior mature?

3. Since the human race is all of one species, how can we account for the fact that certain cultures are more advanced than others?

4. List types of behavior you have recently seen which you consider immature. Give reasons for your judgment.

5. Refer to studies of heredity such as are given in biological science textbooks. Find out what a hybrid is. What happens when hybrids mate? Are human beings hybrids?

6. Try to obtain pictures of your ancestors. Consider their biographies, and try to find any traceable inherited characteristics.

7. In what ways are you an individual? Which of the ways can be traced to heredity? Which to environmental influences?

A.   KINDS OF MATURITY
B.   HEREDITARY CHARACTERISTICS OF MAN

● C. THE PATTERN OF HUMAN DEVELOPMENT

Since we do not entirely know the limits of our individual capacities, we cannot know whether we ever reach our limits. We may have the potential to grow to be six feet tall, as far as our genes are concerned, but we also need good food, rest, and exercise if we are to reach that height. Disease may affect our stature, and accidents may interfere with our growth. On the other hand, the best of environmental conditions cannot make a person taller than his hereditary potential will permit. Heredity sets limits within which we may grow and develop. Environment helps to determine the extent to which these limits will be approached.

Thus, we cannot change the color of our eyes which is determined by heredity, but we can learn to make better visual discriminations. We cannot change the shapes of our noses without plastic surgery, but we may learn to appreciate perfumes by training our sensory discriminations. We cannot change our fundamental body structures, but we can make the most of the structures with which we were endowed by learning to use them properly. Although each of us inherits a unique combination of genes and develops in his own way, we can learn to use our individuality to its best advantage.

The processes of growth, maturation, and development are, of course, important factors in determining our adult characteristics. Because of the difficulty in differentiating these terms, they are often used loosely by laymen. Although they are defined on page 110, further explanation is needed here if they are to be properly understood.

Growth, as we use the term, refers only to increase in physical size. It is thought of as increase in the size or mass of such structures as the muscles, skin, glands, bones, nerves, and brain. Longer arms, larger muscles, more skin, longer and heavier bones, a larger heart, a longer spinal cord, and increased mass of the brain are products of growth. As we shall show later, growth does not occur evenly throughout the body. At birth some structures have reached stages much more advanced than others, and some do not begin to grow markedly even then.

Maturation results from increase in size and strength of physical structures but also involves hereditary factors which "unfold" as the organism becomes older. It refers to the orderly sequences or progressions in behavior that become possible as we mature. The child's muscles, bones, and nervous system grow, and when they reach various points of maturation the relationships between them are such that he can take his first upright step, can learn to run, jump, hop, and skip. Functions characteristic of the human species thus emerge in the maturation process, infancy to adulthood.

Learning to walk represents a change in the way a child's body functions, and the change comes about as a result of growth and maturation. These processes involve not only a change in size, but also a difference in what the child can do. Although learning may be involved in these changes in function, it is obvious that one cannot learn to do what his growth and maturation will not permit.

As a person grows up, his glands grow and change in function. Some, which have been producing hormones, for example, the thymus, may cease their function. Others, like the gonads or sex glands, grow slowly until early adolescence, when they increase rapidly in size and change their output of hormones. These in turn affect many other areas of growth and physiological functioning.

The hereditary process apparently sets the patterns for sequences in maturation. In every child throughout the world we find that the growth and maturation patterns from conception to birth require approximately 280 days and the various body structures appear in the embryo and fetus in the same order. Although individuals differ somewhat in their patterns of growth and maturation after birth, even these patterns are still enough alike for us to recognize certain common stages.

Development is the result of growth, maturation, *and* learning. Thus we may say that a child develops the ability to swim; that is, even though he has sufficiently mature body structures to perform the acts involved in swimming, he still must learn how. If he never has the chance to learn, he probably will not be able to swim on his first attempt — if, for example, as an adult, he should fall from a boat. The same holds true for many other abilities, such as those involved in playing a musical instrument, dancing in rhythm to music, and reading.

A child *develops* skill in handwriting. Here, too, the physical structures must first be ready before the teaching can begin. It is the same with speaking; children often speak words distinctly at the age of fifteen months as a result of maturation, but the language they speak depends on what they are taught.

Performances, then, depend on development — the result of growth, maturation, *and* learning.

We shall now examine the major patterns in physical development from birth to senescence and then present three principles useful in relating the entire progression. To understand the progression better, let us discuss the course of development under the following heads:

Infancy — from birth to about age two.

Early childhood — about ages two to six.

Middle and later childhood — about age six until the preadolescent spurt in height; for girls, an average age of ten, and for boys, of eleven or twelve.

Adolescence — from the appearance of pubic hair to the cessation of growth in height and sex organs. For girls adolescence ends at about age eighteen; for boys, at about twenty.

Adulthood — ages eighteen and twenty through fifty-five to seventy, depending upon the individual.

Senescence — Individuals vary, but most begin to show marked physical decline not later than age seventy.

Infancy

At no other time in the existence of the individual is growth so rapid as during prenatal life. During the first month after conception, the human embryo shows the beginnings of arms and legs, lungs, liver, kidneys, glands, and rudimentary sense organs. Some of these organs begin to function in the second month. By the end of the sixth month the unborn child (fetus) is mature enough to have a good chance of

FERTILIZATION
Sperm penetrates egg

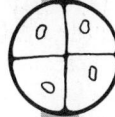

9 days

2 to 8 weeks
Embryo

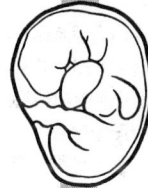

9 months
Fetus

Early stages in human development. *The prenatal period, or period of gestation, is 280 days or nine months.*

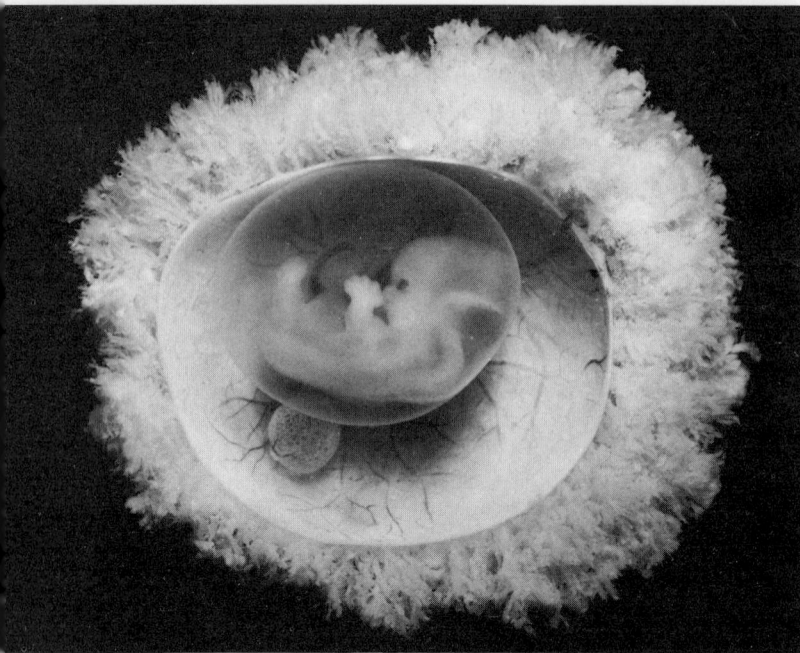

The human embryo at six weeks. *The inner membrane surrounding the embryo is the* amnion, *filled with the protective* amniotic *fluid. The small yolk sac, below the amnion, nourishes the embryo in early growth. The larger sac would have become the* placenta, *bringing nourishment and eliminating wastes through the mother's circulatory system. This embryo was removed because of illness during pregnancy. (Courtesy of the Department of Embryology, Carnegie Institution of Washington.)*

survival even if he were to be born at that stage. The last three months of normal pregnancy are devoted largely to increase in size and integration of body functions, preparing the child for the relatively more rigorous life it will experience in the outside world.

The newborn baby is called a *neonate*. He has a very large head in proportion to the rest of his body, and his arms and legs are short. Development proceeds from the head to the lower extremities (in a cephalo-caudal direction) and from the trunk outward (proximo-distal). Thus the neonate is better able to control his head for suckling than to control his bodily elimination. He achieves control over arms and legs before fingers and toes. His head is about one-fourth his total length, in contrast to the head of an adult, which is one-seventh of his total height. With development, the trunk and legs become proportionately longer than the head.

Someone has characterized the infant as "an alimentary canal with a loud noise at one end and no responsibility at the other." This may seem a bit heartless, but we all agree that the young infant spends a good deal of his time eating and that his elimination processes are uncontrolled. He has some mastery over activities which involve his head — eating and crying, for example — but the parts of his body involved in elimination are not yet under voluntary control.

Muscular activity in the very young infant is characterized by mass move-ment. If his toes are pricked, he responds with whole-body movements, involv-ing the trunk, legs, arms, and head. As he matures, his movements become more specialized, so that when his toes are pricked, he withdraws only his legs. This process of differentiation is largely a function of maturation, although some learning is involved.

The neonate can grasp your finger with surprising strength, using his whole hand, but he cannot release quickly. At about the age of six months he normally begins to exhibit prehensile grasping, that is, he uses his fingers and thumbs rather than his whole hand when he tries to secure small objects.

James (6) has said that to a new baby the world is "one great big blooming buzzing confusion." The newborn child cannot localize sounds or focus his eyes. He cannot interpret what he hears or sees. He can cry as tensions mount, for food, warmth, or other needs; but he cannot indicate or perhaps even recog-nize what he wants or why he cries. But he grows rapidly, even though it may seem that he does not change much from day to day. It is not uncommon for the infant to triple his weight during the first year of life and to increase his height by one-third. The cartilage in his skeletal structure, having served its purpose of flexibility during birth, must now give way to more rigid bone.

Along with physical growth and skeletal development occur those inner processes of growth which bring about maturation, and with growth and maturation the ability to learn increases.

During the second year the infant is still growing fairly rapidly. What can he do now that he could not do at birth? The most important activities include talking, walking, using the toilet, eating solid foods, using his knife, fork, and spoon, and expressing specifically such feelings as anger, fear, or affection. No longer is the world a "big blooming buzzing confusion," but many parts of it have taken on definite meaning.

Early childhood

The rate of growth in height and weight begins to diminish between the ages of two and six. Consequently, Junior eats less than he did earlier. This may become a problem, for parents may not understand that he is simply less hun-gry and does not need as much food. He may show preferences for particular foods, but his parents may wish him to eat foods which are "good for him." He may refuse to cooperate simply because he isn't hungry.

Young children are active. The large muscles are still growing quite rapidly and need exercise. Wise parents try to provide plenty of space and large play equipment so that the child can exercise his muscles without marring living-room furniture or having to beg his parents continually for something to do.

As he begins to expand his environment by going outside his home and asso-ciating with other children, he typically gets such childhood diseases as measles and chicken pox. There seems to be no reasonable way to avoid these illnesses,

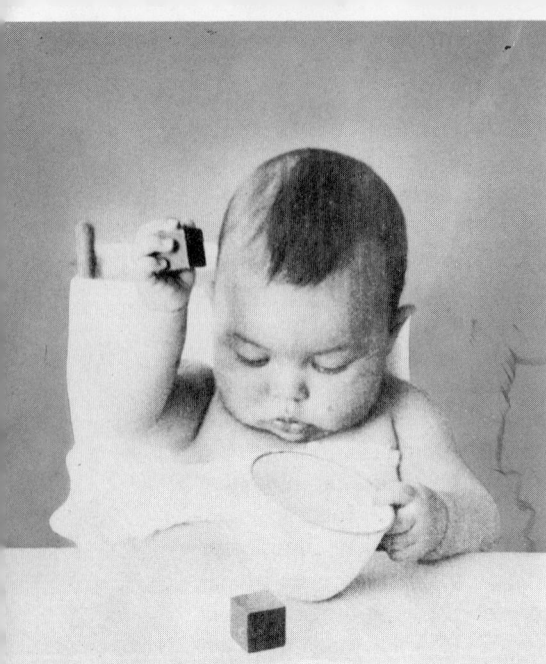

Maturation and the ability to grasp. *The child at left, 28 weeks old, pulls at a cup with his fingers and does not hold the block firmly. The muscles and nerves have not matured enough for the thumb to function with appropriate strength. At 52 weeks, the thumb can be used in opposition to the fingers with sureness and skill. (Gesell Institute of Child Development.)*

but children should have good medical care when they do contract such illnesses, and when they catch cold, in order to prevent any damaging after-effects.

What can the child do at six that he could not do so well at two? He is much stronger. He has more endurance for activities like running and jumping. He has much better co-ordination, not only in walking but also in running rapidly, hopping, skipping, and getting around in general. His finer muscles are now under better control, and he can use his knife and fork quite adeptly in eating. His senses are usually keener, and he has finer discrimination in seeing and hearing. For some time now he has had no toilet problems. His physical proportions are coming into balance. Although his fingers, toes, arms, and legs are still comparatively short in relation to trunk and head, they are more adequate for the many physical tasks he now attempts.

The young child is not without problems. At birth an injury may have occurred, leaving physical scars or brain damage. Later, illnesses may have impaired his mental processes. Other major difficulties may have arisen if his parents wanted him to behave in a more mature manner than his capabilities permitted in such matters as obedience, weaning, toilet training, table manners, and speaking clearly. Modern parents, however, do not expect as much from the infant as those of other generations did. More often than formerly they feed him when he is hungry rather than according to schedule. They usually do not wean him before nine months and may still give him a bottle after two years. Since modern facilities make laundering relatively easy, the child is allowed to wear diapers until he can walk and talk and understand what the bathroom is for, usually when he is about two years old. He is not urged to talk, for he will begin to speak when he feels a need and has matured enough. When he does begin to talk, he is taught to speak clearly by hearing others speak clearly to him.

Modern parents differ in the kind and amount of obedience they expect; but too great insistence will probably result in more, not in fewer, behavior problems and anxiety on the part of the child. More often than not, disobedience is related to an unsatisfied physical need. For example, when parents want the child to sit at the table after finishing his meals, he may need activity and so may disobey them to get it. A mother may want him to sit quietly during a visit to grandparents, but after a car ride he wants and needs exercise. At six o'clock in the morning the child is rested and requires physical movement and activity, but his parents may want to sleep. After a nap in the afternoon, the little boy is ready to romp and play in the evening, but his father comes home from work tired and wants to read the paper. You may find it interesting to recall some of your own childhood experiences or to take care of an infant for a few days.

Middle and later childhood

From ages six to twelve, the years of the first to the sixth grades in school, children are gaining rapidly in the ability to coordinate, but their rate of growth in height and weight and the development of their muscles and glands is tapering off.

Increase in height is very steady from age six to a period just prior to puberty

Muscle control and coordination. *Note how awkwardly the baby holds his spoon. The little girl at right has become adept, not only at holding a pitcher and steadying a cup, but also in coordinating her movements so that she can pour the milk without spilling it. (Gerber Baby Foods.)*

when a spurt of growth occurs. Boys are usually taller than girls except during the ages of ten to fourteen. Of course, there are wide differences within each sex, but the typical superiority of girls over boys during this period is due to the fact that girls mature about two years earlier than boys.

Children reflect the structures and growth rates of their parents. The child of large, early-maturing parents is likely to be large and to mature rapidly, while the opposite is true of children of smaller parents.

The ossification or hardening of the bones is a better indicator than height or weight of a child's rate of growth. The rate at which the wrist and hand cartilage changes to bone and the time when certain bones appear in the joints are reliable indicators of rate of growth. X-ray photographs can be used quite accurately to indicate months of carpal age. If one ten-year-old child has a bone development equal to that expected of a typical ten-year-old and another child of the same age has the development only of an eight-year-old, we can be quite sure that the former will enter into puberty sooner than the latter.

Between the ages of six and twelve children show marked improvement in motor skills. At six most children can begin to learn manuscript handwriting. At twelve they write in the cursive form — some of them about as well as they ever will. At six some children use crayons and paints awkwardly, but at twelve they handle the paint brush, charcoal, or other instruments of art with assurance and skill.

The games of six-year-olds are not highly organized. But eleven- or twelve-year-olds play volleyball, softball, football, basketball, soccer, and many other games according to children's rules and standards. Individual sports like bicycle riding, skating, and swimming are accomplished with a fairly high level of skill .

The steady increase in structures and strength during childhood, with accompanying integration of function, lays the basis for the rapid learning of many motor activities during the first six grades of school. The eyes and hands work better together in handwriting, playing a musical instrument, or batting a baseball. Walking, running, and jumping become more efficient, and the various parts of the body seem to work more smoothly together. These are active years. The Brownies and the Cub Scouts are groups providing opportunities for constructive uses of surplus energy, and the new and exciting games and tasks lead the children into interests which may occupy them for years to come.

What problems related to physical growth do children experience during these years? Besides illness and injuries and possible malnutrition, the main problems of childhood are of three types:

1. Marked deviation from others of the same age in size or appearance. The child may feel unacceptable to others and may be excluded from games or conversation. Often the very tall or fat child or the very thin, weak, or short child may be left out and may feel shy or seek attention through aggressive actions.

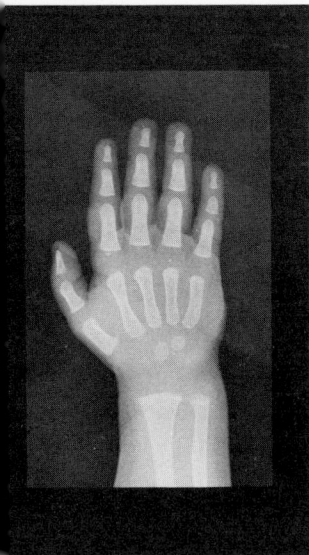

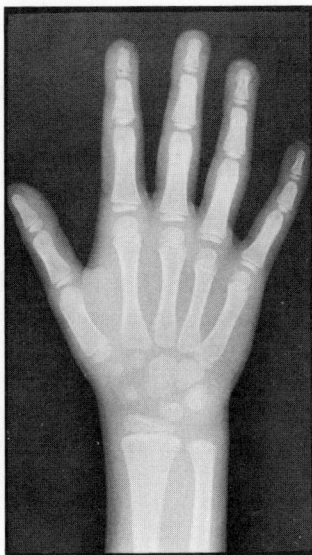

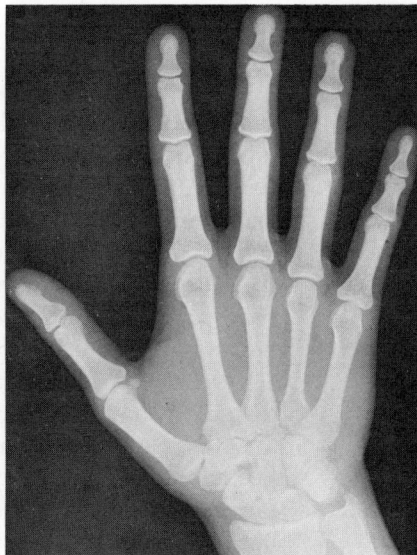

Bone ossification. *The stages in the ossification of a girl's hand are shown in consecutive order: one year, 6½ years, 11 years, 16 years. (Courtesy of Dr. George Erickson, Harvard Medical School.)*

2. Inability to play games as well as other children or to perform handwriting, art, music, or other school tasks involving coordination. The child may feel different. He may be pointed out by his classmates, jeered at, or made a butt of jokes. Sometimes he is compared to his disadvantage with his more favored siblings. Unless children with poor coordination have teachers and parents who recognize differences in rate and level of growth and treat each child accordingly, they may be left out of many enjoyable activities and feel rejected by their peers.

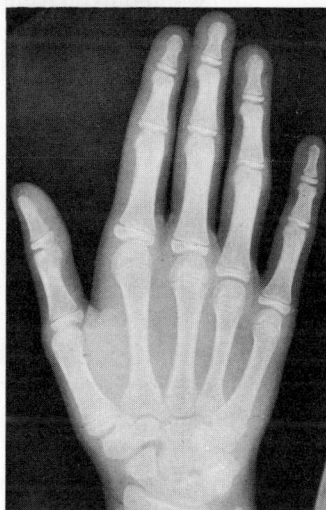

3. Confusion over the roles of the sexes. Our culture imposes many restrictions on girls' activities and places demands on boys to be superior in many kinds of games. Some girls of ten or twelve, however, can play softball or basketball, can wrestle, swim, ride a horse, climb trees, or fight as well as boys. Such behavior is often discouraged by their mothers and teachers. Some girls resent adult attitudes and expectations and often wish they were boys. They may become quite tomboyish in spite of or in reaction to adult standards. Conversely, boys with a great interest in reading, art, music, or even crocheting may have little ability or interest in football and other contact sports, and may be classed as "sissies." They too are sometimes dissatisfied and unhappy because they cannot do what they prefer without social disapproval. For them, sometimes, being a girl might have its advantages.

The most important result of all these facets of childhood development is the self-concept of the child which is its outcome. Does he think himself satisfactory or unsatisfactory? Does he feel happy or unhappy about himself as a person? From rather obvious superiority or lack of ability in certain activities and from the most frequent reactions of others toward him, he will either feel good about himself or feel inadequate, guilty, or rejected. If, in addition to his out-of-school play group experiences, he also finds life in school difficult, the feelings will be reinforced. He may have no area of compensation for his weaknesses in physique and motor coordination.

Try to recall your own physique, appearance, and ability in group and individual games during your elementary school years. Were you like most of the other children of your sex, or were you quite different in physique and appearance? Did you enjoy group games, swimming, riding a bicycle, playing a musical instrument, or singing? Did you learn good health habits — like keeping clean and brushing your hair — because you were pleased with yourself and wanted to take good care of your body? Can you see that some of the bases for the way you now perceive yourself were laid in your childhood years? Keep these ideas in mind for use in bringing up your own children, working with smaller brothers and sisters or the neighbors' children, or working with children as a teacher or in some other occupation.

Adolescence

The beginning of adolescence, from the physical standpoint, is usually marked by two characteristics: the appearance of pubic hair and a rapid increase in height and weight. Adolescence ends with complete maturity of the sex organs and the achievement of adult height. There is wide variation among normally developing individuals in the time when this sequence in development begins; in fact, as many as seven years may separate early and late maturers. The time range is equally wide in achieving full maturity. A very early-maturing girl may be as far along physically at the age of ten as a very slow but normally developing boy aged seventeen. With social or emotional maturity, the range can be much wider. Some adolescents at age sixteen are more mature emotionally than some adults aged thirty-five.

According to Jones (7), our society during the last fifty years has tended to induce more rapid physical development. Boys and girls reach sexual maturity about six months earlier, on the average, than they did at the turn of the century. Though physical development is more rapid, most adolescents are now unable to support themselves, single or married, until long after they have achieved physical maturity.

Adolescence is not a period of violent changes for most people. Rather, it is a period of changes as orderly as those occurring at other times of life. At the beginning there is rapid growth in structure and rapid development in the functioning of the sex glands, but the actual rate of increase in height and weight is not so high as in the first year of life.

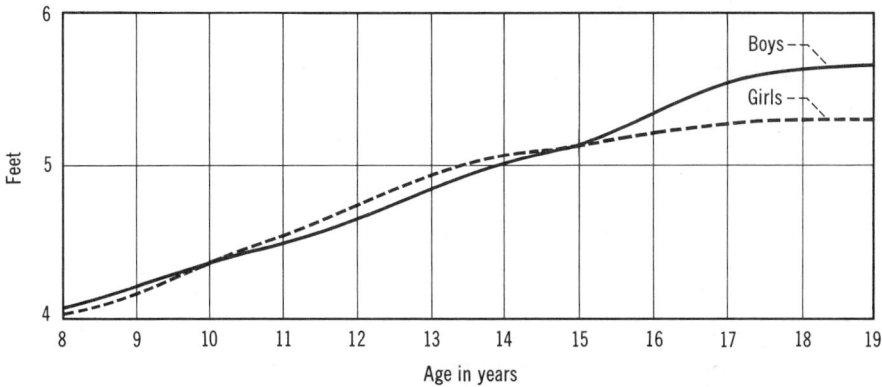

Rate of growth in childhood and adolescence. (*From* Adolescence, *Part I of the Forty-third Yearbook of the National Society for the Study of Education.*)

When the ovaries in the female and the testes in the male start their rapid growth, secondary sex characteristics begin to appear. For girls the most pronounced of these are the appearance of pubic hair, development of the breasts, and widening of the hips; for men, deepening of the voice, widening of the chest, appearance of pubic and facial hair. Girls increase rapidly in height before menarche, the time of first menstruation. Both boys and girls find their strength and weight increasing rapidly. A weight increase tends to change body proportions and may be quite conspicuous. Understanding these bodily changes and accepting them as part of the growing-up process is a major need of adolescents.

The actual size of the individual is important in determining his attitude toward himself and his relationship to others. The experience of growing slowly and steadily throughout childhood and then suddenly reaching near-adult stature in a period of two to four years may cause problems, the most severe being those of girls who reach menarche at the age of ten or eleven and develop very early, of girls and boys who are late in developing and still

Height in boys and girls. *The girls shown here are taller and more mature physically than boys of the same age. What effects might this difference have on personality and social development? (E.I. du Pont de Nemours and Company.)*

look like children when their classmates have become adolescents, and of those who are considerably above or below average size even at maturity. Some of the difficulties of the short or thin boy and the tall or heavy girl stem from the great prestige given in our society to tall, strong athletes in competitive events and to well-formed girls of medium height in terms of popularity. These value judgments are played up in television, movies, and advertising. They tend to foster an ideal body size and shape out of all relation to its true incidence in our population.

Deviations during adolescence are likely to be greater and more noticeable than during childhood. Changes in proportions are closely related to changes in height and weight. Arms and legs increase in length quite rapidly. We have already mentioned the changes in physique of boys and girls, and these contribute to certain ideals of masculinity and feminity which adolescents set for themselves in their groups. The self-concepts of group members are drastically affected, for all wish to be like the ideal. Girls whose heredity causes them to be tall, heavy, or small-breasted but who want to be average in height and proportions may isolate themselves from the group if dieting, exercises, and perhaps reducing pills fail. The short, stout, narrow-shouldered boy and the extremely tall thin boy may likewise have difficulty in accepting themselves. The nicknames coined in high school shower rooms and the heavy absenteeism of girls from physical education classes are indications of the extent of the adolescent concern with physique. So too are the use of cosmetics, lifter shoes, shoulder padding, and a multitude of other forms of disguise in dress and grooming.

The marked changes of adolescence are also apparent in glandular functions. Sweat glands begin to act profusely. Sex organs, heretofore dormant, begin their secretions. If the idea of being capable of reproduction, and all its ramifications and responsibilities, is difficult for some adults to grasp, it is even harder for adolescents. Understanding the nature and implications of such functional changes is one of the pressing problems of this age group. Parents and school workers can aid young people in understanding, preparing for, and accepting these changes.

Stolz and Stolz (8) found that of 93 boys and 83 girls, 31 per cent of the boys and 41 per cent of the girls experienced anxieties concerning physical development. Among those manifestations which disturbed boys most frequently were smallness, obesity, poor physique, lack of muscular strength, unusual facial features, and unusual development in the nipple area. For the girls, tallness, excess weight, facial features, general physical appearance, tallness combined with heaviness, and smallness combined with heaviness were problems.

Although some people still have the notion that adolescence is a period of great awkwardness, it is not based on conclusive evidence. Espenschade (9) tested 165 boys and girls aged thirteen to seventeen over a four-year period. In the 50-yard dash, the jump and reach, broad jump, and throwing a ball the boys and girls were about equal in ability at age thirteen, with the boys showing slight superiority. Thereafter the boys increased in skill until about age sixteen, when a leveling-off or decline began. The girls maintained their relative position until about age fourteen or fifteen, when they began to level off or decline except in the ability to jump and reach. Thus increase in skill apparently continues until the age of about sixteen for boys and fourteen or fifteen for girls.

Brace (10) developed a test of motor abilities measuring such complex skills as making a full turn of the body while jumping, and kicking to shoulder height. He found that nine-year-olds performed about seven of the twenty tasks; thirteen-year-olds, about twelve; and eighteen-year-olds, fifteen. Thus coordination increases throughout adolescence. Perhaps the awkwardness sometimes ascribed to teen-agers may arise from their appearance. Although the adolescent may actually possess better coordination than the child, he may *appear* awkward in many social activities because of self-consciousness and not knowing how to conduct himself.

What can an adolescent in his last years of high school do that he could not do as a sixth-grade child? First of all, he is usually capable of reproduction. He can perform complex motor tasks with much higher precision. His strength is greater, and so is his endurance.

What were your adolescent years like? Were you one of the many fortunate ones who matured about the same time as most of your classmates with an appearance not markedly different from theirs? If you did deviate noticeably from the group or if you were not satisfied with your appearance or skills, can you now look back with objectivity on any unpleasant experiences? Have you come to a better understanding of yourself, and are you more relaxed with whatever you possess in the way of health and appearance? Can you assess your strong points and capitalize on or improve them? Can you improve your skills, health, and appearance?

Adulthood

A person is physically an adult when he has achieved his mature height, when the ossification of his bones is complete, and when there is no further growth in his physical structure. Most college students are physically adult; they are about as agile, strong, and healthy as they will ever be. In young adulthood, rather than later, the possibility is greatest for learning new physical skills and for perfecting those which are partly learned already. If you want to learn to swim, play golf or tennis, or play a musical instrument, you will do well to start as soon as possible. From this point on, you will go downhill in your physical abilities, slowly at first but later more rapidly. A baseball player thirty-eight or forty years old is considered to be rather advanced in age. A prize fighter in his early thirties may be past his peak. Of course, in one sense we are aging from the moment of conception, and we may be declining in certain abilities from the time of birth. But, generally speaking, most of us are at or near our physical peak in the twenties and have reached maximum sensory acuity prior to age twenty. For example, Miles (11) reported that visual perception, as measured by tachistoscopic presentations of letters, figures, and other symbols and signs, reached its peak between ages 10 and 17, and that visual perception at 18–29 was 95 per cent that of ages 10–17. At 30–49 it was 92 per cent, at 50–69 it was 76 per cent and at 70–89 only 46 per cent of what it had been at 10–17 years of age.

Fisher and Birren (12) found that among 552 male industrial workers the peak of strength came during the twenties, with a gradual decline thereafter until age sixty, when the average strength was about 16.5 per cent less than at twenty. Kay (13), studying serial learning performances, reported that the difference between twenty-year-olds and thirty-year-olds was primarily a matter of speed, with the thirty-year-olds showing a loss; the difference between the thirty- and forty-year-olds was more nearly a matter of accuracy with the older group again showing the loss.

Thus after the twenties and in middle adulthood there is a decline in sensory acuity (*e.g.,* vision and hearing), in strength, and in various types of motor performance. Many older people, however, can offset the natural decline to some extent by daily exercise of certain physical abilities, for example, those involved in carpentry or bricklaying, and continue at a relatively high level of physical performance until well beyond the age of fifty.

Problems related to physical development frequently encountered by young adults include the complete acceptance of the physical self and the satisfactory release of sex impulses. Meeting society's expectations by finding gainful employment, by marrying and raising a family, and by becoming completely self-reliant in emotional and economic life poses closely related problems.

The young adult must appraise his physical appearance, motor abilities, and health, and then work toward making the best of what he has, trying to be happy with the results. While body proportions and size may be anything but ideal, they are unchangeable; and while they may have caused unhappiness during childhood or adolescence, in adult life they assume much less importance. The college environment can help the student develop whatever physical talents he has.

In solving problems of satisfactory sex release, marriage and raising a family, gainful employment, and complete independence from parents, some college students experience frustration. As we shall see in succeeding chapters on the social and emotional areas of development, people adjust in their own individual ways.

Senescence

Unlike the "one-hoss shay," the human body does not degenerate suddenly and collapse in all parts simultaneously. Decline in functions like seeing and hearing is fairly rapid in many sixty-year-olds while the rate of decline in walking or sitting may be much slower. Just as full sexual maturity is a clue to physical adulthood, so menopause in the female is one indication that senescence is in the offing. The cessation of sex-gland functioning in the female is the most significant and the most sudden glandular change known to accompany the process of aging. For most American women menopause occurs between the ages of forty-five and fifty-five. They are then no longer capable of reproduction. Knowledge of this fact, along with the effects of certain chemical changes, seems to have a disturbing effect on many women. Some interpret loss of the ability to reproduce as a real sign of old age, especially those who feel that they are no longer attractive to men.

In men there is no such abrupt cessation of sex functions. Many are capable of reproduction at sixty-five or even later. However, except for the marked difference in sex functioning, women of sixty to eighty are no more senescent than men of that age. All the signs of aging in both men and women are becoming better understood through the sciences of gerontology and geriatrics. Study of the aging is particularly important at present because more people are living beyond the age of sixty-five.

Sensory deterioration is very marked in senescence. The digestion is no longer as efficient as it was earlier. The heart and blood vessels degenerate rapidly in many older people. After age fifty-five, disorders of the cardiovascular system cause more deaths than cancer, nephritis, and diabetes combined. Glands other than those of sex also show decided decline in activity. Senescence results, generally speaking, in lower resistance to disease, slower healing of wounds, less awareness of and interest in the environment, slower reaction time (14), wrinkled skin, and other characteristics.

Senescence is not often given serious consideration by young adults whose lives are still ahead of them. And this is understandable. But, though a young person may be quite unconcerned with his own old age, he should still consider the importance of the problem to his grandparents or even his parents, and recognize that a satisfying life is much more difficult for them to achieve now than when they were younger.

Gumpert (15) found that 7.7 per cent of the population was sixty-five years of age or older in 1950. By 1960 the percentage should rise to 9.2, and by 1980 to 11 per cent. With the increasing proportion of aged people, local and state governments and public and private agencies will have to spend more money for their care. Young married adults nowadays do not habitually take care of their aged relatives, often because the need comes at the same time they are raising their families and paying for a home, car, and other conveniences. Many aged persons are not happy. Some do not have proper medical care. Many are spending their last years at a very low level of existence. Whereas the parents of a child look forward to his development with enthusiasm and hope, they often do not have a comparable attitude of affection and interest in their own aging parents.

You may wish to study these problems more widely (16), for they will affect you either now in relation to your parents or later in relation to yourself.

Principles of development

In the previous sections we have traced some of the general trends in physical development from conception through adulthood and into senescence. Psychology attempts to discover general principles which can be used to correlate many individual facts. From the previous discussion and the research which underlies it we can now list some of the principles of development. They should be useful to you because they can help you think through your own development and thus attain a better understanding of yourself and others — your own children someday or other young people you may know and work with. Consider their likenesses and differences in terms of the following principles:

1. *Development proceeds according to an orderly pattern.*
2. *Individuals develop and decline at their own individual rates.*
3. *Development and decline of various parts of the body and their functions do not proceed at the same rate within the individual.*

These principles point to the fact that people are both alike and different. We must judge each person's growth or development, not only in relation to group norms but also in relation to his own particular pattern of development. We must learn to expect differences among people. And once a person has matured, he must accept himself as he is and learn to make the most of his body structure and physical abilities, whatever they may be.

SUMMARY

People develop mature behavior in part through learning. There are many areas of maturity: physical, intellectual, emotional, social, and moral. A person does not mature in all these ways simultaneously. Because both heredity and environment have roles in the development of the individual, there is an almost infinite combination of tendencies and experiences which exert their influence. We can therefore be sure that no two of us are exactly alike, not even identical twins.

Although we are individuals, scientists can detect general patterns of development which hold true for all people. When marked deviations from these patterns occur in an individual, he is a subject of concern not only to scientists but to parents, educators, physicians, and others, including himself. Heredity plays its part in individual development at conception, but environment, both in the physical sense (nutrition, disease, accidents) and in terms of learning, has a great effect on behavior.

The differences in performance between men and animals are great. Man possesses a structure which is superior in many ways. At the same time, we may all wonder whether we are living up to the potential with which we are endowed.

The general pattern of human development has been investigated widely, and certain terms and sequences to express it have emerged. *Growth* is defined as increase in size, length, weight, and mass. The term *maturation* describes progressive changes in the functioning of the various tissues of the body, due in part to the unfolding of bodily structures at the proper time. The interaction of growth and maturation, and learning, results in *development*. Rapid growth occurs in prenatal life, infancy, and early adolescence. These can be critical periods in the life of the individual because of the rapid changes occurring in his body. Intervening periods, when growth is slower, may be looked upon not as periods of rest, but as times when structures are becoming coordinated. For example, after the rapid growth of muscle tissue, there is a period when the increased tissue is brought under control through activity and learning. Development, uneven as it is for various functions of the body and for various people, may bring stresses and strains of an emotional, social, and physical nature. The psychological aspects of the development process profoundly affect behavior and adjustment.

Most college students are physically mature, but many are probably not mature in every way. While reading this chapter you may have said to yourself many times, "Why, that's what happened to me." You are now beginning to see the various forces which made you what you are now. You recognize the difficulties you encountered in your own developmental process, but now you realize that others may have had the same problems or others equally difficult. You begin to see that heredity and learning had a share in molding your total personality, and you recognize that you can still change in many ways. As you begin to understand your hereditary endowment, your physical growth and maturation, and your previous experiences, none of which you can change and all of which help to make your personality what it is, you begin to face reality and assess yourself more accurately. If you cannot change, you must accept yourself as you are, find the proper ways to put your assets to use, and adjust to life as you find it. If you can change or improve you should assess the nature of the changes you want to make and proceed to find ways to make them. You must look at yourself as objectively as possible. Part Two is concerned with understanding how we learn.

Suggested activities

1. Identify the major sequences of development in your life. Were you a rapid maturer? Slow? What psychological correlates were the result?

2. Study the effect of developmental patterns on the lives of various people in case studies and biographies. What influences a person to become the particular kind of adult he becomes?

3. Study juvenile delinquency, school drop-outs, and students with poor

school adjustment. What are some of the primary causes for such problems of youth?

4. Look at your daily schedule. How have you provided for food, rest, and exercise?

5. What activities have you undertaken today? How are they related to physical growth and development?

6. Obtain measures of age, height, and weight of an eighth-grade class. What differences do you find among the children? Can you detect any social or emotional differences related to age, height, and weight?

7. Observe an infant. What can he do? What can he not do? In what ways does he look different from older children? How does your knowledge of development affect your outlook toward bringing up children?

8. Go to a junior or senior high school gathering. What differences in physique do you see? How do boys and girls compare in physical maturity? Is there an observable relationship between maturational level and behavior?

9. Do any of the problems you face today originate in your childhood or adolescence?

REFERENCES

1. L. Cole, *Attaining Maturity*, Rinehart, New York, 1944. See also L. Cole, *Psychology of Adolescence*, Rinehart, New York, fourth ed., 1954, Chapter XX.
2. W. N. Kellogg and K. S. Kellogg, *The Ape and the Child, A Study of Environmental Influences Upon Early Behavior*, Whittlesey House, New York, 1933.
3. J. Huxley, *Man in the Modern World*, Mentor Books, New American Library of World Literature, New York, 1943, p. 75 ff.
4. H. S. Jennings, *Biological Basis of Human Nature*, Norton, New York, 1930.
5. C. R. Stockard, "The Artificial Production of a Single Median Eye in the Fish Embryo by Means of Salt Water Solutions of Magnesium Chloride," *J. Comp. Neurol. Psychol.*, 1909, 17, pp. 191–192.
6. W. James, *Principles of Psychology*, Holt, New York, 1890.
7. H. E. Jones, *Development in Adolescence*, Appleton-Century-Crofts, New York, 1943, p. 23.
8. H. R. Stolz and L. M. Stolz, "Adolescent Problems Related to Somatic Variations," *National Society for the Study of Education 43rd Yearbook*, University of Chicago Press, Chicago, 1944, pp. 86–88.
9. A. Espenschade, "A Motor Performance in Adolescence," *Monographs of the Society for Research in Child Development*, 1940, No. 2, pp. 49–53.
10. D. C. Brace, *Measuring Motor Ability*, Barnes, New York, 1927.
11. W. R. Miles, "Age and Human Ability," *Psych. Rev.*, 1933, 40, pp. 99–123.
12. M. B. Fisher and J. E. Birren, "Age and Strength," *J. Appl. Psychol.*, 1944, 28, pp. 504–519.
13. H. Kay, "Learning of a Serial Task by Different Age Groups," *Quart. J. Exper. Psychol.*, 1951, 3, pp. 166–183.

14. R. W. Kleemeier, "Age Changes in Psychomotor Capacity and Productivity," *J. Business*, 1953, 26, pp. 146–155.

15. M. Gumpert, "Our 'Inca' Ideas About Retirement," *New York Times*, 1952, July 27. Copyright 1952, The New York Times Corp.

16. J. Tuckman and I. Lorge, "The Influence of a Course in the Psychology of the Aging Adult on Attitudes Toward Old People and Older Workers," *J. Educ. Psychol.*, 1952, 43, pp. 400–427.

SUGGESTIONS FOR FURTHER READING

Bookwalter, K. W., et al., "The Relationship of Body Size and Shape to Physical Performance," *Res. Quart. Amer. Ass. Hlth. Phys. Educ.*, 1952, 23, pp. 271–279.

Dennis, W., *Age and Behavior*, U.S.A.F. Sch. Aviat. Med. Proj. Rept., Proj. 21–0202–0005, Washington, 1953, Rep. No. 1, VII.

Garrett, H. E., *General Psychology*, American, New York, 1955, Chapter 2.

Ikin, A. G., "Psychological Problems of Maturity," *Pastoral Psychol.*, 1954, 5, pp. 49–54.

Jaynes, J., "Imprinting: the Interaction of Learned and Innate Behavior: II. The Critical Period," *J. Comp. Physiol. Psychol.*, 1957, 50, pp. 6–10.

Kuhlen, R. G., and G. H. Johnson, "Changes in Goals with Adult Increasing Age," *J. Consult. Psychol.*, 1952, 16, pp. 1–4.

May, R., *Man's Search for Himself*, Norton, New York, 1953, Chapters 3, 4.

Pressey, S. L., and R. G. Kuhlen, *Psychological Development through the Life Span*, Harper, New York, 1957, Chapter 12.

Pugh, M. C., "Charting Growth with the Wetzel Grid," *Res. Quart. Amer. Ass. Hlth. Phys. Educ.*, 1954, 25, pp. 47–53.

Smith, W. J., "Family Plans for Later Years," *Marriage Fam. Living*, 1954, 16, pp. 36–40.

Stagner, R., and T. F. Karwoski, *Psychology*, McGraw Hill, New York, 1952, Chapter 15.

Zuk, G. H., "The Plasticity of the Physique from Early Adolescence through Adulthood," *J. Genet. Psychol.*, 1958, 92, pp. 205–214.

Learning

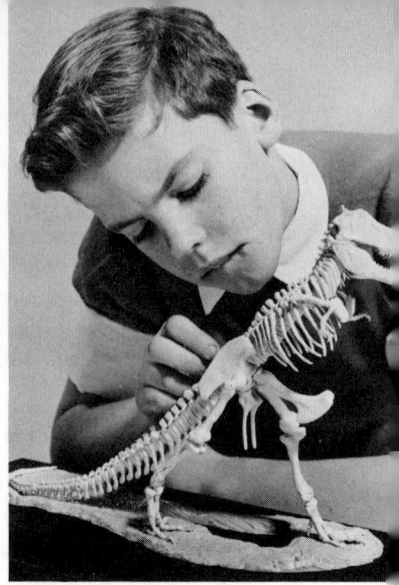

Visualize a student walking across the campus, meeting a friend, and saying, "Hello." A rather simple act, you think, and one that does not require much learning. But let us examine the action more closely to see how much learning really is involved.

That the student is walking across the campus implies that he knows how to walk — an ability not completely inborn but acquired by maturation and partly by learning during the early years of life. He is presumably wearing campus attire: the socialization of the individual which causes him to wear appropriate clothes also begins shortly after birth and continues over a period of time. Note also that the student has to have a reason for walking across the campus or for being on the campus at all. What is he doing there? If he answers, the very act of speaking will not only imply knowledge of what words mean but also something of social custom, and it will necessitate the control of complex muscular activities. If he can tell us who his friend is, he must have some system of values, which has also been learned. Knowledge of friends also implies ability in judging people. If he remembers a friend's face and recognizes him with a greeting, the memory of a previous experience is again the effect of learning. If he shakes hands, he is demonstrating social learning again as well as motor control. Since he has a certain taste in clothes, he has learned to appreciate dress, color, and style. He took enough interest in clothes to dress as an individual, and probably he wears his clothing distinctively, the result of complex learning.

5

Theories and Application

What is learning? Why is it important? What are the different types of learning? How does learning occur? What are some of the factors which have a positive influence on learning? What are the different theories of learning? How are they similar, and how different? What is conditioning? What is meant by transfer of learning? How can you apply principles of learning?

Even such a simple example of human learning could be extended almost indefinitely, but you can already realize that a great deal of learning is involved in almost everything you do, no matter how simple it seems. Heredity may affect your body structure, environment may influence your growth, and accidents may befall you, but the specific ways in which you behave are largely the result of various kinds of experiences from which you have learned something.

So commonplace is learning throughout life that we often overlook its significance. But to understand our behavior we must ask such questions as "What do we learn?" "How do we learn?" "Why do we learn?" Answers to such questions will tell us a great deal about ourselves and should help us solve many of our everyday problems.

A. PURPOSEFUL LEARNING

For our purposes we shall define learning as *a process whereby a change in behavior results from an experience,* an activity, special training, or observation. Such behavior may be mental, emotional, or physical, or some combination of these.

For truly effective learning the change in behavior should be permanent. It may be argued that a change in behavior occurring for the first time indicates

137

learning. Many changes in behavior, however, come about through maturation, and others are acquired quite at random and do not persist. Therefore, the first time a person does something in a different way, it does not necessarily mean he has *learned* a new kind of behavior. The criterion of whether learning has occurred is that the behavior can be repeated.

Maturation, disease, and accidents can cause modifications of behavior because they change body structure and functions. When a muscle grows, when the eyes of an aged person lose their acuity, or when a person is drugged by alcohol, behavior changes. Such changes are obviously not a result of learning.

But learning *may* bring about a change in the organism. Electrical or chemical changes in nervous tissue may occur during learning, but this is a hypothesis which has not been established well enough to permit us to say that we know exactly what takes place. We hope some day to understand learning better and perhaps even to be able to explain it in terms of body changes. For the present, however, we must be content with observing the effects of learning and, through inference, try to understand, predict, and control learning in practical situations.

A sequence in purposeful learning

We presume that most students have come to college with the purpose of learning. In fact, purposeful learning characterizes most of our mature behavior. To clarify the learning process, let us take a practical situation such as learning to play a piano solo for the college music department. In purposeful learning there are certain clearly definable stages.

1. The student must be ready to learn. Maturation, intelligence, and physical ability are involved in this problem situation. The student must have a background of previous piano-playing so that he can learn the new and more difficult material. He must want to learn; it is not likely that he will perform well if he has no particular desire to do so. Readiness to learn implies an overall satisfactory state in the learner in relation to his learning task; that is, he must have the necessary mental and physical ability, the experience, and the motivation to learn.

2. The student meets and interprets the problem. In this case, the problem is to learn to play the piano solo. There is a piano present, as well as sheet music and an instructor. The learner looks over the music, thinking about it in ways determined partly by his previous background. He listens to the instructor and tries to get an idea of precisely what is expected of him and how he might attack the problem. His attitudes also may be involved. For example, he may learn much more readily if he interprets the situation with self-confidence and not with fear. Moreover, if he has a proper understanding of the music he will be more likely to play it well than if he misinterprets the composer's intention. In any event he interprets the task as he sees it.

3. The learner responds to the situation as he perceives it. In this case he practices the music, probably taking the more difficult parts separately. He may perform the easier parts well without much practice, but he may try a passage first in one way, then in another, judging and comparing results.

4. *The student's responses are confirmed, reinforced, or perhaps found to be wrong.* As he practices, the student will get some ideas of whether or not his responses are correct. Perhaps the music will not sound right, and he may modify his methods. Perhaps the passages will not feel right to his hands or fingers. Undoubtedly the instructor will make comments. On parts which he can play correctly, the learner may still wish to practice in order to make his learning more nearly permanent. There will be a tendency for him to repeat the responses which seem correct and which the instructor says are good. Thus the responses which the student considers correct will be confirmed and reinforced; those which he deems incorrect will be criticized, then corrected.

5. *Lack of successful learning may bring frustration.* So far it has been implied that the student can learn to play this piano solo; but in some instances a learning task may be impossible for the particular person in question. Perhaps the student and his instructor disagree over a rendition. The student's responses may not have satisfied his teacher or himself. The pupil may then react by getting angry, stopping the lessons, or continuing to practice without making much improvement. On the other hand, he may change his methods and practice until he attains success.

The foregoing steps in learning, which in general follow a sequence described by Cronbach (1), illustrate the idea that purposeful learning can be analyzed. You will no doubt wonder whether the sequence is the same in all kinds of learning. We believe that the above steps are typical of most purposeful learning; however, some responses are not learned purposefully, as we shall see later in this and subsequent chapters.

The learning process as we have described it is not significantly different from what we called problem-solving in Chapter 1. You may wish to compare these sequences to note their similarity, especially that both involve setting a goal for oneself. In purposeful learning a goal or purpose has actually been set by the learner. He is faced with a situation to which he responds in terms of his goals. He must respond if he is to reach the goal, and the nature of his responses will determine whether or not he is successful. Success will reinforce but lack of success will negate the tendency to repeat the responses. Thus purposeful learning may be thought of as a problem-solving process, with, however, many of its steps implied or less formally set forth than in a deliberate use of problem-solving techniques.

Outcomes of learning

Learning leads to a change in behavior: mental, physical, or emotional. We must now consider just how this change may be manifested. It may exhibit itself in several common outcomes.

Concepts and information. A concept is the *meaning* a person attaches to symbols, like words and signs, and to sensory experiences. When you were very small, your concept or idea of a man was rather vague. Probably your father represented your best picture of man. As time went on, you extended this concept to include the whole category of adult human males. Men were big. Men had deep voices. Men worked for a living, drove automobiles, fought in wars, and so on. At the present time your concept of man, or the meanings you attach to the word when you see or hear it, is such that it enables you *a.* to classify man as different from other objects and *b.* to associate the word with your previous experiences.

One intelligence test used with children under seven years of age is the Goodenough Draw-A-Man Test (2). It is based on the assumption that children draw what they know about a thing rather than what is actually true about it. Small children may draw a man with an incorrect number of fingers, they may fail to distinguish between chest and abdomen, they may omit eyebrows. As they get older, children tend to become more certain about details and show them in their drawings. The test implies that all children have the ability to perceive "man" characteristics, but this ability varies among children and according to age. Thus, a point scale which takes into account the inclusion of certain details provides some measure of mental maturity or intelligence based upon the child's concept of man.

If you think of the fable of the blind men and the elephant (3), you may recall that one of the men felt that the elephant was "very like a rope" since he held the animal's tail. Another, feeling the elephant's leg, thought the elephant "very like a tree." And a third, touching the animal's side, found it "very like a wall." A concept grows and develops. It represents the entire body of a person's knowledge, idea, and understandings about something. In college much of your study involves the acquisition of an increasing number of accurate concepts. Practically all reading, laboratory work, and lectures are devoted to improving your concepts. That is what we are doing here. We are trying to improve your concept of the symbol, "concept."

Let us now attempt to clarify two additional terms — *self-concept* and *personality* — so that you may understand them in the sense used here.

A person's self-concept is the totality of meanings which he has about himself. More simply, it is the complete pattern of what he thinks of himself as an individual. The self-concept develops over a period of time; that is, it is the result of learning. The infant is not aware of himself as a person, but as he grows and learns, he acquires a self-awareness from his experiences. This awareness includes his intepretations of his physical self, his attitudes, his goals, his social relationships — everything he thinks of as making up "him."

Susan, for example, thinks she is attractive, has acceptable social attitudes and clear-cut goals, and is fairly congenial — with enough independence to maintain her self-esteem and individuality in thought and action. Since Susan is able to accept herself as a desirable person and interrelate the various

OUTCOMES OF LEARNING. *Learning can have various outcomes: new concepts and information, new motor skills, new types of emotional expression or control.*

CONCEPTS AND INFORMATION. The drawing at left for the Draw-a-Man Test is by a boy aged 4 years, 9 months. His mental age was determined at 4 years, 9 months. The other drawing by a girl, aged 5 years, 8 months received a score equal to a mental age of 7 years. Note the details in the second drawing. (From F. L. Goodenough, *The Measurement of Intelligence by Drawings*, World Book Company.)

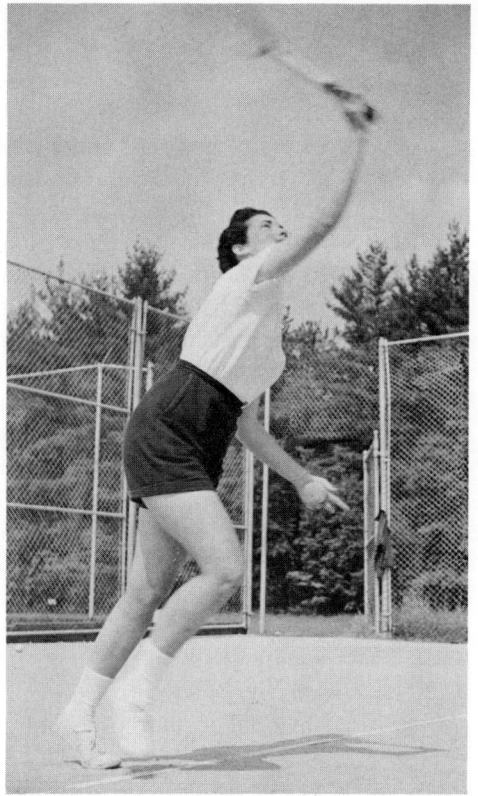

MOTOR SKILLS. The tennis serve is a learned skill involving muscular control and coordination. (Boston University Photo Service.)

EMOTIONAL RESPONSES. Dr. Charles Munch, conductor of the Boston Symphony orchestra, has learned an emotional response of appreciation for music, as well as musical techniques and skills. (Courtesy of Boston Symphony.)

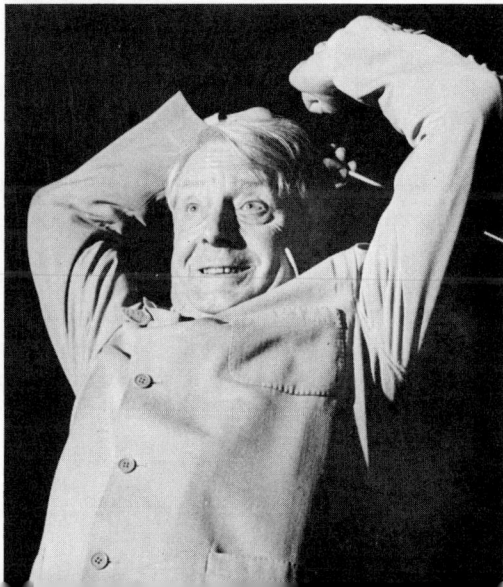

facets of her self, and because her idea of herself corresponds with the way others see her, Susan may be said to have an adequate, well-organized self-concept.

The term *personality* is more difficult to define. It includes the self-concept as one of its aspects but it goes beyond that. Personality, in part, represents the characteristics of a person as he appears to other people, as when we say, "He has a pleasing personality, he seems kind, and he is attractive."

Personality may also, in part, represent the manner in which a person responds to certain situations. For example, we generally think in terms of personality traits, such as, "He gets angry quickly," or "He is always running himself down." First, then, personality represents a person's *stimulus value* — the way he affects others. Secondly, personality may represent a *response pattern* — the way he generally acts in a certain type of situation.

A third aspect of personality takes into account one's motivational and value systems. Allport (4), for example, considers one's inner system of beliefs, expectancies, desires, and values as part of his personality. He suggests that this inner system affects both one's stimulus and his response characteristics. According to Allport (5), "Personality is the dynamic organization within the individual of those psychophysical systems that determine his unique adjustment to his environment." This implies that personality is changeable (dynamic), yet stable and well organized enough so that in an individual it can be described and interpreted (psychophysical systems). It also suggests that personality is the medium between the environment as we sense it and our resulting behavior. In this sense, personality is an *intervening variable;* it is the reason we interpret our environment as we do and adjust to it in our own particular way.

Stagner has summed up the problem of the necessary complexity of any definition of personality by saying, "The question, What is his real personality? . . . cannot be answered in any direct manner. We can only state that a man's real personality includes what he wishes to be, how he wishes to appear, how he appears to others, and how he appears to himself. It involves his evaluation of his environment, of other people, and of himself. It also includes the manner in which these inner patterns are concretized in action. . . . Personality is intrinsically complex; we can offer no simple formula for reducing its rich variety to a dry definition." (6)

The writers of this book tend to accept Allport's definition of personality, but recognize that a definition must depend on one's theoretical preferences (7).

Because the self-concept, like many of our other concepts, is acquired developmentally, these definitions are included in this chapter on learning. The self-concept will be discussed further in succeeding chapters.

Motor skills. Another outcome of successful learning may be increased skill in motor activity, that is, overt behavior involving the skeletal muscles. Many motor activities involve coordination of the eyes with the hands, the guiding of muscles through the sense of touch, and the guiding of muscles through the feel of the muscles themselves as they react.

Many motor skills are either improved or learned for the first time at college. For example, athletes may improve performances like passing a football, balancing in gymnastics, or making a basket in basketball. Art students may improve their use of the potter's wheel; music students, their instrumental or vocal techniques; and commerce students, their skill in the use of a calculating machine. Many undergraduates improve their dancing, handwriting, golf, or bowling. Such improvements may involve accuracy, strength, endurance, speed, or form.

Attitudes, values, interests, and motives. When we are born we have basic physical needs for food and rest, for example. But as you learned in Chapter 4, we have social needs as well. Social development includes the acquisition of sets of values — interests, attitudes, and motives — as well as the growth of desires for affection and for recognition of our individual worth. Chapter 8 will develop more fully some of the factors in emotion and motivation. For the present we shall be content with pointing out that many emotional responses are *learned,* both the ways in which we react and the things *to* which we react.

In college you may change your attitudes toward religion, toward social problems, and toward political parties. You may develop interests in the subject matter of various courses, or other areas of life. You may expand your value structure, or you may alter your sense of values as you broaden your experience and live with a variety of persons.

Social and emotional controls. As we mature, we develop control over our emotions. We learn what to respond to and what not to respond to. We learn mature ways of expressing emotions; for example, we may get very angry over social injustice, but instead of stamping our feet and yelling about it we may take concrete steps to do something about certain problems. We may discover that we cannot overcome some of our fears, so we learn to accept them. On the other hand, we learn to respond with enjoyment to poetry, drama, or music, where we may formerly have been indifferent to them.

Problem-solving techniques. These techniques have been discussed in the earlier pages of this chapter and in Chapter 1. Some of the problems you meet and solve rather formally in college are those you meet in your courses of study — mathematics, the physical and biological sciences, the social sciences, and so on. Others are of a social nature, the kind you meet every day on a less formal basis.

Problem-solving techniques can be learned. We will do well to note the processes involved in solving problems and become more fully aware of the ones we use in our own attempts. Most of the steps in problem-solving, such as the formation of hypotheses and the gathering of data, can be improved by an evaluation of our own results. Attempts to solve problems can be made more efficient: that is one thesis of this book.

Now we have seen the various outcomes which may result from purposeful learning. The student who learned to play the piano solo may have improved his skills, developed a better concept of some musical symbols, developed a more favorable attitude toward practice, learned to express or control his emotions, and improved his techniques for solving technical problems of musical performance. Thus all the typical outcomes can be observed from one learning situation.

Theories of learning

To clarify further the sequence of purposeful learning, we must now consider some theories regarding the learning process. A *theory of learning* is a systematic statement in which evidence from psychological laboratories and elsewhere is organized into a meaningful framework to explain the essential features of learning. Of the various theories of learning none has been entirely proved. Much more research is needed before we can definitely say, "This is how learning takes place." The theories, nevertheless, are useful in helping us think about learning problems, in developing further research, and in solving practical problems. The various theories have much in common, but exponents of any given theory feel that theirs is scientifically more fruitful than others.

Hilgard (8) points out that theorists continue to disagree on such questions as: *1.* Is learning primarily a matter of acquiring responses to stimuli in a mechanical way through trial and error, with repetition and reinforcement of correct responses (association theory); or is learning primarily a matter of identifying a problem, seeking a solution, and in the process of active seeking, using one's intelligence in arriving at the solution (Gestalt theory)? *2.* Does the correct response need to be reinforced in order to be learned, or does merely associating a response with a stimulus result in learning? *3.* Is there more than one kind of learning? If so, do we need more than one systematic learning theory? Though these questions are not adequately answered at the present time, Hilgard further states that a comprehensive learning theory ought to seek and supply answers to the following questions which might be raised by any intelligent person:

1. *What are the limits of learning?* Here is raised the question of the capacity to learn, of individual differences among learners of the same species and of unlike species. There are questions not only of persistent differences in capacity, but of change in capacity with age. Who can learn what? Are the limits set at birth? Do people get more or less alike with practice? These are the sorts of questions which it is natural to raise.

2. *What is the rôle of practice in learning?* The old adage that practice makes perfect has considerable racial wisdom behind it. Surely one learns to roller skate or to play the piano only by engaging in the activity. But what do we know about practice in detail? Does improvement depend directly on the amount of repeti-

tion? If not, what are its conditions? What are the most favorable circumstances of practice? Can repetitive drill be harmful as well as helpful to the learner?

3. *How important are drives and incentives, rewards and punishments?* Everybody knows in a general way that learning can be controlled by rewards and punishments, and that it is easier to learn something which is interesting than something which is dull. But are the consequences of rewards and punishments equal and opposite? Is there a difference between intrinsic and extrinsic motives in their effect upon learning? How do goals and purposes affect the process?

4. *What is the place of understanding and insight?* Some things are learned more readily if we know what we are about. We are better off as travelers if we can understand a time-table or a road map. We are helpless with differential equations unless we understand the symbols and the rules for their manipulation. But we can form vowels satisfactorily without knowing how we place our tongues, and we can read without being aware of our eye movements. Some things we appear to acquire blindly and automatically; some things we struggle hard to understand, and can finally master only as we understand them. Is learning in one case different from what it is in the other?

5. *Does learning one thing help you learn something else?* This is the problem of formal discipline, as it used to be called, or of transfer of training, to use a more familiar contemporary designation. Some transfer of training must occur or there would be no use in developing a foundation for later learning. Nobody denies that it is easier to build a vocabulary in a language after you have a start in it, or that higher mathematics profits from mastery of basic concepts. The question is really one of how much transfer takes place and what its nature is.

6. *What happens when we remember and when we forget?* The ordinary facts of memory are mysterious enough, but in addition to familiar remembering and forgetting our memories may play peculiar tricks on us. Some things we wish to remember are forgotten; some things we would be willing to forget continue to plague us. In cases of amnesia there are often gaps in memory, with earlier and later events remembered. Then there are the distortions of memory, in which we remember what did not happen, as is so strikingly demonstrated in testimony experiments. What is taking place? What control have we over the processes involved?

With these emphases in mind, we are ready to consider the *association* theories, the *cognitive* theories, and the *purposive* theories of learning.

Association theory. According to such theories we begin our learning by reference to empirical knowledge, that is, knowledge derived from experience. As we look at the clock, we may realize that it is nearly time for lunch. Or the picture of a house may remind us to write home to our parents. The sight of a dog may make us recall our own pet. And, as we see a police car, we slow down because it reminds us of the laws against speeding.

In this way we make *associations* between stimuli and responses which result in changes in behavior. Presumably the various factors of a situation are connected through a mental process so that a stimulus from this particular situation calls forth the response given previously on a similar occasion. Of course, precisely the *same* situation can never recur, but one situation can be enough like another so that what we did in the first case can also be applied here, that is, we have *learned* a response. Such evidence of learning is shown when one tries to remember a person's name. If he can create a situation similar to the original one by remembering the occasion when he last met the person, other people who were present, a detail of clothing, or some of the conversation, he is more likely to recall the name. In other words, a *stimulus*, the person, and a *response*, the recalling of his name, have been in some way *associated* with each other. Such association is a form of learning.

Associations occur in various ways. Some of them may seem to be accidental, and one may not be consciously aware of them. Such associations are not purposeful in our sense of the word, and we shall discuss them later. But many associations are purposefully made, for example, when we try to remember names, telephone numbers, or facts from a textbook. These associations involve first the stimulus, then some form of response, personal motives and readiness, and evaluation of the response. Focus of attention, the degree of awareness of the problem, appropriate stimuli and responses, and the effect of the experience in terms of satisfying the learner's needs — all these affect the nature of the association.

Writers in the past have usually considered the aspects of association to be primarily environmental and not particularly related to the inward state of the individual, except insofar as the satisfaction of a personal need made the occurrence and permanence of learning more likely.

In attempting to explain how association does occur in purposeful learning, let us examine some of the ideas of Edward L. Thorndike (9).* Thorndike believed that association could occur by chance, but he felt that this theory alone did not explain much of what happened in many learning situations. He emphasized what is called the law of effect. Simply stated, this means that, if a state of satisfaction, such as occurs with a real or symbolic reward, ensues when a certain response is made to a stimulus, it aids learning.

Thorndike experimented with animals, especially cats. By placing a cat in a puzzle box and observing its behavior, he was aided in deducing his laws of learning. The puzzle box contained a lever or device which a cat could operate in order to release a door for escape. On the first trial, a cat placed in the box was likely to try previously acquired escape behavior — meowing, crawling all over the box, clawing, smelling, and the like. Eventually it would trip the lever which released it from the box. This behavior was probably accidental in the first trial, for the animal had no way of knowing that the lever could be used to open the door.

After a few trials which ended in apparently accidental success, the cat began to identify the lever with the opening of the box. Various cats would try different ways to operate the lever — biting, clawing, or pushing. Although at first the cats might spend some time in useless effort, as trials proceeded the sub-

* For an extensive treatment of Thorndike and his ideas, examine Hilgard (8).

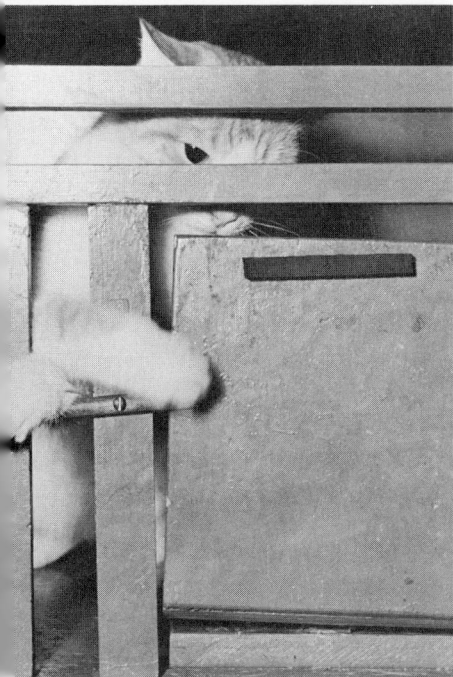

Trial-and-error learning in animals. *The cat tries many kinds of escape behavior before tripping a lever which opens the door. After a few trials, the cat begins to associate the lever with opening the box. (Nina Leen, Pix.)*

jects became increasingly adept at short-cutting useless movements and attaining their goal. In time they could go directly to the lever, move it, and immediately gain their release.

Chance trial-and-error learning of the sort described above is rare among adult human beings, for most of us have previously learned responses to help us gain our objectives in new situations. Past experience will usually furnish some general plan of the way to proceed, even though we do not know exactly what to do. Here is an example of human behavior using trial and error, but it is not wholly trial and error, for the trials have some direction.

Suppose that you return home from college unexpectedly one night. Not wishing to wake the family, you do not turn on the lights. Your purpose is to reach your bedroom and retire for the night, a purpose which ordinarily would be easily and quietly accomplished. However, while you were away, the living room furniture has been rearranged. As you attempt to pass through the living room, you stumble against a chair that had been moved to a different spot.

Now you are forced into trial-and-error behavior. You move to avoid the chair but hit a table. You avoid the table but bump a lamp. This sort of thing goes on until you either have avoided all the obstacles in your way and reached the bedroom or else have given up in disgust and turned on the light. If you repeatedly came into the dark living room and never saw it in the light, and if the furniture remained in the same position, you would soon learn to avoid it. Your trials would become progressively successful until you finally could steer a proper course.

In substance, trial-and-error learning in human beings beyond the ages of infancy implies that the learner has a goal in mind and tries various kinds of actions to attain it. Mentally or physically he responds to the stimulus situation in terms of his goals. Success in his efforts tends to facilitate the acquisition of a response, but failure simply leads him to reconsider that particular response. He evaluates the results of his actions and typically improves them through repeated effort until he can finally obtain his goals directly.

Finding your way through the rearranged living room did not involve merely chance trial and error, for you had some idea of the shape of the room, the direction of your bedroom from the front door, the nature of the furniture, and so on. It is this way with most learning which is purposeful in character. Some idea of how to proceed is present, based on earlier learning.

The small child learns a great deal by trial and error. He discovers what is good to eat by putting things into his mouth. He soon finds out what is naughty and what is nice by experiencing his parents' reactions to his conduct. He learns to walk by trying a few steps and to talk by approximating adult sounds.

As we grow older, our behavior becomes more directed, so much so that at times past knowledge may actually interfere with success in new ventures or improvement of present skills. Take bowling, for example. Many of us bowl, but few of us have had lessons. Undoubtedly our bowling skill would improve if our form could be altered, but to change it might necessitate the "unlearning" of inefficient actions — a difficult task. "Unlearning" would be required, too, when the relatively crude arm and hand movements used in driving a car interfere with the finer coordinations needed to fly an airplane.

Trial-and-error learning in human beings. *Children learn many things through trial and error. If the little boy burns himself, spills something, or gets a spanking, he will learn not to behave this way again. (Photograph by Harold M. Lambert.)*

As adults, we frequently engage in rational and intelligent trial-and-error learning. Most motor skills — athletics, music, writing, typewriting, dancing — involve trial and error. Solving mathematics problems, writing a theme, and learning social skills may also involve this sort of learning.

Thorndike's early position on association learning can be summarized as follows:

1. Learning depends on the number of *stimulus–response bonds* which are made and on the capacity of the individual to form such bonds. An intelligent person has the capacity to produce more such bonds than a dull person.

2. *Practice,* in learning, is effective primarily if stimulus–response connections are rewarded. If no effect (need-satisfaction) is noted, or if a response is punished, as in spanking a child for getting at the cookie jar, learning tends not to occur or at least not to remain. Thorndike later modified his theory on the effects of punishment and recognized that punishing an incorrect response might not lead to its extinction.

3. *Understanding* is not the central focus in learning. However, if enough elements from previous situations are directly relevant to the present one, a person can use connections or bonds which he has already established. New situations are not understood until they are related to past connections; and if such a relationship cannot be established, trial-and-error learning can provide the means of acquiring new responses.

4. Learning is primarily a matter of *acquiring specific responses;* thus the learning of a total response occurs through connecting its more specific components and parts. Since Thorndike worked primarily with animals, it is not surprising that he studied learning by analyzing specific responses and isolating such phenomena as the effects of rewards, punishments, and practice.

5. The learning process is primarily *mechanistic.* Definite stimulus–response connections are made. Hence the same stimulus or set of stimuli should later call forth the same response.

6. The role of the organism in *interpreting situations* depends primarily on how it relates the bonds it has already acquired to the present stimuli.

Suggested activities

1. Practice throwing playing cards into a hat. Notice the trial-and-error learning involved.

2. Attempt to learn a new skill like dancing a new step, bowling, or shooting a bow and arrow. To what extent are random trial and error involved? To what extent has prior learning influenced the new learning?

3. If you drive your car to a distant city, under what conditions might random trial-and-error learning be demonstrated? Directed trial-and-error learning?

4. If a proper maze is available, let a white rat or other small animal run it.

How does he proceed? Do you conclude that he is exhibiting a certain amount of trial-and-error learning?

    Cognitive theory. Whereas associationists emphasize the rather direct response of the organism to specific external and internal stimuli, *cognitive theorists* believe that environment per se is not enough to evoke the kinds of responses people make in various situations. To them no two persons have an identical experience of objective reality. They emphasize what every psychologist knows, that an individual responds *not* directly to stimuli but to what *he* perceives as a result of stimulation and in the light of his own motives. Thus we may respond to certain parts of our environment and ignore others. We interpret or perceive our environment not only in terms of a situation existing outside ourselves, but we bring to the situation our goals and motives, our past experiences, our capacities and abilities, and our levels of maturation and health. We are more aware of some things in the environment than of others. Some parts are clearly in focus — these we call *figures*. Other parts are in the background and we are less aware of them — these we call the *ground*.

    Chapter 6 takes cognitive theory as its starting point and develops it further than it has been described here. There the main emphasis is on perception. We believe that most attempts at learning, and their outcomes, are not accidental but are organized in ways meaningful to the subject. By discovering how to organize an experience meaningfully, the learner is able to make better responses and to learn with understanding. From this point of view, as we have implied, the perceptual fields of individuals are not identical. Since the stimuli are not the same, neither are the responses. However, as we shall see later in this chapter, this theory may not explain certain kinds of learning in which we are not even aware that learning has occurred.

    For adherents of cognitive theory, learning involves *differentiating* various aspects of the environment and of the possible responses. In this sense, we pick out things to respond to and select the responses which might be suitable. From the vast number of experiences available to us we recall certain ones which appear to be applicable to the present situation. Also we differentiate certain goals which we desire to pursue more closely or more immediately than others. Thus, if we can understand a person's perceptual field, everything he knows of himself and his environment, we can understand why he responds as he does in various instances of learning and other daily activities.

    Insight is the term applied to a specific, high-level, problem-solving phenomenon. The Gestalt school of psychologists, which originated in Germany, coined this term in connection with a unique characteristic they observed in some learning situations. It seemed to them that a sudden flash of understanding may occur when we have been trying for some time to work out solution to a problem without seeming to get anywhere. Then all at once we seem to grasp the nature of the problem and its solution; this is insight. The Gestalt psychologists feel that, in the work which precedes a solution, our

mental processes have been busy restructuring the learning situation until a combination of perceptions of the present experience and suitable reproductions of past experiences have provided opportunity for insight into the problem and its solution. The learner has perceived a relationship among his goals, the environmental situation, and ways in which he might proceed.

During World War I, Köhler (10), a German psychologist, was interned by the Allies on the Island of Teneriffe. Finding some rather large apes on the island, Köhler attempted to study their intelligence and, perhaps incidentally, learned much about insightful learning.

On occasion he would swing a bunch of bananas suspended from the ceiling of the ape cage, high enough so that the animals could not reach the fruit by jumping from the floor. They soon found, however, that they could climb the bars of the cage, and by timing the swing of the bananas, jump to them and attain their goal. They also learned to pile boxes on each other to attain a height from which to jump. The piling up of boxes was a solution widely adopted by these apes, although they never seemed to understand the need for balancing a stack of boxes in such a way that they would not tip over from their own weight.

In replications of Köhler's study of apes, there was evidence that mental

Insight learning. *Köhler found that apes can think before acting; or "size up" a simple situation and find a solution. Note that, as the ape stacks the boxes, he is no longer looking at the bananas. He has formulated a plan and can keep his goal in mind. (Lilo Hess, Three Lions Inc.)*

activity took place *before* the physical activity was undertaken. The animals seemed to "size up" the situation, discarding obviously useless behavior without putting it into practice. Suddenly, it appeared, they would understand. They would then immediately try something which showed they had reached a correct solution to their problem. Once the solution was found, the apes repeated it in subsequent similar situations without intervening practice.

Gestaltists feel that the sudden appearance of the solution is the result of restructuring the situation so that elements are correctly related and understanding can occur. Others have said that this so-called insight is merely a mental trial-and-error process in which one solution after another has been mentally tried in imagination and discarded until the correct solution is evident.

In summary cognitive theorists may be considered to base their concept of learning on the following ideas:

1. The higher forms of learning depend on *natural capacities*. Although environment modifies the ability to learn, learning is the differentiation and restructuring of fields and as such is closely related to the organism's innate *ability* to differentiate.

2. *Analyzing outward responses to situational stimuli does not provide a sufficiently complete basis for inferring the learning process.* In a sense, "the whole is greater than the sum of its parts." Simply viewing a pile of nuts and bolts and wheels would not lead us to the concept of an automobile. The same is true with learning.

3. The *organism* is central in the learning process. The ways in which it perceives and structures a situation determine what and how well it learns.

4. Learning is a *dynamic process*. It occurs with purposeful repetition but not as a mere result of the repetition. Specific stimulus–response bonds are inadequate for describing the nature of learning outcomes or of the acquisition of learned behavior.

5. The *structuring of a situation* determines the learning that will occur. People respond to their perception of fields rather than to specific objects in their environment.

Suggested activity

Using six matches or toothpicks, build four equal equilateral triangles. Your solution of this problem illustrates insight. Now, with twelve toothpicks or matches, build four equal squares. Does insight transfer?

Purposive theory. Stephens (11) indicates that *purposive* psychologists emphasize that in learning there is always a variety of ways of achieving the same results: the important element is purpose not method. In other words, people can wash their hands, comb their hair, or study history in different ways, but all these variant methods lead to the same relatively specific goals and satisfy the same motives. When conditions (internal or external) act on an individual, a goal is determined. The individual may utilize any of several available means in his environment to satisfy the need. If he is hungry and only hamburgers are present, he eats hamburgers. If it becomes absolutely necessary, he may eat roots, insects, or reptiles as, for example, survivors of a shipwreck are sometimes forced to do. In our modern society he might eat only steaks if he so desired, or no meat at all, but he would still satisfy his basic need for food.

The focus of attention and the ways of perceiving situations are functions of the needs of the individual. These physiological or psychological needs which are most pressing in terms of the individual's well-being will be satisfied first; and his energies will be devoted to finding ways, within the context of the environmental situation as well as in terms of his own capabilities, to satisfy them.

Learning represents the finding of ways to satisfy a need. Some of these ways are acceptable to the individual and to those with whom he lives, i.e., they actually do satisfy his need and at the same time are socially accepted or tolerated. Other ways may be satisfactory to the individual but not to society — for example, direct aggression like burglary or assault as a way of obtaining food. If the need cannot be directly satisfied, frustrations occur. Conflicts may exist within the individual. He may try to escape conflicts and frustrations through such processes as rationalizing, substituting the eating of food for attainment of affection (compulsive eating), identifying himself with others as a means of building up his self-esteem, and in other indirect ways.

Sigmund Freud is classified as a *purposivist*. He had little to say about learning but much to say about defense and escape mechanisms, discussed in Chapter 8, and about mental health and illness, treated in Chapter 13. However, Freud surmised that the techniques of maintaining physical and psychological security are acquired after birth and that they may become habitual. Thus types of behavior which have been confirmed by whole or partial need-satisfaction tend to be repeated. Those which have not been confirmed are discarded, and other more suitable modes of behavior are sought. As an example, we may think of a young man who has a need for being recognized as a person of worth and ability. He may set himself the goal of fulfilling this need by becoming a dramatic star. However, if he finds that he has little acting ability or that some other circumstance will prevent his reaching that particular goal, he may become a stage-set designer, a cinema photographer, or a make-up artist and achieve satisfaction in that way. Or, on the contrary, he may give up the theater entirely and rationalize his action by becoming extremely critical of acting and actors.

We may sum up the purposive views on learning as follows:

1. *Persons of high intelligence are able to find more satisfactory ways of fulfilling their needs than those of less intelligence.*

2. *Introspection, aided by such techniques as word association and interviews, furnishes a great deal of information about human behavior and learn-*

ing. External observation may tell what a person is doing; we can only infer why he is doing it.

3. *Human beings interpret situations primarily in terms of their needs.* The environment is only a vehicle for attaining need-satisfaction, and it is focused upon only with that end in view.

4. *Human beings are dynamic, rather than mechanistic.* It is this dynamic characteristic which makes for the variety of means of satisfying needs and many of the difficulties involved in obtaining satisfaction. Freud, for example, pictured the various specific drives or needs as practically warring with each other for attention within the individual.

5. *The way in which a problem is seen is determined by the needs of the individual at the time.* Thus the same situation, viewed in two different conditions of need, would be seen differently. Two situations, however, could both be seen as satisfying the same need, but perhaps in different ways.

Suggested activities

1. Assume that you are a second Robinson Crusoe, cast away on a desert island. One of your basic needs is for food. Another is to escape from the island and find your way home. You will require shelter from the elements and protection from hostile animals. What are some of the activities you might undertake? How do they illustrate the purposivist point of view?

2. You are given the problem of leading one of your social clubs in a drive for money to finance the club program. How might you proceed? What, if any, learning may take place? What factors would influence the behavior and learning of the club members?

A. PURPOSEFUL LEARNING

● B. NON–PURPOSEFUL LEARNING

Do you really desire to learn everything that you learn? Or can certain types of behavior be acquired incidentally without your being aware that you have learned or changed your way of behaving? Certain psychological theories suggest that some learning takes place without the individual being aware of it. Conditioning is the term commonly applied to this form of learning.

Conditioning

The pupil of the eye contracts when a beam of light is directed into it. This contraction occurs without the knowledge or consent of the subject; it is a reflex action. It has been demonstrated that if a bell is rung shortly before the beam of light is used, the pupil will contract at the sound of the bell alone after several trials. The response (pupillary contraction) has been connected in some way to the new stimulus of the bell.

Pavlov (12), a Russian psychologist, used dogs'in conditioning experiments. Food was placed on a dog's tongue, causing his mouth to water. When Pavlov rang a small bell just prior to introducing the food, he was able eventually to get the dogs to produce saliva at the ringing sound alone.

Watson (13) used a young boy and his pet, a white rat, to study conditioning. Children normally exhibit a startled response to loud sudden noises, and Watson found that if he made a loud noise behind the child while the rat was present, eventually the child showed distress at the sight of the rat alone. Indeed, the response became so generalized that the sight of other furry objects — including a fur coat — brought forth the signs of distress in the child.

Watson did not leave the child in fear of furry things. Through a process of providing the pleasant stimulus of food, and then introducing the furry objects into the room, the child was returned to his normal state of pleasure at the sight of them.

The above illustrations show *conditioning.* In its first form the term *conditioned reflex* was used to indicate the process in which a previously neutral stimulus called forth a reflex action. Conditioning, however, is found to occur not only in connection with reflexes but also with more complex forms of behavior. Some emotional response patterns and certain aspects of motor skills like typewriting may be interpreted in terms of conditioning. Mowrer (14) believes that learning a language can also be thus explained, and some writers have considered that conditioning is the basis for learning in many forms of behavior. With the concept of the process now so much broader we can no longer think only of the *conditioned reflex* but must also consider the term *conditioned response.*

Let us now further examine conditioning. Conditioning of the pupil of the eye which results in a reflex action may be diagrammed in this way:

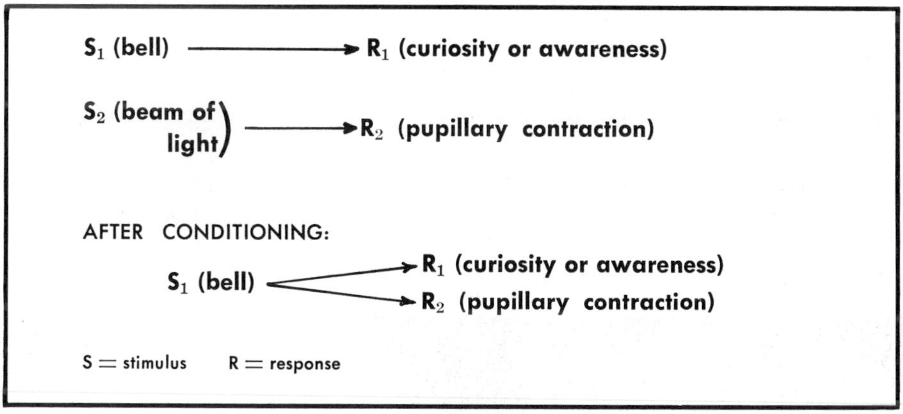

S_1 (bell) —————————➤ R_1 (curiosity or awareness)

S_2 (beam of light) —————➤ R_2 (pupillary contraction)

AFTER CONDITIONING:

S_1 (bell) ⟨ ➤ R_1 (curiosity or awareness)
                ➤ R_2 (pupillary contraction)

S = stimulus R = response

---

1. At first the bell is a "neutral stimulus." The only response it produces is that of curiosity or awareness.

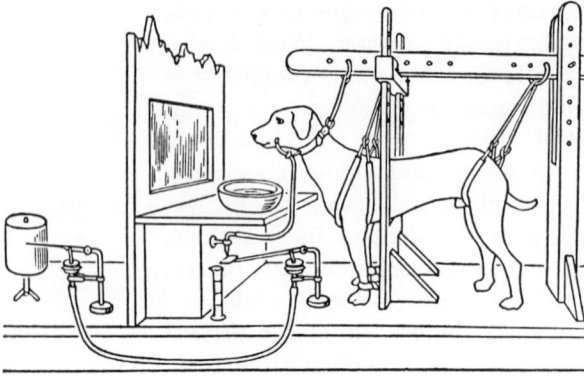

Pavlov's experiment. *In conditioning the salivary response of a dog, Pavlov used a platform on which each drop of saliva would activate a recording mechanism, leaving a mark on a moving smoked drum. (From R. M. Yerkes and S. Morgulis, "The Method of Pavlov in Animal Psychology," Psychol. Bull., 1909, Vol. 6, p. 257.)*

2. The beam of light calls forth the pupillary reflex. This is automatic and the subject does not even know it occurs.

3. The bell is rung shortly before the light is flashed into the eye.

4. After repeated trials the pupil will contract at the sound of the bell alone, so that the light is no longer necessary. Conditioning has now occurred.

The beam of light is called the *unconditioned stimulus,* since it is the natural stimulus to which the *unconditioned response,* the pupillary contraction, is related. The ringing of the bell is called the *neutral stimulus* (also unconditioned, in effect) which brings forth only the response of curiosity or awareness. After conditioning has occurred, the bell sound is called the *conditioned stimulus* and the eye reflex the *conditioned response,* since a new response has now become attached to the bell sound.

When Watson conditioned the child to react emotionally at the sight of a pet rat, "stimulus generalization" operated so that any furry object brought forth the same response. Responses tend to generalize also. Thus Pavlov's dogs not only exhibited salivation but their posture and movements in general showed a response to the ringing of the bell.

Learning through conditioning may be relatively permanent. However, in time, if the learning is not *reinforced* by occasional use of the unconditioned

Reinforcement of learning. *When the rat presses the lever, a small pellet of food falls into the tray. The reward is a motivation to repeat the act. This experiment uses a modified form of the Skinner Conditioning Box, designed by Dr. B. F. Skinner of Harvard. (From the film, "Motivation and Reward in Learning," by Neal E. Miller and Gardner Hart.)*

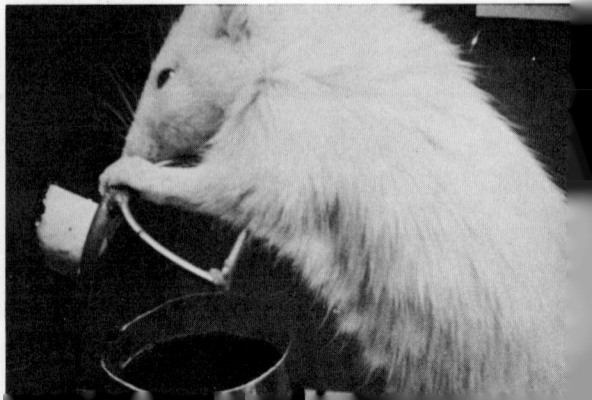

stimulus (such as the beam of light or the food), the response will no longer be made to the new or conditioned stimulus. The response becomes extinct. If rest is given, the response will return but will wear out in a shorter period of time, and finally the conditioned stimulus will no longer call forth the conditioned response.

Probably in our everyday lives the kind of conditioning most prevalent is that which results in emotional response patterns and in attitudes. Many of these — toward people, toward school subjects, and toward different foods or drinks — carry over into adult life from conditioning in earlier years. For example, when you first went to the dentist, your reaction was probably curiosity. He drilled a tooth, and you felt pain. You may now fear going to a dentist, or at least, his use of the needle or drill. You did not start by wanting to fear the dentist, and you did not react with anxiety to words like "fill" or "drill," and yet you may be doing so now as a result of your experience.

As a child you approached a dog, intending to pat it. He growled and bit you. You were afraid thereafter of strange dogs and even now may exhibit an emotional response pattern of fear. In the classroom you may have had teachers who frightened you; if so you may still be timid in the presence of your instructors.

In summary, we can say of non-purposeful learning that:

1. Environment plays a leading role.

2. Observation, rather than introspection, aids us in understanding this kind of learning, and such learning may be analyzed into component factors.

3. Perception is not of central importance in non-purposeful learning, although sensory awareness without a high level of differentiation is important. This kind of learning can and does take place without the association of meanings with sensory experiences.

4. A mechanistic stimulus–response bond is involved, rather than dynamic interaction of various elements in the learning situation and the learner.

5. Specific stimuli call forth specific responses. Problem-solving is not implied in non-purposeful learning.

Suggested activities

1. Try this simple conditioning experiment with a young child: Tell him that every time you raise your right arm he is to raise his right arm. Then tap with your pencil about one-half second before you raise your arm. The order of events is: You tap — you raise your arm — the child raises his arm. Repeat this about ten times, and then merely tap *without* raising your arm. Usually the child will continue to raise his arm. This is simple conditioning.

2. If there are ex-servicemen in your room someone may suddenly call out in a military manner, "Ten-shun!" Servicemen have been conditioned to leap to their feet — you may see an example of conditioning in real life.

3. Train your dog to perform some action. Give the command, guide him

through the act, and reward him with a tidbit. Repeat until he responds at your command.

4. Try waiting until your dog performs some action. Then reward him. Command him after he has performed the act. What is the difference between this arrangement and that described in Activity 3?

5. If possible set up a laboratory experiment in which white mice are given an electric shock whenever they approach a piece of cheese. Eventually they will respond to the cheese alone in the same way that they respond to the shock — by withdrawing.

    A.   NON–PURPOSEFUL LEARNING
    B.   PURPOSEFUL LEARNING

● **C. SEARCH FOR A COMPREHENSIVE THEORY**

As you have seen, various theorists have differing ideas on the nature of learning. All the concepts we have mentioned have different implications for classroom and everyday situations in learning and teaching. Psychologists have made attempts to resolve their differences in the hope that a single theory, embracing the known phenomena about learning, might be evolved which could take the place of the various views and explanations now current. Some psychologists have felt that we are working toward theories of human behavior in general which would include as one aspect, theories of learning. Others have felt that, though unable to proceed that far, they could offer reasonable theories to account for the differences in thinking concerning the nature of learning. Some have attempted to do this by considering learning to be a *dual process*. Among them are O. H. Mowrer (15) and Dewey and Humber (16). To show such a resolution, we quote from Dewey and Humber:

> . . . The aspects of personality which we call secondary drives or learned motives are acquired under conditions in which associational learning including conditioning is adequate, and involve the autonomic[1] nervous system and the visceral-vascular[2] responses. The aspects of personality which we call purposive or problem-solving are learned through the intervention of the central nervous system and find responses in the skeletal musculature and mental or thought habits of the organism. In this latter development associational learning is essential but oftentimes not adequate, because the stimulus–response bonds are retained best if they meet certain felt needs of the person. The former process is largely unconscious,

[1] The autonomic nervous system regulates the various inner organs of the body, like the heart, stomach, and glands. It comprises the sympathetic and parasympathetic systems. The sympathetic system plays a predominant role in emotion and functions in opposition to the parasympathetic system.

[2] The *viscera* are organs of the body cavity, like the stomach, spleen, and intestines. Visceral reactions include stomach contractions, secretion of adrenin, and other responses of visceral organs. *Vascular* refers to blood vessels.

whereas the latter is, for the most part, conscious; the former involves the involuntary muscles, the latter the voluntary ones. That which we *want* or *will* to do is largely a function of innate drives or needs, and of secondary drives or needs which are for the most part unconsciously acquired or learned, primarily through the operation of the autonomic nervous system. That which we actually *do*, on the other hand, is learned primarily through the central nervous system, and is largely a function of conscious behavior. The innate or acquired drives of the autonomic system set the problems; the central nervous system attempts to solve these problems or, as some prefer to say, reduce tensions.

Thus, to illustrate briefly, when one sees another car bearing down on his own in the middle of an intersection, the fear of collision, learned by association, acts as a motivating force. The action of stepping on the brake and swerving out of the way is a response learned originally as a problem-solving activity. Both types of learning are thus represented in a single situation.

You may wish to refer to the material in this section after you have learned more about emotions and motivation, which will be discussed in Chapter 8.

The writers of this book, as suggested earlier, emphasize purposeful learning. They do not deny, however, that many attitudes, emotions, and methods of expression may be acquired without conscious intent.

    A.   PURPOSEFUL LEARNING
    B.   NON–PURPOSEFUL LEARNING
    C.   SEARCH FOR A COMPREHENSIVE THEORY

● D. FACTORS IN READINESS

Some techniques for aiding your learning at college were presented in Chapter 2. They are based on the ideas discussed in this chapter and on others which will be presented in Chapters 6–9. Earlier in the present chapter, in connection with the sequence of purposeful learning, we mentioned *readiness*. Now we shall consider the main elements of this prerequisite to profitable learning. They are: developmental level, intelligence, previous related experiences, socio-emotional setting, and motivation.

Developmental level

A child does not walk until his legs are strong enough to carry him (until maturation has proceeded far enough) and until he can move his legs in response to his will. The same conditions apply to other motor skills and learning outcomes dependent on developmental level.

Experiments have been performed (17) in which one of a pair of identical twins was given training in a task like climbing stairs. It was found that after a certain level of maturation had been reached, the one who had no training learned to climb stairs about as well and as quickly as the one with several weeks of practice beforehand. If learning is attempted at the proper time, it

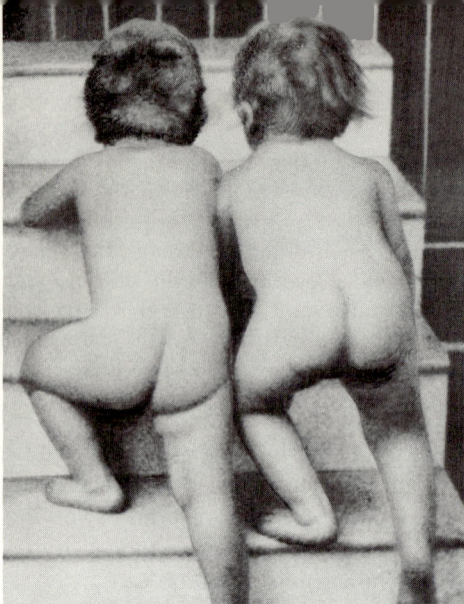

Maturation as a factor in learning. *Physical readiness is essential to many types of learning. At the proper point of maturation the identical twin with no training (at right) learned as quickly to climb stairs as did the one who had been given several weeks of practice. (Gesell Institute of Child Development.)*

can be accomplished economically, but practice is relatively useless if it is undertaken too early. It can also be frustrating and even harmful.

Students can acquire many kinds of learning more efficiently at college age than earlier or later in life. However, certain other kinds of learning, e.g., skill in a foreign language, swimming, and playing a musical instrument, might be developed to a higher level if learning had started in earlier years.

Intelligence

A full discussion of intelligence will appear in Chapter 9. It is enough here to point out that some learning requires a higher level of abstract mental ability than some other types. An Einstein, for example, can develop a theory of relativity, while some idiots cannot talk or dress themselves. A five-year-old may learn to read more readily than a less intelligent child of seven.

Previous related experiences

Once we have learned to drive a car, learning to drive a tractor is not difficult. Once a musician knows how to finger a clarinet, it is not hard for him to learn to play the saxophone. Once the concepts of color and form in art have been learned, they may be applied to clothing design or sales promotion.

In teaching the small child to read, some teachers first give him a background of experiences related to the things he will read about — they take him to the post office, fire station, or grocery store. They show him pictures and movies and help him to express orally the words that he will soon try to read.

Can you learn calculus without knowing algebra? Or algebra without knowing arithmetic? Concepts, vocabulary, and other forms of background are needed in most kinds of college learning, hence the stress placed upon your high school preparation.

Socio-emotional setting

If a person is distracted, for example, by unexpected loud noises, thoughts of the coming party, dislike of his neighbor, or disgust with himself, he cannot concentrate very well on his study. He cannot learn to drive a car well if he is afraid of traffic. Deer-hunters often suffer from "buck fever" and fail to get their deer.

These illustrations show why professors like to have a classroom which offers a pleasant physical environment free from distractions. For the same reasons it is good to have a library not only quiet but also attractively decorated. Most people learn best in a classroom which is not too crowded, where they like their classmates and enjoy their instructor's teaching. A person *can* learn under less suitable conditions, but learning will be more difficult as well as slower and less efficient. He *can* study when he is worried about family troubles or when he is having difficulty with his girl friend, but he will probably do a better job if he solves these problems first.

Motivation

This is part of the subject of Chapter 8. But the current chapter, insofar as it deals with purposeful learning, definitely involves motivation. For example, if you have a clear idea of your *goals* in studying, and accept them as worth while, you will find it easier to direct your attention to the task at hand and your learning will be both more permanent and more meaningful.

Try this exercise: Have a friend hold a picture containing many persons or objects in front of another person. After one minute, have him put the picture away, and ask the other person to list as many of the items in the picture as he

The importance of environment to learning. *Learning is more effective when attempted under suitable conditions, with good light, proper ventilation, and no noise and distractions. (Pittsburgh Corning Corp.)*

can. Try this again with another picture, but this time tell the subject to keep in mind the fact that he is going to be asked to make the list. Compare the two lists. What do you surmise?

Try this exercise: Have someone read a short poem to you. Now attempt to recite it. Does what you learn have anything to do with what you were looking for in the poem? Can you describe its meter? Did you understand the content? The symbolism? Did you appreciate the beauty of the words? Does what you learn depend upon what you were *attempting* to learn?

Your motives influence your attention, strengthen or weaken your persistence in activities, and affect your retention and application of newly acquired learning. If you are working merely for a good mark in class, might you cease when you think you have learned enough to get the good mark? Would you work as hard if the instructor should tell you that everyone will get the same mark? If you have no goal other than to receive a good mark, will you remember and apply what you have learned?

    A.   PURPOSEFUL LEARNING
    B.   NON–PURPOSEFUL LEARNING
    C.   SEARCH FOR A COMPREHENSIVE THEORY
    D.   FACTORS IN READINESS

● **E. THE NEED FOR PRACTICE**

Learning will occur in varying degrees of permanence, and with economy of time and effort, in direct relation to the learner's readiness, the ways in which he attacks the learning task, the difficulty of the task, and other factors — including active practice. As the basis for practice, one may employ association, intelligent trial and error, or problem-solving techniques, depending on the nature of the learning. When a person wants to acquire proficiency through

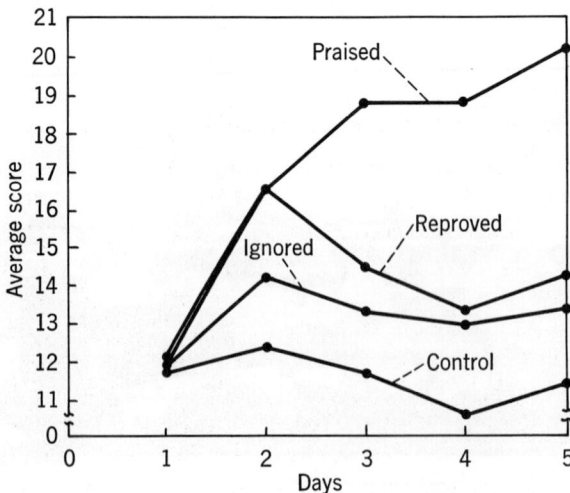

The effect of motivation. *Students who initially made equivalent scores in solving arithmetic problems were found to make higher or lower scores as they were praised, reproved, or ignored. (From E. B. Hurlock, "The Evaluation of Certain Incentives Used in School Work," J. Educ. Psychol., 1925, Vol. 16, Warwick and York, Inc., p. 149.)*

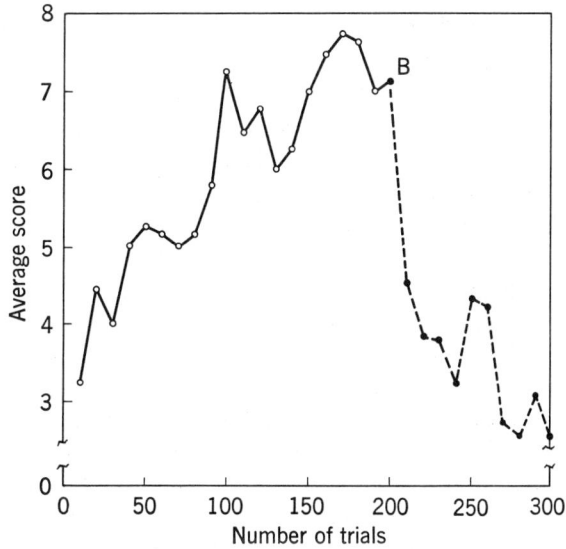

Knowledge of progress. *Subjects were instructed to try to throw a spot of light on a target. For 200 trials they were able to see their results, but thereafter did not know whether or not they had succeeded. Note the sharp decline in average performance. (From J. L. Elwell and G. C. Grindley, "The Effect of Knowledge of Results on Learning and Performance," Brit. J. Psychol., 1938, Vol. 29, p. 41.)*

practice, it may be helpful for him to consider his own progress, the frequency of his practice, whole–part relationships, distribution of practice periods, and the nature of learning curves as they relate to practice.

Knowledge of progress

Efficiency in active practice depends in part on how the individual uses cues to guide his responses. In practicing some tasks, such as theme writing, singing, or speaking French, he himself can perceive the cues to guide his actions, eliminating incorrect responses and improving or repeating correct ones. In other instances learning is more rapid if someone helps him to identify and follow cues. In any event he must somehow learn to evaluate his actions and to experience some measure of improvement if practice is to remain efficient and be continued.

Try this activity: Draw a circle the size of a dime in the center of a sheet of paper. Have a friend hold another sheet so that you cannot see the circle. Tap with your pencil, attempting to make the dots fall within the circle. After ten trials, look to see where they fell. Were you successful? Repeat, having your partner tell you after each trial whether your taps were too high, too low, to the right, or to the left of the circle. How much do these cues improve your performance? Did knowledge of coming closer or of hitting the circle encourage you to continue?

One function of tests and examinations in class should be to indicate to the instructor how well you are learning and how well he is teaching. Test results can thus serve both as cues for you to improve your learning and as cues for him to improve his teaching. Another function of tests is to show *you* how you are progressing with learning important for the course. Thus tests should also help you to decide how well you are learning and how you may improve.

Overlearning

Theoretically, the first time a person makes a correct response to a learning problem, he has learned. The correct response may occur during the first attempt, or it may not take place until after many practice sessions. After a correct response is once made, e.g., spelling a word correctly, the student may continue to practice it. The term used to describe this process is *overlearning*. The fact that responses may not change during overlearning does not mean that nothing is going on within the learner. On the contrary, something *is* happening: overlearning increases retention, thereby lessening the likelihood of mistakes and reducing the amount of time and concentration needed to call forth the desired response. Habitual responses reflect overlearning — you may take out a cigarette and light it without even being fully aware that you have done so, responding to small cues in your environment or within yourself. You do not need to concentrate on the writing or spelling of most words — you "just write them," reacting almost instantaneously to cues as you write.

Overlearning is most needed when responses which are not highly meaningful must be permanently retained. For example, foreign language vocabularies, multiplication tables, the spelling of certain words, dates, and formulas are types of material which typically must be overlearned.

Overlearning, of course, does not in itself further learning. It must have a purpose. It is possible to continue practice on a task and actually get worse instead of better unless the practice is based on successful, rather than random or unsuccessful, responses. It is possible to repeat errors or poor responses instead of correct ones.

Whole-part-whole learning

The amount of material to be learned in one practice session affects the efficiency of learning. Sometimes things are too extensive or too complicated to be learned all at once. Relatively simple skills like memorizing a short poem may best be learned by practicing the entire task at one time. Learning a long poem, however, may be better accomplished by first reading through it to understand it as a whole, then dividing it into manageable parts to be memorized one at a time, always adding to each learned part until eventually one has learned the whole poem. Some fields of study, like chemistry or English literature, are so broad that we may not be able to get a complete understanding early in the course. A manageable unit or part might be the best starting point.

Much yet remains to be discovered concerning the best attack on various learning tasks. Your own experiences in previous study may serve as a guide; also, your instructor may be able to advise you. Generally, the sequence of attempting to understand the whole task first, then dividing it into manageable parts for practice, and relating the part learnings to the whole has been accepted as an efficient way of acquiring comprehensive learning, needed in swimming, handwriting, foreign language vocabulary, and playing a musical instrument.

Distributed vs. massed practice

Fatigue and loss of motivation make it hard to practice any learning task efficiently for a sustained period. Furthermore, a rest period may result in improved performance. This may be due to mental processes at work without our awareness or, in younger children and adolescents, to maturation. In any case, if one is able to space his practice periods so that he can give full attention and effort to the learning for a period, rest a while, and then return, he often learns better than if he attempts very long, uninterrupted practice sessions. In studying a chapter in this book, for example, it is better to get an overview to see how it is organized, then attack one section at a time, review it after study, and continue thus until finished. An hour's study twice a day, for some people, may be better than a two-hour session once a day.

Especially in the early stages of acquiring a skill, short practice periods with guidance appear to produce the best results. In typewriting, for example, the shorter practice session results in less fatigue (and typewriting *is* fatiguing when one has to try hard to strike letters correctly), gives more opportunity for the instructor to note and attempt to correct errors before they are practiced, allows the learner to analyze his performance early in his practice, and provides the learner more opportunity to identify useful cues.

The effect of rest on retention of learning. *Subjects allowed an interval of sleep were able to recall a larger number of syllables learned than those who remained awake for the same length of time. (From J. G. Jenkins and K. M. Dallenbach,* Amer. J. Psychol., 35, 1924, pp. 605–612.)

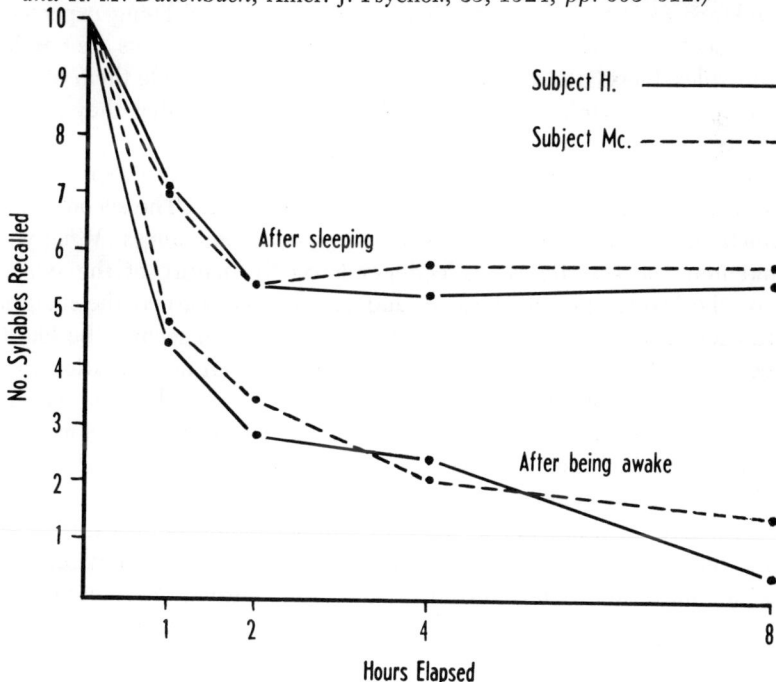

While the above advice is generally applicable, the length of an efficient practice session varies with the individual. One college student can apparently practice his beginning Spanish for an hour with little fatigue and acquire many correct responses throughout this period of time, while another student may show fatigue and decreased efficiency in thirty minutes. Also, as skills are developed, we find that some individuals can stay with tasks productively for several hours with only brief rest or relaxing periods. Assembly-line production of goods, for example, is based on the assumption that many individuals can perform in this way. It is interesting to note, in this connection, that not only assembly-line workers but also clerical workers are being given "breaks" in the morning and afternoon. This practice tends to improve not only morale but also productivity.

    A.   PURPOSEFUL LEARNING
    B.   NON–PURPOSEFUL LEARNING
    C.   SEARCH FOR A COMPREHENSIVE THEORY
    D.   FACTORS IN READINESS
    E.   THE NEED FOR PRACTICE

● F. TRANSFER OF LEARNING

If skills or other products of learning were useful only in the exact context in which they were learned, there would be little point to going to school. The best preparation for everyday life would then be to *lead* everyday life — with guidance from parents and other adults. Instead of being expected to learn from such relatively unguided experience, however, students are taught theories, principles, facts, attitudes, and ideas of all kinds to enable them to fit efficiently into the adult work-a-day world. The usefulness of what they are taught depends entirely on *transfer of learning.*

Transfer of learning occurs when an individual can apply some or all of what he has learned in one situation to another situation. The second may be very much like the first, or it may show only remote resemblances. *What* will transfer and *how* the transfer is made depends on the nature of the two situations, how the learner perceives them, and the way he learned the material. Some transfer is positive — that is, factors of one situation seem to be like those of a second, and behavior can be readily modified from one situation to the other. In other cases, little transfer may be present. In still other cases negative transfer or interference may occur. That is, a form of behavior learned to be appropriate for one situation may *not* apply to another, and yet may block off the proper responses.

Principles of problem-solving, for example, should be of value in almost any situation where problems need to be solved. Courteous behavior, although the details may vary, is recognized by any group through its thoughtful and considerate application. Mathematics can be applied to commerce, to the shop, or to research statistics. On the other hand, learning to play the piano well may interfere with playing the organ insofar as manual and pedal skills are different, although the ability to read music is advantageous to both. Knowing how to fly an airplane may interfere with learning to drive an automobile, for the touch on the controls is different for each.

What will help you, as a student, to transfer your academic learning to situations you meet outside the classroom? The following points should be useful.

1. Learning material in a meaningful way, rather than by rote.

2. Learning principles and generalizations, rather than specific facts only.

3. Trying, as you study, to relate your learning to various aspects of living, looking for applications and generalizations.

4. Forming many broad associations concerning the material you are studying.

5. Using the material; applying it.

6. Learning better methods of studying and attacking problems, rather than using a specific technique like memorization, regardless of its relevance. For example, problem-solving is a good method which can be used in many situations. Memorizing is helpful for some kinds of material but not for all.

7. Having the instructor guide you in finding applications for your new learning, in relating situations and procedures to each other, and in showing how principles and generalizations can be used.

General learning curve. *Student telegraphers were given weekly tests on their rates of sending and receiving messages in Morse Code. In general, five stages can be observed in all learning: slow initial gain, rapid gain, plateau, moderate gain, and approach to the limit of ability. In sending messages they steadily rose to the limit of their ability with no plateau period. The only plateau in this chart is the relatively horizontal portion of the curve for receiving connected discourse, because it precedes a new gain in learning. (From W. L. Bryan and N. Harter, Psych. Rev., 1899, 6, p. 350.)*

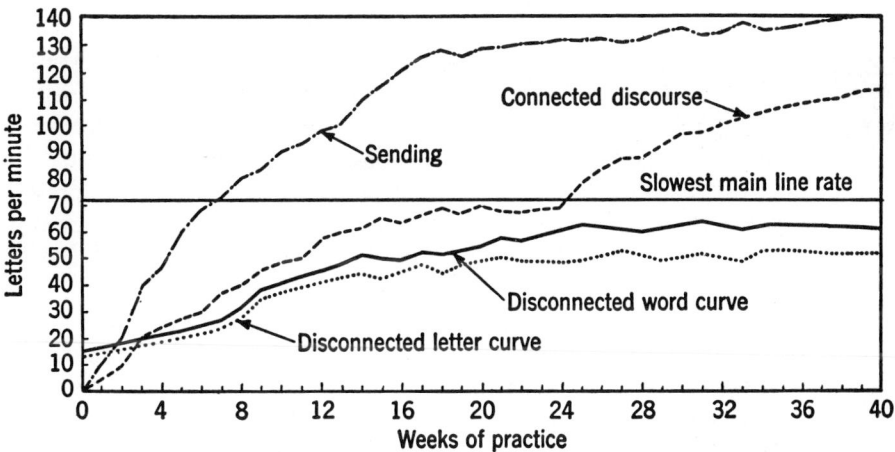

8. Learning the material well, so that it will be retained. Practice, motivation, readiness, careful perception, overlearning, and whole rather than fragmentary learning are all important.

Perhaps, as you read this, you will feel that certain subjects or materials you have studied are more practical than others. This is true. However, you should consider not only immediate practicality but also the effect of less practical and more theoretical subject matter on your attitudes, interests, creativeness, appreciation, and ability to think. Do you find people interesting who know something of art, music, and literature? Would you consider those subjects always practical? Often, too, a seemingly vague theory leads to general principles which can be useful in many practical situations. If you understand the *why* of things, you not only proceed more accurately and successfully but you also may be able to improve on current methods.

SUMMARY

Most of man's behavior is learned or is influenced by learning. For this reason knowledge of the learning process should be useful — a person can control his learning and make it more efficient if he knows how it takes place. Much learning is purposeful. Inherent in any purposeful learning are readiness, interpretation of a problem situation, response, and result. If the results are favorable, the response may be repeated and improved; if unfavorable, the response may be discontinued or changed, or it may lead to emotional reactions. Learning has various outcomes — concepts or information, motor skills, attitudes, values, interests, motives, social and emotional controls, and techniques of thinking or problem-solving.

Psychologists have drawn various inferences about learning. Each theory appears to have some limitations as well as useful applications to human learning. No one theory, however, presents a complete basis for understanding human learning; if so, it would no longer be a theory. Differences among the theories involve considerations of whether the inherent nature of the organism, or heredity, is more or less important than the environmental stimuli in the learning process; whether we can understand learning better by treating relatively isolated components or by considering total responses; whether learning is a matter of making mental connections or of acquiring insights into means–ends relationships, and how past experiences are related to present performances. The association, cognitive, and purposive theories represent some of the points of view brought to bear on these questions. Each has its notable adherents.

Not all learning seems to be purposeful. We find, for example, that a conditioned response does not require a purpose on the part of the learner, and, indeed, that involuntary types of behavior like salivation and the eye reflex are subject to learning. Some emotional reactions and some direct associations of stimuli and responses are not acquired purposefully. The writers of this book, rather than considering purposeful and non-purposeful learning as two completely different processes, think of them in terms of a continuum which embraces various parts of the nervous system, various organs and muscles, varying degrees of differentiation, and varying degrees of purposefulness on the part of the learner. It is the interaction of the organism with its environment that produces learning.

For efficient learning of a particular task the learner must have the necessary level of intelligence, previous experiences essential to the job, a socio-emotional setting conducive to learning, and motivation. Knowledge of progress, frequency and distribution of practice, learning of the whole in which the parts are interrelated, and other factors influence efficiency of learning.

Principles and procedures learned in one situation may transfer to others, as well as attitudes, interests, concepts, facts, and motor skills. Some learning transfers negatively; that is, what is learned in one situation prevents efficient learning in another.

We have examined a lengthy, technical, and controversial subject. Learning theory is the subject of many books and college courses and the main life-work of many psychologists. We have deliberately introduced you to some of the controversies in the hope that you will now read this and other books more critically and recognize the difference between principles and theory in psychology. For while psychologists do not completely agree on the adequacy of a particular theory, there appears to be considerable agreement among them on such principles as those which relate to readiness, practice, and transfer. As more factual evidence is gathered, both theories and principles will change. Arriving at a more complete and accurate understanding of human learning is a major goal of many psychologists.

Suggested activities

1. How did you proceed to study this chapter? Choose one of the three theoretical viewpoints on learning, and interpret your procedures in the light of that theory.

2. If you wanted to teach a child to drive a car, how might you employ conditioning, trial and error, insight, transfer, and readiness?

3. List as many things as you can which you have learned thus far today. What factors have influenced this learning? Undoubtedly you were exposed to opportunities to learn which did not result in learning. What factors influenced the lack of learning?

REFERENCES

1. L. J. Cronbach, *Educational Psychology*, Harcourt, Brace, New York, 1954, Chapter 3.
2. F. Goodenough, *Measurement of Intelligence by Drawings*, World Book, Yonkers-on-Hudson, 1926.

3. J. G. Saxe, "The Blind Men and the Elephant (A Hindu Fable)," *Anthology of New England Poets from Colonial Times to the Present Day*, Random House, New York, 1948.

4. G. W. Allport, *Personality: A Psychological Interpretation*, Holt, New York, 1937.

5. *Ibid.*, p. 48.

6. R. Stagner, *Psychology of Personality*, McGraw-Hill, New York, 1948, p. 7.

7. C. S. Hall and G. Lindzey, *Theories of Personality*, Wiley, New York, 1957, pp. 7–10.

8. From *Theories of Learning*, by Ernest R. Hilgard, second edition. Copyright ©, 1956, Appleton-Century-Crofts, Inc.

9. *Ibid.*

10. W. Köhler, *The Mentality of Apes*, Harcourt, Brace, New York, 1925.

11. J. M. Stephens, *Educational Psychology*, Holt, New York, Rev. 1956, Chapter 8.

12. I. P. Pavlov, *Conditioned Reflexes*, Oxford University Press, Oxford, Great Britain, 1927.

13. J. B. Watson, *Psychologies of 1925*, Clark University Press, Worcester, Mass., 1926.

14. O. H. Mowrer, "The Psychologist Looks at Language," *Amer. Psychol.*, 1945, 9, pp. 660–694.

15. O. H. Mowrer, "On the Dual Nature of Learning — A Re-Interpretation of 'Conditioning and Problem-Solving,'" *Harvard Educ. Rev.*, 1947, 17, pp. 102–148.

16. R. Dewey and W. J. Humber, *The Development of Human Behavior*, Macmillan, New York, 1951, p. 135.

17. A. Gesell and H. Thompson, "Twins T and C From Infancy to Adolescence: A Biogenetic Study of Individual Differences," *Gen. Psychol. Monogr.*, 1941, 24, p. 3–122.

SUGGESTIONS FOR FURTHER READING

Barlow, M. C., "Transfer of Training in Reasoning," *J. Educ. Psychol.*, 1937, 28, pp. 122–128.

Forgus, R. H., and R. J. Schwartz, "Efficient Retention and Transfer as Affected by Learning Method," *J. Psychol.*, 1957, 43, pp. 135–139.

Harlow, H. F., "Mice, Monkeys, Men and Motives," *Psychol. Rev.*, 1953, 60, pp. 28–32.

Hilgard, E. R., *Introduction to Psychology*, Harcourt, Brace, New York, 1953, Chapter 10.

Kendler, H. H., "Verbal Factors in Problem-Solving Behavior," *Acta Psychol.*, 1955, 11, pp. 214–215.

Poulton, E. C., "Memorization and Recall," *Br. J. Psychol.*, 1953, 44, pp. 173–176.

Reed, H. B., "Factors Influencing the Learning and Retention of Concepts. 1. The Influence of Set," *J. Exp. Psychol.*, 1946, 36, pp. 71–87.

Rhine, R. J., "The Effect on Problem Solving of Success or Failure as a Function of Cue Specificity," *J. Exp. Psychol.*, 1957, 53, pp. 121–125

Saugstad, P., "Incidental Memory and Problem Solving," *Psychol. Rev.*, 1952, 59, pp. 221–226.

Spitzer, H. F., "Studies in Retention," *J. Educ. Psychol.*, 1939, 30, pp. 641–656.

Stagner, R., and T. F. Karwoski, *Psychology*, McGraw-Hill, New York, 1952, Chapter 10.

Underwood, B. J., "Studies of Distributed Practice: XII. Retention Following Varying Degrees of Original Learning," *J. Exp. Psychol.*, 1954, 47, pp. 294–300.

Witzig, J. S., "A Study of the Comparative Effect on Retention of Mythological and Factual Prose," *J. Gen. Psychol.*, 1956, 55, pp. 173–187.

Perception

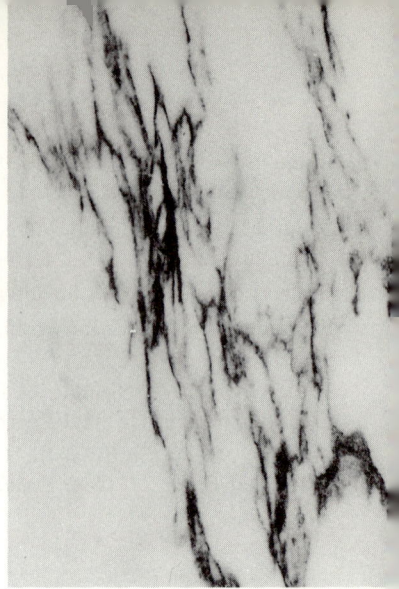

It is a common legal saying that no two people have exactly the same understanding of what goes on in a given situation, whether it be an accident, a crime, or some ordinary daily event. We can dismiss some of the differences in legal testimony by ascribing motives of self-interest to the witnesses. Other discrepancies may be due to faulty memory, excitement, poor vision, and like causes. But the question still remains unanswered how several people, all unbiased and entirely normal in sensory equipment and memory, may understand a situation differently. Consider the following examples:

Your pet German Shepherd dog bristles and growls at the milkman. The milkman thereupon refuses to deliver to your house until "that vicious dog is tied up." You smile and tell him that Max is only a pet and never bites. You are sure that Max is only bluffing.

You may be sure that your brother looks just like you, though strangers can see no family resemblance.

Suppose you see a shadow move across the window shade at night. Because you have been reading mystery stories, you get a thrill of alarm at the "prowler" you are sure is present. Your friend, studying biology, perceives the shadow as that of an owl. Investigation shows that it is only a tree, moving in the wind.

Have you ever mistaken a street sign? Misread your watch? Overheard snatches of conversation and gained erroneous impressions? Do pictures of iced soft drinks really look cold to you? Do knives look sharp? Have you guessed that the picture on this page is of a piece of marble?

6

How We Know the World Around Us

How do we know our environment? How do we know how others see the same environment? Why do different people attend to different aspects of the same environment? What is the nature of seeing and hearing? In what other ways do we sense the environment? What factors influence perception? How is it possible to improve sensory discrimination?

In each of these situations at least two things are occurring. *1.* You are receiving sensory impressions from the stimuli presented to your sense organs, and *2.* you are interpreting them in terms of your past experiences, expectations, and other factors which affect their meaning. This process of endowing sensory impressions with meaning is called *perception.*

Quite obviously your knowledge of your environment will differ from that of someone else. Your eyes, ears, or other sense organs may differ — for example, you or he may be color blind, astigmatic, or tone deaf. You may pay attention to various aspects of the environment in a way quite different from that of other people. Even while sensing and attending to the same parts of your surroundings, two persons may perceive them differently, due to their past experiences, expectations, motives or goals, and ability levels. Thus two persons' interpretations of the environment will always vary because of these sensory and perceptual differences. Two of us can never have completely the same view of objective reality. However, we are able to interact socially with understanding because there are enough similarities between our perceptions and those of others to permit successful communication.

This idea of each individual's unique perception is developed by Snygg and Combs (1) in their discussion of the phenomenological theory of human behavior. According to their view, a person's behavior is determined, not by the objective environment, but by a personal, individual field which is not identical with that of any other person. The phenomenal field is defined as the entire universe — including the individual himself — as experienced by a person

173

at a particular point in time. Thus one's field, or what is real to him at a given moment, includes not merely his perceptions of the physical environment but also the memories, motives, and emotions that he is experiencing at the same time.

Actually, the only reality any of us can know is that which we sense and perceive. We may feel that the phenomenal field of another person is subject to much error and illusion and that he seems to have only an *interpretation* of reality rather than an awareness of reality itself. But to that individual, as to yourself, the field *is* reality; and, the behavior he exhibits must always be in conformity with his phenomenal field.

Thus, to the milkman, your dog is threatening, whereas to you he is playful. Who is correct can be learned only from the dog's subsequent actions, but the milkman will behave as if the dog were dangerous. The shadow across the window affects you as vividly as if it *were* made by a prowler. And when you misread a street sign, you act just as you would if the sign really said what you thought it said.

We do not have the same degree of awareness of all parts of our phenomenal field. At any particular time an individual will concentrate on the things having most meaning for him and will tend to ignore everything else. During the kickoff at a football game most of us watch the ball and the ball carrier, ignoring the line play. To a football player, in terms of his position, this may not be very appropriate. He had better watch the man he is supposed to block. If a girl at the game is waiting for her date to arrive, she may even ignore the kickoff completely and concentrate on her personal appearance. After her friend arrives, she may concentrate on him. So, in addition to being unique to each individual, the phenomenal field is fluid and constantly changing. It remains sufficiently stable, however, so that we do not feel as though we were witnessing a series of disconnected events.

Since one's behavior is a function of his phenomenal field, it follows that one can better understand his own and other people's behavior by knowing, at least partially, how he and others sense and interpret the environment. This will be our concern in this chapter and the next. What governs what we sense, observe, and experience? Why do our impressions and understandings change? Why does one person *differentiate* (2) certain aspects of the environment so that they become clear and important to him, while another does not? Why does an interest in a certain subject area, such as classical music, become more intense while concern with popular music wanes? These questions involve the problems of sensation, perception, and communication. Attention, organization, and meaning are related subjects.

Let us set the stage for our study of sensing and perceiving by giving some examples. Think of the last time you had a toothache. Did you actually know which tooth the dentist was going to fill — or did your whole jaw feel as if someone had banged it with a hammer? Could you guarantee that you felt the same amount of pain as your friend did when he had a toothache?

Even if we all agree that sight, hearing, or other senses tell us much the same things, there are always problems that arise with a change in environmental conditions. For example, there is an old saying that "at night all cats are gray." As far as perception is concerned, what this really means is that at night we tend to lose color vision and can detect only brightness or darkness. Why does the moon look larger when it is near the horizon than when it is high in the sky? Why does its position affect our judgment of its size?

Now that such problems have been set for you, you may feel that you need to know more about the mechanics of sensation and perception. Since your previous experiences in biology or health classes will have taught you something about the sense organs, some of the material presented here will be a review. However, you should now try to keep in mind the psychological importance of the sense organs. This means that we should concentrate on how they function and how their function influences behavior.

● A. VISION, HEARING, AND OTHER SENSES

The only direct contact we have with the physical world is through our sense organs, or receptors. So-called intuitive knowledge (that gained by thinking) must depend on former sensations related to the action of the receptors and perceived more or less consciously. We are accustomed to thinking of "five senses," yet research has isolated, among others, the following: vision, hearing, the olfactory sense (smell), the gustatory sense (taste), the cutaneous senses (heat, cold, pain, pressure), the kinesthetic senses (muscle movement), the labyrinthine sense (balance).

The sense organs are generally referred to as the receptor system. These organs are of three kinds, the *exteroceptors* which receive stimulation from the exterior of the body, the *interoceptors* which receive stimulation from the internal organs of the body, and the *proprioceptors* which receive stimulation from gross movements of the body. The following list indicates the main systems of sense organs according to this classification:

CLASSIFICATION OF RECEPTORS
1. Exteroceptors
   Distance receptors; organs of vision, audition, and smell
   Contact receptors; organs of touch and pressure, warmth, cold, and pain.
2. Interoceptors
   Receptors in the digestive system, circulatory system, respiratory system, and reproductive system
3. Proprioceptors
   Organs of position and equilibrium — in the internal ear; organs in muscles, tendons, and joints.

Basically, all our senses act in similar ways. A form of energy such as light, heat, or pressure acts as a stimulus. These forms of energy are produced by *stimulus objects* such as light bulbs, stoves, or bells. The stimulus meets receptor cells such as those in the eye or ear, and these activated receptor cells in turn start impulses in nerve cells. Tiny electrical charges accompany the nerve impulses. These activities are sent via nerves to the brain. The active brain, in turn, is influenced by these "inputs" from sensory nerves. Then the subject reports that he has an experience of sight, sound, etc.

There are some interesting controls over the senses. For example, not every stimulus leads to sensory activity. For a stimulus to start processes related to sensation, it must be strong enough to be above the *threshold* or *limen* of the receptor cells (3) — for instance, light below a certain intensity will not activate the cells of the eye and start impulses along the optic nerve. Besides the threshold provided by the receptor cells, there are others, one of which is the *difference* threshold. It is possible, for example, to detect a sound but not be able to distinguish it from one closely similar. Musicians with "perfect pitch" have the ability to discriminate between sounds much more accurately than most people. Their difference thresholds are low. Finally, there is an *attentional* threshold. A slight sound may be strong enough to be heard if we listened carefully, but it may not bring itself to our notice. If we concentrate on trying to listen for that sound, however, it is quite audible. People who

Structure of a neuron. *The unit of the nervous system is the single nerve cell, or* neuron. *While there are many kinds of neurons, each consists of a cell body and nerve fibers. A typical efferent neuron and three types of neurons showing the pattern of conduction of a nervous impulse are shown below. Afferent neurons are those which bear sensory impulses to the central nervous system. Those which bear motor impulses to muscles, glands, or other organs are called* efferent. *Association neurons of various types conduct impulses from one neuron to others within the nervous system. (From Munn,* Psychology, *Houghton Mifflin.)*

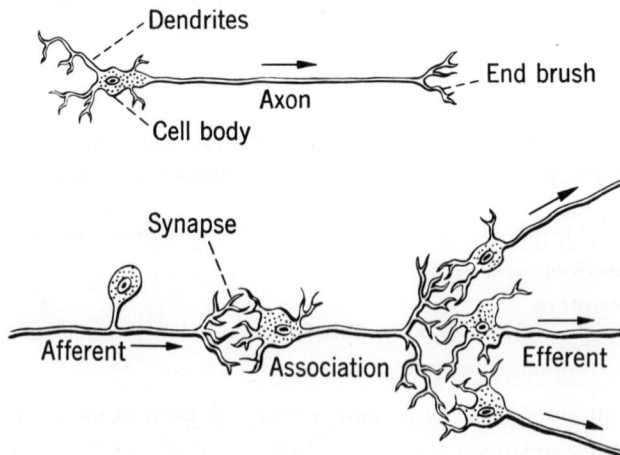

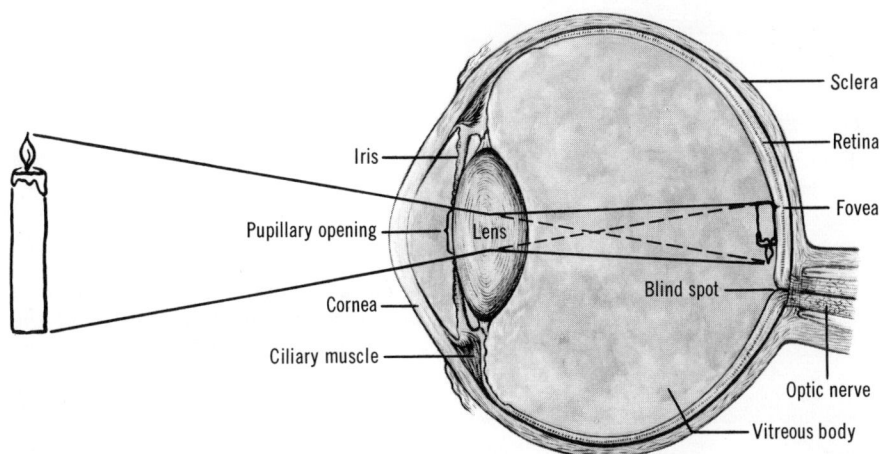

The human eye. *The image is produced on the* fovea, *the area of the* retina *which contains the greatest concentration of sensitive cells known as rods and cones. Light rays entering the eye pass through the tough outer surface, the* cornea, *a watery liquid known as the* aqueous humor, *the* pupil, *and the* lens. *The* iris *gives the eye its color, and controls the size of the pupillary opening.*

live near busy streets may become so accustomed to traffic noises that only something unusual will make them aware of the sounds. Psychologists have worked out a number of these *determiners of attention,* such as movement, a familiar item in an unfamiliar background, brightness, size, and others.

Our sensory processes produce only those sensations of which an organ is capable, no matter how it is stimulated. Pressure on the eyeball causes us to "see stars" even though the eye responded to pressure and not to light. Surgeons performing brain operations find that their patients report experiences of light when certain nerves or areas of the brain are stimulated by electricity or instruments. Thus each receptor sends its own peculiar messages to the brain, and the related brain areas deal with those messages in special ways.

Finally, most receptor organs are acted on by different aspects of the external world. Vision is not merely a general sensation of light. Visual experiences may have such components as intensity, hue, and saturation of color. In hearing we can distinguish loudness, pitch, and timbre. As we examine the sense organs in more detail, we shall see how this can happen.

Vision

You may remember from your study of biology that the eye is somewhat like a camera (4). Examine the diagram of the eye shown above. You will see that it contains a lens that focuses light energy on the retina (the sensitive back part of the eye). Muscles are provided which either contract to thicken or stretch to thin the lens so that the eye can focus on nearer or farther objects.

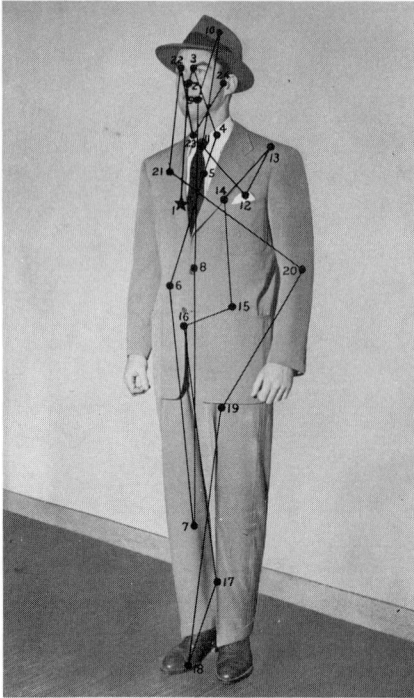

Eye movements of a woman looking at a man. *The dots indicate fixations of the eye, numbered in the order of occurrence. Movements of the woman's eye were followed by a special camera which photographed the location, duration, and sequence of fixations. (Courtesy of the copyright owners, Marshall Field and Co., and* Look *magazine. Research by Dr. H. F. Brandt.)*

The iris contracts or expands to provide the proper amount of light for the retina, much like the diaphragm of a camera.

The retina is the most interesting part of the eye. It is composed of light-sensitive cells called *rods* and *cones* which start impulses in the nerve cells going in to the brain. The cones are effective in daylight and are basic to color vision. They are very numerous and are most highly concentrated near the center of the retina at a spot known as the *fovea*. The fovea provides the sharpest images. In daylight we not only see color, but we see objects very clearly. The rods are fewer in number than the cones and less concentrated in position. Although not sensitive to the stimulus characteristic related to color (wave length), they do provide sensations of brightness.

In the dark of night the cones cease to work and the rods take over the entire function of seeing. Becoming adapted to the dark requires some time — 15 to 30 minutes or more, depending on the individual and on a variety of conditions.

In seeing, it is believed that light causes a change in a chemical component of the retinal cells known as *visual purple,* giving rise to neural activity in the process. The particular cells affected cannot discharge or "see" again until the visual purple has been reconstituted. In the meantime, other cells take over the function of starting visual messages. Each cell responds according to the "all-or-none principle," which means that, if it discharges at all, it does so with its maximum intensity. The reason some lights are seen as brighter than others may be related to an increase in the total number of cells affected.

Imagine that you are on a naval ship during wartime black-out conditions.

As you stand on the bridge at twilight, your ability to see objects at sea diminishes with the coming of darkness. Your ability to see certain colored objects may change. This is known as the Purkinje effect. Sensitivity to the color red is lost first; the brightest color becomes green, not yellow as in full light. Eventually you will be using only the rods of the retina, and then you will be able to distinguish only shapes and different degrees of brightness. Other ships will appear as indistinct shadowy masses passing by.

To conserve your dark adapted visual powers as much as possible when you must go into the interior of the ship it will be lighted only in red. The red light will not as fully desensitize your eyes to seeing shapes.

The fovea contains many more cones than rods, so it is not particularly effective for night vision. Thus men in military service are taught to see objects out of the "corner" of the eye, using the peripheral areas of the retina which contain relatively more rods.

To recognize shapes it is necessary for the eyes to *fixate,* or cease movement, and to focus on the object to be identified. For example, in reading, word shapes must be distinguished. Depending on his reading ability and the kind of material to be read, a person will fixate from one to fifteen or twenty times per line of type. Thus, one technique to increase the speed of reading is to teach the reader to take in more words per fixation. Thereby he comes to read phrases or even whole sentences at a time rather than single words. This ability to take in larger units is, in part, a result of training the eye to stop fewer times per line and to move to the next point more rapidly. Rapid reading is thus related to quick comprehension of units larger than single words.

There are various eye defects which result from faults in the mechanical structure of the eye. Improper focusing of the lens may produce near- or farsightedness or astigmatism. A further explanation of how these defects are brought about is given in the illustration on page 180.

Color blindness

Another eye defect, one which has attracted the interest of everyone from the highly trained scientist down to the ordinary man on the street, is color blindness. Perhaps nothing seems more curious — and even fascinating — to those who have normal vision than the fact that someone else may not have the same color sense.

Color is such an integral part of our everyday experience that it is usually taken for granted. Nevertheless, we do not all experience it in the same way. The person who is partially color blind may not be aware that he has an eye defect. What he sees as "red" has come to *be* red, since "red" is the verbal symbol he has come to associate with the color he sees and the object of which it is an attribute.

The principal characteristic of color blindness is the inability to distinguish between hues — or, in a case of total color blindness, the inability to make any color distinctions. Partial color blindness appears to be the result of a deficiency in the cones of the eye, while total color blindness is probably due to a complete lack of cones in the retina.

Partial color blindness occurs in about four per cent of the male population. It is much less prevalent in women than in men; only about one woman in a thousand is color blind. Total color blindness, on the other hand, is very rare. It is estimated that only one person in about forty thousand is completely color blind. People who are totally color blind experience discomfort in very bright light. They are usually completely blind in the fovea, which is normally the area of greatest color-sensitivity.

The term *dichromatic color vision* is sometimes used to describe partial color blindness. A person with this sort of vision will have the normal experience

Structural differences in the eye. *Farsightedness and nearsightedness may occur when the shape of the eye is such that images do not focus on the retina. The image on the retina is inverted, as in a camera; we actually see the world upside down and without depth, but through mental adjustments based on knowledge we are able to discern depth, distance, and position.*

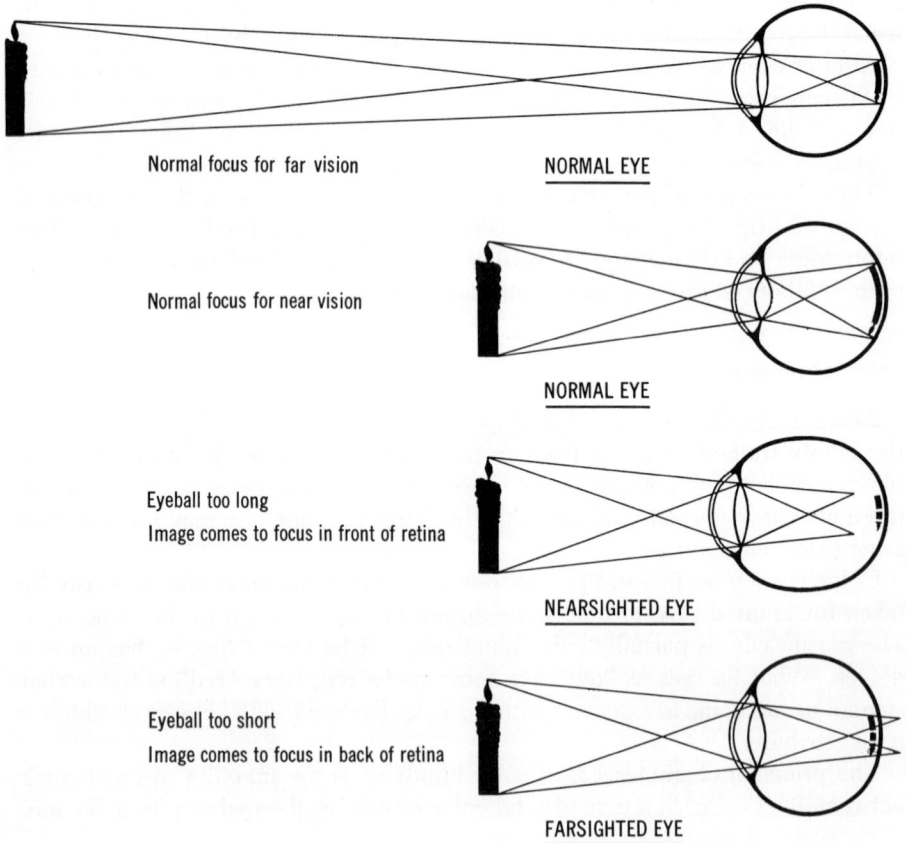

Normal focus for far vision   NORMAL EYE

Normal focus for near vision

NORMAL EYE

Eyeball too long
Image comes to focus in front of retina

NEARSIGHTED EYE

Eyeball too short
Image comes to focus in back of retina

FARSIGHTED EYE

of yellow and blue in all their degrees (and also for the varying shades of gray from white to black). His "blindness" occurs with red and green. Often this defect is known simply as "red-green color blindness."

More information about color blindness is included inside the front cover of this book, along with specimens of the charts which are used in testing for this defect. Turn there and test your own color perception.

There are, of course, methods of treatment for some eye defects. Eyeglasses help most people; operations (for cataracts, crossed eyes, etc.) help others. Still other defects, such as color blindness, cannot be cured.

Thus, because human eyes are not alike in their ability to focus or be stimulated by different wave lengths and intensities of stimulus energies, we do not all see the same things even though we are looking at the same light sources. Of course, there are other than structural reasons for our not seeing exactly the same things, but we will save these for a later discussion.

Suggested activities

1. Sensitize your eyes to darkness. Determine your ability to see reflected colors in near darkness.

2. Check the optical charts inside the back cover of this book to distinguish your visual acuity.

3. Examine the color blindness test plates inside the front cover of this book to test your own color vision.

4. Take driver-training tests to discover your ability to see the shapes and colors of road signs.

5. Try experiments with colored lights in mixing colors. Try mixing paints. The departments of physics or fine arts may be willing to demonstrate the principles of color-mixing.

Hearing

The ear responds to *sound waves,* or alternate compressions and rarefactions of air pressure on the ear drum. When the compressions and rarefactions follow each other rapidly, the sensation of high-pitched sound is produced. When the waves are of lower frequency, the sounds are lower in pitch. We detect intensity of sound by the strength of the pressure on our ear drums, and we are able to judge the distance and location of sound in part by the relative strengths of the waves on the two ears.

Sound waves enter through the opening in the outer ear, vibrating the ear drum which in turn activates the three small bones of the middle ear — the hammer, anvil, and stirrup. The stirrup presses against the oval window of the inner ear, varying the pressure in the cochlea. The cochlear canal is filled with liquid and contains the hair cells which are, in turn, connected to nerve cells or *neurons.* These cells send messages to the brain, which are interpreted as sounds. Collectively, these neurons make up the *auditory nerves*. The various hair cells in the cochlear canal respond to different frequencies of vibrations. This starts the differential processes related to our ability to detect pitch. Other characteristics of the impulses in the auditory nerves relate to other aspects of auditory experience, such as loudness and softness. Look at the diagram of the ear shown below, and find the parts we have mentioned. See if you can trace the hearing process.

Because of defects in the ear, whole or partial deafness may occur. Hearing aids have been devised whereby a relatively insensitive ear drum can be made to vibrate more vigorously by stepping up the volume of sound. In cases where certain structures of the ear have been completely destroyed, hearing can be provided by vibrations in the bones of the head. These vibrations are then communicated to the cochlea and activate the hair cells as in normal hearing. In persons who are "tone deaf" or respond only to certain sounds of certain pitch, the hair cells of the cochlear canal may be defective. Some people, of course, can distinguish a greater range in pitch than others.

Dogs can hear sounds above the range of the human ear, and they are sometimes summoned by whistles that cannot be heard by the people who use them. The bat, it has been found, actually uses a sonar principle, for it emits high-pitched sounds inaudible to the human ear and judges its distance from a wall by the tiny echo which it detects. Naval sonar equipment, based on this prin-

Diagram of the ear. *Sound waves pass through the external canal and strike the ear drum, or tympanic membrane. The resulting vibration activates the three small bones known as the* hammer, anvil, *and* stirrup. *After passing through the canals of the* cochlea, *the sound waves are eventually transmitted through the* eighth nerve *to the brain.*

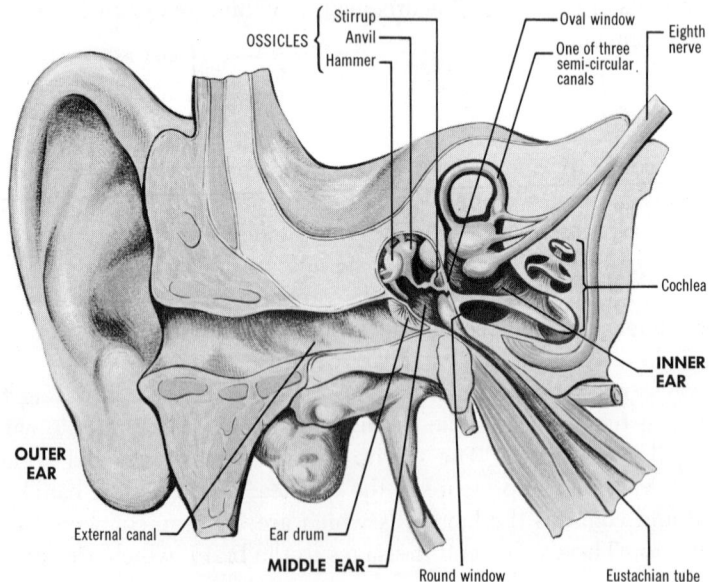

ciple, sends out sounds and measures the time and direction of the echo which returns from an object such as a submarine.

Some persons suffer from partial deafness without knowing it. As small children, they may have appeared dull or unintelligent because they could not understand much of what was going on about them. Even high school and college students may suffer partial deafness without realizing it. The speech department, speech correctionists, and medical centers of many colleges are equipped to check hearing. The audiometer, an electrical device for measuring hearing ability, can often point to specific defects if any are present.

Suggested activities

1. Secure an audiometer demonstration.
2. Blindfold a subject. Place him in a strange room. How does his ability to avoid walls or other objects compare with that which he shows when his ears are plugged with cotton or rubber ear plugs?
3. Talk to a teacher of the blind. How do the blind utilize their sense of hearing to make up for the absence of sight?
4. Find a musician with perfect pitch. Can you distinguish tones as well as he can? Could you learn to do so?

Cutaneous senses

Heat and cold. We do not feel heat and cold with the same receptors. Although cold is merely the absence of heat, the body reacts differently to cold and hot objects. Actually, body temperature is the base from which we judge. When we touch an object which is colder than our body temperature, the cold-sensitive receptors in the skin react. When we touch an object warmer than the body, the heat-sensitive receptors respond. The hot- and cold-sensitive areas on the skin can be mapped, and it has been found that some parts of the body contain more of them than others. In most areas there are more cold-sensitive than heat-sensitive spots.

When we hold an object on a sensitive area of the skin, the character of the object helps to determine whether we will sense that its temperature varies from that of the skin. A non-conductor such as woolen cloth does not allow body heat to be conducted away so rapidly as do metals or other good conductors, for the cloth does not absorb body heat, whereas metal does. This means that, if both cloth and metal of the same coolness are held against the skin, the cloth does not feel as cool as the metal.

It is possible to stimulate various receptors with inappropriate stimuli. We can hold dry ice in the hands and feel a sensation of burning, and at certain temperatures we can receive the sensation of cold from objects which are actually warm. This phenomenon is called "paradoxical warmth" or "paradoxical cold."

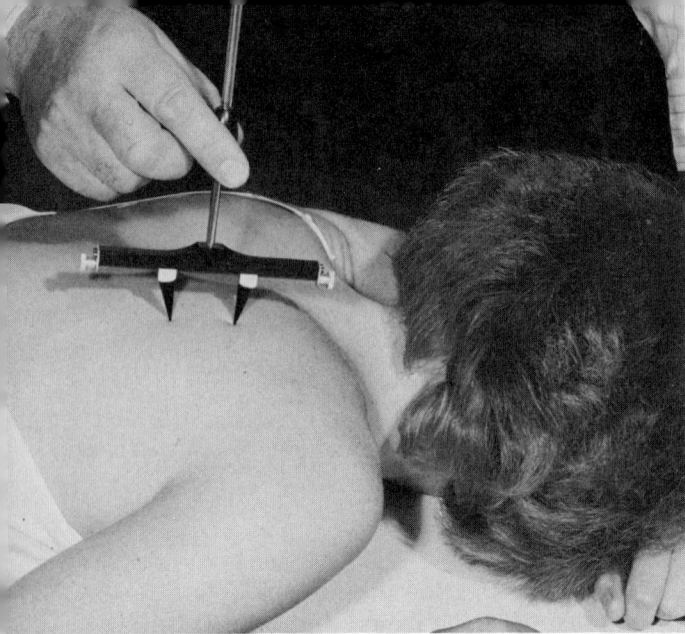

Cutaneous space perception. *An instrument known as the* esthesiometer *is used to study the "two-point threshold," the minimum distance at which a person can tell that he is being touched by two stimuli rather than one. On certain portions of the body, notably the back and the forearm, the space between points must be surprisingly wide. (From Munn,* Psychology, *Houghton Mifflin, 1956, p. 389.)*

Pressure. Pressure-sensitive spots can be found all over the body. They are not the same as those for heat or cold. Again, the number per square inch varies from location to location. The back has so few that it is possible to touch many areas with the points of a partially opened pair of scissors and feel as though the scissors were closed — we sense one point instead of two.

In some respects the sense of pressure is actually one of relationship rather than of the stimulus *per se.* Thus when we have put on a shirt or a blouse, we may at first be quite sensitive to its weight because of the pressure it exerts. After a short time, however, the senses adjust to a new equilibrium, and the shirt is no longer felt though additional wearing apparel or a slight tap on the shoulder would be felt. To illustrate this, if you hold your pencil in the palm of your hand for a short while, you will soon be unable to tell by feeling alone whether it is in your hand or not. But pressure on the pencil would of course be felt promptly.

Pain. Pain, in the skin, is felt at numerous sensitive spots. When any stimulus like heat, pressure, or certain chemicals becomes so strong that danger to the body is likely, the pain receptors warn us. While the external areas of the body are extremely sensitive to pain, the inner portions are less sensitive and many of the internal organs seem to exhibit almost no pain reaction. This makes it very difficult to localize the precise internal organ which may be causing pain within the body.

Kinesthetic senses

You are aware of most of your muscular movements, because receptors or nerve endings located in the various muscles and joints give warning of pressure or tension. In the moving of a finger, various receptors are acting to tell you that this bone is being pushed, that one is being pulled, and this or that muscle is contracting. These various receptors aid in such learning activities as typing or playing football. Much of our understanding of bodily position and activity is, in fact, the result of our kinesthetic senses. It is through the knowledge thus gained — rather than merely through seeing the words their pencils are making — that many children learn to write. To play ball well one must learn to develop "form," which is largely a matter of "feeling" that one is performing correctly. Coordination must be relearned each time a new sensory-motor skill is attempted. The various cues given by our kinesthetic senses help us to perform the act efficiently, constantly correcting poor or wrong responses and repeating correct ones.

Labyrinthine senses

The inner ear contains the semicircular canals, which are filled with fluid. These run in three different directions. Roughly, one of them lies in a horizontal plane, the second in a vertical plane, and the third is perpendicular to both the others. When we are sitting upright, a position held by the interplay of various sets of muscles, we are not relaxed but are constantly falling and catching ourselves. When we start to topple over in one direction, muscles come to our aid to enable us to move back upright again. Movements cause changes

The nonauditory labyrinth. *This structure often called the semicircular canals, is the organ of balance. It contains a liquid known as the* endolymph, *which moves with changes in position, and enables a person to know when he is right side up, upside down, rising or falling. (From Munn, Psychology, Houghton Mifflin, 1956, p. 389.)*

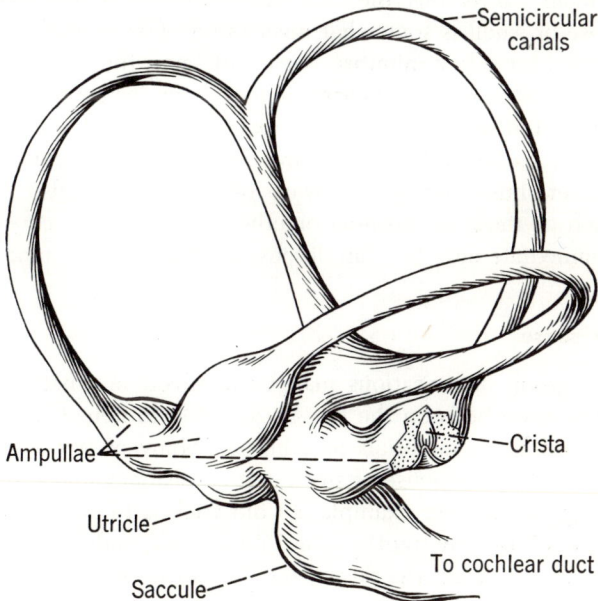

Semicircular canals

Ampullae

Crista

Utricle

Saccule

To cochlear duct

in the positions of the semicircular canals, which in turn cause the fluid within them to activate sensory receptors, thus informing us that we are off balance. Normally, correction occurs without our being aware of it, but in activities like walking a tight-wire, and other acrobatics, conscious effort may be needed to help us keep our balance.

When the labyrinthine receptors are disturbed too much, dizziness may occur — for example, when we are rapidly whirled around. Motion sickness may occur when two or more of the senses conflict — seasickness is often related to the conflict between the eyes as they see the stable horizon and the labyrinthine senses which feel the motion of the boat.

Olfactory sense

The nasal passages are moist and contain small cells sensitive to various smell stimuli. An odor is actually composed of tiny solid or gaseous particles which must be dissolved in moisture in order to stimulate the sensory cells. Thus any tiny particles in the air which are not soluble cannot be smelled; some, like pepper, can be smelled and also irritate the nose and cause reflex sneezing, an action to remove the source of the irritation.

We can distinguish several basic types of odors, although the exact number is somewhat in question. One classification lists fruity, flowery, spicy, resinous, smoky, and putrid. Experiments have been made by movie-makers in providing several scents which could be blended and fanned down into the audience, thus adding to the variety of sensory impressions and to the realism of the show. To date, however, because of problems of ventilation, cost, and for other technical reasons, the idea has not proved widely feasible.

The sense of smell is somewhat misleading. For example, most odors, after being smelled for a few minutes, "wear out," and thus, even though still present are no longer noticed. During a party, for instance, a living room may become saturated with the smell of tobacco smoke or food, but the odors will not ordinarily be noticed by those present. An outsider coming into the room will, however, immediately be aware of them. It is also true that certain smells, such as those of gasoline or ether, can not only cover up less strong and less immediate ones but can desensitize the nose for some time.

Gustatory sense

A whole group of sensations may be involved in what we ordinarily call "taste." The taste buds on the tongue are able to detect the flavors of sweet, salt, sour, and bitter materials in solution. Many of our so-called tastes are, in fact, affected by the sense of smell, the consistency and texture of food, and even the sight of it. For example, an old trick is to show a person an apple, ask him to hold his nose tightly, blindfold himself, and then feed him an onion. Often he will not detect the deception. Food that looks good is often thought to taste good, and vice versa. Experiments in which cooked meat has been served under a green light have shown such food to be distinctly distasteful to many subjects.

Different taste buds are sensitive to each of the four basic flavors. More subtle flavors are tasted through combinations of the reactions of the taste buds. Material that does not dissolve enough in the saliva to activate the taste buds has no taste — e.g., sand or certain powders.

As we get older our taste buds tend to lose their sensitivity, so that an adult often cannot distinguish flavors as well as a child. Excessive smoking, certain types of illness, or other circumstances may cause the partial or complete loss of the sense of taste.

Suggested activities

1. Fill different containers with cold, hot, and lukewarm water. Place one hand in hot water first, then in lukewarm water. How does the latter feel? Repeat, first using cold water, then lukewarm. Describe the effect.

2. Using blunt scissors, touch a blindfolded subject with the points. What areas of the body contain most pressure-sensitive spots?

3. Test your thresholds for feeling pressure, using a boar's bristle fastened to a wooden peg (esthesiometer).

4. Taste an onion, a potato, and an apple without using the sense of smell. What do you notice?

5. At a children's playground observe a platform on which people can stand and be whirled around. What does rapid motion do to their sense of balance?

6. Procure four pure flavors — salt, bitter, sweet, and sour. Mix them to produce other taste sensations.

A.   VISION, HEARING, AND OTHER SENSES

● B.   ATTENTION AND DIFFERENTIATION

The parts of our phenomenal fields do not all reach our awareness with equal clarity. We pay more attention to some aspects of our universe than to others. In psychological terms, we say that what we focus on at any given moment with any of the sense organs is the *figure*. That which is not the focus but is experienced to a lesser degree is known as the *ground*. To clarify these terms, think of the room in which you are sitting. You are reading; the book is the focus of your attention. You see the words clearly. The printed words, therefore, represent figure and the white pages are ground. You focus on the words but pay little attention to the paper, or ground. Visualize the marching band at football games. In its music the melody is the figure, and the accompaniment is the ground. On the other hand, to one of the musicians his own part might be figure, the other parts ground.

In order to understand figure–ground relationships, one must know something about the process of *differentiation,* referred to in chapter 5. In this context, differentiation is the bringing into focus of certain aspects of the total field of sensory experience. You do this when you try to recall the high spot of the junior prom. When you first look at a printed page, it may be only a mass of type on paper, but when you start to read, you must differentiate the words from the page as a whole. When you glance quickly at a painting, you may see just a blur of color, but when you really look at it, you begin to see details in the picture. At first, the parts of the painting were at a low level of differentiation, but now they are at a higher level.

To differentiate anything a person must *attend* to that part of his environment which contains it; that is, pay *attention* to it. One can daydream in class to such an extent that the instructor and his words, rather than being the focus or figure, become ground — not highly differentiated. This we call "lack of attention." The figure, in a sense would then be the thoughts of the individual — for they are what he is attending to.

Attention can be described in various ways. It may, for instance, be considered from the viewpoint of posture. When a deer stands near the highway and watches an oncoming car, his whole attitude indicates attention. He seems tense, his ears are cocked forward, his head and neck are stretched in the direction of the car, and he is ready to run if it seems necessary. In the classroom, if you are paying close attention to a lecture, you will probably find yourself sitting upright, rather tense, and even — if sufficiently rapt — with your head a bit forward and turned so that you can hear to best advantage. It is also easy, on the basis of posture, to detect those whose attention is wandering. Posture is thus related to the focus of attention and what we may call "strength of concentration." It depends, in part, on physical effort.

The level of differentiation is clearly related to attention. When we are paying careful attention to something, we are clearly differentiating between figure and ground. When our attention is wandering, we may daydream. Our

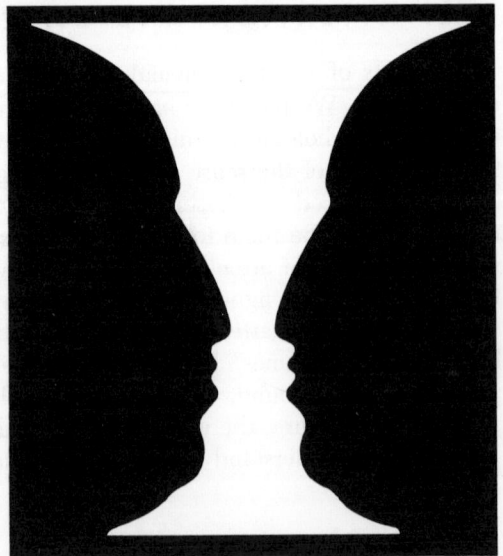

Figure-ground relationships. *Can you see this picture in two ways? The white area can be either the main figure for one illustration or the background for another.*

thoughts may flit idly from topic to topic, and we may feel somewhat hazy about what is happening around us. We are differentiating our experiences at a *low* level.

Attention may also be described in terms of "set" — or readiness to perceive certain things. If you are asked to be ready to leave the room when you hear a fire bell, your attention will be focused on trying to hear it. A mother reading in a room next to the nursery can focus her attention on a book, yet her "set" will be such that any sound from the next room will take her to her baby.

Attention may be involuntary, voluntary, or habitual. For example, you may not *want* to pay attention to the road-machine working outside your home, but the noise and activity surrounding it can make it difficult to do anything else. On the other hand, if a classroom is relatively quiet, it is possible to sleep through lectures, but if you are trying to learn something, you *voluntarily* pay attention to the instruction. *Habitual* attention is that given to stairways, traffic lights, and similar objects which no longer require concentrated awareness because of familiarity. You may not particularly want to attend to them, yet you habitually do so. Habitual attention can often be extended over a longer period of time than voluntary or involuntary attention.

What are some of the important factors of attention? Why do we differentiate certain aspects of the environment as opposed to others?

Kingsley (5) refers to *primary* and *acquired* determiners of attention. Certain characteristics of objects or stimuli are potent for securing attention, he feels — these are *primary*. *Acquired determiners* are those which an object has assumed because of the meaning given to it by past experiences. To distinguish between these terms, think of the yellow blinking light at a stop sign. Because it is colorful and because it is blinking, the light itself has *primary* attention-gaining powers. Because it means "Caution," and we have *learned* what it means, it also has *acquired* attention-gaining characteristics. Now let us consider the *primary* and *acquired* characteristics of attention more closely, giving some examples of each.

Primary determiners of attention

Strength of stimulus. When we are not focusing on anything in particular, we are likely to notice first the brighter lights among the store fronts at night, the loudest auto horn, the most pungent perfume. These are examples of strong stimuli which evoke attention.

Unusual quality of stimulus. We readily notice an odd accent or tone of voice, a new suit or hat, the smell of smoke where there usually is none, and other unusual qualities of a stimulus. A normally neutral stimulus in a unique situation gets attention — and sometimes laughter. Recall what always happens when a dog runs onto the football field during a game.

The unusual as a factor in attention. *A Chase Manhattan Bank advertisement makes use of the unusual to gain attention. The large "nest-egg" seems so incongruous that it immediately rouses curiosity. (Courtesy of the Chase Manhattan Bank.)*

Repetition of the stimulus. If you want to be sure that the driver of a car in front of you hears you so you will be able to pass, give him several toots on the horn rather than one long one. A flashing light or repeated taps on the shoulder are other ways of attracting attention more surely than a single signal in either case.

Size or volume of stimulus. We notice a large rain cloud before a small one. We see a truck on the highway before a bicycle. Other things being equal, larger objects attract our attention before small ones.

Size and movement as factors in attention. *The 225-foot-long, million-watt Pepsi-Cola sign at Times Square uses 35,000 light bulbs and features two bottles each five stories high, a bottle crown 50 feet in diameter, and a moving waterfall. (Ross Photos, courtesy of Douglas Leigh, Inc.)*

Changing quality of stimulus. A stimulus which remains the same tends to lose its attention-getting quality. For example, traffic noises on a busy street are not noticed after a while, but if the volume of traffic decreases, the very lessening of the noise may attract attention.

Movement of the stimulus. A moving object is more likely to be noticed than a still one. One moving boat in a harbor full of anchored craft will immediately be noticed. Advertisers take full advantage of the value of motion by their use of "moving" electric signs.

The start or stop of a process. The intermittent low hum of the motor of an electric refrigerator goes entirely unnoticed except when it starts and stops. The ticking of a clock may not be noticed until it happens to stop, but then the very cessation of sound attracts attention.

Acquired determiners of attention

Motivation. As do all acquired determiners of attention, motivation rests primarily within the individual responding rather than in the stimulus. It is acquired by different persons in varying degrees. In general, that is, people attend to those things for which they are searching or which have meaning for them. If we are hungry, for example, we tend to look for restaurant signs, ignoring those of other places of business. If we wish to keep an appointment on time, we may be attracted to clocks, or attend to our watch more closely than we ordinarily would. In a crowd we tend to seek out the faces of friends.

Social suggestion. If we are in a group of people paying close attention to a speaker, we often follow the suggestion of their postures and also pay attention ourselves. If someone yawns or acts bored, we may do so too. There is an old trick in which several students gazing raptly at a notice on the bulletin board collect a crowd, although the notice may not be particularly striking in itself.

Interests. These are learned or acquired also, and phenomena relating to them attract attention. The person who has bird watching as a hobby pays more attention to birds than does the person with no such interest. One who knows football may watch different players from those the casual spectator will attend to.

Acquired determiners of attention, then, are gained principally through learning. When a stimulus-object has meaning for us or we have expectations concerning it, we attend to it in terms of those meanings or expectations. One of the purposes of education is to acquire meanings for many of the stimuli we may seek or meet. Attending closely to your class work, lectures, and other learning situations will more likely occur if you have already learned to attend to such matters in high school classes.

Attention span

The length of time anyone can give his full attention to a single object is limited. Various estimates of the span of attention for school activities have been given, although such figures are not highly meaningful because of the varying conditions of the studies. However, we know that small children are "mercurial," and their attention usually wanders after 5 to 10 minutes of unvaried activity in school. High school students may spend 20 minutes or more in a given activity with a high level of attention. College students may reasonably be expected to attend for longer periods, but even professional football players, who must practice to earn a living, find it inefficient to practice for more than an hour and a half at a time. However, a study reported by Carmichael and Dearborn (6) shows that high school and college students have worked for as long as six hours without showing signs of fatigue. It appears that when one feels that he is tired by working on mental (as opposed to physical) jobs, he is in effect saying that he is bored and lacks motivation. That is, if one is stimulated enough by his work, he *can* give long periods of sustained attention to the task at hand.

Attention is governed in part by the primary qualities of stimuli outlined previously; also, those stimuli which appear to relate to fulfilling a need hold the individual's attention while the need is felt. When the need is satisfied, however, his attention shifts or wavers. Attention is also likely to shift — even though a need is being met — when a competing stimulus is stronger or in some way unusual, or when it appears to be related to a more pressing need than the one which is presently being satisfied.

It follows that you, as college students feeling a need for achievement in your academic work, would do well to limit the number of competing stimuli which might take your attention from study. Also, a period of warming up to your work — controlling your attention and developing a readiness for study — should be useful.

Attention objects

Since everyone is potentially a stimulus for some other person, each person should consider the kind of attention he attracts. Grooming, dress, voice, and carriage are important in deciding whether you hold the attention of your present friends and attract new ones. One can be unnoticed, thought to be boring, or can attract attention of either a good or a bad sort.

People usually desire to attract and be attracted by others. We may use various primary stimulus determiners to attract attention; however, to retain it we must show motives toward others and interests in them which go deeper than surface attraction.

What first catches our attention may be mere window dressing, and — though outward appearance provides some clues to personality — judging others by that alone is likely to be misleading. Thus we should be wary of the first impressions we gain of others. We must look beyond their techniques to get attention. The same is true of groups of people, of college classes, and of school activities. Does a class have a rather bizarre appeal? — is it unusual or different? If so, your attention may be attracted and perhaps held for a time. But if the real meat of the subject matter is not being presented carefully, you may find you are enjoying surface impressions at the expense of satisfying a real need for knowledge and understanding.

Suggested activities

1. Rate your study room on distracting stimuli. Can you improve its usefulness for study?

2. Rate yourself on your ability to attract favorable attention. Examine yourself in a mirror. Clothing manufacturers call attention to such details as shoes, belts, and socks that match a shirt or tie. How does your appearance rate in such matters?

3. Study newspaper or magazine advertisements to see the devices used to attract attention.

4. What stimuli have recently attracted — but not held — your attention? Why?

5. What is the effect of voices in attracting and holding attention? Ask several students to hide behind a screen while speaking. Which persons interest you most? Why?

    A.   VISION, HEARING, AND OTHER SENSES
    B.   ATTENTION AND DIFFERENTIATION

● C. INFLUENCES ON PERCEPTION

Although the owner and an observer look at the same car at the same time and the light stimuli impinging upon their respective retinas are very similar, they do not *perceive* exactly the same car. Each may recognize it as the same model and they both may notice certain other characteristics, but it looks somewhat different to each of them. Assume that you are the owner and that you have owned the car for several years. The other person is a casual acquaintance. Both of you see the color and general outlines of the car, and you may hear the same engine noises. But to you, it is not merely a car; it is a possession of yours which has provided good service and many pleasurable driving experiences. The other person cannot perceive this in your car. He receives sensory impressions, but he does not attach the same meanings to them. That scratch on the fender which to you recalls a pleasant picnic, to him is just a scratch on the fender and nothing more.

In other words, phenomena in our environment may have stimulus qualities which are not inherent in the stimuli themselves. Our past experiences often produce expectations which in turn govern our *perceptions* — that is, the meanings we associate with sensory impressions or experiences, and the interpretations we make of our environment. A knife *looks* sharp, ice *looks* cold, and a pillow *looks* soft, even though we cannot actually see sharpness, coldness, or softness as such (7). We also endow certain objects with positions in space, size, and motion or lack of motion as a result of our actual past experiences with them. For example, a person can close his eyes and visualize a motionless or a moving auto, truck, or helicopter. With what characteristics does he endow these objects — simply through his perception? Color, size, motion?

Perceptual patterning

Some of the factors which affect our perceptions are worth considering in more detail. To begin with, the individual typically organizes his sensory experiences into a pattern which is meaningful to him. In this process of perceptual patterning he sometimes focuses on the details of the sensation, whereas at other times he does not notice details, or he discards them as unimportant. Further, sometimes he tries to bring every available meaning to bear in establishing a fully organized pattern; at other times he disregards many possible meanings to satisfy the particular needs of the moment. Our patterning is dependent on ourselves and our environment.

Whether focusing on details or on the whole, whether bringing into action all

Factors in perception. *We do not always sense and perceive accurately. Although the center circles in each drawing are the same size, they appear to be different because of their surroundings.*

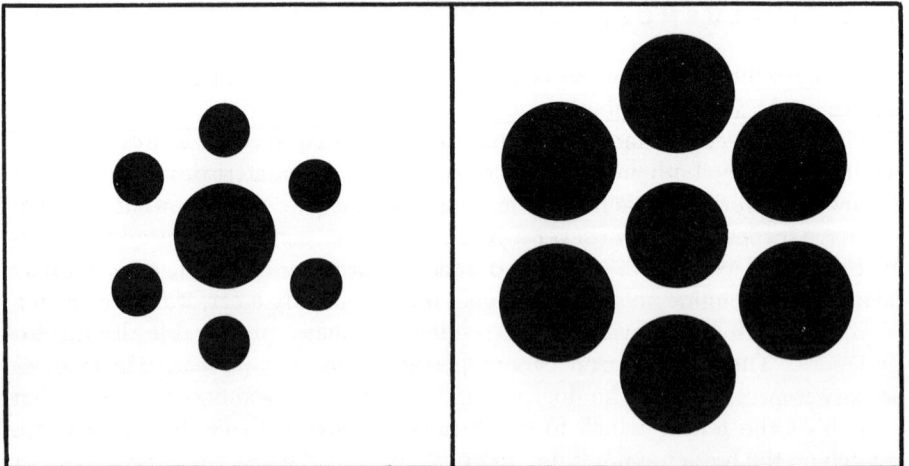

possible meanings or selecting and discarding some, the individual acts in an effort to organize his sensory experiences. Perhaps an example will make these processes clearer.

Because the artist's signature on a painting is obviously not part of the composition, you usually do not mention it when you describe a picture. It does not fit your pattern of organization, and you discard it, although once your attention is drawn to it, you will attempt to make it a part of your pattern.

The illustration on page 188 may clarify the meaning of figure–ground relationship discussed in Part B of this chapter. Your differentiation of figure and ground may have shifted as you examined the picture, but if you concentrate, you will attempt to organize it into a pattern. Let us now examine the characteristics of the organization of a field.

The whole–part relationship

Certain magazines occasionally publish photographs of unidentified objects, and the reader is asked to guess what they are. In many cases he finds that he is looking at a rather small object magnified to a larger size and presented out of context. For example, he sees what look like fish nets but really are small magnified areas of nylon stockings. Or he sees a deeply pitted surface resembling the effects of soil erosion and finds he is actually examining a common bath sponge. This sort of illusion shows how we may look at *parts* of an object and interpret them as a complete or *whole* object. Some typical pictures of this sort are shown on page 196. See if you can tell what they are.

We all know the expression, "He cannot see the forest for the trees." It means simply that a person has focused on the *part* of the forest (or situation) to such an extent that he cannot see it as a whole. On the contrary, to him the part *becomes* the whole. In the same way we may not see the tree for the leaves, the leaves for the cells, or the cells for the granules. Each is a part of a larger object, but each can be a whole in itself.

We tend first to perceive wholes and then proceed to differentiate parts as we feel the need to, or as we become more familiar with the object perceived. For example, it is hard for most of us to distinguish between identical twins, but their parents find it easy to tell them apart. Or consider a figured shirt or dress — do you first get an over-all impression, or do you first examine the details of the tiny figures making up the pattern? Do you learn the details of a lesson as quickly as you grasp the general idea? When you are practicing golf or tennis, do you find the broad, general body movements easier than the details of footwork and grip? Typically we observe the whole, with further attention we differentiate the parts, then we integrate the parts and the whole becomes more meaningful.

The diagrams on page 197 further illustrate whole–part relationships. As you can see, stimuli tend to form patterns, and it is the pattern rather than the

Whole–part relationships. *Here are enlarged photos of some parts of everyday objects. Can you name the "whole" of which each is a "part"?* [1] *(Photos by John A. Murray.)*

individual stimuli which we perceive. The first diagram illustrates the effect of closeness or *proximity* of objects in patterning — that is, you see a triangle rather than separate dots. The second demonstrates the effect of likeness or *similarity,* and the third illustrates the effect of *closure,* or the tendency of the perceptual process to fill in the gaps in an open pattern. Thus the manner in which stimuli themselves are organized affects what we perceive. But there are variations also in the ways in which individuals organize any one perceptual field, and even the same individual may perceive a thing differently at different times.

Established habits

Another influence on perception is likely to be the individual's "set" or expectancies, which may provide him with a certain predisposition to perceive things in certain ways (8). For example, if you were given a calendar to hang on the wall, a tack, and a milk bottle, would you perceive the milk bottle as a light and fragile hammer? If you were given two six-foot boards and two C-clamps such as carpenters use, could you construct a coat rack? That is, would you perceive the clamps as useful instruments both to fasten the boards together so they could be wedged between the floor and ceiling and also to serve as the coat hangers? We recognize that this involves problem-solving as well as perception, but the problem could not be solved if the clamps were perceived only as clamps and not also as hangers.

Other factors in perception

Perception may also be influenced by *organic conditions.* If one is near starvation, many formerly neutral or definitely unpleasant objects (like grasshoppers, sea urchins, or decaying food) may be perceived as edible. Certain *drugs,* too, may influence one's perceptions.

The *emotional status* of the individual markedly affects his perception. For

[1] Answers: paper clips, cellophane, match sticks.

example, under threatening conditions, perception becomes much more variable and erratic, and it is often delayed. Cowan and Beier (9) found this to be true in an experiment in which students were to decipher words, some of which were considered threatening and others neutral. If the students were alerted to forthcoming threatening words, however, the variance in perception decreased.

Age and development, of course, are other influencing factors. Cronbach (10) points out that the perception of events or objects tends toward the simplest pattern that will summarize the main observations. He mentions some young children who, on a western trip, shouted "Howdy Oats!" to a cowboy. This, he found, was their perception of "adios" as heard on the Lone Ranger program. The two English words made sense; the unknown Spanish word did not.

Suggested activities

1. Have someone do magic tricks. What is the role of sensation? Of perception?

2. How is Helen Keller's world different from our own? Read biographies and articles about her.

3. What is the principle of Cinerama? Of 3–D?

4. What is the role of perfume in industry (11)?

5. To what illusions are we regularly accustomed?

6. Blindfold a subject. Rest a board on two blocks about an inch high, and stand the subject on the board. Place the subject's hands on the shoulders of someone standing in front of him. Have two men pick up the board (and the subject), as the person in front slowly squats. Have the men raise the board about two inches and move it gently about. Ask the subject to jump. What does the subject perceive?

Patterns in perceiving. *In the first diagram you see a triangle rather than six dots separately. You probably see the second diagram as five horizontal rows rather than as five vertical rows. The third is an example of the perceiver's tendency to fill in gaps in an open pattern.*

Proximity	Similarity	Closure

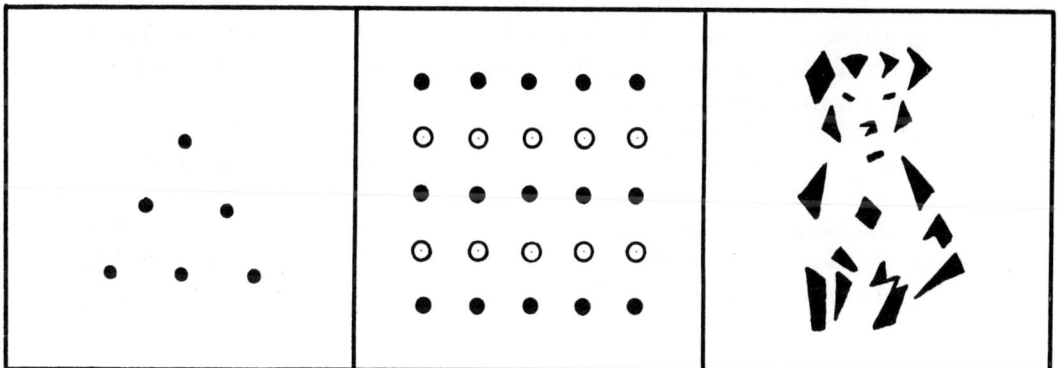

A. VISION, HEARING, AND OTHER SENSES
B. ATTENTION AND DIFFERENTIATION
C. INFLUENCES ON PERCEPTION

● **D. IMPROVING PERCEPTION**

Knowledge about sensing and perceiving would be of little value to us if it were only of medical or laboratory interest. We are interested in the application of such knowledge to our everyday lives. One of the goals of education may very properly be to help us gain a clearer and more objective view of our environment — to help us understand things as they objectively are, rather than as they may have seemed to us in the past.

Improving sensory discriminations

Discrimination and judgment of sensory impressions are partly learned. We continually subject ourselves to the re-learning and evaluation of our impressions. Thus we already have one clue toward how to improve sensory discrimination — that is, by learning.

Visual discrimination is needed in reading — to see the difference between "house" and "horse" for example. It is also needed in distinguishing between shades of color — in paintings, home decorations, clothes, or cosmetics. Such discrimination can be improved by close comparison of nearly identical words or colors, by striving to see differences between similar objects, and by taking time for careful observation of what we are seeing. For example, do you find it difficult to distinguish between some of your classmates? Why not form as many associations with each of them individually as you can? Look for details — facial contour, coloring, hair line, scars, tastes in clothing or cosmetics. Do their voices sound exactly alike? Are their postures alike? What differences are there in size and proportions?

We also need to improve our auditory discrimination. Some people never get tired of listening to classical music, because each time they hear a selection they discover some new melody, counterpoint, tonal quality, or shading. Such fine discriminations can come about partly through musical education or coaching and partly through definitely intending to seek new details or figures.

Touch discrimination is needed in typewriting, hitting a golf ball accurately, playing the piano, or catching a fish with skill. Kinesthetic discrimination is needed in most motor activities — for example, throwing a forward pass, writing by hand, or dancing.

Patterns can be made more meaningful by attention to details and an attempt to understand the stimulus as a whole. The way to get the most enjoyment from watching football is to learn the various T-formations and wing-backs and more of the fine points of the game. Knowledge of specific aspects, coupled with a general knowledge of the possible plays that can be run or what may next occur, will give you a better idea of what is happening on the field. Symbols used in mathematics or chemistry books may be confusing until you learn something about the subjects themselves. It is the same with words in foreign languages, musical notes on the staff, or keys on the typewriter. In every case the symbols will become more meaningful with careful and detailed observation, comparison with other confusing symbols, practice in distinguishing differences, coaching, and acquiring general knowledge related to the subject.

He who would read with more understanding might first slow his reading rate and think more carefully about the words and phrases. Knowledge of precise meanings, not only in relation to reading but elsewhere, is essential. If an instructor or coach is present, he can help by pointing out details and calling attention to minor variations as well as by giving exercises in comparing very similar objects. For example, beginners in music may confuse sixteenth, thirty-second, and sixty-fourth notes, since all have two or more "flags." An instructor can emphasize the number of flags and the appearance of the notes, and practice soon overcomes the difficulty. Music students will recall other similar examples.

Improving social perceptions

Man is a social animal. Can some of our social perceptions be improved? How do we form impressions of other people, and how do they form impressions of us? Can we improve our *empathy* — our ability to identify or feel ourselves in the same state of mind as another person or a group? Can we help ourselves develop social sensitivity and awareness?

In perceiving social situations we always have a starting place — a point of view. People are always related to situations, which in turn differ in time, place, and content. The *part* must be judged in relation to the *whole*. *Context* and *frame of reference* must always be considered.

The word *context* is usually used in referring to the words in a sentence which surround and help to define a new or unknown word. Thus if the word "bow" is seen alone, we do not know whether it refers to a device for shooting arrows, the front of a ship, or a polite gesture. But when the word occurs in a sentence like "The girl wore a *bow* in her hair," the meaning is apparent from the context.

We may expand the meaning of the word *context* to refer to a situation in which a person finds himself. Thus, to understand why a professor gives low grades to the whole class on a certain test, one needs to know the context — the environmental factors affecting him. Perhaps the college has been described as a "diploma mill," and administrators have told instructors to be less lenient in grading. Or maybe the professor feels that a little extrinsic motivation for study is needed. Is he working in an area where near-perfect recitations are required? In other words, one is not just a person — he is a person related to a certain setting, or context.

When you are trying to interpret the way one of your friends is behaving in a certain social situation, you must examine the entire set of factors which led to his being there. What is the physical environment? What persons are present? Is his position that of a leader or a subordinate? What restrictions are put upon his actions? He might act quite differently if you met him down at Clancy's garage or out fishing on Lake Michigan.

At any particular time we tend to portray a role suitable to the social situation as we understand it. We act from a *personal* frame of reference in a variety of *social* contexts. Thus in a given situation, we may assume one role with its attitudes, motivations, expectations, and tendencies for action as opposed to other possible roles. For example:

George, a college senior, is asked to come to the instructor's office after class to make up an examination. What might be George's frame of reference?

He may act like the usual student — he is expected to comply with the reasonable request of the instructor, so he shows up as a matter of course and takes the test.

He may, however, be a campus hero — an outstanding football player and potential All-American. If he operates from this frame of reference, he may complain to the instructor, because football practice is more important to him than the make-up examination at that particular time.

On the other hand, if he is an ex-GI, who has served in a rather unpleasant area of the world and "lost" a few years of his young adulthood, he may feel that the world has taken unfair advantage of him. He may therefore think the instructor is "picking on him," and although he takes the test, may harbor resentment at having to do so.

George may have other frames of reference, based on his past experience and the attitudes and motives he has devloped over a period of time. Which frame of reference will most influence his behavior depends in part on his motives and his established roles.

Thus our social perceptions vary, depending on the frame of reference from which we operate. Since the frames of reference of different individuals vary, our actions do not always seem consistent to other people, nor do theirs to us. If we are to maintain adequate social- and self-perceptions, it is sometimes necessary to rethink our own roles and to study those of others carefully. As an illustration consider the matter of *stereotypes*.

For purposes of handy reference and convenience each of us tends to group people into classes with a common denominator. Thus we save ourselves the trouble of really studying an individual to know him as he is. Instead we attribute to him those qualities which his group possesses, or with which it is traditionally endowed. For example, when you hear the word "Communist" do you think of a particular type of person — one who is dangerous, threatening, and bent on destroying our form of government? Or does the word connote a family man, deeply committed to his work and devoted to his country? The latter idea, of course, is not part of our stereotype. Might it be, however, part of that of a citizen of another country? When the word "pastor" is mentioned, do you think of a gentle person, willing and unselfish and ready to do good through self-sacrifice? You probably do not think of a greedy, grasping person, intent on self-aggrandizement.

Stereotypes can be dangerous. Most of us do not wish to be labeled; we prefer to be considered as individuals. Yet such generalizations exist in modern society, especially in relation to national, racial, and religious groups — three very significant areas of everyday living. Our stereotypes may become so strong that even what we see, hear, and experience directly is not accepted as truth because it does not conform to them. College living and study should enable us not only to get rid of present incorrect notions but also to develop an open attitude toward all new objects, facts, persons, and situations.

Here are four suggestions for improving your perceptions. It will require conscious effort on your part to carry out these suggestions until you begin to feel at home with them and form the habits they imply.

1. Learn to pay closer attention to what you and others say. This involves gaining a better vocabulary and knowledge of written and oral English, and also thinking and talking more clearly. Such abilities can be improved, not only in speech or English classes, but in every area of college work. Simply being more attentive and critical of what you say, read, or hear is of great value. While it is not necessary to be extremely precise or pedantic, it is important to listen carefully to others and to communicate clearly with them.

2. Observe carefully. Some people are experts at sensing the sentiment of a crowd and playing carefully on its emotions. Others may disregard all such signs. Some people cannot take hints, for example. You can improve your ability to sense people's moods by careful attention to others and by trying to infer their feelings. Concentrate on others rather than on yourself.

In essay examinations it is interesting to see how students' answers vary. Some miss significant details. Others include mostly details but interpret them differently or do not organize them into a meaningful total answer. Ask yourself the following questions about any important situation you have found yourself in recently:

1. Did you observe the entire situation or merely a small part of it?
2. How much can you remember of what you observed?
3. Did you observe only generalities, or did you notice details?
4. Are you sure you recognized what you observed?
5. Are you objective? Or did you put things into the situation which were not actually there?

3. Broaden your experiences. Although imagination is helpful, we cannot really "know" things unless we have experienced them. For example, it would be difficult for you to imagine the color "ambiflex" even though we tell you it is a combination of purple, green, orange, and white. To know that color, you will have to see it. The same is true with emotions. Although we can imagine great sorrow, anger, or fear, we do not really sense their broadest import until we have experienced them actually rather than vicariously. Actors are said to want to undergo many emotional experiences so that they can better interpret them to audiences. Although this may not be the best way of learning to act, it is quite true that unless we have experienced such feelings as sympathy and negativism we cannot portray them successfully.

Broadening your experience through studying new fields, entering new activities, traveling, and reading will provide a good basis for meaningful perception and for reserving judgment. The statement is often made that the more education one has, the less sure he is of anything. In a sense this is true. When we have only a little knowledge, we fail to see the various alternatives involved in a situation. A professor who has great knowledge of his subject is often less willing than his students to be dogmatic. The more you know, the less likely you are to think of statements as being unequivocably true or false, black or white. Statements involving attitudes, beliefs, values, and theories are more correctly "various shades of gray."

4. Reserve judgment or opinion. It often seems easiest to make a snap judgment about people or events. Drawing quick conclusions enables us to categorize a situation and handle it more easily in our immediate thinking and acting. Until we know it fairly well, however, we are quite likely to be faulty in our judgments.

In college it becomes increasingly important to ask ourselves: "Are my own goals, prejudices, stereotypes, or other personal factors clouding my judgment? Does my own frame of reference preclude my making a good judgment? In what context are we — the other fellow and I — operating? How does he see the situation? What are his goals, past experiences, and expectations?"

SUMMARY

We sense the environment through seeing, hearing, touching, tasting, and other sensations. We attach meaning to our sensory experiences and, in the process, we learn. To some extent individuals do not acquire identical impressions from or attach identical meanings to their various sensory experiences. They interpret any environment somewhat differently. Communication is possible to the extent of the similarity of sensory experiences and interpretations. Perfect understanding is probably impossible, for two people apparently cannot sense precisely the same reality. In addition, the "sensed" world of individuals varies according to their sensory equipment, cumulative experiences, goals, and environment.

Improvement of sensory discrimination and perception is possible. Success in the academic area of college life demands it. To communicate more effectively and to understand others better, we should attend closely to what we and others say, observe carefully, broaden our sensory experiences, and reserve judgment until we have adequate knowledge.

REFERENCES

1. D. Snygg, and A. W. Combs, *Individual Behavior*, Harper, New York, 1944, Chapter 2.
2. *Ibid.*, p. 36.
3. R. Stagner, and T. F. Karwoski, *Psychology*, McGraw-Hill, New York, 1952, p. 110.
4. J. L. Falk, "Theories of Visual Acuity and Their Physiological Bases," *Psychol. Bull.*, 1956, 53, p. 110. (Explains varying differences between the eye and the camera.)
5. See H. L. Kingsley, *Nature and Conditions of Learning*, Prentice-Hall, New York, 1946, chapters on attending and perceiving. See especially the discussion of "set" in perceiving.
6. See L. Carmichael and W. F. Dearborn, *Reading and Visual Fatigue*, Houghton Mifflin, 1947.
7. See N. L. Munn, *Psychology: The Fundamentals of Human Adjustment*, Houghton Mifflin, Boston, Rev. 1957, Chapter 12.
8. N. R. F. Maier, "Reasoning in Humans, III. The Mechanisms of Equivalent Stimuli and of Reasoning," *J. Exper. Psychol.*, 1945, 35, pp. 349–360.
9. E. Cowan and E. G. Beier, "Threat-expectancy, Word Frequencies, and Perceptual Pre-recognition Hypothesis," *J. Abnorm. Soc. Psychol.*, 1954, 49, pp. 178–182.
10. L. J. Cronbach, *Educational Psychology*, Harcourt, Brace, New York, 1954, p. 279.
11. L. Aikman, "Perfume, the Business of Illusion," *Nat. Geogr.*, 1951, April, pp. 531–550.

SUGGESTIONS FOR FURTHER READING

Garrett, H. E., *General Psychology*, American, New York, 1955, Chapter 5.
Harlow, H. F., "The Formation of Learning Sets," *Psychol. Rev.*, 1949, 56, pp. 51–65.
Havemann, E., *The Age of Psychology*, Simon, New York, 1957, Chapter 2.
Heider, F., *The Psychology of Interpersonal Relations*, Wiley, New York, 1958, Chapters 2, 3.
Kepner, H. W., *Psychology Applied to Life and Work*, Prentice-Hall, Englewood Cliffs, N. J., 1950, Chapter 25.
Mowbray, G. H., "Simultaneous Vision and Audition. The Comprehension of Prose Passages with Varying Levels of Difficulty," *J. Exp. Psychol.*, 1953, 46, pp. 365–372.
Munn, N. L., *Psychology: The Fundamentals of Human Adjustment*, Houghton Mifflin, Boston, third edition, 1956, Chapter 12.
Smith, K. U., and W. M. Smith, *The Behavior of Man: Introduction to Psychology*, Holt, New York, 1958, Chapter 9.
Wenger, M. A., F. M. Jones, and M. H. Jones, *Physiological Psychology*, Holt, New York, 1956, Chapters 6–14.

Thinking and

Communication

You have probably been in English classes most of your school life. Most likely you were successful in them, for here you are at college. Some of the requirements may have seemed like chores. They may not have seemed as useful as you might have wished. Grammar, spelling, definitions, and punctuation do not always seem interesting enough to deserve the attention you must give them. But they are nonetheless important. This chapter will attempt to demonstrate the importance of language in independent thinking and in communicating with others. Have you ever considered how language aids thinking? Stop reading for a minute and try to think of something — anything you please — without using words. Can you do it?

● A. LANGUAGE AND THINKING

When a person thinks, he usually uses words because words are representations of his experiences. It is possible to recall a scene or project a dress pattern into the idea of the completed article without using words, but this thinking is fairly concrete and simple. It does not involve abstractions or stress complicated relationships between things or ideas. It is at a relatively low level.

Apes and similar animals seem to be capable of low-level thinking. However, since they do not possess language, they apparently cannot recall complex experiences other than those in the immediate past, or project plans

7

Language Skills and Personal Growth

What is the process of thought? Is language neces-
sary for thinking? What are the different concepts of
thinking? What are some deterrents to thinking? How
does a child learn to use language? How can a person
improve his ability to communicate through the use of
words in speaking and in writing? What are some of
the pitfalls of communication? What makes a good in-
terview?

except for the immediate future. Apes evidently lack the intelligence needed
for developing language and high-level thinking.

The human neonate, although potentially capable of thinking and speech
development, does not use language. The mentally deficient adult is characterized by the inability to acquire extensive verbal language or to use other
symbols meaningfully. Like apes and young children, he cannot recall experiences or plan future projects as well as normally developed human adults.

The precise level at which rudimentary mental activity like that of young
children, apes, or mentally deficient persons may be called *thinking* is unknown.
Language and thinking with the use of symbols emerged gradually in the
evolution of the human species. So, also, in the developmental pattern of human beings there is probably a gradual emergence of thinking with the use
of symbols from what was previously rather random, undirected mental activity. Russell (1), in a discussion of thinking in children, finds that there are
as many as six distinguishable levels, although he does not insist that all of
them are involved in thinking at any one time.

Conscious critical thinking, using words and other symbols commonly employed in everyday activities, is our main concern in this chapter. Because
thinking is not fully understood, we shall examine other writers' ideas concerning the nature of thinking, thus giving you a basis for forming your own opinion.

Two definitions are necessary, first: those of *sign* and *symbol*. Following
Young's (2) terminology, a *sign* is "any cue or learned stimulus which sets off

or leads to a response." Thus we can teach a dog to come when we whistle, for the sound is a sign indicating to the dog that he will be petted or fed. When a cat learns that opening the refrigerator door means "food is coming," he is constantly underfoot in the kitchen. *Symbols* for our purposes here are special kinds of signs which have social meaning. By this we mean that they are signs agreed on by members of a society. Words, used both in speaking and writing are symbols, with meanings which depend on *social agreement.* "Democracy," as a symbol, may have various meanings to various groups of people, but there is general agreement within any group on what it means. Our musical notation, number system, and proofreader's marks are also symbols, but the sound of a door-bell is a sign. Some methods of teaching foreign languages include the use of cartoons in which stick figures perform various movements with the proper descriptive words placed near the drawings. This method uses *signs* to teach *symbols.*

Animals — for example, apes, dogs, cats, and chickens — can understand certain signs. They do *not* understand symbols, at least not in a meaningful way. When your dog responds to different words, he is responding to changes in your tone of voice and manner of speaking, rather than to the meanings implied by the words.

The nature of thinking

Munn (3) states that "We think with symbols . . . . They may be words, gestures, or images. . . . Thinking is typically a sequential arousal of symbols. We think of one thing; that starts us thinking of another; that of still another; and so on. In this way we manipulate and rearrange, as it were, the various aspects of the world which have fallen within the range of our experience."

Munn's concept of thinking is a comprehensive one. It includes such low-level mental activities as reverie or daydreaming as well as high-level reasoning like that involved in the purposefully directed solution of complex problems.

> **Visual symbols.** *Many objects during the history of man have acquired symbolic meanings apart from their actual physical properties. How many of these symbols do you recognize? What do they mean to you — to other individuals or groups? Is there any danger of irrational thinking due to emotional suggestion?*

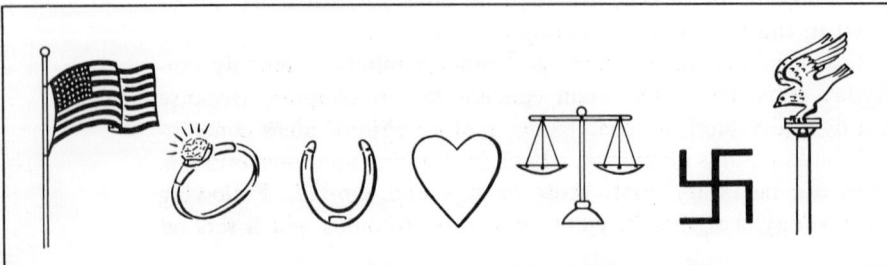

Other writers differentiate high-level thought processes from mere random recall of experiences and daydreaming by using such terms as "reflective thinking," and "elaborative thinking." In the next few pages we shall present some definitions of thinking and a summary of the elements they have in common.

Reflective thinking. According to John Dewey (4) reflective thinking "involves (1) a state of doubt, hesitation, perplexity, mental difficulty, in which the thinking originates, and (2) an act of searching, hunting, inquiring to find material that will resolve the doubt, settle and dispose of the perplexity." Notice that reflective thinking involves "searching, hunting, and inquiring" for a *purpose* — namely, "to resolve the doubt, settle and dispose of the perplexity." Dewey (5) in further elaboration, identified five phases or aspects of reflective thinking:

(1) suggestions, in which the mind leaps forward to a possible solution;

(2) an intellectualization of the difficulty or perplexity that has been *felt* (directly experienced) into a problem to be solved, a question for which the answer must be sought;

(3) the use of one suggestion after another as a leading idea, or hypothesis, to initiate and guide observation and other operations in the collection of factual materials;

(4) the mental elaboration of the idea or supposition . . . ; and

(5) testing the hypothesis by overt or imaginative action.

The above sequence should not be considered as fixed, according to Dewey, and points are not given in order of importance. If you will at this point accept the question, "What is thinking?" as merely a perplexing problem, then try to come to a solution through further reading and thinking, and finally come back to Dewey's outline, you will undoubtedly understand it as clearly as can be expected.

Productive thinking. Wertheimer (6) presented a cognitive point of view concerning thought processes. (See the learning theory discussed in Chapter 5.) He emphasized securing a consistent understanding of the whole problem situation and seeing what the structure of the whole required for the parts. You will recall the similar importance attached to figure–ground relationships in cognitive theory and the significance of individual perception in structuring one's field. Wertheimer's emphasis on meaningful structural patterns is apparent in the following summary of the nature of thinking:

. . . in the desire to get at real understanding, requestioning and investigation start.

A certain region in the field becomes crucial, is focused; but does not become isolated.

A new, deeper structural view of the situation develops, involving changes in the functional meaning, the grouping, etc., of the items.

Directed by what is required by the structure of a situation for a crucial region, one is led to a reasonable prediction, which — like the other parts of the structure — calls for verification, direct or indirect.

In the above analysis the desire to get at real understanding seems to initiate productive thinking; the requestioning and investigating start. This leads to a focus on some portion of the field, from which one sees the whole structure with more insight. It is in the process of acquiring better perception and meanings, predicting solutions, and correlating them that thinking may be characterized as productive.

Elaborative thinking. Kingsley (7) restricted elaborative thinking to "the process of working out a solution to a problem . . . by the use of signs, symbols, or clues." He listed six stages in the process:

First, a difficulty is felt;
second, the problem is clarified and defined;
third, a search for clues is made;
fourth, various suggestions appear and are evaluated or tried out;
fifth, a suggested solution is accepted or the thinker gives up in defeat;
sixth, *the solution is tested* by checking its applicability to the problem and by verifying the fact that it is a real "solution."

In Kingsley's analysis, as in Dewey's, the thinker feels a difficulty; and this, like Wertheimer's desire to get at real understanding, is the originating point in the thinking process. Whereas Kingsley's sequence called for stating and defining the problem, Dewey would have "intellectualization of the difficulty or perplexity that has been felt" and Wertheimer states that "a certain region in the field is focused." These seem to be different ways of phrasing an idea which seems to be generally agreed on by the theorists.

Other concepts of thinking. Humphrey (8) identified the following characteristics of thought processes:

1. A problem is thrust upon the thinker. His activities are interrupted until a solution is found . . .
2. The intermediate processes, between the perception of the problem and the solution, include the thinking . . .
3. There are successive stages in working out the solution.
4. The thinker is using his senses to find out the trouble. He stops, looks and listens. The thinking is not done in a vacuum, but in close touch with reality.
5. He forms mental images.
6. By a remarkable power of the mind, all these activities are kept relevant to the point at issue.

As in the previous analysis, Humphrey identifies the experiencing of a problem as the origin of thinking. This implies that the thinker must be *capable* of experiencing a problem. Humphrey's emphasis on the fact that thinking does not occur in a vacuum but in close touch with reality suggests that the thinker must be *aware* of reality. Elsewhere however, he states that the "human *or animal* organism" can think.

Johnson (9) examines thought as a content of consciousness, as problem-solving, and as judgment. He feels that all the important aspects of thought can be treated as problem-solving and as judgment. Thought as a content of consciousness, according to his view, cannot be fully investigated. You may wish to read some of the references cited at the end of this chapter concerning the nature of thinking, for it is a fascinating subject. Part of its fascination stems from our everyday experiences in thinking, and part from the fact that we lack precise knowledge of what occurs internally when we think. Our best judgments about thinking originate from our observation of the outward effects or results of thinking and from recalling our own inward experiences.

Though persons who apparently think efficiently have attempted to describe their thought processes, there is not complete agreement in their accounts. The various definitions we have cited result probably from the particular writer's own introspection as well as his analysis of the results of experiments. The common elements in thinking which we shall now discuss result from the use of basically the same techniques.

Common Elements in Definitions

1. All the definitions seem to agree that thinking involves mental activity which originates with a feeling of tension about something. This state may be caused by simply being asked a question. Or a person may perceive something, decide it is not satisfactory, and therefore attempt to improve the condition. From the phenomenological and Gestalt point of view, whether the "problem" arises from an outside circumstance, another person, or the subject's own analysis, it will result in thinking — if he perceives his field as no longer well organized (a situation which would normally lead to tension) and if he desires to achieve better organization. For example, you might be asked, "How can thinking be improved?" or you might ask yourself that question. Once you accept it as a problem and see no immediate solution to it, you will begin to think about it — that is, your field is no longer satisfactorily organized (because you do not have the answer) and you seek to organize it (by finding an answer).

2. For thinking to produce a constructive result the problem must be intellectualized, formulated, or stated in such a way that it is clear to the thinker. A problem in mathematics may involve signs and symbols other than words, as may one in painting or music. The clarity with which any such signs and symbols can be formulated to get at the essentials of the problem is directly related to success in solving it. Further, some adults apparently can identify and formulate more complex problems than others. You may find it interest-

ing at this time to attempt to recall what you considered complex problems five and ten years ago. If you have younger brothers or sisters, or can observe younger children, note the problems which they consider challenging.

3. Once the problem is intellectualized, thinking is directed toward its solution. Possible answers, of course, may originate in close temporal proximity to the intellectualizing process. If the problem can be readily solved, little thinking occurs. If it cannot, however, the individual will gather pertinent information, consciously attend to the problem by focusing his thoughts on it, and eventually develop possible solutions or hypotheses. Terms such as "creative thinking," "critical thinking," and others already mentioned, are used to describe this phase and level of thinking. For example, the person who does not accept answers someone else has already obtained but searches for a better one of his own might be described as thinking creatively, reflectively, or productively. Persons who invent new solutions or markedly improve old and accepted ones in such fields as the sciences and the arts have obviously not accepted all known solutions as satisfactory. They question some critically; they experiment with others, do research, and reserve judgment.

4. The *testing* of hypotheses also requires experimentation, questioning, and reserving judgment. In solving more complex problems, one cannot always concentrate on possible solutions without interruption. One's present information, his hypotheses, and the particular context in which he is operating may not seem to be in harmony. This feeling that the "pieces do not fit" may apply to a theme or term paper, a musical composition, a painting, or a social, political, or economic problem. Relaxing in the pool, taking a walk, or pursuing a different activity may be useful in eventually arriving at a solution. With the passage of time the pieces or parts that previously did not fit may come together as one gains a better perspective.

Failure to find acceptable solutions to problems is frustrating. Many people are willing to accept solutions of others rather than to experience continued high tension; others convince themselves that the unsolved problem really does not exist. While some of this behavior is undoubtedly necessary to maintain peace with oneself, it results in considerable inefficiency in thinking. Let us now turn to some characteristics which are associated with inefficient thinking and problem-solving.

Deterrents to thinking

Three main deterrents or impediments to the thinking of intelligent persons include the desire for social approval, rigidity, and inaccuracy in the use of symbols. The last of these matters will be treated briefly here, along with the others, but will be discussed more fully later in the chapter.

Social approval. The desire to be approved by others may be an impediment as well as an incentive to thinking. It becomes an impediment in smaller groups like the home or classroom when a person either denies the

Effect of social opinion on thinking. *In an experiment by Dr. Solomon E. Asch subjects were asked to tell which of the three lines on the card pictured below equalled in length the single line on the other card. Everyone except the person tested (the boy in the middle) was instructed to persist in giving a wrong answer. From top to bottom: 1. The subject listens to the rules of the experiment, 2. makes his first judgment, disagreeing with everyone else, 3. leans forward to look at another pair of cards, 4. shows strain of repeatedly disagreeing with majority, 5. retains original opinion after 12 pairs of cards have been shown. Seventy-five per cent of subjects changed their opinions to agree with the majority. (William Vandivert, Scientific American.)*

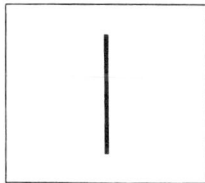

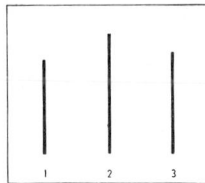

existence of a real, existing problem or will not attempt a new or better solution to an old one for fear of losing the approval of those in his social context. This fear can become general throughout a larger community such as the college campus, state, or nation.

As we saw in Chapter 3, there are many values to be derived from group living, but it also creates problems. If one persistently cannot seek solutions to his individual difficulties and those related to the group for fear of losing the respect or admiration of those near him, he will tend not to identify problems or not to think productively about solving them. To some extent, the fear of proposing new and different solutions to the problems of world peace characterized our national life following World War II. Fear of losing approval permeated instruction in many colleges and universities. Controversial issues, in many instances those which vitally affect all people, were removed from debate and discussion. Many questions involving religion, race, and politics are side-stepped today for the same reason. As a result, there is a danger that creative solutions will not emerge.

Rigidity. This deterrent to efficient thinking involves the inability to change one's methods of approaching a problem when its nature demands a new kind of attack. The precise cause of mental rigidity in normally developing, bright young adults has not been determined. Experiments, however, have been conducted in which rigidity was induced in the subjects or perhaps was already present (10). These experiments show quite conclusively that a person who has acquired a habitual method of dealing with such problems as measuring amounts of water in a laboratory situation does not change with the presentation of a new problem which needs a different method of solution. The same is true in the use of certain objects to perform tasks. Reid (11) found that one way to help college students overcome the possible effects of rigidity was to give them aids in identifying a problem and working towards its solution. Cowen (12), experimenting with college students, found that reducing anxiety and psychological stress resulted in less rigid and more productive problem-solving.

From these experiments and other evidence it seems that productive thinking requires that one must be free from intense psychological stress, examine carefully his habitual methods of dealing with problems, be willing to accept change and novel solutions, decide the point at which the desire for approval blunts his zest for thinking, and develop the symbols essential for dealing with complex problems.

Inaccuracy in the use of symbols. A word of caution is needed in respect to the development of symbols, especially those which we call "words." If one is not careful, he is likely, after a time, to accept the symbol as the object for which it stands. He thus may begin to think erroneously, for he will have in mind not the actual object, but only what it has come to mean to him through its symbol. For example, if we ascribe to George the terms "dull" or "unintelligent," we may act as if he actually were that way all the time when, in fact, he may be quite the opposite. We tend to think of the symbol "America" as being the United States only, and we may act as though all Americans are alike. We say, "Americans are freedom-loving. Americans are honest and sincere. Americans will do so-and-so in a certain world situation." Yet thought will show us that none of these is necessarily true. Other symbols take on a threatening connotation — atom bomb, dentist's chair, death. Yet the threat may not be inherent in the situation or object at all. Thus symbols must continually be reassessed if one's thinking is to be dependable. It is equally important to recognize, as discussed in the next section, that the use of symbols is a necessary part of all high-level thinking.

Suggested activities

1. Compare what we have said in previous chapters about problem-solving and the scientific method with the definitions of thinking given in this chapter.

2. Have children eight to ten years old define for you such words as "economy," "television," and "patriotic." What limitations in their thinking can you detect? How do you explain these limitations?

3. How well can you think without symbols? Try to plan tomorrow's activities without using words.

4. Invent new symbols for the words "the," "dog," "brown," "is," "and," "black." Make a sentence from these symbols. What difficulties arise? Why do they arise?

A.   LANGUAGE AND THINKING

● B.   THE DEVELOPMENT OF LANGUAGE

Have you ever wondered whether a very smart parrot might some day carry on a real conversation with you instead of merely repeating phrases he had been taught? Have you ever speculated about the stories of Mowgli and Tarzan, wondering whether it might not be possible for people to talk with animals? Or have you ever wondered whether a fox being pursued might be able to tell other foxes that hunters were on his trail? We are really raising questions about the nature of language. What is involved in developing language?

Gestures and language

For a highly interesting account of the language of early man and a consideration of communication among subhuman species, you may wish to read some of the writings of Kimball Young (2, Chap. 6) and Köhler (13). Young emphasizes the importance of the gesture in communication and shows how mankind is particularly well adapted in physical structure for the use of ges-

tures. He points out that the acquisition of upright posture and the elaboration of the cerebral cortex are among the great turning-points in animal evolution. The freeing of the hands, permitting the creation and improvement of
tools and new ways of manipulating the environment, the postural relationships
of men to one another (face-to-face), the release of the mouth and larynx from
its nearly exclusive earlier concern with food-getting — all led to the development of better communication through gestures and with the voice.

In the above context, gestural forms of communication include crying, grunt-
ing, and yelling, as well as such motions as waving, beckoning, and motioning
others away. The subhuman species use the following gestures widely — cries
of danger, growls of anger or fright, bristling of the hair on the neck, wagging
of the tail, twitching of the ear, licking, and, purring. In sensing the gestures
of others, animals participate in communication also, even though on a primitive level.

Apes, having like men the freedom of arm movement, can communicate
through motions of the hands as well as orally. Their vocal expressions, however, are not true speech. They can communicate only matters of immediate
concern and those in specific situational contexts. Though showing some evidence of making individual plans, apes cannot make plans in concert. Neither
do they appear to recall experiences except those of the immediate past, or to
plan except for the immediate future. Even these kinds of recall and projection
seem to be limited to sensory experiences and do not appear to include concepts or abstractions.

Language development in infancy and early childhood

The development of language in the human infant results from maturation
and learning but follows a fairly uniform sequence in all human beings. Merry
and Merry (14) organize this sequence into the following periods: 1. reflex
sounds, 2. babbling, 3. word using, 4. one-word sentences, 5. words combined
into thought units, and 6. uninflected speech forms. Various writers outline
the sequence in different ways. The above presentation, however, is a useful
one for gaining an understanding of the progression in language development
and its importance in thinking.

Gesture. *Leonard Bernstein, famous conductor, communicates directions to an orchestra in gestures
even clearer than words. (CBS,
TV.)*

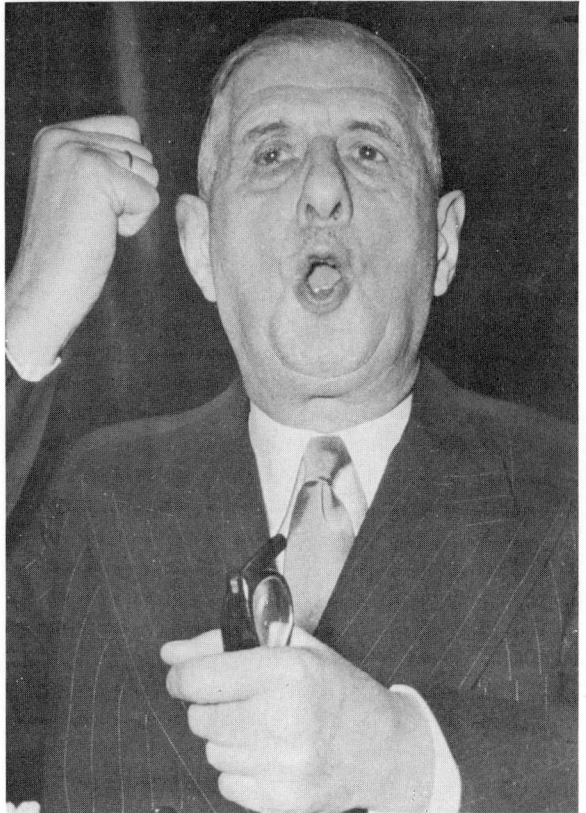

The importance of gesture in communication. *French leader Charles de Gaulle emphasizes his words in a press conference. (Black Star.)*

Reflex sounds. Reflex sounds are those emitted orally as the direct response to stimuli (either external or internal) without conscious or purposive effort. Immediately after birth, cries are produced as the air strikes the membranes of the breathing organs. This seems to be a reflex act which all normal infants express as a result of the first intake and expulsion of air, and it aids in clearing the breathing organs of obstructing materials. The obstetrician typically holds the infant by the legs and slaps him gently to make him cry, thus performing a necessary part of the preparation for the infant's new life in a different environment.

At about the fourth week of life the infant begins to differentiate his crying sounds according to his needs. Hunger, discomfort from being wet, cold, pain (as from a pin prick), being held or wrapped too tightly all produce characteristic cries which the mother may learn to identify. These noises are still primarily, if not totally, reflex actions, but maturation allows for some differentiation in them. The infant is also able to make various sounds resulting from excitement and sensory satisfactions. Later, as he begins to realize that his cries get attention, he cries purposefully. At this level of development, then, his crying may be a reflex activity (to pain, for example), or it may be purposeful (as when he wants attention). Much as in lower animals, the communication of the young infant is by gestures and oral sounds not involving symbols.

The "babbling" stage. Chance sounds that may include imitation of adult words become interesting and entertaining to the infant. He may repeat them as soon as he hears himself or others express them. A certain sound becomes a stimulus for him to reproduce it. Whether to interpret this as a circular form of reflex activity or as purposive learning is debatable. As yet it has not been ascertained what is the earliest age at which an infant tries to speak words in order to express a feeling or idea. However, at about the age of four months he may make sounds such as "ah," "ma," and others. Vowel sounds, which do not involve lip or tongue movements, usually precede consonant sounds. At this stage some parents think their child is beginning to talk with meaning. (Who wouldn't like to interpret "da-da" as "Daddy"?) However, they are certain to be disappointed, for these sounds are not words. They are not attached to a person or object, and they have no objective meaning for the infant.

The word stage. At about nine or ten months the infant begins to utter word sounds in response to external stimuli. These are spoken in imitation of older persons, and like the parrot, the child repeats them without a very clear idea of their meaning. As maturation and learning proceed, however, he pronounces words more accurately and associates them with objects. "Ma-ma" is associated with Mother, "da-da" with Daddy, "muk" with milk, and so on. This is the beginning of speech and vocabulary, the rudiments of verbal language.

Some parents are too quick to respond to the infant's sounds that may resemble speech; others may revert to "baby talk" with him, feeling that he can learn it more readily than correct speech. Some parents reward the child for using baby talk or even for inventing his own words, and cases have been known where an older brother or sister was needed to interpret the baby's language to the parents. We cannot expect the small child to speak excellently, but we should not force him to relearn his vocabulary as he grows older and wishes to communicate in the accepted language. Rather, we should speak clearly and correctly to him from the beginning and thereby show him that we expect him at least to approximate adult words.

Language development. *According to the circular-reflex theory, the child learns to associate syllables or words with the objects they represent through: A. articulation of syllables at random and then a fixation of these syllables through hearing himself say them; B. imitation in response to another person; C. and D. frequently seeing the object while hearing the sound. The baby's response thus becomes conditioned to the stimulus. (From Allport,* Social Psychology, *Houghton Mifflin, 1924, p. 184.)*

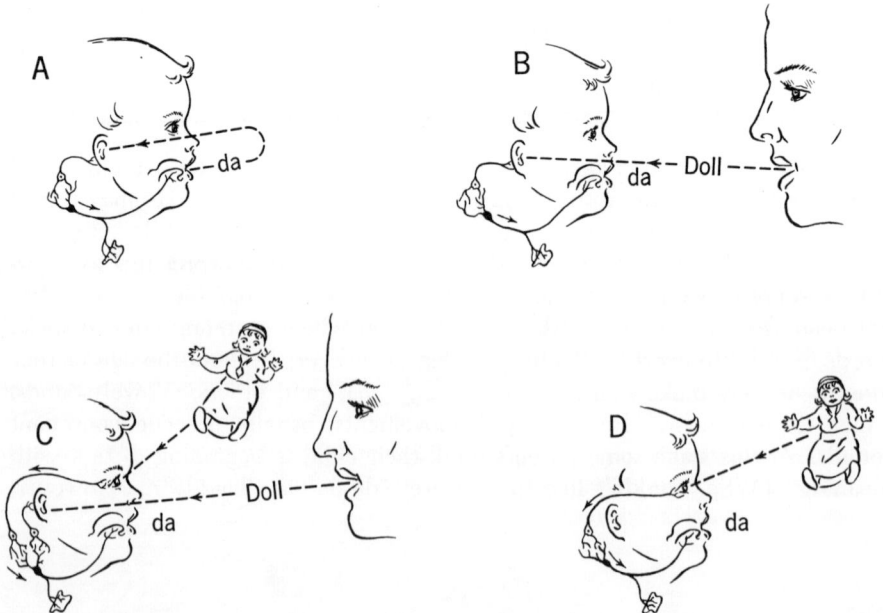

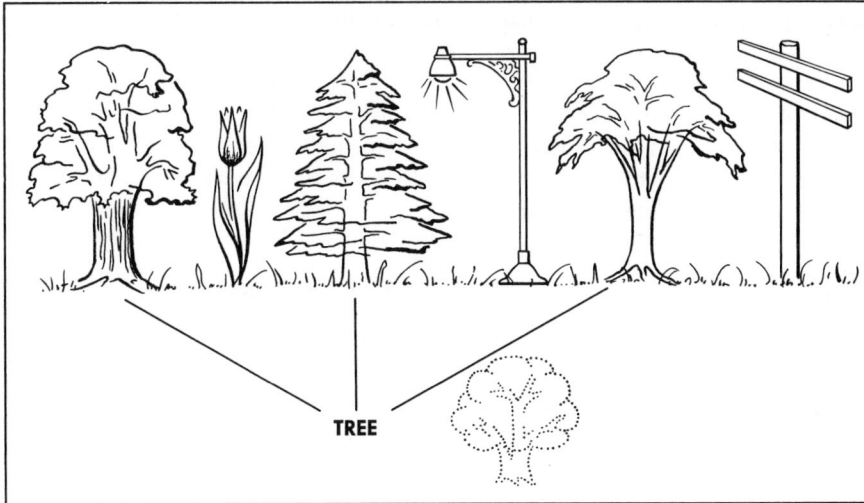

Differentiation in developing concepts. *The child hears the word* tree *and begins to associate the word symbol with a general concept of an object with certain characteristics (height, branches, wooden trunk, etc.). He must determine the unique characteristics of a tree, and of certain kinds of trees, in order to distinguish a tree from similar objects.*

One-word sentences. At some time between the ages of fifteen and eighteen months the child begins to use words to express complete ideas rather than in a merely imitative or purely recognitive sense. For example, "Mama" may mean "Please come to me, Mama," or "There goes Mama," or something else. Since children understand words before they speak them, we may expect at this age to find Johnny gesturing, crying, or moving toward a toy rather than expressing a desire for it by calling it by name.

Combining words. The transition from single-word to two- or three-word sentences expressing complete ideas is gradual and often goes unnoticed by parents. Two- and three-year-olds are adept with such short sentences. Such expressions as "Johnny crying," meaning, "Johnny is crying," or "Baby eat," meaning "I want to eat," manage to get the young child what he wants, or at least to express his meanings to older persons.

Uninflected speech forms. Once a speaking vocabulary sufficient for expressing ideas in two- or three-word sentences has been attained, it develops very rapidly and sentences quickly lengthen. The child of four has a listening vocabulary much larger than his speaking one. He responds to words and understands them before he is sufficiently mature to speak them. His attention to the speech of others, and his repetition of what he hears, are a key to the rapidity of language development in children from the age of four to six. Parents who set an excellent example for their children without demanding unduly high levels of perfection find that their child develops a broad vocabulary and speaks quite well before entering first grade. Contrary to popular belief, the only child often learns to talk better than one with older brothers and sisters. This is partly because imitation of incorrect or immature expressions of siblings does not occur. Parents who talk to and with their children stimulate the need for oral communication; and beyond the age of six they should discourage the child's continuing immature vocabulary and infantile gestures as substitutes for real words.

Language development in middle childhood and adolescence

As the child enters school and progresses through the grades, emphasis is placed on verbal communication in such activities as the "sharing period," reading, music, and games. Oral expression is characterized by continued expansion of vocabulary, increasing length of sentences, and the use of adult pronunciations. Teachers and classmates often serve as sources of new words and models for imitation. Reading is a further source of learning, especially as it relates to sentence structure and correct usage. Oral reading, choral speaking, singing, and discussing in the elementary grades can be very helpful.

Throughout the elementary grades, girls generally are more advanced than boys in language activities. They speak earlier than boys and excel in word usage, correctness of sentence structure, loquacity, and comprehensibility. Their superiority stems from their more rapid rate of maturation and from cultural pressures toward more sedentary and less strenuous physical activities.

Levels of abstraction. *The ability to think in abstract terms is an important factor in human mental development. A person learns some concepts by making generalizations from particular objects in his environment. Thus, a specific dog named Fido might be a child's first experience of "dog," that is, when he learns that there are other animals like Fido. From the concept of dog, his thinking can branch into other categories for purposes of thought.*

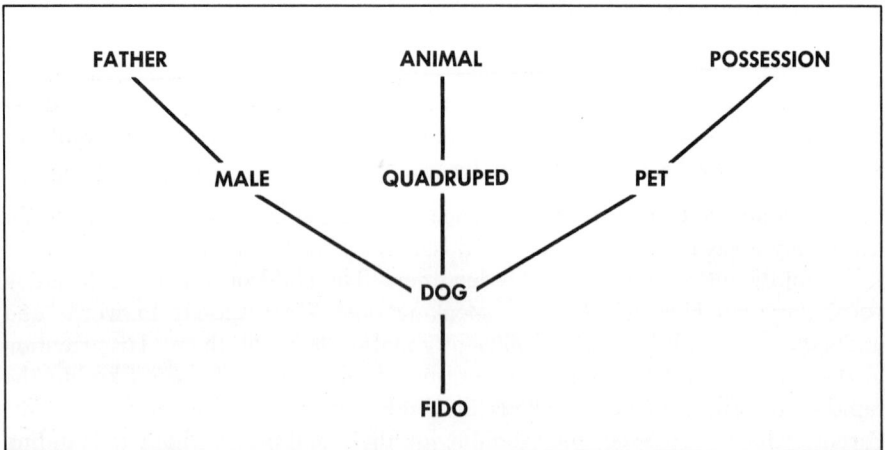

In adolescence, interests become differentiated by members of both sexes and are reflected in vocabulary and speech development. The adolescent who likes to read and to speak before his peers may continue his rapid improvement in language activities, whereas the disinterested one may make relatively little progress even though he has the required English, speech, and drama classes. One factor which influences language development in this period is the very strong need for the adolescent to become affiliated with a peer group. This may lead to unique expressions. Just as blue jeans or Bermuda shorts can sweep a college campus, so also may "jive talk," "rock and roll," "Minnie Pearl and the square dance," or any other theme which unites the interests of an age group.

Adult vocabulary

The common usage vocabulary of adults generally ranges from 13,000 to 15,000 words. However, some studies have shown that college students may recognize as many as 65,000 (15) to 259,000 words and derivatives (16). Thus, the size of adult vocabulary is extremely variable, and reflects three main influences: interests, intelligence, and opportunity to learn. Without discussing these further, since they will be treated elsewhere, we shall simply note that the college environment is an excellent one for the development of proficiency in all forms of language activity — speaking, reading, listening, and writing. It is also an excellent place to improve thinking and communication through vocabulary development and the use of mathematical, musical, and other symbols. Such improvement may continue through middle age.

A.   LANGUAGE AND THINKING
B.   THE DEVELOPMENT OF LANGUAGE

● C.   IMPROVING COMMUNICATION

Communication implies an exchange of ideas. It may be one-way, as in a class lecture by an instructor or a book silently read by one person. Or it may be an interchange, as in casual conversation with friends. We considered in Chapter 6 how successful communication with another person requires some knowledge on our part of his phenomenal field. Communication with him, in turn, can lead to a better understanding of his field. Improving our skills in speaking, listening, reading, and writing can result in clearer and more satisfying interchange of ideas with one another. Without communication, in fact, understanding and exchange of ideas is impossible.

Two people who understand each other very well may say the same thing at the same time on occasion, and they can carry on a conversation freely. Talking with a stranger, on the other hand, often calls for a cautious exploration of his motives, interests, and other personality characteristics. People without a previous understanding relationship often open their conversation with neutral topics like baseball scores, the weather, new car styles, and other commonplace subjects.

Communication is a primary concern in modern society; improved understanding and unifying goals are essential in domestic, local, national, and international affairs. The Armed Forces employ specialists in the cultures, attitudes, and procedures of people in other countries to improve relations between them and the U.S. Servicemen stationed in their lands. The government also hires trained workers to assist in the preparation of radio programs to be transmitted to foreign countries. For a striking illustration of the value placed on effective communication we have only to look at national advertising, with its highly paid employees making continual decisions on what will appeal to potential customers. The marriage counselor, too, achieves success partly through his ability to help two people understand and communicate with each other.

The improvement of our own communication may be approached from the standpoint of specific reading, writing, speaking, and listening techniques. In the following discussion, we shall present ideas applicable to these skills in a variety of everyday situations. Let us therefore put the primary focus on the *stages of communication:*

1. Setting the stage
2. Organizing your ideas
3. Discovering ways to present your ideas
4. Presenting the ideas
5. The art of listening
6. Evaluating the communication.

Setting the stage

Two people apply for the same position with a large industrial concern. One of them, George, knows one of the vice-presidents of X Company. He feels that possibly there is a position open which he could handle, so Monday morning he goes to the executive's office, gives his name to the secretary, and gains admittance on the basis of family acquaintanceship. Not knowing what positions are open, or even the particular work he is best fitted for, he takes much of the vice-president's time. Finally he leaves, having been told to return in a few months if he has not yet found suitable employment.

Herbert, the other prospective employee, goes about it in a different way. First he decides the kind of work he can do. He writes a letter to the personnel manager of the X Company, giving a brief outline of his qualifications and asking for an appointment. He dresses carefully. Beforehand, he has in mind the questions he may be asked and those to which he would like answers. With the conclusion of a pleasant interview, he is offered a position. He asks for a short period in which to decide and leaves the office with pleasant expectations.

These two examples illustrate what is meant by setting the stage. George did not see the proper person. He presumed upon family acquaintanceship. He did not know which, if any, positions were open, nor did he have in mind his own qualifications for any particular job. He came during a busy Monday morning, without having made an appointment. He was not offered a position, even on the strength of family friendship. He did not set the stage properly for good communication and as a result did not achieve his aims.

It would seem obvious that there are times and places in which to conduct not only business interviews but other formal and informal types of oral communication. In many instances the appropriate procedure is prescribed by the nature of the society in which we live: professors and deans may be seen at certain hours or by previous arrangement; doctors' and dentists' appointments are usually at specified times in an office; and business is typically carried on at the place of business during working hours. As an adolescent you learned not to ask for an increase in allowance immediately after your parents had had a tough session with the budget. In school you learned not to request permission to go to the library immediately after your teacher had emphasized the necessity for completing an assignment in the classroom. Time and place should be carefully considered in both formal and informal situations if you are to achieve success in communication as well as other aspects of your life in society.

Setting the stage involves several other factors besides time and place. For example, would you dress for church the way you dress for a class? Are you emotionally ready for a particular kind of communication you may wish to make? Can you talk your girl friend into a date if you are angry with your roommate? What do you know about a situation you may be ready to enter?

Communication in an interview. *Effective communication is important in an interview for a job. Would a prospective employer get an accurate picture of your personality, motives, attitudes, and ambitions from talking to you? You also need to understand his views of the job, its opportunities and demands. (Hays, from Monkmeyer.)*

While we are not advocating that you need to investigate exhaustively, you will find that background information about persons you are going to meet or converse with may help you in many instances to decide how and where to approach them. For example, it may be embarrassing to discuss the values of fraternity life with someone who has not had the opportunity to pledge — or to invite to the same party people who have widely divergent points of view.

In summary, setting the stage involves trying to find out something about the backgrounds, interests, prejudices, and ideas of those with whom you will be communicating. It also includes arranging the time, place, and manner of approach which will be most useful in helping you gain the results you want.

Organizing your ideas

The following selection from Mark Twain (17) may be enough to convince you that organization of ideas is important. Read it and laugh if you will, but then start asking yourself questions about the organization of your own thinking.

Mr. Bixby placed me as a steersman for a while under a pilot whose feats of memory were a constant marvel to me. However, his memory was born in him, I think, not built. For instance, somebody would mention a name. Instantly Mr. Brown would break in:

"Oh, I knew *him*. Sallow-faced, red-headed fellow, with a little scar on the side of his throat, like a splinter under the flesh. He was only in the Southern trade six months. That was thirteen years ago. I made a trip with him. There was five feet in the upper river then; the Henry Blake grounded at the foot of Tower Island drawing four and half; the George Elliott unshipped her rudder on the wreck of the Sunflower!" "Why the Sunflower didn't sink until . . ."

"I know when she sunk; it was three years before that, on the 2nd of December; Asa Hardy was captain of her, and his brother John was first clerk; and it was his first trip in her, too; Tom Jones told me these things a week afterward in New Orleans; he was first mate of the Sunflower. Captain Hardy stuck a nail in his foot the 6th of July of the next year, and died of the lockjaw on the 16th. His brother John died two years after, March 3rd, erysipelas. I never saw either of the Hardys — they were Allegheny River men — but people who know them told me all these things. And they said Captain Hardy wore yarn socks winter and summer just the same, and his first wife's name was Jane Shook — she was from New England — and his second one died in a lunatic asylum. It was in the blood. She was from Lexington, Kentucky. Name was Horton before she was married."

. . . Moreover, he cannot stick to his subject. He picks up every little grain of memory he discerns in his way, and so is led aside. Mr. Brown would start out with the honest intention of telling you a vastly funny anecdote about a dog. He would be "so full of laugh" that he could hardly begin; then his memory would start with the dog's breed and personal appearance; drift into a history of his owner; of his owner's family, with descriptions of weddings and burials that had occurred in it, together with recitals of congratulatory verses and obituary poetry provoked by the same; then this memory would recollect that one of these events occurred during the celebrated "hard winter" of such-and-such a year, and a minute description of that winter would follow, along with the names of people who were frozen to death, and statistics showing the high figures which pork and hay went up to. Pork and hay would suggest corn and fodder; corn and fodder would suggest cows and horses; cows and horses would suggest the circus and certain celebrated bare-back riders; the transition from the circus to the menagerie was easy and natural; to the elephant in equatorial Africa was but a step; then of course the heathen savages would suggest religion; and at the end of three or four hours' tedious jaw, the watch would change, and Brown would go out of the pilot-house muttering extracts from sermons he had heard years before about the efficacy of prayer as a means of grace. And the original first mention would be all you had learned about that dog, after all this waiting and hungering.

Twain accounts for this lack of coherence in terms of a too-detailed memory. We account for it as a deficiency in organizing one's thought. Perhaps none of us are in danger of being like Mr. Brown . . . or *are* we?

How can you learn to organize your thinking? Maybe the newspaper axiom of "What? How? Why? Who? When? Where?" is an answer. When the outcome of what you are going to say will be very important, it may be useful preparation to write answers to these questions:

1. What am I trying to accomplish?
2. What is my reasoning or the steps in my thinking?
3. What are the main points? Sub-points?
4. What will I probably be asked?
5. What will I want to ask?

Then, before actually engaging in the exchange of ideas, a brief review of these questions and your possible answers may be helpful. A speech, for example, is often more enjoyable if the speaker does not read from his notes; yet it is more meaningful to the listeners if he has studied his material, has organized the sequence of the presentation, and has the main ideas well in mind. We are not striving for stiffness or formality. Neither are we asking you to prepare all your communication. But we do believe that one should communicate in an organized way and that practice will be of value.

Discovering possible ways to present your ideas

We now turn to a consideration of some of the problems inherent in the actual communication itself — the way one asks questions, provides answers, and exchanges ideas.

We are indebted to Doob (18) for examples of interview questions which capably illustrate the need for careful presentation of ideas. He discusses seven possible sources of difficulty in interviewing, which we believe may exist in all other forms of communication as well:

1. Problems of definition. That is, do the main terms mean the same for all the persons involved?

Example: "Should all educators be compelled to take a loyalty oath?"

Problem: What are "educators"? What is a "loyalty oath"?

2. Double-barreled questions. These involve ambiguity of questions and answers.

Example: "Most Americans believe their country is the best in the world. Do you agree?"

Problem: What does the answer "Yes" mean? That the answerer thinks most Americans have this belief? Or that he himself believes "their country is the best"?

3. Loaded questions. The answer depends upon the wording of the question.

Example: "Do you hold the treasonous view that American generals may be criticized by our newspapers in time of war?"

Problem: How would you answer in view of the word "treasonous"?

4. Complicated language or phrasing. Question may be misunderstood.

Example: "Do you believe that the categorical imperative should be the source of deportment and ethics in the conduct of affairs by a government subscribing generally to the principle of commonality, a predicament — according to most geopoliticians — in which the United States finds itself almost all the time?"

Problem: What does this mean?

5. Order of questions. Doob discusses this factor in relation especially to a poll or interview. He recommends a few "ice-breakers" which can be answered with ease and without tension. For example, think of the techniques used with new contestants on TV give-away shows. The remarks and questions that will produce tension are withheld until the time comes when they are necessary.

6. Ignorance or confusion. Doob refers to the use in polls and interviews of certain questions which will "filter out" informants who are ignorant or confused. Otherwise, he feels, the information obtained will be meaningless. Do you know of people who think they can tell you exactly how to do a problem in mathematics, who know all the answers to social issues, who can presumably answer any question — according to *their* opinion — but who actually do *not* know what they are talking about? These people are more harmful than helpful.

7. Bias. Doob says this can be prevented by arranging alternative answers to poll questions skillfully. In our context, we can eliminate bias in answers (if we really want honesty) by phrasing our question carefully.

Example: "I have a new hair do. Don't I look nice today?" As against the less-biased "I am not sure which way I prefer my hair — the way it was or the way it is. What do *you* think?"

Most of us empirically learn enough social "know-how" to communicate quite well with others. However, we are not always aware of how much about ourselves we are communicating. Take the following examples from Proshansky (19). The subjects, college students, were shown a picture clipped from a newspaper or magazine and asked to respond to or interpret it. Here are two of the descriptions.

1. "Home of a man on relief — shabby, dresses poorly. Scene is probably of a shack down South. Also might be the home of some unemployed laborer. Horrible housing condition. Why doesn't the government provide for these people? The ordinary worker is always forgotten and allowed to rot."

2. "Picture of one room, very messy, stove in center, woman on the left, man standing next to stove, couple of children near them. This is a room of what we call 'poor people.' They seem to be messy, sloppy people, who seem to enjoy dwelling in their own trash."

What opinions do you have of the two responses? What opinions do you form about the students who gave them?

Even your sense of humor may affect the way others judge you. Cattell of the University of Illinois, devised a personality test which examined the responses individuals make to various jokes. Look at the following (not Cattell's):

1. "John fell down and did he ever look silly!"

2. "Men are all alike." "Men are all Ah like, too."

3. "If you drink a quart of milk every day for 1200 months, you'll be 100 years old."

What do you feel about people who laugh at each of these jokes? One's sense of humor can reflect kindness or cruelty, love of verbal play, intellectual dullness or sharpness, and a surprising variety of other characteristics.

Your presentation of an argument or a discussion and your conversation may also tell things about you which you never knew were being told. Someone once said, "What you are speaks so loudly I cannot hear what you say." Before you present your ideas, you should ask yourself: "Should I use humor? Be sympathetic? Flattering?" "How can I best word this?" "Does he know what my definition of . . . is?" "Is this a loaded question?" "Am I being ambiguous?"

You will probably want to know more about how communication reveals your personality. For this purpose you may wish to take a course in public speaking or to read some relevant books. Many works in social psychology contain information about attitudes, public opinion, and propaganda; and books on industrial psychology discuss relationships between employers, foremen, and workmen. These subjects are both interesting and useful. Since our purpose here, however, is simply to make you aware of some of the problems of communication, we shall merely point out the value of consulting experts in the fields of speech, social and industrial psychology, English, journalism, and other related areas for further examination of the subject.

Presenting the ideas

If you have prepared for an interview or a speech, it should not be difficult to make an adequate presentation and thereby communicate effectively with your audience. Besides preparation, however, the main points to observe include the following:

1. Have your mode of presentation well in mind.
2. Try to control your emotions — both the external signs and the inner feelings.
3. Try to understand how your audience is reacting and govern your presentation accordingly.
4. Present the material in a manner showing that you are interested in the subject and competent to discuss it. Try to make your listeners feel that listening to you will be worth while.
5. Speak in such a manner that you are pleasing to listen to, easily heard, and clearly understood.

The first of these points has already been discussed. On the difficult matter of controlling your emotions, Chapter 8 will be of further help. We should mention here, however, that a very important factor in being able to control emotions is being so well-prepared and so convinced of the value of your message that you can get your mind off yourself and talk with confidence. Practice, of course, is invaluable, and courses in public speaking are well worth any effort they require, including that of trying to overcome the fear of reciting. The mechanics of diction, voice projection, and certain other techniques of clear and effective speaking can also be learned in classes in drama, public speaking, and related fields. The third and fourth points, however — relating to the audience and understanding their reactions — imply the need for personal experience in talking to others and also mean that you must focus your attention on them rather than yourself.

The art of listening

What we have said about speaking may apply in reverse to listening. It is probable that many times during the course of a day you are not fully aware of what is being said, how it is being said, or what is meant or implied by the speaker. Do you concentrate on the lecture during the entire class period? Do you hear and fully understand the sermon in church? Are you aware of the import of a political speech you have heard on television? Test yourself on how well you listen by answering the following questions:

1. Can I hear clearly what is said?
2. Am I fully alert and listening carefully?
3. Do I understand the terminology and definitions used?
4. Can I remember the main- and sub-points?
5. In recalling discussions, have I a good idea of who said what?
6. Did I inflict my own biases on what I heard?

7. What was said? What was implied? What did I deduce?

8. What was the purpose of the speaker?

Try the following activity: Pick an article on a somewhat controversial and complex topic, perhaps one of a political nature, and construct a series of questions designed to reveal students' attitudes or biases. Have someone read the article aloud carefully and clearly. Then ask students to write on a sheet of paper as many things as they can remember about it and its content, numbering their statements. Administer the attitude test. Re-read the article, and have students check their correct and their erroneous statements. Compare the results of the attitude test and the statements which were right and wrong. You may expect to find that the accuracy with which the students hear the oral reading of the article will depend on their own biases and viewpoints. In effect, they are hearing largely what they wish to hear — in other words — they are hearing themselves.

You are familiar with the distortions produced by gossip. Someone says something about someone else, who in turn passes on a more extreme statement, and so on until finally the original account may be misrepresented entirely. If you wish to improve the accuracy of what you hear, practice checking your understanding of a lecture against that of other students, compare notes, make tapes of speeches on the radio and play them back after trying to remember what was said, summarize talks and addresses and ask the speaker for corrections. Obviously these techniques will not apply to everyday conversations as well as to more formal and carefully prepared talks. But the practice of listening closely, asking for a repetition of things not clearly heard, raising questions when you do not understand, and probing for definitions should help you in everyday communication as well as in formal situations.

Evaluating the communication

The value of a communication is, of course, a matter of how effectively those concerned are able to understand each other's ideas. It is not necessary that all purposes of the communication be achieved, but merely that the interchange of ideas be successfully accomplished. Success or failure can be checked in various ways — judging from subsequent remarks or activities of others, watching their expressions, and so on. Teachers often make use of discussion periods to see whether readings or lectures have been successful in communicating ideas. Advertisers and political groups conduct polls for similar reasons. If the person being addressed receives the message, he usually indicates in some way that he has done so. If not, he usually lets you know that.

If your ideas are not accepted or at least carefully considered, perhaps you are not getting them across. The views of few people are so useless that they should be continually ignored. For example, various concerns whose products are sold from door to door show much interest in consumers' reactions. Some companies teach their salesmen exactly what sales talks to use, including the proper replies to various questions or objections from prospective buyers. Specialists in improving sales techniques for department stores and other businesses have given a great deal of attention to the way clerks assist customers to buy items that they may have forgotten or that they did not plan to purchase. For example, when you buy shaving cream, the clerk may ask whether you want razor blades too. But he won't say, "Will that be all?" if he knows the psychological effect which a negative leading question will have. An efficient salesman will probably ask "You'll need blades too, won't you? We have a special on them today" — or something similar — to make it easy for you to agree and to buy more. When you ask for toothpaste, he may recommend "the large *economy* size," and so on.

Any phraseology, manner, or intonation usually gets results if it reassures the other person, makes it evident that you are agreeing with him, and makes it easy for him to agree with you. In contrast, think of the unfavorable reactions you have had to conversations with people who are truculent or overbearing, who use distasteful language or poor English, or who have harsh and raucous voices.

SUMMARY

Thinking, language, and communication are all related, and it is largely these qualities that differentiate man from the lower animals. The development of language is not a function of vocal cords, lips, and tongue so much as it is one of mental ability. Intelligence is needed for language development, and language is essential to high-level thinking and meaningful, rapid communication.

Thinking usually involves the use of symbols which we call words. It implies purposeful handling of ideas rather than mere daydreaming or aimless random thoughts. Precisely when real thinking becomes part of the mental activity of an infant is unknown. The infant does not have adequate speech and language to convey whatever thoughts he may have.

Not a sudden development, the use of language in human beings proceeds gradually with maturation and learning. The general sequence includes reflex sounds, babbling, use of words, use of one-word sentences, of thought units, and finally the mastery of inflected speech forms. In adolescence and adult life, the acquisition of a broader vocabulary and the more efficient use of language in both spoken and written forms become related to one's interests, intelligence, and education. Colleges and universities provide an excellent environment in which to build competence in such essential skills as reading, writing, speaking, and listening.

Communication can be improved. Giving thought to such aspects of the communication process as organizing your ideas clearly, deciding what ideas or opinions you want to express, determining how your subject can best be presented, including the kind of language which will be most suitable and the emotional tone you want to convey, and anticipating the probable effects you will have on others — all these matters are important in every form of communication, written or spoken.

In conversation and other oral exchange of ideas, listening is as important as speaking. The ability to interpret correctly what is being said must be cultivated, but your efforts in this direction will pay large dividends.

Suggested activities

1. Try to poll student opinion on some topic. Interview some of your subjects to try to discover how they interpreted the questions, what their true opinions were, and why they answered as they did.

2. Examine the writings of various authors. What points, according to some of the principles mentioned above, were adequately handled? Which were not? Why?

3. After a lecture in one of your classes, check with your instructor to see whether you are adequately obtaining the information he is presenting. Compare your understanding with that of your classmates. Compare your notebooks.

4. Record an informal interview with a child of six. Compare this interview with another you have had with a child of twelve and a youth of sixteen. What differences in vocabulary, mode of self-expression, and other factors can you distinguish?

5. Study a research report, such as those found in the references following this chapter. Compare the report with its abstracts in such a volume as *Psychological Abstracts*. Insofar as communication is concerned, how do the report and its abstract compare? How does each compare with less formal writing?

REFERENCES

1. D. H. Russell, *Children's Thinking*, Ginn, Boston, 1956, pp. 15–16.
2. K. Young, *Personality and Problems of Adjustment*, Appleton-Century-Crofts, New York, Rev. 1952, p. 201.
3. N. L. Munn, *Psychology*, Houghton Mifflin, Boston, Rev. 1956, p. 284.
4. J. Dewey, *How We Think*, Heath, Boston, 1933, p. 12.
5. *Ibid.*, p. 107
6. M. Wertheimer, *Productive Thinking*, Harper, New York, 1945, p. 167.
7. Howard L. Kingsley and Ralph Garry, *The Nature and Conditions of Learning*, second edition, pp. 422–424. Copyright, 1946, 1957, by Prentice-Hall, Inc., Englewood Cliffs, N. J. Reproduced by permission of the publisher.
8. Reprinted by permission of Dodd, Mead & Company from *Directed Thinking*, by George Humphrey. Copyright, 1948, by George Humphrey.
9. D. M. Johnson, *The Psychology of Thought and Judgment*, Harper, New York, 1955, pp. 19–20.

10. D. W. Taylor and O. W. McNemar, "Problem Solving and Thinking," *Ann. Rev. Psychol.*, 1955, 6, pp. 455–482.

11. J. W. Reid, "An Experimental Study of 'Analysis of the Goal' in Problem-Solving," *J. Gen. Psychol.*, 1951, 44, pp. 51–59.

12. E. L. Cowen, "Stress Reduction and Problem-Solving Rigidity," *J. Consult. Psychol.*, 1952, 16, pp. 425–428.

13. W. Köhler, *The Mentality of Apes,* Harcourt, Brace, New York, 1927.

14. F. K. Merry and R. V. Merry, *The First Two Decades of Life,* Harper, New York, 1940, Chapter 6.

15. R. H. Seashore, "The Measurement and Analysis of Extent of Vocabulary," *Psychol. Bull.*, 1933, 30, pp. 709–710.

16. G. W. Hartmann, "Further Evidence of the Unexpected Large Size of Recognition Vocabularies Among College Students," *J. Educ. Psychol.*, 1946, 37, pp. 436–439.

17. S. Clemens (Mark Twain), *Life on the Mississippi,* Harper, New York, various copyrights given, pp. 110–113.

18. L. W. Doob, *Social Psychology,* Holt, New York, 1952, pp. 142–143.

19. H. M. Proshansky, "A Projective Method for the Study of Attitudes," *J. Abn. Psychol.*, 1943, and quoted in Doob, *op. cit.*, p. 74.

SUGGESTIONS FOR FURTHER READING

Bram, J., *Language and Society,* Doubleday, Garden City, 1955.

Chisholm, F. P., "A New Kind of Comprehension Test," *J. Communication,* 1955, 5, pp. 83–88.

Erickson, A. G., "Can Listening Efficiency Be Improved?" *J. Communication,* 1954, 4, pp. 128–132.

Guilford, J. P., et al., "The Nature of the General Reasoning Factor," *Psychol. Rev.*, 1956, 3, pp. 169–172.

Harrell, L. E., *A Comparison of the Development of Oral and Written Language in School-Age Children,* Child Development Publications, Purdue University, Vol. 22, No. 3, 1957.

Helson, H., et al., "An Experimental Investigation of the Effectiveness of the 'Big Lie' in Shifting Attitudes," *J. Soc. Psychol.*, 1958, 48, pp. 51–60.

Irvin, E. C., "Activities Designed to Improve Listening Skill," *J. Communication,* 1954, 4, pp. 14–16.

Lorge, I., "How the Psychologist Views Communication," *Teach. Coll. Rec.*, 1955, 57, pp. 72–74.

Miller, J. G., "Brainwashing: Present and Future," *J. Soc. Issues,* 1957, 3, pp. 48–55.

Munn, N. L., *Psychology: The Fundamentals of Human Adjustment,* Houghton Mifflin, Boston, third edition, 1956, Chapter 11.

Nakamura, C. Y., "Conformity and Problem Solving," *J. Abnorm. Soc. Psychol.*, 1958, 56, pp. 315–320.

Nichols, R. C., "Ten Components of Effective Listening," *Education,* 1955, 75, pp. 292–302.

Phifer, G., "Propaganda and Critical Listening," *J. Communication,* 1953, 3, pp. 38–42.

"Preparation for Brainwashing," *Time,* April 30, 1956, 67, p. 48.

Rogers, C. R., and F. J. Roethlisberger, "Barriers and Gateways to Communication," *Harvard Bus. Rev.*, 1952, 30, pp. 46–52.

Stagner, R., and T. F. Karwoski, *Psychology*, McGraw-Hill, New York, 1952, Chapter 11.

Emotions and

Motivation

There are few better opportunities for watching people expressing their emotions and reacting to strong motives than a football game. Not only are the players highly motivated to win, some even to the extent that they will try to play with injuries, but they express triumph, disgust, happiness, and anger in unmistakable ways. Spectators, identifying themselves with the team and wanting their side to win, throw their hats into the air, slap each other on the back, and cheer wildly — or with different emotions, complain violently about the referee and even fight in the stands.

When the opponents are closely matched, the players on both teams, and the spectators, are kept at a high pitch of feeling. But if one team is clearly superior to the other, the game may seem dull and uninteresting. The winners feel little triumph; the losers, little disappointment. The general feeling may be that it was "not really a game at all."

So, too, life without emotion would have much less meaning. Typically we experience both pleasant and unpleasant emotions. While pleasant ones are enjoyable, they cannot be experienced continuously even by those who make pleasure their main goal in life. Neither can unpleasant emotions be endured for a long time without interruption. They are necessary, however, to some extent. A certain amount of fear, for example, is needed to prevent us from doing foolish things like driving too fast or taking dangerous chances while swimming. Mild anger, too, may lead us to seek constructive ways to attain some of our goals. Thus while emotions may be pleasant or unpleasant, mild or intense,

8

Factors in Development and Learning

What are emotions? What are motives? How do we develop feelings and attitudes? How can we facilitate the expression of pleasant emotions? How can we eliminate or control unpleasant emotions? What are the physiological and psychological aspects of emotion? What characterizes emotional maturity? What are adjustment mechanisms? How do motives and emotions affect learning?

transitory or lasting, their expressions, in terms of effect, cannot be classed as wholly good or bad. They may also have different effects at different times.

Emotions and motives have similar psychological bases. Both are involved in a person's adjustment to his environment and the satisfaction of his needs. Both stem from the biological and social aims of maintaining phyical existence and maintaining and enhancing the self-concept.

The self-concept, you will remember, comprises the ideas a person has of himself as a unique individual. Everybody thinks of himself as a certain kind of person — intelligent, brave, socially acceptable, popular, ambitious, highly desirable. Or perhaps he sees himself as insecure, inefficient, unwanted, and unloved. Every person's self-concept is largely a reflection of his inner interpretation of the reactions of others to him and of his own success in achieving his goals. When we try to enchance our self-concepts, we are really trying to improve our ideas of ourselves so that we may feel better about ourselves. Sometimes we even forego physical security to maintain or enhance the concept we already have, for instance, the football player who plays while injured, the girl who goes hungry while on a strict diet, the man who starves rather than steal, or the soldier who dies in battle rather than seek safety in flight.

A college student's goals are not only to do well in academic work and to explore and expand his environment, but also to maintain or improve his social relationships. If he is emotionally mature, he commits himself to what he believes are worthwhile goals. He shares his feelings of happiness with others freely but not unrestrainedly. He meets potentially frustrating situations with vigor, but he does not allow himself to be dominated by them. He gains mastery over unpleasant emotions like fear and anger, or he finds socially approved methods of expressing them.

● **A. PHYSIOLOGY AND PSYCHOLOGY OF EMOTION**

Emotions have been studied intensively by psychologists, physicians, and other scientists. From different points of view they have also been considered by writers and musicians. Yet we still do not know precisely what occurs internally during intense emotion or why emotional expression is more intense in some people than in others. There is considerable disagreement concerning the cause–effect relationships of the physiological and psychological components of emotion.

The James–Lange (1) theory of emotion implies that physiological changes occur first and precede the psychological (or "feeling") state. That is, "We meet a lion, run, and then feel frightened."

The Cannon–Bard (2) theory implies that certain brain centers below the cortex, when aroused, set off impulses in two directions at the same time. One goes to the cerebral cortex, the part of the brain involved in complex thought processes, and the other to the autonomic and other motor nerves, causing physiological changes inside the body itself and in its adjustment in space. Thus, "We meet a lion, then run and feel frightened simultaneously."

Physiological aspects of emotion

The autonomic nervous system, which controls the action of the internal organs such as the heart, stomach, bladder, and reproductive organs, largely controls physiological functioning during intense emotion. The two parts of this system, known as the sympathetic and the parasympathetic systems, are both involved during emotional states, and there is simultaneous neural discharge in both. The effects of the parasympathetic system are generally less observable, because of the more dominant excitatory effects of the sympathetic. But, whether an emotion is pleasant or unpleasant, both systems are active. Apparently the physiological changes which occur in emotion may also involve a structure known as the hypothalamus, and to the degree that we become consciously aroused, the cerebral cortex is also involved. Once a person is intensely aroused, he seems to be unable to prevent some physiological changes from running their course. This indicates that whatever changes are set in motion are controlled by parts of the nervous system which are not under the domination of the cortex, the center of consciousness. For example, it takes long special training to be able to slow down the heartbeat, alter for a long period the

Emotions at a football game. *What emotions and motivations may the players have? How may the concern of the girls differ? To what extent are the coach's livelihood and reputation dependent on the performance of the team? What are the motivations of the spectators? (Above: Harvard Alumni Bulletin, Inc.; left: A. Pione and St. Louis Post-Dispatch, from Black Star; below: Boston University Photo Service.)*

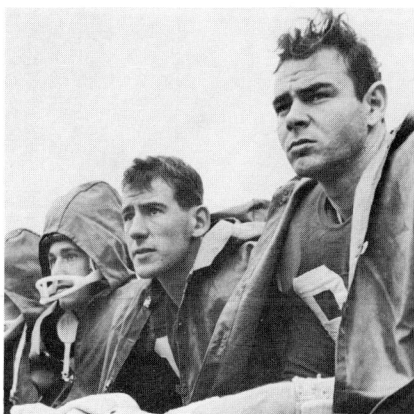

respiratory rate, or increase the flow of saliva and gastric juices. Neither can we think clearly about a situation while intensely aroused emotionally.

In order to survive, primitive man needed to respond to threatening situations with increased ability to run, hit, see, and hear. The autonomic nervous system, in conjunction with glandular action, enabled him to do such things under stress. Modern men, too, are sometimes able to rescue people from burning buildings or automobile accidents by the unusual strength they are able to exert under intense emotion. They also, however, sometimes experience social problems because of their inability to maintain cortical control over their aroused feelings.

Let us see what happens when we encounter a situation which seems threatening. Messages received by the senses pass through the cortex, and stimulate other messages which pass through the autonomic nervous system to the glands and organs of the body, including the adrenal glands. The liver releases a supply of blood sugar, known as glycogen, the fuel which the muscles use in bodily action. The heart beats more rapidly to move this supply of fuel to the points

The autonomic nervous system. *The parasympathetic connections between the autonomic nervous system and various organs of the body are represented by wavy lines; straight lines represent connections of the sympathetic nervous system. The two divisions of the nervous system tend to accelerate or retard functions of visceral and other internal organs. In general, the sympathetic division seems to effect bodily changes in times of emotion and stress. The parasympathetic speeds up digestive processes and other vegetative functions.*

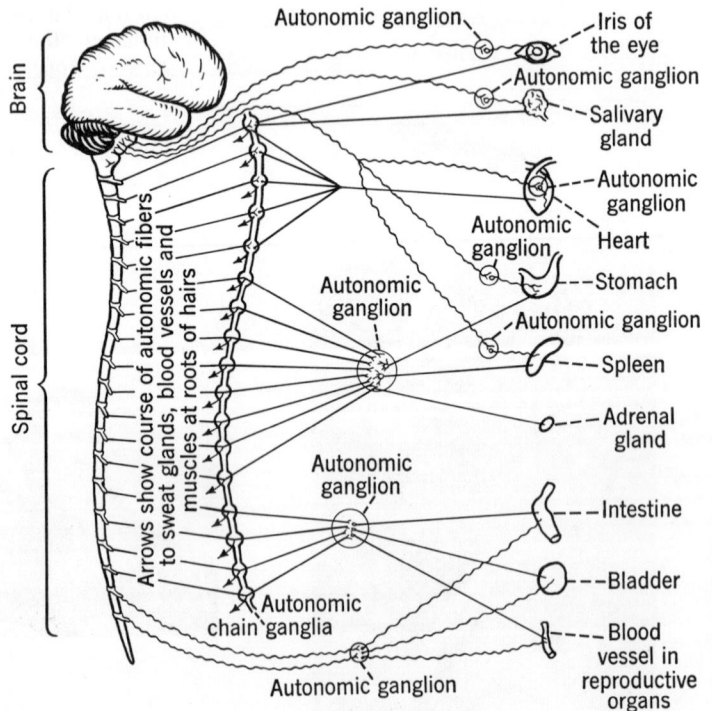

Lie detector. *As a subject answers questions, the Polygraph or lie detector records respiration, blood pressure and pulse, and skin resistance. Since a consciousness of guilt usually engenders fear, the subject often gives himself away in answering crucial questions. (Associated Research, Inc.)*

where it is needed, and the rate of breathing increases to bring into the body more oxygen, a chemical substance essential to rapid or prolonged activity.

The adrenal glands release adrenalin into the blood. This is a quick-acting, powerful hormone which aids in dilating the air passages of the lungs to admit more oxygen. Blood flows from the visceral region to the skeletal muscles, sugar is released from the liver, heart beat and blood pressure increase, and digestive processes slow down. The pupils of the eyes may dilate, and the person may get "goose flesh," which is similar to the rising of hair on a dog's neck as he prepares to fight. The combined effect of adrenalin and nerve impulses to various parts of the body is preparation for a state of emergency.

The outward signs of these internal changes can be seen in a person who tries to stand quietly and talk calmly while he is intensely angry. Salivation has decreased so that his mouth is dry and it is difficult for him to speak. Sweat appears on his palms and forehead. His hands and knees tremble because the muscles, prepared to act, are not allowed to do so. Thus he is ready in every way to meet the situation through an expenditure of extra energy, but he cannot release this energy by simply standing quietly and speaking.

A similar manifestation of heightened energy not completely under the control of the higher brain centers is present also in petting situations. When two people feel strong physical attraction for each other and express their emotion

TABLE 8.1
Physical Symptoms of the Emotion of Fear — Emotion in Aerial Combat [1]

These are the symptoms most often reported in a group of 4,504 flyers returned from aerial combat missions.

Symptom	Per cent reporting
Pounding heart	86
Muscular tenseness	83
Irritability	80
Dryness of throat and mouth	80
Cold sweat	79
Butterflies in stomach	76
Feeling of unreality	69
Frequent urination	65
Trembling	64
Confused and rattled	53
Feeling weak or faint	41
Poor memory for what happened on mission	39
Feeling sick to stomach	38
Poor ability to concentrate	35
Wetting or soiling pants	5

The following are delayed effects:

Tired out	92
Restlessness	89
Feeling depressed	80
Jumpy at loud or sudden noise	76
Grouchiness	65
Poor appetite	63
Bad dreams	58

[1] From Laurance F. Shaffer, "Fear and Courage in Aerial Combat," *J. Consulting Psychology*, 1947, 11, p. 139. Used by permission.

physically, the physiological components of intense emotion may be aroused. Once this process has begun, cortical control is not readily retained. The body is ready for physical activity. Even though the higher brain centers successfully exert control, there still may be other effects related to endocrine overactivity, such as digestive disturbances, allergies, anxieties, or headaches.

A good practice to follow when emotionally aroused is to release tension through physical activity involving large muscles. There is a story about a farmer who chopped wood when he was angry at his wife, whereas she swept the floor vigorously when angry at her husband. According to the fable, one winter they both became so angry at the government over crop-rationing that the woodpile had never been so big nor the floor so clean. Walking, swimming, and other types of strenuous exercise may be of value in relieving emotional strain.

In summary, modern man, like his ancestors, is equipped physiologically to experience intense emotions. Some people, apparently due to heredity, are more excitable than others, but all have some potentiality for strongly pleasant and unpleasant feelings. Whether your emotions will enrich your daily living or lead to unhappiness and perhaps ill health is important for you to consider. While it is seemingly impossible to alter the *physiological* aspects of intense emotion, it is possible to prepare for certain situations in advance and decide how to meet or avoid them. It is the *psychological* aspects of emotion over which we can gain most control.

Psychological aspects of emotion

As we suggested previously, it is difficult to discover the time difference between the physiological and psychological reactions to emotion — if, indeed, such a difference exists. We feel afraid, angry, jealous, sad, or affectionate at about the same time the accompanying physiological changes are occurring.

Unpleasant and unhappy feelings denoted by such words as fear, anger, and hate usually are experienced when a situation is perceived as threatening to the maintenance or enhancement of our phenomenal selves, that is, our physical selves and our self-concepts. On the other hand, we experience happy, pleasant feelings when a situation seems to enhance us in some way. It is entirely possible, however, that a situation seemingly neutral to an instructor may produce unpleasant feelings in one student and pleasant ones in another. For example, the instructor may make an assignment for each student to prepare a three-minute talk on "What Emotions Mean to Me." Reactions will vary. Student A may perceive the situation as one in which he can express himself freely and become favorably recognized by his classmates. He will be happy if he sees it as a chance to enhance his concept of himself as a worthwhile person. Student B, however, may perceive the situation as threatening. Perhaps he has recently had some unhappy experiences and does not want to share them with the class. He will probably be anxious while preparing the report and may show intense fear when his turn comes to give it.

Swimming instructors encounter similar reactions. Some students have a strong desire to learn to swim and to enjoy the pleasures of swimming. Others are afraid of drowning. The first group, again, perceive the situation as one to enhance their phenomenal selves, while the others see it as threatening.

We do not want you to infer from our description that a person can feel as he chooses. If you are angry about a family problem or a campus situation, you cannot simply decide to be happy and relaxed. And if a car is rapidly bearing down on you in the middle of an intersection, you will not experience pleasure. In other words, you cannot turn your feelings on and off like a light switch. The nature of your feelings about yourself and others, as well as your way of expressing them, is something which has been developing since birth. The extent to which adults can modify their emotions is not completely known.

It is true, however, that we can change our perceptions. We learn what is threatening to us and what is pleasant. Just as a dog does not fear a moving automobile unless he has been bumped by it, so we do not develop stage fright or fear of public speaking unless we have been laughed at or become identified with others who are afraid. We normally do not fear snakes or get angry at ourselves for missing a test question until we have experienced the effects of either situation. Our interpretations of previous events tell us what stimuli we should fear, hate, or love, and thereby they influence the nature of our future perceptions.

Suggested activities

1. Do your actions give your emotions away? Try telling an obvious false-hood with a straight face. Try to work up a feeling of anger against some real or imagined injustice, but keep smiling happily during the attempt.

2. Collect pictures from newspapers or magazines. Show only those of expressive faces, and ask your friends to guess what emotions are being displayed. Then read the captions aloud to test whether the facial expressions were interpreted correctly.

3. Obtain a demonstration of the galvanic skin response. You will need a psycho-galvanometer for this purpose. As you read a word list to the subject, observe the deflection on the meter. Words related to experiences in the subject's immediate past often call forth a measurable change in response.

4. Does experiencing an emotion too frequently tend to extinguish it? Have a joke-telling session some night. What finally happens?

5. Collect anecdotes about members of your class. Through appropriate questioning, see whether they will give themselves away when you touch on an emotional subject.

A.   PHYSIOLOGY AND PSYCHOLOGY OF EMOTION

● B.   EMOTIONAL DEVELOPMENT

In 1917, Watson (3) reported a study of emotions in neonates; he was firmly convinced that there were three unlearned emotional responses present at birth: fear, rage, and love. Loud sounds or sudden loss of support evoked *fear*, characterized by trembling, catching of breath, clutching of hands, puckering of lips, and later by crying. Restraint of body movements brought forth *rage*, indicated by flushing of the face, holding of the breath, stiffening of the body, agitated moving of the limbs, and screaming. Tickling, rocking, and other tactile stimulation of sensitive regions of the body brought forth a *love* response exemplified in smiling, cooing, and extending the arms.

Some researchers have not reached the same conclusion that Watson did. Taylor (4) for example, reported that he could not identify the response pat-

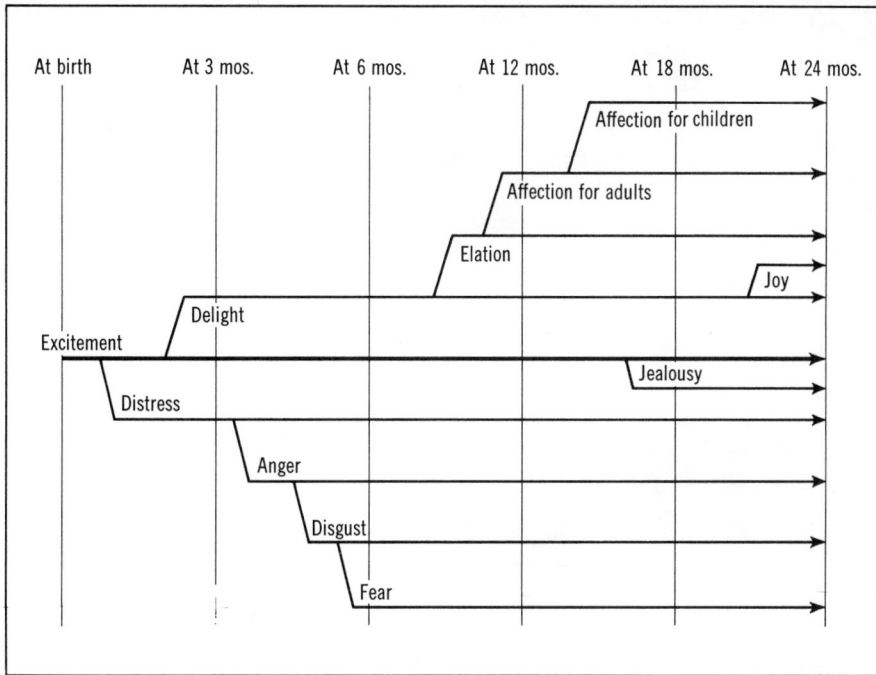

Emotional development in infancy. *This chart shows the approximate ages when specific emotions are differentiated. (Adapted from K. M. Banham-Bridges,* Child Development, *1932, 3, p. 340.)*

terns suggested by Watson. He concluded that emotional behavior in infants consisted of undifferentiated, generalized muscular reactions to many stimuli rather than particular responses to specific stimuli. His view appears to be generally accepted at present.

In 1932, Bridges (5) outlined a schema of emotional development based on her studies of babies in a foundling home from birth to age two. She observed that the young infants responded to emotional stimuli with undifferentiated excitement, and that from this state the various specific emotions emerged as maturation and learning proceeded. The illustrations on the next page show children in different stages of emotional development.

This concept of the differentiation of distinct and definable emotions from a more generalized emotional state correlates with the principle of differentiation in the development of motives, motor activities, perception, intelligence, and social behavior. It will be clarified in the ensuing discussions of anger, fear, and affection, and of the role of maturation and learning in the development of emotional responses.

Anger

Anger becomes differentiated from distress when the child is about six months old, according to Bridges. It occurs more frequently than other emotions in children of preschool age. Many restraints are placed on the young child by adults during the period of weaning, toilet training, teaching safety

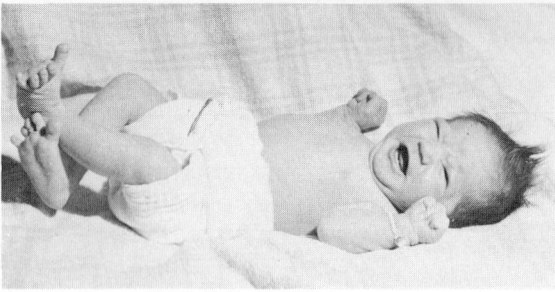

Emotional development. *It is difficult to identify emotions expressed in the first few days of life. We can only say the infant at left, 4 days old, shows excitement. In the second picture a slightly older child expresses an indefinite emotion, but definitely a type of distress. At the age of the little girl, emotions are more specific. (Children's Bureau photo by Philip Bonn; Roy Goin; Bell Telephone System, photo by Harold Halma.)*

in the home and on the streets, and establishing eating habits and table manners. The child's needs for food, elimination, activity or rest, and his routines are often frustrated by his elders, and he responds with anger. When other children take things from him or do not allow him to do as he wishes, he frequently has the same reaction. Even an object which will not work as he wants it to is provoking. In his first two years the child typically expresses his feeling of anger without restraint. He cries, moves his body, and — when his motor control has sufficiently matured — kicks, hits, bites, pulls, and scratches. It is not unusual to observe such behavior among three-, four-, and five-year-olds. Temper tantrums, in fact, are most common in the third and fourth years of life. But by age five and even earlier, physical expression is giving way to verbal outbursts, and feelings of anger are being inhibited. The home situation and the nature of the child largely determine how he expresses his anger.

Children of elementary school age show and feel anger less often than younger children. Still, restraints placed on their activities in school and at home by both adults and agemates are a common source of irritation. Because the child is usually with people his own age as soon as he starts to school, many frustrating situations arise in such contacts. Agemates may not allow him in their group or may not share a desired article or activity with him. Or they may say unkind words to him. Though boys more frequently than girls continue to express their anger physically, they too generally have learned not to fight back in that way, especially against adults or stronger agemates. In some schools and homes, the angry elementary-age child fears to strike back verbally as well — especially against adults. Thus he may desist even from that form of retaliation.

Thus children around the ages of ten to twelve may sometimes transfer their feelings of aggression toward adults or agemates to a pet or an inanimate object which cannot strike back. They sometimes repress their true feelings and exhibit apathy or moodiness. And some become angry with themselves. Many, however, have learned how to handle at least some frustrating situations without becoming angry and to interpret other situations without feeling that aggression is being directed toward them. For example, a six-year-old may become very angry at being called away from his play; the eleven-year-old on the other hand, will accept the summons as reasonable and does not get upset. As children mature and learn during the elementary school years, the causes and expressions of anger become more social and less physical.

In adolescence situations which arouse anger are generally social. Usually they involve siblings, agemates, and adults. A social situation which seems unfair and thwarting to psychological need is a common source of anger. Another is the inability to perform an activity as well as one might wish. By the age of sixteen, physical fighting has virtually ceased, but impertinent remarks and sulkiness as symptoms of anger are increasing.

In young adults the arousal of anger continues to occur, usually in relation to society and the feeling of being thwarted. Further, situations which seem to violate one's ideals — such as discrimination against minority groups, rough treatment of children or animals, poverty, and neglect of the aged — lead to this strong emotion. Few adults express their anger through physical aggression against people. They discuss, debate, and write to convey their feelings and sometimes use various means of repression. They may direct much constructive energy toward improving conditions of life for themselves and others as a result of being somewhat but not extremely angry.

Fear

Fear becomes differentiated from distress at about the same time as anger, near the sixth month of life. It is incited by loud noises, falling, and loss of support. More specific fears in connection with objects, persons, and events become differentiated during the pre-school years. Fears are caused in the young child by sudden and abrupt actions, such as a dog's unexpected jump or bark; by unfamiliarity, as by the appearance of a witch disguise at Halloween; and by pain-producing events, such as being burned, hit, or bitten. Once a child has developed fears in a concrete setting, he is old enough to verbalize and conceive of other frightening situations. Thus the fears of imaginary creatures and events begin increasing sharply from about the age of three. They become less prevalent at ages nine to twelve.

A summary of the causes of fear from infancy to adulthood, as developed by Wake (6), is presented in Table 8.2. He groups fears into three categories: concrete fears, fears of personal inadequacy, and imaginative fears. The concrete fears include those aroused by noises, falling, accidents, strange objects, persons or situations, and by animals. Those in the area of personal inadequacy include fears of personal failure, loss of friends or relatives, of sexual inadequacy, and of public performances. Imaginative fears are stimulated by the supernatural and mysterious, imaginary situations and creatures, being alone.

The figures in the table indicate that concrete fears are most prevalent in early life and continue into adulthood. Fears connected with personal inadequacies increase at successive age levels, while those of the imaginative type reach their peak at ages five to twelve. Since concrete fears persist after age six, some early childhood fears may be quite permanent and not easily eradicated. Imaginative fears, on the other hand, largely disappear as the individual gains maturity and a better understanding of himself and the world. The incidence of fears connected with personal inadequacies rises continually from early childhood into young adulthood. This is the time when the self-concept becomes more highly differentiated, and the individual tends to set higher goals for himself to meet it. If the goals are too high, there is likely to be a strong fear that they will not be attained.

Besides the causes of fear discussed above, physiological changes associated with glandular functioning in both sexes at puberty and in females at menopause may cause an upsurge of fears and anxieties.

The expression of fear, like that of anger, is direct and physical in young children, and there is a similar gradual change to indirect expression and repression in young adults.

TABLE 8.2

Age Changes in Types of Fears Between Infancy and Adulthood [1]

Types of fears	Jersild's boys and girls, ages 0–8	Jersild's subjects, ages 5–12		Wake's subjects, ages 11–16		Wake's subjects, ages 18–24	
		Boys	Girls	Boys	Girls	Men	Women
Concrete, per cent	83.8	45.1	40.0	56.2	59.4	50.8	56.4
Personal inadequacies, per cent	4.7	4.6	5.5	28.8	21.6	43.1	28.2
Imaginative, per cent	11.4	50.2	54.5	13.6	16.2	6.1	15.0

[1] From F. R. Wake, *Changes in Fear with Age*, Doctor's dissertation, McGill University, 1950, p. 44. Used by permission.

Affection

Affection becomes differentiated from the more general emotions of elation and delight between six and twelve months of age. It ranges from mild to intense, just as do anger and fear. However, although intense anger and fear are usually experienced during the pre-school years, children of that age probably do not feel intense affection. Rather, it appears that affection is not accompanied by any physiological aspects, outlined earlier, until adolescence when strong feeling emerges for members of the opposite sex. In general, objects of affection can include not only persons but also animals and inanimate objects.

Affection toward parents or parent substitutes is strongest early in life when the individual is most dependent on the adults who take care of him. When the child begins to attend school and widens his social environment, affection toward father and mother probably decreases. And with puberty there are many ups and downs in the feelings of the adolescent toward his parents. As he seeks emotional and intellectual independence from adults and also begins to experience love for agemates of the opposite sex, there may be times when he hates rather than loves his parents. This is particularly true if the parents seem to be trying to prevent an association with a girl or boy friend. Once the adolescent has had some love affairs and perhaps has concentrated for a while on one person of his age, he appears to be able to reinterpret his emotional relationships with his parents and to love them more deeply than before. As with other emotions, there are individual differences in the intensity of affectional states. How a particular child feels toward his parents at any one age is highly dependent upon the parent–child interactions from infancy onward.

Affection in early childhood toward agemates of the same sex depends partly on their number and proximity. We note a gradual increase in early childhood in this kind of attachment, and a sharp increase from six to about nine when both girls and boys begin to form strong ties with other persons of the same sex. Many of these relationships persist throughout adolescence. High school girls, particularly, have strong affections toward one another, and until one of them begins to focus attention on a member of the opposite sex, their bond with each other remains intact. Parents of a teen-age daughter often feel that her girl friend has replaced them as the primary object of her affection.

Until they are about eight years old, young children express their affection as freely to one sex as to the other. Then as the feeling for their own sex heightens, that for the opposite sex typically decreases — until puberty. With sexual maturation adolescents usually begin to experience strong physical attraction to persons of the opposite sex and intense, though often short-lived, affection. As the individual proceeds to understand himself and others better, he concentrates on one person of the opposite sex. If the attraction and affection are mutual, a marriage may eventually result. This is the outcome expected by society.

The feeling that children develop for their parents and agemates lays the basis for the filial love represented in the concept of the brotherhood of man.

American fiction, movies, television, and radio tend to give prominent attention to erotic love, such as that of husband and wife, love of things, such as money and fine possessions, and love of self in the form of success and prestige. Civilized living, however, appears to be based largely on the idea of filial love and affection. It is entirely possible that an unmarried adult who feels love for many different persons of all ages and both sexes may find as much satisfaction, or more, as one who is married or one who is dominated by love for self and things. Unmarried young adults in our society may also find satisfying affectional outlets, as do some unmarried older people.

Other emotions

The following is not intended to be a complete listing of emotions but simply a brief résumé of a few easily recognizable ones — jealousy, disgust, anxiety, and worry.

Jealousy is experienced in connection with someone loved; intense disgust is usually felt for oneself or for someone previously admired. Jealousy does not arise in connection with mere acquaintances. It may be felt by younger

Causes of worry in adolescence. *Note that by the freshman year most students seem to have reached decisions so that there is little worry over morals in succeeding years. Girls tend to lose their worry over appearance after the first year of college. How can you explain this — and other features of the chart? Is it valid according to your own experience? (From Pressey and Kuhlen,* Psychological Development through the Life Span, *Harper, New York, 1957, p. 343, Fig. 80.)*

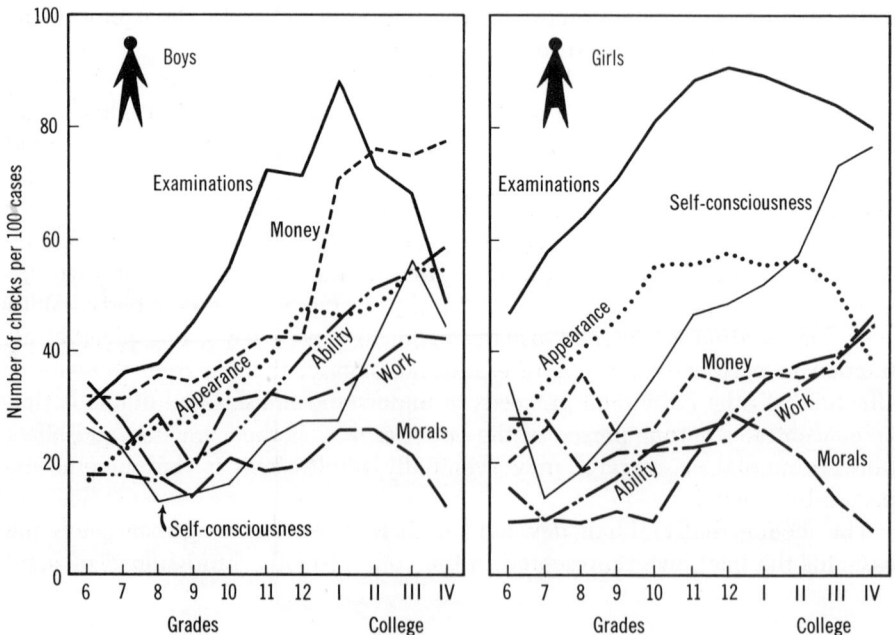

children toward a sibling, by adolescents toward sibling or agemate, and by older persons toward agemates. Disgust occurs with oneself when one does not behave as he thinks he should. We also experience intense disgust with a loved or esteemed agemate whose actions are different or less admirable than we anticipated.

Anxiety and intense worry apparently emerge at about age eight to ten. Worries about money, appearance, ability, and work increase among males during their last years of college, while self-consciousness and concern over work and abilities become more prevalent among females. This fact may suggest that when people receive more education, their self-concepts or interpretation of environmental situations make them less secure rather than more so. It may be that our society overemphasizes the importance of making a good marriage, being successful in a career, and securing the things money can buy. The college senior wants to achieve in these areas to enhance his self-concepts; therefore, he may set his goals higher than he should. Realistic appraisal of himself may lead to worry about his ability to become what he wants to be.

While worry is commonly directed toward a specific object, the source of *anxiety* is less tangible. An individual can usually identify his worries, but he often cannot tell what is making him anxious. The cause of anxiety may be no single factor, but a generalized situation or state. The danger of hydrogen warfare with its resultant destruction, the threat to the college male of having to forsake his career for a while to engage in military service, the recognition that one's parents will die and one will be alone if he is not married — all these may not be seen as threats by the anxiety-ridden person; he may simply experience a vague feeling that the future is not promising, that something will go wrong, that things will not turn out well for him. Although unable to name the cause of his insecurity, he may nevertheless spend increasing portions of his waking hours thinking about himself and the uncertain future. Anxiety is typically a mild emotion without intense physiological components, but its low-level persistence over an extended period may lead to listlessness, physical illness, and a warped concept of reality. The neurotic person usually exhibits the cumulative effects of anxiety.

Maturation and learning in emotional expression

In Chapter 4 you learned that the first appearance of certain motor activities common to the human species (such as prehensile grasping, walking upright, and skipping) results primarily from maturation, not from learning. The age at which the young child takes his first steps, for example, apparently cannot be markedly "speeded up" through practice or training. Some emotional responses likewise may be common to human beings: temper tantrums during anger, the facial expression of sadness, running away or "freezing" in extreme fear. Thompson (7) compared the facial expressions of twenty-six blind and twenty-nine seeing children. He reported that both groups showed similar responses in anger, sulkiness, annoyance, and sadness. More uniform responses, however, were given by the ones who could see than by those who could not. To the extent that the expressions of the blind and seeing children were alike, we may infer that the response is primarily maturational, not learned.

But, learning is known to affect the *patterns* of emotional response. The child learns to differentiate situations and his relationships to them. In this way certain stimuli become more feared and others may become less feared. Singing before a kindergarten group is pleasurable, singing in the seventh-grade chorus when one's voice is changing is frightening, and singing before an audience as a college junior may be again entirely pleasant. The difference in the singing may be due to maturation, but the emotion which accompanies it is learned through experience.

Some patterns of emotional response result from conditioning and identification, especially among children. Adults can change a child's affection for a toy or pet into fear by presenting the affectional object simultaneously with a feared condition such as an electric shock. Imitative learning, like that which occurs when a four-year-old girl identifies with her mother, may lead to smiles or the use of certain gestures or words to show happiness. Imitative learning probably is the principal basis for the varying modes of expressing emotion used in different cultures to greet loved ones or to express feeling.

Many adolescents and young adults can and do learn to express some emotions outwardly and to conceal others. For instance, those who prepare for dramatic careers must learn to convey the feelings which are represented in a particular role and simultaneously to conceal their own. Learning how to experience and express pleasant emotions and how to meet, without intense reactions, situations which are potentially threatening, unpleasant, and unavoidable represents a major step in development.

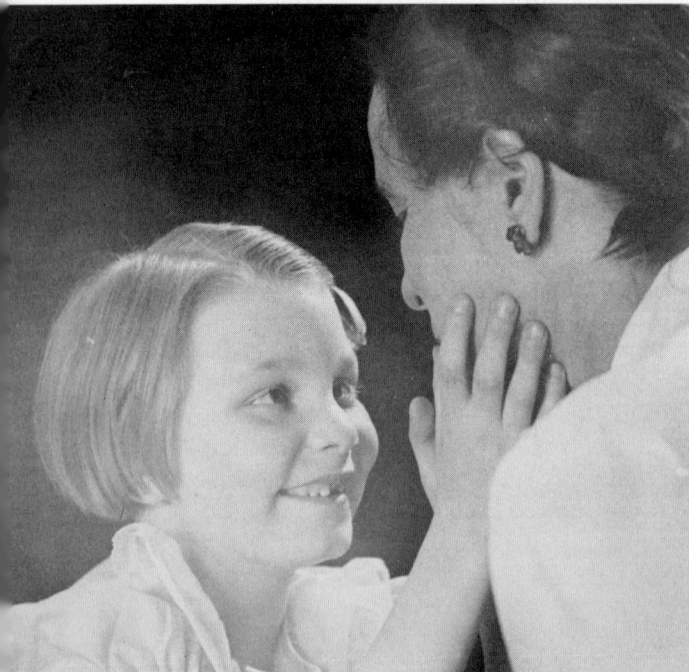

Emotional expression in deaf-blind children. *Although children with normal eyesight show more uniform emotional responses, the facial and vocal expressions of children who are deaf and blind are still very similar to normal, even though they have never seen or heard the expressions of others. (Perkins School for the Blind.)*

Learned emotions. *Children do not fear rats and other animals unless they have been negatively conditioned to them. Many fears are learned from others. (Children's Bureau photo by Esther Bubley.)*

Suggested activities

1. Collect anecdotes concerning immature behavior which you have observed on the campus. Ask your friends to judge whether or not they feel that the behavior is immature.

2. Some of your friends may have small children. Observe the children, keeping a record of their emotional behavior. Compare the behavior of children of various ages.

3. Visit a high school. What evidences of adolescent emotionality do you see at a football game, at a dance, in the halls, etc.?

    A.   PHYSIOLOGY AND PSYCHOLOGY OF EMOTION
    B.   EMOTIONAL DEVELOPMENT

● C. MATURE EMOTIONAL BEHAVIOR

Young people are not always immature. On the contrary, many students are quite mature in their emotional reactions, and so are many high school graduates not in college. Likewise, it is not *only* young people who are sometimes immature. Some adults experience much unhappiness through their emotional difficulties, and some contribute to the unhappiness of others.

An emotionally immature adult *can* find ways which will enable him to enjoy pleasant emotions more deeply and to encounter with less discomfort emotional situations that may be unpleasant and frustrating. Chapter 13, on mental health, will present a more complete discussion of the characteristics of emotional disturbances. At this point, we shall simply describe some of the means of dealing with potentially frustrating situations, under the following headings: 1. developing skills to meet frustrating situations, 2. reinterpreting self-situation relationships, 3. avoiding frustration and substituting goals, 4. finding socially approved ways to release unpleasant emotions, 5. recognizing various forms of adjustment mechanisms, and 6. securing specialized assistance for disturbing problems.

Developing skills to meet frustration

The college student who lacks such skills as dancing, swimming, skiing, and others common to his agemates may experience emotional problems in his early attempts to engage in these activities, or he may feel left out if he does not try to participate. Social activities — teas, formal dinners and dances, receptions, and group occasions of many types — also require certain skills. Appearing before an audience requires skill in speaking, appropriate dress, and some knowledge of the social amenities.

If the student recognizes his inadequacy, he may approach the problem by simply withdrawing or avoiding these situations. A more satisfying solution, however, is to develop the skills he needs. The college environment is an excellent one for learning the activities required for socialized living. An individual who takes the opportunity to develop a variety of abilities finds that many situations which previously led to unpleasant emotions are now sources of satisfaction.

Reinterpreting self–situation relationships

One difficulty in developing needed skills is that a person may feel he cannot maintain his self-esteem while learning. The student who has never served as a host or hostess, for example, may feel that, if he should ask for help from an instructor or roommate, he would lower himself in that person's opinion. Another may not enter a beginning class in dancing, swimming, skiing, or speech because he does not want to show his inabilities in the presence of others.

In many circumstances involving the fear of appearing before a group, the individual may need to reinterpret himself and the situation. Spectators usually want to hear or see a good performance. And in most instances college classmates want the less skillful person to do his best. Usually they are generous in praise and not too critical. Often they are so interested in themselves and their own progress that they give brief notice to the beginner. Many fearful situations could be overcome if the person who is afraid of not doing well could convince himself somehow that others will accept him and his best efforts.

Anger often arises in the person who experiences feelings of inadequacy and loss of self-esteem. In part, this is due to his feeling that others are trying to make him seem foolish or inadequate. It is perhaps true that an adult may sometimes deliberately try to provoke those around him to anger. We are certain, however, that most often the person who frequently gets angry has either developed the response as a habitual means of defending his self-concept or has interpreted a situation as more threatening than it really is.

Avoidance and substitution

The need to preserve physical existence demands that we avoid those situations that might destroy us. For example, we will not dive into deep water, no matter how inviting it looks, if we do not know how to swim. Nor will we take off in an automobile if we do not know how to drive. Sometimes we must also avoid emotional situations which might damage the self-concept. The psychologist with no knowledge of local politics, for example, would probably not accept an invitation to appear on a television quiz program on the subject. Many people deliberately avoid debates and arguments when they know their opponent is likely to become violently upset or abusive. If a person perceives a situation as one that will arouse intense and unpleasant emotion, he reasonably avoids it until he can develop the skills to meet it more adequately or interpret it more favorably. An individual who becomes threatened by a great many unavoidable situations may live in constant terror and anxiety.

Sometimes it is possible when avoiding a potentially damaging emotional situation to substitute at the same time an acceptable and attainable goal. For instance, the psychologist who rightly declined an invitation to appear on a quiz program on politics might very reasonably volunteer to participate in a proposed panel discussion on juvenile delinquency or some other topic lying to some extent within his field. By substituting a community service within his capability for one of which he is incapable, he attains emotional satisfaction and does not harm his self-concept.

Ways to release unpleasant emotions

Complete repression of anger, fear, jealousy, worry, and resentment may lead to greater social acceptance but not to personal satisfaction and happiness. Adults expect one another to become angry, fearful, or jealous at times, and to show these feelings openly. The person who is intensely aroused will probably experience better physical and mental health if he can find some means of using his available energy and expressing his feelings rather than always trying to repress them. From the standpoint of cooperative living, it is better to release unpleasant emotions through physical and mental activity not directed against other persons. When one begins to feel angry, he can excuse himself and engage in physical activity such as a brisk walk. Walking may not only release energy, it may also allow opportunity for thinking about the self–situation relationship; one can actually smile at himself for having become angry after energy is released and he has reinterpreted the situation. For instance, a student may feel annoyed when a classmate asks him to go over a difficult problem with him. He may think it is too much trouble or feel that the other person should do his own work. After walking to another class and thinking over the situation, however, he may realize that going over the problem with his classmate may help him to clarify his own thinking. Thus he would be helping himself as well. He may also realize that actually his fellow student has paid him a compliment. With physical energy released and the self–situation relationship straightened out, he will then be ready to enter into the cooperative effort whole-heartedly.

While adult Americans too often escape from unpleasant life-situations through watching television, reading "thrillers," and doing other things that involve low-level mental activity, the technique of becoming vitally absorbed in something suggests that close attention to some elements of the environment focuses the attention away from self, including unpleasant emotions. Physical and mental activity, directed toward useful pursuits, is one means of escaping some of the undesirable effects of resentment, fear, worry, jealousy, and grief. When such activity leads to the development of new interests and skills, and an interpretation of self–situation relationships whereby the unpleasant feeling no longer exists, the technique is especially constructive.

Recognizing adjustment mechanisms

Three of the procedures just described are socially approved, constructive ways of dealing with unpleasant emotions in our society. The deliberate avoidance of potentially frustrating situations and the substitution of goals as a means of avoiding frustrations are withdrawal procedures. If these responses become habitual, they may eventually produce emotional problems more intense than the unpleasantness being avoided.

Not all procedures can be classified as either direct attack, or avoidances. Among the more divergent ways of dealing with situations which produce emotions are fantasy, regression, negativism, projection, rationalization, and compensation. All these are adjustment mechanisms, so-called because they are means of adjusting to frustrating circumstances without meeting them directly, and at the same time of protecting one's self-concept. To some extent normal adults use these mechanisms, although they do not usually describe their own behavior as "negativistic," "regressive," "compensatory," and the like. There are many other such mechanisms, but these are among the most common. As we have said, you should note that adjustment mechanisms are found in the behavior of well-adjusted adults as well as maladjusted ones, and are experienced by most, if not all, normally developing children.

Fantasy. In fantasy, which can include day-dreaming or losing oneself in a television program or a movie, a person can be whatever he chooses and thus escape from reality. If a person's self-concept is deflated as a result of a

Displaced emotions. *Just as children sometimes take out aggressive feelings toward people on a pet or inanimate object, adults may also choose a less dominant object on which to release emotion.*

low test grade, a rebuff by a friend, or inability to make the team, he can dream and in his dreaming become an athletic star, an "A" student, a highly desired lover, a conquering hero, or a suffering hero; in short he can assume any of a number of roles, whichever soothes his injured ego best. In day-dreaming, identifying with heroic characters in a novel, and other forms of fantasy, the self-concept is greatly enhanced.

Fantasy as a way of dealing with a deflated self-concept is neither good nor bad in itself, neither a constructive nor a destructive mechanism. It may be either, depending on how often it is used and for what purposes. The student with a low test mark may possibly think of a new and useful way for improving his work. But he may also escape from reality without identifying any constructive means of dealing with the real problem. The person who daily day-dreams himself out of unpleasant reality and who uses no constructive methods for dealing with his problems may require specialized help, which we will describe in more detail later. A person may create a world in his fantasies which is real to him but very unreal to others. He may in the process become completely incompetent to deal with his life situation.

Regression. Regression ranges from *simple* to *primitive.* A frustrated young woman who cries to get what she wants is exhibiting simple regression. She is simply using a technique that worked when she was a child as a means of getting her wishes satisfied by someone else. Children typically cry to get adults to accede to their demands. Adults who cry for the same purpose are said to regress to a childhood level of behavior. But the severely maladjusted adult can regress beyond forms of behavior characteristic of human infancy. That is, he may exhibit subhuman behavior, such as caring for his biological needs at the level of the ape or lower animals. As a child matures in our society, he often encounters controls by adults or by other children which he interprets as threatening. He may cry, scratch, bite, scream, yell, hit. We expect such behavior in younger children. The young adult, however, whose responses to frustrating situations are frequently regressive and characteristic of childhood needs help in meeting his life-problems more maturely. Regression is predominantly a mechanism for avoiding important realities in life.

Negativism. Many children between the ages of two and four exhibit negativism, which operates in much the same way as does regression. When mother says "Put the doll away," little Mary yells, "No." When mother says it a second time, Mary screams louder. With a typical mother, such persistent loud yelling accomplishes Mary's purpose of retaining the doll. Also, temporarily, Mary gains control over her mother by not doing as commanded. Negativism characteristically accomplishes these purposes and sometimes adults use it deliberately. A filibuster by one Senator in the United States Senate allows him to control the other ninety-seven and at the same time to delay voting by others on a bill which is undesirable to him. In both formal and informal group meetings, the vociferous dissenter accomplishes two purposes in that he controls the actions of his more courteous fellows and at the same time does not commit himself to action he dislikes.

The adult who exhibits negativism is difficult to deal with socially. He uses this mechanism to maintain and enhance his self-concept and becomes greatly disturbed if not allowed to do so. We must recognize our own uses of negativism and also be aware of this mechanism in any members of groups we are interested in.

Projection. The harassed saleswoman in the Christmas rush would like to tell the customer that he is unreasonable, unfair, and a nuisance. She cannot do so for fear of losing her job. Social expectations require her to control and repress her aggressive feelings. This saleslady goes home and reads in the evening paper a report that the police had jailed a woman for using profane language and kicking a male shopper. Identifying her true feelings with the jailed woman, she nonetheless writes a letter to the "Readers' Column" of the newspaper, berating the woman and lauding the policeman.

This saleswoman is projecting her own self-concept in the process of criticizing the jailed woman. She divests herself of guilt feelings concerning her

own previous aggressive thoughts against the customer through openly criticizing the aggressive actions of the other woman. Why did the clergy in the
witch hunts in Salem in early colonial times persist so long in condemning
innocent people? It may be that after experiencing threats to themselves from
the non-conformists and from their own base desires to get rid of the non-
conformists, the clergy identified with the imaginary destructive powers of the
witches and carried their base feelings to the limit with open accusations
against the witches. Through projection, the clergy were apparently able to
live comfortably with themselves and for a long time to escape the usual controls placed on the behavior of most other persons. Oliver Cromwell, Adolf
Hitler, and other national leaders have used this mechanism to enhance their
self-concepts while performing atrocious deeds against others in the name of
righteousness, nationalism, or some other cause.

Rationalization. Though we often rationalize, we are probably unaware
that we have done so until afterward, and then we recognize our rationalization
mainly by introspection or by discussion with others. In an examination situation, for example, Bill doubts his ability to make a high grade but wants to; he
also wants to be honest, and he usually is. However, other students are sitting
close to him, so that it is easy to compare answers, and Bill does so as do many
others. Bill rationalizes thus: "My score on this exam will be considered in relation to other students' scores. They are comparing answers and will thus
raise their scores. To be fair to myself, I should compare answers, too. Everyone else is doing the same thing." Bill thus protects his self-esteem on two
counts: he is not really dishonest but is merely doing what the others do; his
score will be better than it would be if he had not compared answers.

We could probably not live comfortably with ourselves without some re-
course to rationalization, but carried to the extreme and used repeatedly in
dealing with important life situations, rationalizing may be disastrous. Persons
of moderate income can rationalize the purchase of expensive automobiles,
home furnishings, and clothing until they have nothing left for food, clothing,
medical care, and the education of their children. The expenditures of some
college students during the first semester for "important" things — expensive
clothing, parties, taxis — can be rationalized until the unavailable money is
needed to pay for tuition and housing at the beginning of the second semester. Tact and diplomacy can be rationalized to the point where the individual
loses his integrity. Extensive and repeated rationalization can lead eventually
to serious emotional problems.

Compensation. Compensation may be direct or indirect. The direct
form is exemplified by the 5-foot, 6-inch athlete who makes the high school and
college basketball teams only through many more hours of practice than most
of his team mates put in. Indirect compensation is illustrated in another 5-foot,
6-inch student who gives up basketball and concentrates, for example, on
wrestling or on academic success. Compensation is widely acclaimed in our

success-conscious society. The man who was born in poverty and quit school before high school graduation to sink an oil well or build a successful business receives much praise as an adult. Some of the most respected people in our society are those who achieve education or wealth despite unfavorable child-hood circumstances.

In extreme forms of direct compensation, the individual often denies the existence of a weakness or a handicap which clearly exists. The one-armed man who insists on preparing for a career as a typist, the person with poor voice who is bent on becoming a singer, and the college student who slaved to make D's in high school chemistry and physics but persists in a science major in college — such people will almost inevitably meet intense disappointment. However much they may be praised for their valiant efforts, eventually the moment of in-tense frustration arrives. Note that the three people we described have handi-caps which cannot be overcome. The severely handicapped adult who denies his handicap usually needs specialized help.

Securing specialized assistance. As we suggested earlier in this chapter, some childhood fears persists into adulthood. Some children who develop the temper-tantrum technique to gain mastery over others continue to use it into adult life. Some adults are constantly anxious about the future without quite knowing why or what about. Many young adults are troubled because they seem unable to share their feelings of happiness and affection satisfactorily with others. Whenever one feels that an emotional state such as worry, anger, fear, or depression prevents him from living efficiently and happily, he might well seek specialized assistance. This assistance is often available to college students in the counseling center, the medical center, through advisers, and in the offices of private psychiatrists. Colleges and universities are recognizing that emotional problems in bright young people can lead to poor academic work as well as to inefficient and unhappy living.

Thorpe (9) describes the need for specialized assistance to college and uni-versity students as follows:

> Although the majority of college and university students maintain a normal state of mental health, many institutions of higher learning have a substantial number who at times manifest anxiety or depression, who are disturbed by recur-ring fears or conflicts, or who are victims of psychosomatic disorders of varying degrees of severity. . . .
>
> Furthermore, virtually every college has its quota of more severely maladjusted personalities. Some students are withdrawn, others are indifferent, and still others are antisocial or overly hostile. There also are students who are psychoneurotic and whose anxieties and tensions are apparent to both their classmates and instructors. . . . It should be evident that these disorders constitute a serious handicap to the individual, to the school, and to the stability of society itself.

Psychologists, psychiatrists, and counselors who work with college students feel very often that they can be much more helpful to the student if the student will come voluntarily for help rather than wait to be referred by a faculty adviser, an instructor, a housemother, or someone else. In many of our institutions of higher learning, students are beginning to go as freely to the health or counseling center with their emotional problems as they do with physical illnesses. Society in general is recognizing that mental illness can be as incapacitating as are many physical ailments.

Suggested activities

1. Collect anecdotes illustrating fantasy, rationalization, projection, etc. Discuss them in class, attempting to discover why they were used.

2. What might excessive or inappropriate use of escape or defense mechanisms lead to?

3. How would you attempt to teach a person to overcome his fear of the water so that he might learn to swim?

A.   PHYSIOLOGY AND PSYCHOLOGY OF EMOTION
B.   EMOTIONAL DEVELOPMENT
C.   MATURE EMOTIONAL BEHAVIOR

● D.   MOTIVES AND EMOTIONS IN LEARNING

Why does one student decide to continue in college and another quit and marry? Why does one student seek high marks while another is satisfied with average marks? Why does one person spend hours sunbathing while another gives his time to working with children in a social agency? The answers to these questions involve motives and emotions.

Earlier in this chapter we pointed out that motives emerge in connection with the various needs for maintaining physical existence and for maintaining and enhancing the self-concept. Emotions, moreover, emerge with maturation and learning, and emotional expression is closely related to maintaining physical existence and enhancing the self-concept. Thus when we consider why Mary gave up her career in order to marry we are concerned with both her motives and her emotions. No sharp or fine line can be drawn between motives and emotions as initiators of action. Mary may have chosen marriage in order to give fuller expression to pleasant emotions, to secure a home of her own without having to work for it, or to contribute to her husband's career. Or all of these things may have influenced her.

Some psychologists (10) believe that the need to preserve and enhance the phenomenal self is the basic human need — the principal motive for all human behavior, including learning. In this context, those emotional states as well as other conditions within the individual which initiate and direct activity toward a goal are motives. While the present writers accept this view, they would group the needs and resulting tension states within the individual which predominantly initiate and direct activity toward goals into four categories: (1) the need to experience sensory gratification, (2) the need to explore, (3) the need to participate and secure approval in social groups, and (4) the need to achieve. These four needs are not mutually exclusive, and each can be identified in the behavior of human beings from birth to maturity.

The need to experience sensory gratification

The human neonate, like other organisms, struggles to maintain his organization, prevent death, and preserve life. While his early reactions are largely, if not totally, at the reflex level, as he grows into early infancy the child responds to sensory stimulations which are pleasant or painful. Much of his early activity is in response to sensory stimulations: he cries when he is hungry, when he is wet or soiled, or when he is too hot or too cold; he responds with mass movements of the body under the same or other stimulating conditions. Inherent in the human neonate, as in subhuman organisms, are actions which maintain the total organization as a fully functioning organism.

As the human infant matures and learns, he has a good many experiences which yield feelings of satisfaction. Among these are being caressed, hearing certain pleasant sounds, seeing certain pleasant sights, tasting foods and liquids to allay hunger, securing rest and sleep when tired, and, eventually, experiencing sexual gratification in adolescence and adulthood. Securing such satisfactions and avoiding painful stimulations continue to serve him as motives throughout life. Without such motives, mankind would not survive.

Among adults the available forms of gratification are highly varied, and such terms as tastes, preferences, desires, urges, and drives are sometimes used to designate motives related to what are mainly sensory gratifications. While an adult turns on a hi-fi record partly to satisfy other motives, a principal one is to experience sensory satisfaction through listening. Attendance at movies, athletic contests, concerts, recitals, and other recreational activities are typically iniated by and directed toward sensory gratification. Some persons also may attend these events for social approval or social exploration.

The need to explore

Children early in life exhibit the exploratory motive. When the child can walk, he explores his environment exhaustively. He leaves his room, the house, and the play area to explore the bright objects elsewhere, to learn what makes the different sounds, to find out where the streets lead. With his hands he explores materials and with his mouth he tries new sounds and new foods.

Because of restrictions placed by parents, teachers, and others upon the movements and activities of young children, the child may lose some of his urge to explore; many persons are less exploratory as adolescents than they were as young children. Punishment for getting into trouble, and rewards for not exploring the new and different, may eventually deaden the exploratory motive.

College education, however, is usually committed to the idea of encouraging students to explore in many intellectual areas. Instructors often urge the student to investigate many topics and problems. As the younger child's curiosity leads to numerous and varied activities, so the college student who is exploratory perceives many challenges, both mental and physical, in his environment.

The need to achieve

The widespread efforts of children to learn to ride a bicycle, to skate, to read, to write, to speak suggest that achievement is a powerful motive. To secure mastery over things is perhaps the most prevalent and persistent motive for learning in our society. To achieve mastery over people is also a strong motive in some children and adults.

Much of the learning of college students is initiated and directed by the achievement motive. When the need to master a topic, a question, a problem, or a physical activity becomes so strong that the individual is not satisfied with himself until he achieves mastery or at least substantial improvement, the amount of energy he expends toward improvement is high. So long as he feels a need to master in order to feel comfortable with himself, the individual is likely to learn. The student who studies or practices in order to gain mastery of a subject may learn more, and learn it better, than the one who is motivated to secure approval from others — for example, from the instructor.

The achievement motive can be defined broadly enough to include the other three we have mentioned — sensory gratification, exploration, and social participation and approval. In a very broad sense, the student who listens for recreation, manages his affairs so that he can participate and receive approval in social groups, or explores the meaning of a formula is achieving mastery over some aspects of himself and his environment.

The need for social participation and approval

Sue, a college freshman, desires social approval. Though she does not wish to explore deeply or to master thoroughly the subject matter of her science class, she does want the approval of her instructor and also of the young man she is going with. The instructor approves only good work, and Sue's boy friend thinks she should master the work of the course; so to secure their approval, Sue works industriously in the course.

The need to participate with others and to receive their approval develops early in most children, though it is not present in early infancy and is of varying strength among adults. Although some adults are not often motivated to participate with others and can remain satisfied with themselves even while they are being condemned by others, most adults attempt to affiliate with others in groups such as the home, the church, clubs, and other more informal agencies. In most people the motive of securing approval initiates and directs many daily activities, including those associated with clothing, speech, food, social amenities, and most interactions with others. The need to secure social approval acts both to initiate some activities and to restrain others.

Acquisition and retention in learning

As suggested in Chapter 2, academic success is closely related to motivation and emotional adjustment. Other things being equal, the student who is strongly motivated to achieve success and who is well adjusted emotionally learns more efficiently and retains what he learns better than does the student with low motivation or poor adjustment. Both motivation and adjustment are associated with the goals the individual sets for himself and his progress toward them. The college freshman whose long-term goal is to become a dentist and who makes satisfactory progress with his intermediate goals — the various courses and other requirements for dentistry — may work persistently and well throughout his college career toward his ultimate goal. Another college freshman who has the same goal but who does poorly or fails the required courses not only gives up the goal voluntarily or by advice, but also may experience an emotional upset in the process.

Of the many research studies conducted to ascertain the relationship between motivation and success, we need cite only three to indicate that there is a very close connection.

Brown and others (11) identified ninety-seven second-semester freshmen on the "Dean's Honor List" and forty-six on the "Scholastic Probation List." The students in both groups were invited by letter to attend any of twelve study sessions during a two-day period. More than three-fourths of the honor-list students attended one of these sessions, whereas only one-eighth of the probationers did. A second letter and a telephone call were used to follow up those students of both groups who did not attend one of the first sessions. Thereafter, 97 per cent of the honor-list students attended, and 50 per cent of those on probation. It had already been determined on a psychological test that all the students in both groups were in the same range of ability, all above the probation level. The researchers concluded that in this case motivation was the important factor contributing to high and low grades.

Lowell (12) investigated the relationship between strength of motivation and speed, both in learning two tasks and in persistence at the tasks. Forty students were divided into two groups on the basis of their motivation toward high or low achievement. The group motivated toward high achievement was found to produce more work during a given period of time and to continue longer in their efforts than did the group not so motivated.

Finally, Willerman (13) hypothesized that active members in a sorority are more strongly motivated to participate, that they become more involved in sorority affairs and derive more satisfaction from the organization than do passive members. Forty-one sorority women were designated as active members by their sorority sisters, and thirty-seven as passive members. The active members, more than the passive, were found to hold offices in student organizations, to feel that the group regarded them as important, to express feelings of belonging to the group, and to agree with group decisions. Apparently the motive of social participation and approval led to more activity and also to more satisfaction from group activities.

While this entire discussion has been pointed toward the desirable effects of high motivation, we have also noted that some persons are so strongly motivated by the desire for achievement and social approval that they set their goals too high. Only the individual can set realistic goals for himself. He can, however, secure help with motivational as well as with emotional problems. Eventually, as we pointed out in Chapter 2, each individual must decide for himself which goals are most worthwhile for him, as well as deciding the level of achievement, social participation, and sensory gratifications he desires for himself.

SUMMARY

Emotions and motives have a similar psychological basis. Motives stem from biological and social needs to maintain physical existence and to maintain and enhance self-concepts. Emotions such as happiness, anger, affection, and fear are learned primarily in social settings and also are closely related to maintaining and improving the self-concept, and to a lesser extent, maintaining physical existence. A person's motives and the manner in which he expresses emotions emerge developmentally and are dependent on both maturation and learning.

Emotions have physiological and psychological aspects. During intense emotion, the entire organism is aroused and the activity of the individual's autonomic nervous system changes his total physiological functioning. Once he is intensely aroused, as in fear or anger, the individual cannot readily gain deliberate control over his internal processes. How he feels about a situation is largely determined by how he interprets it in relation to maintaining physical existence and his self-concept. When an adult perceives a situation as threatening, he typically experiences unpleasant feelings such as anger, fear, worry, grief, and jealousy; when he interprets situations as enhancing rather than threatening to his self-concept, he experiences pleasant feelings such as happiness and delight.

While many adults express their happy emotions freely and fully, many also frequently experience unpleasant feelings. Since the unpleasant feelings are experienced in connection with situations which the individual perceives as threatening to him, he may attempt to build skills to secure mastery over more situations and reinterpret others so that they are less threatening. These are constructive adult attacks upon emotional problems. Sometimes the best way to deal with a potentially unpleasant situation is to avoid it until needed skills are acquired, or to set up a goal which will allow the individual to achieve satisfactions without encountering the situation which produces the unpleasant emotion. However, withdrawal from too many situations, and the use of adjustment mechanisms as habitual ways of meeting life situations, lead to maladjustment. Seeking specialized assistance with emotional problems before they become incapacitating is becoming more prevalent among college students.

To maintain physical existence and to enhance the self-concept, four motives or needs must be satisfied: sensory gratification, exploration, achievement, and social participation and approval. These motives exist in varying strength in different people, and the resulting activities also vary widely. The goals which individuals set for themselves in connection with these motives largely determine the direction and consistency of their daily learning and living activities.

Suggested activities

1. What symbols of recognition do you receive for your efforts? Would you work as hard as you do if you did not get money, football letters, honor society keys, etc.?

2. Examine the college newspaper or annual. What forms of motivation do you find implied in its pages?

3. Examine some magazines and newspapers. What motives and emotions are appealed to in their advertising? Their news and other articles?

4. Go without your next meal. Describe the thoughts and emotions about food that subsequently go through your mind.

5. List your weekly activities to ascertain the extent to which the need for sensory gratification and for social approval initiated your various activities. Include such activities as eating, sleeping, any listening you do for recreation, any visual experience you have for recreation, and other activities which lead to sensory gratifications and to social approval.

REFERENCES

1. W. James, *Principles of Psychology,* Holt, New York, 1890, Vol. II.
2. W. B. Cannon, *Bodily Changes in Pain, Hunger, Fear, and Rage,* Appleton-Century-Crofts, New York, 1929.
3. J. B. Watson and J. J. W. Morgan, "Emotional Reactions and Psychological Experimentation," *Amer. J. Psychol.,* 1917, 28, pp. 163–174.
4. J. H. Taylor, *Innate Emotional Responses in Infants,* University of Ohio Press, Columbus, 1934. Ohio State University Contributions in Psychology, Studies in Infant Behavior, No. 12, pp. 69–93.
5. K. M. B.-Bridges, "Emotional Development in Early Infancy," *Child Develop.,* 1932, 3, pp. 324–341.
6. F. R. Wake, *Changes in Fear with Age,* Doctoral dissertation, McGill University, 1950.

7. S. L. Pressey, in R. G. Kuhlen, *The Psychology of Adolescent Development,* Harper, New York, 1952.
8. J. Thompson, "Development of Facial Expression of Emotion in Blind and Seeing Children," *Arch. Psychol.,* 1941, No. 264.
9. L. P. Thorpe, "Mental Health Practices at the College Level," in National Society for the Study of Education, *Mental Health in Modern Education,* University of Chicago Press, Chicago, 54th Yearbook, Part II, 1955. Copyright, 1955, by the University of Chicago.
10. D. Snygg, and A. Combs, *Individual Behavior,* Harper, New York, 1949.
11. W. F. Brown, *et al.,* "Motivational Differences between High and Low Scholarship Students," *J. Educ. Psychol.,* 1954, 45, pp. 215–223.
12. E. L. Lowell, "The Effect of Need for Achievement on Learning and Speed of Performance," *J. Psychol.,* 1952, 33, pp. 31–40.
13. B. Willerman, "The Relation of Motivation and Skill to Active and Passive Participation in the Group," *J. Appl. Psychol.,* 1953, 37, pp. 387–390.

SUGGESTIONS FOR FURTHER READING

Barklay, K. L., "Influence of College Science on the Development of Attitudes Toward Evolution," *J. Appl. Psychol.,* 1948, 32, pp. 21–28.
Brand, H., *The Study of Personality: A Book of Readings,* Wiley, New York, 1954.
Diller, L., "Conscious and Unconscious Self-Attitudes After Success and Failure," *J. Pers.,* 1954, 23, pp. 1–12.
Dollard, J., et al., *Frustration and Aggression,* Yale Univ. Press, New Haven, 1939.
Eysenck, H. J., *The Structure of Human Personality,* Methuen, London, 1953.
Harvey, O. J., et al., "Reactions to Unfavorable Evaluations of the Self Made by Other Persons," *J. Pers.,* 1956, 25, pp. 393–411.
Hirsch, S. G., *The Fears Men Live By,* Harper, New York, 1955.
Kidd, J. W., "Personality Traits as Barriers to Acceptability in a College Men's Residence Hall," *J. Soc. Psychol.,* 1953, 38, pp. 127–130.
Kluckhohn, C., and H. A. Murray, *Personality in Nature, Society and Culture,* Knopf, New York, 1949.
Lehner, G. F. J., and E. Kube, *The Dynamics of Personal Adjustment,* Prentice-Hall, Englewood Cliffs, 1955, chaps. 4, 5.
McClelland, D. C., *Studies in Motivation,* Appleton-Century-Crofts, New York, 1955.
Mohsin, S. M., "Effect of Frustration on Problem-Solving Behavior," *J. Abnorm. Soc. Psychol.,* 1954, 16, pp. 425–428.
Munn, N. L., *Psychology: The Fundamentals of Human Adjustment,* Houghton Mifflin, Boston, third edition, 1956, Chapters 5, 6.
Sears, R. R., et al., "Some Child-Rearing Antecedents of Aggression and Dependency in Young Children," *Genet. Psychol. Monogr.,* 1953, 47, pp. 135–234.
Walter, L. M., "The Relation of Sex, Age, and School Achievement to Level of Aspiration," *J. Educ. Psychol.,* 1951, 42, pp. 285–292.

Intelligence and
Special Abilities

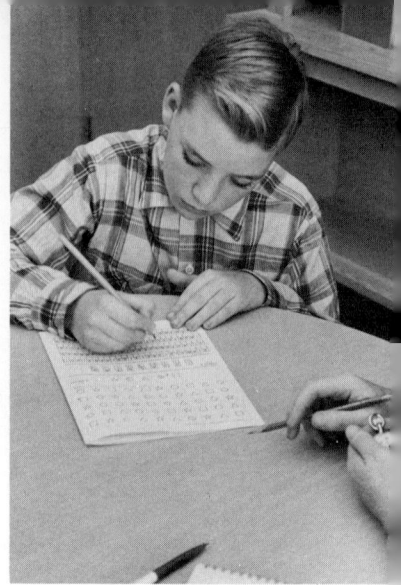

From a variety of sources you probably have some idea of the level of your intelligence. For example, you may know your IQ, or intelligence quotient, which is measured by testing. In earlier school years you had ample opportunity to compare the ease and efficiency with which you learned with that of your fellow students. You probably formed a more or less specific opinion of whether you are average, bright, or gifted. And this opinion probably influenced your decision to go to college.

Though everyone probably has some idea on the subject, we get a variety of answers when we ask different people to explain what they mean by intelligence or mental ability. You may be surprised to learn that this is true not only among lay people but even among experts in intelligence testing.

This chapter will present some of the major definitions of intelligence. It should help you to clarify and explain such expressions as "So-and-so is smart," or "I'm pretty sharp in math, but I'm no good with words." Gaining a better understanding of intelligence may make a difference in what you decide concerning your scholastic program and your future vocation.

Here is part of an obsolete intelligence test. After trying it out, see whether you can detect the concept of intelligence represented by the types of items included [1]:

With your pencil make a dot over any one of these letters
F G H I J, and a comma after the longest of these words: boy mother girl. Then,

[1] Source unknown.

9

Doing the Best with What You Have

What is intelligence? What are mental abilities? What are some factors which affect intelligence and intelligent behavior? How can intelligence be assessed? Can we improve our mental abilities? What are some particular aptitudes and abilities which belong to some · individuals? How can they be measured? What is the relationship of intelligence to scholastic and vocational success?

if Christmas comes in March, make a cross right here . . . but if not, pass along to the next question, and tell where the sun rises . . . If you believe that Edison discovered America, cross out what you just wrote, but if it was someone else, put a number to complete this sentence: "A horse has . . . feet." Write "yes" no matter whether China is in Africa or not . . . ; and then give a wrong answer to this question: "How many days are there in the week?"

The test is longer, but the general plan is apparent. Would you say that the maker of the test felt that the ability to follow directions shows intelligence? Does the amount of factual information a person has accumulated seem to him to be directly related to intelligence? Does he seem to believe that the ability to think clearly without becoming confused also indicates intelligence?

Intelligence is probably more than just the ability to think clearly or to remember what one has learned. And intelligent people are not alike in all respects — some rebuild autos into "hot rods," others can compose music, and still others can write well or do mathematical problems with apparent ease. How can we tell which ones are highly intelligent and which are not?

● A. DEFINITIONS OF INTELLIGENCE

Before we can come to a working definition of intelligence we must consider some of the concepts employed by experts in this area. We begin by discussing the hypotheses that intelligence is *general mental ability*.

Intelligence as general mental ability

Early in the twentieth century, Simon, a French physician, and Binet, a French psychologist, were given the problem of classifying the bright and dull children in the city of Paris. They proceeded by asking school teachers to point out children who were considered to be bright, average, and dull. Working with data obtained from the study of these groups of children, Binet and Simon developed what is commonly accepted as the first real intelligence test, designed to be administered to individual children rather than to groups.

Later, other workers including Goddard, Terman, and Merrill brought this test to America and revised it, producing the well-known Stanford-Binet Tests of Intelligence. The present form of this test represents a revision which was made in 1937, though a still newer revision is now in process.

The revised Stanford-Binet Tests of Intelligence are based on the belief that intelligence is an *over-all* or *general intellectual ability* which is reflected in almost any activity we may undertake. Thus a main requirement of items selected for use in these tests is that they sample this general intellectual ability. The items vary somewhat in kind, according to the age of the subjects for whom the test is intended. The tests were developed for ages two to fourteen and for average and superior adults.

The tests are based on age norms. This means that for every chronological age (CA) there are certain tasks which the average child of this age can complete successfully. Bright children might be expected to perform harder tasks than the average child of their age. Dull children might be expected to fail at tasks considered suitable for their age group.

The term "mental age" (MA) has been coined to reflect the idea that a child may perform tasks suitable to a given age group, regardless of his own chronological age. Thus, if he performs tasks at an average fourteen-year level and none beyond that, his MA is 14 — whether he is actually twelve years old or twenty.

From the testing of many individuals, tasks suitable for each CA were discovered and developed. When an individual passes all subtests at a given CA it means simply that he has an MA equal to that CA. We should note, however, that the difference between MA's 5 and 6 is not qualitatively the same, for example, as between MA's 10 and 11. The five-year-old with an MA of 6 has an IQ of 120; the 10-year-old with an MA of 11 has an IQ of 110. The Revised Stanford-Binet Intelligence Tests assume that the rate of mental development slows down as children approach the age of fourteen, and that mental development ceases at the age of sixteen. Thus it is implied that individuals master material of the kind contained in the tests more readily at age sixteen than during any previous or subsequent year.

Because the MA represents the level of the subject's intellectual functioning, we can readily compare one person with another of a different CA by computing the IQ. To obtain the IQ we divide the MA by the CA and multiply by 100. In actual practice, the age is taken in months, rather than in years. For example, if we have a 10-year-old whose MA is 12, we divide 144 by 120 and get 1.20. This, multiplied by 100, is 120. This means that at the time of testing, the subject is functioning intellectually at the same level as the average 12-year-old. It *does not* mean that he is 1.20 times as intelligent as a 12-year-old with an MA of 12 and an IQ of 100.

We should be careful not to think of an IQ as an exact quantitative measurement like height or weight. We can be quite certain that a child of 66 inches is taller than a child of 63 inches, whether they are measured by the same person or by two different persons. We are much less certain, however, that a college student with an IQ of 122 is more intelligent than one with an IQ of 119 even when both are measured by the same skilled tester using the same intelligence test. Moreover, the IQ does not provide an exact prediction of success. Only through careful investigation of the relationship between IQ's and success in particular courses and careers can anyone decide on the minimum IQ required for successful work.

Attempts have been made to describe persons of varying IQ's. In Table 9.1 appears such a classification developed by Wechsler (1), whose concept of intelligence is discussed in the next section. The categories — defective, border-line, etc. — apply to adults as well as to children. While the range in capability between IQ's 80 and 90 may not represent exactly the same variation in capacity as does the range between 110 and 119, we can see that 8.9 per cent of the entire population have IQ's below 80, and 8.9 per cent have IQ's of 120 or higher. If a person's IQ is in the 120 to 127 range, he is among the top 9.7 per cent of the total population. If he has an IQ of 66 to 79, he is among the lowest 9.7 per cent, according to the Wechsler Intelligence Scale.

You may be interested in examining representative test items from the earlier Stanford-Binet Scale (2).

YEAR VIII.

1. Answering such simple problem-questions as the following: "What should a man do if he comes home and finds a burglar has robbed his house?" . . . "Why is a train harder to stop than an automobile?" . . .

2. Ability to tell how two things are similar. Any real likeness, whether fundamental or superficial is considered satisfactory. . . . "In what way are a mosquito and a sparrow alike?" "In what way are a door and a window alike?" . . .

3. Detecting verbal absurdities. "What is wrong with this? A man had flu (influenza) twice. The first time it killed him, but the second time he got well quickly." . . . "Walter now had to write with his left hand because two years ago he lost both arms in an accident." . . .

4. Naming the days of the week.

5. Solving problem situations . . . "About two o'clock one afternoon a number of boys and girls, dressed in their best clothes, rang the bell at Alice's house. Alice opened the door. What was happening?"

Not all the tests involve verbal situations like these, because some children have had insufficient schooling or speak a foreign language at home or, due to hearing handicaps, have not become well accustomed to language. Hence the test also includes non-verbal (performance) items such as copying a diamond-shaped figure, counting blocks in a picture, copying a chain of beads made by the examiner, and others.

TABLE 9.1

Wechsler's Intelligence Scale

Classification	IQ Limits	Percentage of Population
Defective	65 and below	2.2
Borderline	66–79	6.7
Dull normal	80–90	16.1
Average	91–110	50.0
Bright normal	111–119	16.1
Superior	120–127	6.7
Very superior	128 and over	2.2

Intelligence as a global capacity

David Wechsler, chief psychologist at Bellevue Psychiatric Hospital in New York, became interested in the testing of adult intelligence. Traditionally, this was done with the Revised Stanford-Binet Intelligence Tests, using the CA of 16 for computing adult IQ's, but Wechsler felt that this was not entirely valid for testing adults. In the first place, the Binet had not been standardized on a large enough sample of adults (it had been used primarily with school children) and, when a trial of the Binet test was used in the Army, the average MA of adults turned out to be 13.08 instead of the 16 expected. He also felt that the material used in typical tests for children was not suitable for adults. Problems of motivation and suspicion, emphasis on speed as compared to accuracy, and emphasis on ability to manipulate words all conspired to make such tests less than valid or reliable. Wechsler differed also from Terman in regard to the nature of intelligence. As a result he developed the Wechsler Adult Intelligence Scale, which we shall now consider briefly. This test is now widely used for testing adult intelligence.

The Wechsler test was originally designed for adults of ages 16 to 70, but there is now in use a form for children, called the Wechsler Intelligence Scale for Children (WISC). The tests are administered individually by trained examiners, as is the Stanford-Binet, and scores are provided on subtests. The tester is given an opportunity to gain rapport with the subject and observe his ways of attacking the problems.

According to Wechsler (3),

Intelligence, operationally defined, is the aggregate or global capacity of the individual to act purposefully, to think rationally and to deal effectively with his environment. It is aggregate or global because it is composed of elements or abilities which, though not entirely independent, are qualitatively differentiable. By measurement of these abilities, we ultimately evaluate intelligence. But intelligence is not identical with the mere sum of these abilities, however inclusive. There are three important reasons for this: (1) The ultimate products of intelligent behavior are a function not only of the number of abilities or their quality but also of the way in which they are combined, that is, their configuration. (2) Factors other than intellectual ability, for example, those of drive and incentive, are involved in intelligent behavior. (3) Finally, while different orders of intelligent behavior may require varying degrees of intellectual ability, an excess of any given ability may add relatively little to the effectiveness of the behavior as a whole. It would seem that, so far as general intelligence is concerned, intellectual ability, *per se*, merely enters as a necessary minimum. Thus, to act intelligently one must be able to recall numerous items, *i.e.*, have a retentive memory. But beyond a certain point this ability will not help much in coping with life situations successfully. This is true of even more important capacities, such as the ability to reason, particularly when specialized. The unusual reasoning abilities of the mathematician are more highly correlated with the thing that we ultimately measure as intelligence than sheer memory is, but possession of this ability is no guarantee that behavior as a whole will be very intelligent in the sense defined above. Every reader will be able to recall persons of high intellectual ability in some particular field whom they would unhesitatingly characterize as below average in general intelligence.

Thus it is possible for people with equal IQ's to have quite different patterns of abilities — or somewhat different *kinds* of intelligence.

The derivation of the IQ for the Wechsler test is statistical in nature, and the examiner reads it from tables which are already set up, rather than calculating it by a formula. While the IQ's thus gained are not exactly the same in meaning as those for the Binet test, it is possible to obtain comparable quotients and to screen the varying degrees of intellectual ability into categories like those in Table 9.1 on the opposite page. Wechsler felt that the adult's intelligence, too, should be compared with that of others his own age. He also recognized that mental ability does not remain constant after age sixteen. We shall explain later what changes occur. Let us simply say here that the various age groups and the abilities that normally characterize them were considered in the construction of the Wechsler tables.

The test consists of different parts, each scaled to provide a number of points for correct responses. Verbal, performance, and full-scale IQ's can be determined by using the tables included in the test manual. The separate divisions of the test are:

1. An information test
2. A general comprehension test
3. A combined memory-span test for remembering digits and their sequence, forward and backward
4. A similarities test

TESTING FOR INTELLIGENCE AND ABIL-ITIES. *A great contribution of psychology has been the development of standard-ized tests to determine and measure in-telligence and aptitudes. Such tests are helpful to both the individual and society.*

WECHSLER-BELLEVUE INTELLIGENCE SCALE, FORM 1. The block design test is one of a number of items in the Wechsler test. The object is to reproduce a pictured pattern with colored blocks. (A. M. Love, Jr. Cour-tesy of the Psychological Corporation.)

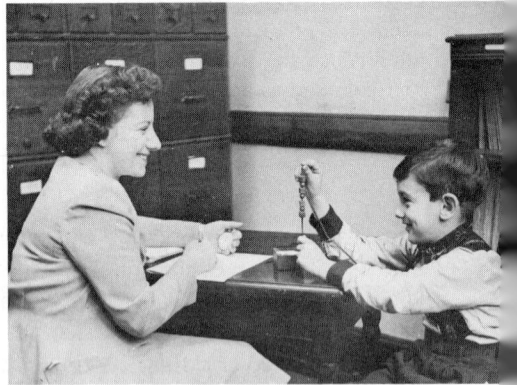

THE STANFORD-BINET TEST. A 6-year-old tries to duplicate a bead pattern threaded by the tester. Note the importance of the relationship between the child and the tester. (City College Educational Clinic.)

GROUP TESTING. It is often more feasible to test a large group at one time. These high school seniors have been given a series of questionnaires which will help to analyze their potential abilities. (*St. Louis Post-Dispatch,* from Black Star.)

5. An arithmetical reasoning test
6. A picture arrangement test
7. A picture completion test
8. A block design test
9. An object assembly test
10. A digit symbol test
11. Alternate — a vocabulary test

We have illustrated only a part of the Wechsler test, because you may some-day wish to be tested. From the pictures on pages 270 and 264, you can get some idea of what it is like. The test provides four separate but intercor-related scales: one for adults aged 16 to 60; one for adolescents aged 10 to 16; a performance or non-verbal scale; and a verbal scale. Non-verbal or performance tests do not seem to measure intelligence as a whole, perhaps because of dif-ferences in individual perception and attention (See Chapter 6.). However, non-verbal tasks are included so that cultural influences may not give one undue advantages or handicaps, for example, with subjects whose native language is not English. The block design, picture arrangement, picture com-pletion, object assembly, and digit symbol tests are non-verbal and relatively free of cultural limitations. They can thus test specific aspects of mental ability.

Intelligence as primary mental ability

Of the many group intelligence tests available, we have chosen to consider briefly the Primary Mental Abilities Tests because they are based on still an-other concept of the nature of intelligence. Group tests, of course, have both advantages and disadvantages. Their advantages are that they can be used by relatively unskilled examiners, they can save time since many subjects can be tested at once, and they require little equipment, usually only pencil and paper. On the other hand, it is usually not possible to gain rapport with all the subjects and because of the nature of the tests, they may not adequately tap every aspect of intelligence. They are widely used, however, for a variety of purposes.

The Primary Mental Abilities Tests were developed by L. L. and Thelma Gwinn Thurstone (4). They are based on results of the statistical technique called factor analysis. Working with the results of various tests, fifty-six at first, the Thurstones found that various *factors* could be isolated. That is, they discovered that the tests were actually testing particular kinds of mental be-havior rather than one single general behavior. The PMA tests were based on several studies of this kind. The form of the test used for subjects aged 11 to 17 includes subtests in verbal-meaning, space, reasoning, number, and word flu-ency. Although IQ's can be calculated from the test results, the *main* purpose of the tests is to provide a profile of these special mental abilities. Scores are changed into percentile ranks in each area. The tests are available in various

Equipment used in testing. *Pictured is some of the equipment used in non-verbal performance tests for pre-school children. (C. H. Stoelting Co., Chicago.)*

forms for different ages. Although 17 is the top age bracket, the tests appear to be useful also for older subjects. The tests are designed to assess mental ability in the following areas (5):

Verbal-meaning. The ability to understand ideas expressed in words is generally believed to be of special value in such courses as English, languages, the social sciences, the physical and biological sciences, and for work as a secretary, teacher, editor, scientist, librarian, or executive.

Space. The ability to think about objects in two or three dimensions is useful in blueprint reading, electrical work, piloting, engineering, and the like. It is also helpful in courses in geometry, mechanical drawing, art, radar, physics, and others.

Reasoning. The ability to solve logical problems, to foresee and plan, is necessary for inventors, doctors, teachers, statesmen, and scientists as well as for students of mathematics and science.

Number. The ability to work with figures is required in accounting, banking, sales, and bookkeeping, among other activities.

Word fluency. The ability to write and talk easily is of special value for careers such as acting, reporting, saleswork, writing, and publicity. It is also helpful in courses in drama, speech, writing, and journalism.

A person who has any of these abilities to a high degree will reflect it in his percentile rank. If his score falls at the fiftieth percentile, we know that he is doing as well as 50 per cent of those on whom the test was standardized, but less well than the other 50 per cent. If it falls at the seventy-fifth percentile, it means that he does as well as 75 per cent but less well than the upper 25 per cent. Careful interpretation of such ratings can give a good indication of the particular abilities of a person, in the areas specified by the PMA tests.

What is intelligence?

We may now return to the question we raised earlier: *What is intelligence?* We have taken a rapid look at three different theories of the nature of intelligence. Having done so, we should hesitate to equate the results of one intelligence test with those of another without first considering the assumptions underlying each, that is, the definition of intelligence which each assumes at the beginning. We should not blindly accept the IQ as a specific, entirely accurate, and absolute rating as we may have thought before. On the other hand, *if* we understand the ideas behind the different tests, we can use the scores as an aid in choosing a vocation or a college program. But we should use these tests as an aid, not as an absolute determiner, of our programs.

Guilford (6) makes the interesting point that intelligence tests should emphasize some of the socially important factors having to do with productive thinking. This is in line with the belief of the authors that intelligence involves more than native ability. Rather, it is whatever native endowment one has, *interacting in a social pattern.* As Guilford says, intelligence is probably not one "unique, solitary phenomenon." Thus the term "intelligence," while useful, is a semi-popular word without a really definite and precise meaning. We would perhaps do better to specify intelligences of different kinds — "Intelligence A," "Intelligence B," etc.

In summary, the writers believe that to understand one's mental abilities it is necessary to consider the results of various kinds of tests and to interpret them with care. With such care, however, it is possible to gain a fairly complete picture of one's mental abilities which will be valuable in choosing school courses and an ultimate vocation. Such interpretations should be made only by qualified personnel. If you should accidentally learn your own IQ, you must be extremely careful in drawing any conclusions from it.

Suggested activities

1. Examine an individual intelligence test or witness a demonstration of testing. What are the advantages of such a test? What are the disadvantages?
2. Can you think of any "culture-free" ways of determining intelligence?
3. Calculate the following:

MA	CA	IQ
108 months	108 months	?
108 months	96 months	?
?	108 months	133

4. Perhaps your instructor has access to group intelligence tests. The class may want to take such tests, score them, and attempt to interpret the scores with his assistance.

A.   DEFINITIONS OF INTELLIGENCE

● B.   **FACTORS IN INTELLIGENT BEHAVIOR**

There is a long-standing question whether intelligence is largely inherited or whether it can be greatly affected by the environment. This brings us to a consideration of the terms *capacity* and *ability*. Any kind of test is designed to sample ability, that is, to give us a picture of how the subject actually performs. We can only infer capacity, or hereditary endowment, from performance. We have no precise way of measuring the limits of capacity — that is, what one theoretically *could* do if circumstances permitted. If we take two one-quart milk bottles and place them side by side, we can see that each has a capacity of one quart; each can hold one quart of liquid. This is roughly analogous to the theoretical limits of intelligence as determined by heredity. To continue the analogy, one milk bottle may have been completely filled, whereas the other may have been only partly filled. If so, the *ability* of the two bottles to supply milk will be different, though their *capacity* is the same. Somewhat the same relationship applies to human capacities and abilities. If a person's health has been good all his life, if his education has been of the best quality, if he is emotionally stable, it is likely that his mental ability will approach and conceivably even reach the limit of capacity imposed by his heredity. But if he is deprived of certain advantages by living in an impoverished environment, by poor health, by scant education — all factors of environment — he may never approach his capacity; the bottle may be less than half full. This does not mean, of course, that all persons are born with the same capacity; it means simply that through accidents of environment many persons never have the chance to develop their full capacities.

In general, while we may find differences in the average intelligence of one social group and another, we also find wide variations among the members of any particular group, and great overlapping from one group to another. For these reasons it is difficult to measure the intelligence of persons from differing racial or national backgrounds, and hence obviously difficult to make any meaningful comparisons between such groups or members of them. For example, it would be impossible to say whether an Eskimo who performed miserably on one of our standard intelligence tests did so because of a defect in capacity or because his environment had not prepared him for the test. Until we are better able to develop tests which do not depend on elements of culture, we shall not be able to say that one social or racial group is generally more, or less, intelligent than another.

Heredity and environment

Psychologists have long wondered whether heredity or environment was the more important in determining intelligence. This is a practical question of real importance to society.

Many studies have been made in an attempt to determine the relative effects of environment and heredity on intelligence. Skodak and Skeels (7, 8) studied children who were placed in adoptive homes before the age of six months. The children were given Stanford-Binet tests at the time of adoption and during succeeding years, the latest test when the children averaged thirteen years and six months of age. The mean (average) IQ of the children's true or natural mothers was 87, but the mean IQ of the children at age thirteen was 107 or 117, depending upon which form of the test was used. Environmental factors, including the education and occupation of the foster parents, seemed to be of more significance than heredity in determining the mental growth of these children.

Later, Skeels and Harms (9) made a study of the mental development of children selected on the basis of inferior social histories and placed in adoptive homes before the age of two. Here again it was concluded that it was the environment more than the child's heredity which determined his intelligence.

Burks (10), on the other hand, studied adopted children but used a control group of parents and their natural children for comparison. The two groups of children were matched for age and sex. The natio-racial criterion was the same for both groups of parents, and they were matched for locality, type of neighborhood, and the occupational fields of the fathers. It was found that the mean IQ of the foster children was 107.4, whereas that of the control group (natural children) was 115.4. Burks assumed that the difference favoring the control group over the foster children was due to more favorable heredity. But since the foster children tested above 100 IQ (100 IQ is expected for random groups of children), Burks felt that this 7-point advantage might well be due to the superior environment of the foster homes.

Leahy (11), also studying true and adopted children, drew the conclusion that variation in IQ is accounted for by variation in home environment to the extent of not more than 4 per cent, the other 96 per cent is accounted for by other factors such as heredity. Hereditary factors apparently caused greater variation than environment.

Newman, Freeman, and Holzinger (12) studied identical (one-egg) twins, who of course have identical heredity, and who happened to be living apart. It was found that the average difference between the twins was about 8 IQ points — and this is approximately the difference we would expect to find between two tests given to the same individual several years apart.

Finally, children who have been transferred from poor environments to better ones at various ages have been studied. Reymert (13) found that if the change is made before the child is more than six years old the IQ can be increased as much as 6 or 7 points, but in children who are older the increase is markedly less and a slight decrease can actually take place.

Thus intelligence is obviously affected by both heredity and environment, and the latter is apparently more influential in the earlier than the later years of childhood. However, the weight of evidence indicates that heredity is of greater importance than environment in accounting for such vast differences in intelligence as represented by IQ's of 50 and 150. Certainly one is endowed at conception with capacity for intelligent behavior and other characteristics. To some extent, this endowment will determine what he will transmit to his children. But for both the individual and his children, improvement in the environment is the main way to higher achievement as far as is now known. It is possible, of course, that ways may be found to alter the effects of heredity as knowledge of endocrine glands and of the central nervous system expands. But this may be far off.

Characteristics of highly intelligent individuals

Are geniuses likely to become neurotic or insane? Are intelligent people likely to be physically weak? Is lack of intelligence usually compensated for by a strong back? The answer is "No" to all these questions. Many studies of gifted children have been made, among them that of Terman (14). In general they tend to show that the brighter children are physically as capable as other children, tend to live more emotionally well-balanced lives, are more successful in earning a living, have fewer divorces and happier marriages, and show more leadership in school, business, and community life. This seems to bear out the view that a general quality of "good" or "poor" inheritance affects not only the general physique but the brain and nervous system as well and determines whether a person is likely to be generally good in all respects or generally poor. (We must not forget, of course, that good health is necessary for the most efficient functioning both mentally and emotionally.) Of course there are exceptions — some very athletic and healthy people are not highly intelligent, and some intelligent people are sickly, but this is not the general rule. An intelligent person is ordinarily a good risk for a long life, a happy marriage, and a successful career.

Physical conditions and intelligence

Certain deficiencies in glandular secretions, notably that of the thyroid, may produce feeble-mindedness. *Cretins,* as the victims of this condition are called, are dull and lethargic, and their intelligence does not have a chance to develop fully. Institutions for the feeble-minded have experimented by providing such children with thyroid extract and have achieved good results with some of the children when they have been treated early enough.

Head injuries (possibly received at birth) may lead to brain damage. Certain diseases also damage the brain. Thus people who inherited superior mental potentialities may not be able to do well on tests after such injuries or diseases. If the damage is severe enough, inability to function well mentally may be noted. Even insanity may occur as a result of some diseases, such as syphilis, which act on the brain. When the brain tissue in one area is damaged, some other part of the brain may "take over" to some degree. Lashley (15), experimenting with animals, removed bits of brain tissue. He found that change in ability to function was more related to the amount of damage than to the location of the area where damage occurred. This indicated that the remaining tissue tended to work toward restoring normal functioning. But when damage went beyond a certain limit, the animal became unable to function properly or it died. Some areas of the brain, such as those related to vision, are quite specific and when they are removed the function is lost.

Unlike some other tissue, the brain does not renew itself. When brain cells have been destroyed by accident, drugs, disease, or poisons, those cells are gone forever. If the damage is not excessive, the patient may lead quite a normal life, but, as with animals, if the damage is extensive there is mental impairment.

Age and intelligence

Although young children obviously do not have the same level of mental ability as adults, it is not true that they cannot reason. The child actually has the various mental abilities that the adult has, but they function at his own level of experience and maturity. In size and development of nervous tissue, the brain is fairly well developed by age six. The child grows in mental abilities and has many learning experiences through which to acquire knowledge and skills. As he learns new concepts and gains new vocabulary, and as he gains experience in problem-solving, discrimination, and generalization, his ability to think and act intelligently increases.

As is suggested by the IQ, bright children develop faster mentally than average or dull children. They also tend to develop mentally for a longer period. The dull child not only develops more slowly but probably ceases to develop sooner than the bright child.

By the time a person is about twenty he has reached the peak of general mental ability as measured by most intelligence tests, and college students are near their prime in their ability to translate their intelligence into achievement in many areas of subject matter. Will you stay that way, or will you deteriorate?

The answer is — not quite either. You will tend to improve in some abilities and to deteriorate slowly in others. Capacity for rote memory reaches its peak about the fifteenth year, but vocabulary and general information test scores improve until about the middle forties. Speed in responding to items on intelligence tests declines with age, but power to deal with problem-solving situations declines much more slowly.

Achievement is somewhat related to the emergence and decline of general and more specific mental abilities. In chemistry, mathematics, and poetry, individuals generally make their most significant contributions between ages twenty and forty; whereas the executive heads of state and federal governments, business corporations, and learned societies usually range from near forty to as much as seventy. Much research yet needs to be done to ascertain how much such factors as motivation, physical stamina, sex, and occupation affect achievement in adults at various ages in comparison with measured mental abilities.

One's ability to learn in his own fields of interest appears to continue throughout life. This is partly because he builds up a background of facts and ideas which enables him to continue to study in his field with an ever increasing backlog of enriching data and experience. You *can* teach an old dog new tricks, but it is better to teach him variations of tricks he learned while he was young.

Productivity — the ability of an author to write books, of a composer to produce music, or of an artist to paint many pictures — seems to reach a peak in the early thirties and to decline thereafter, though naturally there are exceptions to this general rule. Probably physical vigor and the ability to withstand long hours of hard work are related to this phenomenon.

Accuracy and good judgment appear to continue and even to improve throughout life. Older heads are likely to be wiser and more careful than young ones. Thus industry and the arts and professions have room for both the young man and the older one. The young man is quicker to learn new things. He may be more adaptable and should gain many kinds of experience early in life. The young man is highly productive, in part because of his physical energy and stamina. But the older man has judgment and knowledge of his field which enables him to oversee the work of his younger fellows. In the Army the generals make the plans and the lieutenants and captains carry them out. In business the executives can be older men and the salesmen and productive workers younger ones. On college faculties both kinds of workers can be fully utilized.

Occupations and intelligence

Since strong motivation, hard work, health, and other related qualities may be found in persons of various levels of intelligence, it is not out of place to discuss these intelligence levels and to indicate some typical kinds of jobs held by people within them. You will bear in mind, of course, that any individual may be an exception to the generalizations which follow.

If you refer to page 268 you will see that, according to the Wechsler classification, 2.2 per cent of our general population are mentally defective. These persons are sometimes classed as imbeciles, morons, and idiots. Broadly speaking, morons are the "brightest" of the three, imbeciles next, and idiots the dullest. Idiots cannot care for themselves. They need to be fed, cleaned, dressed, and in all ways taken care of, much like small children. Some must remain in bed or sit in chairs, more like vegetables than human beings. Imbeciles, the next grade of defective, can learn to talk a bit, and can often learn to do simple work such as cleaning floors, raking yards, and the like, under supervision. Morons can learn to read and write simple material, and some probably go undetected in our society, perhaps even marrying and raising families. They can do simple routine jobs, such as certain kinds of factory work. Because they are unable to foresee the consequences of their acts, they may become criminals, delinquents, parents of illegitimate children, or other socially offensive types.

Table 9.2 shows average intelligence quotients possessed by various working groups in our society. The IQ range from 60 to 90 includes many workers who are not in business for themselves — the unskilled, the semi-skilled, and some skilled labor. A few in that range own small businesses. The group with 90–110 IQ represents the average intelligence group which makes up the largest segment of the population. It should be emphasized that this table gives rough averages only. For example, some barbers probably have higher IQ's than some bankers, and some farmers are probably brighter than some research workers.

TABLE 9.2

Average IQ's of Various Working Groups

IQ	Occupation
120 plus	Research, statistical work, inventing of the highest order.
110–120	Public school teaching, medicine, law, banking, and big business.
90–110	Small business, secretarial work, bookkeeping, nursing, teaching music.
80–90	Mechanics, bus drivers, policemen, plumbers, hairdressers, telephone operators, clerks, barbers, and farmers.
70–80	Semi-skilled workers requiring little planning and versatility.
60–70	Lumbermen, sailors, cobblers, and miners — those who do routine, crude manual labor.
60 or below	Capable of only the simplest, most routine work, if any.

From R. W. Husband, *Applied Psychology*, Rev., Harper, New York, 1949, Table 11, p. 67. Used by permission.

In the group with IQ of 120 and above are most executives and professional people — the highly successful businessmen, the doctors, lawyers, ministers, teachers, and the like. Most college students (varying from college to college, of course) have IQ's of 110 or higher.

Suggested activities

1. Debate the following:

   a. Elementary school classes should be divided into sections based on IQ's.

   b. Very bright students should be excused from certain class work or courses.

   c. Girls with high IQ's should be selected as filing clerks in a large insurance office.

2. Examine biographies and autobiographies of prominent persons in science,

arts, or statesmanship. What happens to their productivity as they get older?

3. Collect pictures of both intelligent and unintelligent people. Can the class recognize from the pictures which are the intelligent and which are the unintelligent?

4. Study books or articles on the mentally retarded. What are some of the factors in mental retardation?

A.   DEFINITIONS OF INTELLIGENCE
B.   FACTORS IN INTELLIGENT BEHAVIOR

● C. SPECIAL APTITUDES AND SUCCESS

Are there special athletic, musical, or artistic abilities? Although relatively few studies of such special abilities have been made, it appears certain that many factors are involved in outstanding success in these fields. We can draw a few inferences from the available data.

Athletic ability

Motor skills involved in athletic performances include coordination, strength, speed, endurance, and steadiness. Some of these abilities are related to body build and hence are affected by innate or hereditary factors, but all respond somewhat to training.

As you participated in gym classes you undoubtedly took various strength tests or tests of physical fitness, including chinning yourself on the bar, climbing a rope using your arms and hands only, doing push-ups, and the like. If so you noticed that some of your classmates could do some of these things quite well but could not do others. This specialization is apparent in such fields as circus performance, professional athletics, and dancing. Some persons appear to have excellent balance, others have exceptional timing, others strength, or speed. The all-around athlete does exist, however, and is perhaps more common than is usually believed, and may remain unnoticed because he is likely to take part in certain sports, rather than in all.

Are there natural athletes? Jim Thorpe was thought to be one. He seemed able to outdo almost all men in whatever sport he participated. But in the main, there are different kinds of athletic ability, which are largely subject to training. Muscles can be developed. Coordination can be improved. And the kind of thinking required of top-notch competitors can be sharpened. Many of our champions began their practice early in life, with expert instruction from parents or teachers. But in spite of expert instruction, not all can be top performers, as we all know.

For the usual student, the proper course is to find a physical activity in which he is interested and in which he has some ability. Since most students do not compete in team sports after they leave college, consideration should be given to develop skill in individual sports such as golf, swimming, tennis, dancing, or skating. These can be enjoyed throughout one's entire lifetime, and they not only keep one in condition but afford recreation throughout the mature years.

Musical ability

Musical tests such as the Seashore Measures of Musical Talents (16) have been developed to try to assess music aptitude. The Seashore tests include listening to phonograph records with various sounds which sample the ability to discriminate pitch, loudness, rhythm, time, timbre, and tonal memory. Because these discriminatory abilities are useful in music, they provide some measure of the minimum abilities required of musicians. However, the requirements of musicianship involve much more than these tests can assess. For example, if a musician is expected to be creative, if he is expected to provide emotional feeling through his interpretations of music, if he is expected to have the superb motor skills of a fine pianist, then these must be tested differently. Musical ability does not appear to be a single ability. Both sensory and motor skills are involved, as well as keenness of perception and expression, and training affects the ability to perform. The skills needed for playing the piano are not the same as those required for playing the violin, and the skills necessary for these performances are somewhat different from those the composer or vocalist may employ.

Is musical aptitude inherited? At least to the extent that body structures are inherited, we can be fairly certain that it is. Can everyone learn music? Except perhaps for persons described as tone-deaf, practically everyone can learn to express himself through music in one form or another. Here again, for emotional enjoyment, release, and recreation, each person should develop whatever aptitudes he has.

A musical profile. *The aptitude test devised by Seashore involves the testing of a subject's discrimination of pitch, intensity, time interval, and other qualities of musical sounds on records. This profile represents one person's specific abilities as well as an over-all picture of his musical ability. Scores are represented by vertical lines. (Courtesy of State University of Iowa.)*

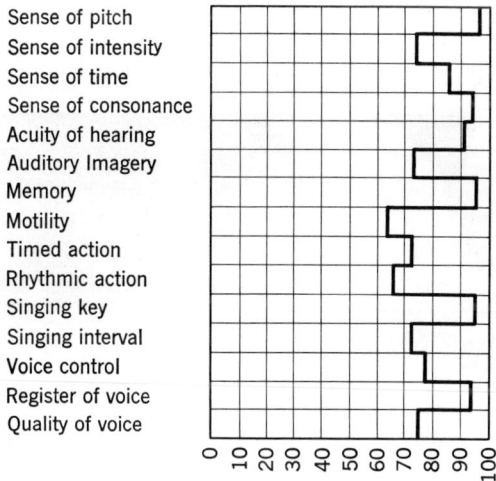

Sense of pitch
Sense of intensity
Sense of time
Sense of consonance
Acuity of hearing
Auditory Imagery
Memory
Motility
Timed action
Rhythmic action
Singing key
Singing interval
Voice control
Register of voice
Quality of voice

0 10 20 30 40 50 60 70 80 90 100

Mechanical aptitude

Motor dexterity, ability to sense distance and space, mechanical reasoning, and mechanical information all may be parts of mechanical aptitude. Discrimination, perceptual abilities, and manipulation all play a part in most mechanical aptitude tests. It appears, however, that different kinds of mechanical aptitudes involve different kinds of abilities. Many persons who are not gifted academically do well in shop courses or can repair appliances or motor cars. On the other hand, schools have found that *it does not follow that a person who does not do well in academic subjects should study shop courses,* for he may not do well in them either. The practice of dumping students with low grades into home economics, shop, or typing classes is diminishing because it has been found that the type of instruction, rather than the particular subject matter, is most important in educating persons of low intelligence. It is true that home economics and shop subjects may be more interesting than the usual academic subject to students who do not have high verbal or mathematical ability, and hence that such students may have sufficient motivation to do well in these subjects. It is true, too, that the brightest student can find challenging learning activities in the so-called vocational subjects.

Is mechanical ability innate? Again we cannot be sure, except that, insofar as body build affects ability to manipulate, hereditary factors may operate. However, during World War II many persons (often women) who did not believe they had any mechanical ability went to work in defense plants and showed that they could perform complex mechanical tasks. Most students can probably improve their mechanical skills. Many persons, for example, like wood-working as a hobby, and later find that they are able to save money when building a house.

Artistic ability

Artistic talent also represents not a simple ability, but a host of skills. The poet, the painter, and the interior decorator all display differing talents, as do

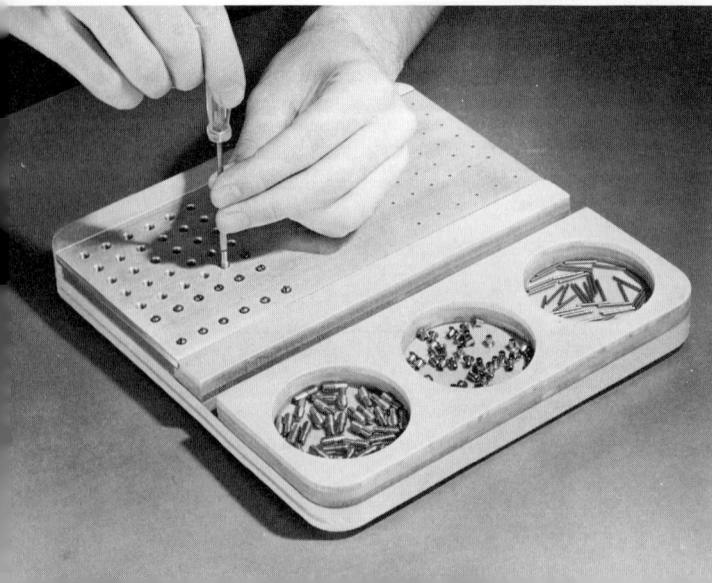

Aptitude testing. *The Crawford Small Parts Dexterity Test, and other similar tests, determine abilities such as manual dexterity and coordination. (Psychological Corporation.)*

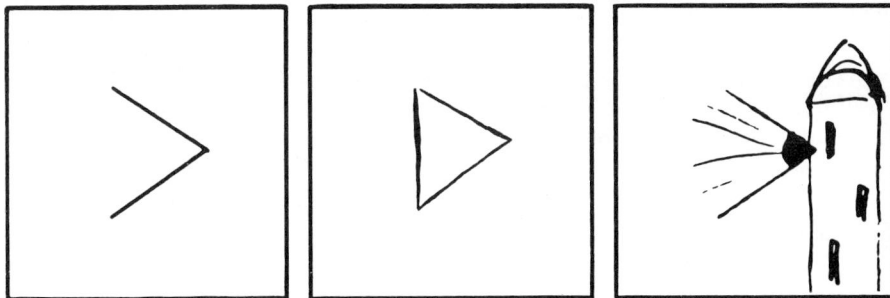

Creativity. *A drawing-completion test, devised by Kate Franck, requires that subjects elaborate on a simple figure like that at left. A typical response of a subject chosen at random is the middle figure. At right is the response of a creative individual. (Frank Barron, Institute of Personality Assessment and Research, University of California.)*

the teacher, the critic, and the collector. Appreciation does not require a high level of creative ability; creation in the arts, however, should carry with it the ability to judge and appreciate.

Tests of artistic ability (and comparable literary or musical ability) may include tests of knowledge, judgment and discrimination, sensory processes, and the like. Although many tests have been devised, they have not always been successful. Probably the failure to devise successful tests in these areas is attributable to the wide variety of elements which make for success in art, music, or literature.

How can a person determine whether or not he can become an artist? Interest, evaluation of one's work, ability to appreciate and discriminate — all these help him to find out. Most people can learn to appreciate; many, with training and practice, can learn to create; and all can probably benefit from instruction in the arts. But a person who really wishes to make a vocation of music, art, or literature must compare the results of his work to date with that of persons who have already demonstrated talent in the field. A Grandma Moses may not start painting until her later years, but few can hope to be like her in that respect.

Almost all of us can improve our tastes and creative efforts in the fine arts, and most of us can profit by studying them as cultural rather than vocational subjects. We can all gain emotional enjoyment, increase our aesthetic pleasure, and improve our daily living by some knowledge and appreciation of the arts. Besides, we may discover latent interests which lead us to hobbies, or we may discover that we have enough talent to become dealers or collectors, even if we cannot become prominent portrait painters or dramatic critics.

Suggested activities

1. Arrange demonstrations of various aptitude and ability tests. How do they help one to ascertain his fitness for a given occupation? In what ways should they be supplemented in order to provide the most helpful guidance?

2. How would you attempt to validate an aptitude test, i.e., show that it was a useful measure of that aptitude? How would you proceed in devising a test to determine aptitude for motor car driving?

3. Can persons without particular aptitudes succeed in professions in which there is keen competition, such as the stage, the concert hall, the art gallery? If so, how can you account for their success?

A. DEFINITIONS OF INTELLIGENCE
B. FACTORS IN INTELLIGENT BEHAVIOR
C. SPECIAL APTITUDES AND SUCCESS

● D. APPRAISING AND USING ABILITIES

In the last analysis, capacity and aptitude alone, whatever they may be, do not determine success. Rather, it is the way in which a person uses the abilities he possesses or may develop that decides whether or not he will achieve success as it is defined in our society.

More people, it is said, fail in their work because of their inability to get along with others than for any other reason. The ability to perceive the attitudes and sense the feelings of others, and to act accordingly, can be developed. The essential requirement is a feeling of empathy, of understanding the emotions and states of mind of others.

Physical soundness — endurance, good health, freedom from time-wasting illness, and real pep and "life" — is needed for success in any line of work. Endurance, strength, quickness, steadiness, accuracy, vitality are essential to many kinds of jobs; it is impossible to work the long hours often required for completion of many jobs without them. One's motivation suffers if he continually "enjoys poor health," and mental activity cannot be carried on satisfactorily if one has aches and pains, although there are exceptional people who, though ill a great deal of the time, have overcome this difficulty and contributed to our literature, art, and science.

Some people aim higher than others. Their levels of aspiration are such that they are spurred on to do as good a job in their field as they possibly can. People with average abilities often make a success of their work because they are willing to put in long hours, to take menial jobs that others reject, and to study their work and "put more into it." But while it is possible in such ways to compensate up to a point, lack of ability is nevertheless a handicap to the person in competition with those of considerably higher abilities.

Clarence was a high school physics student. He did good work on the drawings and notebooks that were required, and he was able to perform mechanical tasks such as making simple motors and building simple apparatus for demonstrations. But Clarence was not successful at working problems in physics, nor in his tests. He got "C" grades only because of the former activities, and because of his apparent effort.

Clarence wanted to go to the state university and become a physicist. We asked him how long he spent each day studying his physics. He told us "between three and four hours each day." This, plus his other studies and his chores around home, took almost all his waking hours outside of school.

You can imagine what Clarence's problem would be like in college, where the competition is stiffer — there just wouldn't be enough hours in the day for him to study, let alone have time for recreation or other pursuits. We encouraged Clarence to enter a mechanical line of work instead of attending college. He is now mechanical assistant to the school custodian — he repairs motors and machinery, and is happy and doing well.

Where can you find out about your intelligence and other abilities? You can get an *interpretation* from the college counselor, psychologist, or testing bureau. You will probably not be given your exact IQ because there are too many variables involved and many people take such scores too literally. You can also examine your past scholastic record. Have you received high marks in most fields without having to work unduly hard for them? Have you been able to keep up with out-of-class activities, hobbies, or part-time jobs without letting your classwork suffer? If so, you are undoubtedly of average intelligence or above, and should have no great difficulty in college, assuming that you have learned to study. If you played too much and worked too little in high school, you may have to work harder in college for a time, until you have built up a background for your courses. You may wish to re-read Chapter 2 to improve your study habits.

For information about special abilities, you may be able to get from your college counselor tests of aptitude in music, art, mechanics, and the like. He can also help you assess your personality, interests, and background, in comparison with those of other students. For information about abilities in such areas as art, music, and athletics, you might also talk to your coach, and your music or art instructors; and you may show them what you have done, for they are good judges of talent in their fields.

Suggested activity

1. Write a short sketch, summarizing your abilities, interests, and lack of knowledge about certain abilities you may wish to possess. Attempt to discover whether your self-estimate is realistic by consulting test results, or through the counseling bureau of your college. In making such a self-estimate, consider how your abilities compare with those of persons representing various occupations, and with those of other college students.

SUMMARY

Intelligence is a name for the mental capacities that are needed for getting along in this world. Other things being equal, the more intelligent person will adjust to life situations better than the dull one. Terman's study showed that persons of high intelligence usually turn out well in adult life: they are likely to make good marriages, be vocationally successful, be leaders, good citizens, and generally exhibit useful behavior. These accomplishments in part result from high abilities, in part from good environment, in part from other socially desirable characteristics.

Mental ability or intelligence is hard to define. Binet felt that there was an over-all ability, which would be manifest in most situations. Wechsler feels that intelligence is a configuration of various mental abilities, while the Thurstones based the PMA on the belief that mental ability can best be described as a profile of special factors. In any case, through properly administered tests, it is possible to gain an idea of one's intellectual position in the general population. Some people have more ability of one kind than others do; and these same people probably have less ability of certain other kinds. An assessment of one's abilities as well as the over-all picture of his intelligence can help him to decide on school courses and a vocational career.

Intellectual capacities are determined largely by the genes, but inborn effective intelligence is modified by environmental influences. Mental abilities do not remain constant throughout life; most abilities develop rapidly in early life; some begin to decline in the late teens, while others remain relatively stable or actually increase, at least insofar as effective use is concerned.

A person may possess special talents in such fields as art, music, literature, or athletics. In aptitudes related to physical structure, heredity is probably important. These special talents, like intelligence, are distributed unequally among human beings. Most people, though not championship material in these special areas, can develop understandings, higher levels of skill, and appreciations which will serve them well in their careers, for recreation, and in other activities of daily living.

Because motivation, hard work, physical health, and emotional stability affect achievements, capacity alone is not sufficient to assure success in school subjects or in vocations. Furthermore, most subjects and careers demand many abilities rather than a few. College students, like other people, need to appraise their strengths and weaknesses in order to select appropriate careers and other goals.

REFERENCES

1. D. Wechsler, *The Measurement of Adult Intelligence*, Williams and Wilkins, Baltimore, fourth edition, 1944, p. 7.
2. L. M. Terman, *The Measurement of Intelligence*, Houghton Mifflin, Boston, 1916, pp. 99–102.
3. Wechsler, *op. cit.*, p. 3.
4. L. and T. G. Thurstone, *The Chicago Tests of Primary Mental Abilities*, Science Research Associates, Chicago, 1943.

5. L. and T. G. Thurstone, *Student Interpreting Profile for the SRA Primary Mental Abilities,* Science Research Associates, Chicago, 1947. (A paraphrase by the authors from this manual.)

6. J. P. Guilford, "The Structure of Intellect," *Psychol. Bull.,* 1956, 33, pp. 267–293.

7. M. Skodak and H. M. Skeels, "A Follow-up Study of Children in Adoptive Homes," *J. Genet. Psychol.,* 1945, 66, pp. 21–58, and

8. M. Skodak and H. M. Skeels, "A Final Follow-up Study of One Hundred Adopted Children," *J. Genet. Psychol.,* 1949, 75, pp. 85–117.

9. M. Skeels and I. Harms, "Children with Inferior Social Histories; Their Mental Development in Adoptive Homes," *J. Genet. Psychol.,* 1948, 72, pp. 283–284.

10. B. Burks, "Foster Family Resemblances in Intelligence," in R. G. Barker, J. S. Kounin, and H. F. Wright, *Child Behavior and Development,* McGraw-Hill, New York, 1940, pp. 245–257.

11. A. M. Leahy, "Nature-Nurture and Intelligence," *Gen. Psychol. Monogr.,* 1935, 17, pp. 235–308.

12. H. Newman, F. N. Freeman, and K. J. Holzinger, *Twins: A Study of Heredity and Environment,* University of Chicago Press, Chicago, 1927.

13. M. L. Reymert and R. T. Hinton, Jr., "The Effect of Change to a Relatively Superior Environment upon the I.Q.'s of One Hundred Children," *39th Yearbook of National Society for the Study of Education,* University of Chicago Press, Chicago, 1940.

14. L. M. Terman and M. N. Odom, *The Gifted Child Grows Up,* Stanford University Press, Stanford, 1947.

15. V. S. Lashley, *Brain Mechanisms and Intelligence,* Research Monograph, University of Chicago Press, Chicago, 1929.

16. J. G. Saetreit, D. Lewis, and C. E. Seashore, *Revision of the Seashore Measures of Musical Talents,* University of Iowa Studies, Aims Progr. Res., University of Iowa Press, Iowa City, 1940.

SUGGESTIONS FOR FURTHER READING

Barbe, W. B., "Characteristics of Gifted Children," *Educ. Adm. Superv.,* 1955, 41, pp. 207–217.

Bayley, N., "On the Growth of Intelligence," *Amer. Psychologist,* 1955, 10, pp. 805–818.

Burt, C., "The Inheritance of Mental Abilities," *Amer. Psychologist,* 1958, 13, pp. 1–15.

Carmichael, L., *The Making of the Modern Mind,* Elsevier Press, Houston, 1956.

Corsini, R. J., and K. K. Fassett, "Intelligence and Aging," *J. Genet. Psychol.,* 1953, 83, pp. 249–264.

Gallagher, J. J., *A Comparison of Brain-Injured and Non-Brain-Injured Children on Several Psychological Variables,* Purdue Univ., Child Development Publications, Vol. 22, No. 2, 1957, 79 pp.

Guilford, J. P., "Creative Abilities in the Arts," *Psychol. Rev.,* 1957, 64, pp. 110–118.

Lehman, H. C., *Age and Achievement,* Princeton, Princeton Univ. Press, 1953.

Munn, N. L., *Psychology: The Fundamentals of Human Adjustment,* Houghton Mifflin, Boston, third edition, 1956, Chapter 3.

Owens, W. A., Jr., "Age and Mental Abilities: A Longitudinal Study," *Genet. Psychol. Monogr.*, 1953, 48, pp. 3–54.

Sontag, L. W., *et al.*, *Mental Growth and Personality Development*, Child Development Publications, Purdue Univ., Vol. 23, No. 2, 1958, 143 pp.

Stagner, R., and T. F. Karwoski, *Psychology*, McGraw-Hill, New York, 1952, Chapter 12.

Strother, C. R., *et al.*, "The Relationship Between Advanced Age and Mental Abilities," *J. Abnorm. Soc. Psychol.*, 1957, 55, pp. 166–170.

PART THREE •

PSYCHOLOGY

AND SOCIETY

Social Influences

on Behavior

Few of you will ever live entirely alone for any length of time. Even if you do, you will not escape the influences which living in a society has already had upon you. The particular segment of American society in which you have grown and developed has influenced the way you perceive things, your approach to people, your codes of conduct, values, and attitudes. Your behavior is the result of the interaction of hereditary tendencies and environment, and the social aspects of your environment have been especially important in making you the particular human being you are.

Social psychology, which studies both man *in* society and the psychology of groups, provides insight into the behavior of man as a social being. Sociology and anthropology have also developed methods of investigating human behavior in group and cultural contexts. This chapter will reflect some of the pertinent findings of all these disciplines. To understand them it is first necessary to be clear on the meanings of some important terms.

As we shall use the word here, *culture* "consists of the customs and traditions of man, his ways of thinking and acting which have largely come down from the past and which he shares with his fellows" (1). A *society* is "an association of people, large or small in number, who have a common set of habits, attitudes, and ideas sufficient to hold them together" (2).

Within societies, smaller groups may be found which are called *sub-societies*. If various groupings within these sub-societies have significantly different attitudes, values, and customs among themselves, we may classify them as

How Society Molds the Individual

What is culture? What is society? How does society influence our behavior? To what extent does society influence our behavior? What are the stages of social development? What are some of the problems of social living? What is the role of psychology in helping to solve social problems? How has society changed in recent years? How can you benefit by a knowledge of how society influences your behavior?

social classes. A *social caste* is an extension of a social class, or a more rigidly separate class. In a caste system there is little communication between one caste and another. Marriage between members of different castes, for example, is disapproved throughout the society.

Culture includes the ideas which have become part of the human heritage, and, of course, the products of those ideas. Inventions such as the wheel and the many uses man has made if it, the evolution of clothing, the cultivation of crops and the domestication of animals, the development of tools, shelters, and weapons for hunting and fighting all are parts of our total culture. But the term implies much more than physical or tangible phenomena. The languages we speak, our ways of expressing ourselves, and our attitudes and ways of thinking are also part of culture. So are our social institutions: our laws, religions, folk ways, and codes of conduct as well as marriage ceremonies, football games, public schools, and business methods. In short, culture implies everything that man has invented or discovered and has taken to his own use in a particularly human way. Culture is transmitted from generation to generation, from family to family and person to person. Thus it is not necessary for every generation, or every individual, to discover fire or invent the telephone. These and countless other elements of our civilization are the result of accumulated learning and experience which dates back many centuries, even many thousands of years.

But we not only speak of culture in this collective sense, in reference to the total human inheritance. We also speak of *particular* cultures, such as those of ancient Egypt, the later Roman Republic, the United States in the twentieth century, or the Navajo Indians of Arizona and New Mexico. In this sense, all human cultures possess certain elements in common. They all, for instance, possess a language, use fire, employ tools and instruments, have clothing, and make use of shelter. But they may differ radically in the kind of language, the way they use fire, the complexity and efficiency of their tools and instruments, and the sophistication and elaborateness of their clothing and shelter. And there are many elements in the culture of the midtown New Yorker which the Navajo has never dreamed of. And yet there is a great deal of borrowing and overlapping between one culture and another, as few nations have better reason to know than the United States, where English, Irish, German, Polish, Russian, and Chinese can all rub elbows on a city street.

Because cultures develop over countless years, and because peoples of various cultures have from time immemorial traded with each other, fought, and intermingled in other ways, the culture in which we in this country live today is a conglomeration of ideas and behaviors gained from various groups and many historical eras. Some of our cultural traditions, the use of a wedding ring and a bridal veil, for example, are widely used by people who have no idea of their original purpose and meaning. Some aspects of culture, such as the development of atomic power, may arise before society has gained the ability to use them successfully. Others, however, such as the continuation of prohibition into the 1930's may linger although many segments of society feel they are outdated and decide to abide by them no longer.

According to our definition, the term *society* could be used to designate a band of nomads on the Sahara desert. If this band were affiliated with other bands, we might also say that their society was part of a much larger society. A certain political area can also constitute a society, while some such areas may include more than one society. For example, we may consider the Norwegians and the Laplanders as two separate societies, since their cultures are somewhat different, although insofar as they inhabit overlapping geographical areas, they might be called one society.

Sub-societies, of course, exist all around us. In America there are many subgroups in large cities where people come from a variety of nations and heritages. Various Indian tribes, Mexican-American people, and the Puerto Ricans in America represent other sub-societies.

How is society important to us? What aspects of culture influence us? Our first problem is to determine what types of behavior our society demands. A second problem is to determine which of these demands must be heeded and which ones may be ignored; moreover, we often find that the demands conflict. On the other hand, some cultural institutions can aid us in solving our problems. Which types of behavior should we disregard or cultivate? College students often pride themselves on being "modern," but what *is* modern and acceptable?

SOCIAL INSTITUTIONS IN DIFFERENT CULTURES. *Marriage customs are a distinctive part of cultural patterns.*

UNITED STATES. Tossing the bride's bouquet is a traditional custom following the usual wedding ceremony in America. (Arkansas Industrial Development Commission.)

YUGOSLAVIA. Behind the banner-carrier is a horse loaded with the bride's trousseau. (Dever, from Black Star.)

GERMANY. A spirited band goes to announce the approaching wedding parade. (Dever, from Black Star.)

INDONESIA. The bride's father holds the bride and the groom on his lap and to the question from his wife, "Which is heavier?" he answers, "They are of equal weight." This means that the groom will be given rights and position equal to the bride by his in-laws. (Pan-Asia Photo News, from Black Star.)

● A. SOCIETY, PERSONALITY, AND BEHAVIOR

The observable influences of culture are well known. All of us know something about the mode of dress, implements, housing, customs, and behavior of the early American Indians. Most of us are somewhat familiar with the cultures of the Chinese and Japanese, the ancient Romans, the peoples of Mexico, Western cowboys, Southern planters, and so on. But to *study* societies and cultures in order to determine how they influence personality and behavior is quite another story. Such anthropologists as Margaret Mead and Ruth Benedict have made careful analyses of primitive societies which suggest that these peoples have considerably different outlooks on life than those of contemporary Americans. And you probably already realize from your own experience that people who were brought up in other parts of the world do not view situations in the same way you do, and that people of greatly different cultural backgrounds often do not understand each other.

For example, in the United States we may raise our voices to emphasize a point. To the Chinese, however, loudness is associated chiefly with anger and loss of self-control. Another example is that we in America usually try to respond promptly to appointments made for a definite time, yet the Arabians feel that such strict adherence to a schedule is unnecessary. In Arab countries, too, one must stay at least three days when paying a call to the house of a sheik. The first day is for preparing the feast, the second for enjoying it, and the third for tapering off and saying good-by (3). India has its unique ideas on cleanliness. We are told that Indian women viewing a film of a baby being bathed in a bathinette felt sorry for the child. How could Americans be so inhuman as to bathe a child in stagnant (not running) water?

Cultures not only influence manners, time schedules, and ideas of cleanliness but they also determine motivations and expressions of emotions. Consider the following illustrations.

Salteaux Indian society

The Salteaux (4) live near Lake Winnipeg in Canada. The population consists largely of hunters and fishermen by trade, and numbers between nine hundred and a thousand persons. Few white people come in contact with these Indians, and those are chiefly traders, trappers, missionaries, or prospectors. The Salteaux are a patient, peace-loving, placid people. They seem to be characterized by cooperation, laughter, harmony, and self-control. They do not engage in war with white people or with other Indians. Murder, suicide, and theft are almost unknown among them. Open expressions of anger seldom occur. There is a mutual helpfulness and a sharing of goods so that no one is much better off than his neighbor.

Yet this picture of an idyllic people needs further examination; such a lack of aggressiveness seems to us unnatural. Further study showed that hostility and aggression *are* prevalent among the Salteaux. These feelings are expressed through rather unusual and indirect channels so that they simply were not easily recognized at first. The Salteaux frequently gossip about each other and say unpleasant things behind each other's backs that they would not say face to face. They express aggression through sorcery and magic, in the belief that thus a man can injure his enemy without the enemy's knowledge, so that he will not retaliate by displaying anger or seeking revenge. They believe they can make an enemy fall ill, lose his economic goods, lose the love and respect of his wife and children, suffer other perils, and even die. Yet when these people meet, they show no hostility. The enemy may suspect antagonism, but he cannot be sure of it. And when a person has the misfortune to meet with an accident or to fall ill, it is only natural for him to suspect that he has an enemy who has been exercising magic upon him. The result is, of course, that the witchdoctor is summoned to exert counter-measures.

After this closer look we begin to picture this society as one in which individuals tend to repress natural hostility and find it difficult to deal with aggressive tendencies, displaying them only in indirect and covert ways. Every cast of ill fortune — the loss of wild game from a trap, sickness, or marital infidelity — is viewed as the working of an enemy. The result of this attitude is a tendency to delusions and even hallucinations. One writer has said that the outlook of the people is almost an invitation to paranoia.[1] Even after this brief description we can readily see that what is normal behavior for the Salteaux is certainly not normal behavior for us.

[1] Hallowell (4) says: "the ground is well prepared . . . for the development of paranoid or pseudo-paranoid trends in individuals." *Paranoia* is a type of mental illness in which the person has delusions, often imagining that people are doing things to him or saying things about him. See Chapter 13 for a further explanation.

Magic as an outlet for aggression. *This Salteaux Indian "doctor," more than 80 years old at the time of this picture, was the oldest man in his village and a head of the medicine lodge. He was believed to have power to cure disease or to cause sickness and death. (A. Irving Hallowell.)*

Arapesh society

This group of New Guinea natives had had little interaction with white persons or other natives when they were first studied. They are a small group and operate as an almost communal society (5). One of their interesting customs is their particular way of training a leader for certain enterprises like warfare, trading with other native tribes, or moving a village to a new location.

The Arapesh avoid leadership or any attempt to influence others to do their will. They seem to be almost afraid of responsibility. Thus small boys are not encouraged to exhibit leadership tendencies, and the adults generally work together cooperatively as a result of group decisions. They disapprove of ownership and hoarding. If one person starts a garden, someone else may till it for him, he in turn working for still another. The produce is stored and shared among the tribe. One does not build his own house — others build it for him, and he cooperates in building theirs.

Since, however, times *do* arise when leadership is needed, the elders of the tribe designate some small boys to train for future leadership. One of the boys will eventually become the leader, while the others will be allowed to go back to the more peaceful existence in the tribe. Meanwhile, however, the boys are encouraged to compete with each other on every level, to boast and show off and call each other names. In a word, they are to demonstrate most of the qualities which the Arapesh generally abhor and consider obnoxious. When the time comes in their development to demonstrate their leadership qualities,

Non-competitive play in the Arapesh society. *The children are playing at being wallabies (small kangaroos). In other games also, they unite as a cooperative group instead of opposing each other as individuals or teams. (Margaret Mead.)*

one of the boys is chosen. He must ever after exhibit the "bad form" of being better than the others through his assumption of leadership.

Children are greatly loved among the Arapesh. They meet friendly and affectionate responses from almost everyone, and they can share homes or dinners with almost any family. As a consequence, they are friendly and generous in return. Concern and thoughtfulness for the children even extends to training them as congenial marital partners. Betrothals are arranged by the parents when children are as young as six, and the girl moves into the home of the boy and lives as a member of his family. The girl is generally the younger member of the pair by some years, and it is part of the boy's responsibility to bring up his own future wife. It is not felt that the parents of the bride-to-be lose their daughter at this tender age; rather that she now has two families, and still belongs to her own household even though she lives in that of her future husband. The system has the immense advantage that because the two young people have so much the same background during the maturing years, they will very likely develop a community of tastes and experiences which is impossible in a culture such as ours.

There are a great many other ways in which the Arapesh culture differs from our own, but it is easy to see how profoundly different from ours their states of mind must be. Their looking with disfavor on competition and leadership and abhorring the wish to assume responsibility gives them a wholly different view of what a person must do to succeed in life. And the fact that their approach to marriage is rational and practical leaves no room for the moonlight-and-roses type of romanticism which gives many of our own young people distorted notions of what love and marriage are really like. Our values about courtship and marriage markedly differ from theirs.

Kwakiutl society

The Kwakiutl Indians, of the northwest coast of America, are of considerable interest because their life values were colored by a wholly different concept of wealth and a wholly different economic system from ours (6). Among the Kwakiutl, economic wealth was not looked upon as a means to gain an equivalent value in economic goods. Rather, their units of wealth were counters of fixed value in a game they played to gain social prestige and personal aggrandizement. They looked upon life as a struggle in which everyone sought to rise socially and to win titles of nobility. Climbing the social ladder required the ability to distribute wealth to others, but not as a gift; rather as a loan which had to be repaid in a year's time with 100 per cent interest.

The main reason these people cared about wealth, titles of nobility, and the prerogatives associated with family names was simply that these were used in a life-long contest in which each sought to shame his rivals and at the same time to rise in the social system. Each person vied constantly with everyone else to distribute the most property. If a person received a gift, which he must

A Kwakiutl potlatch. *This ceremonial feast is an example of the habitual aggression of the Kwakiutl people. From the description in the text, try to predict the next stage in this distribution of blankets. (The Smithsonian Institution.)*

repay with interest, he could not refuse without admitting defeat at the outset. If the repayment time came and he could not do his share, he was shamed and the rival's prestige soared. If he was successful, the struggle went on, involving larger pieces of property. The pervading motive was a desire to show one's success and superiority, as indicated by the singing of vain songs of self-glorification and the reviling of others in scornful language.

At various times a chief might give a *potlatch*. This was a feast in which quantities of goods were consumed, among them large amounts of fish oil. This was fed to the guests and some was poured on the fire. Increasing the fire in this way caused some of the nearer guests to become very warm, and if they moved, they were shamed again. If the feast surpassed any the guest had ever given, he must make immediate preparations for an even more spectacular event, in return. If the guest felt that it had not equalled one he had given, he insulted the host, who in turn tried other measures of self-enhancement. He might destroy a copper coin of some value, kill a slave, destroy some of his canoes, or find other ways of wasting economic goods and wealth.

This society appears to have fostered aggression. The members were brought up with feelings of inferiority and had continually to strive to overcome them; they tried to gain and maintain status, and were notably lacking in feelings of security. This condition is quite different from the emotional tone of the Arapesh, who are dedicated to self-effacement and lack of arrogance.

Understandings from these cultural groups

Many of the characteristics ascribed to these groups have changed as explorers, missionaries, military groups, and others have penetrated their tribal areas and brought outside influences with them. However, in their original unspoiled states, these societies provided enough information so that we could come to understand a good deal about the impacts of a culture upon the entire group which possessed it, and upon its individual members. We should not be surprised to find that societies differ greatly in what can be called normal or abnormal behavior. The normal Arapesh is different in many ways from the normal Kwakiutl or Salteaux in his ethics, values, and related life activities. Thus a person cannot be judged in terms of the conformity of his behavior to *our* standards, but must be considered in relation to the standards of *his own society*. We have learned that not all men are motivated by the same values and goals. What others seek in life may be quite different from what we seek, and their values are as valid and defensible to them as ours are to us. We come to see the futility of attempting to impose our culture forcibly upon an alien society, as various nations have all too often attempted through colonization or missionary efforts. In dealing with other nations in world affairs, whether it be in peace, cold war, or war itself, a deep understanding of their cultures is necessary to an understanding of their actions. We cannot interpret behavior in other cultures as we would the same behavior in our own.

The implications of what we have said about the Arapesh, Kwakiutl, and Salteaux can be applied to the college campus, with of course the appropriate modifications. Judging the actions of others in terms of how *we* would have acted or what *our* motives might have been can often be quite unfair. It is only natural for us to assume that *our* set of values is the proper one, and that the values of others must be wrong if they differ from ours. All too often we attempt to convert others to *our* way of thinking without being willing to consider theirs. We stereotype behavior without considering cultural or individual differences. Although American sub-cultures do not differ so markedly as do those of the primitive groups we have been discussing, real differences in points of view may exist on the campus.

These differences provide one of the advantages of college life. Since you

Understanding cultural groups. *In international relations and world affairs, it is increasingly important that people have a knowledge of the differences among cultures, so that they can understand the attitudes and actions of particular nations. Representatives of Togoland here participate in a meeting of the United Nations Trusteeship Council. (United Nations.)*

will have an opportunity to discuss many things with many different people, your opportunities for understanding others and broadening your own point of view will be enhanced.

Suggested activities

1. Describe "the" American culture. Can you define it?

2. How does the sub-group in which you were raised differ from others?

3. List some of the sub-cultures or sub-societies in your city, on your campus, or in another geographical area.

4. Have you found certain of your ideas to be quite different from those generally held by your classmates? Can you explain why this should be?

5. Anthropological studies other than those discussed have been made by Mead, Benedict, and others. Report orally on some of them.

A.   SOCIETY, PERSONALITY, AND BEHAVIOR

● B.   BECOMING A SOCIAL BEING

Every child is born into a society to which he must learn to adjust. The society in which he lives will pass judgment on whether his actions throughout his life are right or wrong, and it will exert controls over his development as a social being. Because he is a member of a family, the child learns particular standards, mores, and ways of living. He lives in a certain neighborhood and attends a certain church. The schools influence him through the curriculum, the values of his teachers, and his peer groups. His goals are partially set through the influence of the group he belongs to. His language assists him in thinking and communicating. As the child matures, his ways of eating, sleeping, greeting others, and making love depend in part on the social groups or groups of which he is a member. Let us consider now how this process, which may be called *socialization*, proceeds.

Early socialization starts with the family.   The neonate is *asocial*, rather than antisocial, since he is a member of a society but does not yet know how to behave like one. He is wholly selfish in the satisfaction of his needs, for he does not understand the value of cooperating with others for mutual bene-fit. If we consider the physical inadequacies of the infant — his inability to localize sensory stimuli, to control his body effectively, and to interpret his needs specifically, we can scarcely be surprised that he is totally incapable of considering himself as a social being. But he has a vast advantage over the young of other animals in the ability to learn complex behavior, including speech.

Their social innocence notwithstanding, neonates exhibit differing personalities almost from birth (7), probably because of differing heredities. Responses to food, emotional stimuli, and body movements differ even among very young children. Some appear to be nervous, others more calm and even-tempered. They need different amounts of sleep, and they differ in their ability to ingest and digest food. The ability to learn is influenced by heredity, and from birth onward children differ in the amount they learn. Social adjustment may well be much easier for some children than for others.

At birth the neonate cannot identify specific people, indeed, it is questionable whether he can distinguish between people, objects, and himself (8, 9). He does, however, experience social relationships. His mother feeds him, bathes and clothes him, and fondles him. Children who receive affectionate treatment from their parents at an early age are thought to develop more emotional security than those who are treated more impersonally (10). At about the age of two and a half months the child can distinguish people and relate their presence to the feelings of pleasure he associates with the satisfaction of his needs. He begins to "like company." At about the fourth month, the infant is able to smile at people with meaning (11) and to reach out to be picked up. He shows reactions to the emotions and behavior of others. He appears to recognize friends or acquaintances, and reacts differently to strangers and to people he knows. Later the small child attempts to imitate speech and to copy the actions of others, especially those of older children. Shyness is often demonstrated at about the fifteenth month, and when he is about eighteen months old the child may exhibit resistance to the demands of adults (12).

During these early months and years personality is being molded. Overprotection, rejection, or neglect influence personality characteristics; an infant so treated may begin to develop dependency, depression, anxieties, or other abnormal emotional behavior. The emotionally deprived child may exhibit temper tantrums, attention-seeking, defective language development, constant shifting of attention from one person to another, impulsive behavior, and an inability to form normal relationships with others (13).

The mother–child relationship is especially important in personality development. The child soon learns how his mother feels about him through the affection she shows — or fails to show — in handling him, and her quick or slow response to his cries for food or other aid. He learns how to respond to her and she to him, and mutual satisfaction of emotional needs is achieved. In fact, one of the reasons why doctors and psychologists recommend breast feeding rather than bottle-feeding is the emotional satisfaction it accords both mother and child.

As he develops within the family the child is constantly learning to adjust to society. He is given help and encouragement in learning to walk, talk, eat, drink, and in countless other ways. He learns what his particular family considers good or bad behavior. In short, he is forming a basis for a system of values and a basis for his relationships with other people.

At first the child lives rather completely within his own family group. Later he finds that there are other children in the neighborhood, and important adults other than his parents. At first he enjoys playing in the company of other children, rather than actually playing *with* them, although he may explore everything he can about them. Later, perhaps about the age of three, he can begin to share his toys and develop little games or projects with friends.

Early childhood continues the process of socialization. By the age of two most children have developed a small vocabulary and can both formulate and respond to simple language requests (14). Vocabulary development and the use of language increase rapidly, so that by the age of six, children can communicate well with their parents and with each other. They have learned to count and can use abstractions in their language.

Three- and four-year-old children experience a period of heightened emotionality. Their desires are often beyond their ability to satisfy them. They find it hard to dress themselves, they feel that toys do not behave, and that eating properly is difficult. A desire for independence from their parents is coupled with the emotional need for closeness to them. Keep in mind that our furniture and everyday living equipment is usually built for adults, not for children. To realize how significant a problem this can be for a child, drop to your hands and knees and move about. This may give you some idea of how the mere size of household objects dwarfs the child and can profoundly influence his state of mind. Children are extremely active, and as a result, they tire frequently. (Try doing everything a four-year-old child does for an hour or two. Can you keep up with him?)

Children of ages three to six need the opportunity to play with others. A great deal of social learning is attained through such childhood activities. At first the play may be parallel — that is, children may play side by side, yet independently. But as the child develops socially, he becomes more able to take part in cooperative activities. Children at this age are great pretenders. They learn through playing "house," "store," "cops and robbers," or "cowboys." Because the manner in which a person sees himself is a reflection of what others appear to think of him, playmates help to develop the self-concept.

Children who have been subjected to over-stern or authoritarian discipline, who are rejected emotionally, or are overprotected, or who are either more or less rapid in development than their fellows, may not adjust readily to their playmates. The concerns of children between the ages of two and six are still more often related to the attitudes of their parents than to those of other children, however; and if parents are overdemanding, children may develop insecurity and inadequate self-concepts. Parental behavior is copied. Ways of living and attitudes toward behavior are imitated. Social development is either furthered or retarded, sometimes permanently, by the relationships within the home.

School-age children develop socially in a new world. From the age of

Sex roles in society. *Very young children do not understand the differentiation of the sex roles. The child who persists in playing games associated with the opposite sex, however, is likely to be called a "tomboy" or "sissy." (Nationwide Insurance Company; Carroll Seghers II, from Black Star.)*

six to about twelve, the child is in a new and demanding environment. While his family is still the most important social influence upon him, he is finding his teacher and his schoolmates of tremendous importance. Moreover, he may sense that his ways of behavior and attitudes toward his own behavior may need adjusting in terms of this wider social circle. He must learn to adjust to the classroom, the playground, the neighborhood, and the peer group, while seeing his family in an ever more mature light.

For most children the "gang" is paramount, especially during the later years of childhood. The older child is no longer the self-centered individual that he was as a youngster, and is beginning to learn the values of belonging to and cooperating with the group. Usually peer groups develop among children of the same sex (15) — indeed, the boy or girl approaching adolescence may actually tend to "reject" the opposite sex. As we have seen, girls tend to mature more rapidly than boys, and differences in behavior and attitudes inevitably result. At the time girls begin to show interest in social events such as parties or dances, boys of the same age are still in the "rough house" stage. Perhaps the American culture today does not differentiate between the sexes as much as it did formerly — today girls play baseball and even football, they swim, skate, camp, and in general keep up with the boys in many sports and activities. They may even surpass them in some. It is still true, however, that girls are taught a somewhat different role than boys. Girls are expected to enjoy playing with dolls, to like doll houses, and to play "house" or "tea-party." Parents still expect them to be more quiet and lady-like, and to keep their clothes cleaner. They are provided with equipment and opportunities to practice at an early age their future roles as women. Boys are expected not to be "sissies" and to be noisy and grimy and to enjoy rough play. Girls are permitted to express emotions more openly, and they are privileged to cry without shame when hurt or frustrated. Boys are supposed to be "men," and "men don't cry."

From about nine to age twelve the peer group likes to have a place in which to meet, especially if it can be private and unsupervised by adults. Boys may be more troublesome than girls in their activities and often experiment with smoking, drinking, and gambling. Some become delinquent, of course, but mischief, rather than outright law-breaking, is usual. (Girls, of course, may also become members of troublesome gangs. In fact, in certain large cities gangs including both delinquent girls and boys have been known; the girls were sometimes "auxiliaries" to the boys, and carried the weapons when the boys went out to fight rival gangs.) In more normal groups, however, girls are more likely to take an interest in social activities than boys, to have endless discussions of who likes whom, how to interest "so-and-so" and how to win the attention of boys. This is the age of telephone conversations, and parents of children in later childhood and early adolescence often become mystified as well as irritated at the extent and nature of some of these gossip and sparring sessions by remote control.

Conformity to the group is important. Perhaps feeling somewhat insecure in the group, the average youngster will conform wholeheartedly to group standards in dress, language, and behavior. When parents come into conflict with these standards, the latter may often win out in the minds of children nearing adolescence. In the group the child learns to cooperate, to compete with others, to accept responsibility, to control his emotions, to become a leader, and, in general, to adjust socially to his peer group (16).

Adolescence is a period of emancipation from the home. Not only does rapid physical change occur in adolescence, but social and emotional changes accompany this physical maturation. This is a period in which boys and girls learn to accept themselves as nearly mature members of society. It is a time for adjusting to a new view of members of the opposite sex — they are seen not merely as playmates or companions, but as future marital partners. Concern for future vocations, higher education, for religion, politics, and codes of morals which can be accepted intellectually, not merely because of adult pressures, are all concerns of adolescents. Needs for acceptance by the peer group, for learning self-confidence, and for emancipation from childhood behavior are characteristic. Many adolescents, because of physical changes and the knowledge that they soon must accept adult roles, exhibit self-consciousness and heightened emotionality. Some are somewhat preoccupied with sex, at least during the earlier stages of body change. Some may exhibit excessive modesty, others experiment, and many daydream excessively.

The popular boy or girl is one who has several intimate friends, belongs to a clique, and is a member of the school crowd. He is happy and secure and has the self-confidence necessary to develop the social adjustments and leadership abilities which will add even more to his popularity. The popular youths are usually active, extroverted, and aggressive. They are cooperative, considerate of the wishes of others, resourceful, loyal to the group, and contribute to the group the talents they possess. Contrary to popular opinion, such a boy or girl is also likely to be well mannered, neat and clean, and acceptable to parents and other adults as well as to adolescents.

Parties, dances, and other amusements which include both sexes become important. The proper attire (especially as it reflects the current fad) and the proper "line" of talk are needed to prove that one is in the swim. Critical of themselves, adolescents are also critical of others, and are hence often interested in championing social service activities — the improvement of society and the bettering of the lives of "underdogs." Boys enjoy team games, and these help them to build personal prestige. Sports activities in which girls can participate, such as tennis, swimming, ice skating, and dancing, are now also more popular than they used to be with boys alone. Such hobbies as shop work, music, and art are beginning to require a high degree of skill. Many young people enjoy exploring and camping — witness the success of the Youth Hostels in certain parts of the country. Many teen-agers earn a share of their vacation expenses working at summer camps or dude ranches. Others build themselves up physically and earn money in preparation for college through construction jobs, farm work, and factory labor.

Movies, radio, and television influence various modes of self-expression among young people, such as their language, clothing, tastes and even hairdos. Unfortunately the disk jockey is perhaps even more influential in developing the esthetic tastes of adolescents. At many dances adolescents do not attend so much to dance as to observe and enjoy a popular band or a favorite performer. The artist need not be a particularly good musician, but if he exhibits something unique, he frequently has a claim on popularity. Actors, songsters, and other stars influence dress, ways of speaking, and even consciously cultivated mannerisms. The craze for motorcycles, which sprang up after the appearance of certain movies in which they were featured, is a striking example. We may well be deeply concerned with the ultimate effect which the mass media of communication — notably the movies, radio, and television — may have on the quality of our culture and the standards and values of our people, especially the young.

It is also characteristic of young people to think a good deal about the future. Most have ambitions, and want to make something of themselves, although their ideas about what they will do may change fairly often. For most boys a tour of duty in the Armed Forces looms large on the horizon, though this is more often thought of as an interruption than as part of a chosen career. The ambitions of girls frequently center on the world of entertainment, and many think of themselves as potential airline hostesses.

Almost universal among adolescents is the "crush." A member of the opposite sex, the object of affection may be a teacher, an admired adult, a star in sports or entertainment, or a boy friend or girl friend nearer the person's own age. Some adolescent attachments actually ripen into mature affection and even marriage, for teen-age emotions can be as real and lasting as those of any other age. Because interest in the opposite sex arouses the need for attention from the object of interest, adolescents are sometimes prone to show off, tease, exhibit bravado, and make wisecracks, especially during the early teen years.

Young adulthood. College students are going through the early years of maturity, years which produce social problems. One study of college men indicated that common worries included social adjustments (17). Characteristic of these problems are shyness, social sensitivity, worry over making friends and getting along with girls, problems of family adjustment, difficulties in regard to a career, finances, academic problems, sex, and personal adjustment.

Young adults are prone to snobbishness and social discrimination. They are going through a period strongly resistant to adult authority. It is a time during which many young men are called into military service, with consequent frustrations in emotional life related to one's "steady" — frustrations for both women and men. Often, too, there are difficulties in getting the money to finish college, and accompanying worries about the effect of quitting and trying to get a job in business or industry. Marriage, though a desirable and reasonable goal, is possible only for those who can support some sort of home. The desire for an automobile is as great as during the earlier "hot rod" days

Influences in socialization. *Movies and television influence the social behavior of children and adolescents. (Georgia-Pacific Corporation.)*

of high school, except that now the car must be more respectable. School, with its responsibilities and the limitations on action which it imposes, seems to inhibit the freedom young adults crave.

In young adults, feelings of inferiority give way to self-assertiveness, and, as was pointed out above, snobbishness is common. Friends are more carefully chosen, and must be acceptable to both sexes. Athletic, social, and intellectual leaders emerge. Interests include parties, world affairs, appearance, careers, social groups, and sports. Because athletics now demand a higher degree of skill, more people become spectators than participitants. Games which involve thinking are more popular. Hobbies, dancing, and reading assume greater importance. Religious beliefs are questioned and newer concepts developed. Moral behavior is based less on imitation or enforcement than on individual convictions about what is right, developed through discussion with others and attempts at intellectual determination. Dating and going steady increase, and marriage is seriously considered.

While it may seem unecessary for us to characterize your age group, you are now in a position to see the general changes in outlook and behavior which have taken place in you and your friends up to this time. With this basis for comparison with other age groups, it is hoped that you will see the orderly progression of changes which take place as people mature. Changes do not cease at maturity but continue throughout life.

At this point it is perhaps worth saying again that it is important to measure yourself against the criteria of maturity. You cannot influence what has already happened to you. You can, however, change some aspects of your personality, even though such changes are perhaps more difficult now than they would have been earlier. But other important changes are yet to come — as a result of making a home of your own, raising a family, and, later, of growing old.

Middle age and senescence.   The middle years are largely devoted to marrying, raising a family, attaining business or professional success, and preparing for the age of retirement. These years need not here be discussed in detail, for they merely continue the mature functions we have mentioned in connection with young adults. They do, of course, represent a continuous process of adjustment, as does any age. But one has the prime advantage of being accepted as a completely adult member of society whose opinions are valued, whose work is recognized, and who is taking his place in the community as a respected citizen. If one is willing to assume the various adult responsibilities of a community-minded adult, he finds middle age satisfying.

But new problems begin to appear in later middle age and in senescence, roughly from age fifty-five onward. As one becomes less active and as his sensory functions decline, it becomes progressively difficult to engage in active social living, although when the effort is made it is usually satisfying. A grave psychological problem lies in the reactions which some people experience when it becomes apparent that they are growing old. When women realize that they can no longer bear children, one of the main social satisfactions of our civilization, they sometimes feel superannuated and as if life is over. Similarly, men discover that in some respects they can no longer compete with younger men, that certain jobs require physical abilities they no longer have, and they are sometimes disturbed and depressed as a result. Aging appearance is also a source of disappointment and anxiety, especially in our society which idolizes the adolescent and the young adult. In some societies older persons are more respected than in ours. Their opinions — the result of many years of living — are more highly respected, and they take on status and authority as heads of a family group extending down through children, grandchildren, and even beyond.

In our society, with its emphasis on being up-to-date and on holding the newest ideas, older people are in danger of being pushed aside. Friends, neighbors, and children leave, because of the mobility of our population, the growing-up of children (who now have familes of their own), and death. Job opportunities are fewer, and retirement, which often brings with it a feeling of uselessness, is in the offing. Financial difficulties beset many of our old people, for in spite of various pension plans and benefits, most older people do not have an income sufficient to live as comfortably as they did in their earlier years. Eventually it becomes impossible for the older person to live alone because he cannot take care of his needs. This situation creates problems of housing. He may move in with his children, go into a "home," or remain in his own home with paid help; but whatever he does, he lives on a diminished scale.

People growing older who are isolated, less able to communicate, less active, and less useful to society, may develop poor mental health. Some persons become more rigid in their thinking. Others become suspicious, dependent, or hostile, or show emotional disturbances in other ways. Persons in whom physical changes have impaired the supply of blood to the brain may become victims of senile psychoses, requiring hospitalization and expert care. Many become absent-minded, show failing memory and tend to live in the past.

The problems of the aged are receiving increasing attention and study by many groups and individuals, partly because the proportion of older people in our population is steadily increasing. The average life expectancy is now about 70 years, and, because of better public health work and medical care, it is increasing. Such persons as Bernard Baruch, Albert Schweitzer, and others who have remained active and useful well into their later years show that this period of life can be satisfying and effective. Two things are necessary for satisfactory living in these years — planning in advance, and enlightened treatment of the aging. In preparation for older age, many industries are educating for retirement, showing what financial benefits workers will have, where they can live most happily, and how they can remain useful. Hobbies and other recreational pursuits, interest and activity in community welfare programs, opportunities for young and old to enjoy recreation together, and clubs for the aging are among the means employed to help older persons remain happy and useful. Many industries are finding it expedient to keep older workers on the job, for they are often less prone to absenteeism, are more careful, and show greater knowledge of the work than do younger people. Religious groups are also interested in the aging, for a sound religious outlook in old age has considerable psychological benefit.

The immediate importance to you of the problems of aging, as we indicated earlier, is that awareness of these problems can help your present consideration of the older members of your family. Ultimately it can help you in your own preparation for later old age. For yourself, you should maintain your physical health and make your activities conform to your age, especially as you get older. You should consider the problems of older age and prepare to alleviate them or to adjust to them. A hobby, financial solvency, interest in the community, good habits of emotional adjustment, keeping up your circle of friends, making yourself valuable at your work, keeping in touch with your family — these are some of the things which you can consider now, as well as later, in preparation for your later life.

Suggested activities

1. Try a group discussion to see how you and your classmates differ in the ways in which your families and neighborhoods handled such matters as dating, dress, athletics, entertainment, discipline, money matters, books and music, religion, and education.

2. Observe children of various ages. Ascertain the extent to which their behavior conforms to the characteristics we listed for different age levels.

3. Do you agree with our analyses of the characteristics of various ages? What evidence can you gather to support your views?

4. How do poetry, articles, and pictures in high school papers or annuals compare with those in college publications? Do you find that in college books there is evidence of greater maturity?

A.   SOCIETY, PERSONALITY, AND BEHAVIOR

B.   BECOMING A SOCIAL BEING

● C.   PROBLEMS OF SOCIAL LIVING

In general, if a person lives in the United States, the chances are good that we can predict quite a few things about him. For example, he probably has a high standard of living, compared with people of most other nations. Americans have more telephones, automobiles, and electrical appliances, better food, and other material advantages than most other peoples. We probably have more opportunity for education, and for learning from books, magazines, and newspapers. In addition to material advantages, America enjoys certain political values. Founded on the idea of democracy, the United States has developed a political structure which emphasizes the value of the individual and generally

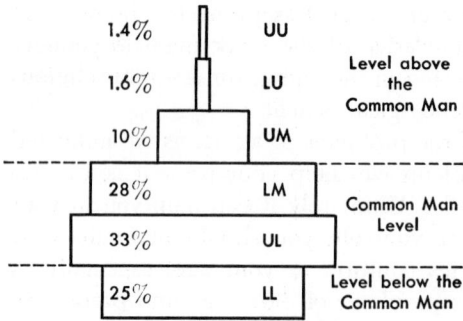

Social classes in a New England city. *The divisions were based on occupation, place of residence, prestige, and club membership. (W. L. Warner:* American Life: Dream and Reality, *revised form of the author's* The Structure of American Life *[Chicago] University of Chicago Press, 1953.)*

attempts to protect his freedom. Freedom of religion, freedom of speech, and equality before the law, while perhaps not yet sufficiently practiced, are probably more in evidence here than in most other parts of the globe.

American society is mobile. Many of our people change their jobs or places of residence frequently. The United States is now preponderantly industrialized and urban. You, as an American, can probably add many other characteristics of Americans to this listing.

Social classes in America

A number of illuminating attempts have been made by sociologists to classify communities according to social class structure. A classification of this sort is usually based on such factors as source and amount of income, kind of housing, type of neighborhood, and cultural advantages offered by the home. For purposes of this kind of study we often recognize upper class, middle class, and lower class groups, each being, in turn, divided into "upper" and "lower," i.e., upper-upper, lower-upper, upper-middle, etc.

The upper social class, comprising a small per cent of the total population, includes mostly business owners and managers, some professional people, and exceptional artists in various fields. The middle class includes white-collar workers, some farmers, skilled workers, and many technicians in the transportation, communication, and service fields. The lower social class includes some skilled, most semi-skilled and unskilled laborers, migrant workers, and the lowest-paid service people. Many factors, besides occupation, are associated with social class status. Extent and kind of education, length of time the family has held a particular class position, and source of income (inherited wealth ranks highest) are all factors in determining class status, though the structure of the various classes varies somewhat.

The purpose of this brief discussion of social classes is to provide some background for a description of the mores and customs of the middle class as compared to those of the upper and lower classes. It should be borne in mind that a person's set of values is in part derived from imitation of his family and friends, and is in part imposed upon him by public opinion. His behavior in different situations will vary as a result of these two sets of influences.

Generally speaking, the American middle class strives upward. Those belonging to the lower middle class attempt to climb to upper middle class, and so on. This upward movement is achieved in part by obtaining an income and a standard of living commensurate with those of a higher class, and in part by achieving some distinction in a field which is ordinarily characteristic of the higher class (18). Obviously, this struggle for betterment puts a premium on education. Children of middle-class parents are encouraged to obtain more education and to achieve higher success than their parents. Emphasis on grades in school, a college education, on the advantages of studying art, music, dancing, etc., is common. The pressure of competition and the constant striving to better oneself may put the middle-class youngster under a special strain. In contrast in some lower-class families education beyond the legal minimum is considered a waste of time, and children are urged to accept adult responsibilities such as getting a job and marrying early.

Members of the middle class tend to be conservative and to look with a degree of suspicion at radical changes in religion, politics, economics, or other aspects of what they may vaguely think of as the "American way of life." This view compares favorably with the upper-class attitude, since these two groups have apparently most to lose in any change, and have been successful in dealing with business or politics as they now exist, so that any change may pose a threat to these groups. On the other hand, a person who belongs to a group which has relatively few advantages may hope to better himself by a change, and so tend to be liberal or radical. Such leanings are, in general, more common in the lower classes, but are not as common in our country at present as in countries that have changed governments more recently. It may be noted that if one has conservative values, a conservative code of conduct and of morals will result. The middle class favors orderly change, perhaps again as a result of pressure to maintain or improve status.

The members of every social class expect their children to follow certain lines of conduct and adhere to certain values. Davis and Havighurst (19) have shown that from class to class, child-rearing differs in regard to child feeding, toilet training, sex training, and other infant and child behavior which psychologists consider of importance to the personality and adjustment of the adult. For example more lower-class children are exclusively breast fed, and are fed at will. Weaning takes place earlier, on the average, among middle-class children. More lower-class children are weaned sharply, at least among Negro families. Middle-class fathers spend more time with their children in educational activities such as reading and taking walks. Middle-class children more often help the parents at home but are not permitted as much freedom outside the home without supervision. Middle-class girls are expected to help with younger children and to sew at an earlier age, but lower-class children are expected to get jobs after school, and to quit school and go to work at an earlier age.

From the above information and from other evidence, certain inferences have been drawn. For instance, middle-class families are more rigorous than lower-class families in training their children in habits of feeding and cleanliness. They generally begin training their children earlier and give them responsibility earlier in life. The middle-class child is apparently subjected to influences which tend to make him orderly, conscientious, responsible, and conservative. As a result he may suffer more frustrations than a lower-class child.

Maccoby and Gibbs (20) found, in a comparison of upper-middle- and upper-lower-class mothers' reports of attitudes toward child rearing, that aggression toward parents is quite strictly controlled in both groups, but that upper-middle-class mothers overlook it more often than do upper-lower-class mothers. Upper-lower-class mothers more often use physical punishment, ridicule, and the denial of privileges in training their children. Although the mothers of both groups are somewhat demonstrative toward their children, upper-middle-class mothers are slightly more so than upper-lower-class mothers. In this study, upper-lower-class families were found, in general, to be more permissive than upper-middle-class families.

The evidence from the Davis and Havighurst and the Maccoby studies conflicts in some ways though not in others, and there are various explanations of this disagreement. The writers of this book believe that the differing samples of parents studied, and the time lapse of about ten years between the two studies, may account for the differences. What is important is that both found significant differences between two classes in the manner of child-rearing.

There is some evidence that lower-class families are less restrictive in attitudes to sex, religion, manners, education, fighting, swearing, and stealing. Children born and reared in this class thus meet fewer situations where they are restricted than do others of different levels. They can therefore be more independent and at least feel that they mature more rapidly.

There is distinct evidence, then, that different social classes rear their young differently. This fact has important implications for the college student. He meets students from other social strata, differently brought up and with somewhat varying values. He quickly finds that as a result of different class backgrounds, the attitudes, goals, and self-concepts of his friends and classmates may differ considerably from his own. Coming for the first time into contact with mannerisms, ways of speech, dress, and conduct which are radically different from what has always seemed acceptable and even advantageous causes severe social and emotional stresses in many students. Religious differences also pose problems; for the boy or girl who was strictly brought up, the relatively great freedom of beliefs found in college and the wide differences in what is considered morally acceptable may come as a severe shock.

The adjustments which students make to all these new experiences vary widely. The recognition of differences which are primarily social may stimulate snobbishness, social-climbing, and the desire for acceptance by those on a higher social level. Conversely, it may stimulate clannishness among those who feel themselves better than others. In either case, the all-too-frequent result is that student groups crystallize along class lines, and belief in the worth of the individual tends to be blurred and even evaluated in terms of class distinction. On matters less social than moral or religious, some students go to extremes in their enthusiasm for greater independence, while others tend to isolate themselves from others whose conduct they disapprove. It seems clear that in the creation of class structures society has created many problems at the same time that it has solved or simplified others.

An extreme case is a freshman girl who was failing to adjust to college. Through counseling, and checking with her dormitory-mates, it was discovered that she sat and smoked cigarettes in her room continuously. The excessive smoking was beginning to affect her health, and her work was being neglected. An interview revealed that her concept of college life included the idea that to be accepted one has to be a really competent smoker. Further counseling enabled her to see a truer picture of herself and of college life, and the problem of pseudo-sophistication disappeared.

Many students find that the theory of evolution comes into conflict with their beliefs about the creation, that new ideas on racial problems run directly counter to their own, and that other philosophical or ethical matters discussed in their classes and informally among students reflect views which shock them deeply, or at the least are very different from what they were brought up to believe. Undergraduates of certain national or ethnic groups may encounter prejudice, even in colleges which pride themselves on a democratic outlook.

Some students must work their way through college. In most colleges this is highly acceptable and in some colleges as many as 50 per cent of the students earn at least a part of their expenses. But the need to work sometimes takes its toll in feelings of inferiority, lack of opportunities for recreation, or inability to compete financially. Of course, others may have too much money to spend, and some seem to find college nothing more than a playground where they can remain immature but happy for a few more years before assuming adult responsibilities. Still other students come from homes where education is not prized; there are students whose parents are strongly opposed to their going to college, deeming it a waste of time and money.

Sexual mores also differ among students. So do attitudes toward petting and necking, drinking, dancing, card-playing, and other social activities. Any of these differences in rearing and in value systems can cause problems which require solution if the student is to make a successful adjustment in college as well as in later life.

Rapid changes in ways of living

Since 1930 the United States has taken part in two wars and a cold war, and has experienced a vast economic depression and tremendous inflation. Since

1930 we have developed television, jet planes, and the hydrogen bomb. The political boundaries of the world have changed considerably, and a struggle for world power has drawn various nations into two large areas of influence. Labor unions have achieved new power. Taxes and controls upon industry have increased. The birth rate has risen markedly, and the strain of rapidly growing population is reflected in schools and colleges, housing, traffic and parking problems, public health, civilian defense measures, and road building. Large elements of the population have shifted from rural to urban and again to suburban living. Many industries have tended to decentralize.

Each of these changes, and many others, produce problems for the individual. It is becoming more difficult to predict the state of one's country a few years hence and to answer such questions about one's own future as the following: "What is the best way of achieving economic security?" "Shall I go to work for a large corporation, or into business for myself?" "Shall I place my savings in insurance, government bonds, or real estate?" "Shall I prepare for stability, inflation, or depression?" It is no easier to answer other questions of broader social implication: "Shall women work?" "What happens to the children when Mother has a job?" "Are we fostering a false standard of living?" "Are more children becoming delinquent?" "What is happening to the self-esteem of men, when women earn part of the living?"

Moral codes have changed rapidly in the last fifty years. During the years of prohibition flouting the law became almost a game for many otherwise law-abiding people — those "in the know" enjoyed being able to rap on a door and be admitted to a "speakeasy" to obtain bootleg whiskey. Especially in periods of stress many people depart from normally accepted codes of behavior. During World War II there was a rash of hoarding, black marketing, cheating with ration stamps, of married people dating while husband or wife was away in

Changes in the role of women. *The rising percentage of married women in the labor force and the new position of women in our society has many consequences relating to personality, social behavior, education, and citizenship. (From William F. Ogburn and Meyer F. Nimkoff,* Sociology, *Houghton Mifflin, 1958, p. 597.)*

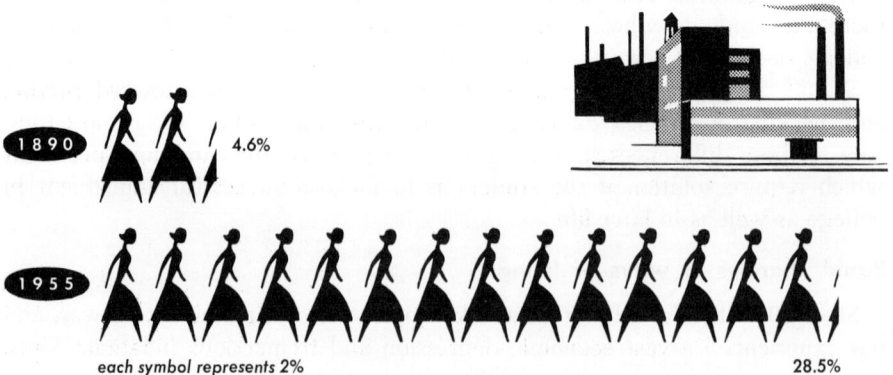

1890   4.6%

1955

each symbol represents 2%   28.5%

service or living in another part of the country, of young people lying about their ages in order to get married, and draft-dodging.

The place of women as upholders of morality is also changing. Traditionally, Americans more or less unconsciously accepted a "double standard," by which men were condoned in certain laxities for which women would have been condemned. For example, men could drink and smoke, but women couldn't do either without seeming "fast." The double standard applied also to sexual promiscuity. However, since women have begun to assume the same responsibilities as men in the business world, there has been a tendency for the double standard to relax.

Technology and automation pose still further problems. In many kinds of work, the person whose specialized talents are in highest demand will be most highly paid. For example during the 1950's engineers and scientists have been in great demand. Both fields require specialized training and developed so rapidly that the individual, either as a student or a practicing engineer or scientist, has to read and study constantly in order to keep abreast of new developments. As Alice was told by the White Queen in *Through the Looking-Glass,* "It takes all the running you can do to stay in the same place."

Competition with others to procure and hold a job produces strains and frustrations not known in earlier eras, as Fromm (21) points out. In contrasting two periods of history, he sees life in the Middle Ages as confining the individual in many ways. The Church imposed taboos upon him, his overlords controlled him, and his guilds prescribed his way of making a living. The son of a peasant could not aspire to become a noble, and the noble did not fear losing his status. There was considerably less freedom than there is today. But, Fromm believes, while the individual was restricted, he was also supported. He knew quite well what to expect from others and was sure of his after-life as well as of the present. Although he was hemmed in, danger was locked out.

Today, on the other hand, there is more freedom to rise in the social structure. Man is free to choose his job and to live where he pleases in this country, but a new threat seems to be emerging. Complex machines, doing much of the work formerly done by skilled or unskilled laborers, now replace many workers in factories, so that one must develop special skills to compensate, and such threats as the lay-off, the strike, seniority, are never far from the consciousness of many workers. In all this there may be no real security or feeling of worth. Knowing that he may be replaced in the near future by a machine and that his present work represents only a small aspect of total production, today's worker is often not satisfied. To some extent, industry is taking steps to alleviate this feeling, but as Fromm points out, modern man has paid for his freedom with a loss of security and feeling of importance.

Labor–management difficulties are often related to the lack of significance which workers feel in their jobs rather than to wages. The Hawthorne plant of Western Electric Company, makers of telephone equipment, tried a series of experiments in which a group of workers was selected to work in a separate area under varying conditions. They were told that they were being observed to see how lighting, temperature, noise, and other factors affected production. Each time conditions were changed, production tended to increase. But when the original conditions were restored, production still climbed. Studying this phenomenon, researchers concluded that these workers developed a group morale because they knew that they were a selected group working in an experiment and so felt important. It was this feeling of personal worth rather than the changed conditions as such which was thought to be responsible for the increase in their production rate.

Family life

Sociologists point out that the family as a social force may not be as strong as it was twenty or thirty years ago. The entertainment and social satisfaction formerly provided within the family circle are now found in movies and other spectator amusements. Television has become in some homes a substitute for conversation. One group of average teen-age boys and girls were found to spend about thirty hours a week watching television — five more hours than they spent in school!

Travel is easier than before, and families move from place to place as fathers seek employment. Neighborhoods are less closely knit. Mothers often work. Financial pressures grow as people try to improve their standard of living. As the life span increases, more older people must live with their children and grandchildren; at the same time modern houses provide less room per person than did the larger houses of past decades.

Thus many of our problems of adjustment are not ours individually, but are imposed upon us by society as a whole. The extent to which any one person can change society is negligible. Therefore, our efforts must often be spent in adjusting to the changes in society, and in endeavoring to maintain or enhance our self-concepts and satisfy our needs through such adjustment.

SUMMARY

We face many problems because of the nature of societies and cultures, some of which we are solving slowly, others more rapidly. As we shall see in later chapters, psychology is an effective tool in developing answers to questions raised by social living.

Human beings are social animals; their attitudes, mores, and actions reflect the society into which they were born. And societies differ. The Salteaux Indians, the Arapesh, and the Kwakiutl of the northwest coast of North America differ from one another in group and in individual behavior because of social and cultural influences, so marked that some forms of behavior considered normal by the Salteaux are considered abnormal by the Kwakiutl.

Children are not born with established patterns of social behavior. Concepts of morality, attitudes, language, symbolic thinking — all are part of the social-ization process. Although children vary as individuals, social development fol-lows a predictable pattern. In America the family is the first and perhaps the most important social influence. Although there appear to be certain innate tendencies which affect personality development, the manner in which the in-fant is accepted into the home has a great deal to do with his subsequent emo-tional and mental health. His emotions are influenced by his early life, and his self-concept is either enhanced (with good chances for future social and emo-tional adjustment) or discouraged (with chances for future maladjustment).

After his first six years or so the child's horizons widen. He now finds the peer group and the school about as important as his immediate family. As he approaches adolescence, peer culture becomes even more important to him in determining his values and behavior — in fact, he enters the stage at which he normally begins to emancipate himself from the home and become a mature individual. Adolescence, like any other stage, is beset with problems, and the person whose social needs are not satisfied at that time may not become a well-adjusted adult and his future may be in some doubt.

College students have their social adjustment problems too, partly because of differences between the cultures in which they and their classmates were reared. Different American social classes have their own ways of bringing up children, and give them differing values and mores. The change from living at home to living at college presents difficulties in that adjustments must be made to these differences among students' backgrounds and ways of life, as well as to the differences that college life itself presents.

American society has been changing rapidly in recent years. Mass media of communication, the world situation, labor–management relations, differences in family life, and modern technology create problems as well as advantages.

What are the implications of all these changes for you as a college student? Perhaps the first is that you should understand that you are in part a product of your culture. As you move into other cultures, you will want to reassess your system of values, attitudes, and behavior. You will want to try to understand others partially in terms of their cultural development, not merely of your own. You may want to reassess your own life-philosophy and consider carefully what the future may hold for you. You will come to understand that many of your problems are really those of society as a whole, and you may want to join some of the organizations or informal groups attempting to solve social prob-lems. As your understanding of social development and cultural influences increases, you should be better able to adjust to the life you are living at college and may expect to live in the future.

Suggested activities

1. Describe the culture in which you were reared. In what ways does it seem to be a special segment of the general American culture?

2. Examine a few issues of your school newspaper. What articles show evidence of a particular college culture?

3. How has society in America changed in your lifetime? What implications might these changes have for your college career?

4. Try predicting what American life may be like in fifty years. Can you attempt to prepare for such changes? In what ways?

REFERENCES

1. K. Young, *Personality and Problems of Adjustment,* Appleton-Century-Crofts, New York, 1952, p.4.
2. *Ibid.*
3. E. T. Hall, Jr., "The Anthropology of Manners," *Scientific American,* April 1955, p. 54. Reprinted and abridged in *Reader's Digest,* July 1955, p. 122, as "What Are Good Manners?"
4. A. I. Hallowell, "Aggression in Salteaux Society," *Psychiatry,* 3, 1940. Abridged and reprinted in C. Kluckhohn and H. A. Murray, *Personality in Nature, Society and Culture,* Knopf, New York, 1940.
5. M. Mead, *Co-Operation and Competition Among Primitive People,* McGraw-Hill, New York, 1937.
6. R. Benedict, *Patterns of Culture,* Mentor Books, New American Library of World Literature, New York, 1934.
7. M. E. Fries, "Psychosomatic Relationships Between Mother and Infant," *Psychosom. Med.,* 1944, 6. Reported in R. W. White, *The Abnormal Personality,* Ronald Press, New York, 1956.
8. F. K. Merry and R. V. Merry, *The First Two Decades of Life,* Harper, New York, 1950, p. 74.
9. R. Stagner, *Psychology of Personality,* McGraw-Hill, New York, second edition, 1948, pp. 167–168.
10. R. W. White, *The Abnormal Personality,* Ronald Press, New York, 1956, p. 144 ff.
11. E. Hurlock, *Developmental Psychology,* McGraw-Hill, New York, 1953, p. 74.
12. F. K. Merry and R. V. Merry, *op. cit.,* p. 378.
13. R. W. White, *op. cit.,* Chapter 3.
14. E. Hurlock, *Adolescent Development,* McGraw-Hill, New York, second edition, 1955, pp. 80–81.
15. *Ibid.,* p. 106.
16. *Ibid.,* p. 136.
17. *Ibid.,* p. 130.
18. K. Davis, *Human Society,* Macmillan, New York, 1949, p. 364 ff.
19. A. Davis and R. J. Havighurst, "Social Class and Color Differences in Child-Rearing," *Amer. Sociol. Rev.,* 1946, 2. Reported in C. Kluckhohn and H. A. Murray, *op. cit.*
20. E. E. Maccoby and P. K. Gibbs, "Methods of Child-Rearing in Two Social Classes." Reported in A. P. Coladarci, *Educational Psychology, A Book of Readings.* Dryden Press, New York, 1955.
21. E. Fromm, *Escape From Freedom,* New York, Farrar and Rinehart, 1941.

SUGGESTIONS FOR FURTHER READING

Allport, G. W., *The Nature of Prejudice,* Addison-Wesley, Cambridge, Mass., 1954.

Beals, R. L., "The Village in an Industrial World," *Science Monthly,* 1953, 77, pp. 65–75.

Buchanan, W., and H. Cantril, *How Nations See Each Other: A Study in Public Opinion,* Univ. of Illinois Press, Urbana, 1953.

Coffin, T. E., "Television's Impact on Society," *Amer. Psychologist,* 1955, 10, pp. 630–641.

Hilgard, E. R., *Introduction to Psychology,* Harcourt, New York, 1953, Chapter 23.

Mead, M., *The Coming of Age in Samoa,* Mentor Books, New American Library of World Literature, New York, 1928.

Mead, M., and N. Calas, *Primitive Heritage: An Anthropological Anthology,* Random House, New York, 1953.

Pressey, S. L., and R. G. Kuhlen, *Psychological Development Through the Life Span,* Harper, New York, 1957, Chapters 11, 12.

Prothro, E. T., "Arab Students' Choices of Ways to Live," *J. Soc. Psychol.,* 1958, 47, pp. 3–7.

Rath, R., and J. P. Das, "Study in Stereotypes of College Freshmen and Service Holders in Orissa, India, Towards Themselves and Four Other Foreign Nationalities," *J. Soc. Psychol.,* 1958, 47, pp. 373–385.

Stagner, R., and T. F. Karwoski, *Psychology,* McGraw-Hill, New York, 1952, Chapter 4.

Wickens, D. D., and D. R. Meyer, *Psychology,* Dryden, New York, 1955, Chapter 13.

Group Dynamics

You, as a student, are a leader in many ways. Not only are you a member of that relatively small group of Americans who attend college, but in order to attend you have demonstrated social competence and academic proficiency. If you are a typical student, you were active in cocurricular activities in high school, and you are probably active in certain organizations now. You may have been a cheer leader, an athlete, a bandsman, active in drama, on the newspaper, or in any of a number of other high school activities. You demonstrated leadership in various ways — by holding a prominent office, guiding committee work, or exerting influence in group decisions.

After graduation from college you will probably assume a position in a community which will keep you in contact with groups of people — business and professional organizations, community projects, church and school groups.

Do the groups with which you are familiar have adequate leaders and followers? Are they functioning successfully? Are you a successful leader? Understanding leadership roles and other factors associated with membership and interaction in groups helps group members function efficiently and pleasantly. This chapter is devoted to this theme; and the stage may be set by quoting S. L. Pressey and D. C. Hanna (1), who describe two distinct types of college classes. As you read these quotations, ask yourself: "How might these different classes affect the learning of the students? How might the class members react in each class? How does group membership affect my own attitudes and behavior?"

The Psychology of Group Interaction

What are primary groups? What are some character-istics and influences of groups? What are some out-comes of group membership? What are the types of leadership, and what types are most effective? How can a person develop leadership? What are some roles of members in a group? How can the dynamics of a group be improved?

A college class is usually thought of as a place where students learn; and the only relationship explicitly fostered there is between the student and instructor rather than between students. In class, the students are supposed to pay attention to the instructor and discuss topics with him; to pay attention to other students or talk with them during the class hour is considered contrary to the classroom ethic. Students are supposed to get acquainted with each other and develop as social beings not in class but at the student union and in fraternities and dormi-tories; and at dances, games and other student affairs. The dichotomy of function is rather sharp. . . .

But it would seem possibly desirable that students should make each other's acquaintance in classes also. There, they might find a common ground of ac-quaintance in shared intellectual or professional interests rather than simply in ath-letic or social diversions. And perhaps, if the instructor felt some responsibility for a student's social as well as intellectual development, a "socialized" class might present exceptional opportunities for him to study each student's social adjust-ment, and help him in his growth as a social being (2).

The authors of this book are not promoting either method of teaching a college class, for each has its advantages and its drawbacks; how the class is taught must depend upon the nature of the situation, the material, the student body, and the instructor. What we are asking is this: How does the manner in which a group functions, such as a college class, affect the members of the group? What are some of the possible effects? Does the interaction of group members influence behavior in and outside the group?

Two types of college classes. *At left is a "socialized" class. The conventional class below is a more formal period with less opportunity for student interaction. (Photos from the University of Wisconsin.)*

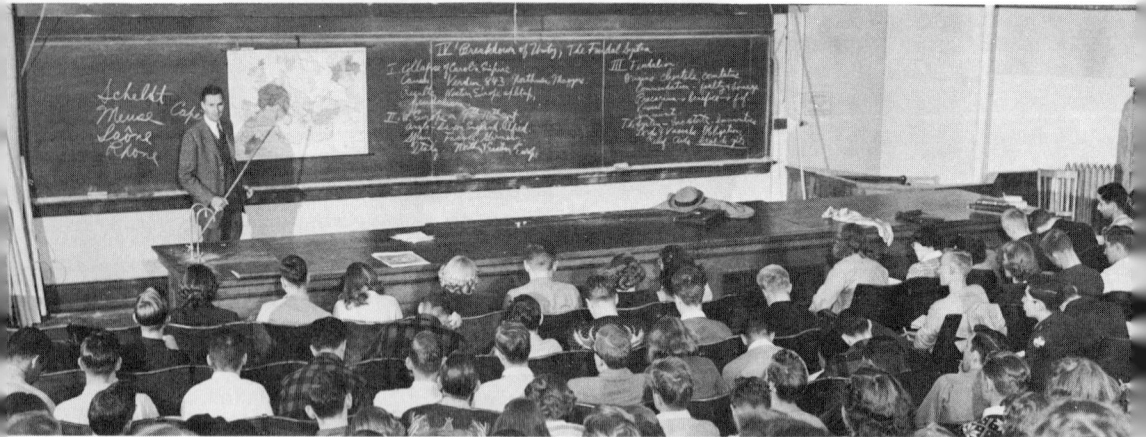

Pressey and Hanna reported interesting results from their study, and we shall return to these later in this chapter. First, however, let us provide some orientation to the dynamics of group processes and interaction, including the characteristics of groups as well as their leaders and members.

● **A. PRIMARY GROUPS**

We shall focus on what the sociologist calls primary groups. Primary groups are characteristically rather small and intimate, in contrast to the larger and more impersonal secondary groups (3). The primary group engenders a "we" feeling. Relationships among its members are largely face-to-face, rather than through secondary media of communication such as newspapers, radio, or television. The bond between members of primary groups is durable and exists because of the similarity of their goals. Furthermore, members of primary groups often share a feeling of responsibility for seeing that the goals of the other members are met. You will recognize your family, fraternity, college crowd, clubs, dormitory, and athletic teams you belong to as primary groups.

The family

Your family was the first and probably the most pervasive group influence in your life. The foremost function of the family is to procreate and care for children until they become self-sufficient. But it has other functions. For example, the family is an economic unit, and the various members function differently in connection with the earning and spending of money for the good of the family and its members. The family is an agency for developing attitudes, religious beliefs, social skills, and community relationships. Recreation, protection of family members, and provision of the material things of life are some of its proper functions.

At one time the family structure of which people in our culture were conscious was much more elaborate than it is now. Family organization extended well beyond the immediate parents and children; cousinships were traced to lengths which most of us today would boggle at; and the family had a patriarchal structure. The type of family relationships indicated by the Scottish clan, the ruling houses of Europe, and the American Indian tribes illustrate similar extensive and patriarchal structures. Such family groups had their own mores and traditions, were controlled mainly through the elders of the family, and exhibited loyalty and support to the members much more strongly than is done in this country today. Many American families, especially in pioneer times, exhibited these characteristics. Cousins, aunts, uncles, grandparents, brothers, and sisters tended to settle near each other in cities, small towns, and rural areas. Certain possessions were practically considered to be family property, and were not to be disposed of outside the larger family group.

Our present family structure is quite different from this earlier pattern. Mass production has weakened family unity, even within the narrower family groups we are accustomed to. The mobility of today's society has caused family members to live far apart from each other, and created a corresponding lack of communication among them. Married women often work outside the home (as many as 50 per cent of them in some areas); and the activities fostered by the community, in the schools, among professional and business groups, in spectator sports, and the like, have further tended to separate family members.

The family is doing less than formerly to facilitate the social development of children. Old-fashioned discipline is rare. Children apparently do not receive as much instruction at home in reading, handicrafts, or non-commercialized recreation as formerly. There are fewer jobs or chores about the house, through which responsibility could be learned and shared. More freedom for children in the use of the automobile and in seeing movies and television weakens, or at least changes, the influence of the family in the formation of attitudes.

Children now receive more formal education and in general have a better material standard of living than before. Families are traveling more, and there is greater access to music, libraries, and art exhibits. Through newspapers, magazines, radio, and television, people across the country can learn how others live; and the increased standardization of food, clothing, housing, and other material conveniences has caused American families to become more interdependent but at the same time less intimate.

The size of families, which diminished for a number of years, has now once more increased. As more parents become better educated and as medical science advances, children are receiving better nutrition and child care. Families thus tend to be healthier, and some even larger, than in previous generations. There are more facilities available to the family which needs emotional, educational, or vocational guidance.

In Chapter 4 we indicated the importance of family influences, especially during the earlier years of childhood. In Chapter 13 we shall relate this fact more directly to mental health. Here we shall briefly consider the interaction of family members as it affects personality development.

Dominance by parents may cause children to be shy, inclined to avoid difficulties with other people, and insecure and dependent, even as adults. Parental dominance may also lead to rebellion and resentment, or, if the child is over-indulged, to over-confidence, bravado, and selfishness. On the other hand, through a careful balance of direction and permissiveness, the parents may assist children to become secure and to control their own emotions in a manner necessary to successful interaction in society; these children in turn are likely to become good marital partners and parents.

Little research is reported about the effect of the child's personality upon the parents. White (4) indicates that children as young as ten days can be classified as displaying active, passive, or median activity. He finds that through hereditary factors children's personalities are partly formed at birth, and that small babies in the same family quite often differ from each other in temperament. This in turn has its effects upon the parents. Bringing up a cooperative, moderately active child has quite different effects on the physical, emotional, and social well-being of the parents than bringing up a fretful, hyperactive child who never lets them sleep and is continually demanding attention. The unresponsive child can be frustrating to his parents. Differences among children can lead to difficulties of various kinds in the household, not necessarily the result of the parents' methods. It is assumed, however, that parents are better able to meet the needs of the infant than is the infant to modify his actions toward his parents.

The childhood play group

In addition to the family, a second group which influences the child is his neighborhood play group. Such groups are in part determined by the propinquity of their members. Temporary interests — playing cowboys and Indians, going to camp, joining certain play organizations, or visiting a group member's yard — may hold small groups of children together for a time. As the children develop and find different interests, membership in these groups may change frequently. Today it is often difficult to see any differences between the play of boys and girls — both may swim, bicycle, play badminton, or act as cowboys, gunmen, or space cadets. Girls are often accepted by boys into childhood play groups for certain kinds of activities. The cultural pressures to bring a girl up differently from a boy have decreased notably in recent years.

Children normally like to play with others nearly their own age — indeed, if we find certain youngsters tending to play to any great extent with much younger children, we may become concerned and try to find the reasons. The older youngsters may be insecure with children of their own age, and development of mature behavior patterns may be hindered through playing with younger children. Equally important, younger children may be dominated by older ones, and as a result may find their way into various activities which might be better left unexplored.

The childhood group, of course, furnishes many opportunities for social development through effective group interaction. It gives practice in social interaction, and the child develops attitudes and opinions from those of the group. Such groups afford the child loyalty, affection, and security. If it exists for any extended period, the play group may broadly influence the thoughts, moral behavior, and activities of its members.

The high school crowd

In comparison with the play group, adolescent crowds are more closely knit and permanent. Hurlock (5) indicates that the crowd selects members who "fit in" in terms of interests, backgrounds, abilities, and friendship, rather than forming spontaneously as does the play group. The clique is a more closely knit subdivision of the crowd, or a crowd may emerge from a clique. Two or three boys or girls who have much in common may form a clique, gradually admitting on varying bases of intimacy and friendship others who, in the aggregate, form the "crowd." Crowd members are carefully selected. They are of both sexes, whereas the childhood groups are sometimes limited to one sex. The crowd is held together by strong feelings of affection and admiration, and its activities are primarily social. The advantages to the members are manifold in relation to the values of group life, as we saw in Chapter 3. To the high school student, crowd life is almost a "must," though there are some difficulties. Crowd life may be so satisfying that the teen-ager neglects his school and home duties. The crowd may exercise undue influence on his code of acceptable behavior, his attitudes, and especially his values. It may encourage snobbishness, and may isolate those who are not members.

Characteristics of primary groups

Groups commonly exert considerable influence on their members, as well as being influenced by their membership.

Primary groups at college. *Though characterized by a bond of relative intimacy and teamwork, primary groups vary in their cohesiveness, organization, and degree of permanence. The pictures above show primary groups which are unstructured with little or no organization. At left and below are pictured a basketball team and a class, primary groups with a more formal structure. (Top right photo from Colby College, Waterville, Maine; bottom photos from University of Connecticut.)*

Formation of attitudes. Various studies indicate the power of the primary group in the formation of attitudes. For example, Garrison (6) concluded that college students differ in their attitudes toward domestic and international problems primarily because of differences in home and community background. Education and intelligence, of course, are also factors in the formation of attitudes (7, 8). According to Klee (9), class discussion among senior high school students was the most important single factor in determining changes in their attitudes toward war and peace. Intercultural workshop experiences affected the reactions of members on questions of ethnic distance. College seniors approximate faculty social values more closely than do freshmen (10). Thus home, community, and classroom experiences, especially through group discussion, affect attitudes. Membership in primary groups, with the accompanying ease and volume of communication, is a prime determiner of both the strength and kind of attitudes the individual will hold.

Motivation. One's level of aspiration, and the strength and persistence of his motives, are also affected by the groups he belongs to. Many studies of motivation have been conducted with pupils in classrooms in which such factors as competition (between groups and among individuals), cooperation, and level of aspiration were considered. Brasch (11), for example, studied the effects of individual and group competition on the achievement of sixth-grade pupils in arithmetic. Setting up a competitive situation in which individual and group prizes were awarded, he found that greater gains were made by pupils working for group prizes.

Hilgard and others (12), studied college students working together in small groups on arithmetic problems and timing themselves competitively for completion of problems. Each student recorded privately the level of aspiration for the next set of problems in terms of the time required to complete a page. It was found that group performances, when announced, affected the aspiration of the individual members. Students who completed more than the group mean tended to move their expectancies downward, and those who did less than the group mean tended to revise their aspirations upward.

Conformity. We have mentioned that in the high school clique (Chapters 3 and 10) a member who does not conform tends to lose social approval. Conformity, on the other hand, leads to acceptance by the group and less conflict with others. Security is thus enhanced, and social motives are more likely to be satisfied. Raw material for the formation of attitudes is present in the form of the ideas expressed by the group and the language it uses. Thus if a member has no particular ideas about a given subject, he is furnished them ready-made. The person who has weak attitudes may find them reinforced; the one with contrary attitudes may find them reversed. The alternative is to be different from the group, and he who is too different runs the danger of being ostracized, forced out, abused, laughed at, or subjected to other group pressures. The needs to be like others and to identify cause children to accept many of the influences of the group, even though previous experiences have taught them other values. For example, in a group prone to smoking and the use of vulgar language, it is almost impossible to avoid at least a modicum of such behavior merely through the need to identify with the group, even if no overt pressure is exerted. Fear of rejection is a powerful coercive force. On the other hand, the tolerance of groups for individual eccentricities in some members who contribute in athletic or other ways must not be forgotten.

Role and personality. Groups tend to develop leaders and followers as we shall see a little later. Since groups provide experience in social interaction, the extent to which members succeed or fail within the group tends to affect their habitual behavior and their self-perceptions. Bedoian (13) found, among sixth-grade pupils, that when sociometric tests were administered and results compared with scores on a mental health analysis test, pupils who were "over-accepted" in social ways had higher scores on criteria of mental health than those who were "under-accepted." Those who enjoyed better mental health were more popular with their peers. We may assume that mental health is conducive to better adjustment, since security, recognition and group status, the feeling of belonging, and other social motives would be better satisfied. The individual with poor acceptance, it follows, would be more likely to have a lower score in mental health. It should be remembered that mental health in this sense is not all-important. Some great men have habitually been in poor mental health.

We have seen that one characteristic of groups is that they influence their members in various ways. What other characteristics do groups have in common?

Need satisfaction. Social needs such as that for participation and approval are satisfied in primary groups. Among campus organizations, you will perhaps discover that some are known for their successful programs and others are not. There are some groups which everybody would like to join, and whose members put in long hours to make a success of their parade float, fund-raising activity, or the election of the political candidate they are sponsoring in a student election. Members of these groups maintain and enhance their self-concepts through active participation for which approval is generously given and shared.

Cohesiveness. People try to join and receive approval from groups which they believe to be important. The more prestige a person has within such a group, the more attractive it is to him. If unable to win approval or prestige, the member tends to withdraw. Once he is a successful group member, identification tends to force the individual to defend the standards of the group, and as a result he tends to evaluate people and behavior in terms of those standards. The college fraternity is a good example of this effect. Professional organizations such as medical or psychological societies also reflect it.

Groups in which there is considerable personal interaction among members are more desirable to many than groups colored by formality, snobbishness, or aggression. Cooperation rather than competition enhances the group spirit. External events, such as an attack on the group from the outside (e.g., the banning of a college fraternity, criticism by authorities, etc.) may increase cohesiveness. Support from the outside, prestige in the eyes of outsiders, and the general reputation of the group make membership more attractive.

Some groups hang together only because there is little motivation for their members to leave. When competing influences appear — when other groups compete for membership, when dues are raised, or when extensive activities are planned which will take added time — members drift away. These groups can enlist only moderate effort from their members. Since personal goals are not achieved, members attend only through habit or feelings of obligation. Disagreement over ways of solving group problems is a frequent source of strain, as are unpleasant experiences in the group. The formation of cliques, attempts by a few to dominate and control, failure of communication among members, inability to formulate and progress with group plans, and ineptness of leaders also lessen cohesiveness.

Differences between primary groups

We need point out only a few of the more obvious differences between primary groups. Purposes vary according to the needs of the members. Memberships differ, of course, and with them the cohesiveness, looseness or tightness of organization, and the kinds of activities undertaken. Some groups are more formal, others less so. Some are temporary, like the childhood play group, others quite permanent, such as the family. As we shall shortly see, groups vary in the kind of leadership they develop and in the roles of their members. They also differ in the influence they exert on their members and the means of controlling them.

Suggested activities

1. Discuss groups to which you have belonged or to which you now belong. What influences do they have on your attitudes, system of values, and overt behavior? How did they influence or control these attitudes or behavior?

2. Compare two rather widely different groups to see how their systems of values, methods of control, attitudes, motivations for joining, and membership requirements vary.

3. Examine a number of issues of your college newspaper or annual. What groups are portrayed? What functions do they serve?

4. Study biographies of prominent families. Perhaps you have read *Cheaper by the Dozen* (14). How did the family influence its members? Could you detect customs, traditions, value systems, and codes of conduct?

5. Visit the high school hangout — the corner drug store, dairy bar, or sandwich shop. Keep a diary of what you observe, including fads, language, behavior, dress, and interaction among the students.

A. PRIMARY GROUPS

● B. LEADERSHIP AND MEMBERSHIP

Among the more obvious yet important qualities of groups are those associated with leaders and members. If as we discuss the qualities of leadership and membership you will apply the principles we mention to a particular structured group you belong to — a college fraternity, a church group, or the drama, music, or literature club — the discussion will be much more meaningful than if you think in terms of the less formal high school crowd, the family, or the neighborhood play group.

Lewin, Lippitt, and White (15) have made widely quoted studies concerning the group behavior of ten-year-old boys engaged in hobby club activities. These researchers attempted to discover how the behavior of members of small groups changed when the leadership role was also changed. In the second of these studies four groups of boys were selected which were roughly equivalent in terms of interpersonal relationships, intellectual and physical ability, socio-economic status, and personality characteristics. Four adult leaders were then trained in so-called democratic, autocratic, and laissez-faire leadership. Every six weeks the leaders were shifted from club to club, or the method of leadership they used was changed from one type to another. These shifts were accomplished so that when the experiment ended each club had experienced each of the three types of leadership — authoritarian, democratic, and laissez-faire — under each leader. In the process the behavior of the members was observed and recorded. The leaders were instructed to conduct themselves in very special ways for each type of leadership, the main features being summarized as follows (16):

Authoritarian
1. All determination of policy was made by the leader.
2. Techniques and activity steps were dictated one at a time by the authority, so that future steps were always to a large degree uncertain.
3. The leader usually dictated the particular work task and work companion of each member.
4. The dominator or leader tended to be "personal" in his praise and criticism of the work of each member; he remained aloof from active group participation except when demonstrating.
Democratic
1. All policies were a matter of group discussion and decision, encouraged and assisted by the leader.
2. Perspective toward activities was gained during discussion periods. General

steps toward the group goal were sketched, and when technical advice was needed, the leader suggested two or more alternative procedures from which a choice could be made.

3. The members were free to work with whomever they chose, and the division of tasks was left up to the group.

4. The leader was "objective" or "fact-minded" in his praise and criticism, and tried to be a regular member of the group in spirit without doing too much of the work.

Laissez-faire

1. Freedom for group or individual decision was complete with a minimum of participation by the leadership.

2. Various materials were supplied by the leader, who made it clear that he would supply information when asked. He took no other part in discussion of the work.

3. The leader was a complete non-participant.

4. He gave few spontaneous comments on activities of the members unless he was questioned, and made no attempt to praise or regulate the course of events.

Work which the boys did under laissez-faire leadership was less well organized, less efficient, and less satisfying to them than the work they did under either the democratic or the autocratic system. Under laissez-faire also, less work was done and the work was poorer. The boys played more, though leadership might have been expected to emerge from the group. In fact some boys made occasional attempts to "get things going," though their attempts were not particularly successful. Common goals were hard to formulate and work was sporadic. "Fooling around" was common. Since little was accomplished and no clear plans were made, the boys felt little identity with the group's work. We may conclude from this experiment that laissez-faire leadership produces little constructive activity.

In these experiments democratic leadership appeared to be most successful of the three types. Motivation appeared to be highest under this type of leadership, since various members contributed to planning, organizing, and assigning the work at hand. When the adult leader left the room (as he occasionally did for experimental purposes), boys tended to keep right on working. This was interpreted as showing that, when group members have a share in planning work, their responsibility for seeing that the work is accomplished transcends any motives for mere play. Group decisions, of course, take time. Yet when the group solidly supports a project, both work and pleasure in it are facilitated. In the democratic situations there was more "we" feeling among the members — the sharing of responsibility for group progress, for helping each other achieve their goals, and of friendliness and higher morale. Sharing of materials and tools, mutual praise and encouragement, friendly horseplay, and other evidences of this "we" feeling were evident.

Authoritarian leadership produced equally high work output as democratic leadership when the leader was present. But authoritarianism produced more aggressiveness, there was some scapegoating, and hostility was shown among the members. Also authoritarian leadership produced submission and dependence. Creativity was stifled, and the boys, forced to follow their work patterns a step at a time without knowing the eventual outcome, felt little satisfaction in their work. Individual goals were less well met than under the other forms of leadership.

In summary, democratic leadership produced the most desirable over-all results and was more efficient in achieving individual and group goals than was autocratic or laissez-faire leadership.

In connection with this experiment it is significant to note that the behavior for the leaders was prescribed rather carefully. You will probably notice that in the groups you yourself belong to, or lead, the techniques of leadership do not ordinarily differ so sharply or fit into such well-defined patterns. For example, many leaders — perhaps your own teachers — are in the main authoritarian, but are benevolent, careful to share knowledge of progress and future plans, and considerate of individual differences so that their behavior does not seem authoritarian at all. Many leaders shift techniques fairly rapidly, depending upon the work to be accomplished. And many use techniques at a given time which might be considered a combination of all three methods.

Leadership in groups is necessary. On the college and adult levels, we may suspect that if leadership is not assigned, it will emerge from the group in the person of one or two people; that group members will formulate plans for their activities; or that the group may act as a collection of individuals who are more or less accidentally in contact. Many organizations have no formal leadership — a bridge club, for example. Members share in planning and making rules. But if the group is to act successfully as a group, leadership must show itself in some way, even if informally.

We must be careful not to over-generalize from the experiment described above. The definitions of authoritarian and democratic leadership on which it was based are rather narrow. Democracy does not imply lack of formal

Leadership and membership roles. *This chart (a sociogram) illustrates a possible sequence of relationships in a group. Paul and George seem to have the most influence. They would probably be good co-leaders. Warren and Stuart work well with each other but have little to do with others. (From Franklyn S. Haiman,* Group Leadership and Democratic Action, *Houghton Mifflin, 1951.)*

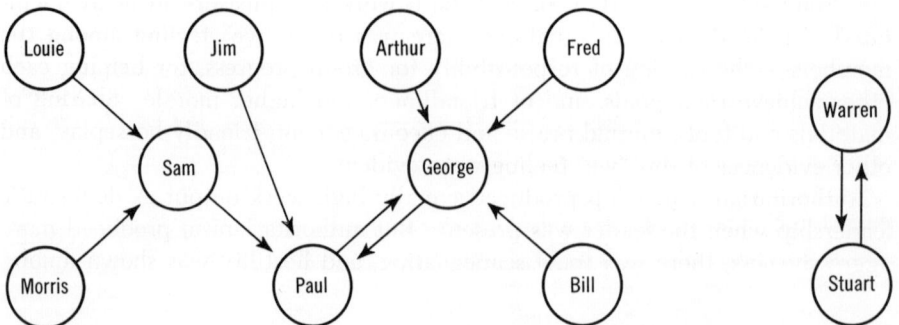

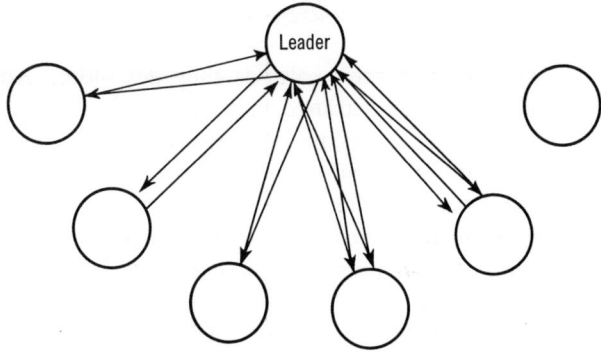

Leader domination. *In this group each person talked directly to the leader rather than participating in a group discussion.* (*From Franklyn S. Haiman,* Group Leadership and Democratic Action, *Houghton Mifflin, 1951.*)

leadership, nor does it imply that *all* planning and goal-setting must be done by the group. There are many instances in democratic behavior where, for purposes of efficiency, certain goals, plans, and checks on progress must rest with a leader because he has specialized knowledge or abilities. Although a schoolroom may represent a segment of democratic society, we would all agree that the teacher has certain responsibilities assigned to him by virtue of his position, and that he has specialized abilities and knowledge that must cause him frequently to assume an authoritarian role. At least he must make clear the area in which democratic activity can be allowed to take place. Indeed, one of the prime bases for a true democracy is the recognition of special responsibilities. Leadership assigned by the group, as in the case of our elected political officers, must be accepted and followed. Democracy does not mean that every member will vote on every issue every time.

Development of leadership

Hurlock (17), in discussing at length the subject of leadership among adolescents, points out that leadership is not a quality common to all situations. Among adolescents, at least, different individuals will function as leaders in different activities. Leaders of various types can be detected. Spaulding (18), who studied junior college leaders, distinguished the social-climbing leader who through prestige has gathered a social following, the intellectual success, the "good fellow" who collects important school positions, the big athlete, and the leader who is interested in athletics and in other activities as well. School leaders tend to participate socially in various activities. Leadership which develops early in children tends to persist, even though a person may not be a leader in all situations.

What are some of the traits of leaders? In general they are likely to be taller than followers, physically superior, and earlier to mature. Because children place great emphasis on physical superiority, and because the early maturer can therefore tend to dominate (or become an object of admiration), we may assume that such children gain an initial advantage. Leadership is practiced by these taller, heavier, more mature children, and in turn, because of this practice and because of social habituation to acceptance as leaders, these children may continue their roles as they get older. Adolescent leaders must make a satisfactory appearance, must be well-groomed and wear becoming clothing. Leaders are likely to be somewhat more intelligent than followers, but not markedly so. Leaders tend to get grades somewhat above average and to be slightly older than followers. Health, physical attractiveness, high energy level, loyalty, sensitivity to the needs of others, creativeness, tact, sense of humor, willingness to assume responsibility and do hard work, and dependability — plus specific abilities or advantages required in a given situation, all help to determine leaders. Although individual leaders differ markedly, we may conclude that the boy or girl who attains early leadership and who possesses to a marked degree those qualities of personality and character which society admires will become a leader in college and in adult life.

This is not to say that leadership cannot be learned or that people who are deficient in certain qualities cannot achieve leadership. Napoleon, largely through aggressiveness and the desire to compensate, achieved power in spite of his stature, his tendency to dominate, and his moodiness. Unexpected skills, such as his military genius, are often brought to light. Motivation to lead sometimes suddenly develops in persons previously willing to follow.

Membership roles

Benne and Sheats (19) have listed various roles of the members of a group. They classify these under three main headings:

> 1. *Group task roles.* These roles are related to the task which the group is undertaking. The purpose of these roles is to facilitate group effort in selection and definition of a common problem, and in the solution of that problem.
> 2. *Group building and maintenance roles.* These are designed to aid the group in functioning as a group — strengthening, making the group more cohesive, regulating, and altering or maintaining the group's way of working.
> 3. *Individual roles.* These roles are necessary to satisfy particular needs of the individual within the group and are not directly related to group task or group building roles.

These categories bring to light a striking concern with furthering the group task. Perhaps you have not given much thought to the idea that a group has problems to solve and that it undertakes certain tasks. Yet a little reflection will indicate that the only group which does not have projects is the one which never does anything. Even purely recreational groups plan their activities. The second group of roles listed above, those directed toward group functioning, raise questions about the kind of leadership the group receives, the sort of communication existing between members and leader and among the members. How does the group arrive at solutions to its problems? Can group thinking be improved on? The individual role is related to the fact that individual members have purposes of their own in addition to those which they share with the group. If the individual member does not receive satisfaction of his needs, as we have shown before, he may not remain active in the group. He may become a passive member or he may leave the group entirely.

The following "group task roles" identified by Benne and Sheats (20) are briefly defined:

1. *The initiator-contributor.* This person suggests or proposes to the group new ideas or a new way of regarding the group problem.

2. *The information seeker.* This person seeks clarification of suggestions which are made. He wants them based on facts, and upon authority relevant to the problem.

3. *The opinion seeker.* This person asks for a clarification of the values which the group holds in relation to the problem.

4. *The information giver.* This person states his opinion in regard to a suggestion.

5. *The elaborator.* This person follows through on suggestions, trying to see what they would mean to the group and how they would work out in practice.

6. *The coordinator.* This person clarifies the various suggestions and tries to pull them together and coordinate them.

7. *The orientor.* This person tries to show the group the position it is now taking and may raise questions about its direction.

8. *The evaluator-critic.* This person subjects the group's activity to some criterion — practicality, logic, etc.

9. *The energizer.* This person stimulates the group to action.

10. *The procedural technician.* This person performs routine tasks for the group — secretary, recorder, treasurer, etc.

The following "group building and maintenance roles" are also enlightening:

1. *The encourager.* This person praises good points, exhibits acceptance, "we" feeling, and group solidarity.

2. *The harmonizer.* This person attempts to mediate differences between members or their points of view.

3. *The compromiser.* This person, when he has stated a suggestion or idea and a conflict has arisen involving his point of view, is willing to compromise or yield, or admit error.

4. *The expediter.* This person attempts to encourage communication, bringing persons into the discussion who have not given their ideas, keeping the discussion to the point, etc.

5. *The standard setter.* This person expresses standards for the group to attempt to achieve, and applies them in evaluating group processes.

6. *The group-observer or commentator.* This person keeps records of the group process in action and brings such data into the discussion as seem pertinent.

7. *The follower.* This person is a more or less passive and accepting person, going along with the ideas of others.

The following "individual roles" are portrayed:

1. *The aggressor.* This person may express disapproval of others, joke excessively, attack the group or the problem, show envy, etc.
2. *The blocker.* This person is negativistic and resistant, disagreeing and opposing beyond reasonable objections.
3. *The recognition-seeker.* This person boasts, talks excessively, acts in unusual ways, to enhance himself.
4. *The self-confessor.* This person brings in personal feelings, ideas, etc., not pertinent or not oriented to the group.
5. *The playboy.* This person does not involve himself in group processes, but sits back in horseplay, whispering, etc.
6. *The dominator.* This person tries to assert authority, giving directions, attesting his "rights," etc.
7. *The help-seeker.* This person attempts to express insecurity, gain sympathy, or in other ways depreciate himself.
8. *The special interest pleader.* This person expresses his own biases or prejudices by pleading for the minority groups within the group.

As you have seen, the "individual" roles described above are not flattering. They leave us with the feeling that members should all be oriented toward the group task and toward helping the group find successful ways of working and maintaining itself. Within this context, those who are self-oriented are considered to be acting more or less against group interests — if not actively disrupting group progress, at least not contributing toward it. Benne and Sheats bring out reasons for the emergence of these individual roles — a low level of training in group skills among members or leaders, the prevalence of authoritarian or laissez-faire (as opposed to democratic) points of view, a low level of group maturity, poor discipline and morale, or an inappropriately chosen or defined task.

The article we have cited was based upon methods of analysis developed at the First National Training Laboratory in Group Development and was concerned with finding whether group membership roles would respond favorably to the training. The authors relate that a group's own self-observation and evaluation of its processes do prove useful in training members; flexibility of roles and the enactment of a wider range of roles can come from commitment by the group to such training.

Pigors (21) sees membership roles from a slightly different point of view. He names the constructive follower, who will assume responsibility and further the work of the group; the routine follower, who is willing to work but lacks initiative; the impulsive follower, whose relationship to the leader is in the nature of an emotional involvement (admiration, a "crush," etc.); and the subservient follower, whose activities are more or less machinations to further his own ends.

As we have seen, some persons act as clowns, using group time for entertainment and self-enhancement. Others are negativistic or destructive; in these the motives of jealousy, a desire to be different, or a desire to attract attention may be operating. If too many members of the group are of the impulsive or subversive types, the group quite naturally lacks cohesiveness. The formation of cliques within the group, the desires and attempts of certain members to dominate and control, sniping at leaders, and ineptness in leaders represent real threats to the group. Failure of communication among members, or between members and leaders, and inability to formulate and progress toward goals weaken the group.

Suggested activities

1. Formulate group membership roles and act them out. Analyze their effect upon the group.

2. Study a group in action. How many of the above roles can you find? Are they apparently related to group success or failure?

3. Study a group of which you are a member. What are the characteristics of its leaders? What are their qualifications? Techniques?

4. Analyze your own roles in various groups. Are you satisfied? Can you deliberately change your roles?

5. Make a tape recording of a portion of a group meeting or class discussion. Discuss this meeting in terms of roles portrayed.

    A.   PRIMARY GROUPS
    B.   LEADERSHIP AND MEMBERSHIP

● C. IMPROVING THE DYNAMICS OF A GROUP

In terms of the values of group activities, group decisions are more likely to be effective than precepts or lectures in overcoming resistance to change of behavior (22). For example, the modern industrial, school, or civic group may act much in the manner of the old-time town meeting, with various members voicing opinions and all cooperating in arriving at a group decision. This decision, because it is the result of group thinking, will probably be carried out wholeheartedly. A case in point is the development of an "ethic" of price-cutting by various dealers of electrical appliances. Decisions by executives of a dealer organization would probably be circumvented or ignored, but if the dealers themselves come to a group agreement as to what should and should not be done about cut-rate merchandising, the decision will probably be carried out more sincerely.

The formulation of the problem, the organization of the discussion, and the successful arrival at a group decision require not only attempts by the group to solve these problems but also excellent leadership. Gibb, Platts, and Miller formulate eight general principles which can be applied to improve group efforts at problem-solving (23). The following listing is based upon these principles:

1. *Atmosphere.* A pleasant, comfortable, and adequate meeting place is important, as is also the equality in placing of members. (Some teachers like to have students and themselves sitting in a circle, facing inward, for purposes of class discussion.) Informality, refreshments, facilities for working (tables, papers, and pencils, etc.), smoking arrangements (in groups where smoking is permitted), a pleasant, well-aired, well-lighted room — these all contribute to the success of group efforts.

2. *Threat reduction.* A small group, informality, use of name plates, devices for getting acquainted, permissiveness in allowing members to speak, encouragement of the timid — such devices all help to reduce the threat to individuals in a group situation.

3. *Distributive leadership.* Sharing the leadership, with consequent sharing of responsibility, more active participation of members, and feelings of belonging, is vital. This sharing of leadership also aids in developing leadership in members and tends to avoidance of status leadership.

4. *Goal formulation.* Within the proper framework of the group, purposes must be formulated, defined, and achieved. A group without purpose shows little progress and induces little of that feeling that the group is worthwhile which is necessary if it is to compete for the time of its members.

5. *Flexibility.* Provision must be made for altering plans. As something new and important comes to the attention of the group, it may wish to change its agenda. Goals must be capable of change, also, as well as procedures. Plans for a meeting are necessary, but plans which are too detailed lack flexibility and become formal and unrealistic.

6. *Consensus.* Majority rule is not always satisfactory, for the needs of the minority are often disregarded. Consensus is desirable, if at all possible. Consensus implies that everyone is in agreement as to the solution to the problem, and the solution thus represents the joint efforts of the group as a whole.

7. *Process awareness.* Groups must become aware of how they arrive at decisions. A decision is of little value if the method of reaching it alienates some of the members. Are the members being easily swayed, dominated, or are problems "solved" merely because the time to close the meeting is drawing near? Are all being heard? Are there snap decisions? Are decisions made from sheer boredom?

8. *Continual evaluation.* A concern for self-evaluation can be a healthy sign. The group will be evaluated anyway — by the members and by outsiders. If evaluation and indicated changes are carried out, group functioning should be improved. The evaluation should be informal and continual, and is coincident with Item 7 above.

As college students, and later as college graduates, most of you are, have been, or will be leaders of one group or another. Think of the Parent-Teachers' meetings called to discuss problems of the schools, the community meetings called to discuss town problems, student meetings called for various purposes, lodge meetings, and business meetings. In any case, groups have meetings, and meetings turn into discussions of problems of some sort. We list here some suggestions for group leaders which help to keep discussions on the track and to come out with successful conclusions:

A. GETTING STARTED
  1. State objectives
  2. Motivate the discussion
     a. Stimulate interest.
     b. Consider different media.
B. BUILDING THE AGENDA
  1. Stick to building the agenda.
  2. Defer details until later.
  3. Simplify statements for the agenda.
C. HANDLING THE EXCESSIVE TALKER
  1. Break in.
  2. Summarize statements.
  3. Relate remarks to the subject.
  4. Invite other opinions.
  5. Maintain human relations.
D. RESOLVING CONFLICTS
  1. Break in early.
  2. Reduce tension by such acts as
     a. clarifying or summarizing.
     b. changing the subject.
     c. bringing in other opinions.
     d. suggesting a recess or break.
E. KEEPING THINGS MOVING
  1. Summarize progress.
  2. Keep the next step in mind.
F. KEEPING ON THE BEAM
  1. Break in on discussion.
  2. Give recognition to speakers.
  3. Remind the group of the point under discussion.
  4. Suggest dropping or postponing discussion.
  5. Restate the problem and invite new comments.
G. WORKING WITH A DOMINATING LEADER
  1. Try to give the leader insight into the effect of his role by
     a. evaluation of group work.
     b. tape recording (for leadership training purposes).
     c. participation count (of members speaking).
  2. Break up into sub-groups.
H. CLOSING THE MEETING
  1. Allow time for summary.
  2. Restate plans or decisions made.

Finally, groups which have successful meetings consider problem-solving from various angles. Arriving at a consensus, rather than decision by a major-

Following a leader. *Will the dynamics of this group be such that the boy can persuade his friends to do as he suggests? Note the types of interest and indifference expressed. (Max Tharpe.)*

ity. contributes to group satisfaction if it can be accomplished. Leadership should be distributed among those who can best fulfill its function and, as we have seen, should change with the situation and goals to be accomplished. Awareness of processes by which decisions are arrived at is important in that it may permit members to prevent decisions which are "forced" by dominating leaders or strong followers, railroaded through by cliques, made hastily because of fatigue, boredom or lack of time, which do not consider minority members and their needs, or are entirely impractical or undesirable. Decisions of these sorts lead only to unfavorable comment outside the meeting, lack of cooperation, inability to achieve group goals, and a consequent drop in the prestige and membership of the group. Rigidity and formality are usually out of place in student groups, although Robert's Rules of Order are often invoked simply to keep decisions organized and facilitate group progress. The formulation of a pleasing and unthreatening emotional climate before group decisions are made is important — humor, emotional support, encouragement, and the "soft language that turneth away wrath" all are needed.

From a practical point of view, each person should ask himself whether the groups to which he belongs serve a real purpose or are being more or less imposed upon him by others. Often people get the idea that there should be such and such a club, and thereupon formulate plans and recruit membership. Forming a club must be a function of the prospective members themselves. If there is a real need to be served, the club will be formed and will survive. If it develops artificially, its membership will not be stable, the artificiality will soon become evident, and the members will find that the time and effort they have given is time wasted.

Now if you will refer again to pages 321–322, you will find that two types of college classes were portrayed. Pressey, in accordance with his opinion that students might profit from a "socialized" class, tried to introduce this method into some of the required educational psychology classes in the College of Education at Ohio State University. Each class, whether "socialized" or conventional, included no more than twenty-five students. In the "socialized" classes, the students spent about half their time working informally and socially about round tables in groups of five or six. There were some field trips. Social, cooperative work was stressed.

In conventional classes he found that by the end of the quarter acquaintance among students had progressed but little. The median student knew only five classmates after eleven weeks, the best acquainted knew only eleven, and 6 per cent still knew none at all. In contrast, informal classes ended with a median acquaintance of eleven, and only 4 per cent knew none or only one. As time went on, most of the students began to spend a share of their out-of-class time together — at lunch, working in the library, meeting at campus hangouts, or dating.

Instructors knew far more about personality and social problems of students in the informal classes, and were in a position to offer help if help was needed.

Do you feel that there are values in working as a member of a group, rather than in participating as an individual among a large group of individuals? Do you feel that one can learn to operate effectively as a group member or leader? Do you feel that groups can successfully formulate and solve problems? Perhaps more knowledge of the theories of group dynamics and of the facts that have been discovered, and more practice as a group member or leader will be valuable experience for you. The fact that you are a college student will provide you with many opportunities to read and practice some of the knowledge of group behavior which is now available.

SUMMARY

Group relationships are a natural concomitant of living in a society. These relationships can be satisfying and can aid materially in helping us achieve our goals and satisfy our needs, or they can be unsatisfying and frustrating. How we handle ourselves as leaders and group members can contribute to the cohesiveness and success of the groups, or it can lead to their destruction. Groups influence their members in many ways, but because groups are so varied, we have been able in this chapter to illustrate only a few of these influences.

Among primary or face-to-face groups, the earliest and perhaps the most influential is the family into which we are born. The family, an institution which has changed markedly from its earlier roles, still exerts influence through training, precept, interaction among members, the formation of attitudes, mores, and character, and exerts force when necessary. Especially because of its influence in early childhood, the family contributes to personality. Patterns of parent–child relationships — indulgence, dominance, rejection — help to determine not only the child's outlook upon life, but help him to learn roles which he will use to attempt to satisfy his needs. Although the parents exert great influence over the child, the reciprocal influence which the child exerts upon the parents is also important.

Groups beyond the family are also potent forces. The childhood play group, informally organized around neighborhood propinquity, is another determiner of patterns of social interaction. It, too, contributes to mores, language, attitudes, moral development, and training in social abilities. High school cliques and crowds, more formal and selective, may even outweigh the home and family in influence during adolescence. These groups provide training in social relationships, recreation, leadership, formation of values and attitudes, and the satisfaction of needs for affection, security, enhancement of the self-concept, recognition, status, and the need for learning courtship behavior.

Organized groups have special functions. They tend to be less recreational, although recreation can be their main purpose. They are relatively formal, and tend to select members carefully. They control and restrict their members in certain ways.

Leadership is important in small groups. The Lewin, Lippitt, and White studies indicate the effects of democratic, authoritarian, and laissez-faire leadership. Various implications arise from these experiments, although we must be careful in applying their findings to our everyday group life, partly because few leadership techniques show such clear-cut separation of methods in actual practice, and the experiments were performed in a society which is predisposed to democratic practices so that these might subconsciously be favored by the subjects. Nevertheless, the experiments suggest that other values in democratic techniques outweigh the disadvantages of fumbling and slowness.

Although certain hereditary traits (early maturation, size, height, good looks, intelligence) may aid children in becoming leaders, the qualities of personality and character necessary to leadership may be learned. Leadership traits tend to persist, but leaders are of various kinds and no one person tends to be a leader in all situations.

Group effectiveness and cohesiveness can be enhanced. As the personal goals of members are furthered, and as members formulate group goals and attempt to achieve them, group effectiveness is increased. Various techniques of leadership can be employed to aid the group in setting and achieving goals, but members have responsibilities for their own actions in terms of personal interaction, assisting the group in various ways, and attempting to further group goals as well as personal ends.

This chapter, of course, does not provide a complete discussion of group dynamics, but it does outline some of its main concerns and indicate its methods. If you are interested in learning more about this subject you should examine some of the references listed below. You may also wish to apply some of the points we have discussed to the activities of the groups to which you belong.

Suggested activities

1. What were your purposes in joining the groups to which you belong? Are you as successful a group member as you desire to be? Analyze your position and try to arrive at hypotheses in regard to your relationship to various groups.

2. How many students in this classroom do you know? Would knowledge of your classmates' names, backgrounds, and interests be of value to you? How could you acquire this knowledge?

3. Tape various group discussions. Analyze them in terms of criteria listed in this chapter.

4. Arrange small group discussions. Try to add to your knowledge of successful group leadership and membership through such discussions.

REFERENCES

1. S. L. Pressey and D. C. Hanna, "The Class as a Psycho-Sociological Unit," *J. Psychol.*, 1943. Quoted in A. P. Coladarci, *Educational Psychology, A Book Of Readings*, Dryden Press, New York, 1955, pp. 246–253.
2. *Ibid.*, p. 246.
3. K. Young, *Personality and Problems of Adjustment*, Appleton-Century-Crofts, New York, Rev. 1952.
4. R. W. White, *The Abnormal Personality*, Ronald Press, New York, second edition, 1956, p. 151.
5. E. Hurlock, *Adolescent Development*, McGraw-Hill, New York, 1955, p. 139 ff.
6. K. C. Garrison, "A Comparative Study of the Attitudes of College Students Toward Certain Domestic and World Problems," *J. Soc. Psychol.*, 1951, 34, pp. 47–54.
7. H. K. Mull, "The Ethical Discrimination of Various Groups of College Women," *J. Soc. Psychol.*, 1952, 35, pp. 69–72.
8. H. G. Gough, "Studies of Social Intolerance: I. Some Psychological and Sociological Correlates of Anti-Semitism," *J. Soc. Psychol.*, 1951, 33, pp. 273–346.
9. L. E. Klee, "How Do You Feel About World Peace?" *J. Educ. Res.*, 1949, 43, pp. 187–196.
10. I. Lazar, "Student-Faculty Similarities in the Choice of Social Values," *Amer. Psychol.*, 1954, 9, p. 413.
11. I. Brasch, "The Effects of Competition, Both Individual and Group, in the Achievement of Sixth-Grade Pupils in Arithmetic," *Abstr. of Grad. Theses in Educ.*, Teachers College, University of Cincinnati, 1940, pp. 65–78.

12. E. R. Hilgard, E. M. Sait, and G. A. Magaret, "Level of Aspirations Affected by Relative Standing in an Experimental Social Group," *J. Exper. Psychol.*, 1940, 27, pp. 411–421.
13. V. N. Bedoian, "Mental Health Analysis of Socially Over-Accepted, Socially Under-Accepted, Over-age, and Under-age Pupils in the Sixth Grade." *J. Educ. Res.*, 1954, 47, pp. 531–548.
14. F. B. G. Gilbreth and E. G. Carey, *Cheaper by the Dozen,* Crowell, New York, 1948.
15. K. Lewin, R. Lippitt, and R. K. White, "Patterns of Aggressive Behavior in Experimentally Created 'Social Climates,'" *J. Soc. Psychol.*, 1939, 10, pp. 271–299.
16. R. Lippitt, "An Experimental Study of the Effect of Democratic and Authoritarian Group Atmospheres," *University of Iowa Studies in Child Welfare,* University of Iowa Press, Iowa City, 1940, 16, pp. 43–195.
17. E. Hurlock, *op. cit.*
18. C. B. Spaulding, "Types of Junior College Leaders," *Sociol. and Soc. Res.*, 1933, 18, pp. 163–168.
19. K. D. Benne and P. Sheats, "Functional Roles of Group Members," *J. Soc. Issues.* Abridged in J. M. Seidman, *Readings in Educational Psychology,* Houghton Mifflin, Boston, 1955.
20. *Ibid.*, p. 15.
21. P. Pigors, *Leadership or Domination,* Houghton Mifflin, Boston, 1935.
22. D. Cartwright and A. Zander, *Group Dynamics,* Row, Peterson, Evanston, 1953, Chapters 20–21.
23. J. R. Gibb, Grace N. Platts, and Lorraine F. Miller, *Dynamics of Participative Groups,* John S. Swift & Company, St. Louis, Mo., 1951.

SUGGESTIONS FOR FURTHER READING

Britt, S. H., *Selected Readings in Social Psychology,* Rinehart, New York, 1950.
Brodbeck, M., "The Role of Small Groups in Mediating the Effects of Propaganda," *J. Abnorm. Soc. Psychol.*, 1956, 52, pp. 166–170.
Brown, W. H., "An Instrument for Studying Viscidity within Small Groups," *Educ. Psychol. Measmt.*, 1953, 13, pp. 402–417.
Cavan, R. S., *The American Family,* Crowell, New York, 1953.
Festinger, L., "Wish, Expectation and Group Performance as Factors Influencing Level of Aspiration," *J. Abn. Psychol.*, 1942, 37, pp. 154–200.
Gilchrist, J. C., "The Formation of Social Groups under Conditions of Success and Failure," *J. Abnorm. Soc. Psychol.*, 1952, 47, pp. 174–187.
Hodges, H. N., Jr., "Campus Leaders and Non-Leaders," *Sociol. Soc. Res.*, 1953, 37, pp. 251–255.
King, B. T., and I. L. Janis, "Comparison of the Effectiveness of Improvised vs. Non-improvised Role-playing in Producing Opinion Changes," *Hum. Relat.*, 1956, 9, pp. 177–186.
Laird, D. A., and E. C. Laird, *The New Psychology for Leadership,* McGraw-Hill, New York, 1956.
Murray, V. P., and C. E. Murray, *Guide Lines for Group Leaders,* Whiteside and Wm. Morrow, New York, 1954.

Shaw, M. E., "Some Effects of Irrelevant Information upon Problem-Solving by Small Groups," *J. Soc. Psychol.*, 1958, 47, pp. 33–37.

Shaw, M. E., and J. C. Gilchrist, "Intra-Group Communication and Leader Choice," *J. Soc. Psychol.*, 1956, 43, pp. 133–138.

Snyder, R., J. R. P. French, Jr., and R. J. Hoehn, *Experiments on Leadership in Small Groups*, U.S.A.F. Personnel Training Research Center Revised Report, Washington, 1955, No. AFPRTC–TN–55–1.

Ziller, R. C., "Four Techniques of Group Decision Making under Uncertainty," *J. Appl. Psychol.*, 1957, 41, pp. 384–388.

Psychology

in Practice

Up to this point we have been considering how a knowledge of psychology can help the individual adjust to forces within himself and his environment. We have sought to demonstrate how the application of psychological principles can aid the individual in understanding himself and others. Now we shall consider how psychology can be of use to society in general.

Although we emphasize the role of professional psychologists, we wish to point out two things: first, psychologists represent many areas of specialization in working toward the solution of various social problems; second, psychologists do not always work alone, for men in other fields contribute much to the prevention and solution of social problems. Consider the following situations:

1. A school principal discovers that Joe Johnson is often absent from school and is failing. There appears to be a family problem and some evidence of delinquency.

2. An industrialist, wishing to establish a plant in a small city, wants to know where to build it. He needs to know about economic factors — transportation, accessibility to raw materials, supply of labor, problems of marketing his product. He also needs to know something about living conditions in a likely town — educational opportunities for workers' children, recreational opportunities, community mores, housing.

3. A paratrooper suddenly complains that he is unable to use his right arm. Although he recalls no injury to the arm, it has become paralyzed. He is suffering, also, from feelings of insecurity: "Can I ever hold a job?" "What will my family think?"

How Psychology Combats Social Problems

How can psychology be of use to society? How does psychology help in the study of delinquency and crime? What has psychology contributed to a knowledge of the causes and cures for various social problems? What principles of psychology have been applied to industrial procedures and techniques? What use has been made of psychology in the Armed Forces? In education? What careers are open to trained psychologists?

4. The "city fathers" discover that their town has an above average incidence of fatal automobile accidents. Insurance companies are highly concerned and are putting pressure on the city government to do something about the problem.

As you consider these representative problems, ask yourself whether they could be solved by any one professional worker or group? Does the psychologist fit into the picture? In what ways? This chapter points out the areas in society in which psychology can be helpful.

● A. THE STUDY OF DELINQUENCY AND CRIME

Recently we have become concerned about the number and seriousness of crimes being committed by youngsters twelve to eighteen years of age. We see an increase in car thefts, in beatings by street corner gangs, in burglary and robbery, and occasionally in more serious offenses. We may wonder what has gone wrong with the younger generation. Because a large percentage of habitual criminals have begun their careers in their early teens, our concern is for young people in particular. Is this a psychological problem? A cultural-social problem? Or a purely legal problem?

In Chapter 10 we examined the variety of customs which exist in various cultures and concluded that an act is not necessarily "good" nor "bad" in itself, but must be interpreted in terms of the sanctions and mores of the culture in which it is committed. Thus a criminal act is one in which the individual does something that is contrary to the sanctions of the society in which he lives. A delinquent act, in turn, is an act contrary to law which, if committed by an adult, would be considered a crime. A delinquent act in one state might be a criminal act in another because of differences in the legal definition of an adult. Also, there is much variability among offenses which lead to arrest. For example, one of the authors of this book examined the police "blotters" in his city to identify the offenses for which young people had been arrested. Offenses varied from fighting, stealing cars, mugging, and armed robbery to such minor offenses as throwing pop bottles in the lake, selling football souvenirs without a license, loitering in public places, and making unnecessary noises in residential areas. Some arrests were for trivial offenses.

It makes some difference who performs the act and under what circumstances it is performed. At college and professional football games the fans often destroy the goal posts after homecoming or championship games. Such practices as "crashing" theaters, setting bonfires in the streets, and making noises throughout the night in residential areas are still observed in a few college towns. These activities are usually considered evidences of the high spirits of students, and do not lead to arrest; or, if the offenders are apprehended, they are soon released. But what would happen if non-college young men and women destroyed college property, "crashed" the theater, built fires, or otherwise disturbed the peace? Almost certainly the consequences for them would be more serious.

Shaw (1) has remarked that, in certain villages, taking watermelons "on the sly" from a farmer's field is almost an expected part of growing up. Taking a melon from a fruit stand, however, is considered to be a theft. Shaw concludes that all of us might have been labeled delinquents if we had been caught in some of our acts.

Causes of delinquency

Psychologists have studied many aspects of juvenile delinquency, but especially its causes. We stated in Chapter 6 that behavior is determined by the phenomenal field of the individual. Applied to the delinquent individual, this means that the way in which he perceives himself and his environment is the cause of his delinquent act. Thus we cannot identify the cause through study of the physical and social environment alone. Instead we must ascertain *why* the child interprets himself and his environment in such a way that his most reasonable response in a particular situation is, knowingly or unknowingly, to commit an offense against society. Evidently his past experiences, present motives, mental health, and adjustment lead to an unsatisfactory self-concept — or he interprets conformity to the customs, mores, and laws of his community as a threat to his self-concept. In some instances, he may even be unaware of the laws and therefore not know that he is violating them.

Although the causes of delinquent acts are different for each individual case, there are certain conditions in the environment and within the individuals who commit offenses which are worthy of examining.

Physical and social environment. In some large cities there are thousands of people living in an area of one square mile, ten city blocks each way. Think of the problems involved in providing adequate housing. Proper schools, recreation areas, sanitation, and privacy are almost non-existent. Tenants are forced to live in congested quarters under unhealthy and unhappy conditions. Teen-age gangs often roam the streets, showing no interest in the meager club and playground facilities or in their schools. Often both parents in a family work. Many of these crowded areas are made up of people of various national origins, races, languages, and creeds. With these groups of such different backgrounds living so close to each other, conflicts often occur. Children sometimes do not know right from wrong, as interpreted in the laws of the

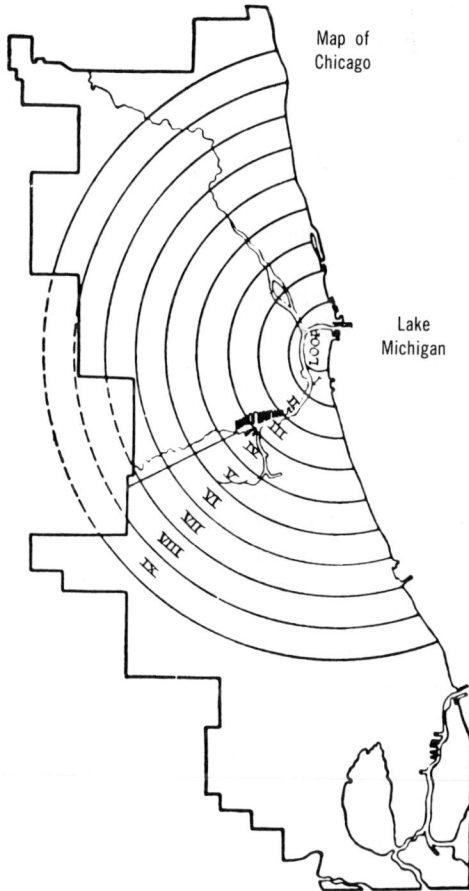

Map of Chicago

Lake Michigan

Delinquency rate and residential standards. *In Chicago, the highest rate of juvenile delinquency is at the center of the city (Zone I on this map) in transitional areas where slums are more prevalent. In Zone I, 15.3 per cent of the segment of the population aged 10 to 16 appeared in the Juvenile Court during a 7-year period, as compared with 3.7 per cent of children of that age group in Zone IX, which includes residential suburban areas. In tabulating data like this, psychology contributes valuable information for solving social problems. (From Clifford R. Shaw,* Delinquency Areas, *Copyright 1929 by the University of Chicago.)*

city; parents sometimes teach the children to disobey laws or at least do little or nothing to prevent disobedience. It is notable that not all, or even most, children in these areas become delinquent. The majority of the parents and children in these neighborhoods are law-abiding. Since there are so many persons per square mile in these congested areas, however, it is inevitable that a high percentage of the total number of delinquents may be expected to come from them as against the more favored residential districts.

Children raised in such impoverished physical and social circumstances may feel that they are inadequate as individuals and that they must fight, steal, or be sexually promiscuous in order to be important — that is, in order to enhance their self-concepts. Moreover, if the child feels that he has little to lose and much to gain by disobeying the law, he may quite logically choose to break the law.

Undoubtedly improved housing, public play areas, better schools, and improved social service work would help more children to become zestful, happy, law-abiding citizens. The rebuilding of slums and the development of housing projects help to improve the environment. Less discrimination throughout our society on such bases as socio-economic status, national origin, race, and religion might also prevent many of the conflicts that lead to delinquency and crime. In this connection, it is interesting to note that some of our most serious conflicts have arisen recently in northern cities where attempts have been made to provide low-cost rental housing without discrimination on any basis. Thus improving physical conditions alone will not lead to the elimination of delinquency; the social environment also must be improved.

Medical or physical factors. Plastic surgery has sometimes been found useful in treating criminals who were dissatisfied with their personal appearance. It has helped some people who were sensitive about their looks to remove scars, straighten noses, and re-shape cauliflower ears. Some criminals have felt that they could not hold jobs because of their appearance. Others actually found that this was true. Treatment has enabled some of these people to lead more normal lives (2).

Children who are undersized or undernourished, who have thyroid difficulties, or who suffer from other physical disabilities may develop a feeling of antagonism toward society. An undersized boy may steal a car to gain status with his gang, thus showing them that his size doesn't make any difference in his importance to the gang. A hyperactive child may not do well in school. He may become a truant and then drift toward delinquency. The undernourished child may be led to steal food.

Treatment of the offender must include medical care to assure his good health so that he has every opportunity to compete physically with his fellows and to accept himself without engaging in disapproved conduct. Prevention of physical disabilities and deficiencies, which is a better solution to the problem of delinquency than the treatment of offenders already warped, can be undertaken in the home, in the schools, in city clinics, by social service workers, and by the churches. The consequences of such defects are often underestimated.

Emotional problems. It is possible that a delinquent may be well adjusted. Indeed, one researcher found delinquents to exhibit more leadership qualities, aggressiveness, courage, and better adjustment than the average child (3). Though these characteristics may appear in a group of delinquents, the individual delinquent who is well adjusted in relation to himself and other delinquents nevertheless has a set of values and ideals which are different from those embodied in our laws. Thus in a broad sense most, if not all, delinquents are maladjusted, for they have antisocial attitudes. This, of course, assumes that antisocial attitudes are indicative of maladjustment. Rationalization of delinquent acts, attention-getting by antisocial means, resentment against society, desire for status with a delinquent gang, and similar behavior can reflect emotional difficulties. Some delinquents may be neurotic; and some may be psychotic. And some may simply have learned ways of satisfying their emotional needs which are not acceptable to society. The study of emotional problems is an area in which the psychiatrist and psychologist are particularly useful. One of the first steps in deciding how to treat a delinquent youngster, in fact, is to give him a psychological examination.

Mental factors. Some delinquent behavior may be partly caused by low mental ability. That is, some criminal acts may be the results of efforts to satisfy needs through unintelligent means. Dull persons lack the knowledge of a variety of techniques for satisfying their needs and so may be quite suggestible. Moreover, they may not be farsighted enough to detect the consequences of their acts. Furthermore, because dull children do not usually do well in school, they tend to play truant and then move on to more serious delinquent activities.

While it is true that measured mental abilities of delinquents in corrective institutions show a somewhat lower mean than those of the population at large, we must be careful in interpreting this generalization. Any person who is forced to take a mental ability test under conditions of fear, worry, or resentment — as is often the case with delinquent children — is not likely to do as well as he would if conditions were normal. Furthermore, mental test scores reflect past learning and school experience, and the delinquent is almost always behind his grade in school, partly because of habitual truancy. The smaller proportion of bright youngsters in corrective institutions than in the normal population may result from the fact that the bright delinquent may not be as often identified as a delinquent, for since he is cleverer than his fellow offenders, he may avoid arrest or be able to talk his way out of trouble when he is caught (4).

Antisocial attitudes and values. Delinquents are social to the extent that they participate in gangs or other social groups. Gangs fulfill the needs of delinquents for status, recognition, affection, and security just as law-abiding groups fulfill these needs for other adolescents. The problem is that the values and attitudes of the delinquent gangs are contrary to the interests of society. The boys and girls in these groups need re-education to bring their values into harmony with those of law-abiding citizens. They need to accept the fact that their sub-culture cannot compete successfully with the culture as a whole.

Some delinquents are, therefore, normal in most respects but conform to certain standards of an abnormal society. Pressures placed upon children by one or two delinquent members of a crowd may turn an otherwise harmless group of youngsters into a vicious gang. For example, four or five boys may get together after a football game. Two "tougher" boys suggest stealing a car and taking a ride. The more honest boys demur, but may enter into the adventure after cries of "Chicken," questions about their loyalty to the group, or threats of beatings by the others. From this point, all are equally delinquent and must hang together to avoid detection by the authorities. Such an adventure, in turn, may lead to more serious ones.

The *asocial* criminal has not developed a conscience or value structure which is socially oriented — he tries to achieve his own ends without considering the cost to others. He does not, however, purposefully transgress against society. The *antisocial* person is against society, for whatever reasons seem logical to him. He may operate as a lone wolf, and he may often be mentally disturbed or psychopathic. His activities may be violent, perverted, or sadistic.

Preventing and treating delinquency

Delinquent youngsters are often the product of a variety of hereditary and environmental factors which predispose them to delinquency and which precipitate delinquent acts. A typical future delinquent is the child raised in a slum area in a large city in which the environment is anything but encouraging. He may be the victim of a broken home. His parents may drink excessively, may themselves be criminal or irresponsible, or may reject him. The delinquent child often knows no home in the true sense of the word. In his home, such as it is, he may not be properly taught or cared for. He may spend a great deal of time roaming the streets, where he may make friends with others whose circumstances are similar to his own, or where he may become a lone wolf.

For such children school is often no pleasure. Emotional problems and possibly a lack of mental ability may make attempts at learning only another source of frustration. Inadequate self-concepts developed from the home environment are reinforced at school, and they may develop feelings of guilt as well as of inadequacy. Needing affection, such children may rebel against society, whereas others might withdraw. Some become psychotic, and practically all are maladjusted.

An excellent film portraying the story of such a child is "The Quiet One" (5), which illustrates the background which led a particular boy to delinquency and the subsequent treatment at a corrective institution which started him on the road to better adjustment. The story reflects the modern policy of considering such children as individuals and providing the specialized help they need.

Often a magazine or newspaper article appears with a panacea for the prevention or treatment of delinquency. One such "cure" is the perennial "get tough" policy, which implies that if children were punished enough, others would learn from their example. Another view is that "parents are responsible for the acts of their children." Some people feel that parents should be punished if their children commit crimes, in the belief that delinquent acts would not occur if more careful supervision were exercised. Some persons stress slum clearance, others the study of religion. Some would-be reformers are of the highly over-sympathetic, "sob sister" type. Yet various cases of delinquency can teach us that there is no one environmental or other sole cause of criminal behavior, but rather a combination of the various factors which make up our phenomenal fields and phenomenal selves.

Psychology can do a great deal in the prevention and treatment of delinquency. It is possible to recognize potential delinquents and to develop patterns of preventive measures. In the case of Donald, the main character in "The Quiet One," the signs pointing toward the possibility of his delinquency were truancy from school and inability to learn. Clinical study might well have detected his problems at an early stage and suggested ways to solve them. Once he was at the training school, Wiltwyck, psychiatric examinations and informal psychotherapy did much to help him improve his outlook toward society and himself. Teachers are being taught to notice students who are friendless, too quiet, or unable to learn, as ones who may need special study. Courts are becoming sensitive to social and psychological factors in the backgrounds of the children brought before them, and disposition of delinquency cases often rests largely upon the recommendations of clinical staffs.

Many states are rapidly moving forward in the treatment of offenders. They are finding that youngsters should not be handled in the usual courtroom manner, for the stigma of being labeled a criminal and the possibility of contact with older delinquents and adult criminals may both be harmful. Thus we are now witnessing the development of special juvenile and family courts, whose purpose is to handle problems dealing with youthful offenders. Trained judges, social workers, psychologists, psychiatrists, medical officers, educators, probation and parole officers, and police are practicing rehabilitation and therapy, rather than punishment alone, for wrong doing.

Judgments are offered to the court concerning the symptomatology and prognosis for the individual, and the court tends to use enlightened judgment in handling these cases. Boys and girls may be institutionalized, given probation, sent to foster homes, returned to their own homes, sent to special schools, held for further examination, or released — depending largely on the opinion of clinical workers. Society thus brings several disciplines together to work on the problem.

City planners, social workers, medical authorities, police, educators, psychologists, and others are trying to introduce factors which will help children to become healthy, happy, and law-abiding citizens. Precipitating causes are being attacked, too, in various ways. Better schools, more adequate playgrounds, boys' clubs, and youth and community centers provide more opportunity for wholesome achievement of emotional and social needs. Such organizations as the YMCA and YWCA, Boy Scouts, Girl Scouts, FFA, FHA, 4-H, and other youth clubs help to foster positive growth and development. Providing more adequate supervision of taverns, dance halls, "red-light districts," hotels and motels, instituting curfew laws, enforcing truancy regulations, checking on child labor practices, and working with churches and schools on incipient cases of delinquency also aid in solving the problem. In the schools, especially, more emphasis is being given to the individual needs of children and to proper guidance and counseling. Parents are being consulted. Opportunities for those both ahead and behind their age-group in school are being found, and handicapped children are receiving special education.

Thus psychology, in cooperation with other fields of study, is aiding society in its attempts to solve the problems of delinquents and criminals. At the time of this writing there is a shortage of social workers, psychiatric social workers, psychometrists, school psychologists, psychiatrists, and other workers in this area. There is also a need for properly educated teachers. Students now considering a life-occupation may wish to know more about these fields. Chapter 14 will provide further information on how such fields may be more fully surveyed as offering possible careers.

Suggested activities

1. What agencies in your town take active part in the prevention or treatment of delinquency?

2. Visit a state (or county) correctional institution. How does it make use of psychology?

3. Survey police records, newspapers, or other sources of information to try to discover the causes of crimes, types of crimes, backgrounds of criminals, and their treatment by society. Does your information bear out the facts and suggestions we have presented?

A.   THE STUDY OF DELINQUENCY AND CRIME

● B.   PSYCHOLOGY IN INDUSTRY

Industrial psychology is one of the most fruitful fields of applied psychology. Besides proving so valuable in its own right, it has produced a considerable amount of research data which has helped other than industrial groups. If you apply for a position with a large corporation, you may be checked for your aptitude for the job by a psychometrist; if you become a supervisor or an executive, you will be given instruction in the psychology of labor relations; if you go into advertising, you will want to know consumer psychology and the psychology of advertising; and in salesmanship you will need to know something of how to develop and maintain good public relations, how to persuade people to buy your products, and perhaps how to handle sales meetings (group psychology).

We have already mentioned the celebrated Western Electric study (p. 315) which reported that increased production by a selected group of workers was more closely related to the fact that they had been set apart as a select experimental group and had subsequently developed a high group morale than it was due to any changes in working conditions.

Psychologists have also studied other conditions in industry, including the effect of color. Certain colors tend to evoke emotional tones in people. Hospitals have found that cool blues and greens tend to have a soothing effect, but that reds are disquieting. Color can also affect safety in an industrial plant. Highlighting danger areas saves accidents. The area around the shears on a steel-cutting machine or around the drill on a drill press may be painted yellow to call attention to the danger. The background parts of the machine may be painted gray, which is not distracting. Switches or controls may be orange or yellow; paths for routing wheelbarrows or hand trucks along the floor can be shown in various colors, and so on. The use of color applies not only to the machines but to the whole factory floor. Fire extinguishers will be red, a traditional, easily spotted color, and so will alarms. The work areas will be well lighted and attractive. Incidentally, some concerns have found that the use of music which fits into the factory rhythms tends to increase production. As a corollary, distracting music or that which does not fit into factory rhythms lowers efficiency.

Some years ago in a particular restaurant customers used to complain of being chilly in an ice-blue dining room. When it was painted a warm shade of red, they felt comfortable even though there was no change in the temperature. In another restaurant it was found that customers tended to linger over luncheon, holding up badly needed table space. When the room was painted a bright red-orange, they moved along faster (6). The appeal of food, too, is affected by color. Restaurateurs are giving considerable attention not only to the arrangement of food on the plate, but also to adding color to the menu.

Returning to psychology and management–labor relations, we find that labor discontent is related not only to pay or fringe benefits but also to the fact that the workers feel insecure, having little voice in the management of many industrial factors which affect them. If management tries to meet their demands for a voice in managing some of their own affairs, employee attitudes improve. Hiring, promotions, and firing are of interest to the working force, and unions demand a share in these matters. It has also been shown that the routine and rather unspectacular jobs of most machine operators may frustrate their desire

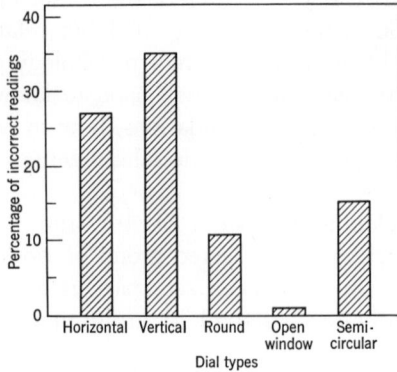

Percentage of incorrect readings

40
30
20
10
0

Horizontal Vertical Round Open window Semi-circular

Dial types

PSYCHOLOGY AIDING INDUS-TRY. *Pictured on these pages are a few of the many ways in which psychology has been valuable to industry.*

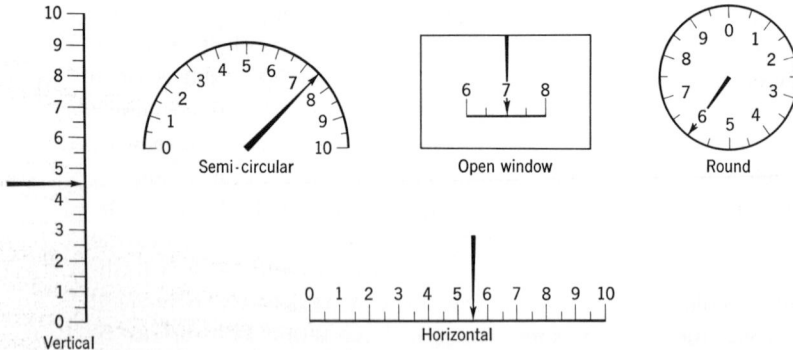

Vertical

10
9
8
7
6
5
4
3
2
1
0

Semi-circular

3 4 5 6 7
2   8
1   9
0   10

Open window

6 7 8

Round

9 0 1
8   2
7   3
6 5 4

0 1 2 3 4 5 6 7 8 9 10

Horizontal

RESEARCH IN PERCEPTION. Tests were used to determine which of these five dials was easiest to read and caused the fewest errors. The numbers, arrows, and spacings are the same; only the shapes are varied. Results of the experiment are shown in the graph above. The open window dial caused the lowest number of incorrect readings. (*Journal of Applied Psychology*, Vol. 32, pp. 177, 182.)

DRAMATIZATION OF WORKER'S PROBLEMS. Management conferences often include role-playing. Here a psychologist plays the part of a worker who is often absent, and an executive acts as the foreman who must decide what to do about it. (*Life* photo by Edward Clark.)

MARKET RESEARCH. Industry uses psychology in studying sales techniques, consumer opinion and demand, and advertising methods. Interviewers study the attitudes of potential buyers and recommend changes in products and methods of distribution. (Gale Tucker.)

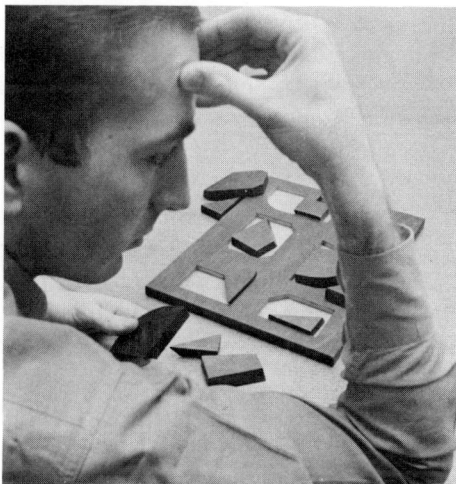

SCREENING APPLICANTS. This man is taking the puzzle board test, a psychological technique being studied by duPont to measure a job applicant's skills and aptitudes. (E. I. duPont de Nemours and Co.)

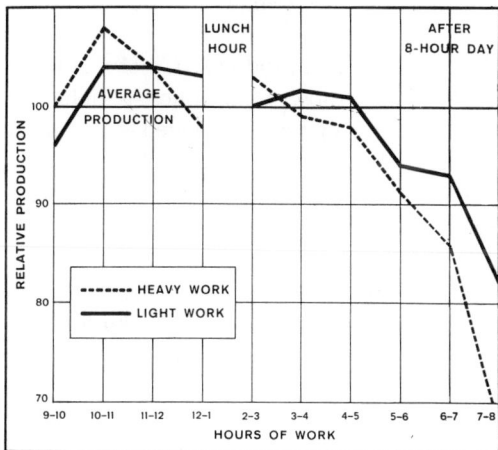

STUDIES OF EFFICIENCY. Psychology can help industrialists to understand the result of fatigue in terms of working efficiency. Since efficiency is reduced after seven hours of work, industry has come to realize that a long day actually causes the average output per hour to fall short. (Courtesy of *Life* magazine, © 1957, Time, Inc.)

for status and recognition. To alleviate this condition, many plants have arranged "field days" so that the workers can see what an important share they have in an entire manufacturing operation and can also show their families and friends the importance of their work.

Coffee breaks, well-equipped cafeterias, recreation programs, company newspapers and magazines which report worker happenings, and adequate lounging facilities improve labor–management relations. Profit-sharing tends to discourage slow-down techniques.

Industry is also providing more education for its supervisors and is selecting them more carefully. There are tactful ways of supervising, and there are driving and dictatorial ways which breed resentment. A supervisor can analyze a worker's performance and help him to improve, or he can merely tell him that he is not doing well. The first, of course, is the desirable way. Techniques of human relationships are being studied in group sessions and by the use of films.

Executives are being taught some techniques for studying the worker and giving him the type of job most suitable for him, of training him carefully, and seeing that he is as happy as possible. It has been found that some workers are inefficient, often ill, or absent because of family problems, including finances and divorces. The executive may counsel with workers, or he may employ specially trained counselors for this service. One of the new benefits furnished in some plants is group and individual counseling and the giving of information relative to preparation for retirement and old age. Men nearing retirement may receive information about health, worker benefits from governmental, factory, and other sources, suitable living conditions, and recreation and hobbies.

Surveys have been made of workers' reactions to various policies of management. Some results are very interesting. For one thing, workers tend to react more strongly to what they consider grievances (7) than to the things that management is doing *for* them. They are concerned with what other workers think of them, and accordingly they prize prestige and respect. Many do not want promotions and resent being given training and pep talks. They tend to protect their jobs and to feel that life is insecure because of layoffs or shutdowns. The immediate supervisor or foreman is the most important person in terms of the workers' reactions to management. A poor foreman can ruin an otherwise excellent management program.

Industry also makes use of psychology in selling its products. Careful surveys of the pulling power of various advertisements show which ones — including the use of color, illustrations, and kind and size of type employed — are most effective. Market surveys, correlated with shrewd estimates of the character and motivations of buyers, pay dividends. Surveys of TV and radio advertising are used to ascertain the market and the effectiveness of the company's advertising.

Finally, industry utilizes psychology to sample public opinion about a particular company and to help build good public relations by the right kind of advertising of the philosophy and activities of the plant. Sales talks which are partly designed to build desirable attitudes are carefully planned. The Bell Telephone System, for example, advertises the services it provides to the consumer and also shows that its employees are public-spirited, "home-town" individuals. Your new automobile was built to specifications determined in part by questioning customers. Safety features, styling, horsepower, and the like are carefully geared to information obtained in polls, advertisements, interviews, and employment of special consultants.

Thus, since business and commerce in one way or another cut across almost every facet of society, psychology is very important in industry. Many psychologists are employed in this field, and their efforts are coordinated with those of other specialists.

Suggested activities

1. Report on studies of how industry uses psychology in selling, labor relations, public relations, safety education, worker efficiency, salesmanship, or supervisory relations.

2. Examine aptitude tests which are used by some local industry in fitting workers to their jobs.

A. THE STUDY OF DELINQUENCY AND CRIME
B. PSYCHOLOGY IN INDUSTRY

● C. PSYCHOLOGY IN THE ARMED FORCES

How does the government get pilots for 300,000 airplanes? That was one problem it faced during World War II. To help determine who should get the expensive necessary training and who should be weeded out for safety's sake before he actually began to fly was the job assigned to Dr. John C. Flanagan, psychologist for the testing service of the American Council on Education (8). Dr. Flanagan had at one time more than a thousand people on his staff, so great was the problem.

Intelligence tests did not successfully distinguish between men who might be expected to become good pilots and those who might not. It was further found that a bad pilot might make a good navigator, and that a man who did well at one type of machine gun or cannon might not do well at another type. And, though reasoning ability, vocabulary, and mathematical skill were required for navigators, they did not help to identify good pilots or bombardiers. Flying, navigating, bombing, and gunnery all seemed to demand special skills. Tests already in use did not screen successfully for these skills.

Tests finally were developed which helped to measure the ability to fly, and these tests dealt with both physical and mental abilities. The development of these tests involved analyzing the job of flying, constructing tests which seemed most likely to assess the required abilities, then trying out the tests and studying

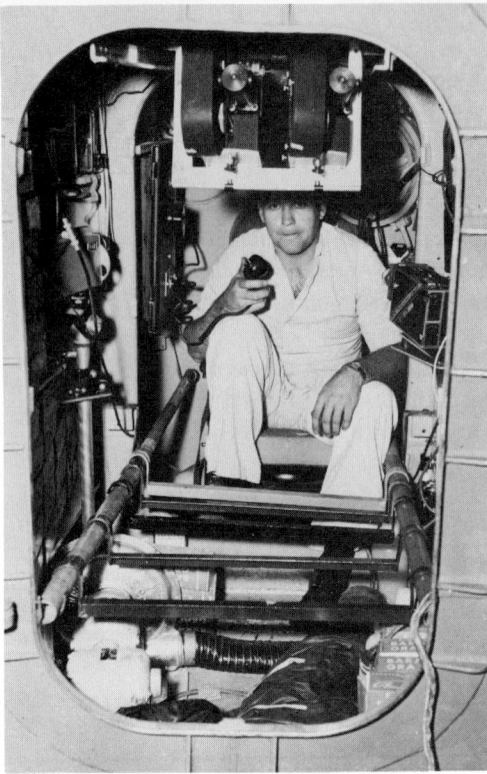

EFFECTS OF SPACE TRAVEL. A unique experimental space cabin was developed by the Air Force School of Aviation Medicine to determine the effects of a week-long flight into outer space.

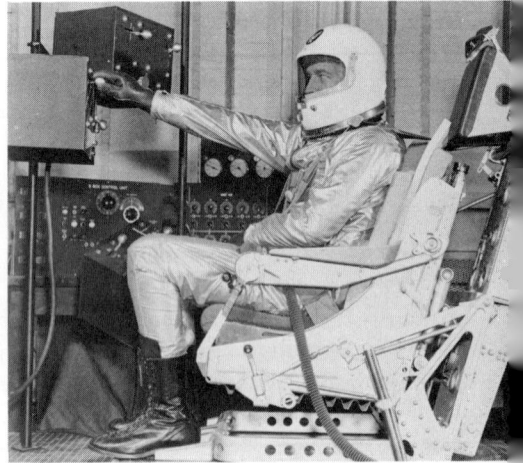

STUDYING MAN'S ABILITY UNDER CONDITIONS OF STRESS. The subject is timed on his speed at turning a knob, flipping a switch, pushing a button, adjusting a lever. Later he will be placed on a centrifuge supported by compressed air to determine how well he can perform the same tasks in a full-pressure suit under conditions of "weightlessness."

DETERMINING INDIVIDUAL ABILITY. To discover whether a man can become a good pilot, the Air Force measures his ability to make decisions under high thermal loads. The subject is placed in a heat chamber and must make complicated comparisons from a fast-moving film.

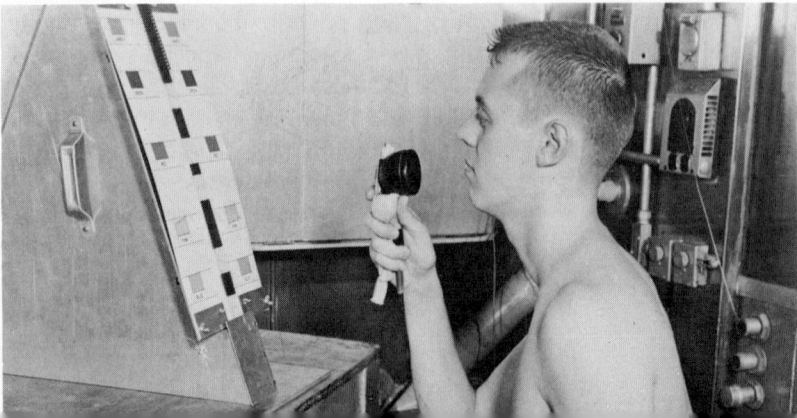

results to see whether the tests actually worked. The tests eventually included appraisal of reaction-time, coordination, judgment of distances, discrimination between positions of objects, education, and motivation for flying. Mechanical testing equipment as well as paper-and-pencil tests were used. The government saved hundreds of thousands of dollars, a great deal of time, and many lives through the use of these tests. Less training was wasted on men who were not likely to become good fliers, and fewer accidents occurred.

Another area of investigation was efficiency of bomber crews. Some flying crews did much better than others, experiencing fewer accidents, and achieving more successful attacks. In certain crews, the members tended to "crack up" emotionally after a few missions, whereas other crews flew mission after mission without a lessening of their effectiveness. Why should these differences exist?

Various studies were made, some of which included interviews and psychiatric devices. One conclusion was that crews in which there was good group morale were likely to be most successful. Teamwork and group feeling seemed important, especially in dangerous nerve-wracking missions. It was found that a good bomber crew functioned as a unit, exhibiting a high degree of interdependence among members. Mutual support of each other psychologically as well as physically and living up to high standards of performance ("don't let us all down") appeared to function in keeping crews stable (9).

Clinical psychology [1] played an active role in World War II and receives a great deal of attention in the Armed Forces today. For a certain percentage of men in dangerous active combat areas, psychological symptoms were likely to develop after varying amounts of strain. One of the symptoms was loss of function of various parts of the body, for psychological reasons. Although the eye, arm, or other organ affected was not actually damaged, it was not capable of its proper function, and the part affected often seemed related to the kind of job the soldier had. Pilots frequently exhibited symptoms related to depth perception or distance judgment (eyes), ground soldiers had difficulties with arms, and so on.

In World War I, this type of hysteria was termed "shell shock" and was thought to be caused by the concussion of bursting shells or the noise of heavy guns. World War II brought new light to the problem. Hysteria, it was learned, can be caused by psychological conflict. In combat, for example, a man is usually afraid and does not want to enter a danger area, especially if he is cold, tired, and hungry and has seen his friends suffer wounds or death. On the other hand, he has a certain self-concept to uphold. He thinks of himself as being unwilling to let his teammates down, he does not want to be known as a coward, he does not want to be a poor soldier. Many men have home problems and perhaps in their past there has been serious emotional stress. A combination of present strains working on weaknesses remaining from past mental scars can result in symptoms of hysteria.

---

[1] Clinical psychology is concerned with diagnosis and treatment of behavior disorders.

Apparently what happens is that a man realizes that if he were ill or injured he would not need to fight. Neither would he be letting his friends down; for cripples and sick men are not expected to fight. If he were blind or deaf, or had lost an arm or a leg, he would have a way out of the conflict. Sometimes a shell bursting nearby, a minor wound, a slight illness, or another casualty brought about overt symptoms of hysteria. At other times hysteria developed without any precipitating event. McDougall (10) refers to a case of war neurosis in which a motorcycle sergeant was found in a large city in France, miles from where he was supposed to be. He had experienced a state of fugue, or amnesia. Apparently while he was riding along an active war front the strain became excessive. He was able to reach the safety of the city which was rather far behind the lines, but he did not realize where he was or how he had arrived there. The behavior of riding to this safe place and neglecting his duty seemed to have been effectively screened from his conscious self by a psychological defense.

In such cases psychologists and psychiatrists were employed to great advantage. Various modes of treatment, depending on the cause, kind, and extent of the emotional problem were used. Giving rest to the patients in a safe place, letting them sleep (including the use of sleeping pills, if necessary), providing comfort, relaxation, and counseling enabled many to return to active duty in a short time. Others actually became worse after reaching hospital areas. They often had deep conflicts and needed more extensive treatment.

Preventive measures were also discovered and found useful. Taking men out of combat as often as possible, building team spirit, and properly screening men for their jobs prevented some severe maladjustments. Probably every person has his "breaking-point" under stress, and it is necessary to avoid this breaking-point if possible in order not only to prevent emotional damage but also to increase efficiency. Men who fight when they are neither physically nor emotionally fit for it are often a danger to themselves — and to others.

Another area in which psychology is useful is psychological warfare. This takes many forms, and is directed at a variety of targets, including the home front, enemy troops and civilian population, and one's own Armed Forces. For example, the Japanese soldier was encouraged to die rather than surrender. To be captured, he was told, was a disgrace and meant that he would no longer be considered a Japanese. Americans used to wonder why, when they captured a Japanese soldier, he would be willing to divulge the number of their troops, arms, and equipment, and in other ways help the Americans. When they learned about his attitude toward surrender, the answer was apparent. Some Japanese soldiers would reason that they might as well help the Americans since they could not return home in good standing. In some cases an actual change of allegiance occurred.

In war propaganda, particularly in China since World War II, there have been allegations that America has used disease germs, or has flown over Chinese territory without permission. These are charges which we do not accept as true but actions which Chinese citizens might consider to be unfair tactics or even atrocities. Stories about enemy treatment of prisoners of war are nearly always rampant in wartime, and with certain notable exceptions are usually about as true of one side as they are of the other. These practices are examples of crude psychological warfare — attempts to bolster morale and to stir up hatred of the enemy by spreading stories about him.

A brutal technique of psychological warfare which has been widely publicized during and since World War II has of late years come to be called "brain washing." While this takes many forms, it essentially consists in erasing a man's former beliefs and convictions and building up in his mind new ones, generally the exact opposite of what he believed before. This is usually a slow process, and apparently an agonizing one. Physical and mental resistance are lowered by long imprisonment, malnutrition, broken sleep, uncomfortable posture long maintained, threats, promises, beatings, enticements, refusals, and every known device of frustration until the self-concept is completely changed and no foundation for former beliefs remains. Bit by bit a new subservient self is created, and new beliefs are erected upon it. Some successful cases of brain washing came to light during and after the Korean War. At that time there were also reported a number of cases in which the technique had failed. We see numerous reports of less extreme uses of what is basically the same technique in the "confessions" of discredited officials in dictatorship countries who publicly accuse themselves of error and even of criminal behavior. Similar pressure, with a similar result but no evidence of successful brainwashing, was exerted in the fall of 1958 on the Russian novelist, Boris Pasternak, who refused the Nobel Prize for his novel, *Doctor Zhivago*, then widely popular outside the Soviet sphere of influence. Clearly the refusal, swift on the heels of a message of gratitude, was strong evidence of coercion. Further evidence was the announcement that Pasternak had been expelled from the Soviet authors' league.

Psychology is used by our Armed Forces in teaching men how to lead and to give orders, how to teach others, how to interview, and how to develop group morale. It is used as a screening device to help men get jobs in the forces which are suited to them, and (in combination with psychiatry, medicine, occupational therapy, and the like) to help those who have emotional problems. It is useful in helping to select men who are likely to make good officers and to help train them for their work. And, through the Veteran's Administration, psychology and psychiatry help refit men for civilian life.

A.   THE STUDY OF DELINQUENCY AND CRIME
B.   PSYCHOLOGY IN INDUSTRY
C.   PSYCHOLOGY IN THE ARMED FORCES

● D. PSYCHOLOGY IN SCHOOLS

You have been in school a good share of your life. As a student, you have seen a great many teachers in action, some excellent and inspiring, some very poor and not likable, and a great many who are simply doing an average job. In our country, teaching is difficult. It consist of far more than merely imparting knowledge to students through lectures, although lectures have their place. The American philosophy of government — indeed, our way of life — places emphasis on the essential worth of the individual, as opposed to the concept of totalitarian countries in which the good of the state is placed above the value of the individual. We have in our schools a wide variety of persons, each of whom has capacities which we should like to develop to the full. In the interest of efficiency and economy, we teach these people in groups — classes, grades, and schools. This is, in a manner of speaking, a form of human mass-production, and a very complex task. Our aim is to turn out people who conform to the demands of society to the degree necessary for satisfactory adjustment to our way of life, but — and this is important — who also retain their individuality, cultivate their own individual talents, and develop unique interests. To carry out this purpose is indeed a difficult task for schools and teachers. How can we encourage individual differences and permit them to develop in a class of twenty to fifty or more? What must a teacher do? What education and experience does he need? What does psychology have to do with the problem?

The aims of education may be stated differently in various schools, but in general they include teaching students to live healthy lives, to develop emotionally mature and healthy ways of behaving, to communicate well with others through reading, writing, speaking, and listening, to make good social adjustments, to fit into our society, to understand the world as it is through the study of sciences, geography, world history, etc., to develop pleasant and useful recreational activities, and to prepare for vocations, marriage, and family life. Obviously, these aims are very broad and, to accomplish them, a person's education must continue over a long period of time. It must include general as well as specialized knowledge of many different aspects of life.

To carry out those tasks which are particularly applicable to a given subject field, the teacher assigned to that field must know this material and how it relates to the total educational program. In addition — and here is where psychology enters the scene — he must understand people and must know how to teach his subject matter so that it will be interesting, understandable, and useful to his students.

Because boys and girls go through various stages of development, the teacher needs to have a basic understanding of child development. The stages of development have a direct bearing on the children's motives, behavior, abilities to learn various concepts and skills, and also on the methods which may be used to help them learn efficiently. Learning, as you have seen, is a complex process. Various types of learning outcomes are possible, and each has its related principles and conditions. The teacher must know a great deal about the nature of the learning process and the way to provide as efficiently as possible the most advantageous conditions for learning.

Teachers must study individual boys and girls. They often are called on for counseling and guidance, and they must be prepared to recognize those children who need the help of specialists — doctors, psychologists, psychiatrists, and others.

Consider some of the tasks a teacher in your college may do in an average day — along with the special areas of psychology to which these tasks are related:

1. He presents subject matter (psychology of learning).
2. He prepares, administers, and evaluates tests (psychology of testing).
3. He advises and counsels students (counseling psychology).
4. He works in committees (psychology of group dynamics).
5. He may administer certain work — oversee research, manage a "bureau," etc. (psychology of personnel work, research, statistics).
6. He may supervise other teachers (supervision, group work, personnel work).
7. He may consider student problems (psychology of adjustment).
8. He may teach courses such as advertising, music, art, or others which employ specialized psychology.

We could undoubtedly expand this list, especially if we take into account certain workers in speech correction, remedial reading, and other specialized areas of education.

To prepare for a career in teaching, one must, of course, study the subject matter of the courses he plans to teach. In preparation for teaching in primary and secondary schools, he also studies curriculum construction, discovering what he will need to teach and how his work is related to that of other teachers. He studies child development, educational psychology, and perhaps adjustment problems of students. He studies the philosophy and history of education to gain a clear idea of the goals toward which he is working. And he studies methods and techniques of teaching so that he may accomplish his educational goals. In addition he must develop his own personality so that he will be mature, well adjusted socially and emotionally, and able to get along well with students, parents, faculty, and administration.

Suggested activities

1. Analyze the teaching in your class from the standpoint of facilitating purposeful learning, as treated in Chapter 5. What aspects of psychology are apparent in functions other than teaching which your professors undertake?

2. Compare the use of psychology in a well-prepared lecture to its use in leading an excellent class discussion.

3. Study the requirements for a teaching certificate in your institution. How much work in psychology is required? How much do you think is desirable?

4. What personal characteristics are desirable for teaching? (Research is available on this point.)

A. THE STUDY OF DELINQUENCY AND CRIME
B. PSYCHOLOGY IN INDUSTRY
C. PSYCHOLOGY IN THE ARMED FORCES
D. PSYCHOLOGY IN SCHOOLS

● E. PSYCHOLOGY AS AN OCCUPATION

Throughout this chapter we have been attempting to show some of the possible uses of psychology to society. We have stated that psychologists do not always attempt to solve social problems by themselves, but that in many instances they work in "teams" with other psychologists, educators, social workers, administrators, physicians, psychiatrists, and others. However, in any problem involving human beings, it is almost certain that psychology can play a part.

Psychology, as a specialty, can form an occupation in and of itself. In other instances a knowledge of psychology is required within the total program of some other professional training, as in such occupations as teaching, personnel work, and certain branches of military service. Table 12.1 shows just what percentage of psychologists are in each type of work related to psychology.

To illustrate how the field of psychology is organized into specialties, we list below the current divisions of the American Psychological Association (11) of which most, though not all, psychologists are members. (The Association has no Division for numerals 4, 6, and 11.)

1. Division of General Psychology
2. Division on the Teaching of Psychology
3. Division of Experimental Psychology
5. Division on Evaluation and Measurement
7. Division on Developmental Psychology
8. Division of Personality and Social Psychology
9. The Society for the Psychological Study of Social Issues — A Division of the APA
10. Division on Esthetics
12. Division of Clinical Psychology
13. Division of Consulting Psychology
14. Division of Industrial and Business Psychology
15. Division of Educational Psychology
16. Division of School Psychologists
17. Division of Counseling Psychology
18. Division of Psychologists in Public Service
19. Division of Military Psychology
20. Division on Maturity and Old Age

The American Psychological Association attempts to maintain high standards and ethics so that quacks or self-styled psychologists will not be able to operate. Laws have been passed to help control unethical practitioners. Psychology is a highly advanced and complex field of study, and much harm can

DIFFERENT CAREERS IN PSYCHOLOGY.

Psychology as an occupation has many specialties. These photographs explain three categories of professional careers in psychology. (Life photos by Walter Sanders.)

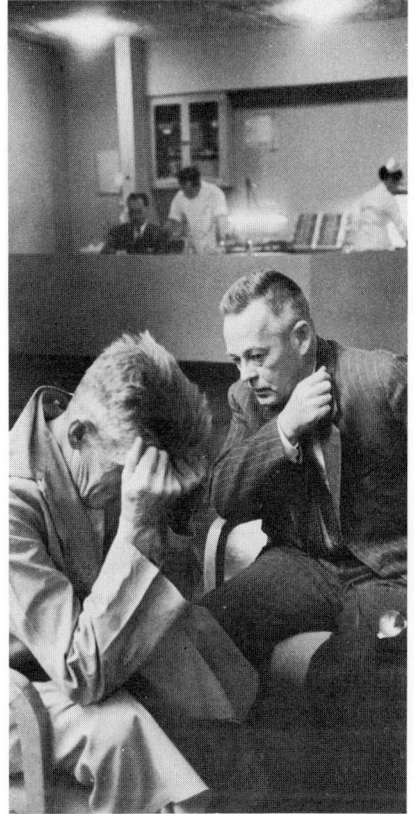

PSYCHIATRIST. The psychiatrist treats mental illness. He must have medical training, and he usually works in a hospital but often has a private practice as well.

PSYCHOLOGIST. Applying scientific methods to the study of human behavior is the job of the psychologist. This man for example is using a machine which charts particular human reactions.

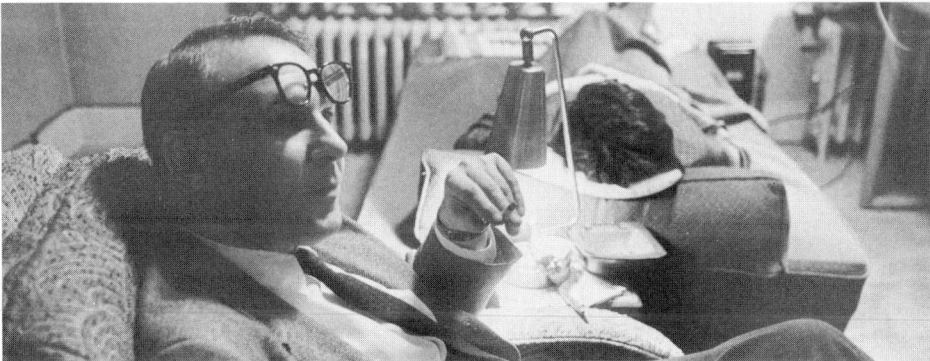

PSYCHOANALYST. The psychoanalyst deals with people who are deeply troubled but usually rational. The object of psychoanalysis is to allow the patient to talk freely about personal problems and to bring out repressed desires, fears, and anxieties. The psychoanalyst then tries to clarify the pattern of discord and lead the patient to an interpretation and recognition of his difficulties.

be done by poorly trained or untrained persons if they are permitted to take part in psychological work.

In addition to college education beyond the baccalaureate degree, other special requirements may be set for the psychologist. For example, a person desiring to be a clinical psychologist must have an internship under supervision. For entrance to graduate work, at least for work toward the Ph.D., most colleges provide various screening and testing devices which must be passed successfully. Psychology is a science and a profession. The usual prerequisites of any scientific or professional occupation — intelligence, the ability to apply learning, and good judgment — are required.

TABLE 12.1

Psychologists Classified According to Agency Employing Them

Source of employment	Men	Women	Total
Colleges and universities Teaching, administration, personnel, etc.	55%	38%	50%
Federal government Veterans Administration, armed services, other agencies	14	7	12
State and city government School systems, hospitals and clinics, other agencies	7	24	12
Private organizations Business and industry, clinics and guidance centers, schools	11	14	12
Self-employed Private practice of psychology	2	3	2
Miscellaneous Student, retired, non-psychological occupation	11	14	12
Total	100	100	100
Number of cases in sample	598	265	863

From D. Wolfle, "Annual Report of the Executive Secretary," *Amer. Psychologist*, 3, 1948, p. 509, Figure 4. Based on a sample of the membership of the American Psychological Association. Used by permission.

For beginning psychologists, especially those without the Ph.D., the pay is not particularly high. With sufficient training and experience, however, financial rewards can be excellent. In addition to a good income, the professional psychologist enjoys social prestige, the ability to be of service to society, challenging work, and the companionship of interesting people.

For more information about psychology as a career, you may consult a college counselor or talk to various psychologists in your community. They will give you an idea of what specific training is required and how it may be obtained. They will help you relate your interests and abilities to a specialty in psychology.

SUMMARY

Psychology as a profession is a useful field of endeavor. This fact is reflected in its many applications to various aspects of life — either as an independent discipline or in combination with other sciences. Because of the general usefulness of the work, the demand for trained psychologists is great and the number currently available is far too small. The jobs, indeed, are seeking the men. However, a career in psychology requires specialized education, like any other profession, a master's degree and often a doctorate. Such work is interesting, profitable, and highly useful.

Psychology is useful to society in studying the problems of delinquency and crime, isolating the factors related to this kind of antisocial behavior, suggesting ways to prevent such behavior, and rehabilitating persons who become involved in criminal and delinquent activities. There is no easy solution to crime and delinquency, because the causes of these serious social problems are numerous and varied and involve the interaction of many factors. The psychologist works with a team of specialists in other fields. Unfortunately, there are not enough specialists in any of these fields, including psychology, to handle the problems adequately. The cost of crime — in terms of the losses of the victims, court fees, the maintenance of penal institutions, and the lost potential of the criminals and delinquents themselves — indicates the great need for trained persons to work toward the prevention of crime and delinquency.

Industry utilizes many psychological services. Employing workers, job placement, supervision, safety, the use of color, and job-training, all have psychological implications. Advertising, selling, and public relations are also based in part on psychological principles.

The Armed Forces employ many psychologists for duties in connection with research for psychological warfare, testing and screening service personnel, diagnosing and working with maladjusted men, and educating personnel.

Psychology has many uses in teaching. Studies of student–teacher adjustment, effective methods for teaching, testing and classifying and counseling students, research, and remediation for exceptional children — all reflect ways in which psychology can be brought to bear on teaching problems. School counselors, psychometrists, and psychologists are in ever-increasing demand in education.

We have only scratched the surface in indicating how psychology is utilized as either a theoretical or an applied science. You may want to read more about how this science can be applied to whatever field you are planning for, or you may be interested in a career in psychology itself. Since human relationships are the basis of society, and since these relationships are often the place where trouble begins, you can readily appreciate the need for as good a knowledge of psychology as you can possibly obtain.

Suggested activities

1. Study state regulations for various positions of a psychological nature.

2. Obtain information concerning the need for psychological workers in various fields.

3. In what areas, other than the four mentioned in this chapter, is psychology used?

4. Collect some magazine advertisements. How do they utilize psychological principles?

5. Examine your college catalog. What psychological training can you obtain at your college? Are scholarships available?

REFERENCES

1. C. Shaw, unpublished lectures, Northern Illinois University, DeKalb, 1952.

2. See R. S. Banay, "Physical Disfigurement as a Factor in Delinquency," *Federal Probation*, Jan.–March, 1943.

3. H. G. Gough and D. R. Peterson, "The Identification and Measurement of Predispositional Factors in Crime and Delinquency," *J. Consult. Psychol.*, 1952, 16, pp. 207–212.

4. N. K. Teeters and J. O. Reinemann, *The Challenge of Delinquency*, Prentice-Hall, New York, 1950, p. 94.

5. *The Quiet One*, Film Documents, Athena Films, New York, 1948.

6. See H. W. Hepner, *Psychology Applied to Life and Work*, Prentice-Hall, New York, 1950, Chapter 19.

7. *Ibid.*, p. 473

8. See F. B. Davies (Ed.), *The AAF Qualifying Examination Report*, Number 6, Army Air Forces Aviation Psychology Program Research Reports, U.S. Government Printing Office, Washington, 1947, (Supt. Documents).

9. R. R. Grinker and J. P. Spiegel, *Men Under Stress*, Blakiston, New York, 1945.

10. W. McDougall, *Outline of Abnormal Psychology*, Scribner, New York, 1926.

11. *Directory*, American Psychological Association, 1955, p. 491.

SUGGESTIONS FOR FURTHER READING

Bennett, E. M., *et al.*, "Emotional Associations with Air and Rail Transportation," *J. Psychol.*, 1957, 43, pp. 65–75.

Davids, A., and J. T. Mahoney, "Personality Dynamics and Accident Proneness in an Industrial Setting," *J. Appl. Psychol.*, 1957, 41, pp. 303–306.

Dubno, P., "The Role of the Psychologist in Labor Unions," *Amer. Psychologist*, 1957, 12, pp. 212–215.

Eysenck, H. J., *Uses and Abuses of Psychology*, Penguin, London, 1953.

Garrett, H. E., *General Psychology*, American, New York, 1955, Chapter 15.

Gill, L. E., *Advertising and Psychology*, Longmans, Green, New York, 1954.

Glueck, S., "The Home, the School, and Delinquency," *Harvard Educ. Rev.*, 1953, 23, pp. 17–32.

Haveman, E., *The Age of Psychology*, Simon, New York, 1957, Chapter 3.

Hilgard, E. R., *Introduction to Psychology*, Harcourt, New York, 1953, Chapter 22.

Katz, D., D. Cartwright, S. Eldersveld, and A. M. Lee, *Public Opinion and Propaganda*, Holt, New York, 1954.

King, M. S., and G. A. Kimble, "Job Opportunities for Undergraduate Psychology Majors," *Amer. Psychologist*, 1958, 13, pp. 23–27.

Linebarger, P. M. A., *Psychological Warfare*, Combat Forces Press, Washington, 1954.

Lowsche, C. H., *Psychology in Industrial Relations*, McGraw-Hill, New York, 1953.

McArthur, C., *et al.*, "The Psychology of Smoking," *J. Abnorm. Soc. Psychol.*, 1958, 56, pp. 267–275.

Maier, N. R. F., *Psychology in Industry*, Houghton Mifflin, Boston, second edition, 1955, Chapter 1.

Miller, H. G., "Effects of High Intensity Noise on Retention," *J. Appl. Psychol.*, 1957, 41, pp. 370–372.

Pressey, S. L., and R. G. Kuhlen, *Psychological Development through the Life Span*, Harper, New York, 1957, Chapter 5.

Menta Health

One focus of this book has been on developing ways of solving problems, both in college and out. For living may be described as solving, or failing to solve, a never-ending succession of problems — which range from such trivial and habitual matters as deciding what to eat for breakfast and whether to study history before dinner or after, to such major concerns as choosing a career and selecting a mate. We have all had times when the problems which faced us seemed either so numerous, or so difficult, that the immediate future seemed hazardous. But some people seem to be in a state of fever, frenzy, or frustration all the time, while others weather their crises and return to a state of reasonable calm. Why is it that some people live, and solve their problems, so much more efficiently and happily than others? In part the difference is that some are better balanced, healthier in mind.

● A. CHARACTERISTICS OF MENTAL HEALTH

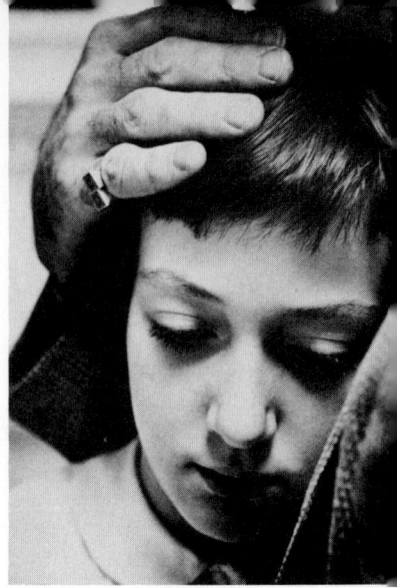

A bulletin of the National Association for Mental Health (1), describes the characteristics of mentally healthy people as follows:

a. They feel comfortable about themselves. They are not bowled over by their own emotions — by their fears, anger, love, jealousy, guilt or worries. They can take life's disappointments in their stride. They have a tolerant, easy-going attitude toward themselves as well as others; they can laugh at themselves. They

13

Types and Prevention of Mental Illness

What are the characteristics of mental health? How prevalent is mental illness in modern society? What are the types of mental illness? How does mental illness develop? How can the mentally ill be helped? What are some ways of diagnosing, classifying, and treating mental illness? What are some principles of mental health? How can you keep mentally healthy?

neither underestimate nor overestimate their abilities. They can accept their own shortcomings. They have self-respect. They feel able to deal with most situations that come their way. They get satisfaction from the simple every-day pleasures. *b. They feel right about other people.* They are able to give love and to consider the interests of others. They have personal relationships that are satisfying and lasting. They expect to like and trust others, and take it for granted that others will like and trust them. They respect the many differences they find in people. They do not push people around, nor do they allow themselves to be pushed around. They can feel they are part of a group. They feel a sense of responsibility to their neighbors and fellow men.

c. They are able to meet the demands of life. They do something about their problems as they arise. They accept their responsibilities. They shape their environment whenever possible; they adjust to it when necessary. They plan ahead but do not fear the future. They welcome new experiences and new ideas. They make use of their natural capacities. They set realistic goals for themselves. They are able to think for themselves and make their own decisions. They put their best effort into what they do, and get satisfaction out of doing it.

Thus mental health is more than just the absence of mental illness. It is related to terms like "peace of mind," "happiness," and "contentment." A stable personality which can accommodate emotional shocks without being overwhelmed is essential for mental health in adults. Mental health involves one's confidence in his ability to handle any problems he may encounter; basically, this means relative freedom from fear and anxiety concerning the future. Self-respect, self-esteem, and a willingness to face reality, rather than to escape by daydreaming, excessive reading, drinking, or gambling, are also indicative of mental health.

Mental health cannot be considered merely in such terms as "introversion" and "extroversion," "dominance" and "submission." By definition the extrovert is sociable and friendly and likes to work and play in the company of others. He spends comparatively little time thinking about himself. Thus judging by his outward expressions, we often think that the extrovert is mentally healthy. It is common, however, for persons who cannot live comfortably with themselves to compensate by being constantly with others. It might be possible, then, for an extrovert to be in poor mental health. On the other hand, the introvert is sometimes self-centered and tends to avoid other people. He may be a lone wolf in many ways. He tends not to share his thoughts or feelings easily with others. He likes solitary pursuits and feels at ease when alone. It is likely that neither the extreme introvert nor the extreme extrovert is mentally healthy, but there are many mentally healthy adults who tend toward either introversion or extroversion. Basically, what *leads* the individual to exhibit more or less introversion or extroversion has more to do with his mental health than has the outward manifestation.

Dominance and submission are also present within and among individuals. A person who insists on having his own way at all times encounters problems. One who is too eager to please or to follow the suggestions of others gets pushed around. Some adults appear to be unhappy unless they can lead others, while some appear to be unhappy if they are placed in a position of leadership. Such outward expressions of dominance or submission cannot be taken as very clear evidence either for or against mental health, although it is probable that the adult who must always lead or must always follow in order to feel comfortable with himself will experience many frustrations.

Mental health is not easy to define, and there is no simple and easy way of distinguishing between healthy and unhealthy behavior. Certain actions of an apparently well-adjusted person, if exercised inappropriately or excessively, may indicate maladjustment or a need to improve mental health. Recall the three main characteristics of mentally healthy persons: "They feel comfortable about themselves," "they feel right about other people," and "they are able to meet the demands of life." The outward expressions and actions of individuals which demonstrate these characteristics vary widely. One person, for example, may feel comfortable about himself and right about others while spending much time in solitary tasks; another may feel the same while spending much time in company with others.

You should not be alarmed if you feel that some of your own behavior resembles that of people we shall discuss in our descriptions of the mentally ill. There probably is nothing wrong with you. Just as medical students often "pick up" physical symptoms from reading their text books, so you may "pick up" mental symptoms when you read about poor adjustment and abnormal psychology. This is perfectly natural, and it probably indicates only that you are identifying somewhat with the illustration and hence may learn the concept better.

A. CHARACTERISTICS OF MENTAL HEALTH

● **B. MENTAL ILLNESS IN MODERN SOCIETY**

It is estimated that more than 600,000 patients occupying hospital beds are mentally (or emotionally) ill — a number exceeding that of all other medical and surgical patients occupying beds at any one time. Mental patients tend to remain in hospitals for longer periods than other patients, although many are cured and returned to the homes of their families. (However, the number being discharged from institutions has increased since 1955, due to new therapies and improved treatment programs.) In addition to the mentally ill persons in hospitals, there are perhaps another half million who could profit from being institutionalized. Finally, there are many people treated in clinics as out-patients living at home, as well as many borderline cases which, although recognized, do not seem to require specialized treatment. We must also not forget those older people who are being cared for in homes for the aged, but who are often so forgetful or disoriented that they may actually be suffering from senile psychoses. Our listing does not include the feeble-minded, who are defined as people of sub-normal intelligence. According to a recent estimate one person in five in the United States will need expert mental treatment during his lifetime and one in ten will need institutionalization for mental illness

How widespread is mental illness? *Mental illness may be more prevalent than you realize. (From the Parke, Davis & Company booklet,* Patterns of Disease, *Copyright 1958.)*

About 1 of every 10 persons (17 million) have some form of mental or emotional disorder requiring treatment.

Over 1 million patients are treated annually in mental hospitals.

About 1½ million adults and children visit psychiatric outpatient clinics and private psychiatrists.

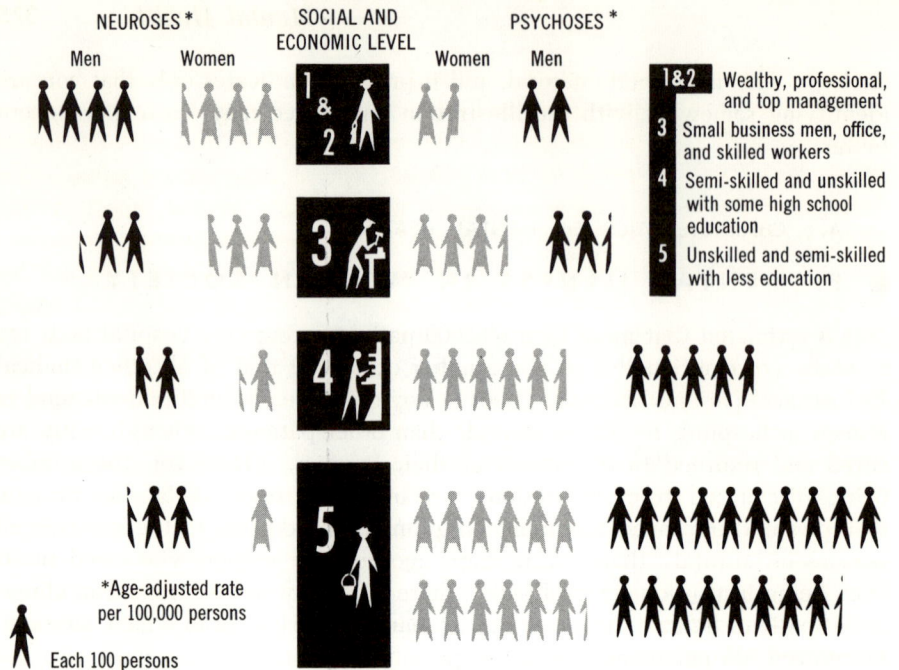

Mental illness in varying socio-economic levels. *The upper social and economic level has the lowest rate for psychoses and the highest rate for neuroses. (From the Parke, Davis & Company booklet,* Patterns of Disease, *Copyright 1958.)*

sometime during his life. Not all of these will, of course, actually receive such aid even though they need it.

Because of the high incidence of mental illness, it is clear that everyone should have some knowledge and understanding of it. Although this book is not concerned primarily with abnormal or clinical psychology, we hope to provide you with a basis for learning some of the concepts of psychopathology. You may wish to take college courses in clinical or abnormal psychology to secure a more complete understanding.

Normal vs. abnormal personality

Behavior or personality disorders range from mild to intense, and may be of short or long duration. Deviations from normal behavior in which the individual does not lose contact with reality and for which he cannot legally be committed to an institution are termed *neuroses* or *psychoneuroses*. The more intense disorders, in which the patient exhibits a fairly complete loss of contact with reality and for which he can legally be committed to an institution are called *psychoses*. There are borderline cases, and expert opinion is necessary in diagnosing an individual's behavior as neurotic or psychotic, or normal or abnormal. *The distinction between normal and abnormal personality is made on the basis of appropriateness and adequacy of the individual's behavior as compared both with his earlier and more usual behavior and with the norms set by the society in which he lives* . In the case of any cultural group — the Arapesh or Kwakiutl, for instance — we would define mental illness in that group partly in terms of its own culture. In our American culture a rancher's keeping a shotgun and several watchdogs would be considered normal behavior, but a student's attempting to do the same in his residence hall would be abnormal, and treated as a symptom of mental illness.

Mentally ill persons do not necessarily exhibit weird or bizarre behavior. Few patients, even in hospitals, think they are Napoleon, despite the cartoonist's stereotypes. More frequently mentally ill patients, compared with healthy individuals, exhibit ordinary types of behavior in an extreme form, with more repetition, or at inappropriate times. Their symptoms may reflect chronic disturbed feelings which most of us experience infrequently if at all. Normal persons are subject to moods, but in the manic-depressive patient these moods are exaggerated. Many persons are suspicious at times, but the paranoid carries his suspicions past the bounds of reasonable behavior so that they dominate his entire thinking and activities.

Of course, some mentally ill patients do exhibit bizarre behavior. In mental hospitals one may find those who are suffering from delusions, hallucinations, delirium, apathy, or paralysis of some of the sense organs or skeletal muscles. But their behavior, however irrational it may sometimes appear, can be interpreted in terms which make it seem logical in view of its causes and the present state of the person. Since this is true, there should be no fear or horror of mental illness. Mentally ill patients are sick — just as are medical patients, but their illnesses primarily originate in their psychological rather than their physiological functioning even though there may be physical causes.

"Unadjusted" behavior, a characteristic of a person who is not mentally ill but who is still not in the best mental health, is rather common. We often see examples of unadjusted behavior without particularly noticing them, because there is not a marked difference from a more healthy kind of behavior. The eccentric storekeeper, the "nervous" lady, or the man who cannot sleep without pills for his insomnia may be unadjusted, tending toward psychoneuroticism, but such a person is probably not really mentally ill. Unadjusted behavior, of course, is less serious and probably more common than psychoneurotic behavior.

Psychotic reactions typically develop over a period of time. Psychotic adults who are certain that they are being persecuted, spied upon, or treated unfairly, for example, may have started feeling this way as children or adolescents. At these earlier ages their behavior may have been little different from that of their age-mates. However, with increasing age and experience the psychotic's behavior becomes increasingly different from that of his age-mates and also perhaps less flexible and more compulsive than formerly. Or the person may have repressed his feelings for many years, when suddenly circumstances will cause him to express his true feelings freely and in abnormal ways. In any event, an accurate diagnosis of the kind and extent of abnormality requires expert knowledge and judgment. The layman is in no better position to appraise his fellow man's mental health than he is to appraise his physical health. If he suspects that someone needs diagnosis or treatment, he must seek expert assistance. "Doctoring" by well-meaning but untrained persons is a very dangerous practice.

The difficulty of classifying mental illnesses

Attempts have been made to classify separate and distinct mental illnesses, each requiring special treatment. Recently, however, classification has become more a matter of describing broad groups of symptoms, for few patients exhibit all the typical or expected syndromes (groups of symptoms). Many people exhibit characteristics which seem to be typical of several classifications. Thus as we discuss some of the illnesses in further detail it should be remembered that each patient in a clinic or hospital must be treated as an individual rather than as a stereotype. We cannot, for example, distinguish between manic-depressive psychoses and involutional melancholia as well as we can between chicken pox and whooping cough. The therapy for two persons exhibiting symptoms of involutional melancholia will probably be more individualized than would be the treatment for two patients who have measles or pneumonia.

The psychoneuroses

The psychoneurotic individual is a person in relatively normal contact with reality, but who makes an abnormal adjustment to his problems. In other words, this kind of person has conflicts in his life which he has not been able to resolve successfully. These conflicts lead to continuing anxiety, an unpleasant emotional state. The patient develops certain responses in an attempt to lessen his distress. These responses are typically defense mechanisms which are often not socially approved, which do not permanently lessen the anxiety, and which do not resolve the conflict. While these reactions to the conflict are somehow acquired, we must emphasize that the individual may not recognize that he has acquired them. As a result he may not understand the nature of his difficulties or of his symptoms. He is not faking or "gold-bricking" ailments such as headaches, backaches, and insomnia; they are as real to him as illnesses which are organically caused. Treatment requires the services of a psychiatrist.

Anxiety reactions.   These symptoms are different from other psychoneurotic manifestations in that they do not minimize anxiety. Instead of putting up a defense against anxiety, the subject experiences it more or less continually. But he does not seem to know what he is afraid of, or what he is anxious about. He may exhibit certain symptoms of fear such as tenseness, uneven heart beat, difficulty in sleeping well. Since the patient does not really know why he is anxious, he may rationalize his symptoms as fear of going insane, fear of death, or a response to some other more realistic fear-provoking aspect of life. We usually find that a real conflict has caused this anxiety, but that the subject may not understand that this conflict is related to his anxiety. The anxiety reaction may continue for some time after the actual conflict or fear-provoking experience has been resolved.

John, a student at Mainline College, was always tense and "nervous." He was unable to concentrate on his studies and could not remember what he had read. At first he rationalized his tenseness as worry about his work, although he knew he was capable of college study and he had done well in high school. He was not only anxious in class, but he also seemed unduly worried and fearful on dates, at sporting events, and in all his daily activities. Through expert diagnosis, John's real conflict was found to be in his relationship with his father and in his being in college against his father's wishes. John had, contrary to his father's desire, made his own way to Mainline and was working to pay his expenses. Although he was sure that he was right in deciding to go to college, his fear of his father's being right and his interpretation of his relationships with his father were producing his anxiety. This state developed even though in John's opinion the conflict had been resolved by his entering college and the argument had been more or less forgotten.

Phobic reactions. Most people have heard of claustrophobia, which is the fear of being confined in any sort of enclosed structure. Some persons are unable to remain in such places as closets and elevators, or even to ride in automobiles. At one time psychological literature abounded with various names for specific phobias — literally hundreds were listed in one book or another. Today we recognize that the phobias which are possible are almost endless and there is little point in attempting to name them. Phobias are psychoneurotic reactions in which the anxiety arising from a conflict is *displaced*. By focusing anxiety reactions on such things as cats, dark places, or high places, *some of the anxiety can be relieved* simply by physically avoiding these concrete objects or situations. This form of displacement allows a person to repress or remain unaware of what he is really anxious about, thus serving as a defense against the real problem.

How do phobias originate? Any very striking fear-provoking incident, early in childhood, may have established the object of the phobia. The incident may have been long forgotten, and if remembered might now seem childish. Nevertheless, the tendency to exhibit a fear of the related object or phenomenon has been established. In phobias, as in other psychoneurotic reactions, the source of the anxiety is an ongoing conflict in the subject's life. Until that conflict is resolved, the patient cannot be truly cured. He may overcome one phobia only to attach himself to another. If not a phobia, probably some other psychoneurotic reaction will develop.

Karen could not ride in a taxicab very long before inventing some excuse to stop and get out. Perhaps it was to buy something in a store, perhaps she saw someone she knew, or it was some other excuse, but stop she must. If friends were with her and tried to talk her out of stopping, she exhibited symptoms of fear — tenseness, rapid breathing, and a pounding heart. Eventually she would become sufficiently ill to require taking her out of the cab and into a place where she could relax and recover.

Karen's troubles began partly as a result of a cab ride during early adolescence. She and a girl friend had been warned against riding with strangers, but one day they were particularly tired and a taxi driver offered them a free ride home. They soon discovered that he was under the influence of liquor and in no condition to drive. They asked to stop and get out, but he insisted upon driving them to their homes, and a very unpleasant scene with parents, cab driver, and girls occurred.

Diagnostic measures revealed that Karen's fear was out of proportion to this incident. It involved conflicts among the members of Karen's family, guilt feelings in Karen whenever she did something she was not sure her parents would approve, and a certain amount of resentful yet dependent behavior on her part. In a sense, she could escape some of these problems when she escaped from riding in taxicabs.

Hysteria. Hysteria, as the term is used in psychology, is not the unrestrained, disconnected behavior that the layman implies when he uses the word. Rather, hysteria denotes physical symptoms resulting from emotional distress. Hysteria may symbolically represent the nature of the conflict within the individual, and it may serve to give him some relief from his anxiety through both *primary* and *secondary gains.* Let us explain these terms further.

You may recall our discussion in Chapter 12 of soldiers who developed paralyzed arms, blindness, or other incapacitating conditions when they found themselves unable to resolve the conflict between their fear of combat and their reluctance to show cowardice or let their buddies down. The *primary gain* evident in these situations is that these soldiers could now be removed from combat areas and be treated at hospitals with no trouble to their consciences. This relieved the fear and also made it possible for them not to shirk their duty or let down their friends.

A *secondary gain* often was present in the form of sympathy from their families and from hospital attendants. Also, it was pleasant to be waited on, to have their infirmity diagnosed and treated, to sleep in good beds, eat good food, and enjoy rest and recreation.

The soldiers' conflicts which we have described result in *actual* disability. A paralyzed arm does not represent pretense or role-playing — the arm actually refuses to function. The patient has not consciously tried to become paralyzed, nor does he understand the nature of his paralysis. He is not practicing a hoax, and in many cases he wants desperately to get well. Often hysteria persists long after the immediate stress is over, and sometimes it even becomes worse after the patient has returned home. For immediate stress may be reinforced by other conflicts in the subject's personality which must therefore be resolved.

Why does the patient have one particular disability rather than another? In some cases actual organic injury may be present at the onset, but in other cases the disability is related to his everyday life. Writers may develop writer's cramp, salesmen may become unable to talk, pilots unable to judge distance, and singers unable to hear notes. Each case is an individual matter and requires careful diagnosis and treatment.

Dissociative reactions. We sometimes hear of a person who finds himself in a strange city, not knowing his name or anything about his past — not knowing even whether he is married or not. Sometimes he begins a new life, and he may be successful in his new role for a long period. Perhaps at some particular time he will suddenly revert to his original personality, forgetting the intervening years. This is *fugue,* often called amnesia. We sometimes find cases of multiple personality, which are fortunately extremely rare, in which the same person has two or more apparently distinct personalities which interchange from time to time and which may or may not know about the "other personality." Some forms of sleep-walking also represent dissociative reactions.

These reactions have a common base — they enable the subject to avoid fear-arousing situations or other unpleasant experiences. They represent *an escape into another personality* which is completely different, a "getting-away-from-it-all." Often there is an underlying conflict between the fear and their sense of duty. In the sense that one part of the personality seems to have "split off" from the main body, these reactions are *dissociative.*

George had been picked up from a railroad boxcar several years ago, penniless and without identification. Attempts by authorities to establish his identity were fruitless. George could remember nothing about his past life and had not been reported as a missing person. Making use of his talents, George became a salesman of used cars and eventually owned a large automobile agency. He married and had two children and became a respected community member.

Later George, wishing to get more knowledge of his former status, undertook psychiatric treatment. Clues were discovered, and his past identity was ascertained. George recovered his memory of his past. He was relieved to find that he had been a respected business man and community member with no family responsibilities. Conflicts in connection with his business, combined with overwork and physical exhaustion, had led to his state of fugue.

Obsessive-compulsive reactions. Deep feelings of guilt may sometimes arise as a result of conflicts represented in repressed but hostile or destructive feelings toward one's family, in regard to one's sex activity, or due to other tensions and feelings which one cannot accept as moral or worthy of himself. A person so affected is not likely to express his hostile feelings or otherwise unacceptable actions overtly, but the fear persists that sometime he may inadvertently give way to these feelings. He attempts to protect himself by using a defense of a symbolic type and *relieves his feelings of guilt by going through certain rituals.* Through focusing on the ritual, the emotional feelings are thus isolated from the person or object against whom they were directed. Guilt is relieved by "undoing."

James often rubbed his hands together as if he were washing them. In times of stress he did this continuously, and attempts to break the habit were unsuccessful. He tried wearing gloves, keeping his hands in his pockets, and carrying something, but these tactics only made him feel uncomfortable.

Examination showed that James had at one time waked in the night to find himself standing near his step-brother's bed, apparently ready to do him violence. The sibling rivalry, in this case, was accentuated by the preferential treatment given his step-brother by his step-father and acceded to by his mother. On this occasion the brother had been bullying James, but James was blamed by the parents as being the cause of the trouble.

A week or two after this incident the step-brother was killed in a bicycle–motor-car accident. James blamed himself for hostile wishes and took onto himself feelings of guilt as having possibly been in some way to blame. The hand-washing was apparently symbolic of a desire to make himself "clean" again.

Depressive reactions. The depressed patient typically feels that he is undeserving, worthless, and unacceptable. He may feel unwarranted fatigue, be rundown and unable to concentrate. Thus his work may be greatly hampered. His appetite may be affected — he may either lose interest in food or eat excessively. He may have a history of moodiness, feelings of inferiority, guilt, or suppressed hostility.

Psychosomatic disorders. In studying the role of the brain and the autonomic nervous system in Chapter 8, we learned that various physiological phenomena occurred during intense emotions. Strong emotions, and those which continue over long periods of time, may produce loss of appetite, indigestion, peptic ulcer, or excessive eating. Loss of appetite is associated with anxiety, whereas excessive eating indicates that food may be a substitute for other psychological needs which have been unfulfilled, such as the need for affection. Other psychosomatic disorders include disarrangement of the eliminative functions, high blood pressure, heart symptoms, asthma, hay fever, tendencies to the common cold, rashes, menstrual problems, headaches, enuresis (bed-wetting), impotence or frigidity, and others. In each case the particular form of psychosomatic symptom seems related to the form of the conflict involved or the anxiety present.

Since this book is not a volume dealing with abnormal psychology in any definitive sense, we shall forego a more complete description of the psychoneuroses. Our intent has been to show briefly some of the chief kinds of psychoneurotic symptoms that have been recognized, and to illustrate how they may be related to conflicts and emotions. You will recognize that within each category the kinds of symptoms and the conflicts causing them can be practically extended without limit. Each case is separate and distinct in its background and we must be on guard against seeing a possible "symptom" and judging its bearer as if we really knew the answer. Only expert examination reveals the true nature of the situation. — Now we shall discuss the various types of psychoses.

The psychoses

Psychoses differ from neuroses in that there is a more or less complete loss of contact with reality. Functional psychoses typically represent reactions to conflicts, feelings of guilt or hostility, or other psychological difficulties as opposed to physical malfunctioning.

Melancholia (involutional [1] psychotic reaction). This reaction involves depression. Patients may feel guilty, unworthy, agitated, unable to sleep. Sometimes they will have delusions in regard to the body, such as believing that an organ is missing or not functioning properly. Melancholia differs from the depression neuroses in that it is a more extensive illness in which the patient has less contact with reality and his personality is more completely disorganized. Since melancholia is an illness of middle age and is more prevalent among women, speculation has arisen as to whether the hormone changes accompanying the menopause or climacteric are associated with it. As a person sees himself (or herself) getting older and thinks about physical decline, perhaps depression is not unlikely, especially if he has achieved few if any of his goals or feels that life thus far has been quite worthless.

Manic-depressive reactions. These reactions lead to varying degrees of disability and have varying prognoses of cure. Manic reactions represent increased activity on the part of the patient and feelings of happiness, confidence, aggressiveness, initiative, and spontaneity. Manic-depressive persons may at first seem to their friends to have taken a turn for the better when the manic stage sets in after a period of depression. In less serious cases they may recover without treatment, but when the reaction is acute or involves delirium the patient becomes a problem to society as well as to himself. He may become uninhibited, profane, obscene, quick to anger He may handle his business affairs wildly and go quickly into projects where his money is easily lost. He can develop delusions of power. More extreme cases may be wild and combative and need restraint and sedation. Apparently the manic state does not represent genuine happiness but is rather defense against such unhappy feelings as inferiority and guilt.

The depressive states also vary in acuteness, ranging from mild depression — in which the patient is discouraged, fatigued, and uninterested in the world, and may contemplate (and attempt) suicide — to the acute stage in which patients may need spoon-feeding and other bodily care, much as if they were small children. In extreme cases they may lie completely motionless in a hospital bed.

Schizophrenia. Various types of schizophrenia (literally, a "splitting of the mind") are distinguishable. *Catatonic* states are those of almost complete stupor. Patients are rather immobile and oblivious to the environment. They

---

[1] In a physiological sense, *involution* means the decline before senility, represented by menopause in women and by the decrease of vital force in both sexes.

may have fixed facial expressions. If they are placed in certain positions, they will tend to remain that way. Apparently they are exhibiting extreme negativism and live a life of fantasy a great deal of the time. But they are not completely out of contact with reality. These patients, oddly enough, are among the schizophrenic patients most likely to be curable.

Hebephrenic patients may exhibit general dishevelment and odd mannerisms. They tend to be silly and to laugh inappropriately. They are disoriented to time and place and are likely to be incoherent and irrelevant in speech. They are easily distracted, and often go around muttering indistinguishable words and phrases.

So-called *simple* schizophrenia represents a retreat of the patient into an autistic (inner) life. The patient apparently is not so ill as some in other categories, but he is not as likely to recover as is the catatonic. Memory, orientation in time and space, and general behavior are often good from a societal viewpoint. These patients are not spectacular — they do not rave or become wild.

Paranoia. Paranoid patients suffer from delusions and hallucinations which serve as defenses for conflicts or threats. Delusions of grandeur may cover up for feelings of inferiority. "Voices" which "tell" some patients how to behave may help them disclaim responsibility for their own actions. Feelings of being persecuted may seem to excuse some of these people for various failures in their attempts to achieve. They may reflect the delusion that plots against their welfare are being perpetrated, and they cannot be convinced that this is not true. Some feel that they are influenced through such media as mental telepathy, hypnosis, or even radio waves. In paranoia a retreat from reality appears to develop over a period of time, not to come suddenly.

Organic illnesses

Up to this point we have been discussing mental illnesses *which originate primarily in the emotional or psychological dynamics of the individual.* These are called *functional disorders.* Not all psychological disturbances come from conflicts or emotions. Various forms of damage to the brain and nervous system may result in behavior disturbances as may other physical impairments. Among the physical conditions associated with mental illness are general paresis (syphilis), brain damage caused by a spirochete usually spread during sexual intercourse; alcoholism (which is, of course, partly psychological in causation); senile psychoses, which are caused by arterial changes during old age; brain tumors; blows on the head; and varieties of disability caused by birth injuries, hormonal imbalance, or physical damage during high fevers. Mental deficiency (not a disease but a lack of mental ability) may be caused by birth injuries, lack of certain hormones, and disease — as well as by inheritance. Mental deficiency is often accompanied by poor emotional adjustment, and the complete picture is thus that of a mentally diseased person.

Mental illnesses which are associated with physical damage are *organic*. On occasion it may be difficult to discover whether a given group of symptoms represents an organic or a functional disorder. For this reason, the diagnosis of a patient typically requires both medical and psychological tests. Treatment in the hospital generally includes medical and psychological or psychiatric assistance.

Suggested activities

1. Look up statistics and prepare a report on the incidence of mental disease. Prepare a list of sources of help in prevention, diagnosis, or treatment.

2. Procure, display, and discuss publications of the National Association for Mental Health.

3. Read and report on books dealing with psychological or emotional problems. Many books of fiction treat such topics in an interesting way.

4. What are your own State's laws in regard to mental health?

5. Investigate and report on the problem of alcoholism, drug addiction, or accident-prone drivers, etc.

A. CHARACTERISTICS OF MENTAL HEALTH
B. MENTAL ILLNESS IN MODERN SOCIETY

● C. CAUSES OF MENTAL ILLNESS

Coleman (2) indicates that each of us may "break down" under sufficient stress — whether physical or psychological. That is, under war conditions, loss of health, certain injuries, loss of loved ones, or other pressures anyone may develop unadjusted, psychoneurotic, or even psychotic disorders.

Some persons, however, seem more predisposed to mental illness than others. They can tolerate less stress than "stronger" persons, and we consider their self-concepts as less stable or less adequate. The extent to which stable and adequate personalities are related to heredity is unknown. The role of development in the formation of a stable personality, with emphasis on the period of early childhood, is receiving considerable attention, especially from psycho-analytically oriented psychiatrists and psychologists. In Chapter 10 we indicated some of the sequences in social development and the problems related to the socializing of the individual. We shall now refer to these problems in relation to mental health.

From the moment of conception the child needs security to maintain and develop organization as a human being. Until birth this security is provided in the uterus; but once he is born, outer environmental stresses and strains become influential — first in maintaining physical existence and later in maintaining and improving psychological adjustment. The infant's physical needs must be attended to, since he cannot minister to them himself. At first he is self-centered and cannot understand the need for waiting for his bottle or waiting to be covered up when he is cold. He may sense neglect or even rejection on the part of his mother if his needs are not attended to reasonably well. This is especially true at feeding time. Feelings of insecurity develop tension and lack of satisfaction in the child. Mothers who are anxious or domineering and inflexible may further this tenseness. Impersonal handling of the child, roughness, or harshness may deprive him of emotional satisfaction. The mother's part in the necessarily close relationship between mother and child tends either to foster a sense of security — the beginning of good mental health — or to impart quite the opposite feeling — insecurity, rejection, and emotional dissatisfaction.

Some believe that toilet training, poorly managed, may lay the groundwork for personality disorders. Too early or too rigorous insistence on approved toilet habits can be harmful, for the child may not be able to satisfy his parents in this regard because of physical immaturity. Since such training is often related to parents' moral values, the child may develop feelings of inferiority, guilt, or perhaps rebellion and resentment. The child is "good" if he controls himself, "bad" if he does not. Rejection by parents may be felt, even if it is not actually present.

As the child learns to cooperate with his parents, siblings, and playmates, he finds that he cannot always do as he wishes. He encounters conflicts between his own desires and those of society. Some parents overindulge a child, and he may turn into a little bully who demands attention to his whims through temper tantrums, rages, and aggressive behavior long after he should have learned to control his emotions. Other parents dominate their children, who thus may become submissive, timid, shy, and dependent. The overprotected child may shrink from new experiences and be "tied to his mother's apron strings." Some parents reject their children emotionally, and this is the most difficult deprivation children have to face. Such children may become seclusive or aggressive, rebellious, and resentful of authority. Note that we have used the word "may" with all the consequences of parental attitudes or treatment which we have mentioned. Fortunately, many children who are subjected to these parental attitudes and behavior remain or become well-adjusted individuals because of other conditions or influences either in the environment or within themselves.

Some parents may be anxious to furnish all the toys, clothing, and other material requirements the child may desire, yet are unable to offer him affection even though they may wish to do so. Sometimes these parents are incapable of showing affection because of some lack in their own personalities. In other cases the parents may actually not want the child or the responsibilities of parenthood.

Poor husband–wife relationships, nagging, discord, worry, anxiety, jealousy of brothers or sisters, or unusual religious or moral attitudes within the home may cause anxiety, hostility, and irritability. Some children face conflicts with their peers because of unusual circumstances in the home.

Other children may face long illnesses or suffer peculiarities of appearance. Because of physical disability, some may not be able to compete physically with their peer group at the stages when this is important. Attitudes and behavior related to sex are often a source of problems. Extreme demands of any kind placed on children who are incapable of satisfying them are sources of inferiority or guilt feelings.

The illustrations we have given are by no means exhaustive. Rather, they are representative. Lest the college student get the idea that it is practically impossible to "bring a child up right," we hasten to point out that long-continuing abnormalities in the home, real lack of affection, and forthright rejection are most damaging to personality development. Children are remarkably flexible, and they can tolerate more stress than one might think. Even some rather extreme traumatic conditions are not likely to damage children, if they feel secure in their family relationships. Interestingly enough, one of the insights that came from World War II is related to the evacuation of British children to the country during the time of the bombing of London. Such children exhibited more stress because of separation from their parents than because of the bombing. They did not exhibit particular fear so long as their parents were with them in a protective role (3).

Childhood is a particularly important period in that the learning which occurs at that time tends to influence the way the individual perceives himself and others for the remainder of his life. Havighurst (4) describes "developmental tasks" as certain physical, mental, emotional, and social learnings which must be accomplished at definite times in the child's life if he is not to be prevented or at least delayed from achieving success in later periods. For example, the child who does not talk at the age at which others usually do is at a disadvantage in communicating not only with parents but with playmates, and eventually he may have difficulty in school. The child who is deprived of the opportunity to learn certain social relationships at an early age (as, for example, how to get on easily with his peers) may never completely adjust socially. The child who has not begun to control his emotions at an early age may never attain social and emotional maturity.

Certain apparent maladjustments appear to be learned purposefully. For example, fatigue syndromes may reflect the attitudes of the parents toward rest, work, or weakness. An insecure child may find that fatigue is a way of controlling others, since a delicate child cannot be expected to exert himself, and others must wait on him and cater to him. Fatigue can represent rationalization, compensation, or an attempt to gain attention.

Anxiety neuroses may be the result of uneasiness in the home (5). If the child is given too much responsibility or criticized too severely or frequently, anxiety is almost certain to appear. Hysteria also may represent escape or attention-getting, and so on.

Thus no child probably ever develops perfectly or in a perfect environment, and — although most abnormal tendencies are overcome by changes in the home, or through the school, playground, or church — some neurotic tendencies of childhood may persist to become adolescent or adult problems. Often the predisposing factors are inherent in the individual, awaiting only a triggering event, such as failure in business, death of a loved one, rejection by a prospective husband or wife, to bring forth full-fledged neuroses or even psychoses.

    A.   CHARACTERISTICS OF MENTAL HEALTH
    B.   MENTAL ILLNESS IN MODERN SOCIETY
    C.   CAUSES OF MENTAL ILLNESS

● D. HELP FOR THE MENTALLY ILL

    Modern clinics for the mentally ill employ the services of various professional workers. A psychiatrist often heads such a clinic and provides diagnostic and therapeutic aid as well as over-all direction of the activities of the clinic. Psychologists offer psychological help — usually that of testing and use of other psychological diagnostic devices. Psychiatric social workers provide social case histories of patients and often work with families or other environmental influences in the lives of the patients. Information about the physical condition of the patient may be supplied by the psychiatrist, since he is a medical doctor, but it may also be provided by other medical sources. Clinics need to know about the patient's intelligence, his home conditions, his marital adjustment, his occupational success, and other sociological information. The workers of the clinic then usually "staff" the patient — discuss him together in their professional group, each contributing the information he has which is relevant to the patient's complaint. Together they arrive at a diagnosis and decide on plans for gathering more data which may be needed and for providing therapy.

    Many ways of obtaining information are available. Sociological data may be obtained by interviews with the patient, his family, school personnel, and others, depending on the age of the patient and the characteristics of his problems. His intelligence, as well as his special abilities and aptitudes, can be assessed through tests. Information about personality traits can be obtained through scales which rate him by his performance on paper-and-pencil tests.

    Because patients may either not know the answers to certain questions or may try to disguise or repress certain answers or symptoms, the information obtained from interviews or tests is often supplemented in other ways. Among them are projective techniques, in which the patient provides information about his inner conflicts and motives by responding to ambiguous or unstructured stimuli. For example, the Rorschach Test (6) consists of pictures which are in reality nothing but ink blots which have no meaning except that with which the patient endows them. The diagnostician can judge something of the patient's inner life by analyzing his reactions to these pictures. The Thematic

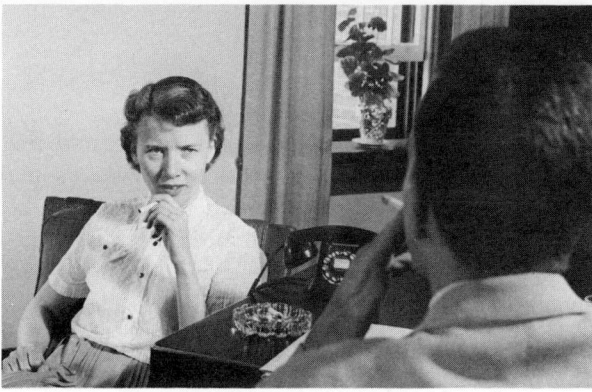

INTERVIEW WITH PATIENT. The interviewer will ask the patient about her family, her job or school, her own feelings about her problems, making careful observations of her conversation and actions.

GAINING INFORMATION ABOUT THE MENTAL PATIENT. *Since the patient often cannot explain the causes of his troubles even to himself, psychological techniques must be used. These pictures were taken at St. Elizabeth's Hospital in Washington, D. C. The woman is not an actual patient. (Photos courtesy of the National Institute of Mental Health.)*

PROJECTIVE TECHNIQUES. For the Rorschach test the patient is asked to comment on ink blots. In such unstructured tests she may unconsciously reveal information about inner conflicts and motives.

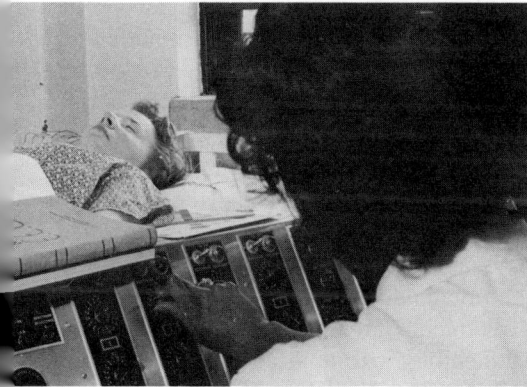

ELECTROENCEPHALOGRAPH. Used in the physical examination and in treatment as well, the electroencephalograph detects and records brain waves.

INTERVIEW WITH FAMILY. The patient's husband is questioned about her personality and behavior, as well as his understanding of her problem.

Apperception Test (7) presents interesting but ambiguous pictures, and the patient is asked to tell a short story about each; in his stories he reveals some of his own fears, memories, problems, and anxieties. The Rosenzweig P-F Test (8), the Make-A-Picture-Story Test (9) and others operate on similar principles.

Further light on the personality of children can be gained by an analysis of their play with a set of dolls especially designed for the purpose. Psychodrama, in which patients act out their problems, can often aid in diagnosis or therapy.

Psychoanalytic techniques are often based on free association. The patient is made comfortable and assisted to relax, often by reclining on a couch. The analyst makes himself a part of the background and is unobstrusive. The patient is asked to mention anything which comes into his mind, and the analyst takes note of the content, things which seem repressed or avoided, the reactions of the patient, and so on. He may be aided by analyzing the patient's dreams, or occasionally by information gained while the patient is under hypnosis or under the influence of certain relaxing drugs.

The physical examination may include neurological tests and tests for diseases like syphilis in addition to more common aspects of physical examination.

There is growing interest in a particular technique called *electroencephalography* (EEG), in which the minute electrical charges given off by the brain are amplified, recorded, and studied. By placing the electrodes of the EEG machine over various areas of the brain, certain kinds of abnormal functioning in these areas can be detected. The brain waves, given off as part of the metabolic processes, include *alpha* waves, which are large, rhythmic, and smooth; the somewhat faster and more irregular *beta* waves; the weak *gamma* waves; and strong, slow *delta* waves. If the specialist in electroencephalography finds differences in these waves from expected patterns — differences in rhythm or amplitude, or other irregularities — he can thus often detect tumors or other difficulties. Such studies are important in helping to determine the nature of factors which may be causing disturbed behavior. For example, both functional and organic diseases may sometimes be diagnosed in this way.

Once sufficient information has been obtained, the next necessary steps are evaluation, diagnosis, and prescribed treatment. Treatment will, of course, depend on the diagnosis. Any medical difficulties will be attacked, for example, syphilis will be treated, brain tumors perhaps excised, etc. Medical treatment may include shock therapy, tranquilizing drugs (see page 392), hydrotherapy, or sedation in certain advanced cases. Massage, diet, or other techniques may be necessary. Psychotherapy may be indicated to help the patient achieve a more adequate personality. Giving the patient an opportunity to release emotions and develop insight into his own problems, re-educating him in emotional behavior through such techniques as psychoanalysis, psychodrama, non-directive counseling, group activity, and occupational therapy, or other such techniques may be employed. Social workers can sometimes improve the environment of the patient — perhaps through provision of an adequate standard of

TREATMENT. *Treatment depends on the diagnosis reached after obtaining data. The woman in these pictures is not an actual patient. (Courtesy of the National Institute of Mental Health.)*

PSYCHODRAMA. The patient may reach a greater understanding of her conflict by participating in a drama about similar problems. Spectators also may identify with a character or situation in the drama.

PLEASANT ENVIRONMENT. The maintenance of family and community ties through visits is important to the patient's progress.

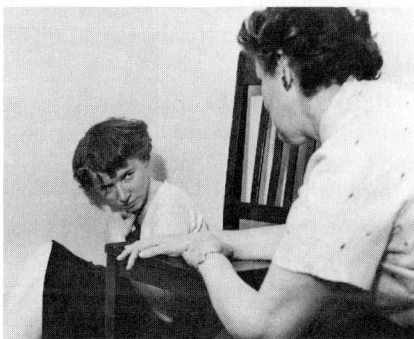

COUNSELING. A psychiatric social worker tries to help the patient develop insight into her problems. The patient should feel understood and accepted.

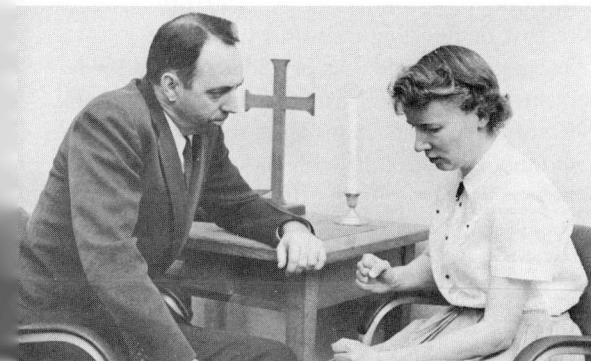

RELIGIOUS GUIDANCE. A pastoral counselor with special clinical training may talk with the patient and her family. Ministers of today are increasingly trying to relate principles of psychology and mental health to religion.

OCCUPATIONAL THERAPY. The hospital provides games, magazines, and arts and crafts supplies.

living, employment, readjustment of marital relationships — and even custodial care can be of assistance.

Of course, not all patients attend clinics. Many see psychiatrists in private practice, interview counselors, or consult other workers who can advise and, if qualified, diagnose and treat. This may be true in cases where work of a highly specialized nature is not needed. Some practitioners depend for some of their information on tests of various kinds. Others depend primarily on psychoanalytic techniques. A variety of privately operated services for helping the patient are available. The primary limitations of these facilities are a shortage of professional workers, heavy case loads, and the expense of private counseling or psychiatry.

Many problems can be treated by experts with beneficial results, yet do not require extended or frequent visits to a therapist. Some college students could profit by some professional aid, but may not be maladjusted enough to require full-scale or extended services. The offices of the deans of men and women, the student counselors, health department, medical clinic, and infirmary can often be of assistance. These services may be able to help some students directly, and they may aid in referral of other students to more expert assistance. Sources of free or inexpensive help can be indicated. Many colleges have established aids to students in the correction of speech and hearing difficulties, sight-saving, and reading and study problems, any of which may have emotional concomitants.

Most large cities have clinical facilities which provide the aid from psychology, psychiatry, social work, and educational guidance. In some instances the city schools provide such facilities. Various states provide free or inexpensive clinical and hospital care. Church organizations may provide pastoral counseling or sponsor the services of clinical personnel. The federal government — particularly through the Veterans' Administration — provides many facilities, including psychiatric help, for veterans. The Armed Services have specially trained staffs working with military personnel. Hospitals are provided for veterans and their families and for members of the armed forces. In addition, there are numerous private clinics and practitioners who cater primarily to those willing and able to bear the cost of the diagnosis and treatment.

The National Mental Health Act, passed in 1946, has provided money for research and related services. Operating through the National Institute of Mental Health of the Public Health Service of the United States Department of Health, Education, and Welfare, the government is working with the various states to make sure each community has the services it requires (10).

A note on tranquilizing drugs

Much publicity has been given to the tranquilizing drugs now being used in mental hospitals and by family physicians. You may have the idea that they are almost a self-evident prescription for headaches, tensions, anxiety, or the "jitters." Will they actually cure mental illness, high blood pressure, migraine headaches, or alcoholism? Are they habit-forming? Safe to use?

There are several kinds of these tranquilizing drugs, derived from various sources. One group is derived from the extract of the rauwolfia (snakeroot) plant from India. Another is synthetic, an antihistamine called Chlorpromazine. A third group comes from derivatives of mephenesin. These drugs can be given by injection or in tablet form. Exactly how they work is not yet definitely known.

In contrast to sedatives, which tend to depress thinking, speech, and physical activity, these drugs tend to exert a calming effect without interfering with a person's mental functioning. They are very helpful in the treatment of those mental patients who must be calmed down before psychotherapy is possible. Other patients may be made more comfortable by using the drugs, even though they perhaps cannot be cured. Patients who are aggressive seem to be helped more than those who are depressed.

Since many patients seen by a physician have ailments that are partially or entirely of an emotional nature (psychosomatic ills, hysteria, etc.) it is evident that in the hands of skilled professional men these drugs, together with other therapies used by the doctors, can be of real service. At the time of this writing, a great deal still remains to be learned about tranquilizers — whether they are going to be habit-forming, what permanent effects may result, whether they are especially useful in treating particular types of disorders, and the like. In any case, *they should be used only under the direction of a physician.* They are not cure-alls and they do not eliminate the causes of the tensions which the patient may have.

Thus tranquilizing drugs are useful insofar as they can relieve the symptoms of anxiety and calm the patient, offering him relief and affording opportunity for medical or psychiatric therapy. As miracle medicines to be sold on an over-the-counter basis to all who feel a need to calm their nerves, their effectiveness and safety have not yet been established.

A. CHARACTERISTICS OF MENTAL HEALTH
B. MENTAL ILLNESS IN MODERN SOCIETY
C. CAUSES OF MENTAL ILLNESS
D. HELP FOR THE MENTALLY ILL

● E. PREVENTING MENTAL ILLNESS

Conflict plays an extremely important role in mental health or illness. As we attempted to show in discussing neuroses, practically all human behavior — mental or physical — is accompanied by emotional changes. Some of these changes are mild, others more striking. Attitudes, goals or motives, conflicts, frustrations, and feelings of guilt, hostility, or inferiority can produce physiological as well as psychological changes — some quite temporary, others more permanent. Such is the case for normal people. For those who are somewhat maladjusted or definitely neurotic or psychotic, these changes reflect inappropriate behavior leading to tension and unsatisfied needs.

In our discussion of motivation in Chapter 8, we stated how tension caused by a pressing drive or need motivates us to goal-seeking activity. When the goal is quickly or easily attained, tension is lessened and we experience satisfaction. But what happens when a strong barrier of some sort prevents our reaching the goal?

Arnold wishes to gain recognition. He wants to be known as "somebody." (Being "somebody" enhances his self-concept and gives him feelings of security.) This is a normal social need. Arnold has chosen to try to make himself important by becoming a radio announcer. Unfortunately, when heard through the microphone, Arnold's voice includes a great number of hisses, clicks, and smacks which are not noticeable in ordinary conversation. These extraneous sounds may be attributable in part to Arnold's nervousness and to his tenseness and concentration in trying to speak carefully, and in part to the fact that the microphone amplifies any small sounds. At any rate, it appears that a radio announcer's career is out for Arnold — his voice is too great a barrier. If he is sufficiently desirous of attaining this particular goal, frustration and conflict may cause him certain anxieties. The way Arnold chooses to get out of this dilemma must depend on how he sees this barrier, how he reacts to the conflict, and how he can utilize his abilities to achieve recognition in a career other than radio announcing.

Conflicts are of three main kinds:

1. Some can be called *push-pull conflicts* because we are both attracted and repelled by the same goal-object. Sometimes we use the word *valence* to indicate the attractiveness (positive valence) or repulsiveness (negative valence) of an object, much as in chemistry. In a push-pull conflict the same object or situation has both positive and negative valences. For example, think of a job in which you are interested. You may be attracted because of the money, prestige, and promise of a successful future. At the same time the job may be a worry to you — it may place strong demands on your time and energy. The work may be confining, and the employer may be a difficult man to please. This push-pull conflict may be resolved by gaining more interest and confidence in your ability to do the work, changing to a different job, etc. Failure to resolve it in some way may result in bad temper, difficulties on the job, poor relations with the boss, or even physical illness or a "nervous breakdown."

2. Some conflicts are *double adient*, that is, both of two conflicting objects or situations have positive valences. You will remember the story of the donkey who starved to death because he could not decide from which of two bales of hay to eat. Life is full of these conflicts — a person wants to finish school, yet he also wants to be married and go to work; he likes athletics and social life, yet he wants to make good grades in order to graduate with honors; he cannot

decide between two excellent job offers, etc. Obviously one will make a choice or other persons or circumstances will eventually force a decision. Vacillating for an extended period of time often leads to anxiety.

3. *"Double avoidant" conflicts* are those in which two objects both have negative valence, yet we must move toward one or the other. We don't want to come to classes when ill, yet we don't want to stay in the dormitory and miss the examination. We don't want to give a talk in class, yet we don't want to fail the speech course. We don't want to work, yet we don't want to get in difficulty for non-payment of bills. We are not quite sure which is the frying pan and which is the fire.

There is an interesting laboratory experiment in which dogs are trained to expect food when a circle of light is thrown on a screen.[1] When the figure of a flat oval is presented, the food is shown, but it is kept behind glass doors and the dogs cannot eat it. The pups soon learn to go toward the food at the sight of a circle, since the glass door will open. Soon they learn to pay no attention to the oval, but they perk up at the presentation of the circle. Finally, a figure exactly halfway between the oval and the circle is displayed. In this situation the dogs become frustrated. The reactions of the dogs vary — some apparently show disgust and confusion and lie down and avoid the figure entirely. Others get very excited and bark and fuss. Some whine and beg. They vary, as people do, in their ability to tolerate frustration and in their responses to the same frustrating situation.

Conflicts can be resolved in at least four ways — by removing the frustrating situation, by attempting to circumvent the problem, by changing the goal-object, or by changing the motivation.

Suppose that you must take an examination for which you are not properly prepared. You need to succeed in the course, yet the barrier of an examination lies before you. You can attack the barrier and thus remove the frustrating situation — study hard tonight instead of going on a date, ask for review or help from your instructor, or get your roommate to help you. You can circumvent the barrier — try to pass the course without passing this particular examination, do extra-credit work, or keep your other marks high, confer with the instructor, asking for a special test. You can change your goal-object — accept failure in this course, change your major, or quit school and get a job. You can change your motives — decide that a college education is a silly whim, merely a salve to your vanity or a means of enhancing your prestige, and thus convince yourself that what you really want is a home and family. Hence you have no need to pass the course at all.

Some of these possible solutions are negative — negative in that they run counter to the expectations of society and are likely to lead you into a deeper kind of frustration. Skipping a class, cheating on the examination, complaining that the examination is not fair — all such techniques may cause you to have guilt feelings and fears, and may lower your concept of yourself. Moreover,

[1] For an interesting film showing such an experiment, see (11), and page 396.

Different reactions to frustration. *The dog at left barks in reaction to the denial of expected food, while the other lies down, distressed and disconsolate, turning away from the stimulus and giving up. The lighted figure which was the stimulator is shown in the background. Humans also react differently to frustration. Contrast Teddy Roosevelt's vigor with the lethargy of a Bowery "bum." (From the film, Of Pups and Puzzles, courtesy of Metro-Goldwyn-Mayer; Underwood & Underwood; Brown Brothers.)*

if unfair tactics are detected, you face added problems in the form of punishment. Negative solutions are good neither for society nor for yourself.

Thus, conflicts may cause unresolved anxieties, tensions, feelings of inferiority, guilt feelings, stark fear, hostility, and a host of other emotions. Some may be directed against other people, some against yourself. Conflicts must be resolved positively to maintain mental health. Most students find it possible to handle the majority of their problems in a sound manner — but some do not. What are some evidences of possible maladjustment in college?

Common evidences of conflicts in college

Academic failure. Classes are often geared to students in the upper fifty per cent according to ability. With the educational background, intelligence, motivation, and study habits similar to that of the upper one-third of high school graduates, college students may complete their classes successfully but with an occasional C or D grade. Some failures are attributable to low intelligence and inadequate previous preparation; however, failures are often symptoms suggesting motivational and emotional problems. Such symptoms can also include missing classes, lateness in handing in work, inability to concentrate, failure to contribute to class discussions, unhappy personal or group relationships, and the like. On the surface, at least, it appears that the student is simply not trying. However, if we could explore the problems more deeply, we would probably find one or more unresolved conflicts related to these surface symptoms in a student, otherwise capable, who fails outright or receives such low grades that he eventually must withdraw from college.

Social isolation, withdrawal. We live in a social world, and the person who withdraws excessively from social interaction is refusing to face reality. We reap certain benefits from society, but we must also contribute to the social benefits of others. Some students wish neither to give nor to take these social benefits. They seem to prefer to be by themselves, cultivating solitary hobbies, attending shows alone, and the like. A few drive their friends away from them by rudeness or failure to offer friendship in return. Some avoid student get-togethers. Others must room alone. Such behavior, if not extreme, may not give rise to much concern. But we are familiar with those who are excessively isolated, and these — even though they may not harm anyone but themselves — may deserve concern. Perhaps their withdrawal is associated with fear of people, feelings of inadequacy, snobbishness, or intellectualization as a form of escape from reality. Whatever the symptoms, social isolation and withdrawal suggest unresolved conflicts.

Excessive moodiness. Adolescents are likely to have their ups and downs, perhaps more than people at any other age. Adults may have somewhat cyclic stages of elation and depression. The problem is not whether we are moody at all, but whether we are excessively so — whether we move too far toward elation or depression, whether we swing too rapidly, or for too little cause. Illness, family problems, boy-and-girl relationships, the weather, success in work, examinations, and many other phenomena contribute to one's emotional moods. Frequent and sharp fluctuations may be a symptom of instability and lack of emotional control.

Rebellion against authority. The mature person conforms to authority because it seems wise to do so. But there are those who almost always have a chip on their shoulders and who cultivate the attitude that "nobody can make me do what I don't want to do." They may get into arguments and other conflicts in a variety of situations. They may deliberately flout authority. To them it appears that the instructors, deans, housemothers, and their own parents are always circumscribing their actions. Why does a person rebel against authority? It may be because he is overdemanding or "spoiled." It may be because he has feelings of inferiority and blames others for his shortcomings. He may have a low tolerance of frustration. There are other causes, of course, many of them related to poor mental health.

Attention-seeking. People normally desire the attention of others, for it contributes to the satisfaction of their needs for affection, status, and recognition. It may also contribute to their feelings of security — they want to feel included in a group. Some use practically any means to attract attention, which will serve them as a substitute for the affection they normally desire and feel they are not getting. Many bolster their feelings of inferiority by continually getting themselves compared favorably to others, calling attention to themselves and hoping for a pat on the back. You know such people, and you see them in classes. They talk too much, have too many wise or intellectual sayings, or argue with their instructors and their classmates. On campus they may wear extreme dress, flash quantities of money and treat others lavishly, contribute to flamboyant parties, or drink too much. Some attention-seeking is normal. Too much may reflect poor mental health.

Rigidity. Rigidity characterizes the person who cannot change his attitudes or actions. His mind is made up. He meets new situations with non-adaptive, inflexible methods and attitudes. He breaks, rather than bends, under strain. He is not willing to accept or consider reasonable alternatives. Perhaps he is afraid of change — new attitudes or ideas terrify him. Perhaps he has such intense conflicts that his reactions are limited and are focused on a narrow segment of life's problems.

Vacillation. A vacillating person may be one who wants today to become a lawyer, tomorrow a doctor. When he is with one person, he is a liberal; with someone else, is conservative. He swings readily from this to that, tries various courses of study, shifts majors and minors frequently, tries out various extra-class activities, perhaps even transfers from college to college. He's friendly today, stand-offish tomorrow. He stands for everything and nothing. He may be immature, with feelings of inferiority. Perhaps he cannot resolve the conflict between the needs for social approval and for personal autonomy. Vacillation can, of course, be as harmful as rigidity.

Financial distress. We list financial distress as an evidence of conflict, because some people exhaust their finances trying to buy happiness rather than earn it. Thus it may indicate that a person is getting rid of his money in an attempt to satisfy a deeper need. You have perhaps heard that when a woman is feeling low, she ought to go out and buy a new hat — her new modishness will raise her spirits. There may be some truth in the comment. Nevertheless, some people spend and spend, trying to relieve a tension that is caused by something far different from a need for what they are buying. Lack of self-control, lack of a sense of proportion, and a desire "to keep up with the Joneses" may be involved. Spending for such purposes may reflect inner conflicts and poor adjustment.

Hypochondria. A hypochondriac is preoccupied much of the time with his health; he worries unduly about uncleanliness, contagious diseases, or contamination. He thinks he suffers from various illnesses and tends to recognize in himself the symptoms of diseases he merely hears or reads about. To him the first sneeze seems to indicate a cold — or worse. Hypochondria indicates a deeper adjustment problem.

We have discussed these nine symptoms in some detail to give you an idea of how certain forms of behavior — carried to an extreme, or used inappropriately — indicate conflict and resulting poor adjustment. Many other symptoms exist, of course. Alcoholism, compulsive eating, continually putting pleasure before work, over-sensitivity and "taking everything personally," refusal to compete, and constant critical attitudes are further symptoms.

Applying principles of mental health

The practice of good mental hygiene can provide a sound basis for a happy, normal, and reasonably successful life. It can help to prevent many problems, and when pressures become too strong, it can keep many people from succumbing fully to emotional disorders. Observing eight principles of mental health will help build a zestful, buoyant personality.

Keep physically healthy. Since good physical health is related to good emotional health, it follows that physical well-being will facilitate healthy personality development. Not only do certain diseases cause or precipitate mental illness, but they can also induce hypochondria, fatigue, and other functional disorders. A person in poor physical condition finds it difficult to participate effectively in a job, in school, or in a social group, and he misses a great deal of the pleasure and excitement of life. Lost time, with its accompanying worry and frustration, the inconvenience and expense of illness, and the actual pain or discomfort involved can produce depression and a biased mental outlook. Regular physical and dental examinations, adequate treatment of illness, and prompt attention to injuries are essential.

The Romans talked about "a sound mind in a sound body." Physical activity may exert a therapeutic effect when we are tired of mental activity, and we are told that sports aid in social adjustment. The practice of good physical hygiene — with its emphasis on rest, activity, and adequate nutrition — is an aid to good mental health. Too few of us maintain a proper balance of activity and rest. Many people also smoke and drink immoderately and ignore nutritional needs in their diet. Frequently, during vacations and weekends we violate most of the principles of physical health.

Physical education teachers are coming to emphasize more activities such as golf, tennis, skiing, skating — which a person can pursue throughout most of his life. Square dancing, social dancing, hunting, fishing, canoeing, swimming, bowling, badminton, handball, volleyball, archery, hiking, and a whole gamut of similar activities are now sponsored in most colleges.

Accept yourself. We have repeatedly stressed that one must like himself and feel good about himself. We do not mean that a person should overestimate himself. We mean that one should accept the fact that he has less ability than others in some areas, but more in other areas. The person who accepts himself recognizes both his abilities and his limitations. He discards guilt feelings about past failures and does not concentrate on such disappointments. He has confidence in his ability to meet situations and does not let feelings of inferiority or inability to compete on every level overwhelm him. He adjusts his level of aspiration to a reasonable limit and does not expect to set the world on fire. He profits by his mistakes and then forgets about them.

Accept the world as it is. Probably most college students are somewhat idealistic and therefore experience occasional disillusionment. We must recognize that not all men are governed by lofty principles and that even our best friends are not perfect. We discover that right does not always win, and that honesty and hard work do not automatically insure success. We see injustice and intolerance and discrimination about us, and we find that dreadful things sometimes happen to the nicest people. We find much evidence around us of unfair competition and intense rivalry, insecurity, dire poverty, and mental illnesses. In many local, national, and international affairs there seems to be no method for determining — much less enforcing — just and humane resolutions of conflicts. We should like to escape and build a fantasy world of our own.

For good mental health we cannot permit this desire for an unreal world to rule our behavior. It is necessary to remind ourselves that things are not usually black or white, but that there are many shades of gray. Every person has some good in him as well as bad. We need to remind ourselves not only that there are many problems in the world which need correcting, but also that some progress is being made in correcting them. We must remember that there are poverty and disease in the world, but also that strides are being made in providing adequate housing, clothing, and education, and that some advances are being made in the area of human relations.

Good mental health implies that we accept reality so that problems can be met squarely. Failure to accept reality leads to escapism of various kinds. Neither over-optimism nor pessimism is desirable. A calm acceptance of things as they are will lead to fewer frustrations and failures. It will also promote emotional health.

Participate in recreational activities. Sometimes we need to do some of the things we really *want* to do — get away from tension-producing situations and enjoy the tonic effects of pleasure and laughter. If one becomes a slave to his job, he risks the danger of staking everything on it. He may become too competitive, aggressive, hostile. He may wear himself down physically, and his social adjustment may suffer. All work and no play does tend to develop an individual into one who cannot leave his work behind and cannot enjoy himself even when he feels he should have some fun. Recreation offers opportunities for releasing tensions and expressing emotions freely, thereby helping to maintain mental health.

Recreation is any activity that one enjoys—maybe a quiet pastime such as reading, playing the piano or listening to music, painting or woodcarving, perhaps a social activity such as playing bridge or dancing, or maybe something more strenuous like an active sport. A certain amount of time should always be allotted to one or more of these forms of recreation.

Develop a social-centered outlook. As we said in Chapter 8, filial love, rather than love of self or erotic love exclusively, is necessary to maintain and extend civilized living. We need to understand and like people. Since we tend to evaluate ourselves by the ways in which others react to us, it is quite obvious that the self-centered person may not be able to obtain a true picture of what he is really like. He depends too much on himself, and his problems seem harder because he has no one to share them with. He misses the security and affection found in friendships. Often, after having achieved a good measure of prestige and financial gain, he finds that his life is really empty and purposeless. Few persons can live happily as islands unto themselves.

Most of us have both introvertive and extrovertive tendencies. To some extent we like to be alone, to have some privacy, and to think things through for ourselves, but most of us also like other people and wish to spend some time with them. We concern ourselves with their exploits and health and well-being. We exchange anecdotes and experiences. Social interaction — whether informal as in dormitory life or more formal as in classes, activities, and par-

ties — should be a definite part of every student's program. Too many studies, out-of-school jobs, or other solitary activities do not permit social
interaction and sensitivity to the needs and feelings of others.

Seek maturity in understanding life. This is not quite the same as accepting the world for what it is. Here we refer to the need for gathering information, analyzing it, and trying to understand it without bias. Uneducated
persons are rather naive and unaware of their biases and superstitions. They
form political opinions without much consideration. They embrace a religious
creed without questioning what it really implies in practice. They choose
friends on superficial bases, enter an occupation on a chance availability; in
other words, they jump to conclusions and accept opinions and attitudes in an
immature manner.

Similar immaturity among college students and other supposedly educated
adults often leads to humiliating or frustrating situations. They may experience
failure because their choice of action and the resulting consequences were not
carefully considered. Religious, social, and economic attitudes conflict with
each other. People fail to reach a mature level of personality integration essentially because various aspects of their living are directly in conflict with
each other or are so unrelated that they produce confusion.

Maturity in understanding life is almost an assurance of successful relationships with others. It aids in avoiding conflicts and frustrations. The books
you read, the classes you attend, and the discussions you hold with your
friends will aid you in attaining maturity. Information alone, of course, is of
little value. A thinking or organizing process must follow the gathering of
facts and information. Then application — that is, using the principles we
have suggested — can be more successful.

Set realistic goals. "He who hitches his wagon to a star may not get
so very far," for he may not have the ability he needs, and his environment may
not be conducive to success. It is quite generally agreed that good mental
health is furthered by success and hindered by failure. There are those in
our society who believe that in school one ought to fail now and then so that
he will be more able to face failures later in life. And it is possible that one
may gain an inflated opinion of himself through universal success. But the
ability to face failure does not depend on practicing failure; rather, on a strong
confidence gained from successes, feelings of security, good mental hygiene,
and a well-integrated personality. Failure can be damaging. Feelings of inferiority, guilt, insecurity, and self-punishment through conscience, fear, timid-
ity, and unwillingness to compete may result from repeated or disastrous
failures.

Hence it is wise to study our own limitations and the limitations placed on
our ambitions by environment. If we set realistic goals and reach them, we
can then set new and higher goals. Few of us aim too low. Those few need

to lift their sights. But more of us set unreachable goals, and when in the middle age we find that we have not attained all our goals, we feel let down, disappointed, and discouraged.

Most college students have a fair idea of their abilities, and a job-counselor can help them gain a more exact estimate of their real talents and interests through the use of tests and other devices. Such a counselor will also help students to discover what opportunities exist for making use of their abilities.

Be temperate. Finally, for a well-balanced personality it is necessary to be temperate — to avoid excesses. The danger of the excessive use of alcohol, tobacco, and drugs is well known, but over-eating and over-exercising can also present problems. We have already seen how the emotions affect physical functioning. Intense anger or fear produces physical disturbances. Prolonged aggression, escapism, and hostility can likewise be harmful.

Just as we recommend a balance between activity and rest, between social and individual activities, so do we recommend temperance in emotional stimulation and expression. Too much sexual excitement, too many thrills, excessive crying, laughing, anger, or fear suggest imbalance in emotional expression. While feelings cannot be turned off and on at will, one can plan his program of daily and long-term activities in order to seek stimulation and expression of pleasant emotions and to avoid and reasonably control his outward expression of unpleasant emotions.

SUMMARY

Mental health is more than freedom from mental illness. People who are mentally healthy feel comfortable about themselves, feel right about other people, and are able to meet the demands of life. They are balanced persons who can withstand stress, and who are usually happy and efficient in their daily living.

Although the number of persons showing symptoms of mental illness or emotional disturbance is very large, mental illnesses are not yet categorized and differentiated as clearly as most physical diseases. The mentally ill may exhibit various degrees of abnormality. *Neurotic* or *psychoneurotic* patients have not lost contact with reality and cannot be legally committed to institutions even though their behaviors deviate from societal expectations. *Psychotic* persons have partially or completely lost contact with reality and can be committed to institutions. Unadjusted individuals, on the other hand, are not seriously ill at all, but neither are they mentally healthy. Many of the symptoms exhibited by ill persons may be only exaggerations of normal behavior, or normal behavior used inappropriately. Only experts can tell with certainty whether a person is normal, unadjusted, neurotic, or psychotic. Psychiatrists do not always agree in their judgments of criminal insanity.

Just as mental illness may differ in degree, so its symptoms may vary, making classification difficult. Some illnesses are functional, stemming largely from psychological conflicts; whereas others are organic, resulting from actual damage or malfunctioning of the nervous, glandular, circulatory, or other systems. The functional diseases include anxiety neuroses, phobic reactions, hysteria, dissociative reactions, obsessive-compulsive reactions, depressive reactions, and psychosomatic disorders. Among the psychoses are melancholia, manic-depressive reactions, schizophrenia, and paranoia. Organic illnesses may stem from syphilis, alcoholism, arterial changes during senility, brain tumors, birth injuries, blows on the head, and the like. Because mental or emotional illnesses can be both organic and functional, diagnoses must include both medical and psychiatric study.

Mental illness seldom develops as a result of a single event or circumstance. Especially in the functional disorders, there can usually be found a fairly long history of the development of the disease. The home, as the earliest and perhaps most powerful social influence, provides both positive and negative forces in personality development. If the needs for affection, independence, control of aggressive impulses, security, status and recognition, and other socially derived motives are satisfied, it is likely that the person will develop a normal personality, well equipped to withstand stress. Since behavioral responses to environmental stimuli are *learned*, the child may develop either healthy or maladjusted ways of behaving, depending on his home situation and the ways in which he perceives himself in it. It is probable that actual neglect and rejection are the greatest dangers a child may face.

The mentally ill are helped in a variety of ways. Diagnosis may involve the measurement of mental abilities, the gathering of social information, a physical examination, assessment of personality traits, a psychiatric interview, and other techniques. A clinic often employs the services of various professional workers — psychiatrists, psychologists, physicians, social workers, and perhaps others. Diagnosis is arrived at by the joint efforts of the clinical personnel, and the course of treatment is decided on in relation to the diagnosis. Various clinical or counseling facilities of governmental, educational, and church-sponsored agencies are available. Private practitioners can be found in most larger cities.

Preferable to diagnosis and treatment of the mentally ill is, of course, the *prevention* of such illness. Among college students, some possible symptoms of impending difficulty might be academic failure, withdrawal, excessive moodiness, rebellion against authority, attention-seeking, rigidity, vacillation, hypochondria, and continual financial distress. Learning to handle conflicts and solve problems can prevent many of these difficulties (and others) and relieve the pressure which might lead to the development of more serious symptoms. Mental health can be positively fostered in several ways — attention to physical health, self-acceptance, acceptance of the world as it is, recreation, development of a social-centered outlook, achievement of maturity in understanding life, setting realistic goals, and observing temperance.

This subject, of course, is an extremely broad one. Many books are devoted to mental illness and mental health. The purpose of this chapter is simply to introduce some basic concepts and to encourage your further study and practice of mental health principles.

REFERENCES

1. *Mental Health is . . . 1 . . . 2 . . . 3*, a copyrighted publication of the National Association for Mental Health, Inc., 10 Columbus Circle, N.Y., 1951.
2. J. C. Coleman, *Abnormal Psychology and Modern Life*, Scott, Foresman, Chicago, 1950, p. 97.
3. A. Freud and D. Burlingham, *War and Children, Medical War Books*, New York, 1943.
4. R. J. Havighurst, *Human Development and Education*, Longmans Green, New York, 1953, p. 2.
5. R. W. White, *The Abnormal Personality*, Ronald Press, New York, second edition, 1956, pp. 240–242.
6. Coleman, *op. cit.*, p. 493 ff.
7. *Ibid.*, p. 494–495.
8. A. Anastasi, *Psychological Testing*, Macmillan, New York, 1954, p. 608.
9. Coleman, *op. cit.*, pp. 495–496.
10. L. F. Shaffer and E. J. Shoben, Jr., *The Psychology of Adjustment*, Houghton Mifflin, Boston, second edition, 1956.
11. *Of Pups and Puzzles*, Teaching Film Custodians, Inc., 25 W. 43rd St., N.Y.

SUGGESTIONS FOR FURTHER READING

Alexander, V. K., "A Case Study of Multiple Personality," *J. Abnorm. Soc. Psychol.*, 1956, 52, pp. 272–276.

Carmichael, L., *Basic Psychology: a Study of the Modern Healthy Mind*, Random House, New York, 1957, Chapter 1.

Davie, J. S., "The Use of a College Mental Hygiene Clinic," *Studies in Medicine*, 1956, 4, pp. 74–83.

Gardner, G. E., "Higher Education and Mental Health," *Ment. Hyg.*, 1953, 37, pp. 354–364.

Garrett, H. E., *General Psychology*, American, New York, 1955, Chapter 14.

Harrison, R. W., "Leaving College Because of Emotional Problems," *Studies in Medicine*, 1956, 4, pp. 49–60.

Hirsch, S. G., *The Fears Men Live By*, Harper, New York, 1955.

Hutt, M. L., and R. G. Gibby, *Patterns of Abnormal Behavior*, Allyn and Bacon, Boston, 1957, Chapters 1, 18.

Katz, B., and L. P. Thorpe, *Understanding People in Distress: Emotional and Mental Disorders — Their Cause, Care and Cure*, Ronald Press, New York, 1955.

Lindgren, H. C., *The Psychology of Personal and Social Adjustment*, American, New York, 1953.

Overholser, W., "Keeping Sane in a Mad World," *J. Pastoral Care*, 1955, 9, pp. 129–136.

Rogers, C. R., "A Process Conception of Psychotherapy," *Amer. Psychologist*, 1958, 13, pp. 142–149.

Shaffer, L. F., and E. J. Shoben, *The Psychology of Adjustment*, Houghton Mifflin, Boston, second edition, 1956.

Steckle, L. C., *Problems of Human Adjustment*, Harper, New York, revised edition, 1957, Chapters 3, 5, 13.

Thorne, F. C., "Life Record Criteria of Psychological Health," *J. Clin. Psychol.*, 1958, 14, pp. 123–132.

White, R. W., *The Abnormal Personality*, Ronald Press, New York, 1956.

PART FOUR •

PSYCHOLOGY AND

YOUR FUTURE

Psychology and

Personal Planning

Students asked to write "educational biographies" telling what influenced their choice of college, courses, and vocation, and estimating their own abilities, make some very revealing answers. Some have chosen a career on the basis of one or two almost accidental experiences. Some have no clear idea how they compare in ability with other people, or what the academic program or vocation they have chosen will require of them. Some are not sure whether they are bright, average, or dull students — in spite of twelve years or so in school, and some guidance and counseling. Some are uncertain whether they are preparing for the right occupation, and are worried that they will not succeed. In short, a number of students exhibit a striking lack of self-confidence and direction.

On the other hand, some students show unusual ability to assess themselves in relation to the future. Such students may have had real help from their parents, or excellent counseling or guidance. Many have had a variety of job experiences and have talked with persons active in the professions they are considering. A good many are eager to secure a good liberal education, not to prepare for a specific profession or vocation.

Hepner (1) believes that the making of lasting (and hence presumably suitable) choices of vocation may have some relation to the kind of training a profession requires. It may be that professions which require long-term specialized education, such as law and medicine, require such an investment in time and money that many students do not feel they can afford to shift even if they want to. It may also be that such professions so carefully screen their applicants

14

Making Choices in Career and Marriage

How can a person use psychological facts and principles in planning his future? What are some guidance resources? How can you assess your talents and abilities? What are some important considerations in choosing a vocation and attempting to obtain a job? What are some important considerations in choosing a wife or husband? How can military service fit into your plans for the future?

that only those students are selected who are sure of their choice and have already begun their specialization. Of course, many occupations open to college graduates do not require extended specialized preparation, and many college students are able and interested enough to succeed in many careers even without specialized graduate education.

Many students are just as uninformed and undirected about marriage as they are about jobs. Many share the common American notion that there is "one boy" or "one girl" in the world for them, and surprisingly few are aware of the extent to which chance factors influence one's acquaintances, friendships, and marriage choices. The rational view that many persons whom one may meet in a lifetime could be successful marital partners is not common among American college students. Yet many young women apparently hope to meet an eventual marriage partner while attending college.

Finally, since most young men will sooner or later spend a period of time in the armed services, they need also to consider how this experience can be made most valuable to them, and at the same time, how it can be made to disrupt their long-range plans as little as possible. What psychological problems will they meet, and how does military life differ from civilian life? How can they find out which is the most suitable branch of the armed services for them? Where will they best fit in?

The purpose of this chapter is to encourage you to think seriously about self-realization in three important and widely experienced areas of young adulthood — career or work, marriage, and required military service. Practically all colleges and universities now provide expert assistance to students who encounter difficulties in these and other areas of daily living.

● A. GUIDANCE RESOURCES AT COLLEGE

The guidance and counseling offered in most colleges is given by highly trained personnel experienced with the problems of college students. It is available at little or no cost, and it is easy to get.

Specially educated personnel

Instructional and advisory staff. Professors, for instance, can give help in many ways besides their classroom teaching. Many teachers consider it a part of their job to help students learn how to study and prepare assignments, and to plan their program of study throughout college. More than anyone else, your professors can help you assess your ability in their particular subjects, and advise whether you should continue or turn to a different field.

Your faculty adviser also can help you with your academic problems. He has your past record including various test scores, and can advise you on matters of curriculum and the mechanics of the college program. His main function is to help you plan your course and to see that you get other help if you need it.

Deans of Students. Many students fear a summons to the Dean's Office, just as many children fear a policeman. The dean may mean trouble, but he needn't. In fact, a Dean of Men or a Dean of Women is much more interested in student success than in student failure. The Dean's Office can help you find out about out-of-school activities, housing, part-time jobs, and sometimes can help with problems at home. Scholarships, loans, fraternity and sorority affairs, and admission to many types of activities are frequently handled through the office of a Dean of Students.

Psychological counselors and physicians. Most colleges have counseling psychologists to confer with students about academic, vocational, and personal problems. Counseling psychologists, clinical psychologists, and psychiatrists prefer that a student come to them voluntarily for interviews, and they are particularly qualified to assist students with emotional problems. A student who is fearful, anxious, or depressed, or one who is not faced with an emotional problem but wonders whether he is temperamentally suited to a particular career, would do well to seek assistance at the counseling center.

Colleges provide medical services, usually at nominal cost. In addition to medical and nursing care, the medical staff gives advice on physical education, diet, allergies, vaccinations, public health, and athletics. The college physician is often a valuable source of information on health as it relates to planning for marriage or a career.

Guidance resources at college. *Most colleges have a placement office which distributes information on careers, provides counseling on vocational choice, and aids in placing students in jobs after graduation. You can also obtain help and advice from other individuals and agencies on your campus. (University of Michigan News Service.)*

Other personnel. There are also rich sources of advice available to you through such people as librarians, staff workers in the business office, the registrar's office, the placement bureau, and through dormitory counselors, speech and reading clinicians, and recreation directors. Your college catalog is one source of information about how best to get in contact with these persons and offices.

Suggested activities

1. Consult your college catalog. Note the specialized services it lists and their sources.

2. Discuss these questions: What should be the point at which a student seeks help, feeling that he cannot solve certain of his problems by himself? How does one know whether he is becoming too dependent on the advice of others, or whether he is attempting to tackle problems for which he lacks necessary training and experience?

3. Why do you think colleges provide counseling and other services for students? Would it be better to screen students carefully, weeding out those who cannot manage their own affairs adequately?

A. GUIDANCE RESOURCES AT COLLEGE

● B. ASSESSING YOURSELF

The amount of assistance students need in assessing themselves in relation to their choice of subjects and careers is variable. Some students apparently have an excellent estimate of their strengths and weaknesses; others seem not to know what they have done well in the past, or what they will be able to do well in the future. Taking advantage of the best resources available, every student should eventually assess himself in relation to his more immediate and long-term goals. A college student can attempt to appraise himself without any assistance from specialists. But he should find out who might give him further information if he needs it.

Scholastic ability

Without knowing your IQ, you can attempt to appraise your intelligence. The important thing to know, of course, is not your IQ but rather how well you can do in various college subjects and in a future career. By comparing your grades with those of others, and the amount of time you spend in study with what others spend, you can get a rough estimate of your ability in different subjects. You must also know how your background for a particular course compares with that of other students. You should also review your grades in high school. In which areas did you do well without great effort, and in which did you do less well with greater effort? When you have made this self-appraisal, you may find it valuable to check your judgments with an adviser or counselor. If you are not sure you have the scholastic ability to succeed in certain subjects or careers, try to get help in your assessment.

Special abilities

You may not be interested in mathematics, yet have real skill in numerical reasoning or computation. Are you good at seeing spatial relationships? It is surprising how many people have special abilities of which they are unaware. Some people feel inadequate in such fields as mathematics and architectural design when their ability is actually high enough for real success. It is hard to identify special abilities in oneself, and you may need expert help, especially if you have had no chance to discover such talents in high school.

Can you sing well or dance well? Are you able to keep a party going? Is painting or drawing, writing, or acting a strong point? Are you a good organizer? Do you like to do detailed work, as in research? You will probably know whether or not you have these abilities if you have had opportunities to use them in high school. But you may not know how you compare with graduates of other high schools — your present classmates. A specialist in any of these fields might help you to appraise your ability.

Interests

Most young adults are aware of interest or lack of interest in things they have done and known. But there are many things they have not done, and cannot judge. For example, it is difficult for a young woman who has taken one ride in a commercial airplane to decide how well she would like such duties of an airline hostess as serving meals, taking care of nauseated adults and crying infants, or living in a variety of hotels.

A college student can experiment to some extent by trying out various courses to determine how much interest he has in them. In deciding on a whole program of courses, however, he has less freedom to experiment. After carefully assessing his present likes and dislikes, it is well for him to identify other possible interests and to relate them to immediate and long-term goals.

Health

How well are you? Do you have any physical defects or allergies? Are you color-blind? Are you frequently ill? Do you have problems of hearing or vision? Does it bother you to stand for periods of time? Health is important to the best performance in all studies and careers. The young adult should immediately secure a careful diagnosis of any health conditions about which he is anxious. Further, if he has any handicap or deficiency, he should take it into consideration in deciding on his career. Some vocations demand much higher vitality and strength than others.

Monetary status and ambitions

Can you afford to attend graduate school? Have you the money to start a business or to get married? Have you been able to save? How many "things" in life do you desire? A college education costs money, as you are fully aware, and you may not be able to get all the education you want without borrowing money or working. Some careers lead to a much higher income than others. Some promise a steady but low income, while others imply more risk but more return. In some professions, the more education that is required, the more secure and the higher the income over a life-span. But this is not necessarily true of teaching or the ministry. Also, would you prefer to make heavy sacrifices to stay in college now or stop with less education and start earning money?

Previous education and achievements

Are there weak spots in your educational background? How do you plan to strengthen them? Are you doing well enough academically so that you can take courses outside your "strength areas," and risk a low mark?

Oddly enough, many students refuse to examine seriously the possible deficiencies in their previous education and achievement. Possibly this is a defense against facing the fact that they are lacking in certain qualities. It may also reflect the hope that they can order their lives in terms of their desires without regard to their qualifications. You may have heard remarks like these: "Well, I know that to be happily married you and your wife ought to have similar interests, but Jane and I love each other and I know it will work out even though we don't particularly like the same things." Or, "I've heard that it takes physical stamina to be a civil engineer, but even though my health isn't good, I'm sure I'll make it if I try hard enough."

Personality

How do you feel about yourself? Are you enthusiastic, satisfied, or somewhat dissatisfied with such things as your physique and personal appearance, your personal relationships, your emotional expression, and your academic work? Are you self-sufficient or do you like to have considerable help? Can you stand criticism?

One's own personality, since it includes all his ideas about himself and others, is difficult to assess. The main reason for attempting to think seriously about oneself as a total personality is that personality appraisal helps in deciding on possible courses and careers and in identifying possible dissatisfactions that might be eliminated with personal effort or assistance.

Suggested activities

1. Make a short assessment of your abilities and interests. Ask your friends to assess you (anonymously). Compare these assessments.

2. Consult members of the college student personnel services. What aids to self-assessment can you obtain?

3. Pick any incident from your life and attempt to explain why you acted as you did.

    A.   GUIDANCE RESOURCES AT COLLEGE
    B.   ASSESSING YOURSELF

● C. CHOOSING A CAREER

Choosing a career today is a very different problem from what it was fifty or a hundred years ago. In those days most occupations were unspecialized, and people were fitted for most jobs by their own home training. Other necessary training could be acquired through an apprenticeship. Competition may have been less keen. Honesty, sharp wits, and hard work often made up for lack of training and experience.

The situation is quite different today. So many kinds of occupations exist that the government has found it necessary to produce a *Dictionary of Job Classifications,* in which over 25,000 job titles are listed. For many of these specialized training is necessary. Often, in professional work particularly, rigorous examinations must be passed.

In addition, almost every occupation requires "on-the-job" training — courses of study, supervisory assistance, plant manuals, lectures, group sessions, and films — all devoted to aiding the employee to fit better into the organization.

Some of us choose our occupations almost by chance, depending on the hope that a job opportunity will present itself when we are ready to go to work. Others choose occupations in response to parental wishes. Parents often reflect their own personal ambitions by seeking to have their children enter professions which they themselves would have liked, regardless of whether the children are interested or prepared. Perhaps Father has a business he wants Junior to take over. Or parents may think they see a particular talent in little Johnny — he appears to be a natural musician or engineer. Or they may stress financial reward, security, or some other virtue which effectively closes the door to a lifework which the child may really desire.

What are some of the criteria, then, to use in choosing an occupation?

Criteria for choosing an occupation

1. Does the vocation satisfy economic needs and desires? Will it provide the standard of living you desire? Entering the ministry can offer the stimulation of working for the good of others, yet few ministers get rich. Selling bonds and stocks, however, is often highly paid. Engineers in routine drafting work get moderate salaries; engineers who own a designing or consulting firm may make large sums of money. To what extent are various occupations equally open and rewarding to women and to men? Whereas teaching ranks quite low in financial return for men, it ranks high for women.

2. What are the working conditions? The work may be indoors or outdoors. It may be in clean, quiet surroundings — or the opposite. What sort of clothing is worn? What kind of people will you associate with? What are the physical requirements? Is there nervous strain in the form of deadlines or other pressures? Working conditions vary widely. Many highly paid salesmen, consultants, and managers must be ready to move frequently on short notice.

3. Is there opportunity for advancement? Many young people decide on a career without considering opportunities for advancement. Where will you be after ten years? No one, of course, can predict the future, but it should not be ignored, either. Many people can live happily for many years without much change in the nature of their responsibilities; others are soon dissatisfied without increasing responsibilities and higher financial rewards.

4. Is there security? Will the work be stable throughout the year? Will you be in demand today and not tomorrow? Will the occupation become outdated? Does the organization which you are considering keep its employees, or does it frequently release them? Are there good relationships between management and employees? Few employers guarantee life-time employment to a beginner, nor does anyone seem able to predict accurately what may happen in many fields of industry or transportation. You can, however, get information from census reports and elsewhere which shows trends in various occupations in past decades. They show, for example, that the percentage of the total population in the professions is steadily rising.

5. Is the work compatible with your interests, abilities, and personality? Some occupations — law, medicine, chemistry — require more than average intelligence. Others, such as selling and professional entertaining, demand perhaps less intellectual ability but more sociability. Verbal ability is required by such vocations as teaching, the ministry, and newspaper work.

Occupations, rightly or wrongly, are held in varying degrees of prestige by the public. Business executives, persons in professions such as medicine and law, and those in high political positions enjoy greater prestige than most farmers, laborers, salesmen, and service personnel. Table 14.1 shows how twenty-five different occupations are rated in social status by a group of graduate students and a group of laborers. It may be interesting to see whether you agree with their evaluations. Notice any differences between the estimates of the two groups, and try to figure out why they would feel differently about the status of any particular job. Whether we like it or not, social status is largely determined by vocation. Therefore, the status of any position should be considered in choosing an occupation. One person may receive enough satisfaction from doing his best in any kind of work, so that he will not be concerned about how his work is regarded by others. Another person may not be satisfied with himself unless his kind of work receives general social approval and unless he is esteemed by others. Finally, members of similar occupational groups tend to live in the same neighborhoods in any given population center and to associate with each other on that basis. The career you choose may thus partly determine the kind of neighborhood you live in.

What about your associates? It has been found that teachers tend to consider their job associates important in deciding on a teaching career (2). Superiors must be considered as well as associates. What sort of assistance and supervision are given and — equally important — how do *you* react to assistance and supervision?

Certain traits of character are associated with success in some occupations. Many, but not all, successful salesmen are more self-sufficient, confident and aggressive than unsuccessful ones (3). Engineers are likely to have exceptional ability at organizing. They are often critical of themselves, open-minded, imaginative, and enthusiastic. Although some traits appear to bear a certain relation to success in particular fields, there is considerable variation in the

Interest profiles of men in different occupations. *Here are resulting profiles of two groups of men, one of high school teachers of social studies and another of airline pilots, rated according to their interests. (From the* Kuder Preference Record, Vocational Form B, *by G. Frederic Kuder. Copyright, 1946, by G. Frederic Kuder. By permission of Science Research Associates, Inc.)*

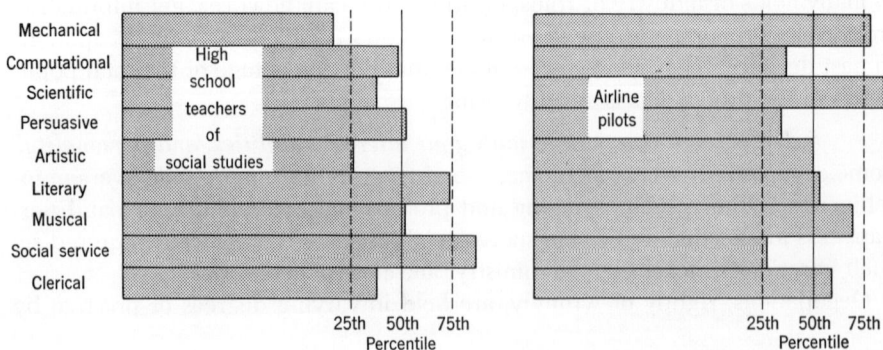

personality traits of successful, happy workers in any occupation. A psychological counselor may be helpful to anyone assessing his personality in relation to career requirements.

Getting a job

Whenever you apply for a job, you may be certain that your prospective employer will want to know a number of things about you, and your success will often depend on how well you can answer his questions.

TABLE 14.1

Social Status of Occupations

	As ranked by:	
Occupation	Graduate students	Laborers
Physicians	1	2.5
Bankers, stock and loan brokers	2	2.5
Superintendents of state institutions	3	5
Officers in Army or Navy	4	4
Managers of business	5	1
Hotelkeepers	6	7
Grade school teachers	7	10
Real estate and insurance agents	8	14
Retail traders	9	9
Commercial travelers	10	8
Bookkeepers, cashiers, and accountants	11	11
Foremen	12	6
Farm proprietors	13	16
Clerks and stenographers	14	12
Policemen	15	13
Skilled factory workers	16	15
Salespeople and clerks	17	17
Train, bus, and streetcar drivers	18	18
Waiters and domestic servants	19	20
Janitors	20	19
Laundry workers	21	24
Unskilled factory workers	22	23
Farm laborers	23	21
Casual laborers	24	25
Coal miners	25	22
Unemployed	26	26

From R. B. Cattell, "The Concept of Social Status," *Journal of Social Psychology*, 15, 1942, pp. 293–308.

1. What education have you had? You may need transcripts of your high school and college records, and recommendations from some of your teachers.

2. Are you legally qualified? Some employers will want to see your license for a particular profession, your birth certificate, military discharge papers, social security card, or other credentials.

3. What experience have you had? Keep a record of jobs held. After leaving a job, get a letter of recommendation soon, while your employer still remembers you clearly. New employers give much weight to earlier successes.

4. What special qualifications do you have? Why should an employer hire you rather than someone else? He has a right to expect that you know your own capabilities well enough so that you can say at once whether you are or are not qualified when he describes the job to you. Many jobs start with a tryout period.

5. How do you feel about yourself and the job? Most large organizations have trained employment officials to evaluate prospective employees. But you should also think how you yourself would feel in the job. If you remember similar jobs, and learn all you can about the new one, this will help you in making such a judgment.

You can begin to find out about yourself in relation to various careers now, and plan your college work to improve your chances. What qualities have you discovered through your courses and outside activities? How can you improve in responsibility, initiative, perseverance, and other qualities needed in most jobs? Any vacation job will help you to develop these traits — and will show you where you are strong and where you are lacking. And simply doing your college work conscientiously will too. While social skills, pleasant appearance, and other externals often help in getting a job, it is usually the more solid qualities such as ability, persistence, dependability, and honesty which keep it — and which give personal satisfaction in the work.

It may surprise you to learn that personality defects are more often to blame for losing a job than lack of ability. Working well usually means working with people — and such traits as enthusiasm, loyalty, the will to work, consideration of others, and sensitivity to their needs and wishes, can go a long way toward oiling the wheels of any organization. Whatever the career you now think is the one for you, you can greatly improve your chances of success in life by learning everything you can about it and about yourself. If you have a realistic view of your own talents and abilities, you will find it vastly easier to decide whether you should be a doctor, lawyer, merchant, or housewife — in short, how to make a life which you can lead with dignity and satisfaction.

Suggested activities

1. Consult the various placement bureaus at your college to see what the current demand may be for occupations in which you are interested.

2. Consult persons active in fields in which you are interested to discover what particular qualifications are needed for persons working in those fields. Inquire about the disadvantages as well as the advantages of such fields.

3. Consult books such as Hepner (listed in the References) for information on applying for a position. Keep an up-to-date record of your achievements, etc., for future use.

A.   GUIDANCE RESOURCES AT COLLEGE
B.   ASSESSING YOURSELF
C.   CHOOSING A CAREER

● D. MAKING A SUCCESSFUL MARRIAGE

A psychology class once taught by one of the writers of this book began to discuss marriage, and soon the students found themselves surprised and bewildered. They had made the usual assumption that people marry for romantic love, and then they were faced with the problem, "How does one know he is in love?" — which seems to be a perennial question among students. It soon became evident to the class that romantic love does not in itself assure marital happiness and is not the main motivating force toward some marriages. Out of this discussion, the students drew up fourteen motives or motivating factors in contemplating marriage. These were:

1. Romantic love.
2. Sexual attraction.
3. Hero worship; an idealized picture of the marriage partner.
4. Economic advancement or security.
5. Love of children.
6. Gaining independence from childhood, home, or parents.
7. Improvement of social status.
8. Proving that one *can* marry — "the crowd is marrying, so I will, too."
9. Housework (for girls) is easier than a business career.
10. Being "talked into" it — submission.
11. Spite against parents or a previous boy or girl friend.
12. Doing what is expected — following social norms.
13. Protection, fear of facing the world alone.
14. Finding a mother- or father-substitute in the marital partner.

Your class can probably add to this list; but it is clear that people marry for a variety of reasons. We can assume that most people are not likely to admit even to themselves that they marry for protection, economic advantage, or other unflattering reasons, but an examination of divorce suits and cases of frequent marriage and divorce tends to indicate that such factors are all too often present.

In our country we have a traditional belief that suddenly one day we will meet our ideal marriage partner, that we will fall completely in love, and that from that point on our "love" will come first in our lives. We are likely to think that it is unsatisfactory or almost immoral to marry for any other reason.

Not all cultures take this attitude. In Europe, especially among the nobility, marriage has been a way of cementing economic or political relationships and maintaining family position. Women were expected to provide a dowry of land or money. Family successions were founded, and wealth and power were concentrated. Love was expected to come *after* marriage, if at all, or was sought outside marriage without disapproval.

The Chinese pay great attention to the suitability of the young man and woman for each other. Marriages are often arranged through an intermediary. The match-makers discuss the personalities of the couple, and if they seem to supplement one another, they are considered a good marriage risk. Accidents of infatuation or sexual attraction play no part in the arrangement. Love is expected to develop through shared family life, and is not expected to spring into being without mutual knowledge as members of the same family.

Among the Arapesh of New Guinea, you will recall, betrothals are arranged by the families, and the girl moves into the house of her future husband while she is still a small child. He thus becomes almost her big brother, and helps to bring her up, so that they are well adjusted to each other by the time they marry.

Hepner (4) makes some interesting observations on how Americans choose their marriage partners. For example, he says

". . . One of the first discoveries about marriage on the part of the psychological investigator is the fact that a boy and girl do not fall into love as a result of deep unfathomable forces. Rather, they fall into love with each other because each answers, or appears to answer, some of the dominant psychological needs of the other. A conventional example is the studious introverted boy, socially awkward, who is anxious to enjoy the company of a girl his own age. He meets an extroverted girl, a poor student, who is vivacious. She helps him to enjoy himself socially. Perhaps she also builds up his feelings of self-worth because she tells him about her own shortcomings as a student and expresses admiration for his intellectual achievements. If he also has feelings of rejection by his parents and she mentions the ways in which her parents do not understand her, he may develop feelings of psychological kinship toward her and identify himself with her, thus forming ties that are likely to lead to further courtship and eventual marriage."

Other factors enter into the choosing of a husband or wife. For example, propinquity is important. If the girl and boy live near each other, as in nearby college dormitories, frequent meeting and acquaintance may lead to closer attachments. Persons of the same social class, interests, and racial or national background have much in common and tend to date each other.

However, courtship may also disclose unexpected common interests. Because of its romantic connotations, courtship performs a very different function in our society than do the more formal and traditional practices of some other cultures like those mentioned above. However, there are also dangers in our pattern. One person may over-idealize the other, and unrealistic expectations are common. Frequently, expectations about the prospective marriage partner may be bitterly disappointed. In marriage, people see each other not only in the favorable circumstances of courtship, but under everyday conditions of living which reveal the bad along with the good. The young person who expects marriage to be compounded entirely of moonlight and roses is in for some rude jolts. Nevertheless, courtship does help people to develop affection for each other, and it is probably the most romantic period of life. In Western civilization it is of value in building strong personal relationships prior to marriage.

The marriage partnership

The nature of love and affection changes with time. As one gets to know his marriage partner, he will discover unsuspected virtues as well as faults. Sharing experiences and working together do a great deal to bring people together. Indeed, the death of a husband or wife some years after marriage is often a more profound loss than death for a newlywed. On the other hand, when there is not sufficient common ground in the form of similar ideals, values, friends, tastes in recreation, intelligence, education, background, standard of living, and so on — early affection may decline into humdrum habit, or even dislike, hos-

Looking toward marriage. *Two people must learn a lot about each other before they are ready to enter into a life-long relationship. Dates should include much time for talking together and getting to know each other. (Gale Tucker.)*

tility, and hatred. Homes in which this happens may be broken psychologically even if not in external fact.

Precarious is the marriage made with the intent to reform someone. The close relationship of marriage can intensify personality problems and weaknesses of character rather than the opposite. The young bride who is too dependent on others will not change overnight into a self-sufficient independent helpmeet who bears her full share of the load. The immature young husband too closely attached to his mother will not immediately become the true head of his own family. The martyred and the insecure will not be magically transformed — though all these weaknesses can be alleviated in time if the weaker vessel is lucky enough to have picked a mate who is sufficiently understanding, forbearing, and strong enough to stand by himself.

Economics. Many things can help to make a marriage work, and one of them is economic security. Today with more marriages in early life, there are more and more working wives. Often this sharing of the economic load brings the couple closer together, but it can raise problems, too. While most people can for a time accept a standard of living below what they are used to, doing without for too long can strain a marriage dangerously. Help from families is often received at the cost of not achieving full emotional independence. The choice may be between waiting until the prospective husband can support a family by himself, and requiring the wife to assume part of the economic load.

There is no question that marriage brings financial responsibilities. It is simply not true that "two can live as cheap as one." Many young people tend to underestimate the cost of living. To set up housekeeping, however humbly, is seldom possible without substantial expense. Food, clothing, and an automobile eat up money with an insatiable appetite. And there are always "extras" — an unexpected doctor bill, a party for an out-of-town friend, a present for somebody's new baby — and so on, and on, and on. All this, of course, makes it hard at the same time to buy life insurance and medical insurance, and to save money to buy a house. The young couple contemplating marriage will do well to work out a budget, and to have it checked by several older and more experienced heads before deciding whether they wish to marry immediately or wait.

When emergencies arise, the optimist may find himself buying on the installment plan, and even borrowing from the finance company where "your signature is enough" but you pay 2 per cent a month. That 2 per cent a month is 24 per cent a year, or almost a quarter of the total loan, is of course cleverly obscured. Financial insecurity, mounting debt, and a declining standard of living are prime causes of fear, anxiety, and humiliation — and, obviously, of strain in marriage.

All this is not meant to discourage young people from marriage even while they are still in college. But we most strongly urge that anyone contemplating such a step assess his resources and analyze his situation carefully.

Similarity of interests. The glamor of formal dates and dances, the fun of coke dates and shared study periods — these are experiences which young people do and should share. But going out with a football hero or a popularity queen is one thing, and living with such a person may be something very different indeed. The girl who falls for a star athlete should be aware that after she marries him he is going to want to spend hours watching sports events which may bore her stiff. And the young man who marries a campus queen should not be unmindful that the easy social sparkle which made her popular with large numbers of people may be accompanied by a hunger for expensive clothes and an appetite for social life which sorts ill with his modest income and desire to stay home evenings and read a book. It is not necessary that two people have exactly the same sets of likes and dislikes, interests and antipathies. But they may find themselves in trouble if they don't have some very substantial interests in common. Many a young person dreams of a husband or wife much like his own mother or father. Perhaps Mother liked to cook and sew, and Dad liked to putter around with tools. Maybe your prospective mate also has a parental image in mind. But if so it's wise to find out whether that image in any important ways resembles yours, or whether it is radically different.

Sex relationships. The Kinsey reports (5, 6) and other studies have thrown considerable light on the sexual behavior of American men and women. The sexual desires of men and women are not always the same, and there is wide variation among individuals within both sexes. Sexual relationships in marriage are very important to happiness. One can approach this phase of marriage with the knowledge that sexual adjustment is not difficult and is in fact entirely natural for normal young adults. However, some college-educated men and women fail to recognize the differences in the intensity of desire between marriage partners. Some also allow a memory of premarital, usually clandestine, sex experiences to interfere with normal sexual functioning early in the marriage.

The notion that two persons can or should be perfectly matched sexually may lead to premarital experimentation with sexual intercourse. This notion is not a sound one in itself, and premarital experimentation is assuredly *not* a sound way to ascertain its validity. The physical, social, and psychological limitations imposed by society on young unmarried people make premarital sexual relationships hazardous and often unpleasant rather than satisfying.

While many men and women have sexual relations before marriage, the majority do not (7). Men, as one might expect, either have had more such experience than women, or are more willing to admit having had it. In any event, the available research suggests that premarital sexual intercourse is more a hazard than an asset to happy marriage, especially in the middle class.

When sex adjustment becomes a problem in marriage, it is not likely to be biologically caused so much as it is to be the result of cultural attitudes and psychological needs or traits. Factual information on the sexual relationship in marriage should be obtained by all who intend to marry; ignorance, lack of patience, and misunderstanding can be very harmful. Health classes, medical counseling, and authoritative literature will all help to give this information.

Religion

Similarity of religious beliefs is helpful in marriage, especially after children are born. Some denominations expect children to be brought up in their particular faith, and maintain schools to further the religious education they feel is necessary. Some church groups place considerable stress on the habits of their members and have stricter codes than others. Interdenominational marriages can work, but they must be entered into with full understanding by both persons. It is easy to marry without considering the religious education of children and the effects on them of a home divided on religious beliefs.

Maturity

If you are planning to be married, how can you tell whether you and your fiancé are really mature enough for marriage? Think in terms of the concepts of maturity we mentioned in Chapter 4. The long discussions and "bull sessions" you frequently have with other young people can give you some information about maturity. Meeting the family of the person you want to marry is also important. How mature is he or she in the family situation? How have other marriages in the family turned out?

One advantage of an engagement is that it provides an opportunity for the two young people to learn more about one another. It permits them to begin adjusting their similarities and differences. If, on a more thorough understanding, they find that a happy marriage seems doubtful, neither person is committed legally. The engagement can be broken. And if understanding leads to deeper respect, enthusiasm, and love, the engagement has been a good preparation for marriage.

Contrary to the fears and doubts of many parents, many persons of college age are mature enough for happy marriages. However, it is true that, once married, the activities and friendships of the young couple may differ from those they had before. Few young men like to see their wives too friendly with former men friends — and vice versa. Many student activities are designed for unmarried students, and economic changes in marriage often make it impossible for a married couple to do things they did singly.

Terman (8) found that some of the factors most predictive of happy marriages were the degree of happiness in the marriage of the parents, happiness in childhood, absence of conflict with parents, firm (but not harsh) family discipline, strong attachment to parents, frankness of parents about sexual matters, mild and not too frequent punishment as a child.

It is interesting to compare Terman's findings with the characteristics which men and women usually look for in prospective marital partners. Young (9) states that American college and university men, in choosing wives, stress sexual attractiveness, sexual purity, beauty, and health. College women in choosing husbands emphasize occupational ambition, ability to make money, and social status. Both men and women usually feel that common race and religion and suitable personality traits are important. Men tend to marry women younger than themselves, and marriage is more likely among persons who live near each other.

Nobody can absolutely guarantee to himself or to anyone else a happy marriage. However, one can and probably should consider marriage as seriously as any career. One should probably know as much, if not more, about the nature of his prospective mate as about a prospective occupation. Since our society attaches a high value to successful marriage, young people may be under increasing pressure to marry rather than to find mutual self-realization and happiness. Simply being married in the early twenties now receives high social approval. This approval may tend to enhance the prospects of a happy marriage, but it is no substitute for a real effort to make the marriage work.

Suggested activities

1. Look up some statistics on marriage and divorce. What reasons are given for most divorces? Do the legal reasons usually seem to be the real reasons? How can you tell?

2. Budget the probable expenses involved in marriage for a young couple. How do the estimates of various members of the class compare with each other?

    A.   GUIDANCE RESOURCES AT COLLEGE
    B.   ASSESSING YOURSELF
    C.   CHOOSING A CAREER
    D.   MAKING A SUCCESSFUL MARRIAGE

● **E. LIFE·IN THE ARMED FORCES**

Sooner or later most young men yet face military service, whether through the draft, the ROTC, or some other form of training. When the Armed Forces were drafting most men, age 18–21, many boys in the junior and senior years of high school developed apathetic attitudes. Some took a "What's the use?" attitude, accompanied by defeatism, escapism, irritability, and lack of power to concentrate. Discipline was hard to enforce. Morals became lax. A few students developed a martyr attitude. These same feelings were not unknown in the colleges.

But life in the Armed Forces can confer many benefits on the young man who will accept them. Most men come back to civilian life in improved physical condition. Most are more mature, more responsible and self-confident. Many are more tolerant; having intermingled with people from many walks of life, they are more understanding of human nature. Those with wide travel have a better grasp of our national responsibility to the world, and a deeper feeling for the virtues of our form of life. More tangible benefits accruing to World War II and Korean War veterans can be listed:

1. Most saved money and bought government life insurance at low rates.

2. Many went to school or are going to school partly or wholly at government expense.

3. They received various tests and counseling and learned more about their interests and abilities.

4. Some received needed medical or dental treatment which they might not have been able to afford as civilians. Almost all gained in vitality, weight, and strength.

5. Many learned either a primary life occupation or an occupation to fall back on in case of need.

6. They built up a basis for pensions, and perhaps for a hobby in later life if they followed reserve training.

7. Many obtained preferential positions in government employment because of their status as veterans.

8. They became eligible for veterans' loans for real estate.

9. In case of necessity they can obtain free treatment in veterans' hospitals, free counseling and employment service, and other like benefits.

Not all these benefits may come to any one man, and some vary in times of war and peace. But in general, military service offers real opportunities for many young men.

Are there also disadvantages? There may be, for some. Some men are not mature enough to benefit from the rigors of military life. Seeking comfort, they gravitate to others equally immature, and make little use of their opportunities. Others, just as in civilian life, suffer accidents, psychological disturbances, and difficulties of social adjustment. Homesickness, worry over family, and other real or fancied problems bother a few. Inability to take criticism and the dislike of being "bossed" are problems for others.

Certainly the way of life is different. Many chafe at discipline and long for privacy. For many there is a succession of petty restraints and annoyances: constant attention to ranks and ratings, perpetually lining up for meals, enduring inoculations, and wearing GI clothing, doing K.P., and "policing" the barracks — all such things can be a source of annoyance.

More important, some people are in danger of becoming too dependent. One can get too accustomed to not worrying about where his food comes from, where to sleep, what to do, and so on. The obverse of military discipline is a kind of paternalism which fosters dependency and, in those who are not too expert at standing on their own feet anyway, intensifies weakness.

Finally, the close living, lack of privacy, absence of feminine companionship, and comparative rough-and-tumble of military life mean that many men are faced with a period of readjustment before they can successfully return either to a job or to college work.

ADVANTAGES		DISADVANTAGES
	Travel	Danger
	Experience with all kinds of people	Commitment to serve for specified period
	Financial benefits	Irregular hours
	Education at government's expense	Lack of contact with civilians
	Tests and guidance	Necessity of doing menial tasks
	Physical development	Absence of choice of clothes, food, etc.
	Training in an occupation	Lack of privacy
	Security	Enforced obedience to orders

Some of the advantages and disadvantages of military service. *Perhaps you can think of other good and bad aspects of military life.*

Educational opportunities in the Armed Forces

The Armed Forces at present offer a variety of chances for specialized training and more general education. Many men acquire high skill in photography, airplane and automobile mechanics, radio and electronics, music, meteorology, and many other subjects which can later be of great use to them in civilian life. The services also can use all the leadership a man can develop. Many men in training for promotions, particularly those who are officers or officer candidates, get experience which cultivates their leadership skills, their understanding of human nature, their ability to teach, and so on.

The services also provide opportunities for additional high school and college education. Through the United States Armed Forces Institute, an important part of the off-duty education program, a wide variety of academic courses, offered on a self-teaching and correspondence basis, are available. The ROTC and the service academies are well known. In addition, men exhibiting special aptitudes may be sent to colleges and universities. Limited numbers of men are given intensive training in foreign languages, and engineering programs are in operation at such institutions as the Massachusetts Institute of Technology and the California Institute of Technology.

Another educational opportunity now available to all the services is the tuition-aid plan. Under this program the services provide 75 per cent of the cost of tuition at colleges or universities near military installations. There is also a final-semester temporary-duty plan whereby service personnel who have attained three and a half years of college credit can be placed on active duty at a college or university with full pay and allowances to complete the final semester.

Opportunities for women in the Armed Forces

The work of the WACS, WAVES, and WAFS is well known. They perform a host of secretarial and clerical duties, serve as chauffeurs, laboratory and technical assistants, help in airport control work, and give instruction to pilots. Members of the Nursing Corps are all commissioned officers. Many civilian women are also employed in purchasing and supply, in fiscal branches, and in Post Exchanges, the USO, and the like. Many overseas branches have openings for women teachers.

Problems of a service family

Because many college students now marry before they enter military service, a word on their special problems may be in order. Most young wives wisely prefer to be with their husbands on or near a military establishment, since separation can put an undue strain on a marriage. Even so, this decision raises problems.

The husband is on call at any time. Leaves or furloughs can be revoked, his duties may take him away from home for extended periods, and extra duties can keep him "over time." Moreover, the pay of most service men is modest, and even with promotions and increases is likely to remain so. Housing on or near military establishments is seldom ideal, the areas are often crowded, and life can be to a degree makeshift. Some young women find that being automatically assigned a social status in accord with their husbands' military rank is annoying and even painful. And finally, one inevitably tends to absorb the military point of view, to feel that civilians are privileged or benighted. While everyone's view of the world is framed by his own niche in it, the military family may find it hard to adjust to civilian life later.

All this does not mean that military life for a young couple is a misfortune. Taken the right way, any experience can be valuable. And the opportunities for travel, meeting people of all kinds, doing new jobs, and for pleasures as well as hardships, may come once in a lifetime. The point is simply that a young couple planning marriage should think about a stint in the armed services just as they should plan for a home, family, and career.

Suggested activities

1. Have any of your class members served in the Armed Forces? Do they agree or disagree with the statements made in this chapter? How?

2. Have some class member visit a recruiting station or obtain information from an education adviser concerning the possibilities of preparing for a civilian occupation while in the Armed Forces, or possibilities of making a career in the Armed Forces.

3. How do the Armed Forces make use of civilian or military psychologists, physicians, statisticians, and other specialized personnel?

SUMMARY

Some people choose a career before they are out of high school; others, equally wisely, not until after college. Today young people exercise more freedom and related responsibility for deciding upon a career than they did a few decades past. In part this freedom results from a large and continuing increase in the number of specialized vocations and jobs. Because more vocations require specialized training, a late decision often means a later start, so that there is often a premium on making an early choice. The urgency to decide early exerts substantial pressure on the college student.

While all young men and many young women are at least nominally preparing for a career, nearly all of them are also looking forward to marriage. Choosing a mate is the most important decision in life, and should be done with as much knowledge, clear-sightedness, and consideration as the individual can muster. Erotic love and romance are important, but the wise young person also thinks carefully about economic matters, common interests, values, intellectual and cultural backgrounds, sex attitudes, ideas on family and religion, and over-all maturity.

Finally, whether by choice or not most young men will probably spend some time in military service. The attitude they take toward this obligation will bear a direct relation to the value they receive from the experience. It can be looked upon as an opportunity for training, travel, adventure, and general experience. On the other hand, problems are often present. Certainly the rational view is to make the best of the necessity — not the worst.

Suggested activities

1. Write a description of yourself which you may use later as a basis for counseling. Describe your general mental ability and special abilities, personality, background, health, financial position, enriching experiences, religious and philosophical beliefs, motives, goals, desires, and education. Study this description. Does putting this information down on paper in an organized form help you to understand your abilities and limitations?

2. Debate the desirability of starting one's own business as opposed to working for a large, established concern.

3. Ask employers or personnel officials for information about their recruitment and selection procedures for various jobs. Compare the procedures used.

4. Write a sample letter of application for a position. What should it include?

5. Start a small card file or record folder of the courses you have taken, your hobbies, job experiences, extra-class activities, honors, special training, etc. Begin to secure legal materials, birth certificates, etc., and high school transcripts. As you progress through college, add to your file descriptions of experiences that may help you later to get a job.

6. Check your college personnel office for information concerning scholarships, grants, jobs around the college, etc. Check the Placement Office for information on the positions now in greatest demand among employers.

REFERENCES

1. Harry Walker Hepner, *Psychology Applied to Life and Work*, second edition, p. 218. Copyright, 1941, 1950, by Prentice-Hall, Inc., Englewood Cliffs, N.J. Reprinted by permission of the publisher.

2. T. A. Ringness, "Relationships Between Certain Attitudes Towards Teaching and Teaching Success," *J. Exper. Educ.*, 1952, 21 pp. 1–56.

3. H. W. Hepner, *op cit.*, Chapter 27.

4. *Ibid.*, pp. 260–261.

5. A. C. Kinsey, W. B. Pomeroy, and C. E. Martin, *Sexual Behavior in the Human Male*, Saunders, Philadelphia, 1948.

6. A. C. Kinsey, W. R. Pomeroy, C. E. Martin, and P. H. Gebhard, *Sexual Behavior in the Human Female*, Saunders, Philadelphia, 1953.

7. A. L. Porterfield and H. E. Salley, "Current Folkways on Sexual Behavior," *Amer. J. Sociol.*, 1946, 52, pp. 209–216.
8. L. M. Terman, *Psychological Factors in Marital Happiness*, McGraw-Hill, New York, 1938.
9. K. Young, *Personality and Problems of Adjustment*, Appleton-Century-Crofts, New York, second edition, 1952.
10. *Catalog, United States Armed Forces Institute*, Madison, Wisconsin, 1956.

SUGGESTIONS FOR FURTHER READING

Baylis, C. A., *Ethics: The Principles of Wise Choice*, Henry Holt, New York, 1958, Chapters 1, 13, 14.

Bee, L. S., "Student Attitudes Toward a Course in Courtship and Marriage," *Marriage and Fam. Liv.*, 1951, 13, pp. 157–159.

Blood, R. O., *Anticipating Your Marriage*, The Free Press, Glencoe, Ill., 1955.

Brayfield, A. H., and R. V. Wells, "Interrelationships among Measures of Job Satisfaction and General Satisfaction," *J. Appl. Psychol.*, 1957, 41, pp. 201–208.

Burgess, E. W., P. Wallin, and G. D. Schultz, *Courtship, Engagement, and Marriage*, Lippincott, Philadelphia, 1954.

Dickinson, C., "What Employers Look for in the College Graduate," *Personn. Guid. J.*, 1955, 33, pp. 460–464.

Eastman, D., "Self Acceptance and Marital Happiness," *J. Consult. Psychol.*, 1958, 22, pp. 95–99.

Ellzey, W. C., *How to Keep Romance in Your Marriage*, Association Press, New York, 1954.

Geddes, D. P., *An Analysis of the Kinsey Report on Sexual Behavior in the Human Male and Female*, Dutton, New York, 1954.

Gellman, W., "Vocation Adjustment and Personality," *Jewish Soc. Serv. Quart.*, 1954, 30, pp. 381–386.

Giedt, F. H., "Changes in Sexual Behavior and Attitudes Following Class Study of the Kinsey Report," *J. Soc. Psychol.*, 1951, 33, pp. 131–141.

Hilgard, E. R., *Introduction to Psychology*, Harcourt, New York, 1953, Chapter 20.

Lehner, G. F. J., and E. Kube, *The Dynamics of Personal Adjustment*, Prentice-Hall, Englewood Cliffs, 1955, Chapter 12.

Pressey, S. L., and R. G. Kuhlen, *Psychological Development through the Life Span*, Harper, New York, 1957, Chapter 9.

Steckle, L. C., *Problems of Human Adjustment*, Harper, New York, revised edition, 1957, Chapter 10.

Sternberg, C., "Personality Trait Patterns of College Students Majoring in Different Fields," *Psychol. Monogr.*, 1955, 69, pp. 1–21.

Psychology and

Your View of Life

Psychology is a science, and like all sciences is concerned with accumulating facts, refining its own methods, developing principles and hypotheses, and discovering laws which will shed new light on the unknown and deepen our understanding. Science is primarily concerned with questions of *what* and *how*, that is, with questions of fact concerning the operations of the universe, not with questions of first cause, moral law, or ultimate purpose. And psychology, as the science of human behavior, is mainly concerned with *what* man is like — *how* he learns, remembers, grows, and develops, interrelates with his fellows and responds to them; *how* he influences and in turn is influenced by the groups he belongs to; *how* he may stay mentally healthy or recover mental health if it has been impaired. These, and others like them, are the kind of questions which the psychologist, *as a scientist*, is concerned with.

But like everybody else, the psychologist is more than a scientist. He is interested in fact, and in his own special area, perhaps more than anybody else. Beyond that, the psychologist, like everybody else, is interested in the answers to questions which are not simply and wholly factual. He too wants to know the why as well as the how and what. Why was the universe created? What kind of being, if any, is its creator? Is this being a principle of good, perhaps existing in opposition to a principle of evil? Or is it totally indifferent to good and evil as human beings understand those qualities? These questions, and many others like them, arise in the mind of every thinking person, and every thinking person does the best he can to reach answers which will square with the facts as he knows them.

432

15

Science and Other Means Toward Truth

What is the difference between science and philosophy? What do psychology and philosophy have in common? What are some common methods of inquiry? What are some fallacious beliefs and examples of inconsistencies in popular thought? How has psychology aided philosophy? What are some basic principles of a psychological view toward human behavior? How can psychology help you to form a sound personal philosophy?

These answers are not scientific; they are beyond the realm of science because they require assumptions which go beyond the facts that science can discover. Both the questions and the answers are philosophical, or religious, or both. That is, they are based on what a person reasons "must" be true on the basis of the facts he knows; if so they are mainly philosophical. Or they are based on faith, in which case they are mainly religious. Both religion and philosophy seek answers to the ultimate questions which science does not yet touch, and the two modes of inquiry intermix and overlap so that they are often hard to separate. Both are clearly distinct from science. But the same person may and often does engage in all three modes of inquiry, just as a business man can also engage in such different activities as playing tennis and collecting funds for a local charity.

To say that science must limit itself to matters of fact is in no sense to impugn its usefulness. A step ladder may not reach the moon, but it can be a highly useful instrument for reaching the ceiling. The benefits of science surround us in such profusion that there is no point in rehearsing them here. But one is worth mentioning, and bears on our present topic: although facts about man and the physical world may not *answer* ultimate questions, everything we can learn *has some bearing* on our ability to answer them more rationally and usefully. In other words, psychology is not philosophy or religion, but it can help our inquiries in both. To see how this can be true, let us first see in somewhat more detail some of the things philosophers, as philosophers, are concerned with.

● A. PHILOSOPHY AND A WORLD VIEW

As we have already suggested, one of the prime concerns of the philosopher is to explain the universe, and to evolve a coherent world view which will account for all the facts as he knows them. In the course of human history these explanations have ranged widely, from the most naive to the most sophisticated and elaborate, and from supreme faith to utter doubt. Most cultures include a belief in one or a number of gods or spirits, which either created the world or at the least, have power over it. These may be evil or good, or both. Among primitive peoples, the principle of fertility was often worshiped, and tended to be male if the society lived off herds of animals, and female if it was agricultural — for the father animal or the mother earth was clearly manifest. The Zoroastrians of ancient Persia conceived of two powers, Mazda (good, light) locked in eternal struggle with Ahriman (evil, darkness). Plato, in the Athens of the fifth century B.C., held that the Good was pure spirit and pure energy, that all material things emanated from it, and that even by intense contemplation we could at best realize its glory but dimly. And a whole host of his successors through the Christian centuries modified his thought in one way or another — the most extreme mystics among them believing that through purification and contemplation the human spirit could re-ascend to the realm of the Good (God) and be absorbed into it.

With the swift growth of modern science after the midpoint of the last century a new view came into existence, known as materialism. In its extreme form, this held that there is no supreme being or creator, that the universe came into existence by chance, that there is no soul or after-life, and that mind and consciousness are a product of purely material and mechanistic forces. Following this line of thought, some philosophers have asserted that the universe is not ruled by good, even that there is no principle of good in it; that good, in so far as it exists, is a product of human development; and that the world is totally indifferent, inert, and unknowing.

Between the extremes of mystical religious faith on the one hand and materialistic, mechanistic skepticism on the other, practically every shade of belief has been expressed at one time or another. It is clear that much of philosophy is often indistinguishable from religious belief — or the lack of it. It is equally clear that a person's moral standards and behavior, his goals, and his whole mode of life can be profoundly affected by the philosophical (or religious) views he holds.

But not all philosophical problems deal with the ultimate imponderables, and there are many ways, in addition to the broad concern with human behavior, in which philosophy and psychology have common interests.

For instance, their methods of inquiry overlap, though they are not identical. Scientific investigation involves observation, experiment, description, and statement of relationships among the facts discovered (1). Philosophy also begins with facts, but interprets them and considers ultimate relationships and meanings.

And as knowledge of the universe expands, for example, into outer space and into the operation of atoms, many questions once philosophical or speculative are now considered scientific.

In this connection and of concern to philosophers and psychological scientists is the nature of knowledge — of how we know what we know, how much we can know, and how dependable is the knowledge of the physical world which we derive through our senses. One striking evidence of concern with this problem was a logical dead-end formulated by an Irish philosopher, Bishop George Berkeley, in the eighteenth century. Berkeley made an excellent case for the view that we have no real evidence of the outside world at all — that as far as we can *prove*, the whole construct which we think of as the world around us could exist within our own hands. Pleasure, pain, heat, cold, knowledge of friends and enemies, work, play, and everything else we ordinarily accept as evidence of outside experience could perfectly well be imagined. Few people think him right, but it is a fascinating logical game to try to *prove* him wrong.

Psychologists also are deeply concerned with the nature and sources of knowledge, as we saw in Chapter 6 on Perception. And the limitations of our senses become an acute problem in the sciences of physics, chemistry, and astronomy. Such instruments as the light microscope and the electron microscope, at one end of the visual range, and the giant telescopes at the other, have pushed back the horizons of our vision immensely. But we still have limitations of our senses, and this fact is of significance to psychologists and philosophers alike.

Both disciplines are also concerned with the nature of thought. Since the time of the ancient Greeks, logic has been a province of philosophy, and until the development of scientific method in modern times was considered the main instrument for finding truth. Most traditional logic started with general propositions believed to be true, and arrived at new propositions which were in turn assumed to be true if the reasoning process followed certain rules. All too frequently the new propositions were derived without reference to facts, and so were dangerously undependable. One of these rules was the appeal to authority. If Aristotle, or one of the Church Fathers, had said that the earth was flat, then it might easily be argued for a good 500 years that this must be true because so great an authority had said so.

But the revival of a spirit of inquiry which began as early as the fifteenth century led ultimately to a wholly new concept of logic and thinking, culminating in the scientific method. This new spirit led men to examine the world about them in order to discover all they could of the facts about it, rather than looking in an ancient book to see what someone had thought hundreds of years before. Men began to experiment. Galileo (1564–1642) dropped heavy and light objects, found that they both fell at the same rate, and thus exploded a misconception that had reigned almost since men started thinking about such things. Sir Francis Bacon (1561–1626) laid the foundation for the scientific method, one of the greatest instruments for thinking which man has developed, when he sketched a plan for repeated experiment, codification of findings, and drawing of generalizations only *after* sufficient evidence had been collected to make a general statement which had good expectation of being sound.

A.   PHILOSOPHY AND A WORLD VIEW

● **B. PSYCHOLOGY AND PHILOSOPHIC METHOD**

Psychology has added vastly to our knowledge of how we think by studying the amazingly complex system of interconnected nerve cells which comprises the nervous system, and by investigating the limitations and capabilities of our senses, the way in which man and the animals learn, remember, associate, create, and reach original inferences and conclusions. In short, philosophy and science, which became separate branches of learning and endeavor in the seventeenth century, are in many ways beginning to merge again, each drawing on the other's findings to assist in refining its own conclusions. Indeed, one writer, in describing the method of philosophy, has also described a good deal of the method of psychology (2):

1.   Extraction of underlying assumptions regarding events or phenomena.

2.   Inference from an assumption to its consequences.

3.   The application of creative imagination, to help synthesize clashing facts or principles.

4.   Detection of fallacies and inconsistencies.

5.   Group efforts to clarify issues and resolve them through disciplined discussion.

6.   Clarification of meanings through analysis of the language employed in arguments or inquiries.

Because of their importance it is worth while to examine these steps in a bit more detail.

Extracting underlying assumptions

To take a simple example, suppose a student fails a test, and argues the value of examinations with his instructor. In this situation, there are a number of underlying assumptions more or less common to the instructor, the student body, and the college administration. Here are some of them: (1) students can pass the test; (2) they *should* pass the test; (3) what is being tested is usefully related to the aims of the course; (4) the results of the test accurately reflect student knowledge. A good many other assumptions are involved in this situation — relating to the instructor, his teaching methods, the content of the course, the whole process of education. Challenging these may raise such questions as: Should tests be given? How much do they reflect real learning? Should this course be taught at all? Serious examination of these questions involves thinking which is scientific and thinking which is philosophical. Scientific thinking helps one to determine the facts and to draw what inferences can be drawn from them. But as soon as the questions concern values — e.g., is the material *worth* learning? — they become philosophical, although the preceding factual steps in the thinking have helped to identify and clarify the value problem.

Inferring consequences

The second step in the method is to infer probable or certain consequences from basic assumptions or verified facts. One of the most famous inferences in philosophy is the statement by the French mathematician and thinker René Descartes (1596-1650), "I think, therefore I am." That is, the evidence of my own consciousness indicates that I am a thinking being. It is therefore a safe inference that I exist. A somewhat similar, but less dependable inference might be from the observation, "He changed his behavior," to the conclusion, "therefore he learned." But the change might have been the result of maturation, (Chapter 4), not of learning; hence the inference is questionable.

In drawing any conclusion from data, we must take into account all other possible inferences that could be drawn from the same data, and we must carefully check all possible assumptions that may underlie our thinking. Today most women students may well question the inference that girls should not attend college because it is too hard on the nervous system — an opinion once common among American educators. The inference might be sound if the hidden assumption were correct that women are less stable in nervous make-up than men, but there is no evidence that this is true.

Creative imagination

Although this quality is popularly associated with literary, artistic, and philosophical activity more than with scientific, there is ample evidence that it is a prime factor in productive thinking of all kinds. One of the most articulate writers on the subject is the French mathematician, Poincaré, who carefully describes the way in which, after protracted thought, the various factors in a complex problem often fall into place with dramatic speed as the result of a sudden flash of insight. There is also a famous story that a complex chemical structure known as the benzene ring, discovered in the last century by August Kekulé, came to him in a flash of intuition while he was riding a bus in London. The essence of creativity in these and countless other moments of discovery is the sudden recognition of a relationship among parts of a problem which has until then remained unseen. And creative imagination is just as important to the scientist as to the philosopher or the artist.

Detecting fallacies

The detection of fallacies (errors in reasoning) and of other inconsistencies in thought is a prime concern of philosophy. For philosophers view the processes of thought as an important means of finding out truth, and have over the centuries worked out elaborate rules to distinguish sound from faulty thinking. These matters are also of course equally important to psychologists and other scientists. Thinking can be *deductive*, that is, from general truths or assumptions to more limited conclusions. Or it can be *inductive*, that is, from particular facts or data to generalizations, hypotheses, and principles. Obviously, inductive thinking is one of the chief tools of the scientist, and he must guard carefully against the temptation to generalize from too few facts. It can be tempting, for instance, to infer that because *twenty* American college students believe that success can be measured in terms of money, *all* college students hold such a belief. The true scientist tries not to generalize beyond his information, and he qualifies his statements as necessary.

A great many faulty and inconsistent beliefs survive in popular thinking in this country as in every other, and it may be illuminating to list a few:

1.   The best way to overcome fear of the dark is to force yourself to stay in a dark room for a while.

2.   Gifted people are less stable emotionally than are those of average intelligence.

3.   A child's personality is inherited from his parents.

4.   A student can learn anything if he tries hard enough.

5.   Personality can't be changed.

6.   One can accomplish anything he desires with sufficient will power.

7.   Psychiatrists have so over-emphasized mental illness that we think everybody is abnormal.

8.   If a mother wants her unborn child to be musical, she should study music during pregnancy.

Detecting fallacies. *Advertisements and political slogans sometimes lead to errors in reasoning.*

9. Mental diseases are always inherited.

10. People with low economic status have low mental ability.

11. Practice leads to perfection; with sufficient practice anyone can perfect his skills.

The above statements are either completely false or true only in part under special circumstances. If someone had not sought after fallacies or inconsistencies, undoubtedly these and many similar misconceptions would still be more generally accepted than they are. Of course, it is possible that, with the gathering of more factual information, we may become less certain than we are now that each of these statements is "false." For at any given moment in history we can determine "truth" only in terms of the knowledge we have.

Discussing and clarifying issues

Group effort to clarify issues and resolve them through disciplined discussion is increasingly common in our culture (see Chapters 3 and 12). Decisions on political, educational, economic, religious, and many other kinds of questions related to social living can be reached through group activity or at least with help from a group. You have no doubt been involved in many such discussions. Recently one of the writers of this book had occasion to act as a member of a group whose purpose was to develop a sequence of courses and activities leading to the professional preparation of school psychologists at a state university. The decisions involved defining the work of school psychologists, identifying the needed abilities and skills, proposing courses or other required educational activities, and securing competent students to pursue the program. Whether the particular program developed by the group is educationally sound can be ascertained only by evaluating the work of the graduates after they have completed their studies and held jobs for a time. At present, however, it seems most likely that as a result of the many group discussions and the pooling of ideas from many minds, the program is more effective than it would have been had it been developed by one person only.

Clarifying meanings

In any investigation or discussion, it is essential to clarify the meaning of all important terms used. Many a heated argument would never occur if the disputants each understood what the other meant by terms pivotal to the dispute. Whether John Jones is "a politician" or "a statesman" is a question which can be argued inconclusively for hours — unless the parties to the argument define their terms. The question then becomes a matter of fact: Did Jones vote for or against the old age tax? Is he for or against low tariffs? Did he or did he not sponsor a bill to allow horse racing in the state? Once these and other questions of fact are answered, it becomes much easier to decide whether Jones is a good public official or a poor one, and the original question, hinging on fuzzy and subjective definitions of words which can be defined in a number of ways, becomes meaningless.

A number of abstract or highly generalized words provide similar traps: *democracy, capitalism, imperialism, liberalism* are just a few. Notice how often arguments in table talk and in bull sessions hinge on the vague use of such words — and how often there is nothing really to argue about once the misunderstanding of words has been cleared up.

Philosophy and science devote a great deal of care and attention to avoiding just this sort of confusion over the meaning of terms. Linnaeus, the great Swedish botanist, made great strides in reducing chaos in the biological sciences when he worked out a system for naming plants and animals. Chemistry, physics, and the social sciences, including psychology, have their specialized vocabularies, in which terms have very precise meanings, and most sciences have dictionaries for their own special terms. A well-known dictionary of psychology contains over 5000 terms, and it has been estimated that a student taking a beginning course in biology may learn as many new words as he would in a first course in a foreign language! In spite of their best efforts, it is not possible for scientists to define all the terms they use as precisely as they could wish. You may, for instance, think the following title of a psychological study is too detailed or specific: "A Study of the Relationship between Emotional Reactions to Learning Situations and Learning Efficiency in Mentally Retarded Children" (3). And yet at least one key term in the title is somewhat elastic, the term "mentally retarded." You have a right to expect, however, that the author will define this term operationally — though another author might define it in a slightly different way.

Propagandists and advertising writers make capital out of this elasticity in language. By subtle appeals to our prejudices and misconceptions, they lead us to think that a foreign country is dangerous because it is "socialistic," that a product is desirable because millions of people use it — or, conversely, because only a few can afford it. It is an important part of your education to learn to see through this kind of language, to resist the pressures that come at you from all sides to make you do what others want you to do, not what you have rationally decided is best.

A.   PHILOSOPHY AND A WORLD VIEW

B.   PSYCHOLOGY AND PHILOSOPHIC METHOD

● **C. PSYCHOLOGY IN THE SEARCH FOR REALITY**

While the six steps in clarifying and checking the validity of our thinking which we have just outlined are essentially the method of philosophy, they are also useful in psychology. Certainly they are far superior to the methods of the Middle Ages, when experiment and verification of knowledge by checking the facts were largely ignored in favor of an appeal to authority. Among the learned men of that time, it was common practice for scholars to sharpen their wits by "disputation." That is, one would propose a question, others would choose the affirmative or the negative side, and they would dispute by citing authorities, from Plato, Aristotle, and other ancient Greek and Roman writers down through such Fathers of the Church as St. Augustine, St. Jerome, and Thomas Aquinas. The man who cited the most impressive authorities usually won the argument. Sir Francis Bacon tells the story that during one such dispute on the number of teeth in a horse's mouth, one naive brother suggested going into the street, opening the mouth of a horse, and counting its teeth. But he was laughed out of countenance, because this was not an accepted method of settling an argument!

In the three and a half centuries since the dawn of the scientific age, we have come a long way from that. In every branch of learning about the nature of the physical world and the creatures in it, men have, by pooling their information and the results of their observations and experiments, accumulated a vast amount of information and gained new insight into the workings of nature. As a result, a great many questions once held subject for dispute are now no longer questions at all: the information to answer them is readily at hand. For example, the characteristics and operations of the human circulatory system are being documented through controlled experimentation and less formal observation, not through mere speculation. Concerning the nature of reality, also, psychology has provided many studies of cognition (that is, of how we know what we know), of the nature of sensation and perception, and of such abnormalities as hallucinations and delusions. Thus we no longer believe, as men once did, that deranged persons are possessed of the devil, and in consequence our treatment of mental illness and disturbance has radically

A scientific approach to mental illness. *The critical examination of superstitious beliefs and notions has led to new methods of treatment. Contrast the therapeutic treatment in a mental hospital of today with Hogarth's drawing of patients of the 18th century. (National Institute of Mental Health photo, not of actual patient; Huntington Library, San Marino, Calif.)*

changed. Seeing these things as physical and not spiritual phenomena, we treat them through science, not through magic. Psychology has also been able to shed light on baffling questions of epistemology, or the nature of knowledge, once solely the province of philosophy. Through studies of the range and limitations of our senses, and of the way they can be supplemented beyond their range by such devices as microscopes and telescopes, science has been able to remove much obscurity from our conception of what we can know. And the nature of values is being clarified by psychological studies of motivation, attitudes, interests, and group dynamics. In short, the sciences, and psychology among them, by amassing an increasing store of knowledge and information about the world and greatly reducing the areas obscured by ignorance, is making it easier to answer a good many of the questions which philosophy had once to answer solely by reasoning and speculation. Some ultimate questions remain beyond the scope of science, but many in the middle range can be answered with a much greater chance of accuracy than ever was true before.

A.   PHILOSOPHY AND A WORLD VIEW
B.   PSYCHOLOGY AND PHILOSOPHIC METHOD
C.   PSYCHOLOGY IN THE SEARCH FOR REALITY

● D.   A PSYCHOLOGICAL VIEW OF BEHAVIOR

The philosophical area in which psychology has been of most help is, of course, that related to the nature of man. Indeed, psychology provides a coherent, rational, and extremely helpful view of man and of human behavior, which should assist you in your relations with others and should also be useful in your thinking on ethical questions. It is hoped that this book has helped you to make a beginning toward this kind of improved understanding, and has contributed to your effectiveness in understanding yourself and others, and in your relationships with them. It should at the very least have given you a point of view about people.

The point of view on which this book is based can be summarized in a few paragraphs. Our basic premise is that *every human being is a unique individual*, even though he acts in a social context much of the time. Hence to be understood, each person must be considered and studied both as an individual and as a member of certain groups, not as a mere "statistic" among hundreds or thousands of others indistinguishable from him. While it is sometimes necessary to consider people in terms of averages and percentiles — and hence in relation to large groups — we can better predict the behavior of any given person if we study him intensively as an individual, and try to understand his particular developmental patterns, motives, and perceptions. This kind of study is not easy, nor can complete understanding always be achieved. But by developing the attitude of trying to understand the individual and how he got to be the way he is, we can learn to improve our insights, and in the process we can often benefit him as well as ourselves by functioning with others more efficiently as members of society. Let us sketch this basic point of view in somewhat more detail.

A *human being* is *a whole and complete organism*. Except for purposes of immediate analysis we cannot separate the physical, emotional, intellectual, social, and motivational aspects of any life. Whatever affects any one of these aspects of an individual, affects the others either directly or indirectly. For instance, if you recall our earlier discussions of such phenomena as hysterical, psychosomatic illnesses, and the physical effects of emotional depression or elation, you will remember that bodily health is often powerfully affected by emotional and mental states. Conversely, mental and emotional states are affected by physical conditions such as a brain tumor, a glandular imbalance, or a drug. Even motor performance is not only related to physique, but is intimately connected to one's self-concept and his emotional adjustment. No important aspect of an individual's make-up is independent of disturbances in any other.

No *two people are alike*. Except for identical or one-egg twins, each individual is born with his own individual genetic make-up. Even children of the same parents can vary immensely in such simple and recognizable traits as color of skin, hair, and eyes, bone structure and musculature, amount of energy, and tendency to introversion or extroversion. In environment also, even brothers and sisters vary considerably. The amount of attention accorded to a first child, for instance, is often much greater than that given a fourth, and the countless influences of so simple a matter make an immense difference in how the person grows up. Once out of the home, environment inevitably varies — different friends, teachers, school experiences; different illnesses and accidents. And the almost infinite variety of experience from one person to another even in the same family make for large variations in personality and achievement. Further, people differ greatly in their tolerance of pain, their ability to persevere, their perception of distance, shape, and color, their ability to withstand cold and physical hardship, and in many other ways which make the outer environment somewhat different from one to another.

Each *person knows his environment through his senses*. The only contact anyone has with the outside world is through sight, hearing, smell, taste, touch, and the sensations of pain and pleasure, heat and cold. The person who is blind or color-blind, whose hearing is impaired, inevitably suffers from his limitation, and at the same time tends to compensate for one deficiency by cultivating greater acuity in his other senses. The person born deaf, for instance, is likely to be remarkably perceptive visually, and to see and understand more through his eyes than does the person who also has hearing to depend on. Such a person does not experience the same reality as the normally endowed.

Different reactions to environmental experiences. *These people are looking at a display of $100,000 in crisp new $1 bills. Some gaze soberly and longingly, others skeptically, others with intense desire or amusement.* (St. Louis Post-Dispatch, Black Star.)

Consider what a unique world Helen Keller, who was born both deaf and blind, must have come to know.

Each person interprets his environment. What a person experiences through his senses becomes meaningful as he relates it to the content of other experiences. The infant senses the sound of sharp thunder, and may be frightened and respond by crying. The adult senses the same sound and attaches meaning to it, but the meaning may vary greatly from person to person. One is frightened and wants to crawl under the nearest bed. Another is curious and elated, and rushes outdoors to watch the storm. In part the present reactions of fear or excitement indicate the way the new event is related to past experience. The way in which a person interprets himself and his environment is a function of such factors as developmental level, intelligence, past learning, emotions, goals and motives, and expectations concerning environmental phenomena. To the extent that individuals associate common meanings with various events, they can share experiences. To the extent that they interpret these things differently, they disagree on the nature of reality and tend to be out of communication with each other.

A person is not aware of all aspects of the environment with the same degree of clarity. One tends to focus on certain things and to be aware of others only as part of the background of his sensory awareness. Thus a person interested in architecture habitually notices buildings. Another, interested in nature, notices scenery. A third, mainly concerned with mechanical matters, may notice neither of these things but may watch how traffic lights are synchronized for maximum efficiency. To a considerable extent, one notices the things he is interested in.

Moreover, the same person will not always be aware of the same things or even the same kinds of thing. A death in one's family may bring to the surface memories seldom recalled, and seeing an old acquaintance may recall an emotional state not experienced in years. Current preoccupations have considerable influence on what is noticed and what is ignored in the immediate field of perception. The figure–ground relationship shifts frequently, mainly as a result of changes in needs and motives, and as a result of changes in the environment. In this sense, one is not living in the same reality for two successive days, or even minutes. Considering also the chemical and biological changes one constantly undergoes, it may be said that he is not quite even the same person for two successive days or even minutes. There are of course threads of continuity which keep us intact as ourselves. Memory is the strand that binds one day to the next and strings together a coherent life; and the self-concept is sufficiently organized and stable so that we not only remember yesterday but remember ourselves as ourselves.

A person can communicate with others only insofar as each understands the other's way of viewing himself and his surroundings. Without a common language, we could communicate only on a primitive level; it is easy to imagine how totally cut off we would be by recalling how difficult it is to begin studying a new subject with all the strange new terms there are to learn. Beyond language, the members of any society understand each other through common customs, a common history, similar moral and ethical standards, and concepts of life and its values. Thus communication is a complex phenomenon, and more psychologists are turning their attention to it. To communicate is to convey or receive information, and information is any message which provides the stimulus to behavior which the sender wishes to provide. An example should clarify this statement. Suppose a biology professor opens a lecture with the statement, "Ontogeny recapitulates phylogeny." Unless you know the meanings of these three words, there is no communication. Even if you know that "ontogeny" means the life history of the individual, and "phylogeny" means the life history of the race or species to which the individual belongs, you may be stuck if you don't know the meaning of "recapitulates." If you do know that word, then you can make the meaning: "The life history of the individual repeats and exemplifies the life history of the race." Only then is there communication, the transmittal of an *intended* meaning which becomes a stimulus to behavior in you. In this case the desired behavior is for you to understand the idea and remember it.

When we consider how differently many people react to the same stimulus — spinach, for instance, or classical music, or cocoanut cake — we can see how complex the business of communication becomes as soon as emotions and prejudices are aroused. In most of us the word "Christmas" immediately calls up warm thoughts of home and the most widely loved and celebrated holiday of the year. To a tribesman it might arouse feelings of antipathy at a "heathen" festival which he dislikes and does not believe in. To the extent that people have different developmental histories, cultures, goals, and motives, each individual finds it difficult to communicate with and understand others. The same statement may be viewed differently by different people. And the situation is further complicated by the fact that different people will act differently, and convey very different messages, in exactly the same situation!

A person's behavior can be changed by changing his understanding of himself, his environment, or both. The normal pattern of healthy behavior is to do what one thinks best for himself as he sees and understands the situation at the time of acting. Behavior, then, is a function of the way a person views himself and his relationship to his environment. It follows that a person can change his behavior by changing this view, and this can be done in a variety of ways. First, it is possible to change oneself or his understanding of himself, by some new learning about himself or his self-concept, or by newly applying what he already knows. Second, it is sometimes possible to change one's environment — this is commonly described as "doing something about it." Or, if that is impossible, one may change his view of the environment — that is,

Developing the self-concept. *Early experiences of constant scolding may lead to a self-concept quite different from that which results from acceptance and encouragement. (Courtesy of American Mutual Liability Insurance Co.; Photo by Rollie McKenna, for Vassar College.)*

he may interpret it as more or less threatening, for example. And third, it is often possible to change himself a little, the environment a little, and at the same time his interpretation of self-environmental relationships. These are all modes of adjustment, and the person in good mental health, who sees his environment and himself clearly, is always in the process of some kind of adjustment.

Obviously, a person's behavior can also be changed by outside forces, mainly other people. This can come about only through communication, and when communication is effective, one person can bring about profound changes in the outlook and behavior of another. Guidance, psychological counseling, and psychiatry are constantly attempting to make such changes through communication. This is their method and their reason for being.

A person acts to preserve or enhance his self-concept. As we have seen, the self-concept is the sum of a person's interpretations of himself, and his way of differentiating himself from others. It is made up of his attitudes toward his physical being, his memories, motives, and goals, his relationships to others, his roles in life, his reputation — in short, everything which he considers a part of himself. One is not born with a self-concept; rather, he develops it gradually as he grows and matures, learns, and has experiences. A large part of the self-concept is made up of his interpretations of what others think of him. He can never know completely what they think, but he is constantly on the alert to find out. Thus if early experiences tended to make him think himself inferior to others, he will always be on the alert for signs that others think him inferior. Such a person may become shy, retiring, self-effacing, miserable on public occasions — and so on. Conversely, the person who interprets the responses of others as favorable to himself tends to have a much happier self-concept. As the old saying has it, "As the twig is bent, so is the tree inclined." This is not to say that change is totally impossible; nevertheless it is true that the self-concept ultimately becomes quite stable and resistant to change.

The ways we choose to satisfy our needs are, in the last analysis, chosen with varying degrees of awareness to maintain or enhance this self-concept. Some of these methods are in accord with social mores. Others may not be; if so, we tend to get into trouble. It is for the sake of our self-concept that we struggle to achieve status, satisfy our curiosity, gain the approval of others, find sensory gratification. Involuntary actions, of course, such as blinking the eyes to shut out a blinding light, or ducking to avoid a blow, may not primarily protect the self-concept, but they are necessary to maintain life, or at least to maintain coherent organization as a being.

Thinking occurs when we attempt to solve a problem. Although the mind in the waking state is perpetually occupied, it may be with little more than random images, sensations, and recollections loosely connected by association or chance stimulus. Structured purposive thinking occurs only when a need arises — that is, when we face a problem. The situation we face may be no more complex than deciding whether to eat hamburger or filet mignon for dinner, and the solution may come almost instantaneously. But even so simple a problem as this may involve an orderly chain of considerations. For instance: "I have only 95 cents; so I have hamburger." Or, a bit more complex: "I don't mind hamburger, but I love filet. I have $5.00. If I eat steak, I can't go to the basketball game, which I also want to do. All things considered, I'll eat steak." Or still more elaborate: "I like both. But the chef in this restaurant buys cheap hamburger which is very greasy. The steak probably isn't too good either, but it comes with mushrooms, and if I order it cooked very rare it probably won't be too bad. So here goes."

While it is possible to think in pictorial images, and by means of non-verbal symbols such as numbers or other mathematical signs, most of our thinking is *done through language*. By using words and other symbolic forms, a person is enabled to use highly abstract concepts — such as beauty, virtue, democracy — to classify and relate various aspects of the problem he is dealing with, and to make judgments about it. It follows that the greater one's mastery of language and other symbols, the more effective his thinking will be. It is a tragic truth that the illiterate and the semi-literate grope dimly in a half-lit mental world compared to the person who is better educated and more highly skilled with the tools of thought. This, of course, is one reason why your college courses include English, mathematics, and (often) some philosophy as well as more obviously practical courses slanted toward business and professional work. For the more one knows the more he thinks; and the more he thinks productively the more fully he lives.

Learning is attempted when a barrier arises to block the reaching of a

goal. Most learning, but not all, is conscious and purposeful. Most learning involves the cerebral cortex, the part of the brain concerned in conscious thought. But some appears to take place in the lower parts of the central nervous system. Primarily, emotional reactions are learned without verbalizing, but much other behavior is learned in relation to the recognized purposes, aims, and goals of the individual which can be stated in words. Learning, as we have seen, is one of the most important factors in determining ways of perceiving and acting. Since learning often represents an attempt to overcome a barrier, it ceases as a purposeful activity when the barrier is overcome.

Some motives as well as responses are learned. Inherent in living organisms is the need to maintain physical organization and life. Sensory gratification, since it is essential to life, is a strong motivational force in the human neonate. As the neonate matures in a society of people, he begins to be influenced by social motives, including the need for social participation, approval, and successful achievement. These biological and social needs become focused eventually, through learning, on the need to maintain and enhance the self-concept. The particular goals which an individual sets for himself result from his perceptions of himself in a physical and social environment. Thus the adult, though he still has biological needs for food, warmth, activity, and the like, has set specific goals for meeting his needs. His goal is not only to secure food and warmth but particular foods in a particular setting in particular attire. While the need for maintaining and enhancing the self-concept appears to be a common over-all motive, the particular goals related to this basic need are heavily influenced by learning.

Not all learning is purposeful. Through imitation and identification with his parents and others, the growing child forms some attitudes without

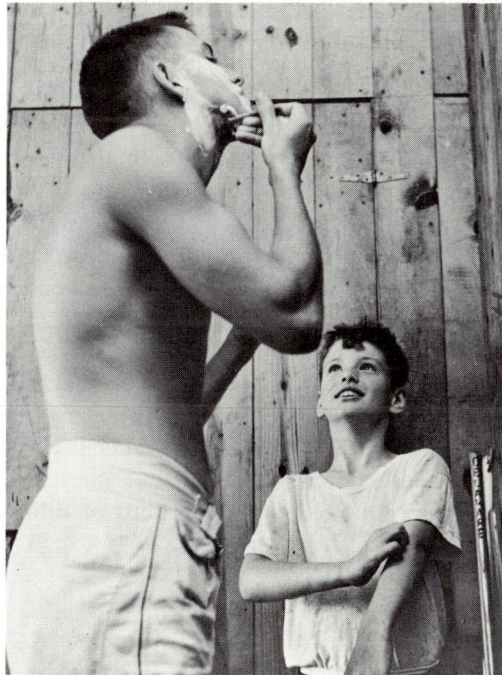

Identification with adults. *Young children learn many attitudes and habits through imitating and identifying with older people. (Photograph by Suzanne Szasz.)*

having deliberately set out to acquire them. Through rewards and punishments, parents and others intentionally or inadvertently foster likes and dislikes in children. It is known, too, that an intense, unpleasant emotional experience may produce a temporary or long-lasting unfavorable attitude or emotional reaction. Pleasant emotional situations likewise may produce pleasant attitudes. As we suggested earlier, people who have unfavorable attitudes and feelings about themselves probably did not acquire them intentionally. As a final example, propaganda techniques and advertising devices ("hidden persuaders") seem to be able to change attitudes and the resulting actions of an individual without his being at all aware of what is occurring. Thus, though many skills, concepts, and techniques for solving problems, as well as some attitudes and emotional reactions, may be learned through purposeful goal-directed activity, this is not always the case. Even so, learning in college will undoubtedly be most efficient if the student does set realistic learning goals.

A. PSYCHOLOGY AND A WORLD VIEW
B. PSYCHOLOGY AND PHILOSOPHIC METHOD
C. PSYCHOLOGY IN THE SEARCH FOR REALITY
D. A PSYCHOLOGICAL VIEW OF BEHAVIOR

● E. PSYCHOLOGY AND YOUR OWN PHILOSOPHY

Let us finally emphasize the importance of the statement that *you should set realistic learning goals.* By this stage in your life your personality and mental abilities have been forming for a number of years, and while there is no reason why you should already have definitely settled on a life career, you do know a good many things about yourself. You already know that you are interested in some subjects and not in others, that certain outside activities are pleasant to you while others are not, and that you have certain talents and certain weaknesses. All that this book has taught you about the nature of the individual and his place in a society should be brought to bear upon your own college experience. If psychology can help you to think rationally about others, and help you to get along with them successfully, it can also help you in assessing yourself and in living with a sense of real satisfaction and accomplishment.

Thus by helping you to understand yourself and others, psychology can help you to understand "what life is all about." For the more clearly you *understand* the nature and make-up of people, the better you will *function* as an individual and a member of society. In this sense, psychology can contribute to your view of life and your own personal philosophy.

Remember, however, that psychology is a science, primarily concerned with the questions of *what* and *how,* much less so with the ultimate questions of *why* and *whether* things should be as they are. It is not, in other words, either philosophy or religion. Questions of ultimate values, of what is most worth while in life for you, what goals you should seek — these we have not attempted to answer. And questions about the ultimate nature of the universe — of good and evil, the nature of deity, and so on — these also are not a major province of psychology. But this behavioral science can help you to achieve a better understanding of yourself, others, and self–other relationships and, less directly, to attack questions involving values and ultimate purposes of life. Having once identified immediate and more remote goals in the areas of academic, social, and emotional life, you can use psychological facts, principles, and methods to achieve them with efficiency and personal satisfaction.

REFERENCES

1. Butler, J. D., *Philosophies and Their Practice in Education and Religion,* Harper, New York, 1951, p. 3.
2. Abstract of a paper of the 1952 Committee on Functions of Philosophy in Education, the Philosophy of Education Society, unpublished.
3. Ringness, T. A., "A Study of the Relationship Between Emotional Reactions to Learning Situations and Learning Efficiency in Mentally Retarded Children." Study in progress under support from U. S. Office of Education, University of Wisconsin Contract SAE 6434, 1957.

SUGGESTIONS FOR FURTHER READING

Allport, G. W., "The Roots of Religion," *Pastoral Psychology,* 1954, 43, pp. 13–24.
Baier, K., *The Moral Point of View: a Rational Basis of Ethics,* Cornell University Press, Ithaca, 1958, Chapters 1, 9, 10.
Bender, I. E., "Changes in Religious Interest: a Retest after 15 Years," *J. Abnorm. Soc. Psychol.,* 1958, 57, pp. 41–46.
Doniger, S. (Ed.), *Religion and Human Behavior,* Association Press, New York, 1954.
Dunham, B., *Giant in Chains,* Little, Brown, Boston, 1953.
Havemann, E., "The Age of Psychology in the United States," *Life,* Vol. 42, Nos. 7 Ja. p. 68, 14 Ja. p. 106, 21 Ja. p. 84, 28 Ja. p. 118, 4 Feb. p. 68.
Lehner, G. F. J., and E. Kube, *The Dynamics of Personal Adjustment,* Prentice-Hall, Englewood Cliffs, 1955, Chapters 15, 16.
Long, M., *The Spirit of Philosophy,* Norton, New York, 1953.
Pressey, S. L., and R. G. Kuhlen, *Psychological Development through the Life Span,* Harper, New York, 1957, Chapter 10.
Riesman, D., *The Lonely Crowd,* Yale University Press, New Haven, 1953, Chapter 12.
Ryle, G., *Dilemmas,* Cambridge University Press, New York, 1954.
Williams, R. M., "Religion, Value-Orientations, and Inter-Group Conflict," *J. Soc. Issues,* 1956, 12, pp. 12–20.

Glossary

ability · present demonstrable performance as in running, playing a musical instrument, solving a problem. Ability refers to what the individual does or can do at the present, as opposed to capacity, which refers to what the individual might do with learning, maturation, and favorable environmental conditions.

achievement test · a test designed to measure present knowledge or skill in any field such as English, science, and typing. Achievement tests in high school subjects are sometimes used to predict the student's subsequent achievement in college, in which case the test is used for prognosis or prediction; if the individual student's responses to items in the test are studied, the achievement test may be useful in diagnosis of the student's strengths and weaknesses in the particular subject field or skill.

acquired determiners of attention · characteristics of stimuli which have meanings for the individual as the result of learning.

adjustment · the relationship between satisfaction of one's needs and the pressures of the environment, as perceived by the individual. Good adjustment implies a harmonious relationship between satisfaction of one's needs and meeting the demands of society. Adjustment implies a higher level of judgment or skill than does adaptation.

adolescence · the period from puberty to maturity, from about ages 12–14 to 20–22.

affective · pertaining to feelings or emotions, as distinguished from *cognitive*.

aggression · behavior of a hostile nature, whether verbal or physical. Action is directed toward or against, rather than avoiding, danger or an adversary.

anthropology · the science devoted to studying man's physical, cultural, and social characteristics, especially those of primitive man. It gives special attention to artifacts, that is, the products of human activity.

antisocial · hostile to society or contradicting social practice.

anvil · small bone in middle ear which, with hammer and stirrup, transmits vibrations to cochlea.

anxiety · an unpleasant emotional state wherein the individual feels threatened but does not seem to know the source or object of the threat. The emotion is of low rather than high intensity.

apathy · a state of disinterest and lethargy in which zest for life has been lost, marked by absence of feeling and emotion.

asocial · without knowledge of society, or without understanding of social values and meanings.

association learning · forming connections and perceiving relationships; learning in which new relations are established among psychological states or activities as a result of experience.

attitude · a learned predisposition to react in a favorable, unfavorable, or neutral way to objects or ideas.

authoritarian character · demanding subordination and obedience, also often implies rigidity.

autonomic nervous system · a major division of the nervous system composed of the sympathetic and parasympathetic systems. The autonomic nervous system regulates the visceral-vascular responses — the heart, blood vessels, lungs and glands.

brainwashing · the processes by which an individual is forcibly brought to depart radically from his strongly held convictions in favor of those held by his enemies.

capacity · full potential for improvement of performance, largely determined by heredity, and inferred from appraisal of present performances.

catatonia · a form of schizophrenia with apathetic or negative behavior, with withdrawal or excessive motor activity.

central nervous system · the brain and spinal cord; the nervous system exclusive of sensory and motor nerves and the autonomic nervous system.

cerebral cortex · nerve cells forming the gray matter or outer layer of the cerebrum.

chromosomes · the bodies within the nucleus of a cell which contain the genes or actual determiners of hereditary tendencies.

chronological age · age as determined by the calendar, counting from birth.

climacteric · the time of menopause or natural cessation of the menstrual cycle.

closure · the tendency to fill in what one expects in his perceptual field, or to complete a perceptual pattern with meaning.

cochlea · spiral bony tube of the inner ear that contains the receptors essential for hearing.

cognitive · pertaining to ideation and knowledge, as distinguished from *affective*.

communal (society) · a primary social group characterized by mutual interests, goals, and customs.

compensatory behavior · a defense mechanism or self-protective behavior to overcome an inadequacy or avoid a block toward a goal. Direct compensation involves an additional effort to reach a particular goal despite inadequacies. Indirect compensation involves a change in the recognized goal which allows for feelings of success.

concept · the meaning or meanings attached to an object, idea, or sensory experience; e.g., the meanings associated with words like *horse* or *thunder*. Concepts are useful in classifying objects and for the association of relationships among objects within and among classes.

conditioned reflex · an acquired reaction of a gland, a smooth muscle or a skeletal muscle to a stimulus which did not originally evoke that reaction; e.g., a hungry dog responds to the sound of a bell with salivation, after the sound has been previously presented with food.

conditioned response · an acquired response to a stimulus which did not originally evoke the response, but of a higher level of performance than the reflex; e.g., a child withdraws from a furry object after the object has been presented at the same time as electrical shock to the child.

conditioned stimulus · a stimulus which, presented with a second stimulus that characteristically evokes a given response, later produces the given response in the absence of the unconditioned stimulus.

conditioning · the process by which conditioned responses are established; more generally, the process by which many attitudes and emotional response patterns are acquired, often unintentionally.

cones · receptors in the retina of the eye essential for color vision.

confirmation · used by Tolman to indicate an individual's awareness and feeling of progress toward a goal. No reinforcement by another person is necessary.

context · the setting or totality of events in which a given activity occurs. Meanings of specific items are in part determined from the larger context, e.g., specific words in a sentence, a sentence in a paragraph, or behavior such as appropriate social life in a college setting.

culture · the products and institutions created by man. Includes language and writings, tools, laws and customs.

cutaneous senses · senses whose receptors are located in or immediately near the skin, i.e., warm, cold, pressure, pain.

daydreaming · the free play of imagination, often of a wishful or adventurous form, while awake.

delirium · a disturbed mental state in which apparently meaningless or disoriented utterances may be made, illusions or hallucinations may be experienced, and actions may be violent and poorly controlled.

delusions · beliefs contrary to fact; e.g., a person may believe that his thoughts are governed by waves from the TV antenna on his house.

depressive reactions · feelings of melancholia, hopelessness, or extreme sadness. May be of mild and temporary or intense and persistent severity.

development · the change in an individual resulting from maturation and learning.

dichotomy · the separation of objects or ideas into two discrete categories such as "black" and "white" or "good" and "bad," with no middle ground between them.

difference threshold · the smallest detectable or noticeable difference between two stimuli.

differentiate · the separating of parts from the whole; developmentally, the refinement and specialization of functions from preceding whole or mass functions, as in the infant's beginning to use thumb and forefinger in grasping, rather than the whole hand.

dissociative reactions · the separation of behaviors or responses which are normally associated; e.g., fugue ("amnesia") states, multiple personality, and certain kinds of apparently meaningless movements.

dominance · the ascendancy of one person over another in face-to-face relationships. Also pertains to higher importance or value.

dominant traits · referring to heredity, those traits which make themselves known, masking the effects of recessive traits.

double adient conflict · a state resulting from a situation in which one must choose between two equally attractive goals.

double avoidant conflict · a state resulting from a situation in which one faces two equally distasteful alternatives.

dream analysis · a pyschoanalytic technique which assumes that dreams symbolically represent needs or desires contributing to the condition of the patient. Manifest content of dream — the items experienced in the dream; latent content — hidden content to be explained by psychoanalysis.

dynamics · moving, flexible relationships. In group dynamics, the interplay of motives, emotions, and actions of group members that affect the structure and behavior of the group.

ego · in Freudian theory, that part of the total personality or psyche most in touch with reality; also more generally, the self or *I* as distinguished from others.

elaborative thinking · according to Kingsley, the process of working out a solution to a problem, using signs, symbols and clues, involving six stages in thought. (See page 208.)

empathy · understanding and acceptance of the feelings of another without experiencing the same emotions.

empirical · pertaining to factual information as contrasted with speculation and deductive reasoning.

environment · everything which surrounds the individual; also used in special instances, i.e., intra-cellular environment, pre-natal external environment, etc., in reference to the surroundings of certain structures.

epistemology · in philosophy, the study of the origin and nature of knowledge.

erotic · related to sex and sexual pleasures.

ethnic · pertaining to national or cultural groups possessing common traits, customs, social history, etc., e.g., the English or French national group, the Jews, or the American Negroes.

extrasensory perception (ESP) · the alleged ability to perceive objects or phenomena without use of the usual sensory cues. Experimentation has included calling the turns of stimulus cards under conditions in which the subject could have no sensory knowledge of their figures or positions. Still controversial and subject to much study.

extroversion · being primarily interested in others and in the external environment, rather than in one's inward thoughts and feelings (introversion).

fantasy · fanciful imagination in which reality or concreteness is ascribed to what is not real.

figure (and ground) · *Figure* refers to that portion of the perceived environment which is focused upon and stands out from the rest, while *ground* refers to the background portion of the perceived environment (not focused upon).

fixating · the act of the eyes in stopping and focusing, as in pauses on a line of print when reading. The eyes do not see clear patterns while in motion.

fovea · the area in the retina which is the point of clearest vision. Contains only cones.

frame of reference · the point of view of a person, reflecting the role he is playing.

free association · a psychoanalytic technique whereby the subject speaks uninhibitedly whatever thoughts occur.

frustration · state of the individual when needs are not satisfied or when goals cannot be achieved.

fugue · the state often called "amnesia" in which one is unable to recall his behavior for certain periods in his life. He may leave home and take up life under a new identity. Also, a flight such as a sleepwalking episode in which the subject does not always seem abnormal to casual observation.

functional disorder · malfunctioning or non-functioning of the subject's normal physical, emotional, or intellectual activities, with no known organic cause. Believed due primarily to conflicts, stress, and frustration, rather than injury to the nervous system or other organic structures.

general paresis · a psychosis resulting from the action on the brain of the specific micro-organism of syphilis, characterized by disorders of reflexes, memory, speech, and judgment; sometimes called general paralysis.

genes · carriers of determiners of hereditary tendencies, located within the chromosomes.

gestalt · a unified whole or a total configuration which cannot be derived from or broken into parts and yet remain whole.

goal · that which the organism seeks or desires to attain in the immediate or remote future.

gonads · sex glands; testes in males and ovaries in females.

growth · increased physical structure resulting from the difference between input and expenditure, occurring in the human organism from shortly after conception until the attainment of mature physical status.

gustatory · referring to the sense of taste.

hallucination · abnormal perception of images or ideas which are then accepted as real by the individual; also experience in the absence of external sensory cues; e.g., an individual perceives harmful objects threatening him when in fact no such objects are present (as in delirium tremens).

hammer · a small bone in the middle ear, helping to carry vibrations to the cochlea.

hebephrenia · a form of schizophrenia characterized by disorganized emotions, silliness, and other bizarre behavior.

heredity · the transmission of characteristics from parent to offspring at the time of conception; all the influences biologically transmitted from parents to offspring.

homeostasis · equilibrium or balance in physiological processes between needs and satisfaction of needs.

hostility · antagonism or enmity, overt or covert.

hypnosis · a trance-like state induced by suggestion, in which the subject carries out commands of the hypnotist.

hypothalamus · a structure at the base of the brain, important in regulating sleep, the emotions, and other physiological functioning.

hypothesis · a statement, intended to show a relationship among facts, not yet proved true or generally accepted.

hysteria · a neurotic and sometimes psychotic condition in which, for example, the function of an organ is lost, even though no physical cause can be found; e.g., a patient cannot walk, even though his legs are not injured.

identification · in personality development, the acceptance and subsequent imitation of another person.

idiot · a mentally deficient individual in the lowest intelligence score range, with IQ below 25, incompetent to provide for own needs and uneducable.

imbecile · a mentally deficient individual in IQ range 26–50. Most are uneducable with usual methods and incompetent socially.

indoctrination · education or training intended to secure acceptance and conformity rather than fact-finding and thinking.

insight · for Gestalt psychologists, the sudden understanding of the solution to a problem, accomplished by perceiving the essential relationships among the various parts or factors of the problem. Also used to describe an individual's recognition of his own limitations or strengths.

integration · the process of bringing parts into an integrated whole; e.g., coordinating discrete facts and skills into typewriting efficiency.

intelligence · the quality or qualities which enable the organism to utilize previous experiences and analyze the present situation in the solution of problems and to project consequences of action into the future. Sometimes related to ability to use abstractions correctly.

intelligence quotient (IQ) · In Binet testing, the formula $\dfrac{\text{MA}}{\text{CA}} \times 100$ is used to determine the IQ, where mental age (MA) is ascertained through interpretation of the test scores. In Wechsler testing, IQ is determined by other statistical techniques. Terman and others felt that IQ represented capacity to learn, but many present-day researchers do not fully accept this definition.

interaction · reciprocal interchange of ideas and feelings among persons.

introversion · perceiving and interpreting phenomena and events in terms of self; also attention to inward thoughts and feelings and apparent tendencies to withdraw from others.

involutional melancholia · a mental disorder, often occurring at menopause, with anxieties, depression, and sometimes delusions.

kinesthetic senses · senses by which one experiences the location and movements of various parts of the body, the receptors of which are located in muscles, tendons, and joints. Sometimes called proprioceptors.

labyrinthine senses · the senses of balance and physical orientation in space, receptors of which are located in the semicircular canals and sacs of the inner ear. Sometimes called static or equilibrium sense.

learning · modification in behavior which tends to persist, as a result of experience rather than of maturation, fatigue, or drugs; related to but more inclusive than habit formation.

Make-A-Picture-Story · a projective test used in assessing certain aspects of personality.

manic-depressive psychosis · a serious mental illness, the symptoms of which may be cyclic periods of elation and depression more extreme than normal.

maturation · progressive change in functions of bodily structures resulting from integration of growth of physical structure, rather than from learning. Certain performances such as the first upright walking and first prehensile grasping appear to result from maturation without guided practice (in a normal, not greatly impoverished environment).

mean · in statistics, the average of a set of scores, calculated by adding all scores and dividing by the number of cases.

mechanistic · proceeding according to established principles of physics and chemistry contrasted with vitalism or teleology. Sometimes *mechanistic* is applied to machine-like, automatic processes as in simple stimulus-response learning.

median · in statistics, the score in a ranked set of scores which has half the scores below and half the scores above it.

memory · the reviving of past experiences with a low to high degree of awareness that the past is being recalled.

menarche · the onset of menstruation in the human female.

menopause · the cessation of menstruation due to age. Marks the end of the human female reproductive period, but not the end of sexual activity.

mental age, or MA · a scale unit developed by Binet to indicate the level of mental maturity in connection with intelligence testing. Terman standardized the Stanford-Binet in such way that the average mental age of children at age six equals six; at age seven, MA equals seven; and so on to age 13.

mode · in statistics, the score made most frequently by subjects within a group or class.

mores · activities or customs which a tribe or social group considers as the only right or correct ones and as vital to the welfare of the individual and group; also, the moral codes of the individual and his groups. Mores tend to be more persist-tent than social customs and styles.

moron · a mentally retarded individual in the IQ range of 51–70. Many persons with IQ's in this range are now being appraised as educable and capable of con-siderable independence in securing a livelihood as adults.

motive · a state within the organism which initiates, directs, and sustains activity, aroused in the interaction between the individual and his environment. The goals which an individual sets in connection with his needs and wishes for sensory gratification, exploration, social participation and approval, and achievement are important determiners of many types of human behavior, including learning.

motor skills · actions involving the muscles and skeletal system, which may be per-formed at varying levels of efficiency, e.g., golf, swimming, handwriting, etc.

negative transfer · a carry-over of an understanding, skill, or attitude from one situation to a second, which reduces efficiency in the second situation; e.g., an individual learns to drive an automobile well, but this may interfere with learning to pilot an airplane.

negativism · a defense mechanism or self-protective behavior characterized by failure to do what is expected and disagreement with others. Resistance to social sugges-tions may result in carrying out opposing activities. Common in early childhood.

neonate · an infant from birth to age one month.

neurology · the scientific study of the structure and functioning of the nervous sys-tem.

neurosis · mental or emotional disorders that are called functional and are not re-lated to any observed change in nerve cells. The term is often used to designate mental disorders that are minor in the sense that they do not involve the character-istics of a psychosis, or severe mental disease. Also referred to as *psychoneurosis*.

neutral stimulus · in conditioning, a stimulus which will be conditioned to a desired response but does not as yet evoke it.

obsessive-compulsive reactions · neurotic reactions, often repeated frequently, in which the subject seems unable to resist certain behavior, e.g., the need to recite certain jingles before taking a test, a compulsive crossing of fingers before making a decision, etc.

olfactory senses · pertaining to smell.

organic illness · illness caused by disease, injury, or failure of an organ or structure of the body in which actual damage to the structure is evident and medical treat-ment is required. As opposed to functional illnesses which also may have an organic base but not one that is sub-microscopic like in the hidden neural changes of pathological learning.

overlearning · learning beyond that required for a first correct response, e.g., con-tinuing to practice spelling a word after it has once been spelled correctly.

overt · visible to observers, as opposed to covert or hidden behavior.

paradoxical warmth or cold · the sensations experienced but called forth by the "wrong" stimulus; e.g., an application of dry ice to the skin may at first produce a burning sensation.

paranoia · a disorder in which a psychotic individual exhibits delusions, including a feeling that others are attempting to harm him or that he is in a grandiose state.

parasympathetic nervous system · the part of the autonomic nervous system which is active in quiescent states, as in the the digestive process. During normal emotional states, both the sympathetic and parasympathetic systems are in equilibrium. It is the cranial and sacral parts of the autonomic nervous system as opposed to the thoracic and lumbar parts.

peer group · a group of individuals of the same age or status who consider one another as equals.

perception · the process of associating meaning with sensory experiences. Also commonly considered to be awareness of external objects and events distinguished from memory or imagination.

personality · a term used to indicate the total behavior and characteristics of the individual, including the organization of any traits or tendencies, which serve to differentiate one person from another. Also, the person as a social rather than a chemical or physical being.

philosophy · a discipline concerned with the nature of reality, knowledge, and values. Also, the attitudes and values one may possess, i.e., philosophy of life.

phobia, phobic reactions · morbid, unrealistic fear of objects or phenomena, in which the reasons for the fear are not present or in which the fear is entirely out of proportion to the danger. Sometimes a result of maladaptive learning.

potentiality · possible performance, not actually existing at present but inferred from the present.

primary determiners of attention · qualities of a stimulus which lead to a person's sensing or experiencing it as figure rather than ground.

primary group · an association of persons with a core of common goals, interests, and mores, who interact frequently with one another in face-to-face relationships.

productive thinking · according to Wertheimer, thinking initiated by the individual's need to find organization and meaning, and resulting in better organization and meaning.

projection · a defense mechanism by which the individual protects his self concept through transferring to others his own socially disapproved motives. Also, a tendency to attribute to the external world or to another person a mental process that is repressed or not recognized as being of personal origin as a result of which the individual's own mental process is mistakenly considered to be an external perception.

psychiatrist · a licensed physician, trained also in psychiatry and psychology and specializing in the prevention, diagnosis, and treatment of mental illness.

psychoanalysis · Freudian theory and method, applied primarily to the treatment of mental illness but also toward reaching an understanding of more normal human development and behavior.

psychoanalyst · synonymous with *analyst* in the United States. Usually a psychiatrist following psychoanalytic theory, although lay analysts not possessing medical training are found in small numbers.

psychodrama · a form of guided role-playing in which the mentally disturbed individual freely acts out roles relevant to his life-situations, especially in his problem areas.

psychology · the scientific study of human behavior and experience including such areas as learning, intelligence, perception, emotion, and many others.

psychometrist · a person who is educated for the administration and interpretation of mental and other psychological tests.

psychoneurosis · See *neurosis*.

psychopathology · the systematic study of mental diseases.

psychosis · a serious form of mental illness, in which the individual has lost partial or complete contact with reality. Ordinarily the legally insane are psychotic and require hospitalization.

psychosomatic · pertaining to mental-physical relations, ordinarily in regard to illnesses, e.g., psychosomatic diseases are those with a symptom or symptoms of physical disfunctioning, such as allergies, migraine headaches, and others. Also, sometimes related to maladaptive emotional learning.

puberty · the period during which the sex organs mature rapidly and secondary sex characteristics start to appear, marking the first phase of adolescence.

Purkinje effect · changing of relative brightness of colors as illumination changes from day to night. Yellow appears relatively bright before sunset, blue after sunset.

push-pull conflict · a state resulting from a situation in which one is both drawn to and repelled by the same idea or object; e.g., one may recognize the need for a vaccination yet be repelled by the needle.

rationalization · a defense mechanism in which the individual justifies irrational, unwise, or unethical behavior by creating a reasonable basis for it; also the elaboration of an ostensible verbal reason to justify an act based on other motives.

recessive traits · referring to heredity, those traits which remain latent when balanced by dominant characteristics. When only recessive genes are present, recessive traits will be demonstrated.

reflective thinking · as defined by Dewey, a method of reasoning, initiated by a question or problem and culminating in a solution, verified by testing.

reflex · a relatively simple and automatic, typically unlearned form of response to stimulation, e.g., the contraction of the pupil of the eye to increased light.

reflex sounds · sounds made by the infant without conscious or purposive effort in response to stimuli.

regression · a response to a perceived threatening circumstance, characterized by a return to an earlier or more primitive form of behavior.

reinforcement · in psychological experimentation, the strengthening or the condition for strengthening a response — in many experiments the presentation of the unconditioned stimulus with the conditioned stimulus, in which case the unconditioned stimulus is the reinforcer. As distinguished from confirmation, reinforcement implies manipulation by the experimenter.

rejection · the process or act of exhibiting lack of affection and acceptance.

reliability · in statistics, the accuracy with which a measure secures the same results when repeated. A test or measure that on two occasions places a large group of individuals in the same order from highest to lowest is highly reliable.

reminiscence · recall, without intervening practice, of something not able to be recalled on a previous occasion.

repression · a defense mechanism or self-protective behavior in which the individual refuses to allow threatening perceptions to be brought into clear focus, or to a high degree of awareness. Some describe this as forcing ideas that would be unacceptable in consciousness into the "dynamic unconscious."

retina · the innermost layer of the eyeball, containing the rods and cones.

reverie · a form of free, random mental activity in which the individual's thoughts are aimless, not focused on any particular goal, circumstance, or event. The associations are under partial control, however, and may give a clue to the individual's hopes and interests.

rods · sense receptors located in the retina of the eye, associated with the light-dark but not the color aspect of vision.

Rorschach test (ink-blot) · a projective technique utilizing 10 cards for assessing personality. The subject looks at the (ink-blot) card and gives his responses or tells "what he sees."

Rosenzweig P. F. test · a psychological "picture-frustration" test used in assessing aspects of personality.

sample · a part of a larger group of persons or objects which constitute a population. A matched sample is drawn in such way that one sample has exactly the same characteristics as the second sample. Subjects in a random sample are drawn by chance (usually using a table of random numbers) in such way that each subject or item in the sampling population has an equal chance of being drawn into the random sample. Random sampling from a population allows generalizing from the sample to the entire population from which the sample is drawn.

schizophrenia · literally, a splitting of the mind; a psychosis, the symptoms of which are variable, including withdrawal from reality in thought processes, bizarre behavior, silliness, assuming of unusual logic or body postures, delusions, hallucinations, and negativism. Old term for schizophrenia was dementia praecox.

self-concept · the ideas one has about himself as a unique individual. The self-concept in normally developing individuals becomes quite stable in later adolescence and early adulthood. In many respects a synonym for ego.

senescence · the period of old age during which a decline in physical and mental functions may be noted.

senility · physiological and psychological impairment of function in old age.

sensory · pertaining to the senses.

signs · any cues or stimuli which set off or lead to a learned response.

social classes · in the United States, subgroups of people in a community who associate together and have common interests and customs. Members of the various social classes sense the status of their own group and ascribe higher or lower status to other classes. Based in part on economic status, source of income, amount of education, and occupation.

society · an association of people who have a common set of habits, attitudes, and ideas sufficient to hold them together.

sociology · the science of group life, social organizations, and institutions.

sociometric tests · tests designed to appraise the direction and intensity of feelings among members of a group.

statistical significance · the degree of probability that a score or measurement obtained is correct or different from another score or measurement. Widely used to indicate the differences between mean scores of two groups, among various distributions among groups, between proportions, and other measures.

statistics · the mathematical treatment of determinate measures to show relationships among the measures, including scores on tests.

stimulus · any condition or phenomenon within or without the organism which activates a receptor or sense organ. Stimulus energies are best described in terms of physics or chemistry (*radiant* energy, for example, acts on rods and cones of the the eye, etc.). The stimulus object is often a percept based on past learning and many types of receptor stimulation.

stirrup · one of the small bones of the inner ear which transmits vibrations to the cochlea.

submission · yielding or conforming to another. The submissive person in a face-to-face situation accepts rather than resists the dominant person's words and actions.

sub-societies · sub-groups having characteristics of the larger society in which they are members, but also certain characteristics of their own, e.g., groups of common national origin living in large American cities. A sub-society may be an ethnic group.

symbols · special kinds of signs which have social meaning, e.g., words, musical notes, etc.

sympathetic nervous system · the part of the autonomic system most active in "emergency" emotional states; the thoracic and lumbar parts of the autonomic nervous system; sometimes, in general terms, a synonym for autonomic nervous system.

syndrome · a constellation or grouping of symptoms; usually the term is used in connection with an illness or disorder.

Thematic Apperception Test (TAT) · a projective test requiring the subject to make up a story in response to viewing each of 19 ambiguous pictures. From these stories inferences are drawn about the subject, his needs and stresses.

theory · a series of statements, usually very generalized, thought to explain the relationships among a large body of facts. Also, a related body of facts and principles for purposes of explanation.

therapy · treatment intended to cure or improve.

thinking · the process of manipulating concepts and ideas, initiated by a feeling of need or questioning about a problem. Thinking is a form of mental activity; but mental activity like that involved in reverie, fantasy, or free association frequently does not involve thinking. Sometimes a synonym for reasoning.

threshold (limen) · a statistic on a stimulus scale reached when a stimulus not previously sensed is sensed because of increased intensity of the stimulus. When a threshold is "high," the effective stimulus must be strong.

threshold of consciousness · as first used by Herbert, the point at which the individual becomes aware of ideas.

thymus · an endocrine gland which grows rapidly during early childhood, and slowly atrophies after the time of puberty.

trait · a more or less permanent characteristic of an individual. Term used widely in literature and personality theory.

transfer · a carry-over of attitudes, habits, skills, or other learning from one situation to another.

unconditioned response · the response originally given to the unconditioned stimulus, or the natural or inborn response to a stimulus.

unconditioned stimulus · any stimulus which arouses a response which is natural or inborn.

uninflected speech forms · according to Merry and Merry, the stage of speech in which the 4- to 6-year-old child begins to use longer sentences and develops a larger vocabulary than the two-or-three-word sentences used by the younger child.

Implies a use of real sentence structure rather than the mere combination of a few simple words.

validity · in statistics, the extent to which a test measures what it purports to measure; more precisely, the extent to which a test can be used to predict subsequent performances.

variable · in experimentation, anything that can be changed. In psychological experiments, the dependent variable is always the response or responses; the independent variable is that which is controlled or manipulated to produce effects upon the dependent or response variable.

whole-part learning · whole learning implies mastery of a complete learning task without practicing on individual parts. Whole-part learning implies mastering the task by learning the parts and then putting them together to make the whole task.

Journal and Magazine Abbreviations

Abstr. of Grad. Theses in Educ.	—Abstracts of Graduate Theses in Education
Acta Psychol.	—Acta Psychologica
Am. Sociol. Rev.	—American Sociological Review
Amer. J. Psychol.	—American Journal of Psychology
Amer. J. Sociol.	—American Journal of Sociology
Amer. Psychologist	—American Psychologist
Ann. Amer. Acad. Polit. Soc. Sci.	—Annals of the American Academy of Political and Social Science
Annu. Rev. Psychol.	—Annual Review of Psychology
Brit. J. Psychol.	—British Journal of Psychology
Calif. J. Educ. Res.	—California Journal of Educational Research
Child Developm.	—Child Development
Dissertation Abstr.	—Dissertation Abstracts
Educ. Adm. Superv.	—Educational Administration and Supervision
Educ. Psychol. Measmt.	—Educational and Psychological Measurement
Educ. Rec. Bull.	—Educational Records Bulletin
Genet. Psychol. Monogr.	—Genetic Psychology Monographs
Harv. Educ. Rev.	—Harvard Educational Review
Hum. Relat.	—Human Relations
Jewish Soc. Serv. Quart.	—Jewish Social Service Quarterly
J. Abnorm. Soc. Psychol.	—Journal of Abnormal and Social Psychology
J. Appl. Psychol.	—Journal of Applied Psychology
J. Communication	—Journal of Communication
J. Consult. Psychol.	—Journal of Consulting Psychology
J. Counsel. Psychol.	—Journal of Counseling Psychology
J. Educ. Psychol.	—Journal of Educational Psychology
J. Educ. Res.	—Journal of Educational Research
J. Engng. Educ.	—Journal of Engineering Education
J. Exp. Educ.	—Journal of Experimental Education
J. Gen. Psychol.	—Journal of General Psychology
J. Genet. Psychol.	—Journal of Genetic Psychology
J. Higher Educ.	—Journal of Higher Education
J. Nerv. Ment. Dis.	—Journal of Nervous and Mental Disease
J. Pers.	—Journal of Personality
J. Soc. Issues	—Journal of Social Issues
J. Soc. Psychol.	—Journal of Social Psychology

Marriage Fam. Living	—Marriage and Family Living
Ment. Hyg.	—Mental Hygiene
Personnel Guid. J.	—Personnel and Guidance Journal
Psychol. Rev.	—Psychological Review
Psychosom. Med.	—Psychosomatic Medicine
Quart. J. Exp. Psychol.	—Quarterly Journal of Experimental Psychology
Res. Quart. Amer. Ass. Hlth. Phys. Educ.	—Research Quarterly of the American Association for Health, Physical Education and Recreation
Rur. Sociol.	—Rural Sociology
Sociol. Soc. Res.	—Sociology and Social Research
Teach. Coll. Rec.	—Teachers College Record

Acknowledgments

Credits for pictures on part opening pages:

Part One, Ward Allan Howe, from Ewing Galloway
Part Two, Max Tharpe
Part Three, Pictorial Parade
Part Four, Max Tharpe

Credits for pictures on chapter opening pages:

Introduction. Hays, from Monkmeyer
 1. Northern Illinois University
 2. Max Tharpe, from Monkmeyer
 3. Lew Merrim, from Monkmeyer
 4. Gary Schultz, University of Wisconsin
 5. Ideal Toy Corporation
 6. American Museum of Natural History
 7. Max Tharpe, from Monkmeyer
 8. Children's Bureau photograph, Esther Bubley
 9. Hays, from Monkmeyer
10. Max Tharpe
11. A. Devaney, Inc., N.Y.
12. *St. Louis Post-Dispatch,* from Monkmeyer
13. The Advertising Council, Inc., and the National Association
    for Better Mental Health, Inc.
14. Gary Schultz, University of Wisconsin
15. Max Tharpe

Drawings on the following pages are by Lilli Mautner:
8, 18, 19, 20, 27, 49, 67, 80, 113, 114, 115, 119, 120,
176, 177, 180, 182, 185, 206, 217, 218, 241, 246,
332, 333, 375, 376, 427, 438, and the title page.

Index

DISTANCE VISION TEST

E P L D

P C D F E

Z C F D E P

F P L O E Z D

P E F E O T D C

PERCEPTION

In these plates you should see one
figure if your color perception is
normal, another if you are red-
green defective. For further discussion of color blindness see page
179. A key to these charts is
given on the back of the title
page of this book.

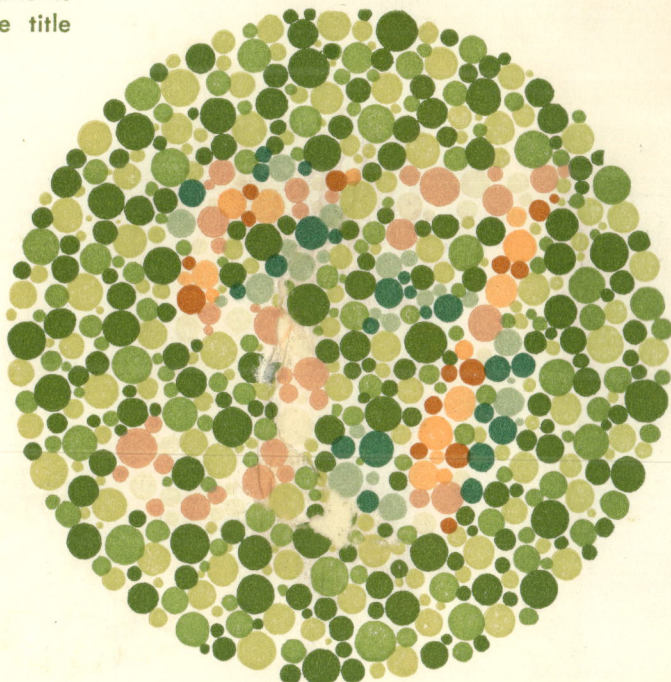

Ringness

Psychology in theory

and practice.